HOLT McDOUGAL

ECONOMICS
Concepts and Choices

HOLT McDOUGAL
a division of Houghton Mifflin Harcourt

HOLT McDOUGAL

ECONOMICS

Concepts and Choices

HOLT McDOUGAL
a division of Houghton Mifflin Harcourt

Consultants and Reviewers

Senior Consultants

Sally Meek has been teaching Economics, AP Microeconomics, and AP Macroeconomics in the Plano Independent School District in Plano, Texas since 1987. She has served as an AP Economics reader since 1998, and is currently a Lead Consultant for AP Economics at Summer Institutes for universities across Texas and a member of the AP Economics Test Development Committee. Additionally, Ms. Meek serves on the National Assessment of Educational Progress Economics Steering Committee and as a test item writer. She served as President of the Global Association of Teachers of Economics and addressed the National Summit on Economic and Financial Literacy in 2005. In 2004, Ms. Meek co-founded the North Texas TINSTAAFL Society and was on the National Council on Economic Education (NCEE) Virtual Economics 3.0 Design Committee. She has received the Southwest College Board Advanced Placement Special Recognition Award and the GATE Distinguished Service Award. Ms. Meek earned her B.A. in political science at the University of Texas at Dallas and her M.Ed. in Secondary Education with a content emphasis on Economics from the University of North Texas.

John Morton is Senior Program Officer for the Arizona Council on Economic Education. He taught economics for 31 years at the high school and university levels. Mr. Morton founded and directed the Center for Economic Education at Governors State University in Illinois for 15 years and founded and served as president of the Arizona Council on Economic Education for 4 years. He served as vice president for program development at the National Council on Economic Education (NCEE) for 5 years. He has authored or co-authored more than 80 publications and chaired the advisory board of *The Wall Street Journal Classroom Edition* from 1991 to 2000. Mr. Morton has won the Leavey Award from the Freedoms Foundation, as well as the Bessie B. Moore Service Award and the John C. Schramm Leadership Award from NCEE and the National Association of Economic Educators. He earned his M.A. from the University of Illinois and pursued postgraduate work at the University of Chicago.

Mark C. Schug is Emeritus Professor and Director of the University of Wisconsin-Milwaukee Center for Economic Education and serves as a Senior Fellow for the National Council for Economic Education. He has taught for over 35 years at the middle school, high school, and university levels. Dr. Schug has written and edited over 180 publications. Additionally, he edited *The Senior Economist* for the National Council on Economic Education (NCEE) from 1986–1996. Dr. Schug often speaks and writes about economic and financial education, market-based reforms in education, and issues in urban schools, and has addressed local, state, national, and international groups. Similarly, he has done training programs for teachers in several states across the nation. Dr. Schug earned his Ph.D. from the University of Minnesota.

Acknowledgments begin on page R79.
ISBN-13: 978-0-547-08294-3   ISBN-10: 0-547-08294-0

Printed in the U.S.A.
1 2 3 4 5 6 7 8 9-1678-15 14 13 12 11 10 09

ECONOMICS: Concepts and Choices

Contents

ECONOMICS: Concepts and Choices

🔊 **Economics Updates** For current economic data and news, go to ClassZone.com

Contents

Animated Economics   For interactive graphs and lessons, go to ClassZone.com

YOUR ECONOMIC CHOICES

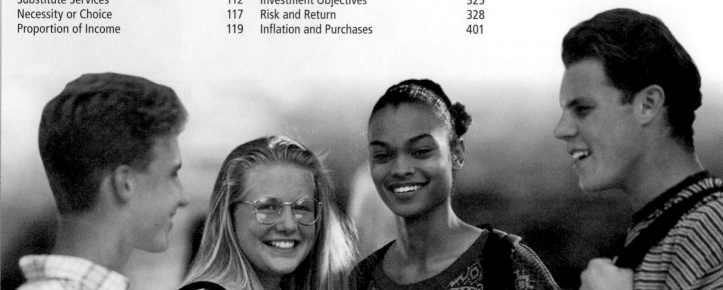

Economics Pacesetters

Global Perspectives

Economics Skillbuilders

Math Challenges

Contents

Graphs, Charts, Tables, and Maps

ECONOMICS: Concepts and Choices

Graphs, Charts, Tables, and Maps (continued)

Contents

RAND McNALLY

Economic Atlas
and Statistics

CONTENTS

United States Maps

World Maps

Data on the U.S. Economy

Data on the World Economy

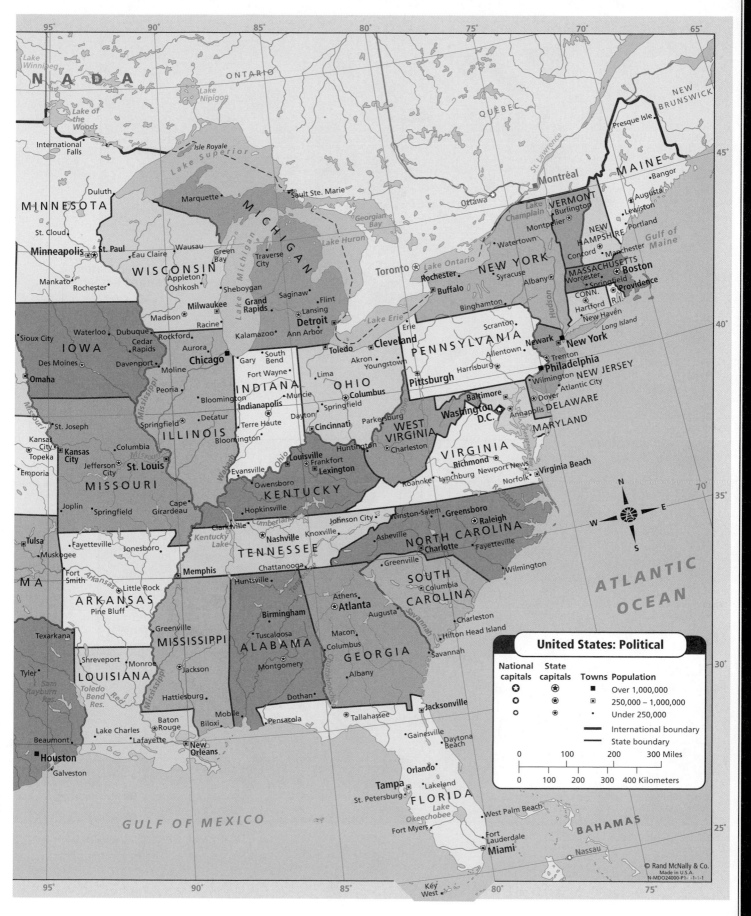

United States: Political

National capitals	State capitals	Towns	Population
⊛	⊛	■	Over 1,000,000
⊙	⊛	▫	250,000 – 1,000,000
⊙	⊛	•	Under 250,000
		▬▬	International boundary
		▬▬	State boundary

0   100   200   300 Miles

0   100   200   300   400 Kilometers

© Rand McNally & Co.
Made in U.S.A.
N-MDO24000-P1-   -1-1-1

RAND M^{c}NALLY

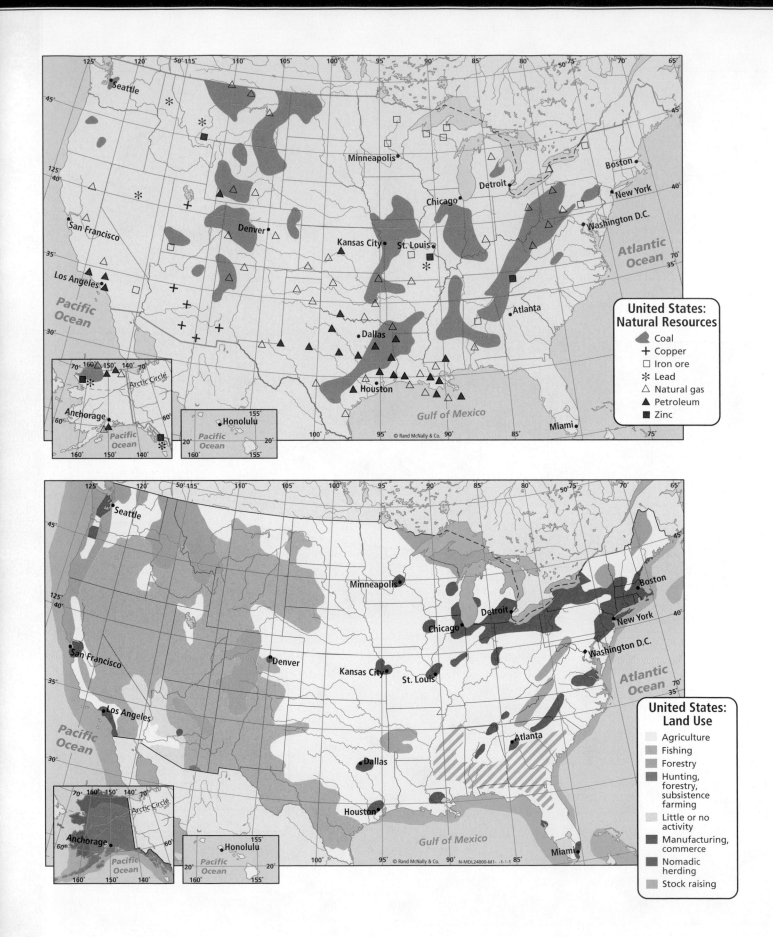

United States:
Natural Resources

- Coal
- + Copper
- □ Iron ore
- ✳ Lead
- △ Natural gas
- ▲ Petroleum
- ■ Zinc

United States:
Land Use

Agriculture
Fishing
Forestry
Hunting, forestry, subsistence farming
Little or no activity
Manufacturing, commerce
Nomadic herding
Stock raising

© Rand McNally & Co.

N-MDL24000-M1- -1-1-1

A4 Economic Atlas and Statistics

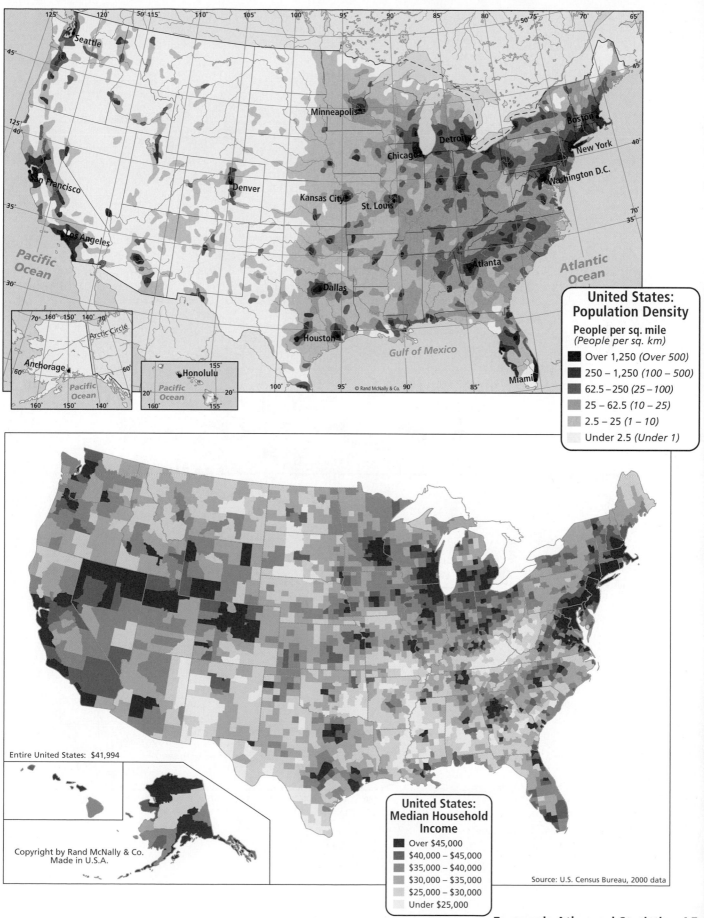

United States:
Population Density

People per sq. mile
(People per sq. km)

■ Over 1,250 (Over 500)
■ 250 – 1,250 (100 – 500)
■ 62.5 – 250 (25 – 100)
■ 25 – 62.5 (10 – 25)
■ 2.5 – 25 (1 – 10)
□ Under 2.5 (Under 1)

Entire United States: $41,994

United States:
Median Household
Income

■ Over $45,000
■ $40,000 – $45,000
■ $35,000 – $40,000
■ $30,000 – $35,000
■ $25,000 – $30,000
□ Under $25,000

Source: U.S. Census Bureau, 2000 data

Economic Atlas and Statistics A5

World: Political

- ⊕ National capital
- · Major city
- — International boundary

0   1000   2000 Miles
0   1000   2000   3000 Kilometers

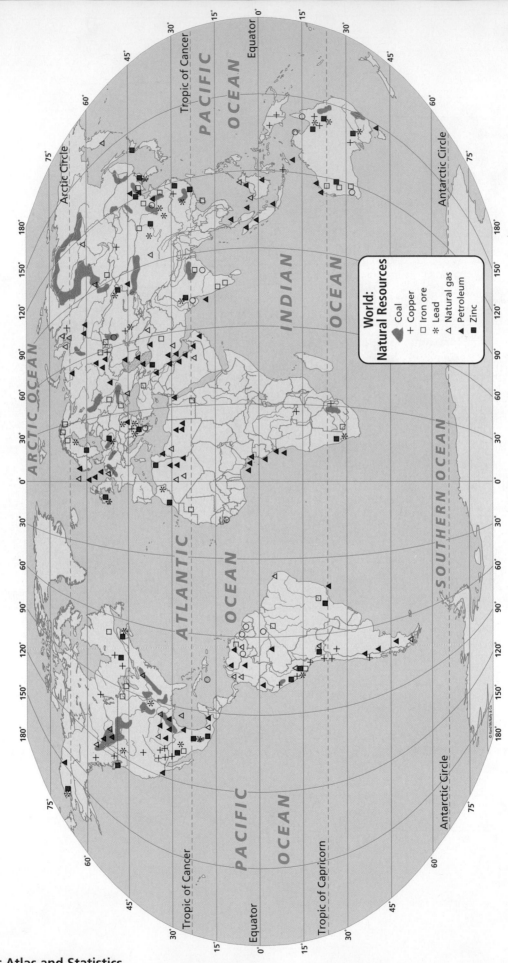

World:
Natural Resources

- ◥ Coal
- + Copper
- □ Iron ore
- * Lead
- △ Natural gas
- ▲ Petroleum
- ■ Zinc

World: Land Use

Agriculture
Fishing
Forestry
Hunting, forestry, subsistence farming
Little or no activity
Manufacturing, commerce
Nomadic herding
Stock raising

PACIFIC OCEAN
ATLANTIC OCEAN
ARCTIC OCEAN
INDIAN OCEAN
SOUTHERN OCEAN
PACIFIC OCEAN

Arctic Circle
Tropic of Cancer
Equator
Tropic of Capricorn
Antarctic Circle

© Rand McNally & Co.

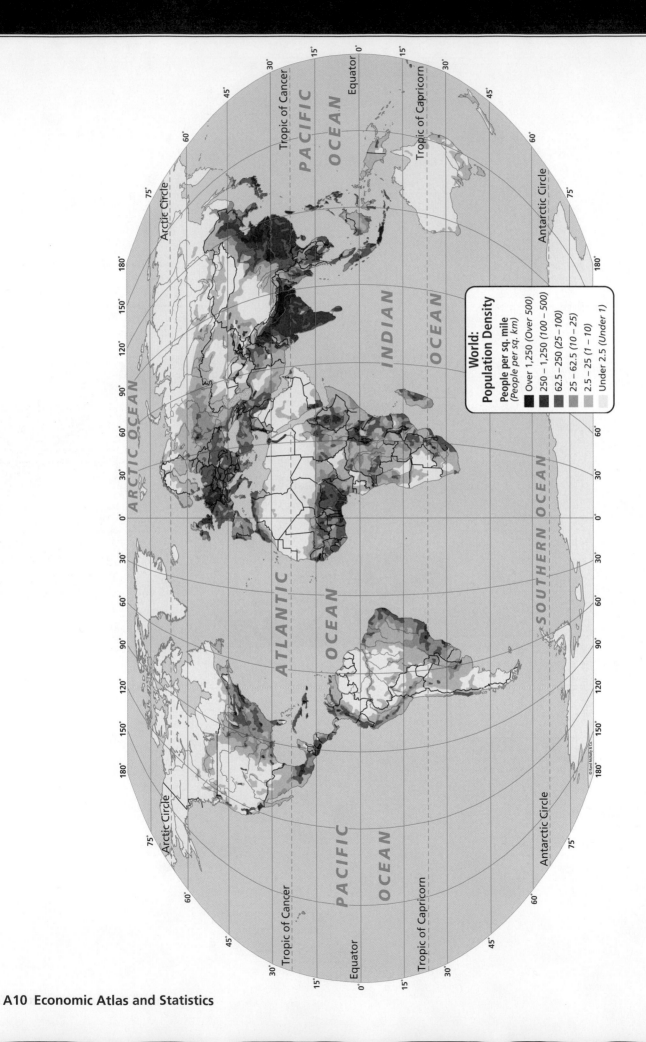

World: Population Density

People per sq. mile
(People per sq. km)

- Over 1,250 *(Over 500)*
- 250 – 1,250 *(100 – 500)*
- 62.5 – 250 *(25 – 100)*
- 25 – 62.5 *(10 – 25)*
- 2.5 – 25 *(1 – 10)*
- Under 2.5 *(Under 1)*

PACIFIC OCEAN

INDIAN OCEAN

ATLANTIC OCEAN

SOUTHERN OCEAN

ARCTIC OCEAN

Tropic of Cancer

Tropic of Capricorn

Equator

Arctic Circle

Antarctic Circle

© Rand McNally & Co.

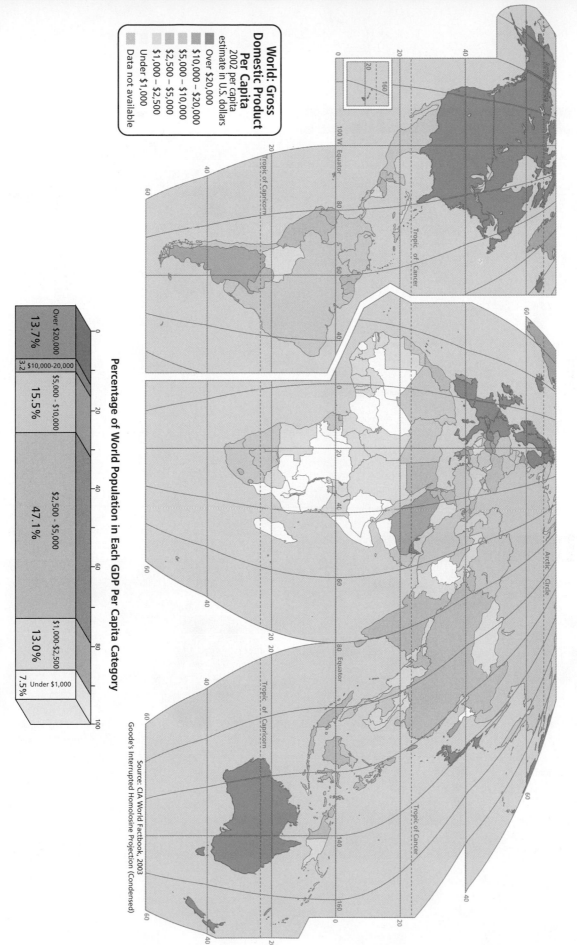

World: Gross Domestic Product Per Capita

2002 per capita estimate in U.S. dollars

- Over $20,000
- $10,000 – $20,000
- $5,000 – $10,000
- $2,500 – $5,000
- $1,000 – $2,500
- Under $1,000
- Data not available

Percentage of World Population in Each GDP Per Capita Category

Over $20,000	$10,000-20,000	$5,000 - $10,000	$2,500 - $5,000	$1,000-$2,500	Under $1,000
13.7%	3.2	15.5%	47.1%	13.0%	7.5%

Source: CIA World Factbook, 2003
Goode's Interrupted Homolosine Projection (Condensed)

RAND MCNALLY

Economic Atlas and Statistics A11

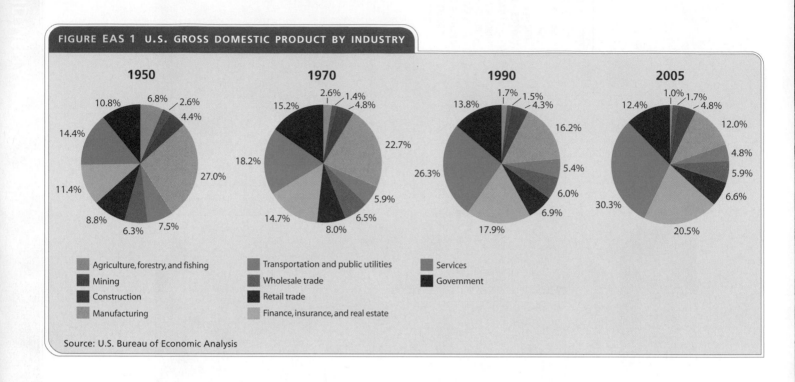

FIGURE EAS 1 U.S. GROSS DOMESTIC PRODUCT BY INDUSTRY

1950
10.8% 6.8% 2.6% 4.4% 27.0% 7.5% 6.3% 8.8% 11.4% 14.4%

1970
2.6% 1.4% 4.8% 22.7% 5.9% 6.5% 8.0% 14.7% 18.2% 15.2%

1990
1.7% 1.5% 4.3% 16.2% 5.4% 6.0% 6.9% 17.9% 26.3% 13.8%

2005
1.0% 1.7% 4.8% 12.0% 4.8% 5.9% 6.6% 20.5% 30.3% 12.4%

- Agriculture, forestry, and fishing
- Mining
- Construction
- Manufacturing
- Transportation and public utilities
- Wholesale trade
- Retail trade
- Finance, insurance, and real estate
- Services
- Government

Source: U.S. Bureau of Economic Analysis

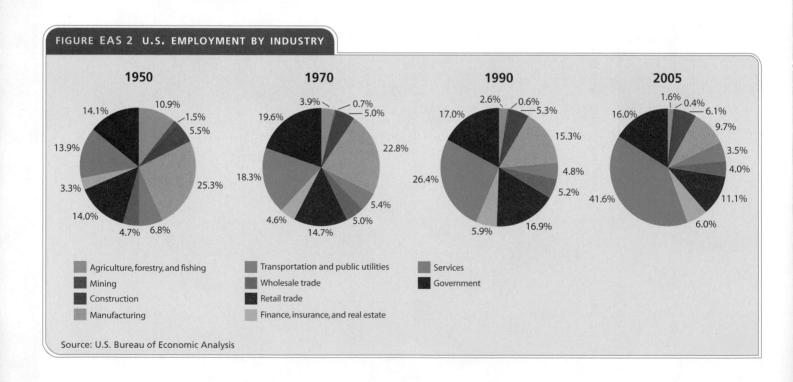

FIGURE EAS 2 U.S. EMPLOYMENT BY INDUSTRY

1950
10.9% 1.5% 5.5% 25.3% 6.8% 4.7% 14.0% 3.3% 13.9% 14.1%

1970
3.9% 0.7% 5.0% 22.8% 5.4% 5.0% 14.7% 4.6% 18.3% 19.6%

1990
2.6% 0.6% 5.3% 15.3% 4.8% 5.2% 16.9% 5.9% 26.4% 17.0%

2005
1.6% 0.4% 6.1% 9.7% 3.5% 4.0% 11.1% 6.0% 41.6% 16.0%

- Agriculture, forestry, and fishing
- Mining
- Construction
- Manufacturing
- Transportation and public utilities
- Wholesale trade
- Retail trade
- Finance, insurance, and real estate
- Services
- Government

Source: U.S. Bureau of Economic Analysis

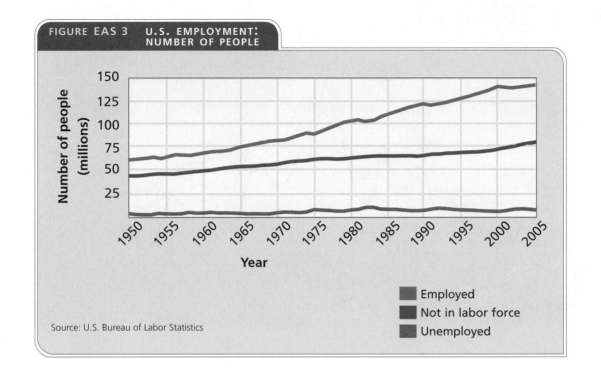

FIGURE EAS 3   U.S. EMPLOYMENT:
NUMBER OF PEOPLE

Number of people (millions)

Year

Employed
Not in labor force
Unemployed

Source: U.S. Bureau of Labor Statistics

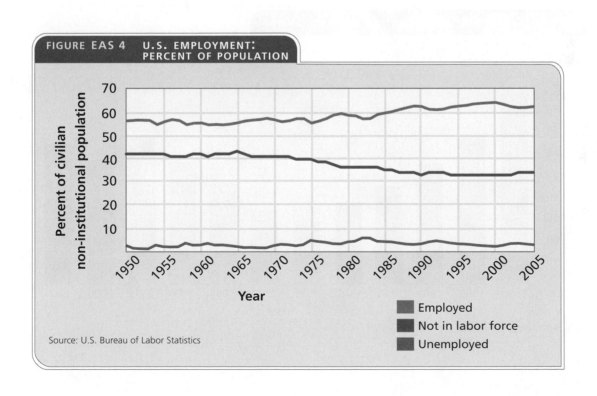

FIGURE EAS 4   U.S. EMPLOYMENT:
PERCENT OF POPULATION

Percent of civilian non-institutional population

Year

Employed
Not in labor force
Unemployed

Source: U.S. Bureau of Labor Statistics

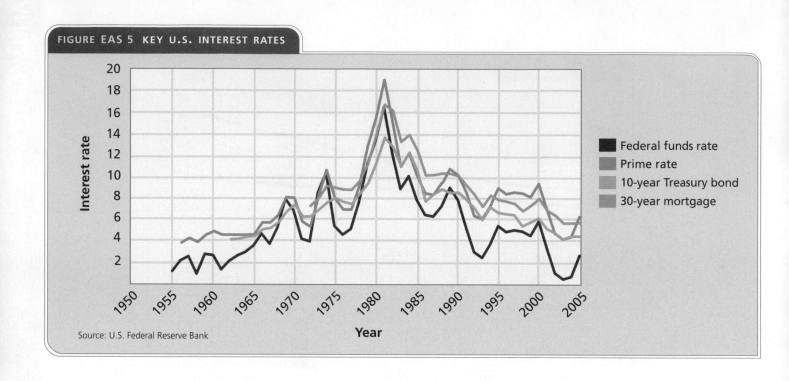

FIGURE EAS 5 KEY U.S. INTEREST RATES

Legend:
- Federal funds rate
- Prime rate
- 10-year Treasury bond
- 30-year mortgage

Interest rate (y-axis)
Year (x-axis)

Source: U.S. Federal Reserve Bank

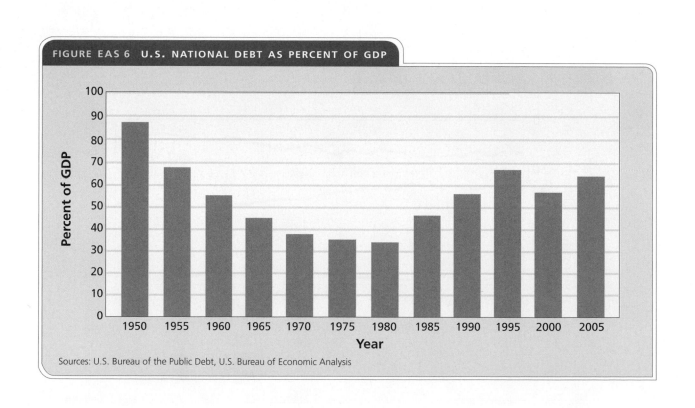

FIGURE EAS 6 U.S. NATIONAL DEBT AS PERCENT OF GDP

Percent of GDP (y-axis)
Year (x-axis)

Sources: U.S. Bureau of the Public Debt, U.S. Bureau of Economic Analysis

FIGURE EAS 7 World Data File

Country	Population	Percent urban / rural	Unemployment rate	GDP (in billions of U.S. dollars)	GDP per capita (in U.S. dollars)	National debt (as percent of GDP)	Inflation rate
China	1,303,701,000	37 / 63	9.0	2,234.1	1,709	24.4	1.8
India	1,103,596,000	28 / 72	8.9	772.0	705	53.8	4.0
United States	296,483,000	79 / 21	5.1	12,455.8	42,000	64.7	3.4
Indonesia	221,932,000	42 / 58	11.8	281.3	1,283	49.9	10.5
Brazil	184,184,000	81 / 19	9.8	795.7	4,320	51.6	6.9
Pakistan	162,420,000	34 / 66	6.6	111.0	728	53.8	9.3
Bangladesh	144,233,000	23 / 77	2.5	60.8	400	44.5	7.0
Russia	143,025,000	73 / 27	7.6	763.3	5,349	12.9	12.6
Nigeria	131,530,000	44 / 56	2.9	99.1	678	11.0	17.9
Japan	127,728,000	79 / 21	4.4	4,567.4	35,757	158.0	−0.6
Mexico	107,029,000	75 / 25	3.6	768.4	7,298	17.4	4.0
Philippines	84,765,000	48 / 52	8.7	98.4	1,168	72.3	7.6
Vietnam	83,305,000	26 / 74	2.4	51.4	618	48.2	8.2
Germany	82,490,000	88 / 12	11.7	2,791.7	33,854	67.3	2.0
Egypt	74,033,000	43 / 57	9.5	89.5	1,265	104.7	11.4
Ethiopia	77,431,000	15 / 85	no data	11.2	153	no data	6.8
Turkey	72,907,000	65 / 35	10.2	362.5	5,062	68.0	8.2
Iran	69,515,000	67 / 33	11.2	192.3	2,767	28.9	12.1
Thailand	65,002,000	31 / 69	1.8	173.1	2,659	47.6	4.5
France	60,742,000	76 / 24	9.9	2,126.7	33,918	66.2	1.9

Sources: International Monetary Func, Population Reference Bureau,
U.S. Central Intelligence Agency; data from 2005 and earlier

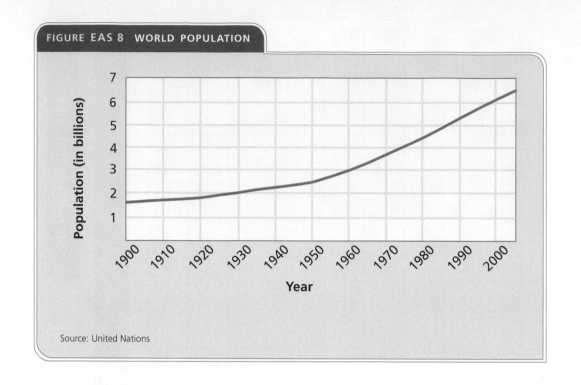

FIGURE EAS 8 WORLD POPULATION

Source: United Nations

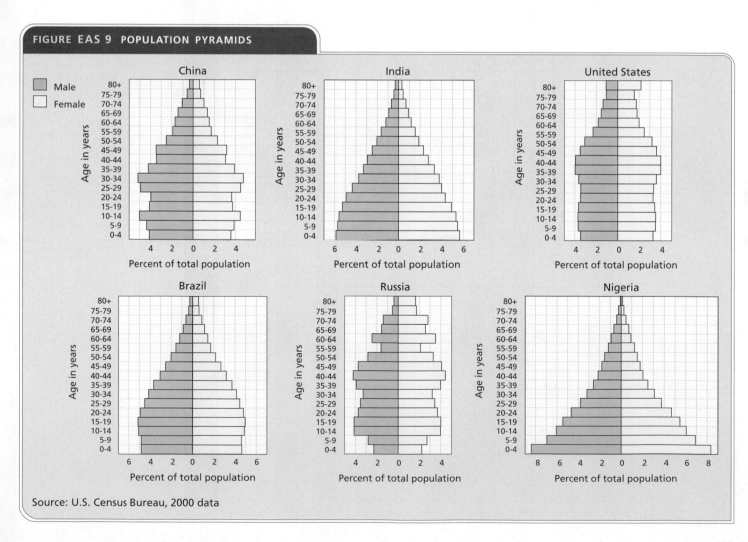

FIGURE EAS 9 POPULATION PYRAMIDS

Male
Female

China

India

United States

Brazil

Russia

Nigeria

Source: U.S. Census Bureau, 2000 data

STRATEGIES FOR TAKING STANDARDIZED TESTS

This section of the textbook helps you develop and practice the skills you need to study economics and to take standardized tests. Part 1, **Strategies for Studying Economics,** takes you through the features of the textbook and offers suggestions on how to use these features to improve your reading and study skills.

Part 2, **Test-Taking Strategies and Practice,** offers specific strategies for tackling many of the items you will find on a standardized test. It gives tips for answering multiple-choice and extended-response questions. In addition, it offers guidelines for analyzing charts and line, bar, and pie graphs that often accompany these questions. Each strategy is followed by a set of questions you can use for practice.

CONTENTS for Strategies for Taking Standardized Tests

Part 1: Strategies for Studying Economics

Reading is the central skill in the effective study of economics or any other subject. You can improve your reading skills by using helpful techniques and by practicing. The better your reading skills, the more you will understand what you read. Below you will find several strategies that involve built-in features of *Economics: Choices and Concepts.* Careful use of these strategies will help you learn and understand economics more effectively.

Preview Chapters Before You Read

Each chapter begins with a two-page chapter opener. Study these pages to help you get ready to read.

1 Read the chapter title and section titles for clues to what will be covered in the chapter.

2 Read the **Concept Review,** which reviews previous learning important to understanding chapter content. Then study the **Key Concept,** which focuses on the main idea explored in the chapter. Finally, read the **Why the Concept Matters** explanation and question. These help place the chapter's main idea in a real-world context.

3 Study the chapter-opening photograph and caption. These provide a visual illustration of the chapter's main idea.

Microeconomics
Unit 2
Market Economies at Work

CHAPTER

4 **1**

Demand

SECTION 1
What Is Demand?

SECTION 2
What Factors Affect Demand?

SECTION 3
What Is Elasticity of Demand?

CASE STUDY
Fueling Automobile Demand

CONCEPT REVIEW **2**

Microeconomics is the study of the economic behaviors and decisions of small units, such as individuals and businesses.

CHAPTER 4 KEY CONCEPT

Demand is the willingness to buy a good or service and the ability to pay for it.

WHY THE CONCEPT MATTERS

The concept of demand is demonstrated every time you buy something. List the last five goods or services that you purchased. Rate each one with a number from 1 (not important to you) to 4 (very important). Which of the goods or services would you stop buying if the price rose sharply? Describe the relationship between your ratings and your willingness to buy at a higher price.

Online Highlights
More at ClassZone.com

Economics Update
Go to **ECONOMICS UPDATE** for chapter updates and current news on demand in the automobile industry. (See Case Study, pages 124–125.) ▶

Animated Economics
Go to **ANIMATED ECONOMICS** for interactive lessons on the graphs and tables in this chapter.

Interactive Review
Go to **INTERACTIVE REVIEW** for concept review and activities.

What caused more people to demand hybrid cars? See the Case Study on pages 124–125.

3 Demand
This computer store customer meets the two requirements of demand—the customer is willing to buy and is able to pay.

96

Demand 97

Preview Sections Before You Read

Each chapter consists of three or four sections. These sections explain and build on the **Key Concept.** Use the section openers to help you prepare to read.

1 Study the information under **Objectives.** This bulleted list tells you the key points discussed in the material you are about to read.

2 Preview the **Key Terms** list. This list identifies the vocabulary you will need to learn in order to understand the material you are about to read. Use the **Taking Notes** graphic to help you organize information presented in the text.

3 Notice the structure of the section. **Blue** heads label the major topics; **red** subheads signal smaller topics within a major topic or illustrative examples of the major topic. Together, these heads provide you with a quick outline of the section.

4 Read the first paragraph under **Key Concepts.** This links the content of the section to previous chapters or sections.

KEY TERMS

demand, *p. 98*
law of demand, *p. 99*
demand schedule,
market demand

STRATEGIES FOR TAKING STANDARDIZED TESTS

Use Active Reading Strategies As You Read

Now you are ready to read the chapter. Read one section at a time, from beginning to end.

1 Read to build your economic vocabulary. Use the marginal **Quick Reference** notes to reinforce your understanding of key economic terms.

2 Use special features and illustrations to reinforce and extend your understanding of content and to apply your knowledge. Study features such as Your Economic Choices, which applies economic concepts to a real-world situation. Look closely at the **figures,** which illustrate economic concepts in table, chart, or graph form. Answer the accompanying **Analyze** questions to test your understanding of the visual and the concept it illustrates.

3 At natural breaks in the section, ask yourself questions about what you have just read. Look for **APPLICATION** headings at the bottom of pages and answer the questions or complete the activities. These provide you with opportunities to apply the knowledge you have gained from your reading.

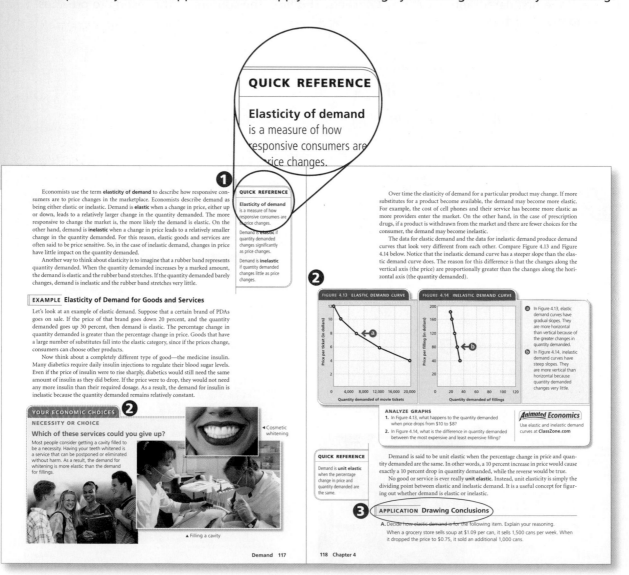

QUICK REFERENCE

Elasticity of demand
is a measure of how responsive consumers are to price changes.

Economists use the term **elasticity of demand** to describe how responsive consumers are to price changes in the marketplace. Economists describe demand as being either elastic or inelastic. Demand is **elastic** when a change in price, either up or down, leads to a relatively larger change in the quantity demanded. The more responsive to change the market is, the more likely the demand is elastic. On the other hand, demand is **inelastic** when a change in price leads to a relatively smaller change in the quantity demanded. For this reason, elastic goods and services are often said to be price sensitive. So, in the case of inelastic demand, changes in price have little impact on the quantity demanded.

Another way to think about elasticity is to imagine that a rubber band represents quantity demanded. When the quantity demanded increases by a marked amount, the demand is elastic and the rubber band stretches. If the quantity demanded barely changes, demand is inelastic and the rubber band stretches very little.

EXAMPLE Elasticity of Demand for Goods and Services

Let's look at an example of elastic demand. Suppose that a certain brand of PDAs goes on sale. If the price of that brand goes down 20 percent, and the quantity demanded goes up 30 percent, then demand is elastic. The percentage change in quantity demanded is greater than the percentage change in price. Goods that have a large number of substitutes fall into the elastic category, since if the prices change, consumers can choose other products.

Now think about a completely different type of good—the medicine insulin. Many diabetics require daily insulin injections to regulate their blood sugar levels. Even if the price of insulin were to rise sharply, diabetics would still need the same amount of insulin as they did before. If the price were to drop, they would not need any more insulin than their required dosage. As a result, the demand for insulin is inelastic because the quantity demanded remains relatively constant.

QUICK REFERENCE

Elasticity of demand
is a measure of how responsive consumers are to price changes.

Demand is **elastic** if quantity demanded changes significantly as price changes.

Demand is **inelastic** if quantity demanded changes little as price changes.

YOUR ECONOMIC CHOICES

NECESSITY OR CHOICE

Which of these services could you give up?

Most people consider getting a cavity filled to be a necessity. Having your teeth whitened is a service that can be postponed or eliminated without harm. As a result, the demand for whitening is more elastic than the demand for fillings.

◄ Cosmetic whitening

▲ Filling a cavity

Demand **117**

Over time the elasticity of demand for a particular product may change. If more substitutes for a product become available, the demand may become more elastic. For example, the cost of cell phones and their service has become more elastic as more providers enter the market. On the other hand, in the case of prescription drugs, if a product is withdrawn from the market and there are fewer choices for the consumer, the demand may become inelastic.

The data for elastic demand and the data for inelastic demand produce demand curves that look very different from each other. Compare Figure 4.13 and Figure 4.14 below. Notice that the inelastic demand curve has a steeper slope than the elastic demand curve does. The reason for this difference is that the changes along the vertical axis (the price) are proportionally greater than the changes along the horizontal axis (the quantity demanded).

FIGURE 4.13 ELASTIC DEMAND CURVE

Price per ticket (in dollars) vs. Quantity demanded of movie tickets

FIGURE 4.14 INELASTIC DEMAND CURVE

Price per filling (in dollars) vs. Quantity demanded of fillings

a In Figure 4.13, elastic demand curves have gradual slopes. They are more horizontal than vertical because of the greater changes in quantity demanded.

b In Figure 4.14, inelastic demand curves have steep slopes. They are more vertical than horizontal because quantity demanded changes very little.

ANALYZE GRAPHS
1. In Figure 4.13, what happens to the quantity demanded when price drops from $10 to $8?
2. In Figure 4.14, what is the difference in quantity demanded between the most expensive and least expensive filling?

Animated Economics
Use elastic and inelastic demand curves at ClassZone.com

QUICK REFERENCE

Demand is **unit elastic** when the percentage change in price and quantity demanded are the same.

Demand is said to be unit elastic when the percentage change in price and quantity demanded are the same. In other words, a 10 percent increase in price would cause exactly a 10 percent drop in quantity demanded, while the reverse would be true.

No good or service is ever really **unit elastic**. Instead, unit elasticity is simply the dividing point between elastic and inelastic demand. It is a useful concept for figuring out whether demand is elastic or inelastic.

3 **APPLICATION Drawing Conclusions**

A. Decide how elastic demand is for the following item. Explain your reasoning.

When a grocery store sells soup at $1.09 per can, it sells 1,500 cans per week. When it dropped the price to $0.75, it sold an additional 1,000 cans.

118 Chapter 4

Review and Summarize What You Have Read

When you finish reading a section, review and summarize what you've read. If necessary, go back and reread information that was not clear the first time through.

1 Look again at the **blue** heads and **red** heads for a quick summary of the major points covered in the section.

2 Study any tables, charts, graphs, and photographs in the section. These visual materials often convey economic information in condensed form.

3 Complete all the questions in the **Section Assessment.** This will help you think critically about the material you have just read.

1 Total Revenue Test

KEY CONCEPTS

QUICK REFERENCE

Total revenue is a company's income from selling its products.

Total revenue test is a method of measuring elasticity by comparing total revenues.

Businesses need to know about elasticity of demand because it influences the amount of revenue they will earn. Economists measure elasticity of demand by calculating a seller's **total revenue**, the amount of money a company receives for selling its products. Total revenue is calculated using the following formula, in which P is the price and Q is the quantity sold: **TOTAL REVENUE = P × Q.**

You can measure elasticity by comparing the total revenue a business would receive when offering its product at various prices. This method is the **total revenue test.**

If total revenue increases after the price of a product drops, then demand for that product is considered elastic. Why? Because even though the seller makes less on each unit sold, the quantity demanded has increased enough to make up for the lower price. For example, if a hot dog stand sells 100 hot dogs for $2.50 each, the total revenue is $250 for the day. However, if the price of hot dogs drops to $2.00 each and 150 are sold, the total revenue for the day will be $300. The demand is elastic.

But if the total revenue decreases after the price is lowered, demand is considered inelastic. If the hot dog stand lowers its price to $1.00 each and sells 200 hot dogs, it makes $200 in total revenue. Clearly, the price reduction has caused only a modest increase in quantities sold, which is not enough to compensate for lower revenues.

1 EXAMPLE Revenue Table

Let's look at an example of demand for movie tickets. In Figure 4.17, you can see how total revenues show whether demand is elastic or inelastic.

FIGURE 4.17 MOVIE TICKET REVENUE TABLE

Price of a Movie Ticket ($)	Quantity Demanded per Month	Total Revenue ($)
12	1,000	12,000
a→ 10	2,000	20,000
b→ 8	6,000	48,000
6	12,000	72,000
4	20,000	80,000

a At $10 a ticket, the quantity demanded is 2,000. Total revenue is $20,000.

b When the price drops to $8, the quantity demanded rises to 6,000. Total revenue rises to $48,000. So, demand is elastic.

ANALYZE TABLES
When the price range changes from $8 to $6, is demand elastic or inelastic? Explain.

APPLICATION Creating Tables

D. Use the information from Figure 4.14 to estimate prices to make a total revenue table.

122 Chapter 4

SECTION 3 Assessment

Online Quiz
ClassZone.com

3 REVIEWING KEY CONCEPTS

1. Use each of the terms below in a sentence that gives an example of the term:
   a. *elastic*   **b.** *inelastic*   **c.** *total revenue*

2. How is total revenue related to elasticity of demand?

3. Why are elastic goods and services said to be price sensitive?

4. What are the factors that affect elasticity of demand and how does each affect elasticity?

5. Analyze the factors that determine elasticity to explain why utilities companies never offer sale prices on their services.

6. **Using Your Notes** How does the concept of unit elasticity relate to the concepts of elasticity and inelasticity? Refer to your completed cluster diagram.
   Use the Graphic Organizer at **Interactive Review @ ClassZone.com**

[elasticity of demand]

CRITICAL THINKING

7. **Analyzing Causes** In early 2004, news articles reported that prescription drug prices were rising almost three times faster than the prices of other products. Identify the factors that explain why the drug companies were able to raise prices so sharply.

8. **Analyzing Data** In June, Snead's Snack Bar sold 1,000 fruit smoothies at a price of $2.50 each. In July, they sold 1,300 fruit smoothies at a price of $2.00. Is the demand for fruit smoothies elastic or inelastic? Use the formula on page 121 to decide. Show the math calculations to support your answer.

9. **Applying Economic Concepts** Suppose the company that runs concession stands at a local sports arena wants to increase revenue on sales of soft drinks. The manager believes the only solution is to charge higher prices. As a business consultant, what advice would you give the manager? Use economic thinking to support your answer.

10. **Challenge** You learned in this section that no product ever has demand that is unit elastic. What possible reasons can you give for that? Draw on what you know about utility, demand, and elasticity as you formulate your answer.

ECONOMICS IN PRACTICE

Calculating Elasticity
Determine the elasticity of bottled water by calculating elasticity and using the revenue table below. Use the information on pages 121 and 122 to help you.

Number of Bottles Sold	Price ($)
35	2.00
75	1.50
100	1.25
120	1.00

Write a Summary After you have determined whether bottled water is elastic or inelastic, think about what factors affect the demand for bottled water. Write a summary of your conclusions explaining whether demand is elastic or inelastic and why, and what factors affect the elasticity of water.

Challenge What effect might the introduction of a new energy drink have on the demand for bottled water? Use economic thinking to support your answer.

Demand 123

STRATEGIES FOR TAKING STANDARDIZED TESTS

Part 2: Test-Taking Strategies and Practice

You can improve your test-taking skills by practicing the strategies discussed in this section. First, read the tips on the left-hand page. Then apply them to the practice items on the right-hand page.

Multiple Choice

1 Read the stem carefully and try to answer the question or complete the sentence before looking at the alternatives.

2 Look for key words and facts in a question. They may direct you to the correct answer.

3 Read each alternative with the stem. Don't make your final decision on the correct answer until you have read all of the alternatives.

4 Eliminate alternatives that you know are wrong.

5 Look for modifiers to help you rule out incorrect alternatives.

6 Carefully consider questions that include *all of the above* as an alternative.

7 Take great care with questions that are stated negatively.

1 | stem

1. The country with the (most) elements of a command economy is

2 *Most* is a key word. China has some elements of a command economy but North Korea has more.

3 | alternatives

A. China
B. North Korea
C. South Korea
D. Japan

4 You can eliminate **D** if you remember that Japan has a market economy.

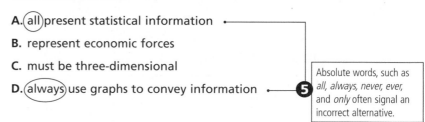

2. Economic models

A. (all) present statistical information
B. represent economic forces
C. must be three-dimensional
D. (always) use graphs to convey information

5 Absolute words, such as *all, always, never, ever,* and *only* often signal an incorrect alternative.

3. Which of these statements about Adam Smith is correct?

A. He is considered to be the founder of modern economics.
B. He was an economic advisor at the Versailles peace conference.
C. He endorsed the trickle-down theory of economics.
D. All of the above.

6 If you select this answer, be sure that all of the alternatives are correct.

4. Which of the following is (not) a factor of production?

A. land
B. labor
C. services
D. capital

7 Eliminate incorrect alternatives by identifying those that are factors of production.

answers: 1 (B), 2 (B), 3 (D), 4 (C)

Directions: Read each question carefully and choose the best answer from the four alternatives.

1. Which of the following is *not* a type of business consolidation?

   A. vertical merger

   B. franchise

   C. conglomerate

   D. multinational corporation

2. Wage rates are influenced by

   A. supply and demand

   B. discrimination

   C. government actions

   D. all of the above

3. As of 2005, the euro had been adopted by

   A. the United Kingdom

   B. all the European countries

   C. some European countries

   D. every member of the European Union

4. The central bank of the United States

   A. has no cash reserves

   B. is the U.S. Treasury

   C. does not lend money

   D. was established by the Federal Reserve Act

STRATEGIES FOR TAKING STANDARDIZED TESTS

Charts

Charts present information in a visual form. Economics textbooks use several types of charts, including tables, flow charts, Venn diagrams, circular flow charts, and infographics. The chart most commonly found in standardized tests, however, is the table. This organizes information in columns and rows for easy viewing.

1 Read the title and identify the broad subject of the chart.

2 Read the column and row headings and any other labels. These will provide more details about the subject of the chart.

3 Note how the information in the chart is organized.

4 Compare and contrast the information from column to column and row to row.

5 Try to draw conclusions from the information in the chart.

6 Read the questions and then study the chart again.

1 | **Gross Domestic Product (GDP)—Percentage Change Over Previous Year—for Selected Countries** | | |
| --- | --- | --- |
| Country | 2002 | 2003 |
| Canada | 3.4 | 2.0 |
| France | 1.1 | 0.5 |
| Germany | 0.1 | -0.1 |
| Italy | 0.4 | 0.3 |
| Japan | -0.3 | 2.5 |
| United Kingdom | 1.8 | 2.2 |
| United States | 1.9 | 3.0 |

Source: *Historical Statistics of the United States*

4 Notice that the rows contain both positive and negative numbers.

3 This chart organizes the countries alphabetically. In some charts, information is organized according to years or the value of the numbers displayed.

5 Think about what trend or trends the data indicates.

6

1. The country that had the greatest percentage change in GDP in 2003 was

A. the United States

B. the United Kingdom

C. Japan

D. Canada

2. In 2002, which country experienced a decline in GDP?

A. France

B. Italy

C. Germany

D. Japan

answers: 1 (A), 2 (D)

PRACTICE

Directions: Use the chart and your knowledge of economics to answer questions 1 through 4.

Refined Copper Production for Selected Countries (in thousands of metric tons)						
	North America			South America		
Year	Canada	Mexico	United States	Brazil	Chile	Peru
1986	493.4	72.3	1,479.9	166.0	783.7	225.6
1987	491.1	128.4	1,541.6	201.7	795.0	224.8
1988	528.7	140.9	1,852.0	185.9	852.9	174.7
1989	515.2	155.8	1,953.8	207.8	1,071.0	224.3
1990	515.8	157.1	2,017.4	201.7	990.8	181.8
1991	538.0	190.1	2,000.0	141.4	1,012.8	244.1
1992	539.3	191.0	2,140.0	158.0	1,242.3	251.1
1993	561.6	197.8	2,250.0	161.1	1,093.2	261.7
1994	527.5	199.5	2,230.0	170.0	1,080.0	253.0
1995	560.0	207.5	2,280.0	165.0	1,288.8	282.0

Source: *2003 Industrial Commodity Statistics Yearbook,* United Nations

1. Which country produced the most refined copper in the years shown?

A. Canada
B. Mexico
C. the United States
D. Chile

2. From 1986 to 1988, Mexico's copper production

A. remained fairly constant
B. nearly doubled
C. decreased slightly
D. almost tripled

3. Which North American country showed an increase in copper production each year from 1987 through 1995?

A. Canada
B. Mexico
C. the United States
D. all of the above

4. Brazil's copper production was greatest in

A. 1995
B. 1994
C. 1990
D. 1989

Line Graphs

Line graphs display information in a visual form. They are particularly useful for showing changes and trends over time.

1 Read the title of the graph to learn what it is about.

2 Study the labels on the vertical and horizontal axes to see the kinds of information presented in the graph. The vertical axis usually shows what is being graphed, while the horizontal axis indicates the time period covered.

3 Review the information in the graph and note any trends or patterns. Look for explanations for these trends or patterns.

4 Carefully read and answer the questions. Note if questions refer to a specific year or time period, or if they focus on trends or explanations for trends.

1 **Nuclear Generation of Electricity in the United States**

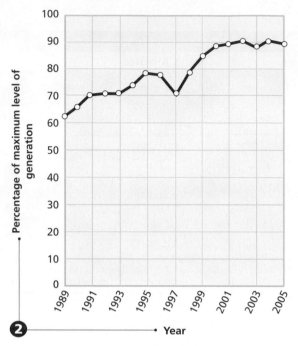

3 One likely explanation for increase in electricity generated is an increase in demand.

Source: U.S. Energy Information Administration

1. Nuclear generation of electricity first exceeded 80 percent of maximum capacity in

   A. 1994

   B. 1995

   C. 1998

   D. 1999

4

2. During which time period did the percentage of maximum capacity increase the most?

   A. 1989–1991

   B. 1993–1995

   C. 1997–1999

   D. 1999–2002

answers: 1 (B), 2 (C)

Directions: Use the graph and your knowledge of economics to answer questions 1 through 4.

Retail Prices for Regular Gasoline

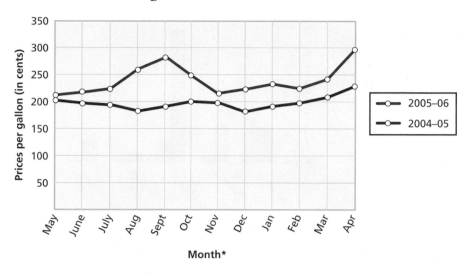

Month*

*Survey taken last week of month

Source: U.S. Energy Information Administration

1. During which period did the price of regular gasoline rise toward its peak?

   A. May–August 2004

   B. November 2004–February 2005

   C. August–November 2005

   D. February–April 2006

2. Which of the following statements most accurately describes the information shown in the graph?

   A. Gas prices were stable during both 12-month periods.

   B. There was a severe spike in price during each 12-month period.

   C. The price of gas was always higher in 2005–2006.

   D. The price of regular gas fluctuated more during 2004–2005.

3. During which period was the price of gasoline lowest?

   A. in December 2004

   B. in December 2005

   C. in May 2004

   D. in May 2005

4. In 2005–2006, the price of gasoline per gallon

   A. nearly reached $3.00

   B. dropped from close to $3.00 to less than $2.20

   C. fluctuated more than in 2004–2005

   D. all of the above

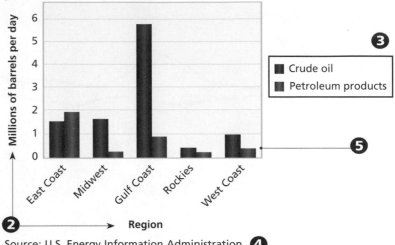

Bar and Pie Graphs

A bar graph allows for comparisons among numbers or sets of numbers. A pie, or circle, graph shows relationships among the parts of a whole. These parts look like slices of a pie. The size of each slice is proportional to the percentage of the whole that it represents.

1 Read the title of the graph to learn what it is about.

2 For a bar graph, study the labels on the vertical and horizontal axes to see the kinds of information presented in the graph. Note the intervals between amounts or years.

3 Study the legend, if there is one. The legend on a bar graph provides information on what is being graphed. The legend on a pie graph shows what each slice of the pie represents.

4 Look at the source line and evaluate the reliability of the information in the graph.

5 Study the data on the graph. Make comparisons among the slices of a pie graph. Draw conclusions and make inferences based on the data.

6 Read the questions carefully and use any words to reject incorrect alternatives.

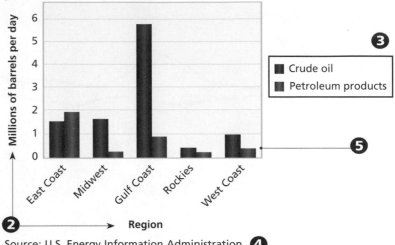

1 **U.S. Imports of Crude Oil and Petroleum Products by Region**

3 Crude oil / Petroleum products

Source: U.S. Energy Information Administration **4**

6 **1.** Which region of the United States imported the most crude oil per day during 2004?

   A. East Coast

   B. West Coast

   C. Gulf Coast

   D. Midwest

1 **Components of M1**

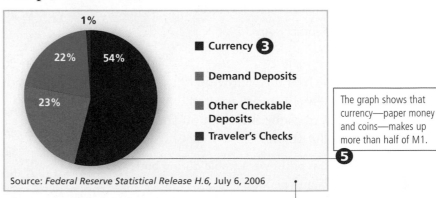

3 Currency

Demand Deposits

Other Checkable Deposits

Traveler's Checks

The graph shows that currency—paper money and coins—makes up more than half of M1. **5**

Source: *Federal Reserve Statistical Release H.6,* July 6, 2006

6 **2.** What is the largest component of M1?

   A. currency

   B. demand deposits

   C. other checkable deposits

   D. traveler's checks

4 Statistics from government agencies, such as the Federal Reserve, tend to be reliable.

answers: 1 (C), 2 (A)

Directions: Use the graphs and your knowledge of economics to answer questions 1 through 4.

New Jobs Added to the U.S. Economy

Source: U.S. Department of Labor

Electricity Generation by Energy Source

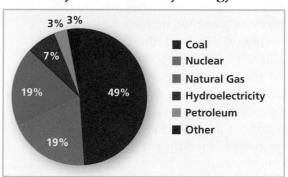

Source: Energy Information Administration, *Electric Power Monthly,* June 2006

1. When was the greatest number of jobs added to the economy?

A. July 2005

B. November 2005

C. February 2006

D. March 2006

2. Which statement is supported by information in the graph?

A. The graph shows that there were greater fluctuations in job creation in the later months of 2005 than there were in the early months of 2006.

B. More jobs were added to the economy in all of 2005 than in all of 2006.

C. The graph shows a steady upward trend in the number of jobs added to the economy.

D. More jobs were added to the economy between January and June of 2006 than between June and December of 2005.

3. Which source of fuel generated nearly half of all electric power?

A. coal

B. natural gas

C. nuclear

D. petroleum

4. Which single source generated the least amount of electricity?

A. coal

B. natural gas

C. nuclear

D. petroleum

STRATEGIES FOR TAKING STANDARDIZED TESTS

Extended Response

Extended-response questions usually focus on an exhibit of some kind—a chart, graph, or diagram, for example. They are more complex than multiple-choice questions and often require a written response.

Some extended-response questions ask you to complete the exhibit. Others require you to present the information in the exhibit in a different form. Still others ask you to write an essay, a report, or some other extended piece of writing. In most standardized tests, exhibits have only one extended-response question.

1 Read the title of the exhibit to get an idea of the subject.

2 Carefully read the extended-response questions. (Question 1 asks you to complete the graph by drawing and labeling a new demand curve. Question 2 asks you to write a brief explanation of what is shown in the completed graph.)

3 Study and analyze the exhibit.

4 If the question requires an extended piece of writing, jot down ideas in outline form to get started.

1 Shifts in Demand

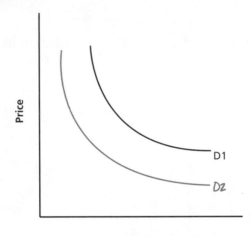

Quantity demanded

2 {
1. The graph above shows the demand for CDs. How would demand for CDs change if the price of CD players rose? Draw a new demand curve to reflect this change. Label the new curve D2.

2. Write a brief explanation of why demand for CDs changed in this way.
}

4 Sample Response CDs and CD players are used together, so they are complements. If demand for one changes, demand for the other will change in the same way. If the price of CD players rises, then demand for CD players and CDs will decrease and the demand curve shifts to the left.

Directions: Use the graph and your knowledge of economics to answer questions 1 and 2.

Shifts in Aggregate Supply

1. The graph above shows an economy at its macroeconomic equilibrium. Copy this graph onto a separate sheet of paper. On the graph, chart how the aggregate supply curve and macroeconomic equilibrium would change if interest rates went up.

2. Write a brief description of these changes and explain why they occurred.

Scarcity and Choices

Economics is about making choices. Even such an ordinary task as deciding what to have for lunch involves economic choice. Should you spend $5 on a hot meal, $3 on a sandwich, or should you save your money and bring lunch from home?

The Economic Way of Thinking

CONCEPT REVIEW

Economics is the study of how individuals and societies satisfy their unlimited wants with limited resources.

CHAPTER 1 KEY CONCEPT

Scarcity is the situation that exists because wants are unlimited and resources are limited.

WHY THE CONCEPT MATTERS

You confront the issue of scarcity constantly in everyday life. Look again at the caption on page 2. Suppose you have $20 to cover the cost of lunches for the week. How will you use your limited funds to meet your wants (lunch for Monday through Friday)? What if you stayed late at school twice a week and bought a $1 snack each day? How would this affect your lunch choices? Identify one or two other examples of scarcity in your everyday life.

Online Highlights
More at ClassZone.com

 Economics Update
Go to **ECONOMICS UPDATE** for chapter updates and current news on the expansion of O'Hare Airport in Chicago. (See Case Study, pp. 32–33.)

 Animated Economics
Go to **ANIMATED ECONOMICS** for interactive lessons on the graphs and tables in this chapter. ▶

Interactive ⟨⟨Review

Go to **INTERACTIVE REVIEW** for concept review and activities.

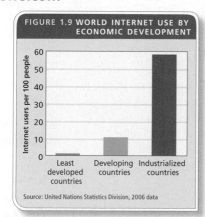

FIGURE 1.9 WORLD INTERNET USE BY ECONOMIC DEVELOPMENT

Source: United Nations Statistics Division, 2006 data

How do economists use graphs? See Section 4 of this chapter.

Scarcity: The Basic Economic Problem

OBJECTIVES	KEY TERMS		TAKING NOTES
In Section 1, you will • explain how the economic definition of scarcity differs from the common definition • understand why scarcity affects everyone • learn three economic questions that societies face because of scarcity • describe the four factors of production and their uses	wants, *p. 4* needs, *p. 4* scarcity, *p. 4* economics, *p. 4* goods, *p. 5* services, *p. 5* consumer, *p. 5* producer, *p. 5* factors of production, *p. 8*	land, *p. 8* labor, *p. 8* capital, *p. 8* entrepreneurship, *p. 9*	As you read Section 1, complete a cluster diagram showing how scarcity is the central concept of economics. Use the Graphic Organizer at **Interactive Review @ ClassZone.com**

What Is Scarcity?

KEY CONCEPTS

QUICK REFERENCE

Wants are desires that can be satisfied by consuming a good or a service.

Needs are things that are necessary for survival.

Scarcity exists when there are not enough resources to satisfy human wants.

Economics is the study of how individuals and societies satisfy their unlimited wants with limited resources.

Have you ever felt you wanted a new cell phone, a car, a new pair of running shoes, or the latest MP3 player? You are not alone. Consumers have many economic wants. **Wants** are desires that can be satisfied by consuming a good or service. When making purchases, people often make a distinction between the things they need and the things they want. Some things that people desire, like a house or an apartment, are more important than other things, like a flat-screen television. **Needs** are things, such as food, clothing, and shelter, that are necessary for survival.

People always want more, no matter how much they have already. In fact, wants are unlimited, but the resources available to satisfy them are limited. The result of this difference is **scarcity**, the situation that exists when there are not enough resources to meet human wants. Scarcity is not a temporary shortage of some desired thing. Rather, it is a fundamental and ongoing tension that confronts individuals, businesses, governments, and societies. Indeed, it is so basic to human experience that a social science has developed to understand and explain it. That social science is **economics**, the study of how people choose to use scarce resources to satisfy their wants. Economics involves

1. **examining** how individuals, businesses, governments, and societies choose to use scarce resources to satisfy their wants
2. **organizing, analyzing, and interpreting data** about those economic behaviors
3. **developing theories and economic laws** that explain how the economy works and to predict what might happen in the future.

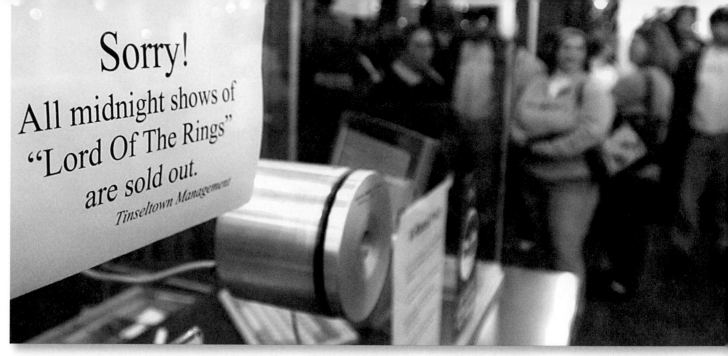

Shortages and Scarcity Shortages often are temporary. Movie tickets may be in short supply today, but in a few days' time they may be easy to come by. Scarcity, however, never ends because wants always exceed the resources available to satisfy them.

PRINCIPLE 1 People Have Wants

Choice is central to the use of scarce resources. People make choices about all the things they desire—both needs and wants. You might think of food as a need, because it is necessary for your survival. Nevertheless, you make choices about food. What do you want for dinner tonight? Will you cook a gourmet creation or heat up a frozen dinner? Or will you treat yourself to a meal at your favorite restaurant? You make choices about other needs too. For example, consider the choices you make about the clothes you wear.

Wants are not only unlimited, they also are ever changing. Twenty-five years ago, for example, few Americans owned a personal computer. Today, however, few Americans can imagine life without computers and computer-related technology.

PRINCIPLE 2 Scarcity Affects Everyone

Because wants are unlimited and resources are scarce, choices have to be made about how best to use these resources. Scarcity, then, affects which goods are made and which services are provided. **Goods** are physical objects that can be purchased, such as food, clothing, and furniture. **Services** are work that one person performs for another for payment. Services include the work of sales clerks, technical support representatives, teachers, nurses, doctors, and lawyers. Scarcity affects the choices of both the **consumer**, a person who buys goods or services for personal use, and the **producer**, a person who makes goods or provides services.

APPLICATION Applying Economic Concepts

A. Identify five wants that you have right now. Describe how scarcity affects your efforts to meet these wants.

Economics Update

Find an update about computer ownership in the United States at **ClassZone.com**

QUICK REFERENCE

Goods are objects, such as food, clothing, and furniture, that can be bought.

Services are work that one person does for another.

A **consumer** is a person who buys or uses goods or services.

A **producer** is a maker of goods or a provider of services.

Scarcity Leads to Three Economic Questions

KEY CONCEPTS

If you have ever had to decide whether something you want is worth the money, then you have experienced scarcity firsthand. Scarcity in the lives of individual consumers—the gap between their unlimited wants and limited resources—is all too easy to understand. Scarcity, however, also confronts producers and whole societies. Indeed, scarcity requires every society to address three basic economic questions: What will be produced? How will it be produced? For whom will it be produced?

QUESTION 1 What Will Be Produced?

To answer the first fundamental economic question, a society must decide the mix of goods and services it will produce. Will it produce mainly food, or will it also produce automobiles, televisions, computers, furniture, and shoes? The goods and services a society chooses to produce depend, in part, on the natural resources it possesses. For example, a country that does not possess oil is unlikely to choose to produce petroleum products. Resources, however, do not completely control what a country produces. Japan does not possess large amounts of the iron ore needed to make steel. Yet Japan is a leading producer of automobiles, whose construction requires a great deal of steel.

What to Produce The availability of natural resources, such as gold in South Africa, influences what a country produces.

Some countries, including the United States, resolve the issue of what goods and services to produce by allowing producers and consumers to decide. For example, if consumers want cars with automatic transmissions, automobile companies would be unwise to make only cars that have manual transmissions. In other countries—Cuba and North Korea, for example—the consumer plays little or no part in answering this question. Rather, the government decides what goods and services will be produced.

This first fundamental economic question involves not only what to produce, but also how much to produce. To answer this, societies must review what their wants are at any time. A country at war, for example, will choose to produce more weapons than it would during peacetime.

How to Produce For some societies, using a large amount of human labor is the most efficient way to produce food (left). For other societies, using a lot of machinery is a more efficient method of production (right).

QUESTION 2 How Will It Be Produced?

Once a society has decided what it will produce, it must then decide how these goods and services will be produced. Answering this second question involves using scarce resources in the most efficient way to satisfy society's wants. Again, decisions on methods of production are influenced, in part, by the natural resources a society possesses.

In deciding how to grow crops, for example, societies adopt different approaches. Societies with a large, relatively unskilled labor force might adopt labor-intensive farming methods. For this society, using many workers and few machines is the most efficient way to farm. The United States, however, has a highly skilled work force. So, using labor-intensive methods would be an inefficient use of labor resources. Therefore, the United States takes a capital-intensive approach to farming. In other words, it uses lots of machinery and few workers.

QUESTION 3 For Whom Will It Be Produced?

The third fundamental economic question involves how goods and services are distributed among people in society. This actually involves two questions. Exactly how much should people get and how should their share be delivered to them?

Should everyone get an equal share of the goods and services? Or should a person's share be determined by how much he or she is willing to pay? Once the question of how much has been decided, societies must then decide exactly how they are going to get these goods and services to people. To do this, societies develop distribution systems, which include road and rail systems, seaports, airports, trucks, trains, ships, airplanes, computer networks—anything that helps move goods and services from producers to consumers in an efficient manner.

APPLICATION Analyzing Cause and Effect

B. Why does the basic problem of scarcity lead societies to ask the three fundamental economic questions?

The Factors of Production

KEY CONCEPTS

To understand how societies answer the first two basic questions—what to produce and how to produce it—economists have identified the **factors of production**, or the economic resources needed to produce goods and services. They divide the factors of production into four broad categories: land, labor, capital, and entrepreneurship. All of these factors have one thing in common—their supply is limited.

FACTOR 1 Land

In everyday terms, the word *land* usually refers to a stretch of ground on the earth's surface. In economic terms, however, **land** includes all the natural resources found on or under the ground that are used to produce goods and services. Water, forests, and all kinds of wildlife belong in the category of land. So, too, do buried deposits of minerals, gas, and oil.

FACTOR 2 Labor

The word *labor* usually brings to mind images of hard physical work. In economic terms, however, its meaning is far broader. **Labor** is all the human time, effort, and talent that go into the making of products. Labor, then, is not only the work done by garbage collectors, factory workers, and construction workers. It also includes the work of architects, teachers, doctors, sales clerks, and government officials.

FACTOR 3 Capital

When you hear the word *capital,* you probably think of money. In economic terms, however, **capital** is all the resources made and used by people to produce and distribute goods and services. Tools, machinery, and factories are all forms of capital. So are offices, warehouses, stores, roads, and airplanes. In other words, capital is all of a producer's physical resources. For this reason capital is sometimes called physical capital, or real capital.

While businesses invest in real capital, workers invest in human capital—the knowledge and skills gained through experience. Human capital includes such things as a college degree or good job training. When workers possess more human capital, they are more productive.

Human Capital Education increases your human capital and makes you more productive in the workplace.

ECONOMICS ESSENTIALS

FIGURE 1.1 Factors of Production

Land All the natural resources found on or under the ground that are used to produce goods and services are considered land.

Labor All the human time, effort, and talent that go into the production of goods and services are considered labor.

What are the Factors of Production?

Entrepreneurship The combination of vision, skill, ingenuity, and willingness to take risks that is needed to create and run new businesses is called entrepreneurship.

Capital All the physical resources made and used by people to produce and distribute goods and services are considered capital. So, too, are the knowledge and skills that make workers more productive.

ANALYZE CHARTS
Two new businesses have opened in your neighborhood—a coffee bar called Lou's Café and a health club called BodyPower. Construct your own Economics Essentials diagram to show how the four factors of production are used in one of these businesses.

FACTOR 4 Entrepreneurship

The fourth factor of production, entrepreneurship, brings the other three factors together. **Entrepreneurship** is the combination of vision, skill, ingenuity, and willingness to take risks that is needed to create and run new businesses. Most entrepreneurs are innovators. They try to anticipate the wants of consumers and then satisfy these wants in new ways. This may involve developing a new product, method of production, or way of marketing or distributing products. Entrepreneurs are also risk takers. They risk their time, energy, creativity, and money in the hope of making a profit. The entrepreneurs who build a massive shopping mall or who open a new health club do so because they think they could profit from these business ventures. The risk they take is that these enterprises might fail.

> **QUICK REFERENCE**
>
> **Entrepreneurship** involves the vision, skills, and risk-taking needed to create and run businesses.

APPLICATION Applying Economic Concepts

C. Think of a product that you recently purchased. How do you think the four factors of production were used to create this product?

For more on cause and effect, see the Skillbuilder Handbook, page R20.

Analyzing Cause and Effect

Causes are the events that explain why something happens and **effects** are what happens. An effect can become the cause of other effects, resulting in a chain of events or conditions. Identifying causes and effects helps economists understand how economic conditions occur. Use the strategies below to help you identify causes and effects using a graphic organizer.

Identify causes by using the word *why* to formulate questions about the topic of the passage. Example: *Why did oil become more scarce in 2003? Why did this situation continue?* The answers you find will be the causes.

Turmoil Reduces Oil Supply

Oil is a scarce resource, but events in the Middle East have made it more so. The invasion of Iraq in 2003 by U.S.- and British-led coalition forces led to an almost immediate shutdown of Iraq's oil exports, thereby reducing the availability of crude oil by some 1.8. million barrels per day. Unrest in Nigeria, Africa's largest oil producer, further added to global scarcity. More than two years later, in part due to continued unrest in the Middle East, oil production was still sluggish. One result of the continued scarcity was a rise in energy prices. Increased energy prices in turn caused shipping costs to rise. The increased costs of shipping led shippers to seek more economical means of transport. Some shippers have decreased their use of planes and trucks. Instead, they have turned to less fuel-dependent modes of transport. One example is the use of double stacked railroad cars that can carry two shipping containers stacked one on top of the other.

Identify effects by looking for results or consequences. These are sometimes indicated by words such as *led to, brought about, thereby,* and *as a result.*

Look for cause-effect chains, where an effect may be the cause of another event and so on.

Diagram the causes and effects in a flowchart like this one.

THINKING ECONOMICALLY Analyzing Causes and Effects

Locate and read an economics-related article in a current affairs magazine, such as *Time, Newsweek,* or *U.S. News & World Report.* Make a diagram to summarize the causes and effects discussed in the article.

Online Quiz
ClassZone.com

REVIEWING KEY CONCEPTS

ECONOMICS IN PRACTICE

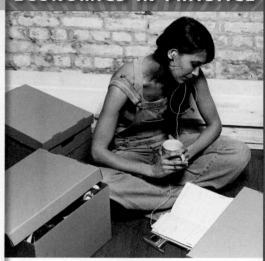

1. Explain the relationship between the terms in each of these pairs:

   a. *wants*   **b.** *consumer*   **c.** *factors of production*
      scarcity   *producer*   *entrepreneurship*

2. What is the difference between needs and wants? Explain how a need may also be a want.

3. How does scarcity affect consumers? Producers?

4. What services that individuals or businesses provide do you use every day?

5. Describe how the owners of a computer repair store might use the four factors of production to run their business.

6. **Using Your Notes** How does scarcity affect methods of production? Refer to your completed cluster diagram.

   Use the Graphic Organizer at **Interactive Review @ ClassZone.com**

CRITICAL THINKING

7. **Drawing Conclusions** Many high schools throughout the United States have faced a serious shortage of math and science teachers. Many prospective teachers choose to go into business and industry because of higher salaries. In some communities, businesses are "loaning" employees who want to teach part-time to schools to fill the math and science teacher gap. Does this scenario illustrate scarcity? Why or why not?

8. **Applying Economic Concepts** Consider the following entrepreneurs: Lucy, who runs an organic farm, and Ron, a sports superstar who owns several restaurants. Describe how they may have used entrepreneurship to establish and run their businesses.

9. **Writing About Economics** Select a 10-minute period of time in your day-to-day life—when you are in the cafeteria at lunchtime, for example. Analyze how scarcity affects your activities during this time period. Write your analysis in a paragraph.

10. **Challenge** At one time or another, you have probably made a choice about how to use your scarce resources that you later regretted. For example, you may have purchased a music download instead of going to the movies. What led you to your choice? What did you learn later that might have led you to a different choice?

Using Scarce Resources
Suppose you are moving into your first apartment like the young woman above. You have saved $1,200 to use for this purpose. When you go shopping, you learn that these are the prices for things you had on your list of furnishings.

Item	Price ($)
Kitchen table and chairs	200
TV set	150
Dishes	45
Silverware	25
Towels	35
Couch	300
Desk & chair	175
Bed	350
Computer	400
Stereo system	300

Make Economic Choices Use these prices to decide how you will spend your budget for furnishings. Make a list of the things you will buy.

Challenge What did you have to give up to get the things you chose? Why did you decide to give those things up?

Economic Choice Today: Opportunity Cost

OBJECTIVES	KEY TERMS	TAKING NOTES
In Section 2, you will • understand why choice is at the heart of economics • explain how incentives and utility influence people's economic choices • consider the role of trade-offs and opportunity costs in making economic choices • demonstrate how to do a cost-benefit analysis	incentives, *p. 12* utility, *p. 12* economize, *p. 12* trade-off, *p. 14* opportunity cost, *p. 14* cost-benefit analysis, *p. 15* marginal cost, *p. 16* marginal benefit, *p. 16*	As you read Section 2, complete a cluster diagram to help you see how the key concepts relate to one another. Use the Graphic Organizer at **Interactive Review @ ClassZone.com** Economic Choice

Making Choices

KEY CONCEPTS

QUICK REFERENCE

Incentives are methods used to encourage people to take certain actions.

Utility is the benefit or satisfaction received from using a good or service.

To **economize** means to make decisions according to the best combination of costs and benefits.

As you recall from Section 1, scarcity forces everyone to choose. But what shapes the economic choices that people make? One factor involves **incentives**, or benefits offered to encourage people to act in certain ways. Grades in school, wages paid to workers, and praise or recognition earned in personal and public life are all incentives. Choice is also influenced by **utility**, or the benefit or satisfaction gained from the use of a good or service. When they economize, people consider both incentives and utility. In common usage, the word *economize* means to "cut costs" or "do something cheaply." In strict economic terms, however, **economize** means to "make decisions according to what you believe is the best combination of costs and benefits."

Incentives The chance of winning a championship trophy serves as an incentive for athletes to train and play hard.

YOUR ECONOMIC CHOICES

MAKING CHOICES

How will you spend time with a friend?

You and a friend have the choice of going to dinner or going to a movie. There is an incentive for choosing the movies, since dinner would surely cost more. On the other hand, your friend has offered to help you with college applications. So dining out, which allows time for conversation, has more utility to you than seeing a movie.

Dinner

Movie

FACTOR 1 Motivations for Choice

Choice powers an economy, but what powers choice? The choices people make are shaped by incentives, by expected utility, and by the desire to economize. For example, look at Your Economic Choices above. How will you decide between the two options? Like other economic decision makers, you weigh the costs against the benefits, and you make your choice purposefully. Perhaps you decide to go out to dinner. Even though you'll spend more money, you feel that the tips your friend can give you on writing your college application essay are invaluable. You've economized by choosing what represents the best mix of costs and benefits.

In making this decision, you were guided by self-interest. This does not mean that you behaved selfishly. Rather, it simply means that you looked for ways to maximize the utility you'd get from spending time with your friend.

FACTOR 2 No Free Lunch

An old saying can sum up the issue of choice in economics: "There is no such thing as a free lunch." Every choice involves costs. These costs can take the form of money, time, or some other thing you value. Let's revisit your choices. If you chose to go to dinner rather than to a movie, you gained the benefit of a satisfying, informative, and beneficial conversation with a friend. Even so, you also paid a cost—you didn't see the movie. On the other hand, if you chose to go to the movie, you gained the benefit of an entertaining evening and having more money to save or spend on something else. Once again, however, your choice involved a cost. You sacrificed the time you could have spent getting advice and guidance on the college application process from your friend.

everything has a cost:
- money
- consequence
- time
- values

APPLICATION Using a Decision-Making Process

A. You have enough money to buy either an MP3 player that is on sale or some fitness equipment you want. What incentives and utility would guide your decision?

The Economic Way of Thinking 13

Trade-Offs and Opportunity Cost

QUICK REFERENCE

A **trade-off** is the alternative people give up when they make choices.

KEY CONCEPTS

Choices, as you have learned, always involve costs. For every choice you make, you give up something. The alternative that you give up when you make an economic choice is called a **trade-off**. Usually, trade-offs do not require all-or-nothing choices. Rather, they involve giving up some of one thing to gain more of another.

EXAMPLE 1 Making Trade-Offs

To understand how trade-offs work, let's take a look at decisions made by Shanti, who has just finished her junior year in high school. Shanti wants to go to summer school to earn some credits she can apply to college. She could take a semester-long course at a local university, or she could take an intensive six-week course at her high school. She decides on the six-week course, even though she'll earn fewer credits. However, she will have several weeks of the summer vacation to have fun and relax.

Trade-Offs All the decisions you make, including selecting school or college courses, involve choosing among alternatives.

EXAMPLE 2 Counting the Opportunity Cost

Shanti's friend Dan, who has just graduated, has decided to take off a year before going to college. He's been offered a full-time job for the whole year. However, he decides to take the job for six months and then spend time traveling.

Dan's choice, like all economic choices, involves an opportunity cost. The **opportunity cost** of a decision is the value of the next-best alternative, or what you give up by choosing one alternative over another. Dan decided to travel around the country and visit friends. The opportunity cost of that decision is the income he could have earned at his job. If, however, Dan had decided to work for the whole year, his opportunity cost would have been the trip around the country that he didn't take. Note that Dan's opportunity cost is not the value of all the things he might have done. Rather, it is the value of his next-best alternative, or what he gave up to get what he most wanted.

QUICK REFERENCE

Opportunity cost is the value of something that is given up to get something else that is wanted.

APPLICATION Applying Economic Concepts

B. Look again at Shanti's decision. What was the opportunity cost of her choice? If she had chosen the semester course, what would her opportunity cost have been?

Analyzing Choices

KEY CONCEPTS

Shanti and Dan did not make their choices randomly. Rather, they carefully looked at the benefits they would gain and the opportunity costs they would incur from their decisions. This practice of examining the costs and the expected benefits of a choice as an aid to decision making is called **cost-benefit analysis**. Cost-benefit analysis is one of the most useful tools for individuals, businesses, and governments when they need to evaluate the relative worth of economic choices.

QUICK REFERENCE

Cost-benefit analysis is an approach that weighs the benefits of an action against its costs.

EXAMPLE Max's Decision-Making Grid

Perhaps the simplest application of cost-benefit analysis is the decision-making grid, which shows what you get and what you give up when you make choices. Look at Max's decision-making grid in Figure 1.2 below. Max has to decide how to spend his scarce time—studying for his government class or going out with his friends. Max likes nothing better than to spend hours talking with his friends at the local juice bar. However, the F he has in the government class at the moment will not look good on his transcript. So he certainly could benefit from some extra study time.

Max knows that he has six hours available for extra study or socializing each week. He begins to build his decision-making grid by listing all the options he has for using these six hours. He then lists the benefits and opportunity costs of each of these options. After reviewing all of this information, he chooses three extra hours of study a week. He feels that the opportunity cost, three hours of time with his friends, is worth the expected benefit, a B grade.

FIGURE 1.2 Max's Decision-Making Grid

A decision-making grid helps you to see what you gain and what you lose when you make choices. Max's decision-making grid shows the costs and benefits of hours spent studying versus time spent socializing.

Choice	Benefit	Opportunity Cost
One hour of extra study	D in government class	One hour with friends
Two hours of extra study	C in government class	Two hours with friends
Three hours of extra study	B in government class	Three hours with friends
Four hours of extra study	B+ in government class	Four hours with friends
Five hours of extra study	A− in government class	Five hours with friends
Six hours of extra study	A in government class	Six hours with friends

ANALYZE TABLES

1. What is Max's opportunity cost of three extra hours of study?
2. Read the information about marginal costs on the next page. What is Max's marginal cost of moving from a grade of B+ to a grade of A−?

Costs and benefits change over time. So do goals and circumstances. Such changes will influence the decisions people make. For instance, Max learns that Pine Tree State, the college he wants to attend, only considers applicants with a 3.4 or better grade point average. If he needs to get a B+ or better to raise his GPA to 3.4, he might decide to spend less time with his friends and study four or five hours per week rather than three.

EXAMPLE Marginal Costs and Benefits

How did Max arrive at his decision? To explain it, economists would look at marginal costs and marginal benefits. **Marginal cost** is the cost of using one more unit of a good or service, while **marginal benefit** refers to the benefit or satisfaction received from using one more unit of a good or service. Max's choice was to study three extra hours, which gave him a B grade at the opportunity cost of three hours with his friends. Look again at Max's decision-making grid in Figure 1.2. What would be the marginal cost of one more hour of study? As you can see, it is the loss of one more hour with his friends. The marginal benefit of that extra hour would be an improvement in grade from B to B+. Max decided that the benefit of a slight improvement in his grade was not worth the cost of one less hour with his friends.

The analysis of marginal costs and marginal benefits is central to the study of economics. It helps to explain the decisions consumers, producers, and governments make as they try to meet their unlimited wants with limited resources.

YOUR ECONOMIC CHOICES

MARGINAL BENEFITS AND COSTS

Which will you do—basketball practice or after-school job?

For every hour you practice basketball, you gain in skill and increase your chances of making the team. However, each hour you practice is an hour you could have spent working at an after-school job to save for a car or college or something else you want.

Basketball practice   Part-time job

APPLICATION Using a Decision-Making Process

C. Look at Your Economic Choices above. Construct a decision-making grid that analyzes the potential choices of attending basketball practice and working at an after-school job. Which option would you choose?

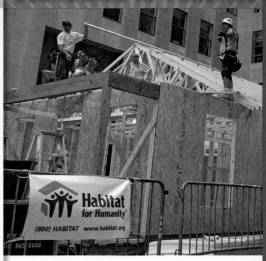
REVIEWING KEY CONCEPTS

1. Explain the relationship between the terms in each of these pairs:

   a. *incentive*
   utility

   b. *trade-off*
   opportunity cost

   c. *marginal cost*
   marginal benefit

2. Two action movies are playing at your movie-theater complex. You have a half-price coupon for one. However, you choose to see the other. How might this still be an example of economizing?

3. Think of some of the options you have for spending time after school—sports practice, hobby clubs, work, or extra study, for example. Which option would you choose? What is the opportunity cost of your choice?

4. How is a decision-making grid an example of cost-benefit analysis?

5. Use the concepts of marginal costs and marginal benefits to explain why some people might see the same movie ten times while others will watch it only once or twice.

6. **Using Your Notes** How do marginal costs and benefits relate to trade-offs? Refer to your completed cluster diagram. Use the Graphic Organizer at **Interactive Review @ ClassZone.com**

Economic Choice

CRITICAL THINKING

7. **Applying Economic Concepts** A Web site reviewing new CDs offers you a free subscription. All you have to do is complete a brief online application. What is the opportunity cost of this "free" offer? Why do you think the offer is being made?

8. **Evaluating Economic Decisions** Explain how self-interest is part of each economic choice. Use an example from your own experience that shows how you purposely served your own self-interest in a choice you made.

9. **Conducting Marginal Cost–Marginal Benefit Analysis** You are on a limited budget and planning a four-day camping trip to a national park. Bus fare is $75 each way and the ride takes 12 hours. Plane fare is $150 each way and the ride takes an hour and a half. Conduct a cost-benefit analysis to help you choose your method of travel.

10. **Challenge** Why are all choices economic choices? Illustrate your answer with examples.

ECONOMICS IN PRACTICE

Making Choices
Some of the incentives that spur people to action are money, recognition, self-esteem, good grades, immediate benefit, future benefit, and altruism (doing good for others, such as working for Habitat for Humanity).

Consider Economic Choices Copy and complete the chart by noting the incentives that might motivate people to take the listed actions. (Several incentives might apply in some cases.)

Action	Incentive
Donate to charity.	
Get a promotion.	
Buy a friend a present.	
Attend a good college.	
Buy organic foods.	
Buy inexpensive imported goods.	

Challenge Have you ever had two or more conflicting incentives for a certain behavior? If so, how would you choose among them? If not, which of the incentives above motivates you most often?

OBJECTIVES	KEY TERMS	TAKING NOTES
In Section 3, you will • describe what a production possibilities curve is and how it is constructed • explain what economists learn from using production possibilities curves • analyze how production possibilities curves show **economic growth**	economic model, *p. 18* production possibilities curve (PPC), *p. 18* efficiency, *p. 20* underutilization, *p. 20* law of increasing opportunity costs, *p. 21*	As you read Section 4, complete a summary chart to identify the most important points on production possibilities. Use the Graphic Organizer at **Interactive Review @ ClassZone.com** **Analyzing Production Possibilities** | PPC	shows impact of scarcity
---	---	

Graphing the Possibilities

QUICK REFERENCE

An **economic model** is a simplified representation of economic forces.

The **production possibilities curve (PPC)** is a graph used by economists to show the impact of scarcity on an economy.

KEY CONCEPTS

In Section 2 you learned that all economic choices involve trade-offs. Economists have created **economic models**—simplified representations of complex economic activities, systems, or problems—to clarify trade-offs. One such model is a **production possibilities curve (PPC)**, a graph used to illustrate the impact of scarcity on an economy by showing the maximum number of goods or services that can be produced using limited resources.

Like all other economic models, the PPC is based on assumptions that simplify the economic interactions. For the PPC these assumptions are:

1. **Resources are fixed.** There is no way to increase the availability of land, labor, capital, and entrepreneurship.

2. **All resources are fully employed.** There is no waste of any of the factors of production. In other words, the economy is running at full production.

3. **Only two things can be produced.** This assumption simplifies the situation and suits the graphic format, with one variable on each axis.

4. **Technology is fixed.** There are no technological breakthroughs to improve methods of production.

Since the curve on a PPC represents the border—or frontier—between what it is possible to produce and what it is not possible to produce, this model is sometimes called a production possibilities frontier. It is a useful tool for businesses and even governments, but it works just as well with individual, small-scale economic decisions. For example, suppose you are preparing food for a soup kitchen and have the ingredients to make 12 loaves of whole wheat bread or 100 bran muffins or some combination of the two. A PPC can help you decide what to make.

Production Possibilities Curve

The production possibilities table in Figure 1.3 below shows five production possibilities for loaves of bread and bran muffins. These production possibilities run from the two extremes of all bread or all muffins through several combinations of the two products. The data in the table also can be plotted on a graph, as in Figure 1.4. The line joining the plotted points is the production possibilities curve. Each point on the curve represents the maximum number of loaves of bread that can be produced relative to the number of bran muffins that are produced.

Further, the PPC shows the opportunity cost of each choice in a visual way. Trace the curve from left to right with your finger. Notice that as you move along the curve you make fewer loaves of bread and more muffins. The opportunity cost of making more muffins is the bread that cannot be made.

Production Possibilities A production possibilities curve can show all the possible combinations for producing muffins and bread.

FIGURE 1.3 PRODUCTION POSSIBILITIES TABLE: BREAD vs. MUFFINS

Loaves of Bread	Bran Muffins
a → 12	0
10	35
b → 7	63
4	84
c → 0	100

FIGURE 1.4 PRODUCTION POSSIBILITIES CURVE: BREAD vs. MUFFINS

a Here you are using all the ingredients to make only bread.

b This point shows a combination of 7 loaves of bread and 63 muffins. The opportunity cost of making the 7 loaves is 37 muffins (100 – 63).

c At this point, you are making all muffins and no bread.

ANALYZE GRAPHS

1. If you decided to make ten loaves of bread, how many bran muffins could you make?
2. What is the opportunity cost of making the ten loaves of bread?

Animated Economics

Use an interactive production possibilities curve at **ClassZone.com**

APPLICATION Interpreting Graphs

A. Look at the production possibilities curve in Figure 1.4. What is the opportunity cost of increasing bread production from four loaves to seven loaves?

What We Learn from PPCs

KEY CONCEPTS

No economy actually operates according to the simplified assumptions underlying the PPC. However, economists use the simplified model because it spotlights concepts that work in the real world of scarce resources.

One important concept revealed in a PPC is **efficiency**, the condition in which economic resources are being used to produce the maximum amount of goods and services. Another is **underutilization**, the condition in which economic resources are not being used to their full potential. As a result, fewer goods and services are being produced than the economy is capable of making. Both of these conditions are easy to see in the PPC.

EXAMPLE Efficiency and Underutilization

Figure 1.5 shows the classic production possibilities model of guns vs. butter. In this model, "guns" is shorthand for military spending and "butter" represents consumer products. Every point along this PPC shows a different combination of military and consumer production. Regardless of the combination, each point represents efficiency, the most that can be produced with the available resources.

Any point inside the curve represents underutilization, or the inefficient use of available resources. Look again at Figure 1.5 and notice that point **3** indicates that all resources are not fully employed. The PPC shows that the economy is capable of producing either 47 million more guns (point **1** on the curve) or 30 million more pounds of butter (point

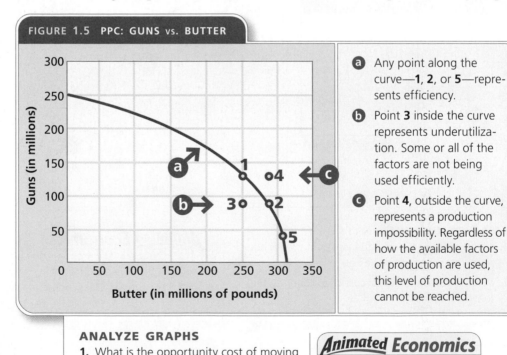

FIGURE 1.5 PPC: GUNS vs. BUTTER

Guns (in millions) / Butter (in millions of pounds)

ⓐ Any point along the curve—**1**, **2**, or **5**—represents efficiency.

ⓑ Point **3** inside the curve represents underutilization. Some or all of the factors are not being used efficiently.

ⓒ Point **4**, outside the curve, represents a production impossibility. Regardless of how the available factors of production are used, this level of production cannot be reached.

ANALYZE GRAPHS

1. What is the opportunity cost of moving butter production from **1** to **2**?

2. At **3**, factors of production are not being used efficiently. Identify a situation where this might occur.

Animated Economics

Use an interactive production possibilities curve at **ClassZone.com**

2 on the curve). Any point outside the curve is impossible to meet because resources are fixed. To produce the number of guns indicated at point **4**, fewer pounds of butter would have to be made (point **1** on the curve). Similarly, to produce the amount of butter indicated at point **4**, fewer guns would have to be made (point **2** on the curve).

The shape of the PPC shows a third important economic concept. This is the **law of increasing opportunity costs**, which states that as production switches from one product to another, increasingly more resources are needed to increase the production of the second product, which causes opportunity costs to rise.

QUICK REFERENCE

The **law of increasing opportunity costs** states that as production switches from one product to another, increasing amounts of resources are needed to increase the production of the second product.

EXAMPLE Increasing Opportunity Costs

Return again to Figure 1.5. A nation makes 250 million pounds of butter (point **1** on the curve), but wants to make 280 million pounds (point **2** on the curve). The opportunity cost of making the extra 30 million pounds of butter is 37 million guns. That works out to a cost of about 1.2 guns for every pound of butter. If the nation increases its output of butter to 312 million pounds (point **5** on the curve), the opportunity cost of the change would be 63 millions guns, nearly 2 guns for every pound of butter. This increase in the opportunity cost—each additional unit costs more to make than the last—explains why the curve is bow-shaped.

Opportunity Cost In the guns vs. butter equation, if more resources are used to make military products, such as stealth bombers, there are fewer resources available for other things, such as butter and other consumer goods. The opportunity cost of making more military products is the other products that cannot be made.

The reason for the increasing costs is fairly straightforward. Making butter involves different resources than making guns. Converting from gun production to butter production is not a simple procedure. New machinery must be produced, new factories must be built, and workers must be retrained. The cost of all these actions will be fewer and fewer guns.

APPLICATION Writing about Economics

B. Write a brief paragraph explaining the concepts a PPC shows graphically.

Changing Production Possibilities

The PPC illustrates a country's present production possibilities as if all resources are fixed. However, a country's supply of resources is likely to change over time. When additional resources become available, new production possibilities beyond the original frontier become attainable, and the PPC moves outward.

EXAMPLE A Shift in the PPC

In the late 1700s, the United States occupied a relatively narrow strip of land along the Atlantic Coast. Yet in less than a hundred years, it had expanded to the Pacific Ocean. This additional land provided the United States with an abundance of natural resources. Similarly, successive waves of immigration have added huge numbers of workers to the labor pool. Also, new technology has made the use of land, labor, and capital more efficient.

The addition of new resources or the more efficient use of resources already available meant that the United States could produce more goods and services. This is shown on the PPC as a shift of the curve outward, or to the right, as Figure 1.6 illustrates. Economists refer to this increase in the economy's total output as economic growth. You'll learn more about this concept in Chapter 12.

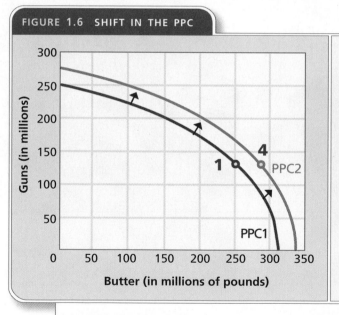

FIGURE 1.6 SHIFT IN THE PPC

More resources or increased productivity shifts the PPC outward, or to the right, from PPC1 to PPC2. This means that the economy can produce more of both guns and butter and point **4**, which was a production impossibility in Figure 1.5 on page 20, now is located on the curve.

ANALYZE GRAPHS

1. If the curve PPC2 represents current production possibilities, what does point **1** represent?

2. What might cause the PPC to shift inward?

Animated Economics

Use an interactive production possibilities curve at **ClassZone.com**

APPLICATION Applying Economic Concepts

C. Identify three developments that would cause the PPC to move outward.

REVIEWING KEY CONCEPTS

1. Explain how each of these terms is illustrated by the production possibilities curve.

   a. *underutilization*   **b.** *efficiency*

2. On what assumptions is the PPC based? Explain how these conditions do not correspond to the real world.

3. What economic data does a PPC bring together?

4. Why do opportunity costs increase as you make more and more butter and fewer guns?

5. Based on what we learn from PPCs, what does an economy need to be able to produce more of both products on the graph?

6. **Using Your Notes** Write a one-paragraph summary of this section. Refer to your completed summary chart for the ideas to use in your summary.

Analyzing Production Possibilities	
PPC	shows impact of scarcity

   Use the Graphic Organizer at **Interactive Review @ ClassZone.com**

CRITICAL THINKING

7. **Applying Economic Concepts** Explain why, in an economy that produces only fish and computers and is working at efficiency, the 500th computer made will cost more in terms of fish than the 450th computer made.

8. **Applying Economic Concepts** Suppose the owners of a car-manufacturing company are thinking of entering the motorcycle production business. How would a PPC model help them make a decision?

9. **Analyzing Cause and Effect** If new technology was introduced but there were not enough skilled workers to use it, where would the nation's production be plotted on the PPC—inside or outside the curve? Explain your answer.

10. **Challenge** During a war, a country suffers massive devastation of its industry. How would the country's PPC change from before the war to after the war? Sketch a PPC to illustrate your answer.

ECONOMICS IN PRACTICE

Creating a PPC
The following information reflects the production possibilities of an economy that makes only corn and television sets. Use the data to create a production possibilities curve.

Bushels of Corn (in thousands)	Television Sets (in thousands)
10	0
9	1
7	2
4	3
0	4

Label Points on a PPC Use the letters to locate the following points on your PPC:

A The point at which the economy makes all TVs and no corn

B A point representing efficiency

C A point representing underutilization

D A point representing an impossible level of production

Challenge Use information from your PPC to explain the law of increasing opportunity costs.

Use **SMART Grapher @ClassZone.com** to complete this activity.

The Economist's Toolbox

OBJECTIVES	KEY TERMS	TAKING NOTES
In Section 4, you will • demonstrate how and why economists use economic models • understand how and why economists use statistics, charts, tables, and graphs • compare macroeconomics to microeconomics • contrast positive economics with normative economics	statistics, *p. 24* microeconomics, *p. 27* macroeconomics, *p. 27* positive economics, *p. 29* normative economics, *p. 29*	As you read Section 4, complete a chart to see similarities and differences between key concepts. Use the Graphic Organizer at **Interactive Review @ ClassZone.com**

Concepts	Similarities	Differences
Charts & Tables vs. Graphs		
Micro vs. Macro		
Positive vs. Normative		

Working with Data

KEY CONCEPTS

An old joke notes that economics is everything we already know expressed in a language we don't understand. While many economists might disagree with the second part of this joke, they probably would have little argument with the first part. Economics is something that everybody engages in every day, and in that way everyone has knowledge of it. Individuals, business owners, and government officials make economic decisions all the time. Economists study these decisions and look for logical ways to explain why some nations are rich while others are poor, or why some consumers want one kind of product while others want another.

Since economists can't interview every person in every nation about economic choices, they rely on **statistics**—numerical data or information—to see patterns of behavior. To help organize and interpret the data they collect, they develop economic models. As you recall from Section 3, an economic model is a simplified representation of complex economic forces. The language of economists—these statistics and models—may sometimes be a little hard to understand. However, it is a more efficient way of explaining economic relationships and interactions than everyday language.

QUICK REFERENCE

Statistics are information in numerical form.

Using Economic Models

In science class, you may have seen a model of a lunar eclipse, which shows how, with the sun behind it, the earth casts a shadow on the moon. The model assumes certain laws of planetary orbit and simplifies the relationships among the objects in the solar system. However, these assumptions and simplifications make the process of the eclipse quite clear.

Economic models work in the same way. They are based on assumptions and are simplified because they focus on a limited number of variables. Economists can express their models in words, graphs, or equations. Models help economists explain why things are as they are. In some cases, models can help economists to predict future economic activity. You've already learned how economists construct and use one important economic model—the production possibilities curve—in Section 3. You'll learn about another, the circular flow model, in Chapter 2.

Using Charts and Tables

Economists study statistics in a particular way, looking for trends, connections, and other interesting relationships. They have several tools to help them with this task. Among the most common tools are charts and tables, in which data are arranged and displayed in rows and columns. (See Figure 1.7 above.) By showing numbers in relation to other numbers, charts and tables can reveal patterns in the data.

FIGURE 1.7 DEVELOPMENT ASSISTANCE

Country	Aid (in millions of U.S. Dollars)	Percentage of Total Economy
Luxembourg	236	0.83
Canada	2,599	0.27

Source: Organization for Economic Co-operation and Development, 2004 Figures

Suppose, for example, you were curious about how much money various developed countries give to help developing countries. In Figure 1.7, if you looked at one set of numbers, you would see that Luxembourg contributed $236 million, while Canada gave more than ten times that, offering nearly $2.6 billion. Your immediate interpretation of these data might be that Canada gives far more in foreign aid than Luxembourg does. But looking at other sets of numbers might suggest a different interpretation. Luxembourg may have contributed far less than Canada in actual dollar amounts. However, the foreign aid Luxembourg gave represented close to 1 percent of the value of all the goods and services the nation produced. Canada's contribution, in contrast, was about 0.3 percent of its total economy. After studying these numbers, you might conclude that in relative terms Luxembourg gives more than Canada in foreign aid.

Economics Update

Find an update on foreign aid at **ClassZone.com**

Using Graphs

When economists are interested in identifying trends in statistics, they often use graphs, or visual representations of numerical relationships. The most common type is the line graph. Line graphs are particularly useful for showing changes over time.

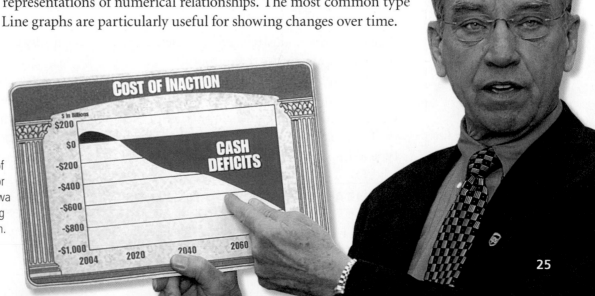

Statistics During a debate in the U.S. Senate on the future of Social Security, Senator Charles Grassley of Iowa illustrates a point using statistics in graph form.

25

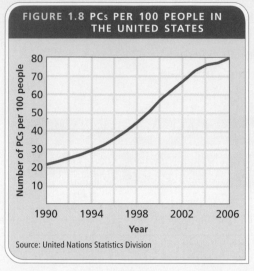

FIGURE 1.8 PCs PER 100 PEOPLE IN THE UNITED STATES

Source: United Nations Statistics Division

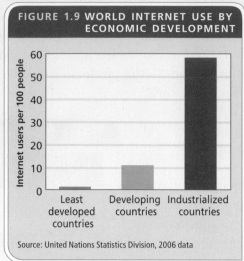

FIGURE 1.9 WORLD INTERNET USE BY ECONOMIC DEVELOPMENT

Source: United Nations Statistics Division, 2006 data

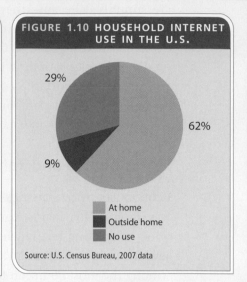

FIGURE 1.10 HOUSEHOLD INTERNET USE IN THE U.S.

Source: U.S. Census Bureau, 2007 data

ANALYZE GRAPHS

Graphs show statistics in a visual form. Line graphs (Figure 1.8) are particularly useful for showing changes over time. Bar graphs (Figure 1.9) make it easy to compare numbers or sets of numbers. Pie, or circle, graphs (Figure 1.10) show relationships among the parts of a whole.

Use a variety of interactive graphs at **ClassZone.com**

All line graphs use at least two sets of numbers, or variables: one plotted along the horizontal axis, running from left to right, the other plotted along the vertical axis, running from bottom to top. On the line graph in Figure 1.8 above, the range of time from 1990 to 2006 is shown on the horizontal axis. The number of PCs (personal computers) per 100 people in the United States is shown on the vertical axis.

For each year, the number of PCs per 100 people is plotted on the graph and then these points are joined to form a line. The line may slope upward, showing an upward trend, or downward, showing a downward trend. The line may be straight, keeping the same slope throughout, or it may be curved, having a varied slope. (In later chapters you'll see that where graphs are used to illustrate economic concepts, lines are referred to as curves whether they are straight or curved.) How would you describe the trend shown in Figure 1.8?

Bar graphs are useful for comparing items by a single measure. For example, Figure 1.9 above shows the number of Internet users per 100 people in least developed, developing, and industrialized countries. The bars make it easy to see the difference in Internet use among the three groups.

Pie graphs, sometimes called circle graphs, show how parts make up a whole. Look at the pie graph in Figure 1.10 above. The whole circle represents all households in the United States. Each segment—or "slice of the pie"—represents where households use the Internet. The size of the segment reflects what percentage of households have that type of Internet use.

NEED HELP?

Throughout this book, you will be asked to interpret and analyze information in graphs. If you need help with these tasks, see "Interpreting Graphs."

 Skillbuilder Handbook, page R29

APPLICATION Interpreting Graphs

A. Look at the line graph in Figure 1.8 above. Write a generalization based on information in the graph.

Microeconomics and Macroeconomics

For scientists, everything in the earth, air, and water—and beyond—is a source of data to be observed and studied. Yet the data often make little sense until they are seen through the lens of a microscope or telescope. Economic information, as with scientific data, takes on meaning when it is viewed through the most useful lens. Two of the lenses through which economists observe economic behavior are microeconomics and macroeconomics. **Microeconomics** is the study of the behavior of individual players in an economy, such as individuals, families, and businesses. **Macroeconomics** is the study of the behavior of the economy as a whole and involves topics such as inflation, unemployment, aggregate demand, and aggregate supply.

QUICK REFERENCE

Microeconomics is the study of individuals, families, and businesses in an economy.

Macroeconomics is the study of the economy as a whole and is concerned with large-scale economic activity.

Microeconomics

As the prefix *micro-*, meaning small, would suggest, microeconomics examines specific, individual elements in an economy. The elements include prices, costs, profits, competition, and the behavior of consumers and producers. Microeconomics can help you understand how the sandwich shop owner arrived at the price of the lunch you bought today, why the neighborhood has several sandwich shops offering the same kinds of food, and why some of these shops flourish while others fail. Microeconomics also can offer explanations for why students decide to work only on the weekends and not on school nights, why some families buy a used car rather than a new car, and why the mom-and-pop grocery store in your neighborhood closed after the superstore opened nearby.

Within the field of microeconomics there are areas of specialized concentration. Business organization, labor markets, agricultural economics, and the economics of environmental issues are among the topics that microeconomists might study. You will study the issues of microeconomics in more depth starting in Chapter 4.

Microeconomics vs. Macroeconomics Microeconomics studies how coffee prices affect competition among coffee shops. Macroeconomics studies how coffee prices affect the whole economy.

Macroeconomics

Macroeconomics, as its prefix *macro-*, meaning large, would suggest, examines the economic "big picture." In other words, macroeconomics is the study of the economy as a whole. While the limited spending power of an unemployed person would be in the realm of microeconomics, the effect of widespread unemployment on the whole nation would be a macroeconomic issue. In a similar way, the rising price of coffee would interest a microeconomist, but a general rise in prices, a sign that the whole economy is experiencing inflation, would be a matter for a macroeconomist.

FIGURE 1.11 The Two Branches of Economics

Economists Study

Macroeconomics
The study of the whole economy

Units of Study

- Economic growth
- Economic stability
- International trade

Topics of Interest

- Money, banking, finance
- Government taxing and spending policies
- Employment and unemployment
- Inflation

Microeconomics
The study of the individual consumer

Units of Study

- Consumer markets
- Business markets
- Labor markets

Topics of Interest

- Markets, prices, costs, profits, competition, government regulation
- Consumer behavior
- Business behavior

ANALYZE CHARTS

The division between microeconomics and macroeconomics is not a fixed one. Some topics fall under both areas of study. For example, a microeconomist might be interested in employment levels in the hotel industry, while a macroeconomist looks at employment levels in the economy as a whole. Identify another topic area that might be of interest to both microeconomists and macroeconomists.

While microeconomics considers the *individual* consumer, macroeconomics studies the consumer *sector*, also called the household sector. A sector is a combination of all the individual units into one larger whole. Macroeconomics also examines the business sector, and the public, or government, sector—that part of the economy that provides public goods and services.

Macroeconomists bring a national or global perspective to their work. They study the monetary system, the ups and downs of business cycles, and the impact of national tax policies on the economy. In addition, they look at such global issues as international trade and its effect on rich and poor nations. You will study macroeconomics in depth beginning in Chapter 10.

APPLICATION Categorizing Economic Information

B. Which does each of the news headlines relate to—microeconomics or macroeconomics?

1. National Unemployment Figures Rise
2. World Trade Organization Meets
3. Shipbuilder Wins Navy Contract
4. Cab Drivers on Strike!
5. Gasoline Prices Jump 25 Cents

Positive Economics and Normative Economics

KEY CONCEPTS

Economics also can be viewed through another pair of lenses. One of those lenses is **positive economics**, a way of describing and explaining economics as it is, not as it should be. Positive economics involves verifiable facts, not value judgments. The other is **normative economics**, a way of describing and explaining what economic behavior ought to be, not what it actually is. Normative economics does involve value judgments because it seeks to make recommendations for actions.

QUICK REFERENCE

Positive economics studies economic behavior as it is.

Normative economics involves judgments of what economic behavior ought to be.

Positive Economics

Positive economics uses the scientific method to observe data, hypothesize, test, refine, and continue testing. Statements made within positive economics can be tested against real-world data and either proved (or at least strongly supported) or disproved (or at least strongly questioned). Suppose, for example, your state is debating the pros and cons of a lottery to raise money for education. In the framework of positive economics, researchers would study data from states with lotteries to see if educational spending increased after the lotteries were begun.

Normative Economics Why is this statement about the North American Free Trade Agreement (NAFTA) an example of normative economics?

Normative Economics

Normative economics, in contrast, is based on value judgments. It goes beyond the facts to ask if actions are good. Since the values of people differ, so do the recommendations based on normative economics.

Consider the issue of using lottery money to fund education. Two economists might agree that the data show that state-run lotteries result in more money for schools, and that many lottery tickets are purchased by people who are poor. Their recommendations, however, might differ because they have different values. One economist might support a lottery because it increases funding for schools. The other might oppose a lottery because it places a burden on the poor.

APPLICATION Applying Economic Concepts

C. Are the following statements examples of positive economics or normative economics?

1. Because of scarcity, everyone must make choices.

2. Americans buy too many cars and do not use mass transit enough.

NAFTA a kinder, gentler way to ruin our economy.

Adam Smith: Founder of Modern Economics

Some 250 years ago, economics as an academic discipline did not even exist. Any discussion of economic issues usually took place in the fields of politics and philosophy. In 1776, however, Adam Smith completely changed this.

Seeing the Invisible

No other economist has had as much influence as Adam Smith, yet he would not have even considered himself an economist. Smith was born in Kirkcaldy, Scotland, in 1723 and studied, and later taught, literature, logic, and moral philosophy. In 1764 he traveled to France and met many European Enlightenment writers and thinkers. His discussions with them encouraged him to look at the world anew. The result was his groundbreaking work, *An Inquiry into the Nature and Causes of the Wealth of Nations,* which he published in 1776.

In *The Wealth of Nations,* Smith challenged the idea that mercantilism—a system by which the government of the homeland controlled trade with its colonies—was economically sound. Instead, he argued, a nation would be wealthier if it engaged in free trade. It was in this market where goods could be exchanged freely that Adam Smith saw a new economic relationship.

He reasoned that people behave in ways that satisfy their economic self-interest. A tailor will make clothes as long as people will buy them at a price that satisfies him. If he makes more clothes than customers wish to buy, he will cut back and make fewer until he finds the balance again. In this way, according to Smith, an "invisible hand" guides the marketplace. In such a free market, both the buyer and the seller benefit from each transaction. Smith's idea of the "invisible hand," as well as many other principles he explained in *The Wealth of Nations,* became the foundation of modern economic theory.

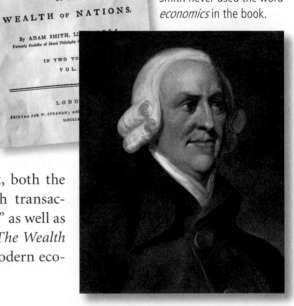

Founder of Economics
The Wealth of Nations is considered the founding work of the subject of economics—even though Smith never used the word *economics* in the book.

APPLICATION Analyzing Effects

D. What impact do you think individual self-interest has on the economy as a whole? Illustrate your answer with examples.

Online Quiz
ClassZone.com

REVIEWING KEY CONCEPTS

1. Explain the differences between the terms in each of these pairs:

   a. *statistics*
      economic model

   b. *macroeconomics*
      microeconomics

   c. *positive economics*
      normative economics

2. Why do economists often choose to present statistics in charts, tables, or graphs?

3. Create a simple model to explain how you decide how much time to study and how much time to unwind each evening. You may use words, charts or graphs, or equations.

4. Think of an example of a macroeconomic issue that affects an individual person, family, or business and explain its effect.

5. Explain the value of statistics and other data to positive economics and to normative economics.

6. **Using Your Notes** In what ways was Adam Smith a microeconomist? In what ways a macroeconomist? Refer to your completed comparison and contrast chart.

Concepts	Similarities	Differences
Charts & Tables vs. Graphs		
Micro vs. Macro		
Positive vs. Normative		

   Use the Graphic Organizer at **Interactive Review @ ClassZone.com**

CRITICAL THINKING

7. **Making Inferences** How do you think politicians might use normative economics statements?

8. **Applying Economic Concepts** In which category does each item below belong—microeconomics or macroeconomics? Why?

   a. Studying statistics to see how well the economy is doing at creating jobs or increasing exports;

   b. Studying statistics on gasoline sales and hotel bookings to explore the impact of higher gas prices on vacation plans.

9. **Distinguishing Fact from Opinion** Consider the example of the state lottery to raise money for education. How might it be possible for two economists to see the same information and arrive at different opinions about what to do?

10. **Challenge** When you go out shopping, do you often worry that there will be a shortage of something you really want? If so, explain why you think there might be a shortage. If not, explain why there seems to be enough of everything you would want to buy.

ECONOMICS IN PRACTICE

Ford Motor Company assembly line, 1913

Using Graphs
Graphs are among the most important tools used by economists.

Create Graphs Use the following information about Model T Fords (shown above) to create two line or bar graphs.

Average price per car
1909 — $904
1911 — $811
1913 — $638
1915 — $626

Number of cars sold
1909 —   12,176
1911 —   40,400
1913 — 179,199
1915 — 355,249

Source: Model T Ford Club of America

Challenge As Henry Ford lowered the price of the Model Ts, he potentially reduced his profit—the amount of money he made—on the sale of each car. Why was that a good economic choice?

Use *SMART Grapher* @ ClassZone.com to complete this activity.

Case Study

Economics Update
Find an update on this Case
Study at **ClassZone.com**

The Real Cost of Expanding O'Hare Airport

Background Chicago's O'Hare airport is one of the busiest airports in the United States. It is a major hub for both domestic and international airlines, and its smooth running is essential if the many airlines that fly in and out of O'Hare are to remain on schedule. However, delays at O'Hare are commonplace, and this sometimes disrupts air travel throughout the United States and abroad.

Two main factors are responsible for delays at O'Hare: turbulent Midwestern weather and the layout of O'Hare's runways. Because all but one of the runways are interconnected, bad weather results in the shutting down of most of the runway system. A modernization plan to improve efficiency at O'Hare was adopted in 2005. This plan generated considerable, and often heated, discussion and debate.

What's the issue? What are the real costs involved in airport expansion? Study these sources to determine the costs tied to the expansion of O'Hare airport.

A. Online Report

This report describes the anticipated benefits of the O'Hare Modernization Plan to redesign the runway system and expand the airport.

Chicago O'Hare Airport Expansion

The modernization plan is estimated to cost $6.6 billion (in 2001 dollars), which will probably be more like $8 billion by completion. . . .

Supporters of the expansion plan say delays could be cut by 79% and that 195,000 jobs and $18 billion would be put into the local economy. In 2004 the airport played host to 69.5 million arriving, departing and connecting passengers and had total aircraft operations at nearly 929,000, an average of one landing or takeoff every 56 seconds. . . .

The airport has 178 gates on eight connected concourses and one freestanding terminal. The realignment [of the runways] and modernization program could make a great deal of difference to the efficiency of the airport. Overall, delays are expected to drop by 79%. The future airfield will be able to accommodate approximately 1.6 million aircraft operations and 76 million [passengers] per year.

Source: Airport-technology.com/projects/chicago

Thinking Economically What factors led to the development of the plan to expand O'Hare? What are the projected costs and benefits?

B. Political Cartoon

Cartoonist Grizelda drew this cartoon about people protesting noise pollution at an airport.

Ssshhhh!

NO MORE NOISE

NO TERMINAL 5

grizelda

Source: www.CartoonStock.com

Thinking Economically
Which opportunity cost does this cartoon address? Explain your answer.

C. Organization Website

The Alliance of Residents Concerning O'Hare (AReCo) addresses problems related to the aviation industry. AReCo's website presents the group's findings and views regarding the expansion of O'Hare.

Area Residents Challenge Wisdom of O'Hare Expansion

AReCo cites health hazards, seeks alternatives to enlarging O'Hare.

The [aviation] industry and airport expansionists consistently try to minimize the impacts of airports and aircraft. One example of the harm that has been . . . understated by the federal government . . . [is the] underreporting [of] the amounts of deadly pollution coming from airports/aircraft.

For example, combined aircraft-related amounts of benzene [a known cause of cancer in humans] totaled 20 tons at Logan, Bradley, and Manchester airports in 1999! . . . Mega airports, such as Chicago's O'Hare, operate more aircraft annually than all of the three above-mentioned airports combined, thus emitting even more harmful and even deadly pollution in heavily urban-populated areas. . . .

In the meantime, there are intelligent steps that Chicago (and others) can take that will really modernize the metropolitan air transportation system and retain Chicago's title of "our nation's transportation hub." Such steps include placing a much stronger emphasis on [more than one type of] transportation, such as medium and high-speed rail, that would link O'Hare airport to other airports (becoming a "virtual hub") and building a new airport in a less populated peripheral area.

Source: Areco.org

Thinking Economically What alternatives does AReCo cite to O'Hare's expansion?

THINKING ECONOMICALLY Synthesizing

1. Explain the real cost of expanding O'Hare airport. Use information presented in the documents to support your answer.

2. Who are the most likely winners and losers as a result of the O'Hare expansion? Explain your answer.

3. How might supporters of expansion use a production possibilities model to strengthen their case?

The Economic Way of Thinking 33

Interactive ◄►Review

Review this chapter using interactive
activities at ClassZone.com

- **Online Summary**
- **Quizzes**
- **Vocabulary Flip Cards**
- **Graphic Organizers**
- **Review and Study Notes**

⟶ Online Summary

Complete the following activity either on your
own paper or online at **ClassZone.com**

**Choose the key concept that best completes
the sentence. Not all key concepts will be used.**

consumer	producer
economic model	production possibilities curve
economics	scarcity
efficiency	statistics
factors of production	trade-off
incentive	underutilization
macroeconomics	utility
microeconomics	wants
opportunity cost	

__1__ is the fundamental economic problem. It arises
because human __2__ are limitless, while resources
are limited. It affects what a __3__ buys and what
a __4__ makes. It affects what is produced, how it is
produced, and who gets what is produced. It affects
how the four __5__ are put to use.

Since people cannot have everything they
want, they have to make choices. Every choice,
however, involves a __6__, something you have to
give up to get what you want. When making an
economic decision, you need to consider the __7__,
the value of the thing you gave up.

Economists often use an __8__, a simplified
representation of reality, to clarify concepts.
Economists use such tools in __9__, the study of the
economic behavior of individual persons, families,
and businesses, and in __10__, the study of the
economy as a whole.

One useful model, the __11__, shows the
maximum amount of goods that an economy
can produce. It also shows __12__, when not all
resources are put to full use.

CHAPTER **1 Assessment**

REVIEWING KEY CONCEPTS

Scarcity: The Basic Economic Problem (pp. 4–11)

1. In what ways does scarcity affect both consumers
   and producers?

2. What are the four factors of production and how
   do they relate to scarcity?

**Economic Choice Today: Opportunity Cost
(pp. 12–17)**

3. What does the phrase "there's no such thing as a
   free lunch" mean in economic terms?

4. Why is it important to consider marginal benefits
   and costs when you do a cost-benefit analysis?

Analyzing Production Possibilities (pp. 18–23)

5. What are three things a PPC shows?

6. What factors could lead to economic growth?

The Economist's Toolbox (pp. 24–33)

7. What are some tools that economists use to draw
   meaning from large amounts of data?

8. What are the differences between microeconomics
   and macroeconomics?

APPLYING ECONOMIC CONCEPTS

Look at the bar graph below showing the relationship
between educational level and weekly wages.

9. Describe the relationship between education and
   earnings for males in 1979.

10. Explain why the earnings gap between college
    and high school graduates might have changed
    between 1979 and 2004.

FIGURE 1.12 EDUCATION AND EARNINGS

Source: U.S Bureau of Labor Statistics

34   Chapter 1

11. **Creating Graphs** Use the following information to create a bar graph showing the weekly wages for females with a high school education and those with a college education in 1979 and 2004.

    1979 High school graduates, no college, $424
          College graduates, $605

    2004 High school graduates, no college, $488
          College graduates, $860

    Source: U.S. Bureau of Labor Statistics

    Use 🚀**SMART**Grapher @ ClassZone.com to complete this activity.

12. **Interpreting Graphs** Compare the graph you created with the one on page 34. Identify three differences between the changes over time for women and for men.

13. **Evaluating Economic Decisions** You plan to open a restaurant that specializes in meals cooked with organic products. You realize that location is very important for this kind of business. You have two options: you can rent an expensive site downtown or you can buy an inexpensive building in a quiet neighborhood. What are the benefits and the opportunity cost for each option?

14. **Conducting Cost-Benefit Analysis** You are considering taking a part-time job after school at a local veterinary surgery. Create a decision-making grid to analyze your potential choices. Include alternative jobs you might take and the costs and benefits of each. Similarly, list activities other than working that you might pursue after school. Indicate which alternative you would choose and explain your choice.

15. **Challenge** You own a small factory that makes widgets and you want to increase production, so you hire new workers. Each new worker increases productivity, but each also must be paid. When will you stop hiring new workers?

Start a Business

Step 1 Team up with a partner or small group of classmates.

Step 2 With your partner or group, decide on a business you want to start. This could be anything that has a realistic chance of succeeding: computer technician, T-shirt printer, caramel-corn producer, dog walker, or anything you think may fulfill a want.

Step 3 On a chart like the one below, list the factors of production you will need to use to start and run your business.

Step 4 Develop a business plan—a way that you can use the factors of production so efficiently that you will be able to make money. Describe your business plan in a paragraph.

Step 5 Present your plan to the rest of the class. When all pairs or groups have made their presentations, hold a class vote to select the best plan.

Factors of Production	
Land	Labor
1.	1.
2.	2.
3.	3.
Capital	Entrepreneurship
1.	1.
2.	2.
3.	3.

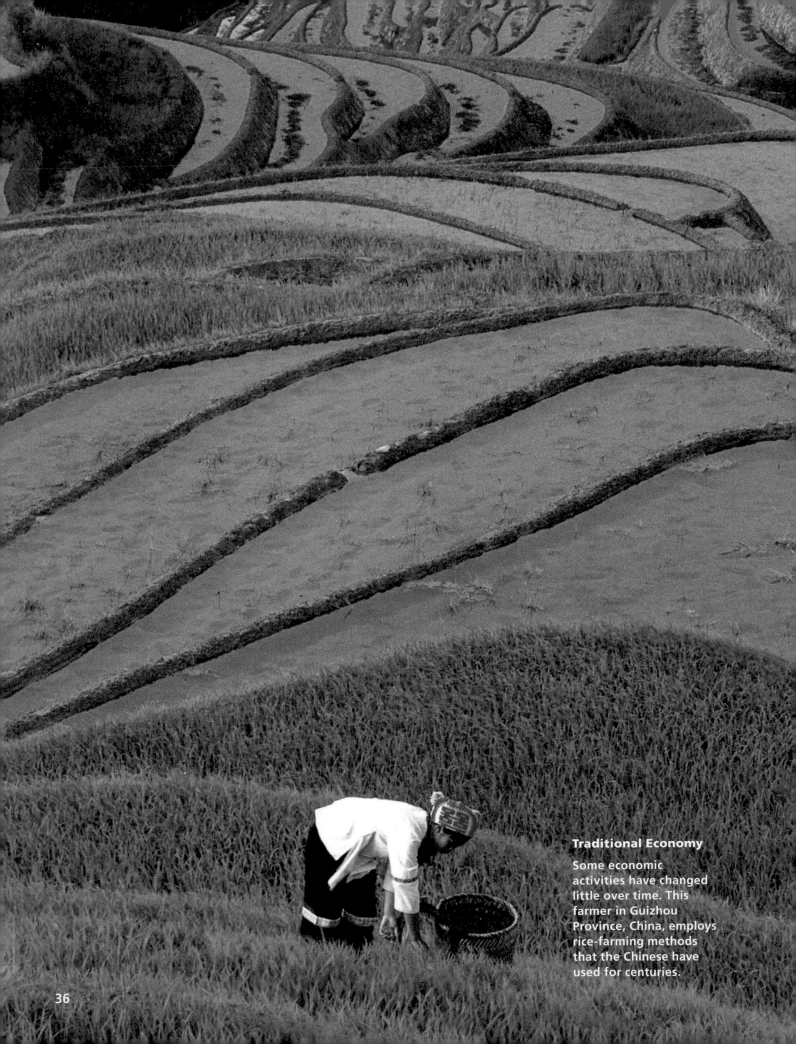

Traditional Economy

Some economic activities have changed little over time. This farmer in Guizhou Province, China, employs rice-farming methods that the Chinese have used for centuries.

Economic Systems

CONCEPT REVIEW

Scarcity is the situation that exists when there are not enough resources to meet human wants.

CHAPTER 2 KEY CONCEPT

An **economic system** is the way in which a society uses its scarce resources to satisfy its people's unlimited wants.

WHY THE CONCEPT MATTERS

How does a society decide the ways to use scarce resources to meet unlimited wants? Its economic system determines what to produce, how to produce, and for whom to produce. Although every country today uses a mixture of economic systems, some mixed systems provide more economic and political freedom and create more wealth than others.

Online Highlights
More at ClassZone.com

 Economics Update

Go to **ECONOMICS UPDATE** for chapter updates and current news on the economies of North Korea and South Korea. (See Case Study, pp. 64–65.) ▶

Animated Economics

Go to **ANIMATED ECONOMICS** for interactive lessons on the graphs and tables in this chapter.

Interactive ◀▶Review

Go to **INTERACTIVE REVIEW** for concept review and activities.

FIGURE 2.7 NORTH AND SOUTH KOREA: GDP PER CAPITA

Source: United Nations Statistics Division

How do the economies of North Korea and South Korea compare? See the Case Study on pages 64–65.

Introduction to Economic Systems

OBJECTIVES	KEY TERMS	TAKING NOTES
In Section 1, you will • identify the three main types of economic systems • understand how a traditional economy operates, including its advantages and disadvantages • analyze how modern forces are changing traditional economies	economic system, *p. 38* traditional economy, *p. 38* command economy, *p. 39* market economy, *p. 39*	As you read Section 1, complete a cluster diagram that provides information on the different kinds of economic systems. Use the Graphic Organizer at **Interactive Review @ ClassZone.com** traditional economy Economic System

Types of Economic Systems

KEY CONCEPTS

In his book *Utopia,* 16th-century writer Thomas More describes a society without scarcity, where wants are limited and easily fulfilled. It is no accident, however, that the word *utopia* means "no place" in Greek. In the real world, scarcity is a fact of life. To address scarcity, societies must answer three questions:

• What should be produced?
• How should it be produced?
• For whom will it be produced?

The answers to these questions shape the economic system a society has. An **economic system** is the way a society uses its scarce resources to satisfy its people's unlimited wants. There are three basic types of economic systems: traditional economies, command economies, and market economies. In this chapter you will learn about these economic systems, as well as "mixed" economies that have features of more than one type.

TYPE 1 Traditional Economy

A **traditional economy** is an economic system in which families, clans, or tribes make economic decisions based on customs and beliefs that have been handed down from generation to generation. The one goal of these societies is survival. Everyone has a set role in this task. Men often are hunters and herders. Women tend the crops and raise children. The youngest help with everyday chores while learning the skills they will need for their adult roles. There is no chance of deviating from this pattern. The good of the group always takes precedence over individual desires.

Traditional The Kavango people of Namibia use fishing techniques passed down from generation to generation.

Command Food was scarce and expensive in this store in the former Soviet Union, a command economy.

Market Advertisements, like these billboards in New York City, are a common sight in a market economy.

TYPE 2 Command Economy

In the second type of economic system, a **command economy**, the government decides what goods and services will be produced, how they will be produced, and how they will be distributed. In a command economy, government officials consider the resources and needs of the country and allocate those resources according to their judgment. The wants of individual consumers are rarely considered. The government also usually owns the means of production—all the resources and factories. North Korea and Cuba are current examples of command economies. Before the collapse of communism in Europe, countries such as the Soviet Union, Poland, and East Germany also were command economies.

QUICK REFERENCE

A **command economy** is an economic system in which the government makes all economic decisions.

A **market economy** is an economic system in which individual choice and voluntary exchange direct economic decisions.

TYPE 3 Market Economy

The third type of economic system, a **market economy**, is based on individual choice, not government directives. In other words, in this system consumers and producers drive the economy. Consumers are free to spend their money as they wish, to enter into business, or to sell their labor to whomever they want. Producers decide what goods or services they will offer. They make choices about how to use their limited resources to earn the most money possible.

In a market economy, then, individuals act in their own self-interest when they make economic choices. However, as they seek to serve their own interests, they benefit others. As a consumer, you choose to buy the products that best meet your wants. However, this benefits the producers who make those products, because they earn money from your purchases. As Adam Smith noted in *The Wealth of Nations* (1776), when you make economic decisions you act in your self-interest, but you are "led by an invisible hand" to promote the interests of others.

Economics Update

Find an update on issues in a market economy at **ClassZone.com**

APPLICATION Applying Economic Concepts

A. How might economic activities within a family with adults, teenagers, and young children represent aspects of traditional, command, and market economies?

Characteristics of Traditional Economies

KEY CONCEPTS

In the earliest times, all societies had traditional economies. Such systems serve the main purpose of traditional societies—survival—very well. The traditional economic system, however, tends to be inefficient and does not adapt to change.

TRAIT 1 Advantages and Disadvantages

The one great advantage of a traditional economy is that it so clearly answers the three economic questions. A traditional society produces what best ensures its survival. The methods of production are the same as they have always been. Systems of distribution are also determined by custom and tradition. In a traditional economy, then, there is little disagreement over economic goals and roles.

Traditional economies have several major disadvantages, too. Because they are based on ritual and custom, traditional economies resist change. Therefore, they are less productive than they might be if they adopted new approaches. Further, while traditionally defined roles eliminate conflict, they also prevent people from doing the jobs they want to do or are best suited to do. People who are in the "wrong" jobs are less productive. The lower productivity in traditional economies means that people do not acquire the material wealth that people in other societies do. As a result, people in traditional economies have a much lower standard of living.

TRAIT 2 Under Pressure to Change

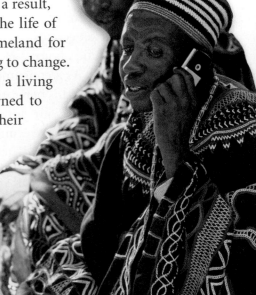

Forces of Change The use of the cell phone has brought changes to many traditional African societies.

Around the world, traditional economies are under pressure from the forces of change. The Kavango people of Namibia in southern Africa, for example, have lived as subsistence farmers for centuries. (Subsistence farmers grow just enough to feed their own families.) Modern telecommunications, however, have bombarded the Kavango with images of the world beyond their homeland. As a result, many young Kavango want something more than the life of subsistence farming. Thousands have left their homeland for the cities. Even the old ways of farming are beginning to change. The vast majority of the Kavango people still make a living from subsistence farming. However, a few have turned to commercial farming, where they grow crops not for their own use, but for sale.

APPLICATION Making Inferences

B. There are no pure traditional economies today. Why do you think this is so?

Online Quiz
ClassZone.com

REVIEWING KEY CONCEPTS

ECONOMICS IN PRACTICE

1. Demonstrate your understanding of the following terms by using each one in a sentence.

   a. *traditional economy*
   b. *command economy*
   c. *market economy*

2. Which is more important in a traditional economy, accumulating individual wealth or honoring tradition? Explain your answer.

3. How are economic decisions made in a command economy?

4. What drives the choices of consumers and producers in a market economy?

5. Does Adam Smith's "invisible hand" also function in traditional and command economies? Explain your answer.

6. **Using Your Notes** What do the three kinds of economic systems have in common? Refer to your completed cluster diagram.

   Use the Graphic Organizer at **Interactive Review @ ClassZone.com**

CRITICAL THINKING

7. **Drawing Conclusions** How might strongly defined economic roles and goals be both a strength and a weakness of traditional economies?

8. **Analyzing Cause and Effect** What effect might mass media have on the erosion of traditional economies in today's world?

9. **Generalizing from Economic Information** You have the following information about an economy: 1) People have little choice in the kinds of jobs they do. 2) Producers are not free to use resources as they wish. 3) People have little, if any, say in how the basic economic questions are answered. What kind of economy might this be? Explain your answer.

10. **Challenge** Most modern economies are a mixture of the three economic systems described in Section 1. Identify elements of traditional, command, and market economic systems in the American economy. (You will learn more about mixed economies in Section 4.)

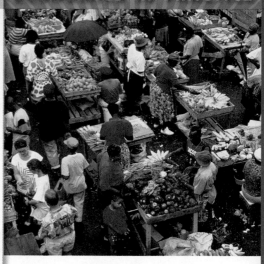

Market economy in action in Mexico

Identifying Economic Systems
The three economic systems may be identified by the way they answer the basic economic questions: What to produce? How to produce? For whom to produce?

Complete a Table Copy the table below. Complete it by noting how each of the three economic systems answers the basic economic questions.

Economic System	Answers to the Basic Economic Questions
Traditional economy	
Command economy	
Market economy	

Challenge Identify modern countries that have economies that closely resemble each of the three economic systems. Explain each of your choices.

Command Economies

| OBJECTIVES | KEY TERMS | TAKING NOTES |

In Section 2, you will
- describe the main features of a command economy
- note how socialism and communism differ
- identify modern examples of command economies
- explain the advantages and disadvantages of a command economy

centrally planned economy, p. 42
socialism, p. 43
communism, p. 43
authoritarian, p. 43

As you read Section 2, complete a hierarchy chart to categorize information about command economic systems. Use the Graphic Organizer at **Interactive Review @ ClassZone.com**

Government Controls

KEY CONCEPTS

In command economies, leaders decide what should be produced and how it should be produced. They also decide for whom it should be produced, in part by setting wages. By determining who earns the highest wages and who the lowest, these leaders decide who has the money to buy available products. A system in which the society's leaders, usually members of the central government, make all economic decisions is called a **centrally planned economy**.

EXAMPLE Government Planning

Think for a moment about how the federal government affects you. If you work, you have to pay taxes. If you're 18 years old and male, you have to register with the Selective Service System. State and local governments exert somewhat more control over your day-to-day life. State laws set both speed limits and the age at which people can drive. Local laws set standards for cleanliness in food stores and restaurants and for honest business practices. And state and local taxes are collected to support such services as police and fire departments and public education.

However, what if the government went further? Suppose that bureaucrats in a government office in Washington, D.C., had the power to decide which businesses could operate in your city. Further, these bureaucrats decided not only what these businesses should produce, but also how much each business should produce each month. Finally, they also decided who could have jobs and set work hours and pay scales for workers. Government controls of this type are a feature of a command, or centrally planned, economy.

EXAMPLE Socialism and Communism

Modern societies that have adopted command economies have done so largely because of the influence of Karl Marx, a 19th-century German philosopher, historian, and economist. According to Marx's analysis, all of history is a struggle between classes. In his own time, the struggle was between the owners of the great industrial factories and the workers who exchanged their labor for wages. While the industrialists grew rich, the workers remained relatively poor. Marx predicted that in time the workers would overthrow this system and transfer ownership of the factories to public hands. With the means of production owned by the government, the class struggle would be resolved and all citizens would share in the wealth.

FIGURE 2.1 Comparing Economic Systems

	Communism	Socialism	Market System
Who owns resources?	Government	Government owns basic resources; the rest are privately owned	All resources privately owned
How are resources allocated?	Government planners decide how resources are used	Government planners allocate basic resources; market forces allocate privately-owned resources	Market forces allocate resources
What role does government play?	Government makes all economic decisions	Government makes decisions in the basic industries	Government's role limited—mostly to ensure market forces are free to work

ANALYZE TABLES
Government involvement varies among economic systems. How do communist systems answer the three basic economic questions?

Socialism, an economic system in which the government owns some or all of the factors of production, developed from the ideas of Marx. Communism, a more extreme form of socialism in which there is no private ownership of property and little or no political freedom, also grew out of Marx's thinking. Essentially, it is authoritarian socialism. An **authoritarian** system requires absolute obedience to authority. Figure 2.1 lists the major characteristics of socialism and communism.

Democratic socialism is established through the democratic political process rather than through the violent overthrow of the government. In this form of socialism, the government owns the basic industries, but other industries are privately owned. Central planners make decisions for government-owned industries. Central planners might also control other sectors—health care, for example—to ensure that everyone has access to these important services.

QUICK REFERENCE

Socialism is an economic system in which the government owns some or all of the factors of production.

Communism is an economic system in which the government owns all the factors of production and there is little or no political freedom.

Authoritarian systems require absolute obedience to those in power.

APPLICATION Comparing and Contrasting

A. How are socialism and communism similar yet different?

Karl Marx: Economic Revolutionary

Millions of lives were affected by the work of Karl Marx. Governments were toppled and new political alliances were forged on the strength of his arguments. What was it in the thousands of difficult-to-read pages he wrote that fueled revolutions?

FAST FACTS

Karl Marx
German philosopher, historian, and economist

Born: May 5, 1818

Died: March 14, 1883

Major Accomplishment:
Detailed analysis of capitalism and foundation for socialist economic theory

Famous Quotation:
Workers of the world unite; you have nothing to lose but your chains.

Influenced:
Russian Revolution, 1917
Chinese Revolution, 1949

Economics Update

Learn more about Karl Marx at **ClassZone.com**

A New View of Economics

Marx was born in what is now Germany in 1818 and grew up in middle-class comfort. In college, however, he became involved in radical politics. In time, his political activism led to his exile from his homeland. He moved from country to country, eventually settling in London. During his travels, he met Friedrich Engels, the son of a factory owner. Through Engels, Marx became aware of the struggles of the working class and he undertook a deep study of economics. He concluded that the Industrial Revolution had created a system of wage slavery.

Factory owners, Marx said, looked upon labor as just another commodity that could be bought. They then used this labor to convert other productive resources into products. The factory owners made a profit by selling products at a higher price than the cost of labor and other resources. By keeping wages low, they could make ever greater profits. The whole industrial system, Marx reasoned, was based on this exploitation of workers.

To Marx, rising tension between worker and owner was an inevitable development in economic history. Over time, more and more wealth would be concentrated in fewer and fewer hands, and dissatisfied workers would revolt and create a new society without economic classes. Marx, assisted by Engels, laid out these ideas in *The Communist Manifesto* (1848). Marx discussed his economic ideas more fully in his enormous study *Das Kapital*, which was published in three volumes between 1867 and 1894.

Because of the way that communist economies worked in practice and the eventual collapse of communism in the early 1990s, Marx's theories have fallen into disfavor. Even so, few people had more impact on 20th-century economic and political thinking than Karl Marx.

Communism Marx's writings influenced revolutionary leaders such as V. I. Lenin in Russia and Mao Zedong in China.

APPLICATION Drawing Conclusions

B. What did Marx think was the logical outcome of the struggle between owners and workers?

Command Economies Today

KEY CONCEPTS

There are no examples of pure command economies today. The forces that have brought changes to traditional economies are also transforming command economies. However, some countries—North Korea, for example—still have economies with mostly command elements.

North Korea

Once under the control of China and later Japan, Korea was split into North Korea and South Korea following World War II. North Korea came under communist control. The government controlled every economic decision. For example, it diverted many of the country's resources to the military, building up an army of more than 1 million soldiers—out of a population of about 22 million. It also developed a nuclear weapons program. However, this military buildup came at the expense of necessities. During the late 1990s and early 2000s, food was so scarce that millions of North Koreans died from hunger and malnutrition. Many North Koreans survived only because of food aid from other countries, most notably South Korea.

The failure to provide food and other important products was just one result of a flawed economic plan. For much of the 1990s, North Korea produced less and less each year, and its economy actually shrank. (See Figure 2.2 below.) In 2003, however, central planners relaxed some restrictions on private ownership and market activity. North Koreans hoped that this experiment with free markets would revive the country's ailing economy. (For more information on North Korea's economy, see the Case Study on pages 64–65.)

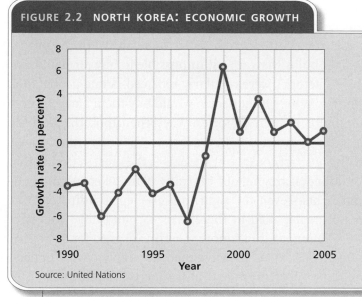

FIGURE 2.2 NORTH KOREA: ECONOMIC GROWTH

Growth rate (in percent) / Year / Source: United Nations

North Korea had a negative growth rate for much of the 1990s. (The red line on the graph marks 0 percent, or no growth.) The average yearly growth rate for all economies during this time period was about 3 percent.

ANALYZE GRAPHS

1. The North Korean economy began to show positive growth after 1999. To what might this development be attributed?

2. During the 1990s, some newspaper reports noted that the North Korean economy was "shrinking." How is this shown in the graph?

Meeting Demand (Left) In communist East Germany, government planners' decisions left this butcher with just one goose to sell. (Right) In West Germany, a market economy, store shelves were laden with consumer goods.

Impact of Command Economies

In theory, command economies have some advantages. For example, they seek to provide for everyone, even the sick and the old who are no longer productive economically. Also, leaders in a command economy can use the nation's resources to produce items that may not make money in a market economy—certain medicines, for example.

In practice, however, the disadvantages of command economies are abundantly clear. To begin with, central planners often have little understanding of local conditions. Because of this, their economic decisions are frequently misguided or wrong. Also, workers often have little motive to improve their productivity, since they know they will be paid the same wages regardless of their output. And because there is no private property, there is no motivation for workers to use resources wisely.

Centrally planned economies often set prices well below those that would be established in a market system. As a result, command economies face shortages. One scene repeated in many command economies is people standing in long lines waiting to buy goods. Such shortages often lead to creative behavior. In the former Soviet Union, for example, light bulbs were almost impossible to buy for home use. However, burned-out bulbs in factories were regularly replaced. Some people took and sold these burned-out bulbs. Why? Other people would buy them and use them to switch out with working bulbs in their factories. They then took the working bulbs to light their homes.

Perhaps the greatest failing of strict command systems is the great suffering that people living under them endured. Carrying out centrally planned economic policies requires that individual rights—even the right to life—be subordinate to the needs of the state. Millions of people died in the efforts to build huge collective farms in China and the Soviet Union. Millions more were imprisoned for exercising their political or economic rights. Estimates suggest that the deeply flawed policies of command economies are responsible for more deaths than two world wars.

APPLICATION Applying Economic Concepts

C. Why are consumer goods often in short supply in a command economy?

REVIEWING KEY CONCEPTS

1. Write a brief paragraph explaining the links between the following three terms.

   a. *centrally planned economy*   **b.** *socialism*   **c.** *communism*

2. Why do communist countries use authoritarian methods to maintain their economic and political system?

3. List and describe some advantages of centrally planned economies.

4. What are some disadvantages of centrally planned economies?

5. What is the relationship between the individual and the state in a communist nation?

6. **Using Your Notes** Write a sentence that makes a generalization about the nature of command economies. Refer to your completed hierarchy chart to complete this question.

Use the Graphic Organizer at **Interactive Review @ ClassZone.com**

CRITICAL THINKING

7. **Making Inferences** Look again at the sentences about Thomas More's *Utopia* on page 38. Do you think that Karl Marx, like Thomas More, was trying to imagine a utopia in his writings? Give reasons for your answer.

8. **Explaining an Economic Concept** How do command societies address the problem of scarcity? Illustrate your answer with examples.

9. **Analyzing Cause and Effect** Read again the information about the North Korean economy on page 45. What factors caused North Korea's serious economic problems? What steps has the North Korean government taken to improve the dire economic situation?

10. **Challenge** Adam Smith used the "invisible hand" as a metaphor for the forces that balance a free market. What might be a good metaphor for the forces at work in a command economy? Explain your answer.

ECONOMICS IN PRACTICE

Celebration of communism in the Soviet Union

Using Graphs
Presenting information in a graph shows economic changes more clearly.

Create a Graph Use the following data to create a line graph.

Household Expenditures in the Soviet Union ($)	
1979	825.2 million
1981	934.7 million
1983	966.7 million
1985	1,017.1 million
1987	1,064.7 million
1989	1,152.3 million

Source: United Nations

Challenge During the 1980s, Soviet leaders introduced market elements into the economy. How might this explain the increase in household expenditures?

Use **SMART Grapher @ClassZone.com** to complete this activity.

Market Economies

OBJECTIVES	KEY TERMS	TAKING NOTES
In Section 3, you will • describe what a market is and how it works • identify the main features of a market economy • analyze how the circular flow model represents economic activity in a market economy • explain the advantages and disadvantages of a market economy	private property rights, *p. 48* market, *p. 48* laissez faire, *p. 49* capitalism, *p. 49* voluntary exchange, *p. 49* profit, *p. 49* competition, *p. 49* consumer sovereignty, *p. 50* specialization, *p. 50* circular flow model, *p. 52* product market, *p. 52* factor market, *p. 52*	As you read Section 3, complete a chart to identify and describe the features of a market economy. Use the Graphic Organizer at **Interactive Review @ ClassZone.com**

Fundamentals of a Market Economy

KEY CONCEPTS

QUICK REFERENCE

Private property rights are the rights of individuals and groups to own businesses and resources.

A **market** is any place where people buy and sell goods and services.

Market economies have several distinct characteristics. Earlier in this chapter you read about the fundamental feature of a market economy—the fact that people's economic behavior is motivated by self-interest. Self-interested behavior is behind two other features of a market economy. One is **private property rights**, the rights of individuals and groups to own property. In economic terms, *property* means everything that an individual owns. This includes factories, offices, clothes, furniture, house, car, and other belongings; money; and even intellectual property, such as songs or ideas developed for inventions. It also includes the labor individuals provide to earn money to buy what they own.

The other feature that stems from self-interest is the **market**, any place or situation in which people buy and sell resources and goods and services. It may be the farmers' market on Saturdays in the town square, or it may be an enormous cybermarket on the Internet, such as eBay. Large or small, real or virtual, the market is where people can exchange their private property for someone else's.

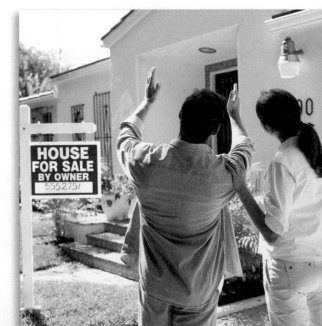

Private Property Rights In a market economy, people are free to own and use private property—houses, for example.

FEATURE 1 Private Property and Markets

For markets to operate efficiently, private property rights need to be well defined and actively enforced by law. If you have ever bought a car, you know that an essential part of the transaction is getting possession of the title. You need proof that the person you are buying it from actually owns it and has the right to sell it. Since clear ownership is vital to any sale or exchange, private property rights are necessary to make markets work properly. If buyers could not trust that the sellers actually had the right to offer their products on the market, trade would break down. Further, suppose you are a musician but know that your songs can be downloaded for free, depriving you of your right to exchange what you own for money. In such a situation, it is doubtful that you would be motivated to record music. In protecting private property rights so that producers have motivation and consumers have trust, the government performs an important role in a market economy.

FEATURE 2 Limited Government Involvement

Sometimes the government's economic role is to stay out of the marketplace. The principle that the government should not interfere in the economy is called **laissez faire**, a French phrase meaning "leave things alone." The concept of laissez faire is often paired with **capitalism**, an economic system that is based on private ownership of the factors of production. Capitalism, the foundation of market economies, operates on the belief that, on their own, producers will create the goods and services that consumers demand. Therefore, according to laissez faire capitalism, there is no need for government involvement in the marketplace. Laissez faire capitalism is a market economy in its pure form. However, there are no pure market economies—all real-world market economies have some degree of government involvement.

FEATURE 3 Voluntary Exchange in Markets

When a buyer and seller agree to do business together, they engage in a **voluntary exchange**, a trade in which the parties involved anticipate that the benefits will outweigh the cost. Both sides in a voluntary exchange believe that what they are getting is worth more than what they are giving up. In a market economy, most trade is based on an exchange of a product for money rather than for another product.

Self-interest guides voluntary exchanges. Suppose you buy a new guitar. Even though you spend a good part of your savings, your self-interest is served because you've wanted this particular model of guitar. The seller's self-interest is likely served by **profit**, a financial gain from a business transaction. If you pay more for the guitar than the seller did, the seller earns money. In voluntary exchange, then, both sides must believe that they are gaining by trading.

FEATURE 4 Competition and Consumer Sovereignty

Market economies are also characterized by **competition**, the effort of two or more people, acting independently, to get the business of others by offering the best deal. You are able to choose today between a Macintosh and a Windows PC operating system because of the competition in the computer market. In the case of these competing systems, each has somewhat different features but mainly performs the same

Laissez faire is the principle that the government should not interfere in the marketplace.

Capitalism is an economic system that is based on private ownership of the factors of production.

Voluntary exchange is a trade in which both traders believe that what they are getting is worth more than what they are giving up.

Profit is a financial gain that a seller makes from a business transaction.

Competition involves all the actions sellers, acting independently, do to get buyers to purchase their products.

COMPETITION

Where will you buy your computer?

You want to buy a new computer. You could buy a "standard package" from the electronics discount store. The price will be very reasonable, but you won't be able to customize the software package or the service program. Alternately, you could buy from a computer specialty store. You'll pay more, but you can choose the extras that you want and the customer support program is excellent.

Computer specialty store

Electronics discount store

functions as the other. You are free to decide which you prefer based on whatever combination of price and value appeals to you more. When you buy over-the-counter medications, you can also clearly see the competitive aspect of the market. Often next to a well-known brand-name product you will see a product with the same ingredients, similar packaging, but a different name and lower price. The producers of the lower priced item are competing for the business established by the brand-name product. If the producers of the brand-name product want to keep your business, they must lower their prices or find a way to add some other value.

That's because you, the consumer, hold the real power in the market place. **Consumer sovereignty** is the idea that because consumers are free to purchase what they want and to refuse products they do not want, they have the ultimate control over what is produced. Sovereignty means supreme authority, which is what consumers exercise as key economic decision-makers. Let's look at the over-the-counter medications again. If there were no competition, the brand-name producers could charge higher prices. It would be in their self-interest to charge as much as they possibly could. Competition, however, acts as a control on self-interested behavior, guiding the market toward a balance between higher value and lower prices. Rather than lose your business, the brand-name producers will either lower their prices or raise the value of their product. Because producers must compete for the consumer's dollar, they have to work at pleasing you, the consumer, while pleasing themselves.

FEATURE 5 Specialization and Markets

A market economy encourages efficient use of resources by allowing people and businesses to specialize in what they do best. **Specialization** is a situation in which people concentrate their efforts in the areas in which they have an advantage. This allows people to trade what they can most efficiently produce for goods and services

Private Property
Buyers and sellers are free to own and use private property.

Government Involvement
Buyers and sellers must be free to operate with minimal government intervention.

Specialization
Buyers and sellers are able to concentrate their efforts in areas where they have an advantage.

Fundamentals of a Market Economy

Voluntary Exchange
When a buyer and seller agree to do business together, each believes that the benefits outweigh the costs.

Consumer Sovereignty
Buyers can exercise their dominance over what is produced by freely deciding whether to buy or not to buy.

Competition
Sellers are free to attempt to get the business of others by offering the best deal.

Profit
Sellers are free to attempt to maximize their profits.

ANALYZE CHARTS

Identify a business in your community. Consider how the fundamentals of a market economy noted in the diagram are illustrated by the operations of that business. Record your ideas in a two-column table.

produced more efficiently by others. Specialization removes the need for households to be self-sufficient, and markets allow households to trade for what they need.

Suppose one adult in your house is a bank teller and another is a welder. Neither banking nor welding needs to happen within your household, but your household does need groceries. By specializing in what they do best—earning money in their jobs—in a market economy these adults are able to trade the dollars they earn for items and services others specialize in. If, however, they had to grow all the family's food themselves, they'd be less efficient than those who specialized in farming. Also, with each hour spent on growing food they would lose an hour's worth of wages from their jobs. Specialization, then, leads to higher-quality yet lower-priced products.

APPLICATION Applying Economic Concepts

A. Which is more important in determining the format in which recordings are offered by the music industry, new technology or consumer sovereignty? Explain.

Circular Flow in Market Economies

QUICK REFERENCE

The **circular flow model** is a tool that economists use to understand how market economies operate.

The **product market** is the market where goods and services are bought and sold.

The **factor market** is the market for the factors of production—land, labor, capital, and entrepreneurship.

KEY CONCEPTS

How do all these fundamental characteristics combine to allow a market economy to function? Economists have developed a model to help them answer this question. Called the **circular flow model**, it visualizes how all interactions occur in a market economy. The model represents the two key economic decision makers in a market economy—households, which are made up of individuals like you, and businesses. It also shows the two markets where households and businesses meet—that for goods and services, and that for resources. (See Figure 2.4 on the next page.)

Product Markets

The market for goods and services is called the **product market**. This is the market you probably know best. The product market isn't a place as much as it is a set of activities. Whenever or wherever individuals purchase goods or services—at a local mall, a dentist's office, the phone company, or an online service selling concert tickets—they are doing so in the product market. The suppliers of the product market are businesses, which offer their goods or services for sale and use the money they earn from the sales to keep their businesses going.

Factor Markets

To run a business, firms must, in turn, purchase what they need from the **factor market**, the market for the factors of production—land, labor, capital, and entrepreneurship. Individuals own all the factors of production. They own some factors of production outright, such as their own labor and entrepreneurship. Others they own indirectly as stockholders in businesses. In the factor market, businesses are the customers and individuals are the producers. A restaurant buys your labor as a server, for example, to serve meals prepared by chefs whose labor they have also bought. The chefs make the meals from products bought from farmers who own the fields and farm equipment.

Circular Flow

This set of interactions between businesses and individuals is illustrated in Figure 2.4 on the next page. On the left and right of the model, you can see the two main economic decision makers, businesses and households. At the top and bottom are the two main markets, product and factor. The green arrows represent the flow of money. The blue arrows represent the flow of resources and products.

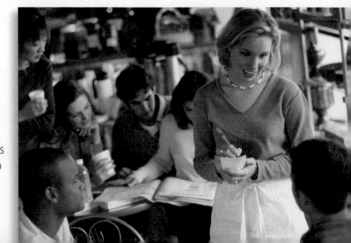

Circular Flow Individuals, such as restaurant servers, sell their labor to businesses in the factor market.

FIGURE 2.4 The Circular Flow Model

Business revenue $

Product Market

Consumer spending $

Sell goods and services

Buy goods and services

Businesses

Sell land, labor, capital, entrepreneurship

Households (Individuals)

Buy productive resources

Payments for resources $

Factor Market

Income from resources $

ANALYZE CHARTS

The circular flow model is a tool for understanding the relationships among economic decision makers and various markets. Why do you think that money always flows in one direction, while resources and products always flow in the opposite direction?

Animated Economics

Use an interactive circular flow model at **ClassZone.com**

Find the "Households" box at the right side of the chart. If you follow the green arrow, you see that individuals spend money in the product market to buy goods and services. From the product market, the money goes to businesses as revenue. The businesses spend this in the factor market, paying for the land, labor, capital, and entrepreneurship needed to produce goods and services. The receivers of that money are individuals who own all the factors of production. With the money they receive, individuals can make more purchases in the product market, and so the cycle continues.

If you look at the blue arrows, you can follow the route of the resources and products in the circular flow model. Once again, start with individuals. They sell their land, capital, labor, and entrepreneurship in the factor market. Follow the arrows to see that these factors of production are bought by businesses. The businesses then use these productive resources to make goods and services. The goods and services are then sold in the product market and flow to individuals who purchase them.

APPLICATION Interpreting Economic Models

B. Think of a good or a service you have recently bought. Using the circular flow model as a guide, write an explanation of the impact of your purchase on the economy.

Impact of Market Economies

Between the late 1940s and the early 1990s, between one-quarter and one-third of the world's population lived under command economic systems. The Soviet Union and its Eastern European neighbors, China and much of Southeast Asia, Cuba, and North Korea all had centrally planned economies. However, with the collapse of communism in the early 1990s, most of these countries have adopted some form of market economy. Also, as you read in Section 2, even those that have clung to communism and central planning have introduced market-economy measures. Why were these countries so ready to embrace the market system?

Advantages

On November 9, 1989, the Berlin Wall, a symbol of the division between the communist and democratic worlds, was finally opened. Over the next few days, hundreds of thousands of East Germans began pouring into West Germany through gates and improvised breaches in the wall. What drew these jubilant East Germans to the west? For most of them, the answer was freedom.

Economic and Political Freedom Freedom is one of the chief advantages of a market economy. A market economy requires that individuals be free to make their own economic choices, since it depends on the consumer's right to buy or refuse products to determine what will be produced. Individuals are also free to develop their interests and talents in work they find satisfying, rather than being assigned to jobs.

Freedom New shopping malls, like this one in Bucharest, Romania, are a common site in many formerly communist countries.

Also, since the government does not use a heavy hand to control the economy, the political process can be much freer, with a diversity of viewpoints and open elections. Government bureaucracy is generally less cumbersome and costly in a market economy than in a command economy, since there are fewer areas of government involvement. A market economy also can be responsive to changes in conditions and accommodate those changes quickly.

Further, individuals in local communities are free to make their own economic choices without the interference of the government. These individuals' better knowledge of the resources and potential of their area leads to better economic decisions and greater productivity.

Profit The profit motive, a key feature of a market economy, insures that resources will be allocated efficiently, since inefficiencies would result in lower profits. It also serves as a reward for hard work and innovation. Knowing you can earn money

Competition Competition among dairy companies ensures that there is a wide variety of milk and other dairy products.

if you come up with a good idea is an incentive to do so, and the more good ideas people have, the more the economy grows. The incentive to come up with good ideas is related to another advantage of a market economy: it encourages competition, letting consumers have the final say. Competition leads to higher-quality products at lower prices. It also helps to create a diverse product market.

Disadvantages

Market economies, however, have disadvantages as well. In a pure market economy, the economic good of the individual is the primary focus. A pure market economy has no mechanism for providing public goods and services, such as national defense, because it would not be profitable from a strictly economic viewpoint to do so.

Another disadvantage is that a pure market economy cannot provide security to those who, because of sickness or age, cannot be economically productive. Nor can it prevent the unequal distribution of wealth, even though that gap may be the result of unequal opportunities.

The industrial boom in the United States in the late 1800s and early 1900s illustrates the problems that can develop in a market economy with little government regulation. During this time, a few business leaders became very rich. At the same time, most of those who worked for these leaders were paid low—but increasing—wages. Further, most business leaders did little at the time to address the negative consequences of industrialization such as pollution. Issues like these led most industrialized societies to adopt some level of government involvement in the economy. The result was economic systems that mix elements of market and command economies. In Section 4, you'll learn more about such mixed economies.

APPLICATION Analyzing Causes

C. Why did many societies feel it necessary to adopt some level of government involvement in market economies?

ECONOMICS SKILLBUILDER

 For more information on comparing and contrasting information, see the Skillbuilder Handbook, page R19.

Comparing and Contrasting Economic Systems

Comparing means looking at the similarities and differences between two or more things. **Contrasting** means examining only the differences between them. To understand economic systems, economists compare and contrast the ways in which societies use their limited resources to meet unlimited wants.

TIPS FOR COMPARING AND CONTRASTING Look for subjects that can be compared and contrasted.

Comparison This passage compares two economic systems that have both similarities and differences.

Contrast To contrast, look for clue words that show how two things differ. Clue words include *however, in contrast, on the other hand,* and *unlike.*

Similarities To find similarities, look for clue words indicating that two things are alike. Clue words include *both, similarly,* and *likewise.*

Economic Systems

An economic system is the way in which a society uses its resources to satisfy its people's needs and wants. Two common economic systems are the market system and the command system. Both systems provide answers to three basic economic questions: What to produce? How to produce? For whom to produce?

In a command economy, government economic planners decide what goods and services will be produced, how they will be produced, and for whom they will be produced. Individuals, then, have little or no influence on how economic decisions are made. In contrast, in a market economy the individual plays the major role in answering the basic economic questions. Consumers spend their money on the goods and services that satisfy them the most. In response, producers supply the goods and services that consumers want.

Few, if any, "pure" economic systems exist today. Most economic systems are "mixed." For example, market economies generally have some limited form of government control—a characteristic of command economies. Most command economic systems are likewise mixed in that they have some elements of market economies.

THINKING ECONOMICALLY Comparing and Contrasting

1. How are market and command economic systems similar?

2. In what ways do these two economic systems differ?

3. Read the paragraphs about North Korea under the heading "Command Economies Today" on page 45. Construct a Venn diagram showing similarities and differences between the economy of North Korea and a typical market economy.

SECTION 3 Assessment

Online Quiz
ClassZone.com

REVIEWING KEY CONCEPTS

1. Explain the relationship between the terms in each of these pairs.

   a. *private property rights*
   market

   c. *specialization*
   profit

   b. *laissez-faire*
   capitalism

   d. *factor market*
   product market

2. What are the essential elements of market economies?

3. What are some advantages of market economies?

4. What are some disadvantages of market economies?

5. How does the profit motive help lead to efficient use of productive resources?

6. **Using Your Notes** Make charts for a traditional economy and a command economy and compare and contrast them with your completed market economy chart.

Market Economy

private property rights

Use the Graphic Organizer at **Interactive Review @ ClassZone.com**

CRITICAL THINKING

7. **Analyzing Cause and Effect** Review the circular flow model on page 53. Based on the model, how do businesses benefit from the wages they pay?

8. **Creating and Interpreting Economic Models** Return to the answer you gave for Application B on page 53. Create a circular flow model to illustrate your answer.

9. **Solving Economic Problems** How do you think the disadvantages of a market economy can be minimized while its advantages continue to operate?

10. **Challenge** On August 29, 2005, Hurricane Katrina devastated regions of the Gulf Coast states of Louisiana, Mississippi, and Alabama. Most of New Orleans, for example, was flooded after the levees protecting the city broke. How would a pure market economy respond to the devastation and loss?

ECONOMICS IN PRACTICE

Employers and employee discuss salary

Understanding the Market Economy
Market economies can be identified by certain fundamental characteristics. These include self-interested behavior, private property rights, voluntary exchange, profit, competition, consumer sovereignty, specialization, and a limited role for government.

Identify Features Each sentence in the chart illustrates one fundamental feature of a market economy. Complete the chart by identifying these features.

Feature	Description
	An author secures a copyright for her latest novel.
	Declining sales signal the end of production for a model of car.
	A prospective employee and a business reach an agreement on salary and benefits.
	Taking advantage of their beautiful natural environment, local planners approve development of new hotels and resorts.

Challenge Write sentences illustrating two fundamental features of market economies not illustrated in the sentences above.

Economic Systems 57

Modern Economies in a Global Age

OBJECTIVES	KEY TERMS	TAKING NOTES
In Section 4, you will • identify the main characteristics of a mixed economy • understand why most modern economies are mixed economies • explain why modern economies are becoming increasingly global	mixed economy, *p. 58* nationalize, *p. 61* privatize, *p. 61* global economy, *p. 61*	As you read Section 4, complete a cluster diagram to record what you learn about modern economies in a global age. Use the Graphic Organizer at **Interactive Review @ ClassZone.com**

Today's Mixed Economies

KEY CONCEPTS

Today, the **mixed economy**—an economic system that has elements of traditional, command, and market economies—is the most common type of economic system. Even the most strongly market-based modern economies have some elements of central planning. Similarly, market influences have penetrated all of today's command economies to some extent. Traditional production methods are still followed in some areas of both market and command systems. And traditional economies everywhere are experiencing greater government involvement and growing pressure from market influences.

Life in a Mixed Economy

Let's look at a farming family in the rural Midwest of the United States to see how elements of all three economic systems may be present in a mixed economy. The family has owned and operated the farm for many generations. While they use the most modern farming methods, family members still cling to some old customs. At harvest time, for example, everybody works to get in the crops. Even the youngest children have their own special tasks to do. The family's crops are sold on the market along with those of their neighbors and of farmers throughout the region. Well-maintained highways connect the farm to the various locations where the crops are sold. Two teenagers in the family attend the public high school. The oldest one works in town at a part-time job during the week, earning the minimum wage. Two grandparents who no longer work full time on the farm each receive a Social Security check every month.

In this scenario, all three types of economic system are blended. The harvest-time customs the family follows represent the influence of a traditional economy. The command aspects of the economy are reflected in the ways that government has become involved. The well-maintained roads, the public high school, the minimum wage, and the Social Security checks are all examples of government benefits and regulations at the local, state, or national level. (You'll learn more about government involvement in the economy, including the minimum wage and Social Security, in later chapters.) The market aspects of the economy are represented in the private property rights and entrepreneurship of the family members. They own their land and have figured out the best ways to use it to make a living. Other aspects of a market economy include the competitive market in which their goods are sold, and the voluntary exchange that takes place when the family sells its crops and when one of the teenagers exchanges labor for wages.

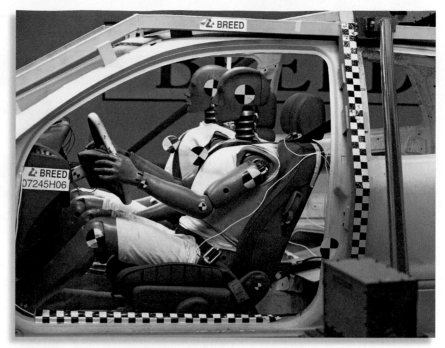

Elements of Command One way the U.S. government intervenes in the economy is to set safety standards for automobiles and other products.

Types of Mixed Economies

Although all modern economies are mixed, they often emphasize one type of system or another. In the scenario you just read, which is based on the economy of the United States, the market economy dominates. Even though there are traditional and command elements, the driving forces of the U.S. economy are such features as private ownership and markets. So, the United States essentially has a market economic system.

Many European countries have a more even mix of market and command economies. France, for example, tried to find a "middle way" between socialism and capitalism. In the years following World War II, its economy emphasized the command system with government ownership of core industries. In the 1980s, however, many people expressed dissatisfaction with the performance of government-owned industry. As a result, the French government pulled back from its ownership role in the economy, privatizing several industries, most notably banking and insurance. Even so, it still has a controlling share of ownership in a number of industries, including energy, automobiles, transportation, communications, and defense. In addition, it provides an array of social services, including health care and education, to the French people.

Sweden, while also a mixed economy, has much greater government involvement. The Swedish government and government-related organizations own about one third of all Swedish companies. In addition, Swedish citizens receive "cradle to grave" social benefits. These include childcare for children ages 1 through 5, schooling for

MATH CHALLENGE

FIGURE 2.5 Calculating Percentages

Economists often use percentages to express the level of government involvement in a country's economy.

Step 1: Read the table, which contains data on the total economy and government consumption—the value of all the goods and services government buys—for three countries.

Step 2: Using Canada as an example, calculate government consumption as a share of the total economy.

Country	Total Economy (in billions of U.S. dollars)	Government Consumption (in billions of U.S. dollars)
Canada	789.8	152.4
Nigeria	48.8	11.4
Sweden	259.2	72.2

Source: Heritage Foundation

$$\frac{\text{Share of economy consumed by government}}{} = \frac{\text{Government consumption}}{\text{Total economy}}$$

$$\frac{\$152.4}{\$789.8} = 0.192960243$$

Step 3: Convert the answer to a percentage by multiplying by 100.

$$0.192960243 \times 100 = 19.2960243\%$$

Step 4: Round your answer to a whole number.

19.2960243 rounded to a whole number ≈ 19%

Comparing Economies To compare government consumption in the economies of two different countries, economists can calculate percentages for each country and compare the percents.

NEED HELP?

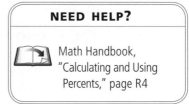

Math Handbook, "Calculating and Using Percents," page R4

children ages 6 through 16, additional years of school and college for those who choose them, health care, dental care, paid time off for raising families, and generous old-age pensions. In return, however, the Swedish pay very high tax rates, in some cases as high as 60 percent of income.

Each country has its own distinct balance of economic types. Namibia, as you read in Section 1, has a large number of people engaged in subsistence farming, following traditional production methods. Since the early 1990s, however, the Namibian government has been encouraging a more market-driven approach, including foreign investment in farming and other businesses. The country's leaders hope that these efforts will help the economy to grow and provide more economic opportunities for all Namibians.

APPLICATION Synthesizing Economic Data

A. Look at the Math Challenge above. What level of government involvement in the economy does each country shown have?

Trends in Modern Economies

KEY CONCEPTS

Economies have changed, and are always changing, in response to changes in natural, social, and political conditions. In the early 1990s, for example, some Eastern European economies experienced abrupt change when their command systems broke down after the collapse of communism in the Soviet Union. Many of these economies have been making reforms to introduce more market elements. (You'll learn more about these economies in Chapter 18.)

TREND 1 Changes in Ownership

Economies in transition often go through predictable processes. Some of the most important relate to changes in ownership. After World War II, some European economies became more centrally planned. For example, the British government, to help the country more effectively recover from the war, nationalized several important industries, including coal, steel, and the railroads. To **nationalize** means to change from private ownership to government or public ownership.

More recently, many economies have moved away from command systems to market systems. In this process, government-owned industries have been privatized. To **privatize** means to change from government or public ownership to private ownership. Poland, for example, is undergoing a transition from a command to a market economy with an extensive privatization program. Since 1990, Poland has privatized a number of manufacturing, construction, trade, and service industries. The Polish government hoped that private ownership of economic resources would provide incentives for greater efficiency, which, in turn, would help the economy to grow.

QUICK REFERENCE

To **nationalize** means to change from private ownership to government or public ownership.

To **privatize** means to change from government or public ownership to private ownership.

The **global economy** refers to all the economic interactions that cross international boundaries.

TREND 2 Increasing Global Ties

One way to help privatize an industry is to open it up to foreign investors. This kind of economic tie between nations is only one example of the global economy. The **global economy** is all the economic interactions that cross international boundaries. Today, American consumers and businesses are actors in a world economy. Businesses now engage in more foreign trade than ever before, and they depend not only on the products they buy from foreign nations, but also on the foreign markets in which they sell their products.

There are several reasons for this surge in economic globalization. One reason is the opening up of the world's markets to trade. Nations have been discussing ways to open trade for many years. The outcome of these talks has been the signing of agreements that ensure that trade among nations flows as

Globalization Some people are opposed to globalization, charging that it results in the loss of national identity.

FIGURE 2.6 The World Student

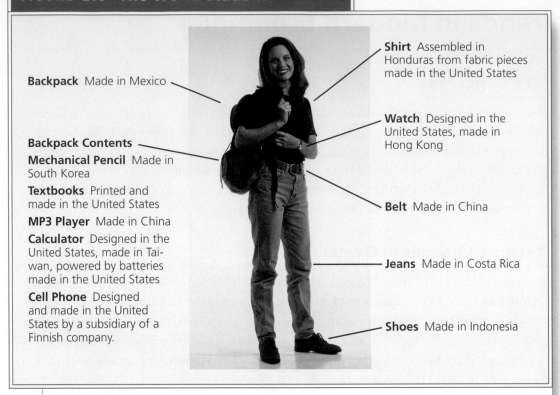

Backpack Made in Mexico

Backpack Contents
Mechanical Pencil Made in South Korea
Textbooks Printed and made in the United States
MP3 Player Made in China
Calculator Designed in the United States, made in Tai-wan, powered by batteries made in the United States
Cell Phone Designed and made in the United States by a subsidiary of a Finnish company.

Shirt Assembled in Honduras from fabric pieces made in the United States

Watch Designed in the United States, made in Hong Kong

Belt Made in China

Jeans Made in Costa Rica

Shoes Made in Indonesia

ANALYZE CHARTS
List all the things that you use in a normal day—the clothes you wear, the foods you eat, the appliances you use, and so on. Identify where each item was made—in the United States or in another country.

smoothly and freely as possible. Another reason for the growth of the global economy is the development of faster, safer, and cheaper transportation. Distribution methods have become so efficient that resources and products can be moved around the world relatively inexpensively. In addition, telephone and computer linkages have made global financial transactions quick, inexpensive, and easy.

Globalization also has been enhanced by cross-border business partnerships. For example, Ford Motor Company of the United States and Mazda Motor Corporation of Japan have long worked as partners. They design and engineer cars together, use each other's distribution systems, and share manufacturing plants. Recently, Ford and Mazda have joined with China's Changan Automotive Group to produce engines for Ford and Mazda cars. Such shared efforts lead to greater efficiency, which results in lower production costs and greater profits.

Other global partnerships have grown out of the need to share the enormous costs of researching and developing new technology. For example, Hitachi of Japan has joined with two American companies, Texas Instruments Incorporated and Integrated Device Technology, to develop smaller and more powerful computer memory chips. Such joint efforts are an illustration of today's economic reality—businesses can cooperate and learn from one another even while pursuing their own interests.

Economics Update
Find an update on global partnerships at **ClassZone.com**

APPLICATION Analyzing Effects

B. How do global business alliances benefit the U.S. economy?

REVIEWING KEY CONCEPTS

1. For each of the following key terms, write a sentence that illustrates its meaning.
   a. *mixed economy*
   b. *nationalize*
   c. *privatize*
   d. *global economy*

2. What is a market-driven mixed economy? Illustrate your answer with examples.

3. In the transition from command to market economies, most economic resources are privatized. What is the expected impact of this action?

4. What forces have contributed to the growth of the global economy?

5. How are you, as an individual, affected by the global economy?

6. **Using Your Notes** Write a four-sentence summary of this section, using your completed cluster diagram as a reference.

   Use the Graphic Organizer at **Interactive Review @ ClassZone.com**

   Today's Mixed Economies — Trends in Modern Economies — Modern Economies

CRITICAL THINKING

7. **Explaining an Economic Concept** Explain, with examples, how the American economy includes elements of traditional, command, and market economic systems.

8. **Analyzing Cause and Effect** Since the fall of communism in the 1990s, countries in Eastern Europe and the former Soviet Union have abandoned command economies in favor of market economies. How do you think economic life in these countries has changed?

9. **Applying Economic Concepts** Many nations import U.S. capital and technology by purchasing equipment that U.S. businesses manufacture. Explain how this development can benefit the American people.

10. **Challenge** How do market forces operate in the global economy? Illustrate your answer with examples.

ECONOMICS IN PRACTICE

Shopping for shoes

Illustrating the Global Economy
How do you participate in the global economy? Study Figure 2.6 opposite and then complete this exercise.

Conduct a Survey Make a survey of class members to identify the "Made in" labels in their clothes, shoes, and other items they use every day. Use a chart similar to the one below to list the items and the countries in which they were produced.

Product	Where Made
Sweaters	
Shirts	
Pants or dresses	
Shoes	
Jackets	
Backpacks	

Challenge Write a short explanation of how this list illustrates the global economy.

Contrasting Economies: North Korea and South Korea

Background Korea was an independent kingdom for nearly 1,000 years. After World War II, the country was divided into two nations, North Korea and South Korea. Since then, the two countries have developed in vastly different ways. After the Korean War ended in 1953, North Korea's communist government followed an economic, political, and military policy of isolation. North Korea has a command economy, though elements of a market system are taking root.

South Korea, in contrast, is a democracy with a market economy. South Korea has achieved incredible economic growth, in part because of its *chaebols* (jeh BOLZ), huge technology conglomerates like Samsung and Hyundai that originated from a single family. Strong government support for businesses has aided the country's economic success.

North Korea

South Korea

What's the issue? How effective are command and market economies? Use these sources to discover how well the economies of North and South Korea function.

A. Online Article

In this article, the United States Institute of Peace (USIP) summarizes the findings of Andrew P. Natsios about the great famine in North Korea. Natsios is the author of *The Great North Korean Famine: Famine, Politics, and Foreign Policy* (2001).

North Korea Suffers Famine

Workers in "unproductive" industries die from lack of food

According to some estimates, . . . three million people died in the North Korean famine of the mid-1990s. . . .

Faced with a massive food shortage, the North Korean government "made a choice," Natsios said. Making the regime's survival its top priority, the government decided that food would go to the country's elite and its military forces. Most citizens, especially those who lived in regions or worked in industries that the government deemed "unproductive," were considered expendable. As many as three million people may have died.

Before the famine, North Korea relied on food and oil subsidies, mostly from the former Soviet Union. When that aid declined and a series of natural disasters occurred, the North Korean government cut food rations to farmers. Many people started hoarding and stealing. The system collapsed. In Natsios' view, North Koreans lost faith in the state.

Source: **"The North Korean Famine."** *Peace Watch Online,* June 2002

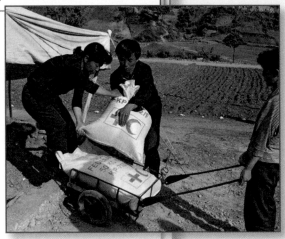

North Koreans receive contributions of rice from an international humanitarian agency.

Thinking Economically What decision described in this document is characteristic of a command economy? Explain your answer.

FIGURE 2.7 NORTH AND SOUTH KOREA: GDP PER CAPITA

B. Graph

This graph compares North Korea's and South Korea's per capita GDP—each person's share of everything produced in the economy—from 1990 to 2005.

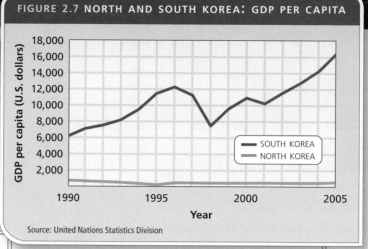

Source: United Nations Statistics Division

Thinking Economically What does this graph suggest about productivity in the two nations?

C. Magazine Article

This article reflects the contributions of corporations like Samsung to South Korea's growing economy.

Samsung and the "Next Great Tech Revolution"

Heading Towards a Digitized Life

Lee Jong Jin, 51, is no couch potato. But lounging in his apartment overlooking the mountains of Seoul, the international trader has little reason to leave his sofa. As he watches an interactive game show, he uses the remote to send in answers. In a corner of the 50-inch plasma screen, he can link to his online bank or control his air conditioner. Lee is one of thousands of Koreans involved in trials of Samsung Electronics' Home Network, which allows digital products to talk to each other. If Samsung has its way, millions around the world will be running their homes from the comfort of their couch within a few years. . . .

Over the last decade, [Samsung] has . . . become the most diverse and profitable consumer-electronics company on the planet. Samsung leads the global market for color televisions, VCRs, liquid crystal displays for electronic devices and digital memory devices. . . . Since 1999, revenues have doubled, and profits have risen 20 times. . . .

In the digital world all these products will finally be networked to each other . . . creating the sort of "smart" living space imagined only in science fiction. That's the idea, anyway. The change, says analyst Keith Woolcock of Westhall Capital in London, will be "the biggest event in technology for the next 10 years."

Source: "Digital Masters," *Newsweek* (International Edition), October 18, 2004

Thinking Economically What aspects of a market economy are illustrated by Samsung's financial success?

THINKING ECONOMICALLY Synthesizing

1. Based on documents A and C, in which country does the government appear to be more involved in controlling business and the economy?

2. Based on documents A and B, what can you infer about the effects of government activities on productivity in the two nations?

3. In today's global economy, is a command economy or a market economy more likely to succeed? Support your answer with information presented in the three documents.

Interactive Review

Review this chapter using interactive activities at ClassZone.com
- **Online Summary**
- **Graphic Organizers**
- **Quizzes**
- **Review and Study Notes**
- **Vocabulary Flip Cards**

Online Summary

Complete the following activity either on your own paper or online at **ClassZone.com**

Choose the key concept that best completes the sentence. Not all key concepts will be used.

capitalism	global economy	private property rights
centrally planned economy	laissez faire	privatize
circular flow model	market	product market
command economy	market economy	profit
competition	mixed economy	socialism
factor market	nationalize	traditional economy
		voluntary exchange

In a __1__, the three basic economic questions of what to produce, how to produce, and for whom to produce are answered in the same way they have been for generations. In a __2__, in contrast, the government makes most economic decisions. Two systems in which government plays a strong role are communism and __3__. In the transition between types of economic systems, the government may __4__ industries, taking them out of private ownership.

A __5__ economy rests on private ownership, however, so __6__ guaranteed by the government are vitally important. A market economy also depends on __7__ to help produce the highest quality goods at the lowest price. Sellers are motivated by the chance to make a __8__, so they try to use their resources as efficiently as possible. The __9__ shows the flow of money as well as the flow of products and resources in the __10__ that takes place between buyers and sellers in a market economy.

The most common kind of economy today is the __11__ which blends elements from all three systems. Each modern economy is also part of the __12__, which entails all the economic interactions that cross international borders.

REVIEWING KEY CONCEPTS

Introduction to Economic Systems (pp. 38–41)

1. What are the three types of economic systems?

2. What are features of a traditional economy?

Command Economies (pp. 42–47)

3. What role does the government play in a command economy?

4. What are the advantages and disadvantages of a command economy?

Market Economies (pp. 48–57)

5. What are the features of a market economy?

6. What are the advantages and disadvantages of a market economy?

Modern Economies in a Global Age (pp. 58–65)

7. What are the features of a mixed economy?

8. What trends are shaping modern economies?

APPLYING ECONOMIC CONCEPTS

Look at the chart below showing statistics for four nations. Answer the following questions.

9. Which country appears to have the most productive economy?

10. Does a high percentage of GDP from agriculture make a country more or less productive? Support your answer with statistics from the chart.

FIGURE 2.8 GROWTH AND PRODUCTIVITY

Country	GDP* Growth Rate	PPP**	% of GDP from Agriculture
North Korea	1.0	1,800	30.0
Poland	3.3	12,700	2.8
Namibia	4.2	7,800	9.3
China	9.2	6,200	14.4

* Gross Domestic Product (value of everything the country produced)
** Purchasing Power Parity (shows a country's productivity relative to its population)
Source: *The CIA World Factbook, 2006*

11. Creating Charts Create a chart showing a continuum of countries with different types of economic systems. At the left will be the nations with the most command elements in their economic systems. On the right will be the nations with the most market elements in their economies. Use the chart below as a model.

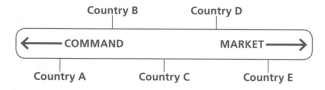

Begin with the countries listed in the chart on the previous page. Then add other countries mentioned in this chapter, such as France, Sweden, and the United States. Conduct extra research if you have difficulty placing these countries on the continuum. One useful source of information is *Economic Freedom of the World Annual Report.*

12. Synthesizing Economic Data Look again at Figure 2.8 on page 66. Why do you think Poland and Namibia had relatively high growth rates? In writing your answer, consider the economic changes that have taken place in these countries in recent years.

13. Evaluating Economic Decisions Using information in Figure 2.8, evaluate Poland's decision to privatize a number of its industries, noting whether you think it was a wise or an unwise action. Explain your evaluation.

14. Explaining an Economic Concept In most of the former command economies in Eastern Europe, one of the first economic changes instituted was establishing the right to own private property. Why do you think the leaders of these countries considered this feature of market economies so important?

15. Challenge Write a brief essay explaining how a country's political system and economic system are intertwined.

Privatize Your Community's Recreation Facilities

Suppose your community felt that its administration of your park district and recreation facilities—pools, gyms, and so on—had become inefficient. As an exercise to understand the issues involved in moving from a government-owned to a privately-owned enterprise, work through the decisions you would face in privatization.

Step 1. With your whole class, divide the recreation facilities into manageable segments. One segment might be park maintenance, another might be fitness classes at the community center, and so on. Then organize pairs or small teams and assign each pair or team one of the segments.

Step 2. In your pairs or teams, discuss how to use the elements of a market economy to make your segment of the project as efficient as possible—to provide the lowest priced services at the highest possible quality.

Step 3. Draw up a plan describing the privately-owned company you think could take over your segment.

Step 4. Share your plans with the teams working on the other segments to see what other ideas came up.

Step 5. With your whole class, discuss whether privatizing services like park district facilities is a beneficial step or not. Discuss possible advantages and possible disadvantages.

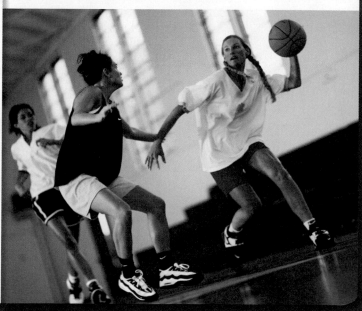

Free Enterprise

In the American free enterprise system, everyone is free to start a business like the couple shown here. Businesses will succeed or fail based on how well they respond to market forces.

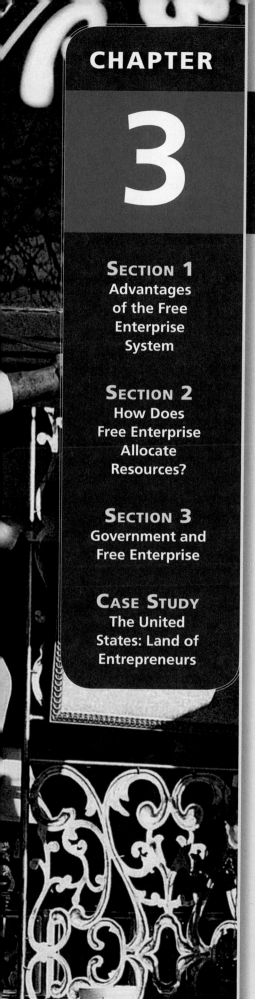

The American Free Enterprise System

CONCEPT REVIEW

A **market economy** is an economic system based on individual choice, voluntary exchange, and the private ownership of resources.

CHAPTER 3 KEY CONCEPT

Free enterprise system is another name for capitalism, an economic system based on private ownership of productive resources. This name is sometimes used because in a capitalist system anyone is free to start a business or enterprise.

WHY THE CONCEPT MATTERS

Free enterprise is all around you, from huge suburban malls to industrial developments to neighborhood corner stores. Think about ways that the American economic system affects your day-to-day life. Consider where you shop, what you buy, where you work, and what you do there. What do you think allows this huge economic engine to run?

Online Highlights
More at ClassZone.com

 Economics Update
Go to **ECONOMICS UPDATE** for chapter updates and current news on entrepreneurs in the United States. (See Case Study, pages 92–93).

Animated Economics
Go to **ANIMATED ECONOMICS** for interactive versions of diagrams in this chapter. ▶

Interactive ◀◀Review
Go to **INTERACTIVE REVIEW** for concept review and activities.

How do households, businesses, and government interact in the economy? See Figure 3.4 in Section 2 of this chapter.

Advantages of the Free Enterprise System

OBJECTIVES	KEY TERMS	TAKING NOTES
In Section 1, you will • explain why the United States is considered to have a capitalist, or free enterprise, system • identify the legal rights that safeguard the free enterprise system • analyze how the profit motive and competition help to make the free enterprise system work	free enterprise system, *p. 70* open opportunity, *p. 73* legal equality, *p. 73* free contract, *p. 73* profit motive, *p. 73*	As you read Section 1, complete a cluster diagram using information on free enterprise. Use the Graphic Organizer at **Interactive Review @ Classzone.com**

What Is a Free Enterprise System?

KEY CONCEPTS

QUICK REFERENCE

Free enterprise system is another name for capitalism, an economic system based on private ownership of productive resources.

As you recall from Chapter 2, the United States has a capitalist economic system. Capitalism is an economic system based on the private ownership of the factors of production. The central idea of capitalism is that producers are free to produce the goods and services that consumers want. Consumers are influenced by the desire to buy the goods and services that satisfy their economic wants. Producers are influenced by the desire to earn profits, the money left over after the costs have been subtracted from business revenues. A capitalist system is also known as a **free enterprise system** because anyone is free to start a business or enterprise.

EXAMPLE United States

Let's take a look at one American who took advantage of that freedom. Monica Ramirez, a makeup consultant for fashion magazines and television, noticed that very few Hispanic women purchased the cosmetics available in stores. She thought that this might present a business opportunity. So, in 2001, she created Zalia Cosmetics, a line of cosmetics specifically for

Latinas. She put her whole savings account into starting the business. Her creativity and energy attracted attention, and she soon had backers willing to invest their money in the business.

By 2004, Zalia Cosmetics had sales outlets in the major Hispanic markets of New York, Miami, Dallas, Los Angeles, San Antonio, and Houston. Today, the business continues to grow and Ramirez is sharing her success. She donates a percentage of her profits to organizations that help and encourage Latina entrepreneurs.

As you can see in Figure 3.1 below, Zalia Cosmetics was just one of more than 585,000 new businesses started in the United States in 2001. No matter where you go in the United States, you can see similar signs of a free enterprise economy at work. If you walk through a suburban shopping mall you'll see national and regional chain stores next to small boutiques and startup shops. Sometimes you'll even see kiosks in the aisles, competing for business. Similarly, on a stroll through a city neighborhood you'll observe corner grocery stores, dry cleaners, and barber shops. At an industrial park you'll see factories that churn out an immense variety of products. In the countryside beyond the city, you'll notice farms with fields of corn or soybeans, orchards of apples or peaches, or grazing areas for livestock.

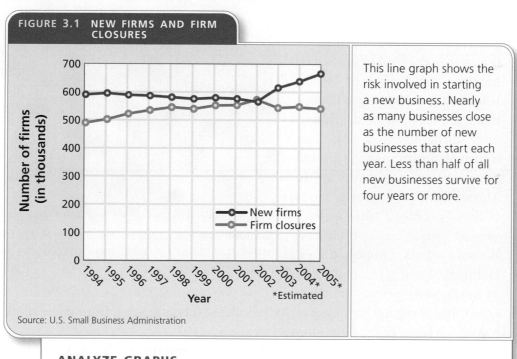

FIGURE 3.1 NEW FIRMS AND FIRM CLOSURES

This line graph shows the risk involved in starting a new business. Nearly as many businesses close as the number of new businesses that start each year. Less than half of all new businesses survive for four years or more.

Source: U.S. Small Business Administration

Economics Update

Find an update on new business firms and business firm closures at **ClassZone.com**

ANALYZE GRAPHS

1. What is notable about 2002 in terms of the relationship between new firms and firm closures?

2. How does this graph illustrate the fact that entrepreneurship involves risk?

What do these examples of free enterprise have in common? They are all illustrations of how individual choices are the basis of a market economy. Business owners freely make the choice to start these enterprises. Also, these owners are free to choose how they will use their scarce productive resources. The managers and workers who operate these businesses voluntarily decide to exchange their labor for the pay the owners offer. Finally, consumers make their own choices on which goods and services they will buy.

The American Free Enterprise System   71

As you recall, government plays a relatively limited role in the American free enterprise system. The government sometimes takes actions that limit free enterprise. For the most part, however, these actions are designed to protect or encourage competition or to enforce contracts.

EXAMPLE Emerging Markets

As you read in Chapter 2, most countries today have mixed economic systems with at least some elements of free enterprise. Each economy has its own balance of tradition, free enterprise, and government involvement and its own distinctive ways in which market forces work. To illustrate this, let's look at the countries of Mexico and Singapore

In the Mexican economy, the government plays a much larger role than in the United States. The Mexican government has established many rules and regulations that make starting a new business quite difficult. As a result, an informal market that gets around these barriers has grown up. In Mexico City, for example, much of the city center is taken up with vendors' stalls, and people jam the streets to buy imported toys, clothing, shoes, CDs, and more at much lower prices than they

Competition Popular stalls on the streets of Mexico City, selling everything from candy to clothes, provide considerable competition for established stores.

could find at regular retail stores. Indeed, the stiff competition from street vendors has driven some of the retail stores out of business.

The country of Singapore has a thriving free enterprise system. However, the government is so closely involved in the economy that the country is sometimes called Singapore Inc. The government establishes what benefits employers must provide to workers. It also requires all workers to put a percentage of income in the Central Provident Fund, a government savings scheme. The fund is used to pay pensions and to finance public projects, such as education, housing, and health care. Even so, the government is considered very supportive of free enterprise. Many of its policies keep business rents, taxes, and other costs low so that Singaporean companies remain competitive in the world economy.

APPLICATION Analyzing Cause and Effect

A. What steps can a government take to support free enterprise?

How a Free Enterprise System Works

KEY CONCEPTS

You learned in Chapter 2 that the right to private property is one of the most fundamental freedoms in a capitalist economy. With that freedom comes the right to exchange that property voluntarily. This exchange lies at the heart of a free enterprise economy. Another key freedom of this type of economy is **open opportunity**, the ability of everyone to enter and compete in the marketplace of his or her own free choice. This ensures that the market will reflect a wide range of interests and talents and will provide incentives to everyone to be efficient and productive.

Free enterprise also requires **legal equality**, a situation in which everyone has the same economic rights under the law. In other words, everyone has the same legal right to succeed or fail in the marketplace. Another important element of a market economy is the **free contract**. For voluntary exchange to work, people must be able to decide for themselves which legal agreements they want to enter into, such as business, job, or purchase commitments.

These freedoms assure that people are able to engage in free enterprise. But what motivates people to start a business? For most people, it is the **profit motive**, the incentive that encourages people and organizations to improve their material well-being by seeking to gain from economic activities. Producers, motivated by profit, seek the highest possible price for their products. Competition offsets the drive to earn profits, since it forces prices down. This helps producers find a price that is not so high that it deters buyers and not so low that it inhibits profits.

QUICK REFERENCE

Open opportunity is the ability of everyone to take part in the market by free choice.

Legal equality is a situation in which everyone has the same economic rights under the law.

A **free contract** is a situation in which people decide which legal agreements to enter into.

The **profit motive** is the force that encourages people and organizations to improve their material well being from economic activities.

EXAMPLE Profit in Rocks

One memorable example of how the various economic freedoms and the profit motive come together in the free enterprise system is the pet rock. Talking with friends in April 1975, advertising executive Gary Dahl joked that regular pets were too much trouble. Pet rocks, he suggested, were much easier to care for. Dahl's friends were amused by the idea. In response, he wrote a manual on pet rocks, showing how they could be house trained and taught to do tricks.

In August, Dahl began packaging his pet rocks, complete with a care manual, for sale at gift shows. Intrigued, a buyer from a major department store ordered 500. In a matter of weeks, Dahl's joke had become a national story. Articles appeared in newspapers and magazines and Dahl did several interviews on television. By the end of the year, Dahl had sold more than two tons of pet rocks and had become a millionaire. However, as 1976 began, consumers lost interest, and it quickly became obvious that the pet rock was last year's fad. Dahl decided to get out of the pet rock business, guided by the same market forces that had brought him into the business and made him rich.

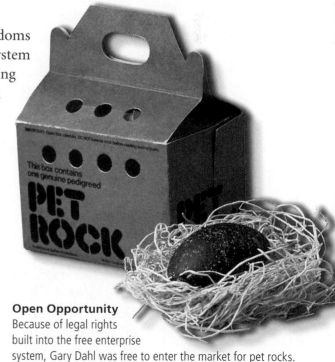

Open Opportunity
Because of legal rights built into the free enterprise system, Gary Dahl was free to enter the market for pet rocks.

Open Opportunity
Everyone should have the ability to enter and compete in any marketplace. Open participation serves as an incentive to be efficient and productive.

Legal Equality
Everyone should have the same economic rights under the law. In other words, the law should not give some people a better chance than others to succeed in the marketplace.

What Legal Rights Are Built into the Free Enterprise System?

Free Contract
Everyone should have the right to decide for themselves which legal economic agreements they want to enter into. Voluntary exchange, a cornerstone of free enterprise, cannot function without freedom of contract.

ANALYZE CHARTS
The American free enterprise system is based on the idea of freedom—producers and consumers are free to pursue their economic self-interest. Certain legal rights have been established to protect and encourage this freedom. Reread the paragraphs on pet rocks on page 73 and those on books on pages 74–75. How do these examples illustrate the legal rights shown in this chart?

EXAMPLE Competition over Books

Gary Dahl did face competition from other producers who jumped into the pet rock market. Competition, however, did not drive him out of business. Rather, consumers simply stopped buying pet rocks. The market for books is somewhat different. Demand for books remains high, but booksellers have been going out of business because of new and fierce competition.

Before 1995, small chain stores and independent neighborhood booksellers dominated the book market. Around 1995, large chain stores such as Barnes & Noble Inc. and Borders Group Inc. began to compete more aggressively. Because of their huge purchasing volume, the large chain stores could buy their books at greatly discounted prices. They passed the savings on to consumers, lowering prices by anywhere from 10 percent to 40 percent. They also created a warm and welcoming atmosphere in their stores, with comfortable reading areas, cafés, and frequent readings and book signings by authors.

The tactics of the large chain stores caused problems for independent book-sellers. In 1991, independent booksellers accounted for more than 30 percent of all book sales in the United States. By 2005, their share of sales had fallen to less than 15 percent. And between 1995 and 2005, about 1,200 independent booksellers went out of business.

Soon, however, the large chains faced a challenge themselves: Amazon.com. The online bookseller opened for business in July, 1995 and within a few months had become an important player in the book market. Amazon's easy-to-use Web site, huge database of titles, quick and reliable delivery, and discounted prices attracted many book buyers. By the end of 2004, Amazon's sales stood at $134 million a week. Now Amazon, however, is looking over its shoulder at a new challenger. Online competitors such as Overstock.com and Buy.com have undercut Amazon's prices on hundreds of books by as much as 25 percent while matching Amazon's level of excellence in service.

Consumers have benefited from all of this competition, for they can now easily and conveniently buy books at the lowest prices. Those independent booksellers who have remained in business cannot match the lower prices offered by the large chains and online sellers. However, they can provide some things that their larger competitors cannot: personal service and a focus on local tastes or specialized subject areas. Consumers benefit from this, too. These independent booksellers who stayed in business illustrate an important aspect of free enterprise. Businesses that keep pace with changes in the market and adjust accordingly thrive. Those that do not eventually fail.

YOUR ECONOMIC CHOICES

FREE ENTERPRISE

Where will you open your restaurant?

You've decided to open a restaurant. You can lease one of two buildings. One is in a busy mall next to a highway exit. However, there are already six restaurants in that mall. The other location is in a small strip mall in a quiet neighborhood with no other restaurants nearby. Consider the chance to make profits and the level of competition, and choose.

Mall food court

Neighborhood strip mall

APPLICATION Analyzing Cause and Effect

B. Explain the chain of cause-and-effect reactions since the mid-1990s that led to lower book prices for American consumers.

Milton Friedman: Promoter of Free Markets

At a glittering White House birthday celebration for Milton Friedman in 2002, President George W. Bush declared that the 90-year-old economist "has shown us that . . . in contrast to the free market's invisible hand . . . the government's invisible foot tramples on people's hopes." Economics professors are rarely guests of honor at White House galas. Why did Friedman receive such a tribute?

Free to Choose

Friedman spent most of his career teaching at the University of Chicago, where he helped develop the free-market ideas now linked with what is called the "Chicago School of Economics." Central to his ideas was the belief that the market should be free to operate in all fields, even such professions as the law and medicine. Easing government restrictions in these fields—lowering licensing standards, for example—would bring more doctors and lawyers into the market. This, in turn, would bring down the cost of legal and medical services. Friedman also put forward the theory that the government's most important economic role was to control the amount of money in circulation. Without this control of the money supply, Friedman noted, the economy would experience inflation—a sustained rise in the general level of prices.

Friedman's ideas were very influential. He advised two U.S. presidents and the heads of state of several other countries on economic policy. He gained worldwide recognition in 1976 when he won the Nobel Prize for Economics. Friedman became well known outside the academic world in 1980 when *Free to Choose*, which he wrote with his wife Rose, became the year's best-selling nonfiction book in the United States.

From 1977 until his death in 2006, Friedman served as a scholar at the Hoover Institution, a conservative public-policy research center at Stanford University. In 1996, he and his wife founded the Milton and Rose D. Friedman Foundation, an organization that promotes school choice.

Economic Freedom
Personal freedom is at the center of Friedman's economic theories.

> "Noteworthy for its clarity, logic, candor and unequivocal stand on political implications." —THE NEW YORK TIMES BOOK REVIEW
>
> # Free to Choose
> ## A PERSONAL STATEMENT
>
> THE CLASSIC INQUIRY INTO THE RELATIONSHIP BETWEEN FREEDOM AND ECONOMICS
>
> ### Milton Friedman
> *Winner of the Nobel Prize*

Economics Update

Find an update on Milton Friedman at **ClassZone.com**

APPLICATION Making Inferences

C. How might Milton Friedman have responded to the problems associated with the informal market in Mexico?

REVIEWING KEY CONCEPTS

1. Explain the differences among the following terms.

   a. *open opportunity*   **b.** *legal equality*   **c.** *free contract*

2. What is the role of the profit motive in the American free enterprise system?

3. How is a free enterprise system linked to economic freedom?

4. Give examples of three different economic freedoms in a free enterprise system.

5. What force acts as a balance to the profit motive in the American free enterprise system?

6. **Using Your Notes** Write two or three paragraphs explaining how a free enterprise system works. Refer to your completed cluster diagram.

   Use the Graphic Organizer at **Interactive Review @ ClassZone.com**

CRITICAL THINKING

7. **Applying Economic Concepts** Explain the role of competition in a free market. Illustrate your answer with examples of businesses in your local economy.

8. **Comparing and Contrasting Economic Information** Monica Ramirez and Gary Dahl both saw business opportunities and started new companies. Compare and contrast Ramirez's response to the market with that of Dahl. Use a Venn diagram to help you organize your ideas.

9. **Predicting Economic Trends** Turn back to page 74 and read again the paragraphs about competitive ideas in the bookselling market. What do you think might be the next new idea to compete with discounted books?

10. **Challenge** In a 1973 magazine interview, Milton Friedman said,

    What kind of society isn't structured on greed? The problem of social organization is how to set up an arrangement under which greed will do the least harm; capitalism is that kind of a system.

    Do you agree with Friedman that societies are structured on greed and that capitalism can reduce the harm caused by greed? Explain your answer.

ECONOMICS IN PRACTICE

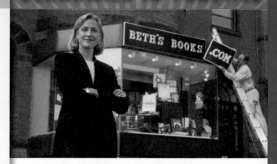

A new business in the United States

Analyzing Economic Information
The following chart gives data about the rules and time for setting up new businesses in six countries. The rules are measured according to the number of government procedures a new business has to go through before it can begin operating. The time is the number of days it takes to complete the process of registering a new business.

Draw Conclusions What is the relationship between the rules and the time for setting up a new business?

Country	Rules (Number of Procedures)	Time (Number of Days)
Canada	2	3
Sweden	3	16
United States	5	5
Singapore	6	6
Germany	9	24
Mexico	9	58
China	13	48

Source: World Bank, 2005

Challenge Use the chart and what you know about the economies of the listed countries to write a short paragraph comparing the ease of entry into the marketplace in three countries of your choice.

How Does Free Enterprise Allocate Resources?

OBJECTIVES	KEY TERMS	TAKING NOTES
In Section 2, you will • explain how consumers help determine the way resources are used • explain how producers help determine the way resources are used • analyze a circular flow model of the U.S. economy	profit, p. 78 modified free enterprise economy, p. 80	As you read Section 2, complete a cluster diagram to show how consumers, producers, and the government interact to allocate resources. Use the Graphic Organizer at **Interactive Review @ ClassZone.com**

The Roles of Producers and Consumers

KEY CONCEPTS

QUICK REFERENCE

Profit is the money left over after the costs of producing a good or service have been subtracted from the revenue gained by selling that good or service.

In the marketplace, consumers buy products for their personal use from producers who make or provide goods or services. In these exchanges, consumers look to get the best deal for the money they spend. Producers, on the other hand, are looking to earn the most profit from these transactions. **Profit** is the money left over after the costs of producing a product are subtracted from the revenue gained by selling that product. Seeking opportunities to earn profits is one way producers help allocate scarce resources in the economy.

EXAMPLE Producers Seek Profit

A new neighborhood coffee shop illustrates how producers help to allocate resources. The owners of the coffee shop, motivated by the desire to earn profits, charge the highest price consumers are willing to pay. The possibilities for good profits encourage other people to open coffee shops of their own. As a result, productive resources that might have been used in some other kind of business are directed toward the coffee shops. The profit seeking of producers, then, has helped in the allocation of resources.

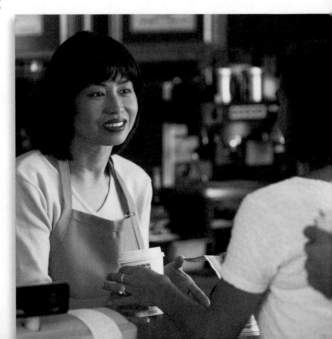

EXAMPLE Consumers Vote with Their Wallets

Consumers also play an important role in allocating resources in a free enterprise system. When consumers choose to buy a product, they are "voting" for their choice against competing products. These "votes" help determine what will be produced in the future, since producers, seeking opportunities to profit, try to provide what consumers want. For example, in the early 2000s, when low-carbohydrate diets were popular, consumers "voted" for low-carb and high-protein foods and against high-carb foods. (Figure 3.3 below illustrates this, showing that between 2002 and 2003 sales of typical low-carb/high-protein products increased, while sales of typical high-carb products fell.) How did food producers respond to these "votes"? They moved some of their productive resources into the low-carb market to try to meet consumer demand.

FIGURE 3.3 SALES OF SELECTED FOOD PRODUCTS

High-Carb Foods			Low-Carb/High-Protein Foods		
Product	Unit Sales, 2003 (in millions)	Percentage Change Over 2002	Product	Unit Sales, 2003 (in millions)	Percentage Change Over 2002
Instant Rice	79.1	−8.2	Frozen Meat/ Seafood	483.5	+7.7
Bulk Rice	180.2	−4.9	Meat Snacks	105.4	+7.6
Cookies	1,839.7	−5.5	Nuts	679.3	+8.8
Regular Carbonated Drinks	7,032.5	−5.9	Diet Carbonated Drinks	2,828.6	+1.0
Dry Pasta	1,227.0	−4.6	Cheese	3,424.0	+4.0
White Bread	1,606.1	−4.7	Wheat Bread	873.1	+4.0

Source: ACNielsen

ANALYZE TABLES

1. Which high-carb item showed the greatest percentage drop in sales between 2002 and 2003? Which low-carb/high-protein item showed the greatest percentage gain?
2. Consumer interest in low-carb diets began to decline after 2004. What differences might you expect to see in a similar table for 2004 and 2005?

Interest in low-carb diets peaked early in 2004, but began to fade thereafter. Once again, consumers had cast their votes in the marketplace, buying fewer low-carb and high-protein products. Producers quickly responded. By the beginning of 2005, some companies had gotten out of the low-carb market completely. Others had significantly cut back production of low-carb products. Consumer actions had caused a reallocation of productive resources.

APPLICATION Analyzing Cause and Effect

A. How would the allocation of resources have been affected if the interest in low-carb diets had continued to increase?

Government in the U.S. Economy

QUICK REFERENCE

A **modified free enterprise economy** is a free enterprise economic system with some government involvement.

KEY CONCEPTS

In Chapter 2 you learned that the United States economy, though based on the market system, is mixed. Government is an important element in the American economic system, but its role is relatively limited. This type of mixed economy, which includes some government protections, provisions, and regulations to adjust the free enterprise system, is sometimes called a **modified free enterprise economy.**

Modified Free Enterprise

In Figure 2.4 on page 53, you saw that the economy could be viewed as a stream of resources and products moving in a circular flow between households and businesses. Money also flows between households and businesses, facilitating this exchange of products and resources. Figure 3.4 shows how the government fits into this circular flow. It also shows how government exacts costs and dispenses benefits. Locate the two main economic decision-makers at the right and left of the chart: households (owners of resources) and businesses (makers of products). The two

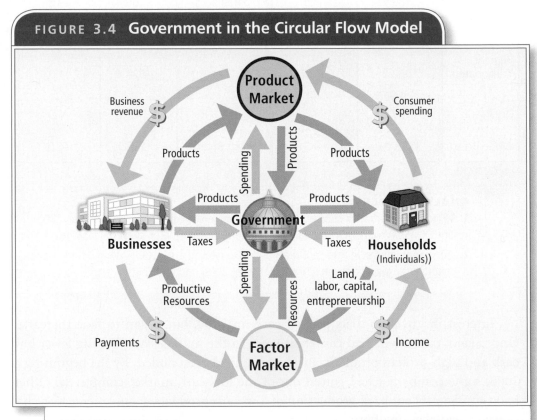

FIGURE 3.4 Government in the Circular Flow Model

ANALYZE CHARTS
This version of the circular flow model shows the flow of resources, products, and money among households, businesses, and the government. Describe the role of government in the economy using information from this chart.

Animated Economics

Use an interactive circular flow model at **ClassZone.com**

markets in the economy, the product market (for goods and services) and the factor market (for economic resources), are located at the top and bottom of the chart. The outer green arrows show the flow of money. The inner blue arrows show the flow of resources and products.

The government is located in the center of the chart. Like the other key actors in the circular flow, the government is both a consumer and a producer. Look at the arrows that run between government and the two markets. The government is a consumer in the resource market, spending money to buy the factors of production. It is also a consumer in the product market, spending money in exchange for products.

Now locate the arrows that run between government and households and government and business firms. Government is a producer here, providing goods and services to both households and businesses. Government collects money from households and businesses, in the form of taxes, as payment for these goods and services. It covers the costs of what it produces with this money. Government also uses this money to make purchases in the resource and product markets, and the cycle continues.

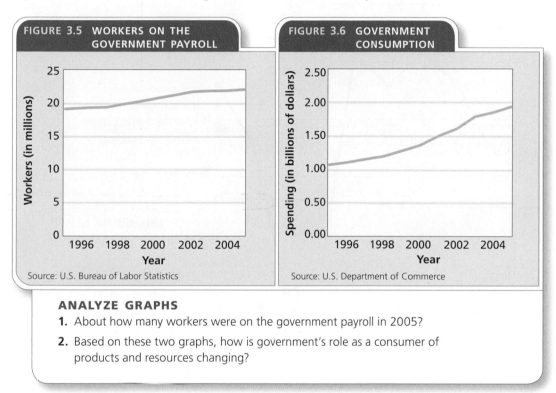

FIGURE 3.5 WORKERS ON THE GOVERNMENT PAYROLL

Source: U.S. Bureau of Labor Statistics

FIGURE 3.6 GOVERNMENT CONSUMPTION

Source: U.S. Department of Commerce

ANALYZE GRAPHS

1. About how many workers were on the government payroll in 2005?

2. Based on these two graphs, how is government's role as a consumer of products and resources changing?

Figures 3.5 and 3.6 above show that government is a major consumer of both resources and products. As you can see in Figure 3.5, all levels of government, local, state, and federal, employ almost 22 million workers. This is equal to about 16 percent of the labor force—all the labor resources available in the United States. Further, if you look at Figure 3.6 you'll see that government consumption—what all levels of government spend on goods and services—is about two trillion dollars.

Economics Update

Find an update on government workers and government consumption at **ClassZone.com**

APPLICATION Applying Economic Concepts

B. The paycheck that you get for working part-time at the pet store shows what you have earned and how much is withheld for taxes. Explain how the paycheck and the taxes withheld are represented in the circular flow model.

For more on interpreting graphs, see the Skillbuilder Handbook, page R29.

Interpreting Graphs: Public Opinion Polls

Public opinion polls are a useful tool for gathering information. Economists frequently use information obtained from opinion polls to measure public response to economic conditions. Polls conducted at regular intervals show changes in public opinion over a given period of time. The graph below shows the results of a poll that tracks consumer confidence. The poll, which is conducted monthly, is based on a representative sample of 5,000 households in the United States.

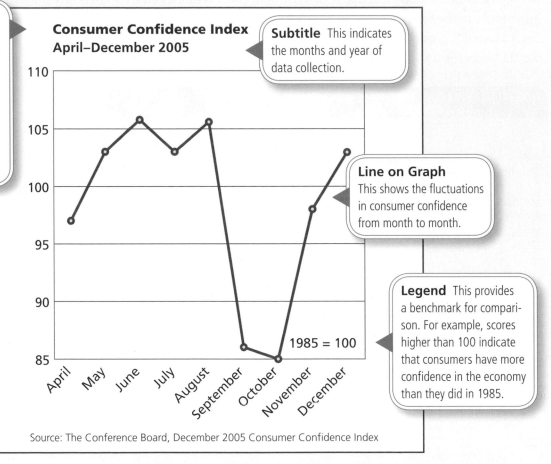

Title This indicates the type of data shown. Consumer confidence refers to the way people feel about the economy. Increasing confidence is likely to result in increased purchases of goods.

Consumer Confidence Index April–December 2005

Subtitle This indicates the months and year of data collection.

Line on Graph This shows the fluctuations in consumer confidence from month to month.

1985 = 100

Legend This provides a benchmark for comparison. For example, scores higher than 100 indicate that consumers have more confidence in the economy than they did in 1985.

Source: The Conference Board, December 2005 Consumer Confidence Index

According to researchers, consumer confidence in the economy tumbled after Hurricane Katrina hit the Gulf Coast in September 2005. Falling gasoline prices and growth in the job market led to a recovery in confidence in November and December.

THINKING ECONOMICALLY Interpreting

1. During which month was consumer confidence the highest? The lowest?
2. Describe the changes in consumer confidence from August through December.
3. The devastation caused by Hurricane Katrina and resulting increase in gasoline prices led to the abrupt drop in consumer confidence shown in the graph. What other events might cause a decline in consumer confidence?

REVIEWING KEY CONCEPTS

1. Why is the U.S. economy sometimes referred to as a modified free enterprise system?

2. How does the profit motive work to allocate resources?

3. How do households and business firms interact in the product and resource markets?

4. Describe how the government interacts with the product and resource markets.

5. Study the circular flow models on pages 53 and 80. How are the two models different?

6. **Using Your Notes** Explain how producers, consumers, and the government interact to allocate resources in a free enterprise system.

Use the Graphic Organizer at
Interactive Review @ ClassZone.com

CRITICAL THINKING

7. **Applying Economic Concepts** Think of several examples in which consumers have voted with their dollars and driven a product from the market or into high demand. Record your ideas in a table like the one below.

Consumers Drive Product from the Market	Consumers Drive Product into High Demand

8. **Comparing and Contrasting Economic Information** Compare and contrast the role of consumers and producers in allocating resources. Which do you think has the greater power?

9 **Interpreting Economic Models** Use the circular flow chart on page 80 and what you have learned from this section to explain the ways in which government allocates resources.

10. **Challenge** What industries in today's world do you think would be wise to make changes given consumers' preferences? Give reasons for your selections.

ECONOMICS IN PRACTICE

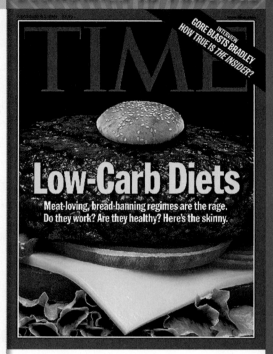

Analyzing Economic Information
Look at the graph below, which shows the sales figures for a company that makes a substance that reduces carbohydrates in baked goods.

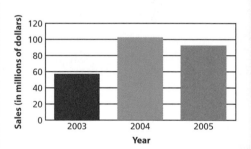

Interpret Information Write a sentence or two explaining the trend that the graph shows.

Challenge If you were the head of the company that made the substance that reduces carbohydrates in baked goods, in what direction would you move your business? How might you reallocate your resources?

Government and Free Enterprise

OBJECTIVES	KEY TERMS	TAKING NOTES
In Section 3, you will • understand that one role of government in the U.S. economy is to address market failures • analyze why governments provide public goods and infrastructure • explain how governments seek to decrease negative externalities and increase positive externalities	market failure, *p. 84* public goods, *p. 84* free rider, *p. 85* infrastructure, *p. 86* externality, *p. 87* negative externality, *p. 87* positive externality, *p. 87* subsidy, *p. 88* safety net, *p. 89* transfer payment, *p. 89* public transfer payment, *p. 89*	As you read Section 3, complete a cluster diagram to show the role of government in free enterprise. Use the Graphic Organizer at **Interactive Review @ ClassZone.com**

Providing Public Goods

KEY CONCEPTS

In the American economic system, most production decisions are made in the marketplace through the interactions of buyers and sellers. This is the free enterprise sector of our economy. Other decisions are made by different levels of government. This is the public sector of our economy. How do we decide which sector of the economy should produce a good or service? If all the costs are borne by, and all benefits go to, the buyer and seller, the free enterprise sector produces it. If people who are not part of a marketplace interaction benefit from it or pay part of the costs, there is a **market failure.** When market failures occur, the government sometimes provides the good or service. Goods and services that are provided by the government and consumed by the public as a group are **public goods.** Public goods are funded with taxes collected by the government.

Public Goods A city street lighting system is an example of a public good.

QUICK REFERENCE

Market failure occurs when people who are not part of a marketplace interaction benefit from it or pay part of its costs.

Public goods are products provided by federal, state, and local governments and consumed by the public as a group.

EXAMPLE Characteristics of Public Goods

Public goods have two characteristics. First, people cannot be excluded from the benefits of the product even though they do not pay for it. Second, one person's use of the product does not reduce its usefulness to others.

Perhaps the simplest example of a public good is street lighting. When the street lighting is on, it is impossible to exclude people from using it. In addition, the benefit you receive from the safety and security street lighting provides is not diminished because others receive it too. There is simply no way for a private business to establish a realistic price for street lighting and then collect it from all users. Rather, local governments provide street lighting, paying for it with taxes.

Another example of a public good is national defense. Everyone benefits from the country being defended. Further, the security you feel knowing that there is a national defense system in place is not diminished because other people feel secure too. Given these benefits, you would readily pay for this sense of security. However, what if you discovered that your neighbors were not paying for national defense? Would you voluntarily pay then? To avoid this problem, everyone is required to pay taxes to the national government, which provides national defense.

EXAMPLE Free Riders

There is no incentive for businesses to produce public goods, because people will not voluntarily pay for them. After all, people receive the benefits of these products whether they pay for them or not. This situation is called the free-rider problem, and it is one type of market failure. A **free rider** is a person who chooses not to pay for a good or service but who benefits from it when it is provided.

QUICK REFERENCE

A **free rider** is a person who avoids paying for a good or service but who benefits from that good or service anyway.

Consider a July 4th fireworks display, which can cost $200,000 or more. If you tried to set up a business to put on such displays, you'd immediately run into problems. There is no way to charge people for watching the display, since it is visible from so many locations. Even if you were able to charge a fee to watch from a particularly good location, many people would still be able to watch it from elsewhere without paying. Those people are free riders—they receive the thrill and enjoyment of the fireworks display, but they do not share in the costs of putting it on. Because of them, there is little interest in providing fireworks displays as a business opportunity.

One way to address the free-rider problem is for government to provide certain goods and services. The city government, for example, could put on the July 4th fireworks display, using taxes to pay for it. In this way, the costs and benefits are shared throughout the community.

Free Riders Free riders will choose not to pay for fireworks displays but will still enjoy the benefits. Because of this, private companies are reluctant to provide such services.

Another example of the free-rider problem is law enforcement. Once a policing system is established, everyone in the community is protected whether they pay for it or not. The best way to ensure that people who benefit from this protection pay a share of the costs is for government to provide the service, paying for it with taxes.

Public and Private Sectors—Shared Responsibilities

Some goods can be provided by either the public sector or the private sector. These often are toll goods—goods consumed by the public as a group, but people can be excluded from using them. For example, toll ways are open for all people to use, but those who do use them have to pay a toll. Similarly, parks are provided for the benefit of everyone, but those who want to enjoy this benefit may have to pay an entrance fee. The initial funding for toll goods is often provided by the public sector. Their day-to-day operation is often the responsibility of the private sector.

QUICK REFERENCE

The **infrastructure** consists of all the goods and services that are necessary for the functioning of society.

The private and public sectors share the responsibility for the nation's **infrastructure**, the goods and services that are necessary for the smooth functioning of society, such as highways; mass transit; power, water, and sewer systems; education and health care systems; and police and fire protection. How important is the infrastructure? Imagine, for example, what the United States would be like without its interstate highways, safe airports and seaports, and passenger and freight train systems. To begin with, the nation's economy would grind to a halt. Further, the nation would lose its ability to move troops in case of attack or to evacuate people in an emergency. A solid infrastructure, then, is essential to economic health.

YOUR ECONOMIC CHOICES

PUBLIC vs. PRIVATE

Will you support tax increases to improve recreational facilities?

The mayor wants to build a water park to attract visitors, who will spend money at your town's restaurants and stores. But what you pay in sales tax will rise by about $100 a year to cover the cost. With that money, you could buy a couple of video games. What will you choose—public wants or private wants?

Water park

Video game

APPLICATION Applying Economic Concepts

A. Identify another example in which the free rider problem makes public goods or services the best solution.

Managing Externalities

Another type of market failure occurs when economic transactions cause externalities. An **externality** is a side effect of a transaction that affects someone other than the producer or the buyer. A **negative externality** is an externality that is a negative effect, or cost, for people who were not involved in the original economic activity. For example, a manufacturing company discharges pollution into a nearby river. The costs of the pollution are borne by everyone who lives by the river, even if they have no connection to the manufacturing company. A **positive externality**, in contrast, is an externality that is a positive effect, or benefit, for people who were not involved in the original economic activity. Another of your neighbors, for example, plants and maintains a beautiful rose garden. All the surrounding homes benefit from the beauty.

EXAMPLE Paying for Negative Externalities

One of the most commonly discussed negative externalities is industrial pollution. The owner of a factory that belches filthy smoke in the air, influenced by such

QUICK REFERENCE

An **externality** is a side effect of a product that affects someone other than the producer or the buyer.

A **negative externality** is an externality that imposes costs on people who were not involved in the original economic activity.

A **positive externality** is an externality that creates benefits for people who were not involved in the original economic activity.

Paying for Pollution

A 1990 amendment to the Clean Air Act set a limit on the amount of sulfur dioxide that industries could release into the air. The government distributed to those industries only enough "pollution permits" to meet that limit. Instead of using their permits, some companies used cleaner production methods and sold the permits to other companies. As the price of these permits rose, more and more companies developed production methods that did not pollute.

FIGURE 3.7 SULFUR DIOXIDE EMISSIONS

Source: Environmental Protection Agency

ANALYZE GRAPHS

1. How would you describe the trend in sulfur-dioxide pollution, especially since changes in government policy in 1990?
2. How did the government take a market approach to the problem of pollution?

The American Free Enterprise System 87

market forces as the profit motive and competition, has little incentive in the short-term to pay the extra money required to reduce the pollution. Everyone living in the surrounding region suffers from this pollution. Not only do they bear the monetary cost of cleaning up the pollution, they suffer other costs too. They are more likely to suffer pollution-related illnesses and, therefore, face higher medical costs.

Limiting negative externalities, then, is one important role of the government in the American economy. The government taxes or fines the polluter, and in the process accomplishes two economic purposes. The money it raises through taxation and fines can offset the higher medical costs. In addition, the cost of the tax or fine to the factory owner provides an incentive to reduce pollution.

EXAMPLE Spreading Positive Externalities

Positive externalities are benefits that extend to people not involved in the original activity. For example, if a new college is built in your town, local businesses benefit from student purchases of goods and services. Workers benefit too, for as business expands to meet students' wants, more and more jobs become available. The community as a whole benefits from all the taxes collected from students. Local government is able to spend some of these funds to provide more public goods. In addition, the whole community benefits from the potential contribution a more skilled and knowledgeable population can make to the economy.

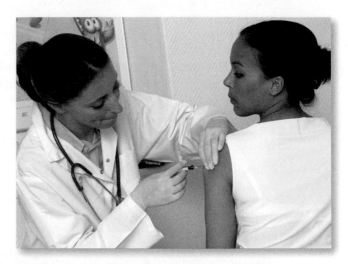

Positive Externalities The government will try to spread the benefit of a flu vaccination program—a healthier population—as widely as possible.

Just as government attempts to limit negative externalities, it tries to increase positive externalities. One way government does this is through subsidies. A **subsidy** is a government payment that helps cover the cost of an economic activity that is considered to be in the public interest. Since subsidies are paid for with taxes, everyone shares in their cost. Subsidies also spread the benefit of a positive externality as widely as possible. For example, the federal government might provide subsidies to drug companies to develop a new vaccine. This benefits the whole population in the long run because once the vaccine is in use there will be fewer and fewer infected people to spread the disease. Similarly, a local government might subsidize influenza shots for the community. Obviously, those people who take advantage of the free or inexpensive shots benefit because they are protected against infection. Even those people who don't get the shot still receive a benefit because they are less likely to encounter someone with the flu and therefore less likely to catch it themselves.

QUICK REFERENCE

A **subsidy** is a government payment that helps cover the cost of an economic activity that has the potential to benefit the public as a whole.

APPLICATION Explaining an Economic Concept

B. How might a drunk-driving law address negative externalities?

Public Transfer Payments

In addition to providing public goods and managing externalities, the government plays another role in the economy. One limitation of free enterprise is that people who are too old or sick to make a full economic contribution do not always have access to all economic opportunities. For these people, and others who are temporarily struggling, there is a public **safety net**, government programs designed to protect people from economic hardships.

Redistributing Income

Although the United States is the world's wealthiest nation, many of its people live in poverty. Since 1966, the proportion of the U.S. population in poverty has ranged from 11 to 15 percent. In 2007, that figure was 12.5 percent—or over 37 million people living in poverty in the United States. About a third of these people are children. Many of the rest cannot work because of age, disability, or other circumstance. Others face temporary poverty due to job loss or economic hardship.

How does a modern society address the issue of poverty? One way is to encourage economic growth. Another is through **transfer payments**, transfers of income from one person or group to another even though the receiver does not provide any goods or services in return. Some transfer payments are between private individuals. When you receive cash and checks from relatives and friends for your birthday or graduation, you are receiving transfer payments. When someone dies, a transfer payment flows to his or her beneficiaries in the form of inheritance. In both cases, the receiver provides nothing in return for the payment.

A **public transfer payment** is a payment in which the government transfers income from taxpayers to recipients who do not provide anything in return. Public transfer payments, since they do not reflect exchanges within a marketplace, are not a characteristic of pure market economies. They are more characteristic of command economies, and their presence in the United States is one feature that makes the U.S. economy a mixed economy.

Most public transfer payments are in the area of social spending—spending designed to address social issues, such as poverty. Social Security benefits, for example, have significantly reduced poverty among the elderly. This program is funded by the contributions of people currently employed. They pay a social security tax to the federal government, which in turn transfers it to people who are at or past retirement age. The Social Security program also provides income for the disabled.

FIGURE 3.8 PUBLIC TRANSFER PAYMENTS

Type	Expenditure (billions of dollars)
Social Security	580.8
Medicare	435.1
Medicaid	190.6
Earned Income Tax Credit	38.3
Food Stamps	34.9
Unemployment Assistance	33.2
Housing Assistance	33.0
Supplemental Income	32.8

Source: Office of Management and Budget, 2007 data

Social Spending in Sweden

Even among countries with free market economies, governments take different approaches to social spending. Sweden, for example, spends more on social welfare than does almost any other country. Around 30 percent of the country's total economic output goes toward such programs as a national health care system, retirement and disability pensions, and free public education—which includes college. The United States, by contrast, spends about 16 percent of its wealth on social welfare. U.S. social programs are not as comprehensive as those of Sweden.

The funds for Sweden's social spending come from higher taxes. The average Swedish household pays about 22 percent of its income in taxes. The average U.S. household, by contrast, pays only about 9 percent of its income in taxes.

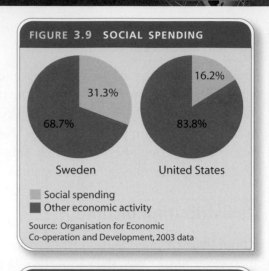

FIGURE 3.9 SOCIAL SPENDING

Sweden: 31.3%, 68.7%
United States: 16.2%, 83.8%

- Social spending
- Other economic activity

Source: Organisation for Economic Co-operation and Development, 2003 data

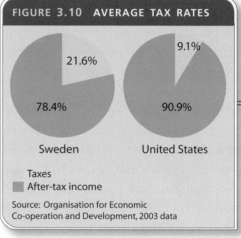

FIGURE 3.10 AVERAGE TAX RATES

Sweden: 21.6%, 78.4%
United States: 9.1%, 90.9%

Taxes
After-tax income

Source: Organisation for Economic Co-operation and Development, 2003 data

CONNECTING ACROSS THE GLOBE

1. **Synthesizing Economic Information** How do tax levels relate to the amount of resources devoted to social spending?

2. **Drawing Conclusions** Which country do you think has more of a market economy, Sweden or the United States? Why?

The government makes transfer payments to the very poor as well as to the aged and disabled. For many years, the program known as welfare made payments to the needy to assure their well-being. A debate developed about whether such a program fostered dependence on the government and removed incentives to break out of poverty. In response to this debate, the government introduced sweeping reforms in the mid-1990s. The new program, widely known as workfare, stressed the importance of helping welfare recipients enter or re-enter the workforce quickly.

Public transfer payments also provide a safety net for people who lose their jobs. Unemployment compensation from a mix of federal and state money tides people over until they can find a new job. While people receive it, they must show that they are making an effort to find another job. (You will learn more about unemployment, poverty, and government social spending in later chapters.)

APPLICATION Applying Economic Concepts

C. What are the opportunity costs of public transfer payments?

REVIEWING KEY CONCEPTS

1. Explain the relationship between the terms in each of these pairs:

   a. *market failure*
   free rider

   b. *negative externality*
   positive externality

   c. *subsidy*
   positive externality

   d. *safety net*
   public transfer payment

2. Illustrate the two characteristics of public goods with examples.

3. How is infrastructure linked to the economy?

4. Give an example of a free rider.

5. How can government limit a negative externality? How can it spread a positive one?

6. **Using Your Notes** Explain how the government gets involved in the economy in a modified free enterprise system. Refer to your completed cluster diagram.

   Use the Graphic Organizer at **Interactive Review @ ClassZone.com**

CRITICAL THINKING

7. **Categorizing Economic Information** Unemployment compensation and payment of living expenses for the disabled are examples of what kind of government involvement in the American economy?

8. **Making Inferences** After several incidents of hallway disputes among students, the board of a high school decides to hire hallway guards. In economic terms, what is the school board doing? How might this decision affect other programs at the school?

9. **Evaluating Economic Decisions** As part of the welfare reform of the mid-1990s, the federal government hired 10,000 people who had been dependent on welfare in an initiative called welfare-to-work. How does this approach differ from transfer payments? What are the costs and benefits of this approach?

10. **Challenge** In 2003, Congress passed laws to encourage private charitable organizations to provide social services. They would compete for government funds to carry out community services through their own networks. Do you think this is an effective way to address social issues? Why or why not? Use economic concepts, such as markets, efficiency, and opportunity costs in developing your response.

ECONOMICS IN PRACTICE

Cleaning up a toxic dump

Categorizing Economic Information Externalities are categorized according to their impact, either positive or negative.

Identify Externalities Decide whether each of the following is a positive or a negative externality and briefly explain its effect.

- A beekeeper establishes a farm next to an apple orchard and the bees move freely into the orchard.

- An airport is constructed near a residential neighborhood.

- A construction company cleans up a toxic dump near a site it is working on.

- Companies pay for programs to help employees get in shape.

Challenge Identify and explain a negative externality and a positive externality that affect you.

Case Study

Economics Update
Find an update on this Case
Study at **ClassZone.com**

The United States: Land of Entrepreneurs

Background The free enterprise system and the belief that everyone has the right to pursue economic success through lawful means is the backbone of American society. Many people achieve that success through working for an employer who provides a place to work, a paycheck, and other benefits. However, an increasing number of people are working for themselves, and for a variety of reasons. These reasons include a desire to market their own products, or to have more freedom.

What's the issue? What are some of the options for opening your own business? Study these sources to learn how others found their way, and the obstacles and opportunities they faced.

A. Magazine Article

This article discusses the development of Fizzy Lizzy, a new soft drink, from initial concept through launch, and introduces the entrepreneur who came up with the idea.

A Business Idea in a Bottle

Getting Fizzy Lizzy Bubbling

[Elizabeth] Marlin . . . got into the beverage business in the summer of 1996, when she set out for a long bicycle ride. . . . Not long into her trip, she realized that her favorite refreshment, which she had packed into a saddlebag—a half-gallon carton of grapefruit juice and a liter bottle of seltzer, which she'd mix together—was not only inconvenient, it was also slowing her down.

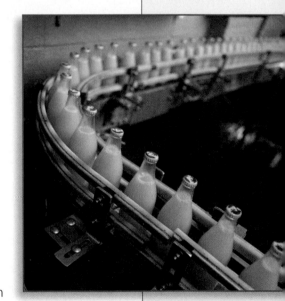

"Juice and seltzer is so simple," Marlin said. "I thought, Why can't I buy this is in a bottle?" She . . . was fixated on the idea of creating a carbonated juice, and began researching the beverage industry. She soon discovered she would need to hire a food scientist to help her. . . .

Although Marlin planned to devote her entire checking account to startup costs, that amount was nowhere near what [Abe] Bakal (consultant with 30 years' experience) was asking for R & D alone. . . . [B]ut he was so impressed by her enthusiasm that he offered to consult in return for a 20-percent stake in the business. . . .

Bakal recalled recently, ". . . one of the things I've learned in product development is that sometimes—not always, but sometimes—you can compensate with enthusiasm and commitment for money."

Source: "The Industry: Message in a Bottle," *New York Times,* June 26, 2005

Thinking Economically How did Elizabeth Marlin and Abe Bakal use their productive resources to start this enterprise?

FIGURE 3.11 SELF-EMPLOYED
WORKERS BY INDUSTRY

B. Chart

The self-employed make up about 7 percent of all U.S. workers. This table shows the number of self-employed workers in different industries.

Industry	Self-Employed Workers	Industry	Self-Employed Workers
Agriculture	856,000	Information technology	135,000
Mining	19,000	Financial services	829,000
Construction	1,890,000	Professional and business services	2,009,000
Manufacturing	348,000	Education and health services	1,102,000
Wholesale and retail trade	1,116,000	Leisure and hospitality	679,000
Transportation and utilities	405,000	Other services	1,026,000

Source: U.S. Bureau of Labor Statistics, 2007 data

Thinking Economically What two fields have the largest number of self-employed workers? Why might these industries attract more entrepreneurs?

C. Newspaper Article

This article discusses franchises, businesses that offer entrepreneurs an option to start their own business by buying into an established company with an existing business model.

Being the Boss with Backup

The Costs and Benefits of Franchising

In Maryland, there were more than 13,000 franchises employing about 179,000 [people] in 2001, according to [a] study, which was commissioned by the International Franchise Association. More than two dozen of those franchises are headquartered in the state, including Educate Inc., with more than 1,000 Sylvan tutoring center franchises worldwide and MaggieMoos's International with 184 ice cream shops, according to the association.

Opening such a business might be just the right fit for Phil Clark, a mortgage consultant from Elkridge. The mortgage business tends to fluctuate, Clark said. A franchise would give Clark more control over his future, a prospect he finds exciting. "A franchise gives me something more stable," he said. . . .

But it comes at a price. The cost of opening a franchise can vary from $25,000 to millions of dollars.

For some, franchising can mean economic empowerment and a chance at the American dream. But buyer beware: There is no guarantee of success, and a franchise requires the same amount of commitment, sacrifice and sweat equity as any independent business. . . .

Source: "Growing Occupation: Being Your Own Boss," *Baltimore Sun,* April 21, 2006

Thinking Economically If you were to start your own business, would you buy a franchise or build a new enterprise based on your own ideas? What factors would help you in making your decision?

THINKING ECONOMICALLY Synthesizing

1. Which of the businesses described in A and C might provide more stability for its owner? Why?
2. How are entrepreneurs important to the economy? Use information from B to support your answer.
3. Compare the businesses described in A and C. Which business requires more creativity to succeed? Why?

The American Free Enterprise System 93

Online Summary

Complete the following activity either on your
own paper or online at **ClassZone.com**

**Choose the key concept that best completes
the sentence. Not all key concepts will be used.**

capitalism	modified free enterprise economy	public goods
externality	negative externality	public transfer payments
free contract	open opportunity	safety net
free enterprise system	positive externality	subsidy
infrastructure	profit	transfer payments
legal equality	profit motive	

  1 is another name for capitalism. Three features
of this type of economy are open opportunity,
legal equality, and **2** , or the right to enter
into agreements of one's choice. The **3** is a
driving force in a free enterprise system, urging
entrepreneurs to enter the market. The market
allocates resources through the activities of both
producers and consumers. Producers, seeking
 4 , move their resources into the most productive
areas. Consumers, through their dollar votes, help
determine which products succeed and which fail.

  Left on its own, however, a free market cannot
address many social issues. The United States has
a **5** , mixing government involvement and market
forces. One role for the government is to provide **6** ,
such as national defense. Without a strong **7** in
place, modern economies cannot function. The
government also addresses problems created by a **8** ,
such as the pollution from a factory that affects all
those living nearby. It furthers a **9** , such as better
health through vaccinations, by offering a **10** for
inoculations. The government also makes direct
 11 in the form of social security, unemployment
compensation, and disability coverage.

CHAPTER 3 Assessment

REVIEWING KEY CONCEPTS

Advantages of the Free Enterprise System
(pp. 70–77)

1. What is a free enterprise system?

2. What are some of the rights that must be protected
for a free enterprise system to work?

How Does Free Enterprise Allocate Resources?
(pp. 78–83)

3. What are the roles of consumers and producers in
allocating resources?

4. What role does the government play in the
economy's circular flow?

Government and Free Enterprise (pp. 84–93)

5. What problem makes public goods necessary?

6. Besides providing public goods, what two purposes
can a government serve in a market economy?

APPLYING ECONOMIC CONCEPTS

Use the information in the table to answer the
following questions about changes in the nation since
the passage of the Clean Air Act in 1970.

Since the passage of the Clean Air Act:
• Nitrogen oxide emissions have declined by 17%
• Sulfur dioxide emissions have declined by 49%
• Lead emissions have declined by 98%
• Carbon monoxide emissions have declined by 41%
• Particulate emissions caused by combustion have declined by 82%

At the same time:
• U.S. population grew by 42%
• Overall energy consumption grew by 43%
• Total U.S. employment grew by 95%
• The number of registered vehicles grew by 111%
• The economy grew by 175%

Source: Foundation for Clean Air Progress

7. How would you use these statistics to argue that
the government has effectively managed a negative
externality?

8. Recently, there has been pressure to loosen clean
air standards. Use economic arguments to support
or oppose this proposed action.

9. **Creating Graphs** Use the statistics below to create a graph titled Businesses in the United States, 1997–2003. Use information from your graph and from Figure 3.1 on page 71 to write a generalization about businesses in the American free enterprise system.

Year	Number of Businesses (in millions)
1997	21.0
1999	21.8
2001	22.6
2003	22.7

Source: U.S. Small Business Administration

Use *SMART Grapher* @ ClassZone.com to complete this activity.

10. **Distinguishing Fact from Opinion** Look again at the information on changes in the United States after the passage of the Clean Air Act. Which of the following statements represents a fact? Which is an opinion? Explain why.

- Pollution has decreased since 1970.
- Pollution has decreased as a result of the Clean Air Act.
- The government can ease restrictions now that pollution is lower.

11. **Applying Economic Concepts** In the 1990s, efforts were made to reform the healthcare system in the United States so that much of it came under government control. Explain in terms of economic concepts you have learned in this chapter why these efforts failed.

12. **Challenge** Milton Friedman wrote,

    Many people want the government to protect the consumer. A much more urgent problem is to protect the consumer from the government.

    Explain what you think Friedman meant by this. Illustrate your answer with examples.

Conducting an Economic Impact Study

A manufacturing company has announced plans to open a factory in your town. The plant will consist of a manufacturing area and a warehouse area and will employ about 500 people. Production will be on a 24-hour basis, with workers working one of three 8-hour shifts. At the same time, a national megastore chain wants to open a store on the outskirts of town. The store will employ 60 people, be open 18 hours a day, and have a 200-car parking lot.

Imagine that you have been asked by local government authorities to conduct an economic impact study to identify the positive and negative externalities that the factory or megastore might create.

Step 1 Form a group with three or four classmates. Conduct research on how a factory or a megastore operates—the materials they use, the byproducts they create, and so on. Then do research to discover the impact a new factory or megastore might have on a community.

Step 2 In your group, review your findings and identify the positive and negative externalities of the factory or megastore. Record the information in a chart similar to the one below.

Externalities Created by the Factory/Megastore	
Positive	Negative

Step 3 Use your chart to write your economic impact report. Note the major externalities and suggest steps that the local government might take to limit negative externalities and to encourage positive externalities.

Demand

CONCEPT REVIEW

Microeconomics is the study of the economic behaviors and decisions of small units, such as individuals and businesses.

CHAPTER 4 KEY CONCEPT

Demand is the willingness to buy a good or service and the ability to pay for it.

WHY THE CONCEPT MATTERS

The concept of demand is demonstrated every time you buy something. List the last five goods or services that you purchased. Rate each one with a number from 1 (not important to you) to 4 (very important). Which of the goods or services would you stop buying if the price rose sharply? Describe the relationship between your ratings and your willingness to buy at a higher price.

Online Highlights
More at ClassZone.com

 Economics Update

Go to **ECONOMICS UPDATE** for chapter updates and current news on demand in the automobile industry. (See Case Study, pages 124–125.) ▶

Animated Economics

Go to **ANIMATED ECONOMICS** for interactive lessons on the graphs and tables in this chapter.

Interactive ◀◀Review

Go to **INTERACTIVE REVIEW** for concept review and activities.

What caused more people to demand hybrid cars? See the Case Study on pages 124–125.

Demand

This computer store customer meets the two requirements of demand—the customer is willing to buy and is able to pay.

What Is Demand?

OBJECTIVES	KEY TERMS	TAKING NOTES
In Section 1, you will • define *demand* and outline what the law of demand says • explain how to interpret and create demand schedules and describe the role of market research in this process • explain how to interpret and create demand curves	demand, *p. 98* law of demand, *p. 99* demand schedule, *p. 100* market demand schedule, *p. 100* demand curve, *p. 102* market demand curve, *p. 102*	As you read Section 1, complete a cluster diagram like this one for each key concept. Use the Graphic Organizer at **Interactive Review @ ClassZone.com** Demand

The Law of Demand

KEY CONCEPTS

In Chapter 3, you learned that the United States has a free enterprise economy. This type of economic system depends on cooperation between producers and consumers. To make a profit, producers provide products at the highest possible price. Consumers serve their own interests by purchasing the best products at the lowest possible price. The forces of supply and demand establish the price that best serves both producers and consumers. In this chapter, you'll learn about the demand side of this equation.

Demand is the desire to have some good or service and the ability to pay for it. You may want to take a round-the-world cruise or to rent a huge apartment that overlooks the ocean. Or you may want to buy a brand-new sports car or a state-of-the-art home entertainment center. However, you may not be able to afford any of these things. Therefore, economists would say that you have no actual demand for them. Even though you want them, you don't have the money needed to buy them. Conversely, you may want the latest CDs by several of your favorite bands. And, at a price of between $12 and $15 each, you can afford them. Since you have both the desire for them and the ability to pay for them, you do have demand for CDs.

Price is one of the major factors that influence demand. The **law of demand** states that when the price of a good or service falls, consumers buy more of it. As the price of a good or service increases, consumers usually buy less of it. In other words, quantity demanded and price have an inverse, or opposite, relationship. This relationship is graphically illustrated in Figure 4.1 below.

FIGURE 4.1 LAW OF DEMAND

As **prices** fall... **quantity demanded** goes up.

As **prices** increase... **quantity demanded** goes down.

EXAMPLE Price and Demand

Let's take a look at an example of demand in action. Cheryl, a senior at Montclair High School, loves movies and enjoys collecting them on DVD. She and Malik, a friend from school, sometimes meet downtown at Montclair Video Mart to look through the DVD stacks. Rafael, the owner of the video mart, often jokes that Cheryl and Malik spend so much time at his store that he might have to give them jobs. Actually, Cheryl already has a job—stocking shelves at her neighborhood supermarket. She worked so many hours this summer that she has extra money to spend. Let's see how DVD prices at Montclair Video Mart affect her spending decisions.

Cheryl has been saving to buy the DVD boxed set of the original *Star Wars* trilogy, one of her favorite series of movies. The set costs $69.95, and Cheryl has the money to buy it this weekend. When Cheryl goes to the Montclair Video Mart, she is disappointed to learn that the *Star Wars* set is sold out and a new shipment won't arrive for a week. She decides to buy some other DVDs so that she won't go home empty-handed, but she also decides to save roughly half of her money toward a future purchase of *Star Wars*.

As she looks through the movie DVDs, she sees that most of those she wants sell for $15. How many will she buy at that price? Let's say she decides to buy three and keep the rest of her money for the *Star Wars* trilogy. But what if each of the DVDs she wants costs just $5? Cheryl might decide that the price is such a good deal that she can buy seven. As you can see, the law of demand is more than just an economic concept. It's also a description of how consumers behave.

Economics Update

Find an update on the demand for CDs and DVDs at **ClassZone.com**

APPLICATION Applying Economic Concepts

A. You have $50 and want to buy some CDs. If prices of CDs rose from $5 each to $10, how would your quantity demanded of CDs change?

Demand Schedules

QUICK REFERENCE

Demand schedule is a listing of how much of an item an individual is willing to purchase at each price.

Market demand schedule is a listing of how much of an item all consumers are willing to purchase at each price.

KEY CONCEPTS

A **demand schedule** is a table that shows how much of a good or service an individual consumer is willing and able to purchase at each price in a market. In other words, a demand schedule shows the law of demand in chart form. A **market demand schedule** shows how much of a good or service all consumers are willing and able to buy at each price in a market.

EXAMPLE Individual Demand Schedule

A demand schedule is a two-column table that follows a predictable format. The left-hand column of the table lists various prices of a good or service. The right-hand column shows the quantity demanded of the good or service at each price.

Cheryl's demand for DVDs can be expressed in a demand schedule. Let's take a look at the price list in Figure 4.2 below. How many DVDs will Cheryl buy if they cost $20 each? How many will she buy when the price stands at $10? Your answers to these questions show one thing very clearly. Cheryl's demand for DVDs depends on their price.

Price and Demand
Storeowners often offer products at sale prices to encourage consumers to make more purchases.

FIGURE 4.2 CHERYL'S DVD DEMAND SCHEDULE

Price per DVD ($)	Quantity Demanded
a → 30	0
25	1
20	2
15	3
b → 10	4
$5	7

ⓐ At the top price of $30, Cheryl is not willing to buy any DVDs.

ⓑ At $10, she will buy four DVDs.

Notice that when the price falls, the number of DVDs Cheryl will buy rises. When the price rises, the number she will buy falls. So quantity demanded and price have an inverse, or opposite, relationship.

ANALYZE TABLES

1. How many DVDs will Cheryl be likely to buy if the price is $15?

2. What is the relationship between Cheryl's demand for DVDs and various quantities demanded shown on this table?

Animated **Economics**

Use an interactive demand schedule at **ClassZone.com**

EXAMPLE Market Demand Schedule

The demand schedule in Figure 4.2 shows how many DVDs an individual, Cheryl, is willing and able to buy at each price in the market. The schedule also shows that the quantity of DVDs that Cheryl demands rises and falls in response to changes in price. Sometimes, however, an individual demand schedule does not give business owners enough information. For example, Rafael, who owns Montclair Video Mart, needs information about more than just one consumer before he can price his merchandise to gain the maximum number of sales. He needs a market demand schedule, which shows the quantity demanded by all the people in a particular market who are willing and able to buy DVDs.

Take a look at the DVD market demand schedule below. Notice that it's similar to the individual demand schedule except that the quantities demanded are much larger. It also shows that, like individual demand, market demand depends on price.

FIGURE 4.3 DVD MARKET DEMAND SCHEDULE

Price per DVD ($)	Quantity Demanded
a → 30	50
25	75
20	100
b → 15	125
10	175
c → 5	300

ⓐ At the top price of $30, Rafael's customers will buy 50 DVDs.

ⓑ At the middle price of $15, the quantity demanded of DVDs is 125.

ⓒ At the low price of $5, the quantity demanded rises to 300.

So, markets behave in the same way as individual consumers. As prices fall, the quantity demanded of DVDs rises. As prices rise, the quantity demanded falls.

ANALYZE TABLES
1. How does the quantity demanded of DVDs change when the price drops from $25 to $10?
2. How does this market demand schedule illustrate the law of demand?

CONNECT TO MATH

How would a merchant use this schedule to decide on a price? First, the merchant would calculate the total revenue at each price. To figure out total revenue, multiply the price per DVD by the quantity demanded.

$30.00	Price
× 50	× Quantity
$1,500.00	Total Revenue

How did Rafael create a market demand schedule? First, he surveyed his customers, asking them how many DVDs they would buy at different prices. Next, he reviewed his sales figures to see how many DVDs he sold at each price. Techniques such as these for investigating a specific market are called market research. Market research involves the gathering and evaluating of information about customer preferences. (You'll learn more about market research in Chapter 7.) By tabulating the results of his market research, Rafael created his market demand schedule.

APPLICATION Applying Economic Concepts

B. Imagine that you have discovered a restaurant that makes the best pizza you have ever tasted. Create a demand schedule showing how many pizzas a month you would buy at the prices of $25, $20, $15, $10, and $5.

Demand Curves

KEY CONCEPTS

QUICK REFERENCE

Demand curve graphically shows the data from a demand schedule.

Market demand curve graphically shows the data from a market demand schedule.

A **demand curve** is a graph that shows how much of a good or service an individual will buy at each price. In other words, it displays the data from an individual demand schedule. Creating a demand curve simply involves transferring data from one format, a table, to another format, a graph.

A **market demand curve** shows the data found in the market demand schedule. In other words, it shows the quantity that all consumers, or the market as a whole, are willing and able to buy at each price. A market demand curve shows the sum of the information on the individual demand curves of all consumers in a market.

EXAMPLE Individual Demand Curve

Study the demand curve (Figure 4.4 below) created from Cheryl's demand schedule. How many DVDs will Cheryl buy at the price of $15? How will Cheryl's quantity demanded change if the price rises by $5 or falls by $5? Find the answers to these questions by running your finger along the curve. As you can see, the demand curve is a visual representation of the law of demand. When prices go up, the quantity demanded goes down; when prices go down, the quantity demanded goes up.

You should note that this demand curve and the schedule on which it is based were created using the assumption that all other economic factors except price remain the same. You'll learn more about these factors and how they affect demand in Section 2.

CONNECT TO MATH

One common mistake people make is to look at the downward-sloping graph and think it means that quantity demanded is decreasing. However, if you move your finger downward and to the right on the demand curve, you'll notice that the quantity demanded is increasing.

FIGURE 4.4 CHERYL'S DVD DEMAND CURVE

Price per DVD ($)	Quantity Demanded
30	0
25	1
20	2
15	3
10	4
5	7

ⓐ The vertical axis of the graph shows prices, with the highest at the top.

ⓑ The horizontal axis shows quantities demanded, with the lowest on the far left.

ⓒ Notice that **demand curves** slope downward from upper left to lower right.

ANALYZE GRAPHS

1. How many DVDs will Cheryl buy when the price is $10?
2. How does this demand curve illustrate the law of demand?

Animated **Economics**

Use an interactive demand curve at **ClassZone.com**

EXAMPLE Market Demand Curve

Like Cheryl's individual demand curve, the market demand curve for Montclair Video Mart shows the quantity demanded at different prices. In other words, the graph shows the quantity of DVDs that all consumers, or the market as a whole, are willing and able to buy at each price. Despite this difference, the market demand curve for Montclair Video Mart (Figure 4.5) is constructed in the same way as Cheryl's individual demand curve. As in Figure 4.4, the vertical axis displays prices and the horizontal axis displays quantities demanded.

FIGURE 4.5 DVD MARKET DEMAND CURVE

Price per DVD ($)	Quantity Demanded
30	50
25	75
20	100
15	125
10	175
5	300

Notice that **market demand curves** slope downward from upper left to lower right, just as individual demand curves do.

The main difference between the two types of demand curves is that the quantities demanded at each price are much larger on a market demand curve. This is because the curve represents a group of consumers (a market), not just one consumer.

ANALYZE GRAPHS

1. At which price will Montclair Video Mart sell 175 DVDs?
2. Cheryl was unwilling to buy any DVDs at $30. Montclair Video Mart can sell 50 DVDs at that price. How do you explain the difference?

NEED HELP?

Throughout this chapter, you will be asked to create and to analyze demand curves. If you need help with those activities, see "Interpreting Graphs."

 Skillbuilder Handbook, page R29

Look at Figure 4.5 above one more time. What is the quantity demanded at the price of $15? How will quantity demanded change if the price increases by $5 or drops by $5? Once again, find the answers to these questions by running your finger along the curve. As you can see, the market demand curve—just like the individual demand curve—vividly illustrates the inverse relationship between price and quantity demanded. If price goes down, the quantity demanded goes up. And if price goes up, the quantity demanded goes down. Also, like the individual demand curve, the market demand curve is constructed on the assumption that all other economic factors remain constant—only the price of DVDs changes.

APPLICATION Applying Economic Concepts

C. Look back at the demand schedule for pizzas you created for Application B on page 101. Use it to create a demand curve.

SMARTGrapher
Create a demand curve at **ClassZone.com**

Vera Wang: Designer in Demand

FAST FACTS

Vera Wang

Title: Chairman and CEO of Vera Wang Ltd.

Born: June 27, 1949, New York, New York

Major Accomplishments: Updated design of wedding gowns and developed thriving fashion business

Other Products: Clothing, perfume, eyewear, shoes, jewelry, home fashions

Books: *Vera Wang on Weddings* (2001)

Notable Quotation: "*I saw women as very modern. I thought, . . . why should you look like the bride on top of a cake?*"

In this section, you've learned about the law of demand. You've also seen demand in action in some hypothetical situations. The story of fashion designer Vera Wang, however, provides a real-world example of demand at work.

When they married, Mariah Carey, Jennifer Lopez, and several other stars turned to Wang for their wedding dresses. What explains the demand for this one woman's gowns?

Responding to Demand

Vera Wang had worked in the fashion industry for more than 15 years by the time she started planning her own wedding in 1989. So she was frustrated when she couldn't find the type of sophisticated bridal gown she wanted. She knew that many modern brides were savvy career women who preferred designer clothing. Yet no one was making wedding dresses for those women.

Changing Styles
Vera Wang designs wedding gowns with a modern flair.

The next year, Wang decided to fill that unmet demand. She created her own line of gowns featuring elegant sleeveless styles rather than the hooped skirts, puffed sleeves, and lace flounces that had dominated wedding-dress designs before.

Soon celebrities such as Uma Thurman were choosing Vera Wang wedding gowns. This generated publicity, and demand for Wang's creations grew. In response, other designers began to create sleeker wedding dresses, and the style spread. Vera Wang is now considered to be one of the country's most influential designers of wedding gowns.

Demand for the sophisticated Wang style has spread beyond weddings. In response, Wang has expanded her product line to include ready-to-wear dresses, perfume, accessories, and home fashions.

Economics Update
Find the latest on Vera Wang's business at **ClassZone.com**

APPLICATION Analyzing Cause and Effect

D. In what ways did Vera Wang respond to consumer demand? In what ways did she generate consumer demand?

SECTION 1 Assessment

Online Quiz
ClassZone.com

REVIEWING KEY CONCEPTS

1. Explain the differences between the terms in each of these pairs:
   a. *demand*
   law of demand

   c. *market demand schedule*
   market demand curve

   b. *demand schedule*
   demand curve

2. Look at Figure 4.1 on page 99. Write a caption for the figure that explains the law of demand.

3. Review the information on Vera Wang on the opposite page. Why is it unlikely that most brides will have demand for an original Vera Wang gown?

4. How might an owner of a bookstore put together a market demand schedule for his or her store?

5. Why does the demand curve slope downward?

6. **Using Your Notes** How are price and quantity demanded related? Refer to your completed cluster diagram.

   Use the Graphic Organizer at **Interactive Review @ ClassZone.com**

   demand

CRITICAL THINKING

7. **Drawing Conclusions** List three products that you are familiar with and the approximate price of each. Which of the products, if any, do you have a demand for? Consider the two requirements of demand as you answer this question.

8. **Making Inferences** Why might Rafael's market demand schedule and curve not be an accurate reflection of the actual market? To answer this question, consider the assumption that was made when the schedule and curve were created.

9. **Applying Economic Concepts** Return to the demand schedule for pizzas you created for Application B on page 101. Assume that your class is the market for pizzas. Tabulate these individual demand schedules to create a market demand schedule. Then use that schedule to draw a market demand curve.

10. **Challenge** Does quantity demanded always fall if the price rises? List several goods or services that you think would remain in demand even if the price rose sharply. Why does demand for those items change very little? (You will learn more about this topic in Section 3.)

ECONOMICS IN PRACTICE

Making a Market Demand Curve
Suppose that you own a store that sells athletic shoes. You survey your customers and analyze your sales data to see how many pairs of shoes you can expect to sell at various prices. Your research enables you to make the following market demand schedule.

Price per Pair of Shoes ($)	Quantity Demanded
175	0
150	10
125	20
100	40
75	70
50	110

Create a Demand Curve Use this market demand schedule to create a market demand curve.

Challenge Write a caption for your market demand curve explaining what it shows.

Use **SMART Grapher** @ClassZone.com to complete this activity.

What Factors Affect Demand?

OBJECTIVES	KEY TERMS	TAKING NOTES
In Section 2, you will • determine a change in quantity demanded • explain the difference between change in quantity demanded and change in demand • determine a change in demand • analyze what factors can cause change in demand	law of diminishing marginal utility, p. 106 income effect, p. 107 substitution effect, p. 107 change in quantity demanded, p. 108 change in demand, p. 109 normal goods, p. 110 inferior goods, p. 110 substitutes, p. 112 complements, p. 112	As you read Section 2, complete a chart that shows each factor that causes change in demand. Use the Graphic Organizer at **Interactive Review @ ClassZone.com**

Factor That Changes Demand	Reason Why Demand Changes

More About Demand Curves

KEY CONCEPTS

The demand schedules and demand curves that you studied in Section 1 were created using the assumption that all other economic factors except the price of DVDs would remain the same. If all other factors remain the same, then the only thing that influences how many DVDs consumers will buy is the price of those DVDs. The demand curve graphically displays that pattern.

Now think about the shape of demand curves. Why do they slope downward? The reason is the **law of diminishing marginal utility**, which states that the mar-

ginal benefit from using each additional unit of a good or service during a given time period tends to decline as each is used. Recall that utility is the satisfaction gained from the use of a good or service. Suppose it is a hot day, and you have just gulped down a glass of lemonade. Would you gain the same benefit from drinking a second glass? How about a third? In all likelihood, you'd find the second glass less satisfying than the first, and the third glass less satisfying than the second.

Because consumers receive less satisfaction from each new glass of lemonade they drink, they don't want to pay as much for additional purchases. So, they will buy

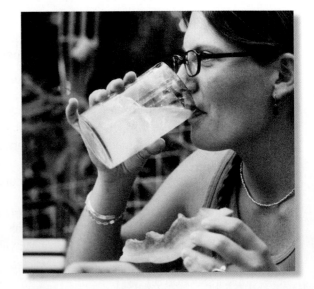

two glasses only if the lemonade is offered at a lower price, and they will buy three only if the price is even lower still. This pattern of behavior, which holds true for most consumer goods and services, creates the downward slope of the demand curve. For another example, see Figure 4.6 below, which displays the demand that a young man named Kent has for video games.

FIGURE 4.6 DIMINISHING MARGINAL UTILITY

This graph displays the demand for video games by a high school senior named Kent.

The demand curve slopes downward because of the **law of diminishing marginal utility**, which states that the marginal benefit of using each additional unit of a product during a given period will decline. Because of that declining satisfaction, Kent will buy additional games only at lower prices.

ANALYZE GRAPHS
How many video games is Kent willing to buy at a price of $45? How does the law of diminishing marginal utility explain his refusal to buy more games at that price?

Why do consumers demand more goods and services at lower prices and fewer at higher prices? Economists have identified two patterns of behavior as causes: the income effect and the substitution effect.

The **income effect** is the term used for a change in the amount of a product that a consumer will buy because the purchasing power of his or her income changes—even though the income itself does not change. For example, you can buy more paperback books if they are priced at $7 than if they are priced at $15. If you buy a $7 book, you will feel $8 "richer" than if you buy a $15 book, so you are more likely to buy another book. The income effect also influences behavior when prices rise. You will feel $8 "poorer" if you buy a $15 book instead of a $7 one, so you will buy fewer books overall.

The **substitution effect** is the pattern of behavior that occurs when consumers react to a change in the price of a good or service by buying a substitute product— one whose price has not changed and that offers a better relative value. For example, if the price of paperback books climbs above $10, consumers might decide to buy fewer books and choose instead to buy $4 magazines.

QUICK REFERENCE

Income effect is the change in the amount that consumers will buy because the purchasing power of their income changes.

Substitution effect is a change in the amount that consumers will buy because they buy substitute goods instead.

APPLICATION Drawing Conclusions

A. Malik goes to the mall to buy a $40 pair of blue jeans and discovers that they are on sale for $25. If Malik buys two pairs, is this an example of the income effect or the substitution effect? Explain your answer.

Change in Quantity Demanded

QUICK REFERENCE

Change in quantity
demanded is an increase
or decrease in the amount
demanded because of
change in price.

KEY CONCEPTS

Remember that each demand curve represents a specific market situation in which price is the only variable. A change in the amount of a product that consumers will buy because of a change in price is called a **change in quantity demanded**. Each change in quantity demanded is shown by a new point on the demand curve. A change in quantity demanded does not shift the demand curve itself.

EXAMPLE Changes Along a Demand Curve

Let's look again at Cheryl's demand curve for DVDs (Figure 4.7 below). Note the quantities demanded at each price. Notice that as quantity demanded changes, the change is shown by the direction of the movement right or left along the demand curve.

FIGURE 4.7 CHANGE IN QUANTITY DEMANDED

Price per DVD (in dollars) vs. Quantity demanded of DVDs

A **change in quantity demanded** doesn't shift the demand curve. The change refers to movement along the curve itself. Each point on the curve represents a new quantity demanded.

a As you move to the right along the curve, the quantity demanded increases.

b As you move to the left, the quantity demanded decreases.

ANALYZE GRAPHS

1. What is the change in quantity demanded when the price drops from $20 to $10?

2. What is the direction of the movement along the demand curve when the quantity decreases?

Animated Economics

Use an interactive demand curve to see changes in quantity demanded at **ClassZone.com**

Figure 4.7 shows change in quantity demanded for one person. A market demand curve provides similar information for an entire market. However, market demand curves have larger quantities demanded and larger changes to quantity demanded because they combine data from all individual demand curves in the market.

APPLICATION Applying Economic Concepts

B. Why do increases or decreases in quantity demanded not shift the position of the demand curve?

Change in Demand

Consider what might happen if you lose your job. If you aren't earning money, you aren't likely to buy many CDs or movie tickets or magazines—no matter how low the price. Similarly, when national unemployment rises, people who are out of work are more likely to spend their limited funds on food and housing than on entertainment. Fewer people would be buying DVDs at every price, so market demand would drop.

This is an example of a **change in demand**, which occurs when a change in the marketplace such as high unemployment prompts consumers to buy different amounts of a good or service at every price. Change in demand is also called a shift in demand because it actually shifts the position of the demand curve.

QUICK REFERENCE

Change in demand occurs when something prompts consumers to buy different amounts at every price.

FIGURES 4.8 AND 4.9 CHANGE IN DEMAND

FIGURE 4.8 DECREASE IN DEMAND

FIGURE 4.9 INCREASE IN DEMAND

When a **change in demand** occurs, the demand curve shifts.

ⓐ As Figure 4.8 shows, a shift to the left (D2) indicates a decrease in demand.

ⓑ As Figure 4.9 shows, a shift to the right (D3) indicates an increase in demand.

ANALYZE GRAPHS

1. In Figure 4.8, how has demand for baseball cards changed at each of these prices: $20, $30, and $40?

2. In Figure 4.9, how has demand for baseball cards changed at each of these prices: $30, $40, and $50?

Animated **Economics**

Use an interactive version of shifting demand curves at **ClassZone.com**

Six factors can cause a change in demand: income, market size, consumer tastes, consumer expectations, substitute goods, and complementary goods. An explanation of each one follows.

FACTOR 1 Income

If a consumer's income changes, either higher or lower, that person's ability to buy goods and services also changes. For example, Tyler works at a garden center. He uses his earnings to buy baseball cards for his collection. In the fall, people garden less and buy fewer gardening products, so Tyler works fewer hours. His smaller paycheck means that he has less money to spend, so he demands fewer baseball cards at every price. Figure 4.8 shows this change. The entire demand curve shifts to the left.

Suppose, however, that Tyler is promoted to supervisor and receives a raise of $2 an hour. Now he has more money to spend, so his demand for baseball cards increases and his demand curve shifts to the right—as shown in Figure 4.9 on page 109.

As you might guess, changes in income also affect market demand curves. When the incomes of most consumers in a market rise or fall, the total demand in that market also usually rises or falls. The market demand curve then shifts to the right or to the left.

Increased income usually increases demand, but in some cases, it causes demand to fall. **Normal goods** are goods that consumers demand more of when their incomes rise. **Inferior goods** are goods that consumers demand less of when their incomes rise. Before his raise, Tyler shopped at discount stores for jeans and T-shirts. Now that he earns more, Tyler can afford to spend more on his wardrobe. As a result, he demands less discounted clothing and buys more name-brand jeans and tees. Discounted clothing is considered an inferior good. Other products that might be considered inferior goods are used books and generic food products.

YOUR ECONOMIC CHOICES

NORMAL GOODS AND INFERIOR GOODS

If your income rises, which car will you choose?

Most people prefer to buy a new car if they can afford it. Used cars are an example of inferior goods—demand for them drops when incomes rise because people prefer new-car quality to getting a bargain.

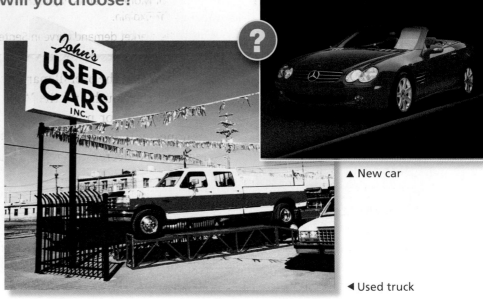

▲ New car

◀ Used truck

FACTOR 2 Market Size

If the number of consumers increases or decreases, the market size also changes. Such a change usually has a corresponding effect on demand. Suppose that the town of Montclair is on the ocean. Each summer, thousands of tourists rent beachfront cottages there. As a result, the size of the population and the market grows. So what do you think happens to the market demand curve for pizza in Montclair in the summer? Check the two graphs at the top of the next page.

Population shifts have often changed the size of markets. For example, in the last 30 years, the Northeast region of the United States lost population as many people moved to the South or the West. The causes of the population shift included the search for a better climate, high-tech jobs, or a less congested area.

FIGURE 4.10 MONTCLAIR'S POPULATION DURING TOURIST SEASON

Y-axis: Population (in thousands); X-axis: Months (Apr., May, June, July, Aug., Sept.)

FIGURE 4.11 CHANGE IN PIZZA MARKET DEMAND CURVE

Y-axis: Price per pizza (in dollars); X-axis: Quantity demanded of pizzas; curves labeled May/D1, August/D2

When a change in market size occurs, it often causes a change in demand.

a Figure 4.10 shows how the population of Montclair changed during the last tourist season. Notice which month had the highest population.

b Notice that the market demand curve (D2) shifts to the right between May and August.

ANALYZE GRAPHS

1. During what month was the population of Montclair at its highest? What happened to the demand for pizzas during that month? Explain.

2. What would you expect to happen to the market demand curve in September? Explain.

One economic result of the migration is that the overall market size of the Northeast has shrunk, while the market size of the South and the West has grown. This change in market size has altered the demand for many products, from essentials such as homes, clothing, and food to nonessentials such as movie tickets. Demand for most items will grow in booming regions and decrease in regions that are shrinking.

FACTOR 3 Consumer Tastes

Because of changing consumer tastes, today's hot trends often become tomorrow's castoffs. When a good or service enjoys high popularity, consumers demand more of it at every price. When a product loses popularity, consumers demand less of it.

Advertising has a strong influence on consumer tastes. Sellers advertise to create demand for the product. For example, some people stop wearing perfectly good pants that still fit because advertising convinces them that the style is no longer popular and that a new style is better.

Think about your own closet. Doesn't it contain some item of clothing that you just had to have a year ago, but would never pay money for now? You've just identified an instance of consumer taste changing demand. Consumer tastes also affect demand for other products besides clothing. When was the last time you saw someone buying a telephone that had to be attached to the wall by a cord?

FACTOR 4 Consumer Expectations

Your expectations for the future can affect your buying habits today. If you think the price of a good or service will change, that expectation can determine whether you buy it now or wait until later.

Economics Update

Find an update on changing consumer tastes at **ClassZone.com**

Let's look at one example of how consumer expectations shape demand. Automobiles usually go on sale at the end of summer because dealers want to get rid of this year's models before the new models arrive. Would you expect demand for new cars to be higher in May, before the sales, or in August, during the sales? It is higher in August because consumers expect the sales and often choose to wait for them.

FACTOR 5 Substitute Goods

QUICK REFERENCE

Substitutes are goods and services that can be used in place of each other.

Goods and services that can be used in place of other goods and services to satisfy consumer wants are called **substitutes**. Because the products are interchangeable, if the price of a substitute drops, people will choose to buy it instead of the original item. Demand for the substitute will increase while demand for the original item decreases. People may also turn to substitutes if the price for the original item becomes too high. Again, demand for the substitute rises while demand for the original item drops.

Substitutes can be used in place of each other. For example, when gasoline prices are high, some people decide to commute to school by bus or train. When gasoline prices are low, a higher number of people choose to drive instead of to take public transportation. As you can see from that example, when the price of one good rises, demand for it will drop while demand for its substitute will rise.

YOUR ECONOMIC CHOICES

SUBSTITUTE SERVICES

How would you decide whether to take a cab or a bus?

Taxis have certain advantages; they will take you to a specific place at a specific time. But if taxi fares rise, you might give up the convenience and go by bus instead.

Taxi   City bus

FACTOR 6 Complementary Goods

QUICK REFERENCE

Complements are goods that are used together, so a rise in demand for one increases the demand for the other.

When the use of one product increases the use of another product, the two products are called **complements**. An increase in the demand for one will cause an increase in the demand for the other. Likewise, a decrease in demand for one will cause a decrease in demand for the other.

In contrast to substitutes, complements are goods or services that work in tandem with each other. An increase in demand for one will cause an increase in demand for the other. One example is CDs and CD players. Consumers who bought CD players

FIGURE 4.12 Factors That Cause a Change in Demand

Income Increased income means consumers can buy more. Decreased income means consumers can buy less.

Complements When the use of one product increases the use of another product, the two are called complements.

Market Size A growing market usually increases demand. A shrinking market usually decreases demand.

What Causes a Change in Demand?

Substitutes Substitutes are goods and services that can be used instead of other goods and services, causing a change in demand.

Consumer Tastes The popularity of a good or service has a strong effect on the demand for it, and in today's marketplace, popularity can change quickly.

Consumer Expectations What you expect prices to do in the future can influence your buying habits today.

ANALYZE CHARTS
Choose a product used by most consumers, and create a hypothetical demand curve showing demand for that product in a town of 1,000 people. Label it A. On the same graph, add a demand curve showing demand if the population drops to 700. Label it B. Which factor on the chart does the shift in the demand curve represent?

also demanded CDs to play on them. And, as CDs became more popular, demand for CD players grew until they began to appear in places they had never been before, such as in the family minivan.

Therefore, with complements, if the price of one product changes, demand for both products will change in exactly the same way. If the price for one product rises, demand for both will drop. Conversely, if the price for one product drops, demand for both will rise.

APPLICATION Categorizing Information

C. Choose one of the following products: soda, hamburgers, pencils, or tennis rackets. On your own paper, list as many substitutes and complements for the product as you can. Compare your lists with those of a classmate.

ECONOMICS
SKILLBUILDER

For more on analyzing political cartoons,
see the Skillbuilder Handbook, page R26.

Analyzing Political Cartoons

Political cartoons often deal with economic themes. Because of this, you will find that
the skill of interpreting political cartoons helps you to understand the economic issues
on people's minds.

TECHNIQUES USED IN POLITICAL CARTOONS Political cartoonists use many
techniques to deliver their message. The techniques used in this cartoon include:

Exaggeration The cartoonist has shown
the automobile as towering over humans to
make the point that some Americans drive big
cars that are gas-guzzlers.

Labels Cartoonists
use written words
to identify people,
groups, or events.
Notice the sign on the
gas pump referring to
OPEC (Organization of
Petroleum Exporting
Countries) and the
license plate on the car.

Source: © *The Economist*

Stereotyping Here
a stereotype image of
a man in Arab robes
stands for OPEC, even
though not all OPEC
countries are in the
Middle East.

Other techniques that political cartoonists use include **caricature**, or
creating a portrait that distorts a person's features; **symbolism**, using an
object or idea to stand for something else; and **satire**, attacking error or
foolishness by ridiculing it.

THINKING ECONOMICALLY Analyzing

1. What does the phrase "Too high!!" mean?

2. What complementary goods are shown in this cartoon? Why are they complementary?

3. How does this cartoon relate to demand? Consider the effect of rising prices,
especially rising prices for complementary goods.

REVIEWING KEY CONCEPTS

1. Explain the differences between the terms in each of the pairs below:

   a. *change in quantity demanded*
   change in demand

   b. *income effect*
   substitution effect

   c. *normal goods*
   inferior goods

   d. *substitutes*
   complements

2. What feature of demand curves is explained by the law of diminishing marginal utility?

3. How does the income effect influence consumer behavior when prices rise?

4. Why might an increase in income result in a decrease in demand?

5. What else besides migration might account for a change in market size?

6. **Using Your Notes** Why does a change in market size affect demand? Refer to your completed chart.

   Use the Graphic Organizer at **Interactive Review @ ClassZone.com**

Factor That Changes Demand	Reason Why Demand Changes

CRITICAL THINKING

7. **Analyzing Causes** A new version of the computer game Big-Hit Football just came out. Malik buys it now because it has improvements over the current version, which he is bored with. Cheryl decides to wait to see if the price drops. Which of the factors shown in the chart on page 113 affected their decisions?

8. **Applying Economic Concepts** The U.S. government has used many strategies to reduce smoking. It banned television ads for cigarettes, ran public service messages about the health risks of smoking, and imposed taxes on cigarettes. Which factors that affect demand was the government trying to influence?

9. **Analyzing Effects** Take out the market demand curve for athletic shoes that you created on page 105. Add a new curve showing how demand would be changed if the most popular basketball player in the NBA endorses a brand of shoes that your store does not sell. Share your graph with a classmate and explain your reasoning.

10. **Challenge** Do you think changes in consumer taste are most often initiated by the consumers themselves or by manufacturers and advertisers? Explain your answer, using real-life examples.

ECONOMICS IN PRACTICE

Explaining Changes in Demand
Think about different types of bicycles: road bikes, mountain bikes, hybrid bikes. What factors affect demand for bicycles?

Identify Factors Affecting Demand The table below lists examples of a change in demand in the market for bicycles. For each example, identify which factor that affects demand is involved.

Example of Change in Demand	Factor That Affected Demand
Electric scooter sales rise, and bike sales fall.	
The cost of aluminum alloy bike frames is about to rise; consumers buy bikes now.	
Using a folding bicycle becomes a fad among commuters. Sales of this type of bike boom.	
The U.S. birth rate declined for 10 years in a row, eventually causing a drop in sales of children's bikes.	

Challenge Identify the two factors affecting demand that do not appear on this table. Provide examples of how these factors might affect demand for bicycles.

What Is Elasticity of Demand?

OBJECTIVES	KEY TERMS	TAKING NOTES
In Section 3, you will • define *elasticity of demand* • identify the difference between elastic and inelastic demand • define *unit elastic* • determine how total revenue is used to identify elasticity	elasticity of demand, *p. 117* elastic, *p. 117* inelastic, *p. 117* unit elastic, *p. 118* total revenue, *p. 122* total revenue test, *p. 122*	As you read Section 3, complete a cluster diagram using the key concepts and other terms. Use the Graphic Organizer at **Interactive Review @ ClassZone.com** Elasticity of Demand

Elasticity of Demand

KEY CONCEPTS

You have learned that there are many factors that influence the demand for a product. However, those factors alone are not the only influences on the sales of goods and services. How does the owner of an electronics store know how to price his or her goods so that the entire inventory of PDAs, or personal digital assistants, are sold?

Store owners know that consumers are responsive to changes in price. Let's examine the relationship between price and demand, and how it affects consumers' buying habits.

Consumer demand is not limitless. It is highly dependent on price. But as you know, demand is seldom fixed. As a result, price is also seldom fixed. Generally, people assume that if prices rise consumers will buy less, and if prices drop consumers will buy more. However, this isn't always the case. The relationship between price and demand is somewhat more complicated than you might think. Change in consumer buying habits is also related to the type of good or service being produced and how important the good or service is to the consumer. The marketplace certainly is very sensitive to changes in price—but not all increases in price will result in a decrease in demand.

Economists use the term **elasticity of demand** to describe how responsive consumers are to price changes in the marketplace. Economists describe demand as being either elastic or inelastic. Demand is **elastic** when a change in price, either up or down, leads to a relatively larger change in the quantity demanded. The more responsive to change the market is, the more likely the demand is elastic. On the other hand, demand is **inelastic** when a change in price leads to a relatively smaller change in the quantity demanded. For this reason, elastic goods and services are often said to be price sensitive. So, in the case of inelastic demand, changes in price have little impact on the quantity demanded.

Another way to think about elasticity is to imagine that a rubber band represents quantity demanded. When the quantity demanded increases by a marked amount, the demand is elastic and the rubber band stretches. If the quantity demanded barely changes, demand is inelastic and the rubber band stretches very little.

QUICK REFERENCE

Elasticity of demand is a measure of how responsive consumers are to price changes.

Demand is **elastic** if quantity demanded changes significantly as price changes.

Demand is **inelastic** if quantity demanded changes little as price changes.

EXAMPLE Elasticity of Demand for Goods and Services

Let's look at an example of elastic demand. Suppose that a certain brand of PDAs goes on sale. If the price of that brand goes down 20 percent, and the quantity demanded goes up 30 percent, then demand is elastic. The percentage change in quantity demanded is greater than the percentage change in price. Goods that have a large number of substitutes fall into the elastic category, since if the prices change, consumers can choose other products.

Now think about a completely different type of good—the medicine insulin. Many diabetics require daily insulin injections to regulate their blood sugar levels. Even if the price of insulin were to rise sharply, diabetics would still need the same amount of insulin as they did before. If the price were to drop, they would not need any more insulin than their required dosage. As a result, the demand for insulin is inelastic because the quantity demanded remains relatively constant.

YOUR ECONOMIC CHOICES

NECESSITY OR CHOICE

Which of these services could you give up?

Most people consider getting a cavity filled to be a necessity. Having your teeth whitened is a service that can be postponed or eliminated without harm. As a result, the demand for whitening is more elastic than the demand for fillings.

◄ Cosmetic whitening

▲ Filling a cavity

Over time the elasticity of demand for a particular product may change. If more substitutes for a product become available, the demand may become more elastic. For example, the cost of cell phones and their service has become more elastic as more providers enter the market. On the other hand, in the case of prescription drugs, if a product is withdrawn from the market and there are fewer choices for the consumer, the demand may become inelastic.

The data for elastic demand and the data for inelastic demand produce demand curves that look very different from each other. Compare Figure 4.13 and Figure 4.14 below. Notice that the inelastic demand curve has a steeper slope than the elastic demand curve does. The reason for this difference is that the changes along the vertical axis (the price) are proportionally greater than the changes along the horizontal axis (the quantity demanded).

FIGURE 4.13 ELASTIC DEMAND CURVE

Price per ticket (in dollars) vs *Quantity demanded of movie tickets (in thousands)*

FIGURE 4.14 INELASTIC DEMAND CURVE

Price per filling (in dollars) vs *Quantity demanded of fillings*

a In Figure 4.13, elastic demand curves have gradual slopes. They are more horizontal than vertical because of the greater changes in quantity demanded.

b In Figure 4.14, inelastic demand curves have steep slopes. They are more vertical than horizontal because quantity demanded changes very little.

ANALYZE GRAPHS

1. In Figure 4.13, what happens to the quantity demanded when price drops from $10 to $8?

2. In Figure 4.14, what is the difference in quantity demanded between the most expensive and least expensive filling?

Animated **Economics**

Use elastic and inelastic demand curves at **ClassZone.com**

Demand is said to be **unit elastic** when the percentage change in price and quantity demanded are the same. In other words, a 10 percent increase in price would cause exactly a 10 percent drop in quantity demanded, while the reverse would be true.

No good or service is ever really unit elastic. Instead, unit elasticity is simply the dividing point between elastic and inelastic demand. It is a useful concept for figuring out whether demand is elastic or inelastic.

APPLICATION Drawing Conclusions

A. Decide how elastic demand is for the following item. Explain your reasoning.

When a grocery store sells soup at $1.09 per can, it sells 1,500 cans per week. When it dropped the price to $0.75, it sold an additional 1,000 cans.

What Determines Elasticity?

Economics Update

Find an update on factors affecting elasticity at **ClassZone.com**

KEY CONCEPTS

Just as there are factors that cause a change in demand, there are also factors that affect the elasticity of demand. The factors that affect elasticity include the availability of substitute goods or services, the proportion of income that is spent on the good or service, and whether the good or service is a necessity or a luxury.

FACTOR 1 Substitute Goods or Services

Generally speaking, if there is no substitute for a good or service, demand for it tends to be inelastic. Think back to the consumers who need insulin to regulate their blood sugar levels. No substitute exists for insulin, so consumers' demand is inelastic even when the price goes up. If many substitutes are available, however, demand tends to be elastic. For example, if the price shoots up for beef, consumers can eat chicken, pork, or fish. In this case, demand is elastic.

FACTOR 2 Proportion of Income

The percentage of your income that you spend on a good or service is another factor that affects elasticity. Suppose that photography is your hobby, and you spend about 10 percent of your income on a digital camera, memory cards, software programs, and lenses. If the price for any of these rises even slightly, your demand will likely fall because you just don't have any more money to spend on your hobby. Your demand is elastic. At the same time, demand for products that cost little of your income tends to be inelastic. For example, if the cost of pencils or ballpoint pens rose, would you buy fewer pencils and pens? Probably not. You spend so little on these items that you could easily pay the increase.

YOUR ECONOMIC CHOICES

PROPORTION OF INCOME

How much would you invest in a hobby?

This amateur photographer spends about 10 percent of her income to pay for her digital camera and supplies. If the costs of taking photographs rise sharply, she won't be able to increase her demand by an equal amount because she won't have enough money to pay for the additional expenses.

If the level of your income increases, you are likely to increase your demand for some goods or services. Suppose you ordinarily see one movie per month. If your income increases, you may choose to attend the movies several times a month.

FACTOR 3 Necessities Versus Luxuries

A necessity is something you must have, such as food or water. Demand for necessities tends to be inelastic. Even if the price rises, consumers will pay whatever they can afford for necessary goods and services.

But that doesn't mean that consumers will buy the same quantities no matter what the price. If the price of a necessity such as milk rises too much, consumers may choose to buy a substitute, such as a cheaper brand of milk or powdered milk. The quantity demanded of milk will change as the law of demand predicts; however, the change in quantity demanded is smaller than the change in price, so demand is inelastic.

In contrast, a luxury is something that you desire but that is not essential to your life, such as a plasma television. The demand for luxuries tends to be elastic. Consumers will think twice about paying a higher price for something they don't truly need. The change in quantity demanded is much greater than the change in price.

FIGURE 4.15 Estimating Elasticity

By examining the three factors that affect elasticity, you can often estimate whether demand for a certain good or service will be elastic or inelastic.

Factors that affect elasticity		Table Salt	Ice Cream	Sports Car	Gasoline	Insulin	Braces on Teeth
Are there good substitutes? yes = elastic, no = inelastic		no	yes	yes	no	no	no
What proportion of income does it use? large = elastic, small = inelastic		small	small	large	small	small	large
Is it a necessity or a luxury? luxury = elastic, necessity = inelastic		necessity	luxury	luxury	necessity	necessity	luxury
Conclusion		inelastic	elastic	elastic	inelastic	inelastic	elastic

(The column group above is labeled **Products**.)

ANALYZE TABLES
What patterns can you see in the factors that affect elasticity? Write a sentence summarizing your answer.

APPLICATION Evaluating

B. Create a chart like the one above for the following products: mountain bikes, airplane tickets, and home heating oil. Determine if the products are elastic or inelastic.

Calculating Elasticity of Demand

Businesses find it useful to figure the elasticity of demand because it helps them to decide whether to make price cuts. If demand for a good or service is elastic, price cuts might help the business earn more. If demand is inelastic, price cuts won't help.

To determine elasticity, economists look at whether the percentage change in quantity demanded is greater than the percentage change in price. To calculate that relationship, economists use mathematical formulas. One such set of formulas is shown below. Another way to determine elasticity is shown on page 122.

MATH CHALLENGE

FIGURE 4.16 Calculating the Elasticity of Demand

Step 1: Calculate percentage change in quantity demanded.
(If the final result is a negative number, treat it as positive.)

Example Calculations

$$\frac{\text{Original quantity} - \text{New quantity}}{\text{Original quantity}} \times 100 = \text{Percentage change in quantity demanded}$$

$$\frac{2,000 - 6,000}{2000} \times 100 = 200\%$$

Step 2: Calculate percentage change in price.
(If the final result is a negative number, treat it as positive.)

$$\frac{\text{Original price} - \text{New price}}{\text{Original price}} \times 100 = \text{Percentage change in price}$$

$$\frac{10 - 8}{10} \times 100 = 20\%$$

Step 3: Calculate elasticity.

$$\frac{\text{Percentage change in quantity demanded}}{\text{Percentage change in price}} = \text{Elasticity}$$

$$\frac{200\%}{20\%} = 10$$

Step 4: After doing your calculations, if the final number is greater than 1, demand is elastic. If the final number is less than 1, demand is inelastic.

Advanced Calculations Economists use a more complex version of these formulas. In Step 1, instead of dividing the change in quantity demanded by the original quantity demanded, they divide it by the average of the original and new quantities. In Step 2, they divide change in price by an average of the original price and new price.

NEED HELP?

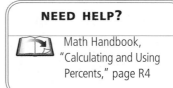
Math Handbook, "Calculating and Using Percents," page R4

C. Choose two points on the demand curve shown in Figure 4.13 and determine the price and quantity demanded for each point. Then use that data to calculate elasticity of demand.

Total Revenue Test

KEY CONCEPTS

Businesses need to know about elasticity of demand because it influences the amount of revenue they will earn. Economists measure elasticity of demand by calculating a seller's **total revenue**, the amount of money a company receives for selling its products. Total revenue is calculated using the following formula, in which P is the price and Q is the quantity sold: **TOTAL REVENUE = P × Q**.

You can measure elasticity by comparing the total revenue a business would receive when offering its product at various prices. This method is the **total revenue test**.

If total revenue increases after the price of a product drops, then demand for that product is considered elastic. Why? Because even though the seller makes less on each unit sold, the quantity demanded has increased enough to make up for the lower price. For example, if a hot dog stand sells 100 hot dogs for $2.50 each, the total revenue is $250 for the day. However, if the price of hot dogs drops to $2.00 each and 150 are sold, the total revenue for the day will be $300. The demand is elastic.

But if the total revenue decreases after the price is lowered, demand is considered inelastic. If the hot dog stand lowers its price to $1.00 each and sells 200 hot dogs, it makes $200 in total revenue. Clearly, the price reduction has caused only a modest increase in quantities sold, which is not enough to compensate for lower revenues.

EXAMPLE Revenue Table

Let's look at an example of demand for movie tickets. In Figure 4.17, you can see how total revenues show whether demand is elastic or inelastic.

FIGURE 4.17 MOVIE TICKET REVENUE TABLE

Price of a Movie Ticket ($)	Quantity Demanded per Month	Total Revenue ($)
12	1,000	12,000
a ➔ 10	2,000	20,000
b ➔ 8	6,000	48,000
6	12,000	72,000
4	20,000	80,000

a At $10 a ticket, the quantity demanded is 2,000. Total revenue is $20,000.

b When the price drops to $8, the quantity demanded rises to 6,000. Total revenue rises to $48,000. So, demand is elastic.

ANALYZE TABLES
When the price range changes from $8 to $6, is demand elastic or inelastic? Explain.

APPLICATION Creating Tables

D. Use the information from Figure 4.14 to estimate prices to make a total revenue table.

REVIEWING KEY CONCEPTS

1. Use each of the terms below in a sentence that gives an example of the term:

   a. *elastic*   **b.** *inelastic*   **c.** *total revenue*

2. How is total revenue related to elasticity of demand?

3. Why are elastic goods and services said to be price sensitive?

4. What are the factors that affect elasticity of demand and how does each affect elasticity?

5. Analyze the factors that determine elasticity to explain why utilities companies never offer sale prices on their services.

6. **Using Your Notes** How does the concept of unit elasticity relate to the concepts of elasticity and inelasticity? Refer to your completed cluster diagram.

   Use the Graphic Organizer at **Interactive Review @ ClassZone.com**

elasticity of demand

CRITICAL THINKING

7. **Analyzing Causes** In early 2004, news articles reported that prescription drug prices were rising almost three times faster than the prices of other products. Identify the factors that explain why the drug companies were able to raise prices so sharply.

8. **Analyzing Data** In June, Snead's Snack Bar sold 1,000 fruit smoothies at a price of $2.50 each. In July, they sold 1,300 fruit smoothies at a price of $2.00. Is the demand for fruit smoothies elastic or inelastic? Use the formula on page 121 to decide. Show the math calculations to support your answer.

9. **Applying Economic Concepts** Suppose the company that runs concession stands at a local sports arena wants to increase revenue on sales of soft drinks. The manager believes the only solution is to charge higher prices. As a business consultant, what advice would you give the manager? Use economic thinking to support your answer.

10. **Challenge** You learned in this section that no product ever has demand that is unit elastic. What possible reasons can you give for that? Draw on what you know about utility, demand, and elasticity as you formulate your answer.

ECONOMICS IN PRACTICE

Calculating Elasticity
Determine the elasticity of bottled water by calculating elasticity and using the revenue table below. Use the information on pages 121 and 122 to help you.

Number of Bottles Sold	Price ($)
35	2.00
75	1.50
100	1.25
120	1.00

Write a Summary After you have determined whether bottled water is elastic or inelastic, think about what factors affect the demand for bottled water. Write a summary of your conclusions explaining whether demand is elastic or inelastic and why, and what factors affect the elasticity of water.

Challenge What effect might the introduction of a new energy drink have on the demand for bottled water? Use economic thinking to support your answer.

Case Study

Economics Update
Find an update on this Case
Study at **ClassZone.com**

Fueling Automobile Demand

Background Automobiles have a huge influence on the U.S. economy. Sales of automobiles and the services connected with them account for 20 to 25 percent of all retail sales. But automobile sales are subject to the same factors that influence demand for any other product.

When the economy is good, demand for automobiles typically goes up. When fuel prices rise, customers tend to favor cars with good gas mileage, rather than trucks or SUVs. When the economy is bad or fuel prices are very high, some people leave the market and use other means of transportation.

Car dealers and manufacturers look for ways to sustain and increase demand for their products. One method is the incentive, an award designed to lure potential buyers into an automobile showroom and to encourage sales. Incentives range from zero percent financing to mountain bikes.

What's the issue? How does consumer demand affect the automobile industry? Study these sources to discover how the law of demand and the factors that affect demand shape the market.

A. Online Article

Car companies often offer incentives to buyers. This article discusses one approach Volkswagen tried to boost sales.

Volkswagen Tries 12 Months of Free Car Insurance to Lure Buyers

To fight slumping sales, Volkswagen introduces a new incentive to attract buyers.

The German automaker . . . will test the program by offering 12 months of free insurance to people with valid driver's licenses who buy or lease new Golfs, Beetle coupes and Beetle convertibles. . . .

"I think it will be a lure for college graduates and first-time buyers," said Harry Nesbitt, sales manager. . . . "It's a way to get people in the dealership without sounding like everyone else."

Automakers in the U.S. have boosted incentive spending 7.2 percent this year, with rebates as high as $8,000 on some models, to lure shoppers conditioned to expect deals. Volkswagen turned to low-interest loans and reduce-priced leases in March for the first time in several years to boost demand as its models aged. . . .

The Volkswagen program would be the first insurance giveaway by an automaker.

Source: Bloomberg.com

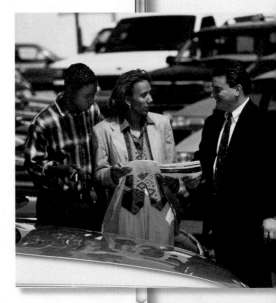

Thinking Economically Do incentives described in this document change the demand for automobiles or the quantity demanded? Explain your answer.

B. Political Cartoon

Brian Duffy, a cartoonist with the *Des Moines Register,* drew this cartoon about the rising price of gasoline.

Thinking Economically Which of the factors that cause a change in demand does this cartoon address? Explain your answer.

C. Online Report

An auto-buying service linking buyers and sellers examines demand for hybrid automobiles. Hybrid cars get power from a combination of batteries and a gas-powered engine.

The Year of the Hybrid

Stellar Fuel Efficiency, Low Emissions, and More Power

Why do we think 2005 will be The Year of the Hybrid? We can sum it up in two words: Power and SUV. There's something reassuring about how auto manufacturers are helping Americans have their cake and eat it too by offering up more fuel-efficient SUVs. Let's face it, America's love affair with the SUV shows no sign of waning. Yet . . . we can't live in denial that the SUV has a fat appetite for gasoline. And then there's the power argument. Despite the crowd pleasing fuel efficiency standards offered by hybrids, there was still the complaint that they lacked juice, or horsepower. . . . 2005's hybrids will appeal to those of us . . . who absolutely demand a lot of horsepower. As if overcompensating for being picked on when they were little, 2005's hybrids are coming out with more horsepower than their gas-only counterparts.

Though hybrids tend to be more expensive than their gas- or diesel-only powered cousins, the savings in fuel (and sometimes in taxes) can more than offset this difference in the long run.

Source: Invoicedealers.com

Thinking Economically Which of the factors affecting demand is evident in this article? Use evidence from the article to support your answer.

THINKING ECONOMICALLY Synthesizing

1. How would the demand for automobiles be affected by information presented in each of these documents? Support your answer with examples from the documents.

2. Identify and discuss the factors that affect elasticity of demand illustrated in these documents.

3. Explain how Documents B and C illustrate a cause and effect relationship in the demand for SUVs. Use evidence from these documents to support your answer.

Review this chapter using interactive activities at **ClassZone.com**

- Online Summary
- Quizzes
- Vocabulary Flip Cards
- Graphic Organizers
- Review and Study Notes

○ ○ ○

⟲ Online Summary

Complete the following activity either on your own paper or online at **ClassZone.com**

Choose the key concept that best completes the sentence. Not all key concepts will be used.

change in demand	law of demand
change in quantity demanded	market demand curve
demand	market demand schedule
demand curve	normal goods
demand schedule	substitutes
elastic	substitution effect
elasticity of demand	total revenue
income effect	total revenue test
inelastic	unit elastic
inferior goods	

1 is the desire for a product and the ability to pay for it. According to the **2**, when price decreases, demand rises, and when price increases, demand falls.

Demand can be displayed in a table called a **3** or on a graph called a **4**. A **5** is a table that shows how much demand all consumers in a market have. When that same information is displayed on a graph, it is called a **6**.

The different points on a demand curve show a **7**. A **8** occurs when consumers are willing to buy different amounts of a product at every price. The six factors that change demand are income, market size, consumer expectations, consumer taste, complement, and **9**.

The term **10** describes how responsive consumers are to price changes. Demand that changes significantly when prices change is **11**. Demand that doesn't change significantly when prices change is **12**. The dividing line between the two is where demand is **13**.

14 is calculated by multiplying price by quantity sold.

CHAPTER 4 Assessment

REVIEWING KEY CONCEPTS

What Is Demand? (pp. 98–105)

1. What two things are necessary for a consumer to have demand for a good or service?

2. What do economists mean when they say that quantity demanded and price have an inverse relationship?

What Factors Affect Demand? (pp. 106–115)

3. What is the difference between change in quantity demanded and change in demand?

4. How do consumer expectations affect demand?

What Is Elasticity of Demand? (pp. 116–125)

5. Explain the difference between elastic and inelastic demand.

6. What are two methods for calculating elasticity of demand?

APPLYING ECONOMIC CONCEPTS

Look at the graph below showing personal spending for two types of products: computers and stationery.

7. What is the general trend of how spending for each of these product types has changed? Are the two trends alike or different?

8. In what way might these products be complements? In what way might they be substitutes?

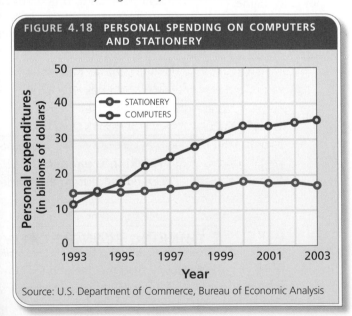

FIGURE 4.18 PERSONAL SPENDING ON COMPUTERS AND STATIONERY

Source: U.S. Department of Commerce, Bureau of Economic Analysis

9. **Creating Graphs** A tornado destroys a town. Think of three goods for which demand will rise in the weeks after the storm and three goods for which demand will fall. For each good, create a graph with two demand curves: curve A representing demand before the storm and curve B representing demand after the storm. Under each graph, write a caption explaining the change in demand.

   Use *SMARTGrapher* @ ClassZone.com to complete this activity.

10. **Identifying Causes** A certain stuffed toy is popular during the holiday season, but sells for half the listed price after the holidays. Which factor in change in demand is at work here? Explain.

11. **Identifying Causes** In the last few decades, demand for ketchup has dropped in the United States, while demand for salsa has risen. Which factors that affect demand account for this?

12. **Using Economic Concepts** Airlines give discounts to travelers who book in advance and stay over a weekend. Travelers who book at the last minute and do not stay over a weekend usually pay full-price. How does the concept of elasticity explain the difference between the two groups' demand for tickets and the airlines' pricing decisions?

13. **Challenge** Suppose that you read the following article in the newspaper:

   Meteorologists announced today that this has been the warmest winter in 57 years. The unusual weather has affected local businesses. According to Pasha Dubrinski, owner of Pasha's Outerwear, sales of winter parkas are 17 percent lower than last year. Dubrinski said, "Instead of buying down-filled parkas, people have been buying substitute items such as leather coats."

   Across town, Michael Ellis, owner of Home Hardware, said that his sales of snow blowers are also down. "Next week, I will cut the price. That will increase demand."

   Are these two storeowners correct in the way they use economic terms? Explain your answer.

Equip Your Team

Step 1 Choose a partner. Imagine you are equipment managers for your school's baseball team. You must equip the nine starters with a budget of $5,000. The equipment supplier sends you the list of prices shown in column A of the table below. Create a list telling how many of each item you will buy.

SPORTING GOODS PRICES

Item	Prices (in dollars)		
	A	B	C
Bat	130	170	200
Baseball	2	3	4
Glove or Mitt	80	130	160
Catcher's Mask	80	90	100
Full Uniform	65	100	135
Jersey Only	30	60	90
Cleats	25	60	90
Sunglasses	20	30	40
Team Jacket	50	75	100

Step 2 When you call in the order, you learn that a big sporting goods factory has burned. Prices have risen to those shown in column B. You must redo your order using the new prices but the same budget.

Step 3 The economy is hit with sudden and severe price hikes. Redo your order using the prices in column C.

Step 4 Share your three purchasing lists with the class. As a class, use the collected data to create a market demand curve for each item.

Step 5 Use the collected data to calculate elasticity for each item. (You may use either method explained in this chapter.) Then as a class discuss your results. What factors influenced elasticity?

Use *SMARTGrapher* @ ClassZone.com to complete this activity.

Supply

The cost of raw materials, the wages paid to workers, and the production decisions made by managers all affect the supply of televisions.

Supply

CONCEPT REVIEW

Demand is the willingness to buy a good or service and the ability
to pay for it.

CHAPTER 5 KEY CONCEPT

Supply is the willingness and ability of producers to offer goods and
services for sale.

WHY THE CONCEPT MATTERS

You may not think of yourself as a producer, but you are. You offer
your labor when you do chores around the house or work at a part-
time job. If you have a car, you sometimes provide transportation
for your friends. Also, if you belong to a sports or academic team,
you supply your skills and knowledge. List five things that you
supply. Then list the costs you incur and the rewards you receive for
supplying them. How would your willingness and ability to supply
these things be affected if these costs and rewards changed?

Online Highlights
More at ClassZone.com

 Economics Update

Go to **ECONOMICS UPDATE** for
chapter updates and current news
on the use of robots in industry.
(See Case Study, pp. 158–159.) ▶

Animated Economics

Go to **ANIMATED ECONOMICS** for
interactive lessons on the graphs and
tables in this chapter.

Interactive ◀◀ Review

Go to **INTERACTIVE REVIEW** for
concept review and activities.

How does the use of robots affect the
supply of goods and services? See the
Case Study on pages 158–159.

What Is Supply?

OBJECTIVES

In Section 1, you will
- define *supply* and outline what the law of supply says
- explain how to create and interpret supply schedules
- explain how to create and interpret supply curves

KEY TERMS

supply, *p. 130*
law of supply, *p. 131*
supply schedule, *p. 132*
market supply schedule, *p. 132*
supply curve, *p. 134*
market supply curve, *p. 134*

TAKING NOTES

As you read Section 1, complete a cluster diagram like the one shown using the key concepts and other helpful words and phrases. Use the Graphic Organizer at **Interactive Review @ ClassZone.com**

The Law of Supply

KEY CONCEPTS

In Chapter 4, you learned about the demand side of market interactions and how consumers serve their interests by purchasing the best products at the lowest possible price. You also discovered that there are other factors that change demand at every price. Demand, however, is only one side of the market equation. In this chapter, you will learn about the supply side of the equation in order to understand why producers want to provide products at the highest possible price.

Supply refers to the willingness and ability of producers to offer goods and services for sale. Anyone who provides goods or services is a producer. Manufacturers who make anything from nutrition bars to automobiles are producers. So, too, are farmers who grow crops, retailers who sell products, and utility companies, airlines, or pet sitters who provide services.

The two key words in the definition of supply are *willingness* and *ability*. For example, the Smith family grows various fruits and vegetables on their small farm. They sell their produce at a local farmers' market. If the prices at the market are too low, the Smiths may not be willing to take on the expense of growing and

QUICK REFERENCE

Supply is the desire and ability to produce and sell a product.

Supplying a Service Service providers, such as utility companies, are producers too.

transporting their produce. Also, if the weather is bad and the Smiths' crops of fruits and vegetables are ruined, they will not be able to supply anything for the market. In other words, they will not offer produce for sale if they do not have both the willingness and the ability to do so.

As is true with demand, price is a major factor that influences supply. The **law of supply** states that producers are willing to sell more of a good or service at a higher price than they are at a lower price. Producers want to earn a profit, so when the price of a good or service rises they are willing to supply more of it. When the price falls, they want to supply less of it. In other words, price and quantity supplied have a direct relationship. This relationship is illustrated in Figure 5.1.

QUICK REFERENCE

The **law of supply** states that when prices decrease, quantity supplied decreases, and when prices increase, quantity supplied increases.

FIGURE 5.1 LAW OF SUPPLY

As **prices** fall... quantity supplied falls.

As **prices** rise... quantity supplied rises.

EXAMPLE Price and Supply

Let's take a closer look at how price and quantity supplied are related by returning to the Smiths and their produce business. The Smiths travel to the Montclair Farmers' Market every Wednesday and Saturday to sell a variety of fruits and vegetables—blueberries, peaches, nectarines, sweet corn, peppers, and cucumbers. However, their specialty crop is the tomato. How should the Smiths decide on the quantity of tomatoes to supply to the farmers' market? The price they can get for their crop is a major consideration.

The Smiths know that the standard price for tomatoes is $1 per pound. What quantity of tomatoes will the Smiths offer for sale at that price? They decide that they are willing to offer 24 pounds. What if the price of tomatoes doubled to $2 per pound? The Smiths might decide that the price is so attractive that they are willing to offer 50 pounds of tomatoes for sale on the market. In contrast, if the price fell to 50 cents, the Smiths might decide to supply only 10 pounds. Furthermore, at prices under 50 cents per pound, they may not be willing to supply any tomatoes. Look again at the definition of the law of supply. As you can see, it provides a concise description of how producers behave.

Economics Update

Find an update on farmers' markets at **ClassZone.com**

APPLICATION Analyzing Effects

A. You sell peppers at the Montclair Farmers' Market. If the price of peppers increased from 40 cents to 60 cents each, how would your quantity supplied of peppers change? How would your quantity supplied change if the price decreased to 25 cents?

Supply Schedules

KEY CONCEPTS

A **supply schedule** is a table that shows how much of a good or service an individual producer is willing and able to offer for sale at each price in a market. In other words, a supply schedule shows the law of supply in table form. A **market supply schedule** is a table that shows how much of a good or service all producers in a market are willing and able to offer for sale at each price.

EXAMPLE Individual Supply Schedule

A supply schedule is a two-column table that is similar in format to a demand schedule. The left-hand column of the table lists various prices of a good or service, and the right-hand column shows the quantity supplied at each price.

The Smiths' supply of tomatoes can be expressed in a supply schedule (Figure 5.2). How many pounds of tomatoes are the Smiths willing to sell when the price is $1.25 per pound? What if the price is $0.50 per pound? Or $2.00 per pound? Your answers to these questions show that the Smiths' quantity supplied of tomatoes depends on the price.

FIGURE 5.2 THE SMITHS' TOMATO SUPPLY SCHEDULE

Price per Pound ($)	Quantity Supplied (in pounds)
a → 2.00	50
1.75	40
1.50	34
1.25	30
1.00	24
0.75	20
b → 0.50	10

a At the top price of $2.00, the Smiths are willing to sell 50 pounds of tomatoes.

b At $0.50, the Smiths are willing to provide only 10 pounds of tomatoes for sale.

Notice that when the price falls, the quantity of tomatoes that the Smiths are willing to sell also falls. When the price rises, the quantity they are willing to sell rises. So quantity supplied and price have a direct relationship.

ANALYZE TABLES

1. How many pounds of tomatoes will the Smiths offer for sale if the price is $1.75?
2. How is this supply schedule different from a demand schedule for tomatoes?

Animated Economics

Use an interactive supply schedule at **ClassZone.com**

EXAMPLE Market Supply Schedule

The supply schedule in Figure 5.2 shows how many pounds of tomatoes an individual producer, the Smith family, is willing and able to offer for sale at each price in the market. The schedule also shows that, in response to changes in price, the Smiths will supply a greater or lesser number of tomatoes. However, sometimes an individual supply schedule does not provide a complete picture of the quantity of a good or service that is being supplied in a given market. For example, several fruit and vegetable stands at the Montclair Farmers' Market sell tomatoes. If you want to know the quantity of tomatoes available for sale at different prices at the entire farmers' market, you need a market supply schedule. This shows the quantity supplied by all of the producers who are willing and able to sell tomatoes.

Take a look at the market supply schedule for tomatoes in Figure 5.3. Notice that it is similar to the Smiths' supply schedule, except that the quantities supplied are much larger. It also shows that, as with individual quantity supplied, market quantity supplied depends on price.

FIGURE 5.3   TOMATO MARKET SUPPLY SCHEDULE

Price per Pound ($)	Quantity Supplied (in pounds)
a → 2.00	350
1.75	300
1.50	250
b → 1.25	200
1.00	150
0.75	100
c → 0.50	50

a At the top price of $2.00, the fruit and vegetable stands will offer 350 pounds of tomatoes for sale.

b At $1.25, the quantity supplied of tomatoes is 200 pounds.

c At the low price of $0.50, the quantity supplied falls to 50 pounds.

So, markets behave in the same way as individual suppliers. As prices decrease, the quantity supplied of tomatoes decreases. As prices increase, the quantity supplied increases.

ANALYZE TABLES

1. How does the quantity supplied of tomatoes change when the price rises from $0.75 a pound to $1.75 a pound?

2. How does this market supply schedule illustrate the law of supply?

In Chapter 4, you learned that Rafael, the owner of Montclair Video Mart, used market research to create a market demand schedule. Market research can also be used to create a market supply schedule. Producers in some markets are able to use research conducted by the government or by trade organizations to learn the prices and quantity supplied by all the producers in a given market.

APPLICATION Applying Economic Concepts

B. Imagine that you own a health food store that sells several brands of nutrition bars. Create a supply schedule showing how many bars you would be willing to sell each month at prices of $5, $4, $3, $2, and $1.

Supply Curves

QUICK REFERENCE

A **supply curve** shows the data from a supply schedule in graph form.

A **market supply curve** shows the data from a market supply schedule in graph form.

KEY CONCEPTS

A **supply curve** is a graph that shows how much of a good or service an individual producer is willing and able to offer for sale at each price. To create a supply curve, transfer the data from a supply schedule to a graph. A **market supply curve** shows the data from the market supply schedule. In other words, it shows how much of a good or service all of the producers in a market are willing and able to offer for sale at each price.

EXAMPLE Individual Supply Curve

Study the supply curve (Figure 5.4) created from the Smiths' supply schedule. How many pounds of tomatoes will the Smiths supply at $1.50 per pound? How will the Smiths' quantity supplied change if the price increases or decreases by 25 cents? Find the answers to these questions by running your finger along the curve. As you can see, the supply curve is a graphic representation of the law of supply. When the price increases, the quantity supplied increases; when the price decreases, the quantity supplied decreases. Note that the supply curve in Figure 5.4, and the schedule on which it is based, were created using the assumption that all other economic factors except price remain the same. You'll learn more about these other factors in Section 3.

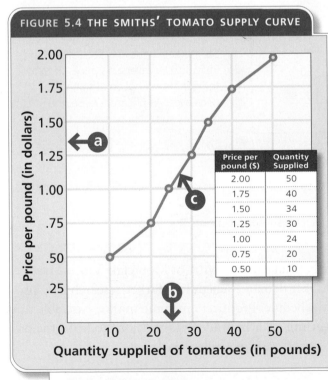

FIGURE 5.4 THE SMITHS' TOMATO SUPPLY CURVE

Price per pound ($)	Quantity Supplied
2.00	50
1.75	40
1.50	34
1.25	30
1.00	24
0.75	20
0.50	10

Notice that **supply curves** always slope upward from lower left to upper right.

a The vertical axis of the graph shows prices, with the highest at the top.

b The horizontal axis shows quantities supplied, with the lowest on the far left.

c The specific quantities supplied at specific prices listed on the supply schedule are plotted as points on the graph and connected to create the supply curve.

ANALYZE GRAPHS

1. How many pounds of tomatoes will the Smiths offer for sale when the price is $1.50?

2. How does this supply curve illustrate the law of supply?

Animated **Economics**

Use an interactive supply curve at **ClassZone.com**

EXAMPLE Market Supply Curve

Like the Smiths' individual supply curve, the market supply curve for all the stands that sell tomatoes at the Montclair Farmers' Market shows the quantity supplied at different prices. In other words, the graph shows the quantity of tomatoes that all of the producers, or the market as a whole, are willing and able to offer for sale at each price. The market supply curve (Figure 5.5) differs in scope from the Smiths' individual supply curve, but it is constructed in the same way. As in Figure 5.4, the vertical axis displays prices and the horizontal axis displays quantities supplied.

FIGURE 5.5 TOMATO MARKET SUPPLY CURVE

Price per Pound ($)	Quantity Supplied
2.00	350
1.75	300
1.50	250
1.25	200
1.00	150
0.75	100
0.50	50

Notice that **market supply curves** slope upward from lower left to upper right, just as individual supply curves do.

The main difference between the two types of curves is that the quantities supplied at each price are much larger on a market supply curve. This is because the curve represents a group of producers (a market), not just one producer.

ANALYZE GRAPHS

1. At which price will all the fruit and vegetable stands want to sell 200 pounds of tomatoes?

2. How is the slope of this supply curve different from the slope of a market demand curve?

Look at Figure 5.5 one more time. What is the quantity supplied at $1.50? How will quantity supplied change if the price increases by 25 cents or decreases by 25 cents? Once again, find the answers to these questions by running your finger along the curve. As you can see, the market supply curve, just like the individual supply curve, vividly illustrates the direct relationship between price and quantity supplied. If the price of tomatoes increases among all of the suppliers at the farmers' market, then the quantity supplied of tomatoes also increases. And, conversely, if the price decreases, then the quantity supplied decreases as well. As with the individual supply curve, the market supply curve is constructed on the assumption that all other economic factors remain constant—only the price per pound of tomatoes changes.

The NBA Goes International

The National Basketball Association (NBA) might consider changing its name to the International Basketball Association. Roughly 20 percent of the players in the NBA come from foreign countries. Notable stars include Dirk Nowitzki from Germany, Yao Ming (far right) from China, and Luol Deng from Sudan. As Figure 5.6 shows, the number of international players in the NBA has risen dramatically. What accounts for this change?

Many factors contributed, including the NBA gaining global popularity and the high salaries earned by NBA stars. A key factor was the increase in talent outside the United States. As better coaching spread throughout the world, the supply of international players talented enough to play in the NBA increased. At the same time, the success of the NBA allowed it to devote more resources to scouting players outside U.S. borders.

FIGURE 5.6 INTERNATIONAL PLAYERS IN THE NBA

Source: National Basketball Association

CONNECTING ACROSS THE GLOBE

1. **Synthesizing Economic Information** How do price and quantity supplied affect who plays in the NBA?
2. **Drawing Conclusions** If European teams offered higher salaries than the NBA, what might happen?

Supply curves for all producers follow the law of supply. Whether the producers are manufacturers, farmers, retailers, or service providers, they are willing to supply more goods and services at higher prices, even though it costs more to produce more. Higher prices signal the potential for higher profits, and the desire to increase profits drives decision making in the market. You will learn more about the costs of production and about maximizing profits in Section 2.

SMART Grapher
Create a supply curve at **ClassZone.com**

APPLICATION Applying Economic Concepts

C. Use the supply schedule you created for Application B on page 133 to create a supply curve.

REVIEWING KEY CONCEPTS

1. Explain the differences between the terms in each of these pairs:
   a. *supply*
   law of supply
   b. *supply schedule*
   supply curve
   c. *market supply schedule*
   market supply curve

2. Why does a supply curve slope upward?

3. What do the points on a market supply curve represent?

4. If the price of a video game increased, what would the law of supply predict about the quantity supplied of the game?

5. How is the law of supply similar to the law of demand? How is it different?

6. **Using Your Notes** How is a supply schedule different from a market supply schedule? Refer to your completed cluster diagram. Use the Graphic Organizer at **Interactive Review @ ClassZone.com**

CRITICAL THINKING

7. **Explaining an Economic Concept** Focus on one item you buy regularly for which the price has changed. How did this shift in price influence supply?

8. **Making Inferences** The market supply schedule on page 133 shows that the quantity supplied of tomatoes priced at 50 cents per pound was 50 pounds. However, market research of customers at the farmers' market showed that the market demand at that price was 250 pounds of tomatoes. How do you explain the difference?

9. **Applying Economic Concepts** Return to the supply schedule for nutrition bars you created for Application B on page 133. Assume that the class represents all the sellers of nutrition bars in the market. Tabulate these individual supply schedules to create a market supply schedule. Then use that schedule to draw a market supply curve.

10. **Challenge** Why might producers not always be able to sell their products at the higher prices they prefer? Think about the laws of demand and supply and the different attitudes that consumers and producers have toward price. How might the market resolve this difference? (You will learn more about this in Chapter 6.)

ECONOMICS IN PRACTICE

Making a Market Supply Curve
Suppose that you are the head of the sporting goods dealers' association in your city. You survey all the stores that sell skis and determine how many pairs of skis they are willing to sell at various prices. Your research enables you to make the following market supply schedule.

Price per Pair ($)	Quantity Supplied
500	600
425	450
350	325
275	225
200	150
125	100

Create a Supply Curve Use this market supply schedule to draw a market supply curve. Be sure to label each axis of your graph.

Challenge Write a caption for your supply curve explaining what it shows.

Use *SMART Grapher* @ ClassZone.com to complete this activity.

ECONOMICS SKILLBUILDER

For more on evaluating sources, see the Skillbuilder Handbook, page R28.

Evaluating Sources

There are many sources of economic information, including news articles, reports, books, and electronic media. Knowing how to interpret sources is how we gain economic information.

TECHNIQUES FOR READING SOURCE MATERIAL The following passage appeared on the Web site of the Portland Cement Association. The passage is a source of information about the supply of cement in the United States in 2004. To interpret this source of information, use the following strategies.

> **Identify** the subject of the passage. Then ask yourself what, if any, economic concept is involved. This passage is about cement. The economic concept discussed is supply.

Cement Supply Falls Short

Several factors have converged to create tight supplies of cement, the key ingredient in concrete, which is used in nearly every type of construction.

First, strong construction markets have increased demand. The flare in demand arrived on the heels of an unusually active winter for construction, traditionally a down period when plants can stockpile cement in anticipation of the spring construction surge. Instead, there was no letup in demand during the 2003/04 winter and little opportunity to prepare a strong inventory for spring when construction activity traditionally increases.

Another factor is freight—limited availability of transport ships and escalating shipping rates. According to figures from the U.S. Geological Survey, 2003 U.S. portland cement consumption was 107.5 million metric tons. Of that total, 23.2 million tons or 21.6 percent was imported cement.

Since the beginning of the spring 2004, shipping rates have skyrocketed and availability of ships is limited. The booming Asian economies are straining worldwide cement capacity and shipping availability.

Source: www.cement.org

> **Identify** economic factors that are relevant to the discussion. The cement shortage is explained in part by an increase in market demand and by the rising cost and limited availability of ships to carry imported cement.

> **Evaluate** the passage's credibility. Do you think the source of the passage is reliable? Are other cited sources reliable? Information from this association and the U.S. Geological Survey is likely to be reliable.

THINKING ECONOMICALLY Interpreting

1. According to the passage, what variables affect the supply of concrete in the United States?

2. Do you think cement will continue to be in short supply in the United States? Explain your answer using information from the passage.

3. Who do you think is most likely to benefit from the information provided in the passage? Why?

REVIEWING KEY CONCEPTS

1. Explain the differences between the terms in each of these groups:

   a. *marginal product*
   profit-maximizing output

   b. *increasing returns*
   diminishing returns

   c. *fixed cost*
   variable cost

2. Why does the marginal cost in Janine's factory decrease as marginal product increases?

3. Explain why marginal revenue and price are the same in Figure 5.9 on page 143.

4. What changes for a company when it reaches the break-even point?

5. How does a business use marginal analysis to decide how many workers to employ?

6. **Using Your Notes** How does a business calculate its total costs? Refer to your completed hierarchy diagram. Use the Graphic Organizer at **Interactive Review @ ClassZone.com**

Production Costs
(main idea) (main idea) (main idea)
(details) (details) (details)

CRITICAL THINKING

7. **Categorizing Economic Information** Categorize the following costs incurred by a bookstore owner as fixed or variable: accountant, electricity for extra holiday hours, wages, clerks' insurance, manager's salary, purchase of books, rent, telephone.

8. **Applying Economic Concepts** Suppose that you own a video store that has total costs of $3,600 per month. If you charge $12 for each DVD you sell, how many do you need to sell each month in order to break even? Explain how you arrived at your answer.

9. **Applying Economic Concepts** The owner of a factory that produces soccer balls determines that his marginal product is at its peak when he has 100 employees. He determines that his marginal cost and marginal revenue are equal when he has 150 employees. What number of employees should he hire in order to maximize his profits? Explain the reason for your answer.

10. **Challenge** Many companies choose to manufacture their products in countries where workers are paid lower wages than in the United States. Which variable costs decrease and which ones increase as a result of this decision? Why do companies make this choice? Consider what you know about the relationship of costs to profits as you formulate your answer.

ECONOMICS IN PRACTICE

Calculating Costs and Revenues
Suppose you are a manufacturer of video games. You have analyzed your costs of production to create the following table.

Total Product	Fixed Cost ($)	Variable Cost ($)
0	500	0
25	500	800
50	500	1,200
100	500	1,800
175	500	2,550
275	500	3,350
350	500	4,250
400	500	5,750

Calculate Costs Copy the information in the table on your own paper and add two columns: Total Costs and Marginal Costs. Use the information given to calculate the values and fill in those two columns.

Challenge You sell the video games for $40 each. Add columns for Marginal Revenue, Total Revenue, and Profit to your chart and calculate the values for each quantity of total product.

What Factors Affect Supply?

OBJECTIVES	KEY TERMS	TAKING NOTES
In Section 3, you will • explain the difference between change in quantity supplied and change in supply • understand how to determine a change in supply • identify the factors that can cause a change in supply	change in quantity supplied, *p. 146* change in supply, *p. 148* input costs, *p. 148* labor productivity, *p. 149* technology, *p. 149* excise tax, *p. 149* regulation, *p. 150*	As you read Section 3, complete a chart like this one showing each factor that causes change in supply. Use the Graphic Organizer at **Interactive Review @ ClassZone.com**

Factor That Changes Supply	Reason Why Supply Changes

Changes in Quantity Supplied

KEY CONCEPTS

The supply schedules and supply curves that you studied in Section 1 were created using the assumption that all other economic factors except the price of tomatoes would remain the same. If all other factors remain the same, then the only thing that influences how many tomatoes producers will offer for sale is the price of those tomatoes. The supply curve shows that pattern.

In Chapter 4, you learned the difference between change in demand and change in quantity demanded. Change in quantity demanded is shown by the points along an existing demand curve, while change in demand actually shifts the demand curve itself. Similarly, the different points on a supply curve show change in quantity supplied. **Change in quantity supplied** is an increase or decrease in the amount of a good or service that producers are willing to sell because of a change in price.

A change in the price of bicycles. . .

. . . causes a change in the quantity supplied.

EXAMPLE Changes Along a Supply Curve

Each new point on the supply curve shows a change in quantity supplied. A change in quantity supplied does not shift the supply curve itself. Let's look again at the Smiths' supply curve for tomatoes (Figure 5.10). Note the quantities supplied at each price. Notice that as quantity supplied changes, the change is shown by the direction of movement, right or left, along the supply curve. A movement to the right indicates an increase in both price and quantity supplied. A movement to the left shows a decrease in both price and quantity supplied.

FIGURE 5.10 CHANGES IN QUANTITY SUPPLIED

A **change in quantity supplied** doesn't shift the supply curve. The change refers to movement along the curve itself. Each point on the curve represents a new quantity supplied.

a As you move to the right along the curve, the quantity supplied increases.

b As you move to the left along the curve, the quantity supplied decreases.

ANALYZE GRAPHS

1. What is the change in quantity supplied when price increases from $0.75 to $1.50?
2. What is the change in price when quantity supplied changes from 50 to 24 pounds?

Animated Economics

Use an interactive supply curve to see changes in quantity supplied at **ClassZone.com**

Just as Figure 5.10 shows change in quantity supplied by one individual, a market supply curve shows similar information for an entire market. However, market supply curves have larger quantities supplied, and therefore larger changes to quantity supplied, because they combine the data from all the individual supply curves in the market. For example, when the price increases from $0.75 to $1.75 on the market supply curve (Figure 5.5), the quantity supplied increases from 100 pounds to 300. Compare this with the change in quantity supplied at those prices in Figure 5.10.

APPLICATION Applying Economic Concepts

A. Changes in quantity supplied do not shift the position of the supply curve. Why?

Changes in Supply

QUICK REFERENCE

Change in supply occurs when a change in the marketplace prompts producers to sell different amounts at every price.

KEY CONCEPTS

Consider what might happen if the workers at an automobile factory negotiate a large wage increase so that it's more expensive to produce each automobile. As the firm's costs increase, it is less willing and able to offer as many automobiles for sale. Any action such as this, which changes the costs of production, will change supply. **Change in supply** occurs when something prompts producers to offer different amounts for sale at every price. When production costs increase, supply decreases; when production costs decrease, supply increases.

Just like change in demand, change in supply actually shifts the supply curve. Six factors cause a change in supply: input costs, labor productivity, technology, government actions, producer expectations, and number of producers.

FACTOR 1 Input Costs

QUICK REFERENCE

Input costs are the price of the resources used to make products.

Input costs are a major factor that affects production costs and, therefore, supply. **Input costs** are the price of the resources needed to produce a good or service. For example, Anna makes nutrition bars that contain peanuts. If the price of peanuts increases, Anna's costs increase. She cannot afford to produce as many nutrition bars, and her supply curve shifts to the left (Figure 5.11). When the price of peanuts decreases, her costs decrease. She is willing and able to increase the quantity she can supply at every price, and the curve shifts to the right (Figure 5.12).

FIGURES 5.11 AND 5.12 SHIFTS IN SUPPLY

FIGURE 5.11 DECREASE IN SUPPLY

FIGURE 5.12 INCREASE IN SUPPLY

When a **change in supply** occurs, the supply curve shifts.

a As Figure 5.11 shows, a shift to the left (S2) indicates a decrease in supply.

b As Figure 5.12 shows, a shift to the right (S3) indicates an increase in supply.

ANALYZE GRAPHS

1. In Figure 5.11, how has the supply of nutrition bars changed at every price?

2. In Figure 5.12, how has the supply of nutrition bars changed at every price?

Animated Economics

Use an interactive version of shifting supply curves at ClassZone.com

FACTOR 2 Labor Productivity

Labor productivity is the amount of goods and services that a person can produce in a given time. Increasing productivity decreases the costs of production and therefore increases supply. For example, a specialized division of labor can allow a producer to make more goods at a lower cost, as was the case at Janine's factory in Section 2. Her marginal costs decreased when there were six workers, each of whom had a separate job to do.

Better-trained and more-skilled workers can usually produce more goods in less time, and therefore at lower costs, than less-educated or less-skilled workers. For example, a business that provides word-processing services can produce more documents if its employees type quickly and have a lot of experience working with word-processing software.

FACTOR 3 Technology

One way that businesses improve their productivity and increase supply is through the use of technology. **Technology** involves the application of scientific methods and discoveries to the production process, resulting in new products or new manufacturing techniques. Influenced by the profit motive, manufacturers have, throughout history, used technology to make goods more efficiently. Increased automation, including the use of industrial robots, has led to increased supplies of automobiles, computers, and many other products. (See the Case Study on pages 158–159.)

Improved technology helps farmers produce more food per acre. It also allows oil refiners to get more gasoline out of every barrel of crude oil and helps to get that gasoline to gas stations more quickly and more safely. In addition, technological innovations, such as the personal computer, enable workers to be more productive. This, in turn, helps businesses to increase the supply of their services, such as processing insurance claims or selling airline tickets.

The Typewriter's End The move from typewriter to computer shows how technology helps to boost productivity.

FACTOR 4 Government Action

Government actions can also affect the costs of production, both positively and negatively. An **excise tax** is a tax on the production or sale of a specific good or service. Excise taxes are often placed on items such as alcohol and tobacco—things whose consumption the government is interested in discouraging. The taxes increase producers' costs and, therefore, decrease the supply of these items.

Taxes tend to decrease supply; subsidies have the opposite effect. You learned in Chapter 3 that a subsidy is a government payment that partially covers the cost of an economic activity. The subsidy's purpose is to encourage or protect that activity. Most forms of energy production in the United States receive some form of subsidy. For example, subsidies helped to double the supply of ethanol, a gasoline substitute made from corn, between 2000 and 2004.

Government **regulation**, the act of controlling business behavior through a set of rules or laws, can also affect supply. Banning a certain pesticide might decrease the supply of the crops that depend on the pesticide. Worker safety regulations might decrease supply by increasing a business's production costs or increase supply by reducing the amount of labor lost to on-the-job injuries.

FACTOR 5 Producer Expectations

If producers expect the price of their product to rise or fall in the future, it may affect how much of that product they are willing and able to supply in the present. Different kinds of producers may react to future price changes differently. For example, if a farmer expects the price of corn to be higher in the future, he or she may store some of the current crop, thereby decreasing supply. A manufacturer who believes the price of his or her product will rise may run the factory for an extra shift or invest in more equipment to increase supply.

FACTOR 6 Number of Producers

When one company develops a successful new idea, whether it's designer wedding gowns, the latest generation of cell phones, or fast-food sushi, other producers soon enter the market and increase the supply of the good or service. When this happens, the supply curve shifts to the right, as you can see in Figure 5.13.

FIGURE 5.13 NUMBER OF PRODUCERS

a This supply curve (S1) shows the number of ice cream cones sold in a week at each price when Casey is the only supplier in the market.

b This curve (S2) shows the number of ice cream cones sold in a week at each price when three more suppliers enter the market.

ANALYZE GRAPHS

1. About how many ice cream cones were sold at $1.00 when Casey was the only producer in the market?
2. How do these two curves show the effect of the number of producers on the supply of ice cream cones in the market?

An increase in the number of producers means increased competition, which may eventually drive less-efficient producers out of the market, decreasing supply. (You'll learn more about competition in Chapter 7.) Competition has a major impact on supply, as producers enter and leave the market constantly.

FIGURE 5.14 Factors That Cause a Change in Supply

Input Costs Input costs, the collective price of the resources that go into producing a good or service, affect supply directly.

Number of Producers A successful new product or service always brings out competitors who initially raise overall supply.

Labor Productivity Better-trained or more-skilled workers are usually more productive. Increased productivity decreases costs and increases supply.

What Causes a Change in Supply?

Producer Expectations The amount of product producers are willing and able to supply may be influenced by whether they believe prices will go up or down.

Technology By applying scientific advances to the production process, producers have learned to generate their goods and services more efficiently.

Government Action Government actions, such as taxes or subsidies, can have a positive or a negative effect on production costs.

ANALYZE CHARTS

A newspaper article states that the supply of snowboards has risen dramatically over the past six months. Choose four of the six factors that cause a change in supply and explain how each might have resulted in the recent influx of snowboards.

Figure 5.13 shows what happens to the supply of ice cream cones in a neighborhood as more producers enter the market. When Casey opened his ice cream store it was the only one in the area. It was an instant success. Within six months, three competing stores had opened in the neighborhood, and the supply of ice cream cones increased at all price levels. A year later, though, this intense competition forced one of the producers to leave the market.

APPLICATION Applying Economic Concepts

B. Choose an item of food or clothing that you buy regularly. List as many input costs as you can that might affect the supply of that product. Compare your list with a classmate's and see if you can add to each other's lists.

Robert Johnson: Supplying African-American Entertainment

In this section, you've learned about the factors that influence supply. You've also seen some examples of how these factors work. The story of media entrepreneur Robert Johnson provides a real-world example of how the entrance of a new supplier can affect a market.

Expanding the Number of Producers

In the late 1970s, Robert Johnson was working as a Washington lobbyist for the National Cable Television Association. He recognized that current suppliers in the cable TV industry were ignoring a substantial market—African Americans. To fill this void, Johnson conceived the idea for Black Entertainment Television (BET), the first cable channel owned by and focused on African Americans.

To launch his dream, Johnson took out a $15,000 bank loan. He also persuaded a major investor to put up $500,000. Next, he secured space on a cable TV satellite for his new channel. BET's first program appeared on January 8, 1980. The company grew from offering two hours of programming per week to round-the-clock programming on five separate channels. Cable operators in the United States, Canada, and the Caribbean saw the value of this kind of targeted programming, and began to buy BET's shows.

At first, BET targeted young viewers with programs similar to those on MTV. As the cable TV industry grew and became more profitable, Johnson invested in more diverse programming. Of this transition he explained, "Now we're a music video channel with a public affairs footprint. . . ." BET could "play music, but also . . . cover issues that are of concern to African Americans." BET.com, the number one Internet portal for African Americans, soon followed.

A Vast Reach BET supplies programming to more than 85 million households in Canada, the United States, and the Caribbean.

In 2001, Johnson sold BET to the giant media company Viacom International Inc. for $3 billion and became the nation's first black billionaire. After the sale, Johnson stayed on at BET and continued to run the company for five more years. His success demonstrated that there was a strong market for African-American entertainment. As a result, many suppliers—some with no traditional ties to the African-American community—now offer the kind of programming Johnson pioneered.

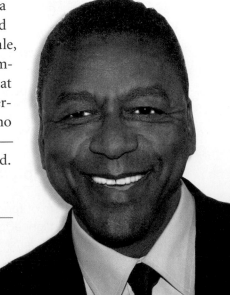

APPLICATION Making Inferences

C. What effects did BET's success have on the supply of African-American programming?

FAST FACTS

Robert L. Johnson

Title: Founder and Chairman of the RLJ Companies

Born: April 8, 1946, Hickory, Mississippi

Major Accomplishment: Founded BET, the leading supplier of cable TV programming aimed at African Americans

RLJ Companies: Real estate, financial services, hotels, Charlotte Bobcats (NBA), Charlotte Sting (WNBA)

Honors: Broadcasting and Cable Magazine Hall of Fame Award (1997), NAACP Image Award

---

Economics Update

Find an update on Robert Johnson at **ClassZone.com**

SECTION 3 Assessment

Online Quiz
ClassZone.com

REVIEWING KEY CONCEPTS

1. Explain the differences between the terms in each of these pairs:

   a. *change in quantity supplied*
   change in supply

   b. *input costs*
   technology

   c. *excise tax*
   regulation

2. What else besides raw materials would be included in input costs?

3. Why might an increase in oil prices lead to a decrease in the supply of fruits and vegetables in your local supermarket?

4. Why do excise taxes and subsidies affect supply differently?

5. Does expectation of a change in price affect supply? Illustrate your answer with examples.

6. **Using Your Notes** How does a change in number of producers affect supply? Refer to your completed chart.

   Use the Graphic Organizer at **Interactive Review @ ClassZone.com**

Factor That Changes Supply	Reason Why Supply Changes

CRITICAL THINKING

7. **Applying Economic Concepts** How do each of these examples of government actions affect the supply of gasoline?

   a. In 2005, the government continued support for ethanol, a gasoline substitute.

   b. The state of California requires a special blend of gasoline that meets stricter environmental standards than other regions in the country.

   c. Many states use gasoline taxes to help fund highway construction and maintenance.

8. **Making Inferences** Why do you think governments want to influence the supply of alcohol and tobacco products by imposing excise taxes?

9. **Analyzing Effects** Take out the market supply curve for skis that you created on page 137. Add new curves showing how supply would be changed in each of the following cases. Share your graph with a classmate and explain your reasoning.

   a. The price of titanium, used in skis, declines dramatically.

   b. A large manufacturer decides to stop producing skis.

10. **Challenge** How does an increased number of producers affect the prices of goods in a market? What is the reason for this effect? Think about what you know about demand and supply and review Figure 5.12 as you formulate your answer.

ECONOMICS IN PRACTICE

Explaining Changes in Supply
Suppose that you are a manufacturer of personal digital music players (PDMPs). What factors affect supply for PDMPs? The chart below lists examples of a change in supply in the market for PDMPs. For each example, identify which factor that affects supply is involved and state whether supply increases or decreases.

Example of Change That Affects Supply	Factor and How It Affected Supply
You give each worker in your factory a specialized job.	
Price of computer chips used in PDMPs rises.	
New machinery speeds up the manufacturing process.	
Your success prompts three new companies to start producing PDMPs.	
A new law requires producers to recycle the wastewater from their factories.	

Challenge Identify which of the six factors that affect supply does not appear on this chart. What would be an example of how that factor might affect the market for PDMPs?

What Is Elasticity of Supply?

OBJECTIVES	KEY TERMS	TAKING NOTES
In Section 4, you will • define the term *elasticity of supply* • explain the difference between elastic and inelastic supply • identify the factors that affect elasticity of supply	elasticity of supply, *p. 154*	As you read Section 4, complete a cluster diagram like the one shown. Use the Graphic Organizer at **Interactive Review @ ClassZone.com**

Elasticity of Supply

KEY CONCEPTS

According to the law of supply, as price increases so will the supply of a good or service. When Toyota Motor Corporation introduced its Prius hybrid in 2000, it was surprised by the automobile's instant popularity. Consumers were willing to pay more than the manufacturer's suggested price. Yet Toyota was not able to increase supply at the same pace that consumer demand and prices rose. Even five years later, Toyota could not meet rising demand. This inability to effectively respond to and meet increased demand suggests that the supply of the Prius was inelastic.

In Chapter 4, you learned that elasticity of demand measures how responsive consumers are to price changes. In a similar way, **elasticity of supply** is also a measure of how responsive producers are to price changes.

If a change in price leads to a relatively larger change in quantity supplied, supply is said to be elastic. In other words, supply is elastic if a 10 percent increase in price causes a greater than 10 percent increase in quantity supplied. If a change in price leads to a relatively smaller change in quantity supplied, supply is said to be inelastic. If the price and the quantity supplied change by exactly the same percentage, supply is unit elastic.

> **QUICK REFERENCE**
>
> **Elasticity of supply** is a measure of how responsive producers are to price changes in the marketplace.

Inelastic Supply The supply of expensive and complicated items, such as this Prius hybrid, is often inelastic.

EXAMPLE Elastic Supply

Let's look at an example of elastic supply. Figure 5.15 illustrates how the quantity supplied of a new style of leather boots was elastic. As the boots gained in popularity, a shortage developed. The boot makers raised the price of the boots from $60 to $150 dollars, and the quantity supplied more than kept up, escalating from 10,000 to 50,000 pairs. The producer was able to rapidly increase the quantity supplied because, unlike car manufacturing for instance, the raw materials needed to make boots are neither particularly expensive nor hard to come by. The actual manufacturing process is also, relatively speaking, fairly uncomplicated and easy to increase.

EXAMPLE Inelastic Supply

In Chapter 4, you learned that demand for gasoline was inelastic. The supply of gasoline is also inelastic. Although gasoline prices rose 20 to 30 percent between 2004 and 2005, producers were not able to increase supply by the same amount because of the limited supply of crude oil and refining capacity.

Figure 5.16 shows how the supply of olive oil is also inelastic. When the price of olive oil rose by a factor of four, supply could not keep pace, as the oil comes from the previous season's olives and is exported from the Mediterranean region.

FIGURE 5.15 ELASTIC SUPPLY CURVE

Quantity supplied of boots (in thousands)

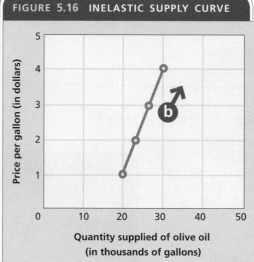

FIGURE 5.16 INELASTIC SUPPLY CURVE

Quantity supplied of olive oil (in thousands of gallons)

a The curve in Figure 5.15 slopes gradually. It slopes more horizontally than vertically because of greater changes in quantity supplied.

b The curve in Figure 5.16 slopes steeply. It slopes more vertically than horizontally because of lesser changes in quantity supplied.

ANALYZE GRAPHS

1. If the price of leather rose dramatically for the boots in Figure 5.15, how might this affect elasticity of supply?

2. In the United States, would the supply of corn oil be more elastic than the supply of olive oil? Why or why not?

Animated Economics

Use elastic and inelastic supply curves at **ClassZone.com**

APPLICATION Drawing Conclusions

A. A bakery produces 200 muffins per week that sell for $1.50 each. When the price increases to $2.00, it produces 300 muffins per week. Is supply elastic or inelastic? Explain your answer.

What Affects Elasticity of Supply?

Just as there are factors that cause a change in supply, there are also factors that affect the elasticity of supply. There are far fewer of these factors than for elasticity of demand. The ease of changing production to respond to price change is the main factor in determining elasticity of supply. Given enough time, the elasticity of supply increases for most goods and services. Supply will be more elastic over a year or several years than it will be if the time frame to respond is a day, a week, or a month.

Industries that are able to respond quickly to changes in price by either increasing or decreasing production are those that don't require a lot of capital, skilled labor, or difficult-to-obtain resources. For example, the quantity supplied of dog-walking services can increase rapidly with the addition of more people to walk dogs. A small business that sells crafts made from recycled materials would be able to respond quickly to changes in the price of its various products by applying its resources to increase the supply of its higher priced items.

For other industries, it takes a great deal of time to shift the resources of production to respond to price changes. Automakers and oil refiners are examples of industries that rely on large capital outlays or difficult-to-obtain resources. It might take such suppliers a considerable amount of time to respond to price changes.

YOUR ECONOMIC CHOICES

ELASTICITY OF SUPPLY

Which supply of cupcakes is more elastic?

You're planning to sell cupcakes at your school's football game to raise funds for a charitable cause, but it's hard to say in advance how many fans will attend the game. You can place an order with a bakery (which you need to do a week early) or have volunteers do the baking the night before the game. Which supply of cupcakes is more elastic? Why?

APPLICATION Applying Economic Concepts

B. Is the elasticity of a farmer's crop of sweet corn greater at the beginning of the growing season or in the middle of the growing season? Why?

REVIEWING KEY CONCEPTS

1. Use each of the following three terms in a sentence that gives an example of the term as it relates to supply:

   a. *elastic*　　　**b.** *inelastic*　　　**c.** *elasticity of supply*

2. How is elasticity of supply similar to elasticity of demand? How is it different?

3. Is the supply of genuine antique furniture elastic or inelastic? Why?

4. What is the difference between industries that have elastic supply and those that have inelastic supply?

5. What is the main factor that affects elasticity of supply and how does it affect elasticity?

6. **Using Your Notes** How is time related to elasticity of supply? Refer to your completed cluster diagram. Use the Graphic Organizer at **Interactive Review @ ClassZone.com**

Elasticity of Supply

CRITICAL THINKING

7. **Analyzing Causes** Between 1997 and 2002, many gold producers cut their budgets for exploring for new sources in order to stay profitable when the price of gold was less than $350 per ounce. When the price rose above $400 per ounce in 2004, gold producers were not able to respond quickly to the increase. Use what you know about elasticity of supply to explain this cause-and-effect relationship.

8. **Analyzing Data** In May, Montclair Electronics sold 100 portable DVD players at $150 each. High consumer demand at the start of the summer travel season increased the price to $180. In June, the store sold 115 DVD players at the higher price. Is the supply of DVD players elastic or inelastic? Show your math calculations to support your answer.

9. **Applying Economic Concepts** Analyze the factors that determine elasticity of supply to explain why it is difficult for orange growers to respond quickly to changes in the price of orange juice.

10. **Challenge** Prices are up 8 percent at the local juice shop. Its raw materials are inexpensive and easy to find, and the labor is unskilled. Should the shop be able to raise quantity supplied more than 8 percent? Why?

ECONOMICS IN PRACTICE

Calculating Elasticity
The growing market for bottled yogurt smoothies is shown in the supply schedule below. Use the information in the table to determine whether the quantity supplied is growing proportionately more than increases in price. Would you expect supply for yogurt smoothies to be elastic or inelastic over a period of six months?

Price ($)	Quantity Supplied of Smoothies
2.00	600
1.75	450
1.50	300
1.25	200

Create a Supply Curve Use the information in the supply schedule to create a supply curve for yogurt smoothies. What does the slope of this curve indicate about elasticity of supply for yogurt smoothies?

Challenge Adapt the information in the Math Challenge on page 121 to calculate the elasticity of supply using the data in the supply schedule above. Substitute quantity supplied for quantity demanded in the formula.

Use **SMART Grapher @ ClassZone.com** to complete this activity.

Economics Update
Find an update on this Case
Study at **ClassZone.com**

Robots—Technology Increases Supply

Background The increasing sophistication of technology continues to have a profound impact on the production and supply of manufactured goods. Robots—machines that can be programmed to perform a variety of tasks—are a prime example of technology's effect on industry.

Today, industrial robots perform a wide variety of functions. Although robots do everything from packaging pharmaceuticals to dispensing genetic material in biotechnical laboratories, half of all industrial robots are used to make automobiles. Robots are ideal for lifting heavy objects and for performing repetitive activities that humans find boring. Lately, though, robots are being used more for tasks that require refined skills.

What's the issue? How does technology increase supply? Study these sources to discover how robots can increase productivity.

A. Online Article

Japan's low birthrate is likely to result in a shortage of workers. This article discusses how Toyota plans to use robots to solve this problem.

Toyota to Use "Super" Robots

As the Japanese labor pool declines, Toyota turns to robots.

Toyota is deploying at all 12 of its domestic plants robots capable of performing several simultaneous operations. It aims to be the first automaker to introduce robots that, in addition to machine work and engine assembly, perform the finishing touches on the assembly line. . . .

In the automobile industry robots mainly perform relatively dangerous tasks such as welding and coating, while, in order to preserve quality, human workers accomplish such complicated final processes as attaching interior trim.

But Toyota plans to introduce robots to final assembly processes after establishing the necessary control technology and safeguards, and developing parts easily assembled by android [robotic] hands.

Even this super robot will not result in the total replacement of man by machine; rather it will reinforce the strengths of the production line and compensate for manpower shortages in a truly Toyota-style production innovation.

The company plans to use robots to keep production costs at the level of those in China. . . . Toyota presently uses between 3,000 and 4,000 standard robots. It expects a total of 1,000 super robots to join them.

Source: japaninc.net

Thinking Economically Will the use of robots as described in this article affect the supply of Toyota automobiles? Explain your answer.

B. Political Cartoon

John Morris drew this cartoon about the use of robots in manufacturing. *Parity* means "equality." In the cartoon, *parity* refers to equal pay and benefits.

"The robots have gone on strike - they want parity with the robots at Ford."

Source: www.CartoonStock.com

Thinking Economically How are the robots in the cartoon affecting productivity?

C. Industry Report

Epson, a maker of industrial robots, presents a case study involving the use of robots in a bakery.

Robots Decorate Cakes

English bakery turns to robots during peak seasons.

Problem: A large English commercial bakery decorates cakes with written messages iced on the top—a task generally undertaken by skilled staff. . . .

During seasonal holiday periods consumer demand for these decorated cakes increases fourfold. Training of additional staff to cope with the expanded demand . . . takes a significant period of time and so volume planning is critical.

Solution: System Devices, the EPSON Robots agent for the [United Kingdom], worked with Integrated Dispensing Systems to design and build a robotic cake decorating cell that . . . used an EPSON SCARA robot. . . .

Cakes are fed to the EPSON robot via a conveyor. A simple optical positioning system ensures that the cakes are presented to the robot in a consistent position.

A CAD [computer-aided design] file of the decoration shape is downloaded to the robot. Because individual cake heights may vary, a laser range finder tells the robot the height of each cake as it enters the work cell. The robot moves over the top of the cake and writes the decorative inscription. . . .

Benefits: Ability to boost production during peak seasonal demand periods; consistently high product quality due to reduced variability on decorations; reduced . . . training costs.

Source: www.robots.epson.com

Thinking Economically In this report, how does the use of robots help the supplier respond to a seasonal change in demand? Would this robotic solution help a department store facing a holiday staffing shortage? Why or why not?

THINKING ECONOMICALLY Synthesizing

1. Which of the six factors that can cause a change in supply is highlighted in the three documents? Does this factor generally increase or decrease supply?

2. Which document, B or C, addresses the issue of elasticity? Explain.

3. In which article, A or C, are the robots an example of variable costs? Why?

Interactive ◀◀Review

Review this chapter using interactive activities at ClassZone.com

- **Online Summary**
- **Quizzes**
- **Vocabulary Flip Cards**
- **Graphic Organizers**
- **Review and Study Notes**

↪ Online Summary

Complete the following activity either on your own paper or online at **ClassZone.com**

Choose the key concept that best completes the sentence. Not all key concepts will be used.

break-even point	marginal product
change in quantity supplied	marginal revenue
change in supply	productivity
diminishing returns	profit-maximizing output
elasticity of supply	supply
fixed cost	supply curve
increasing returns	supply schedule
input costs	total product
law of supply	total revenue
marginal cost	variable cost

__1__ is the quantity of a product that producers are willing and able to offer for sale. According to the __2__, when price increases, quantity supplied increases, and when price decreases, quantity supplied decreases. Quantity supplied can be displayed on a chart called a __3__ or on a graph called a __4__.

__5__ is the change in __6__ caused by hiring one additional worker. When marginal product begins to decrease, production is in the stage of __7__.

Total cost is the sum of __8__ and variable costs. __9__ is the additional cost of producing one more unit. When marginal cost equals __10__, a company has reached __11__.

A __12__ occurs when producers are willing to sell different amounts of a product at every price. The six factors that change supply are input costs, __13__, technology, government action, producer expectations, and number of producers.

The term __14__ describes how responsive producers are to price changes. It is measured by comparing __15__ to change in price.

REVIEWING KEY CONCEPTS

What Is Supply? (pp. 130–137)

1. What two requirements of supply must someone meet to be considered a producer?

2. What does it mean to say that quantity supplied and price have a direct relationship?

What Are the Costs of Production? (pp. 138–145)

3. How does marginal product change during the three stages of production?

4. What is the relationship of total costs to profit?

What Factors Affect Supply? (pp. 146–153)

5. What is the difference between change in quantity supplied and change in supply?

6. How do input costs affect supply?

What Is Elasticity of Supply? (pp. 154–159)

7. How are elastic and inelastic supply different?

8. How might you calculate elasticity of supply?

APPLYING ECONOMIC CONCEPTS

Look at the graph below showing price changes for two commodities: crude oil and gasoline.

9. How is the price of gasoline related to the price of crude oil?

10. What factor that affects the supply of gasoline is shown in this graph? How does this factor affect the supply of gasoline?

FIGURE 5.17   U.S. PRICES OF CRUDE OIL AND GASOLINE

Source: Energy Information Administration, June 2006

11. Analyzing Data Suppose that you own a factory producing backpacks that sell for $20 each. Use the information in this table to calculate marginal cost, total revenue, and profit at each level of output. Identify the break-even point and profit-maximizing output.

BACKPACK PRODUCTION COSTS

Production Costs	
Total Product	Total Cost ($)
100	3,500
200	5,300
300	7,000
400	8,000
500	8,800
600	9,800
700	11,800
800	14,300
900	17,000

12. Analyzing Effects A city puts a new rule into effect about the kinds of beverages that may be sold in schools. Sugary sodas must be replaced by bottled water, fruit juices, and sports drinks. How will this decision affect the supply of each category of beverage at the schools? What factor that affects supply is demonstrated in this situation?

13. Drawing Conclusions Both demand and supply for gasoline are inelastic. Would the elasticity of supply and demand be the same for sports cars? Why or why not?

14. Challenge When a string of hurricanes hit Florida, preparation for and cleanup from the storms increased demand for plywood. Yet prices rose only slightly, partly because large chains shipped plywood from stores around the country in anticipation of the increased demand. How does this story illustrate the law of supply and elasticity of supply?

How Much Are You Willing to Supply?

Choose a partner. Imagine that the two of you run a software company. Your best-selling product is a program that helps businesses manage their inventory. Next year you will produce 20,000 units. The following partial supply schedule shows the prices at which you will likely sell your product during that period.

SOFTWARE SUPPLY SCHEDULE

Price ($)	Quantity Supplied
70	7,500
65	
60	
55	
50	1,000

Step 1 Copy the schedule onto a sheet of paper and fill in the missing amounts in the Quantity Supplied column. Be sure that the amounts you choose adhere to the law of supply.

Step 2 Draw a supply curve to illustrate your schedule. Be sure to label each axis of your curve.

Step 3 Get together with three other groups. These are your competitors. Bring all of your individual supply schedules together to make a market supply schedule. Then convert the market supply schedule into a market supply curve.

Step 4 You and your competitors find out that several other companies are getting ready to introduce similar inventory-control software. On your market supply curve, show how this development causes a shift in supply.

Step 5 Although writing your program was difficult, now that it is written, it is relatively quick and easy to produce copies for sale. Is the supply of your product elastic or inelastic? Why?

Use *SMARTGrapher* @ ClassZone.com to complete this activity.

How are prices set?
Prices greatly influence consumers' buying decisions. A reduced price on this sweater may act as an incentive for these young women to make a purchase.

Demand, Supply, and Prices

CONCEPT REVIEW

Demand is the willingness to buy a good or a service and the ability to pay for it.

Supply is the willingness and ability to produce and sell a product.

CHAPTER 6 KEY CONCEPT

The **equilibrium price** is the price at which quantity demanded and quantity supplied are the same.

WHY THE CONCEPT MATTERS

You've been looking for a vintage concert T-shirt to buy. You see the shirt you want offered on an Internet site, but the price is too high. After exchanging several e-mails, you and the seller set a price. It's higher than you wanted to pay and lower than the seller wanted to receive, but it's acceptable to you both. In a market economy, the forces of demand and supply act in much the same way. They work together to set a price that buyers and sellers find acceptable.

Online Highlights

More at ClassZone.com

 Economics Update

Go to **ECONOMICS UPDATE** for chapter updates and current news on ticketing companies' pricing practices. (See Case Study, pp. 186–187.) ▶

Animated Economics

Go to **ANIMATED ECONOMICS** for interactive lessons on the graphs and tables in this chapter.

Interactive ◀▶ Review

Go to **INTERACTIVE REVIEW** for concept review and activities.

Why have some rock bands questioned the pricing practices of certain ticketing companies? See the Case Study on pages 186–187.

Seeking Equilibrium: Demand and Supply

OBJECTIVES	KEY TERMS	TAKING NOTES
In Section 1, you will • explore market equilibrium and see how it is reached • explain how demand and supply interact to determine equilibrium price • analyze what causes surplus, shortage, and disequilibrium • identify how changes to demand and supply affect the equilibrium price	market equilibrium, *p. 164* equilibrium price, *p. 164* surplus, *p. 167* shortage, *p. 167* disequilibrium, *p. 169*	As you read Section 1, complete a cluster diagram like the one shown using the key concepts and other helpful words and phrases. Use the Graphic Organizer at **Interactive Review @ ClassZone.com**

The Interaction of Demand and Supply

KEY CONCEPTS

In Chapters 4 and 5, you learned about how demand and supply work in the market. Recall that a market is any place or situation in which people buy and sell goods and services. Since the market is the place where buyers and sellers come together, it is also the place where demand and supply interact.

As buyers and sellers interact, the market moves toward **market equilibrium**, a situation in which the quantity demanded of a good or service at a particular price is equal to the quantity supplied at that price. **Equilibrium price** is the price at which the quantity of a product demanded by consumers and the quantity supplied by producers are equal.

EXAMPLE Market Demand and Supply Schedule

Let's look at an example of how this concept works in a particular market. Karen runs a sandwich shop near an office park. Recently, she decided to offer a new product at lunchtime—prepared salads. On the first day, she makes up 40 salads and offers them at $10 each. She is disappointed when she sells only 10 and has to throw the rest away. The next day she is more cautious. She lowers the price to $4 each and makes only 15 salads. She discovers that 35 customers wanted her salads at the lower price. How can Karen find the right price?

Over the course of a week, Karen experiments with different combinations of price and quantity of salads supplied until she discovers market equilibrium at $6 per salad. At that price, she is willing to offer 25 salads for sale, and she sells all of them. When she has either too many or too few salads, she is motivated to change her price. Market equilibrium is the point at which quantity demanded and quantity supplied are in balance.

FIGURE 6.1 KAREN'S MARKET DEMAND AND SUPPLY SCHEDULE

Price per Salad ($)	Quantity Demanded	Quantity Supplied
10	10	40
8	15	(a)→ 35
6	25	←(b)→ 25
4	35	←(c) 15
2	40	10

(a) At prices above $6, quantity supplied exceeds quantity demanded.

(b) At the price of $6, the quantity demanded and the quantity supplied are equal.

(c) At prices below $6, the quantity demanded exceeds the quantity supplied.

Only at the **equilibrium price** of $6 are the quantity demanded and the quantity supplied equal.

ANALYZE TABLES

1. What is the difference between quantity supplied and quantity demanded when the price is $10? What is the difference when the price is $2?

2. How does this market demand and supply schedule illustrate the laws of demand and supply?

Animated Economics

Use an interactive market demand and supply schedule and curve at **ClassZone.com**

Look at Figure 6.1 to see the information that Karen gathered from her first week selling prepared salads. This table is a combined market demand and supply schedule that shows the quantities of salads supplied and demanded at various prices. Notice that quantity demanded and quantity supplied are different at every line of the schedule except one. That line represents market equilibrium and shows the equilibrium price of $6. When Karen offers salads at prices above $6, she produces more salads than she can sell and has to throw some away. When she offers salads at prices below $6, there is unmet demand because people want more salads than Karen is willing to offer at those prices.

Karen's experience shows how the laws of demand and supply interact in the market. She wants to offer more salads at higher prices than at lower prices because she wants to earn more profit. Her costs would make it impossible to earn much, if any, profit if she were to sell the number of salads that the office workers would like to buy at the lower prices. In a similar way, while the office workers may like the idea of fresh salads for lunch, they are not willing to buy the quantity of salads that Karen wants to sell at higher prices.

Economics Update

Find an update on market equilibrium at **ClassZone.com**

EXAMPLE Market Demand and Supply Curve

Just as it is possible to convert a market demand schedule to a market demand curve or a market supply schedule to a market supply curve, it is possible to graph a combined market demand and supply schedule.

Figure 6.2 portrays Karen's market demand and supply schedule on a combined graph. On the graph, the vertical axis shows the various prices at which salads are offered for sale and bought. The horizontal axis shows the quantity of salads, whether it is the quantity demanded or the quantity supplied. The demand curve (D) is plotted using the prices and the quantities demanded (Figure 6.1, columns 1 and 2). The supply curve (S) is plotted using the prices and the quantities supplied from the combined schedule (Figure 6.1, columns 1 and 3). You can read each individual curve the same way that you did in Chapters 4 and 5, when demand and supply were shown on separate graphs. Each point on the demand curve shows the intersection of price and quantity demanded. Each point on the supply curve shows the intersection of price and quantity supplied.

FIGURE 6.2 MARKET DEMAND AND SUPPLY CURVES

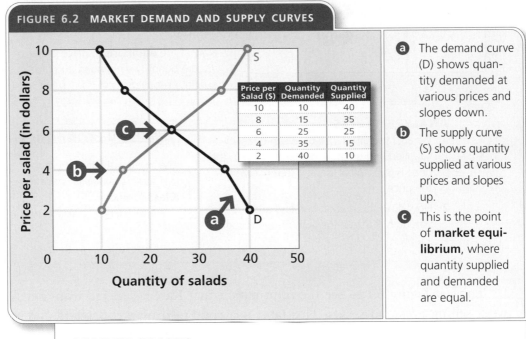

Price per Salad ($)	Quantity Demanded	Quantity Supplied
10	10	40
8	15	35
6	25	25
4	35	15
2	40	10

a The demand curve (D) shows quantity demanded at various prices and slopes down.

b The supply curve (S) shows quantity supplied at various prices and slopes up.

c This is the point of **market equilibrium**, where quantity supplied and demanded are equal.

ANALYZE GRAPHS
1. What is the quantity supplied at $8? What is the quantity demanded at $8?
2. How do these market demand and supply curves illustrate the concept of equilibrium price?

Look at Figure 6.2 again and notice that the two curves intersect at only one point; this is the point of market equilibrium. It occurs when quantity demanded and quantity supplied are the same—25 salads at $6. Showing the two curves together allows you to see the interaction of demand and supply graphically.

APPLICATION Applying Economic Concepts

A. Create a combined market demand and supply schedule for pizza at prices of $25, $20, $15, $10, and $5, where $10 is the price at which there is equilibrium.

Reaching the Equilibrium Price

It's clear from the example of Karen's salads that markets don't arrive at equilibrium price instantly; they often require a process of trial and error. The market may experience a **surplus**, which is the result of quantity supplied being greater than quantity demanded, usually because prices are too high. Or a **shortage** may occur, the result of quantity demanded being greater than quantity supplied, usually because prices are too low.

QUICK REFERENCE

Surplus is the result of quantity supplied being greater than quantity demanded.

Shortage is the result of quantity demanded being greater than quantity supplied.

EXAMPLE Surplus, Shortage, and Equilibrium

In Figure 6.3, we can see how Karen's experience demonstrates the concepts of surplus and shortage. It also shows that equilibrium occurs when there is neither a surplus nor a shortage, because quantity demanded and quantity supplied are equal.

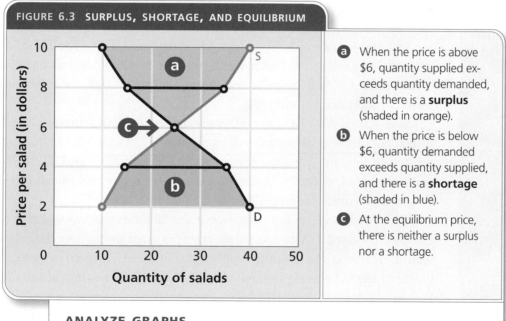

FIGURE 6.3 SURPLUS, SHORTAGE, AND EQUILIBRIUM

ⓐ When the price is above $6, quantity supplied exceeds quantity demanded, and there is a **surplus** (shaded in orange).

ⓑ When the price is below $6, quantity demanded exceeds quantity supplied, and there is a **shortage** (shaded in blue).

ⓒ At the equilibrium price, there is neither a surplus nor a shortage.

ANALYZE GRAPHS

1. Is there a surplus or a shortage when the price is $10? How big is that surplus or shortage? How great is the surplus or shortage when the price is $2?

2. What does this graph illustrate about surplus, shortage, and equilibrium price?

In Figure 6.3, there is a surplus in the area shaded orange. As Karen discovered when she tried to sell salads at prices above $6, she had too many and had to throw some away. The amount of surplus is measured by the horizontal distance between the two curves at each price. For example, at the price of $8, the distance shown by the black line between 15 and 35 shows a surplus of 20 salads.

When there is a surplus, prices tend to fall until the surplus is sold and equilibrium is reached. Producers might also choose to cut back their production to a quantity that is more in line with what consumers demand at the higher prices.

The blue area in Figure 6.3 represents where there is a shortage. When Karen decided to charge less than $6, she had too few salads and lots of unhappy customers who weren't able to get the salads they wanted. As with the surplus, the amount of shortage is measured by the horizontal distance between the two curves at each price. For example, at the price of $4, the distance shown by the black line between 15 and 35 salads shows a shortage of 20 salads.

When there is a shortage, producers raise prices in an attempt to balance quantity supplied and quantity demanded. Producers may also try to increase quantity supplied to meet the quantities demanded at the lower prices.

Holiday Shortages
Consumer tastes often cause spikes in demand for certain items during the holidays.

EXAMPLE Holiday Toys

The concepts of surplus and shortage and the move to equilibrium are active in many markets at different times. Perhaps they are most visible in the market for toys during the holiday shopping season. Toys are often fads, and children's tastes change rapidly. It is difficult for marketers to know how much to supply and at what price to best meet the quantities demanded by consumers. Sometimes they overestimate a toy's popularity and end up with a surplus. If they underestimate popularity, they are faced with a shortage.

In 1996, for example, Tyco Toys Inc. introduced Tickle Me Elmo. The toy included a microchip that made the toy laugh when it was touched. Tyco expected the toy to be popular and ordered about 500,000 for the holiday season. It was priced around $30.

Sales started slowly, and stores thought they might have a surplus. But after several popular television personalities promoted it, Tickle Me Elmo became the hottest toy of that holiday season, and a shortage developed. Even when prices increased markedly, buyers were undeterred. They continued to purchase the toys until they were all gone.

Tyco tried to increase its supply, but the factories that made Tickle Me Elmo were located in Asia, and the shortage persisted throughout the holiday season. By spring, the quantity supplied had doubled. By then, however, the height of the fad was over. Initially, stores tried to sell the toys at the same high prices charged during the holiday season. But consumers were reluctant to buy, and a surplus resulted. Eventually, the market reached equilibrium at a price of about $25.

When you see suppliers reducing prices, it is often because they have a surplus of products to sell. Consider, for example, what happens to the prices of clothing items that are out of season or no longer in fashion. On the other hand, if an item becomes particularly popular or is in short supply for some other reason, suppliers will raise prices. The market does not always reach equilibrium quickly, but it is always moving toward equilibrium.

SMARTGrapher
Create a demand and supply curve at **ClassZone.com**

APPLICATION Applying Economic Concepts

B. Look back at the market demand and supply schedule you created for Application A on p. 166. Use it to create a graph showing the interaction of demand and supply and mark it to show surplus, shortage, and equilibrium.

Equilibrium Price in Real Life

KEY CONCEPTS

In theory, the relationship between demand and supply in the market seems straightforward. The real world, however, is more complex. In earlier chapters, you learned that there are several factors that can cause demand and supply to change. When there is an imbalance between quantity demanded and quantity supplied, a state of **disequilibrium** exists, and the process of finding equilibrium starts over again.

QUICK REFERENCE

Disequilibrium occurs when quantity demanded and quantity supplied are not in balance.

EXAMPLE Change in Demand and Equilibrium Price

Let's take a look at how the market moves from disequilibrium by considering the effect of changes in demand on the equilibrium price for athletic shoes. Recall that a change in demand occurs when one of six factors—income, consumer taste, consumer expectations, market size, substitutes, and complements—prompts consumers to change the quantity demanded at every price.

In Figures 6.4 and 6.5, the intersection of the demand curve (D1) and the supply curves (S) shows an equilibrium price of $75, with quantity demanded and supplied of 3,000 pairs of shoes. When a change in consumer taste causes a decrease in demand for athletic shoes at every price, the demand curve shifts to the left, as shown in Figure 6.4. Notice that this new demand curve (D2) intersects the supply curve at a lower price, around $65. This becomes the new equilibrium price. At this

FIGURES 6.4 AND 6.5 CHANGES IN DEMAND AND EQUILIBRIUM PRICE

FIGURE 6.4 DECREASE IN DEMAND

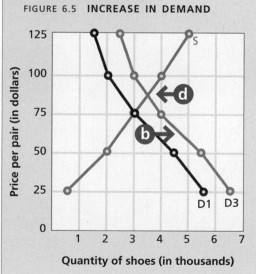

FIGURE 6.5 INCREASE IN DEMAND

a In Figure 6.4, demand decreases; the demand curve shifts left and intersects the supply curve at a lower point.

b In Figure 6.5, demand increases; the demand curve shifts right and intersects the supply curve at a higher point.

c When demand decreases (Fig. 6.4), the equilibrium price falls to about $65.

d When demand increases (Fig. 6.5), the equilibrium price rises to about $90.

ANALYZE GRAPHS

1. What happens to quantity demanded at $100 when demand decreases? What happens to quantity demanded at $100 when demand increases?

2. Does change in demand have a direct or inverse relationship to equilibrium price? Explain your answer.

Animated Economics

Use an interactive market demand and supply curve to see changes in demand, supply, and equilibrium price at **ClassZone.com** new, lower equilibrium price, the quantity demanded decreases to 2,500 pairs of shoes. In other words, when consumers demand fewer goods and services at every price, the equilibrium price will fall and suppliers will sell fewer units—even though the price is lower.

Suppose that an increase in the number of young adults causes demand for athletic shoes to increase. When there is an increase in demand, the demand curve shifts to the right, as shown in Figure 6.5. Notice that the new demand curve (D3) intersects the supply curve at a higher price, around $90. As the equilibrium price increases to this higher level, the quantity demanded also increases to 3,500 pairs of shoes. When consumers demand more goods and services at every price, equilibrium price will rise and suppliers will sell more, even at higher prices.

EXAMPLE Change in Supply and Equilibrium Price

Now let's consider how changes in supply might affect equilibrium price. Recall that a change in supply occurs when something in the market prompts producers to offer different amounts for sale at every price. Remember from Chapter 5 that the six factors that can change supply are input costs, productivity, technology, government action, producer expectations, and number of producers.

In Figures 6.6 and 6.7, the intersection of the supply curve (S1) and the demand curve (D) shows an equilibrium price of $75, with quantity supplied and demanded of 3,000 pairs of shoes. If the price of the raw materials needed to produce athletic shoes increases, the result is a decrease in supply of these shoes at every price.

FIGURES 6.6 AND 6.7 CHANGES IN SUPPLY AND EQUILIBRIUM PRICE

FIGURE 6.6 **DECREASE IN SUPPLY**

FIGURE 6.7 **INCREASE IN SUPPLY**

a In Figure 6.6, supply decreases; the supply curve shifts left and intersects the demand curve at a higher point.

b In Figure 6.7, supply increases; the supply curve shifts right and intersects the demand curve at a lower point.

c When supply decreases (Fig. 6.6) the equilibrium price rises to about $90.

d When supply increases (Fig. 6.7) the equilibrium price falls to about $55.

ANALYZE GRAPHS

1. What happens to quantity supplied at $100 when supply decreases? What happens to quantity supplied at $100 when supply increases?

2. How do these graphs illustrate the relationship between change in supply and change in equilibrium price?

In this situation, the supply curve shifts to the left, as shown in Figure 6.6. Notice that the new supply curve (S2) intersects the demand curve at a higher price, around $90. This is the new equilibrium price. Because of this increase in price, the quantity demanded at equilibrium decreases to 2,500 pairs of shoes. In other words, when there are fewer goods and services available at every price, equilibrium price will rise.

When new technology allows the manufacturer to produce shoes more efficiently, supply increases, and the supply curve shifts to the right, as shown in Figure 6.7. Notice that the new supply curve (S3) intersects the demand curve at a lower price, about

Technology Both supply and equilibrium price are affected when technology improves the manufacturing process.

$55. This is the new equilibrium price. Because of this decrease in price, the quantity demanded at equilibrium increases to about 4,100 pairs of shoes. In other words, when there are more goods and services available at every price, equilibrium price will fall.

Look at Figures 6.4, 6.5, 6.6, and 6.7 once more and notice which situations cause equilibrium price to fall and which cause equilibrium price to rise. The relationships between changes in demand or supply and changes in equilibrium price are illustrated in Figure 6.8. Equilibrium price falls when there is a decrease in demand or an increase in supply. Equilibrium price rises when there is an increase in demand or a decrease in supply. In other words, when consumers want less or producers supply more, prices will fall. When consumers want more or producers supply less, prices will rise.

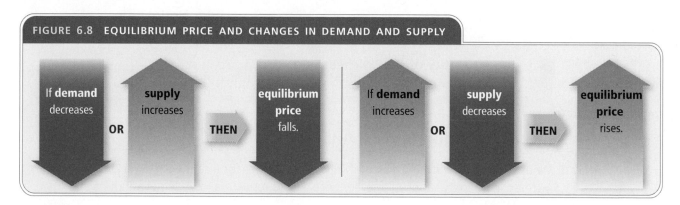

FIGURE 6.8 EQUILIBRIUM PRICE AND CHANGES IN DEMAND AND SUPPLY

If **demand** decreases — OR — **supply** increases — THEN — **equilibrium price** falls.

If **demand** increases — OR — **supply** decreases — THEN — **equilibrium price** rises.

APPLICATION Analyzing Effects

C. If one of the three pizza parlors in your neighborhood closes, what will happen to the supply of pizza? How will that affect the equilibrium price of pizza?

ECONOMICS
SKILLBUILDER

📖 For more on interpreting graphs, see the Skillbuilder Handbook, page R29.

Interpreting Graphs: Shifting Curves

Graphs show statistical information in a visual manner. A graph that shows a shifting curve should immediately alert the reader to one of the following: a change in quantity demanded at every price, or a change in quantity supplied at every price. In Figure 6.9, a change in the number of producers has caused an increase in supply at every price. The sandwich shop across the street from Forest View High School now has a competitor.

TECHNIQUES FOR ANALYZING SHIFTING CURVES Use the following strategies, along with what you learned throughout Section 1, to analyze the graph.

Use the title to identify the main idea of the graph. If supply has shifted, then we know that quantity supplied at every price has either increased or decreased.

Use the annotations to find key elements of the graph. Annotation **a** shows the equilibrium price where curve S1 meets curve D.

FIGURE 6.9 SHIFT IN SUPPLY OF SANDWICHES

a This is the initial equilibrium price.

b Curve shifts to the right.

c This is the new equilibrium price.

Read the axis labels carefully. When both quantity supplied and demanded are present, look for an intersection to find equilibrium price.

Notice that **b** shows a shift to the right. An increase in supply always shows a rightward shift; a decrease in supply always causes a leftward shift.

Notice the new equilibrium price, **c**. An increase in supply results in a lower equilibrium price.

THINKING ECONOMICALLY Analyzing

1. What are the pre-shift and post-shift equilibrium prices for a sandwich? Will an increase in quantity supplied at every price always result in a lower equilibrium price? Why?

2. Imagine that instead of an increase in supply, there is a decrease in demand. How will the equilibrium price change? Why?

3. On a separate sheet of paper, sketch intersecting quantity supplied and demanded curves with an equilibrium price of $4 at 80 sandwiches. How have the curves shifted from those that appear in Figure 6.9?

REVIEWING KEY CONCEPTS

1. Explain the differences between the terms in each of these pairs:

   a. *market equilibrium*   **b.** *surplus*
      disequilibrium   *shortage*

2. How are surplus and shortage related to equilibrium price?

3. Why is equilibrium price represented by the intersection of the supply and demand curves in a particular market?

4. Why do changes in demand or supply cause disequilibrium?

5. Why is the market always moving toward equilibrium?

6. **Using Your Notes** How is equilibrium price related to market equilibrium? Refer to your completed cluster diagram.

   Use the Graphic Organizer at
   Interactive Review @ ClassZone.com

market equilibrium

Equilibrium

dis-equilibrium

CRITICAL THINKING

7. **Analyzing Data** Look at Figures 6.4, 6.5, 6.6, and 6.7 again. What happens to surplus and shortage as equilibrium price changes in each graph? What general conclusions can you draw from this information?

8. **Analyzing Causes** Suppose that the federal government decides to increase the excise tax on cellular phone services by 0.1 percent. Why will this action cause the equilibrium price of cellular phone services to rise?

9. **Applying Economic Concepts** Between 2003 and 2005, there was huge growth in the market for premium blue jeans priced at $200 or more per pair. The growth was largely fueled by popular magazines showing celebrities wearing certain brands. Then, in the summer of 2005, major department stores started cutting prices on the jeans; they were also found on Web sites that offer jeans at discount prices. Use the economic concepts that you learned in this section to describe what is happening in this market.

10. **Challenge** Study Figures 6.4, 6.5, 6.6, and 6.7 again. What would happen if a change in consumer taste caused an increase in demand for athletic shoes and more suppliers entered the market at the same time? Assume that the increases in demand and in supply are proportionately the same. How would this result be different if each of these changes happened separately?

ECONOMICS IN PRACTICE

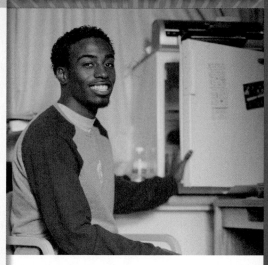

Finding Equilibrium Price
Suppose that you are a manufacturer of a new mini refrigerator for college dorm rooms. You expect your product to be popular because of its compact size and high tech design. After a few weeks in the market you are able to develop the following market demand and supply schedule.

Price per Refrigerator ($)	Quantity Demanded	Quantity Supplied
225	500	6,000
200	1,000	4,500
175	1,500	3,500
150	2,500	2,500
125	4,000	1,500

Create a Demand and Supply Curve Use this market demand and supply schedule to create a market demand and supply curve and determine the equilibrium price.

Challenge Calculate surplus or shortage at every price and suggest ways the manufacturer could try to eliminate the surplus and raise the equilibrium price.

Prices as Signals and Incentives

OBJECTIVES

In Section 2, you will
- analyze how the price system works
- explain how prices provide information about markets
- describe how prices act as incentives to producers

KEY TERMS

competitive pricing, *p. 174*
incentive, *p. 176*

TAKING NOTES

As you read Section 2, complete a chart like the one shown to keep track of how each key concept affects producers and consumers. Use the Graphic Organizer at **Interactive Review @ ClassZone.com**

	Producers	Consumers
Competitive pricing		
Incentive		

How the Price System Works

KEY CONCEPTS

QUICK REFERENCE

Competitive pricing occurs when producers sell products at lower prices to lure customers away from rival producers, while still making a profit.

To better understand how price works in the market, let's look at how one kind of change in supply affects the equilibrium price. More producers in a market increases supply, which leads to increased competition and a lower equilibrium price. **Competitive pricing** occurs when producers sell goods and services at prices that best balance the twin desires of making the highest profit and luring customers away from rival producers. By entering a market at a lower price, a new supplier can add to its customer base while it maintains overall profits by selling more units.

EXAMPLE Competitive Pricing

Let's look at an example of competitive pricing. As winter approaches, Elm Street Hardware prices its snow shovels at $20. But Uptown Automotive sees an opportunity to take some customers (mostly for tools, which both stores sell) from Elm Street. Uptown enters the snow shovel market, raising the overall supply. It also prices the shovels at $13. Uptown has a lower profit margin per shovel, but hopes to sell hundreds of them in order to maintain overall profit. Elm Street can choose to lower its prices as well or risk losing customers.

EXAMPLE Characteristics of the Price System

In a market economy, the price system has four characteristics.

1. It is neutral. Prices do not favor either the producer or consumer because both make choices that help to determine the equilibrium price. The free interactions of consumers (who favor lower prices) and producers (who favor higher prices) determines the equilibrium price in the market.

2. It is market driven. Market forces, not central planning, determine prices, so the system has no oversight or administration costs. In other words, the price system runs itself.

3. It is flexible. When market conditions change, prices are able to change quickly in response. Surpluses and shortages motivate producers to change prices to reach equilibrium.

4. It is efficient. Prices will adjust until the maximum number of goods and services are sold. Producers choose to use their resources to produce certain goods and services based on the profit they can make by doing so.

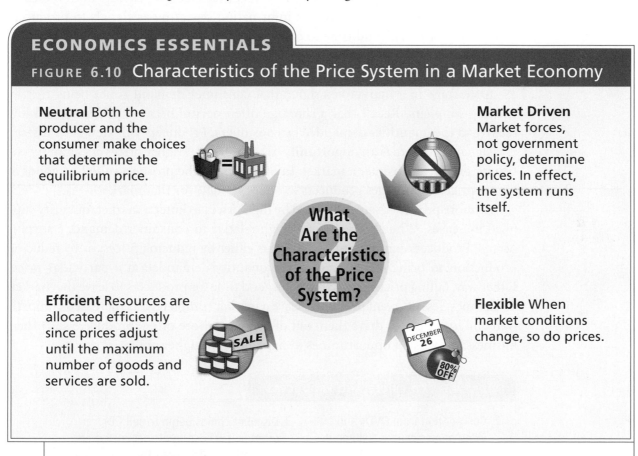

ECONOMICS ESSENTIALS

FIGURE 6.10 Characteristics of the Price System in a Market Economy

Neutral Both the producer and the consumer make choices that determine the equilibrium price.

Market Driven Market forces, not government policy, determine prices. In effect, the system runs itself.

What Are the Characteristics of the Price System?

Efficient Resources are allocated efficiently since prices adjust until the maximum number of goods and services are sold.

Flexible When market conditions change, so do prices.

ANALYZE CHARTS
Choose two of the characteristics of the price system shown in the chart and explain how each is illustrated through the example of competitive pricing.

APPLICATION Analyzing and Interpreting Data

A. If Karen sold 25 salads at $6 each, how many would she need to sell at $5.50 to make at least the same amount of total revenue?

Prices Motivate Producers and Consumers

QUICK REFERENCE

An **incentive** encourages people to act in certain ways.

KEY CONCEPTS

The laws of demand and supply show that consumers and producers have different attitudes toward price. Consumers want to buy at low prices; producers want to sell at high prices. Therefore, prices motivate consumers and producers in different ways. You learned in Chapter 1 that an **incentive** is a way to encourage people to take a certain action. Here, you'll learn that in the price system, incentives encourage producers and consumers to act in certain ways consistent with their best interests.

EXAMPLE Prices and Producers

For producers, the price system has two great advantages: it provides both information and motivation. Prices provide information by acting as signals to producers about whether it is a good time to enter or leave a particular market. Rising prices and the expectation of profits motivate producers to enter a market. Falling prices and the possibility of losses motivate them to leave a market.

A shortage in a market is a signal that consumer demand is not being met by existing suppliers. Recall that a shortage often occurs because prices are too low relative to the quantities demanded by consumers. Producers will view the shortage as a signal that there is an opportunity to raise prices. Higher prices act as an incentive for producers to enter a market. In other words, the prospect of selling goods at higher prices encourages producers to offer products for that market.

As more producers are motivated by high prices to enter a market, quantity supplied increases. When prices are too high relative to consumer demand, a surplus occurs. Producers can respond to a surplus either by reducing prices, or by reducing production to bring it in line with the quantity demanded at a particular price. Either way, falling prices signal that it is a good time for producers to leave the market. Sometimes, less efficient producers leave a market completely, as increased competition and lower prices drive them out of business. More often, producers shift their business to focus on opportunities in markets with higher potential profits.

FIGURE 6.11 CD PRICES AND PRODUCERS

1. Competition from DVDs and video games causes a slump in CD sales—a surplus in CDs.

   CD prices decrease

2. Some CD makers switch production to DVDs, video games; fewer CDs are produced—a shortage of CDs.

3. Discount chains begin to sell CDs, often below cost, to attract customers; competitive pricing of CDs.

   CD prices increase

   CD prices decrease

4. Many small record stores go out of business or devote less shelf space to CDs, more to DVDs and video games.

Competitive pricing in the market often informs the choices made by producers. When a market is growing, and when there is unmet demand, a producer may decide to enter the market with a price that is lower than its competitor's. The new producer can still, however, earn a profit by selling more units at the lower price. So, while prices are the signals that are visible in the market, it is the expectation of profits or the possibility of losses that motivates producers to enter or leave a market.

EXAMPLE Prices and Consumers

Prices also act as signals and incentives for consumers. Surpluses that lead to lower prices tell consumers that it is a good time to buy a particular good or service. Producers often send this signal to consumers through advertising and store displays that draw consumers to certain products. Producers may also suggest that the low prices won't last, encouraging consumers to buy sooner rather than later.

High prices generally discourage consumers from buying a particular product and may signal that it is time for them to switch to a substitute that is available at a lower price. A high price may signal that a particular product is in short supply or has a higher status. Brand marketers rely on the consumer perception that a certain logo is worth a higher price.

Recall what you learned about normal and inferior goods in Chapter 4. Most consumers prefer to buy normal goods at the best possible price. They will buy inferior goods only when they cannot afford something better. While price is a powerful incentive to consumers, the other factors that affect demand also influence consumers' buying habits.

YOUR ECONOMIC CHOICES

PRICES AND CONSUMERS

How Does Price Affect Your Decision?

A new digital video camera with state-of-the-art features costs $500, but you've saved only $250. You can either buy a less expensive substitute with the money you have now, or you can save up to buy the advanced camera later. If other consumers also choose to wait to buy the new camera, a surplus may develop, and the price may decrease.

▲ Buy now

▲ Save for later

APPLICATION Making Inferences

B. A cup of gourmet coffee commands a higher price than a regular coffee. How will this fact influence the take-out coffee market?

Michael Dell: Using Price to Beat the Competition

When he began his company, high-tech entrepreneur Michael Dell used competitive pricing to take business away from larger, more established companies. Later, Dell managed to survive a downturn in sales that hobbled Compaq and drove IBM out of the personal computer market. How did Dell's company thrive as his competitors struggled?

FAST FACTS

Michael S. Dell

Title: Chairman and CEO of Dell Inc.

Born: February 23, 1965, Houston, Texas

Major Accomplishment: Pioneered the direct sale of personal computers to consumers

Key Product Lines: Desktop PCs, notebook computers, workstation systems, servers, printers, flat-screen TVs, PDAs

Honors: Youngest CEO of a Fortune 500 company (1992), America's Most Admired Company (2005)

Lowering Costs to Reduce Prices

Michael Dell began assembling and selling computers as a freshman in college. He became so successful that he quit college in 1984 to focus on his business. He had sales worth $6 million in his first full year.

Dell's success was largely due to his approach to marketing and production. He bypassed computer retailers and sold over the telephone directly to knowledgeable computer users in business and government. Each computer was built to customer requirements and assembled after it was ordered. In this way, Dell lowered his costs significantly and became the low-price leader in the market. The company's sales grew to $69.5 million in 1986 and to almost $258 million in 1989.

Michael Dell In Dell's TechKnow program, students learn to identify and resolve common computer problems.

Dell was also a pioneer in recognizing the potential for sales via the Internet. This strategy allowed the company to maintain close contact with its customers and to adjust its prices frequently, up and down, as market conditions dictated. Competitors who sold only in retail stores found it hard to compete on price because their costs were much higher. In 1999, Dell became the leading supplier of PCs in the United States. In 2005, worldwide sales reached almost $50 billion.

Dell has used his experience with computers to make waves in the market for consumer electronics (televisions, portable electronics, and so forth). He sees a bright future for his company. "We are at the dawn of the connected era, and Dell has never been better positioned to meet the needs of the billions of people who will join us online in the coming years."

Economics Update

Find an update on Michael Dell at **ClassZone.com**

APPLICATION Drawing Conclusions

C. What incentive did Michael Dell have to sell computers at prices lower than those of his competitors?

REVIEWING KEY CONCEPTS

1. Use each of the two terms below in a sentence that illustrates the meaning of the term:

   a. *competitive pricing*   **b.** *incentive*

2. Explain the four characteristics of the price system.

3. Why is the price system an efficient way to allocate resources?

4. How do prices serve as signals and incentives to producers to enter a particular market? to leave a certain market?

5. How does the story of Dell Inc. demonstrate the effects of competitive pricing?

6. **Using Your Notes** How does competitive pricing affect consumers? Refer to your completed chart. Use the Graphic Organizer at **Interactive Review @ ClassZone.com**

	Producers	Consumers
Competitive pricing		
Incentive		

CRITICAL THINKING

7. **Making Inferences** A local supermarket decides to sell a premium brand of meats and cheeses in its deli department. This brand is priced about $2 more per pound than the store brand. About 80 percent of the space in the deli display cases is devoted to the premium brand and 20 percent to the store brand.

   a. How did price serve as an incentive to the supermarket?

   b. What kind of signals is the supermarket sending to its customers with this pricing strategy?

8. **Applying Economic Concepts** A candy company whose products sold in supermarkets for about $3 a bag decided to enter the growing gourmet chocolate market. It purchased two small companies that made premium chocolates that sold for much higher prices. How does this story reveal the way the price system works as an incentive for producers while allocating resources efficiently?

9. **Challenge** A large discount store has built its reputation on offering consumers low prices. However, its customers come from many different income levels. Recently, the store began offering higher priced jewelry and consumer electronics products. What signal might this send to producers of other premium products who have never sold in discount stores before?

ECONOMICS IN PRACTICE

Using Prices as Incentives
As you've learned in Section 2, prices motivate producers to act in certain ways. What actions do producers take in response to rising prices? How about falling prices?

Identify Price Incentives Consider each situation that follows. Decide whether the scenario described is associated with rising prices or with falling prices.

- A farmer switches to organic methods when a report says organic foods are healthier.
- To maintain market share, a car wash adjusts its prices to meet a competitor's.
- After a hot, dry spring, a landscaper decides to get out of the business.
- A retailer decides to begin selling this holiday season's must-have toy.

Challenge Which of the above situations descibes a case of competitive pricing? What might happen to the producer if it did not take the action described?

Intervention in the Price System

OBJECTIVES

In Section 3, you will
- explain how government uses price ceilings to keep prices from rising too high
- describe how government uses price floors to keep prices from going too low
- discuss how government uses rationing to allocate scarce resources and goods

KEY TERMS

price ceiling, *p. 180*
price floor, *p. 182*
minimum wage, *p. 182*
rationing, *p. 183*
black market, *p. 183*

TAKING NOTES

As you read Section 3, complete a hierarchy diagram like this one to track main ideas and supporting details. Use the Graphic Organizer at **Interactive Review @ ClassZone.com**

Imposing Price Ceilings

KEY CONCEPTS

QUICK REFERENCE

A **price ceiling** is the legal maximum price that sellers may charge for a product.

You've seen how prices adjust to changes in demand and supply as the market constantly strives for equilibrium. Sometimes, however, people think it is a good idea to interfere with the free market mechanism in order to keep the price of a good or service from going too high. An established maximum price that sellers may charge for a good or service is called a **price ceiling**. The price ceiling is set below the equilibrium price, so a shortage will result.

EXAMPLE Football Tickets and Price Ceilings

Let's look at an example of a price ceiling in ticket prices for college football. The Trenton University Tigers are a winning team with many loyal fans. The university prints 30,000 tickets for every game and sells them for $15 each. At that price, 60,000 fans want to buy the tickets, so there is a shortage of 30,000 tickets for every game.

The university could resolve the shortage by letting the price rise until quantity demanded and quantity supplied are equal. When this solution is proposed, the university president says she would rather keep the tickets affordable for students. Indeed many students get tickets for $15. On game day, however, ticket scalpers stand outside the stadium and sell some tickets for $50 or more.

Rent Control as a Price Ceiling

In the past, many cities passed rent control laws in an effort to keep housing afford-able for lower-income families. These laws control when rents can be raised and by how much, no matter what is going on in the market. Of course, the people who live in rent-controlled housing appreciate the lower price in the short term.

But rent control can have unexpected consequences. Without the possibility of raising rents to match the market, there is no incentive to increase the supply of rental housing, and a shortage soon develops. In addition, landlords are reluctant to increase their costs by investing money in property maintenance, so housing condi-tions often deteriorate. By 2005, rent control was becoming far less common as most cities realized it made housing shortages worse in the long run.

Santa Monica, California, is an example of a city that had strict rent control laws. In the late 1990s, state legislators passed a law that changed the way local communities could regulate rental housing. As a result, property owners in Santa Monica could let the market determine the initial rent when a new tenant moved in, although the city's rent control board still regulated yearly rent increases thereafter. Figure 6.12 illustrates what happened to rents when the new law fully took effect. Rents increased by 40 to 85 percent, showing that the apartments had been priced artificially low. The increases reflect the shortage that rent control had created.

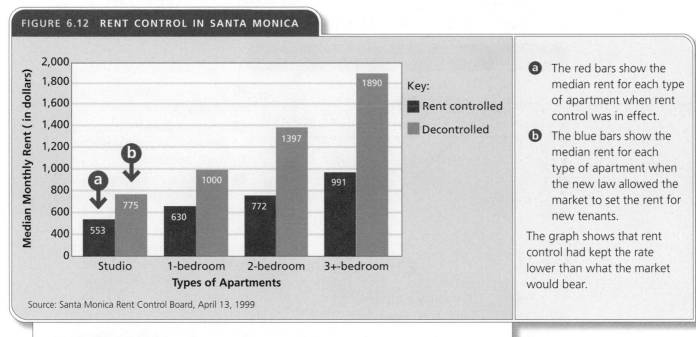

FIGURE 6.12 RENT CONTROL IN SANTA MONICA

Key:
- Rent controlled
- Decontrolled

Source: Santa Monica Rent Control Board, April 13, 1999

ⓐ The red bars show the median rent for each type of apartment when rent control was in effect.

ⓑ The blue bars show the median rent for each type of apartment when the new law allowed the market to set the rent for new tenants.

The graph shows that rent control had kept the rate lower than what the market would bear.

ANALYZE GRAPHS

1. What happened to the rent for one-bedroom apartments when the new law ended rent control?

2. Who would be more in favor of the changes that happened in the rental market in Santa Monica, landlords or tenants? Why?

APPLICATION **Applying Economic Concepts**

A. Create a demand and supply graph for Trenton University football tickets showing how the price ceiling of $15 is below the equilibrium price.

Setting Price Floors

QUICK REFERENCE

A **price floor** is a legal minimum price that buyers must pay for a product.

The **minimum wage** is a legal minimum amount that an employer must pay for one hour of work.

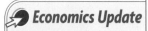

Economics Update

Find an update on the minimum wage at **ClassZone.com**

KEY CONCEPTS

Sometimes the government decides to intervene in the price system to increase income to certain producers. A **price floor** is an established minimum price that buyers must pay for a good or service. For example, the government has used various programs designed to provide price floors under corn, milk, and other agricultural products. The goal of these price floors is to encourage farmers to produce an abundant supply of food.

EXAMPLE Minimum Wage as a Price Floor

One well-known example of a price floor is a minimum wage. A **minimum wage** is the minimum legal price that an employer may pay a worker for one hour of work. The United States government established its first minimum wage in 1938. The 1930s were a period of low wages, and the government hoped to increase the income of workers. If the minimum wage is set above the equilibrium price for certain jobs in a market, employers may decide that paying the higher wages is not profitable. As a result, they may choose to employ fewer workers, and unemployment will increase. If the minimum wage is set below the equilibrium price, then it will have no effect.

FIGURE 6.13   MINIMUM WAGE AS A PRICE FLOOR

Wage rate per hour (y-axis)

Quantity supplied of minimum-wage workers (x-axis)

ⓐ This point shows the equilibrium price for a labor market.

ⓑ The black dotted line shows a minimum wage set above the equilibrium price.

ⓒ The blue dotted line shows a minimum wage set below the equilibrium price.

The length of black dotted line that falls between the demand curve and the supply curve represents a surplus—in other words, unemployment.

ANALYZE GRAPHS

1. Assume the minimum wage is set at the dotted black line. What are the costs and benefits of increasing it?

2. Is the minimum wage set at the dotted blue line an effective price floor? Why?

APPLICATION Analyzing Effects

B. Suppose that the Trenton University Tigers were so bad that only 10,000 people want to buy tickets for $15. What effect would keeping $15 as a price floor have?

Rationing Resources and Products

KEY CONCEPTS

The market uses prices to allocate goods and services. Sometimes in periods of national emergency, such as in wartime, the government decides to use another way to distribute scarce products or resources. **Rationing** is a system in which the government allocates goods and services using factors other than price.

The goods might be rationed on a first-come, first-served basis or on the basis of a lottery. Generally, a system is set up that uses coupons allowing each person a certain amount of a particular item. Or the government may decree that certain resources be used to produce certain goods. When such a system is used, some people try to skirt the rules to get the goods and services they want, creating what is known as a black market. In a **black market**, goods and services are illegally bought and sold in violation of price controls or rationing.

QUICK REFERENCE

Rationing is a government system for allocating goods and services using criteria other than price.

The **black market** involves illegal buying or selling in violation of price controls or rationing.

EXAMPLE Rationing Resources

During World War II, the United States government empowered the Office of Price Administration, which was established in 1941, to ration scarce goods. The hope was that these goods would be distributed to everyone, not just those who could afford the higher market prices born of shortages. It also allocated resources in ways that favored the war effort rather than the consumer market. Figure 6.14 shows some of the goods that were rationed. Rationing also led consumers to look for substitutes. Margarine, a butter substitute, was purchased in huge quantities during the war.

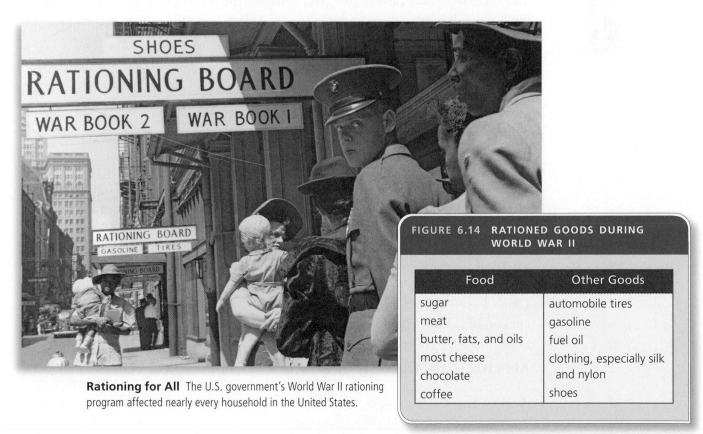

Rationing for All The U.S. government's World War II rationing program affected nearly every household in the United States.

FIGURE 6.14 RATIONED GOODS DURING WORLD WAR II

Food	Other Goods
sugar	automobile tires
meat	gasoline
butter, fats, and oils	fuel oil
most cheese	clothing, especially silk and nylon
chocolate	shoes
coffee	

Rationing in China
Shortages of tofu, a staple of the Chinese diet, led to rationing in 1989.

North Korea maintained a strict rationing system between 1946 and 2002. Most importantly, staple foods—meat, rice, and cabbage—were strictly rationed. However, the system was plagued by inefficiency and corruption. The amount of your ration was generally determined by who you knew, where you lived, and what your occupation was. Government officials in the largest cities often received more than their allotment, while the majority of people got by with less (or received less-nutritious substitutes). Some families had meat or fish only a few times a year.

Between 1996 and 2000, widespread famine in North Korea made the situation desperate. Ration coupons were still distributed, but in most cases, the rations were not. As many as a million people died due to the famine. In response, people established unofficial markets where they traded handicrafts for food. In 2002, the government officially legalized these market activities, and prices rose sharply. Wages also increased. Skeptical of markets, however, the leaders of North Korea were, in 2005, considering a return to the rationing system that failed them in the past.

EXAMPLE Black Markets—An Unplanned Result of Rationing

When rationing is imposed, black markets often come into existence. During World War II, black markets in meat, sugar, and gasoline developed in the United States. Some people found ways, including the use of stolen or counterfeit ration coupons, to secure more of these scarce goods.

During the height of North Korea's rationing system, free trade in grain was expressly forbidden, and most other markets were severely restricted. Prices were very high at the markets that did exist. In 1985, it cost half of the average monthly salary of a typical North Korean to buy a chicken on the black market. Even after the government began allowing some market activities in 2002, the black market flourished because many forms of private property, including homes and cars, were still illegal. Some people started smuggling clothes, televisions, and other goods from China to sell in North Korea. (You'll read more about the black market in the discussion of the underground economy in Chapter 12.)

APPLICATION Making Inferences

C. How does the example of rationing during World War II show that the price system is a more efficient way to allocate resources?

Online Quiz
ClassZone.com

REVIEWING KEY CONCEPTS

1. Explain the relationship between the terms in each of these pairs.

   a. *price floor* **b.** *rationing*
      minimum wage   *black market*

2. What is the difference between a price floor and a price ceiling?

3. What kind of surplus might be created by the minimum wage?

4. How does the existence of the black market work against the intended purpose of rationing?

5. Aside from turning to the black market, how do consumers make up for goods that are rationed?

6. **Using Your Notes** What is the usual result of a price ceiling? Refer to your completed diagram. Use the Graphic Organizer at **Interactive Review @ ClassZone.com**

CRITICAL THINKING

7. **Analyzing Causes** Opponents of rent control cite comparisons of cities that regulate rents with cities that do not. Their evidence shows that there is more moderately priced housing available in cities that let the market set the rates for rent. What would account for the differences in availability?

8. **Making Inferences** The percentage of workers who were paid the minimum wage or less decreased from 6.5 percent in 1988 to 3 percent in 2002 to 2.7 percent in 2004. What does this trend tell you about the relationship of the minimum wage to the equilibrium wage for those kinds of work?

9. **Applying Economic Concepts** In the wake of sharply rising gasoline prices in the summer of 2005, several states considered putting a ceiling on the wholesale price of gasoline. What would be the likely result of such a price control? Would it be an effective strategy for lowering gas prices?

10. **Challenge** Many states have laws against so-called price gouging. These laws make it illegal to sell goods and services at levels significantly above established market prices following a natural disaster. What economic argument might be used against such laws?

ECONOMICS IN PRACTICE

Understanding Price Floors
In agriculture, price floors are known as price supports. The government sets a target price for each crop, and if the market price is below that target, it will pay farmers the difference. Suppose that you are a farmer with 400 acres planted in corn. The following graph shows the supply and demand for your crop.

Calculate the Effect of the Price Support How many bushels of corn will you sell at the equilibrium price? How much revenue will you make? How many bushels do you want to sell at the target price? How many bushels are consumers willing to buy at that price? What is the difference? How much will the government have to pay you for that surplus?

Challenge What changes in supply or demand would move the market equilibrium price closer to the target price?

Prices for Concert Tickets

Background Americans spend billions of dollars on concert tickets yearly—an estimated $3 billion in 2005. With ticket prices for the most popular acts averaging more than $50, most younger or less affluent fans can no longer afford to attend many live concerts. And yet, remarkably, forecasters believe that concert ticket prices have yet to peak.

Ticket prices reflect a number of costs. Performers must cover expenses such as travel, costumes, instruments, and equipment before they reap a profit. Venues, or places where concerts are held, also seek to make a profit, as do ticket distributors. However, in the United States, the sale of concert tickets, along with most other goods and services, is driven by three basic elements of a market economy—demand, supply, and pricing.

What's the issue? How do demand, supply, and pricing affect the concert ticket market? Study these sources to discover the factors that affect demand and supply, and their impact on the price of concert tickets.

A. Congressional Transcript

Pearl Jam believed that TicketMaster Corporation, their ticket distributor, was setting too high a price on the band's concert tickets. This statement, submitted to Congress along with oral testimony on June 30, 1994, explains Pearl Jam's stance.

Pearl Jam Tries to Place Ceiling on Ticket Prices

To keep ticket prices affordable, Pearl Jam appeals to Congress.

Many of Pearl Jam's most loyal fans are teenagers who do not have the money to pay the $50 or more that is often charged today for tickets to a popular concert. Although, given our popularity, we could undoubtedly continue to sell out our concerts with ticket prices at that premium level, we have made a conscious decision that we do not want to put the price of our concerts out of the reach of many of our fans. . . .

For these reasons, we have attempted to keep the ticket prices to our concerts to a maximum of $18. . . . Even where a service charge is imposed, our goal is . . . that no one will pay more than $20 to see a Pearl Jam concert.

Our efforts to try to keep prices . . . to this low level and to limit the possibility of excessive service charge mark-ups have put us at odds with TicketMaster . . . a nationwide computerized ticket distribution service that has a virtual monopoly on the distribution of tickets to concerts in this country.

Thinking Economically How would placing a ceiling on the price of Pearl Jam concert tickets have affected demand and supply? Explain your answer based on the information in the document.

Marie Connolly
and Alan Krueger,
of Princeton
University,
compiled these
data on concert
ticket prices
for their study
"Rockonomics:
The Economics of
Popular Music."

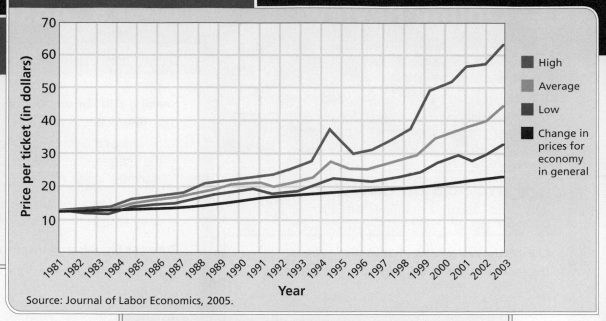

FIGURE 6.15 CONCERT TICKET PRICES

Source: Journal of Labor Economics, 2005.

Thinking Economically In what three years was the high price per ticket about the same as the low price in 2003?

C. Online
Newspaper
Article

TicketMaster
hoped to increase
profits by auc-
tioning tickets
online. This ar-
ticle discusses the
program's poten-
tial effect on ticket
prices.

TicketMaster Plans to Launch Ticket Auction

The sky's the limit, as bidders compete for the best seats in the house.

Fed up with watching ticket scalpers and brokers rake in the huge bucks for prime seats at their venues, TicketMaster plans to debut an online auction program for choice seats to selected concerts and sports events later this year.

The move may drive up the price of front row seats when they start going to the highest bidder, but some analysts say the impact would likely be minimal. . . .

Princeton University economics professor Alan B. Krueger . . . called the open auction a "positive development."

"For the top artists, tickets are still sold below what the market would bear, even though prices have shot up over the last six years," Krueger told POLLSTAR. "This is especially the case for the best seats in the most expensive cities.

"If the auction is widely used, I suspect price variability will increase; we will see greater dispersion in prices across artists, across cities and seats for the same artist." . . .

Source: **Pollstar.com**

Thinking Economically How might TicketMaster's online auction program lead to market equilibrium for the best tickets?

THINKING ECONOMICALLY Synthesizing

1. Do you think TicketMaster's plan in document C would help or harm Pearl Jam's wish "that no one will pay more than $20" to see them (document A)? Explain your answer.

2. What do you think happened to quantity supplied of tickets over the span of the graph in document B? Why?

3. In what year in Figure 6.15 did the high price for concert tickets hit $50—the high price that Pearl Jam speaks of in document A? What year was it $20—the desired price they mention?

Online Review

Review this chapter using interactive
activities at **ClassZone.com**
- Online Summary
- Graphic Organizers
- Quizzes
- Review and Study Notes
- Vocabulary Flip Cards

Online Summary

Complete the following activity either on your
own paper or online at **ClassZone.com**

Choose the key concept that best completes
the sentence. Not all key concepts will be used.

black market	minimum wage
competitive pricing	price ceiling
disequilibrium	price floor
equilibrium price	rationing
incentive	shortage
market equilibrium	surplus

__1__ is a situation that occurs when quantity
demanded and quantity supplied at a particular
price are equal. The price at which that situation
occurs is the __2__. If quantity supplied is greater
than quantity demanded, a __3__ occurs. If quantity demanded exceeds quantity supplied, then
a __4__ occurs.

When a producer enters a market at a lower
price (hoping to increase its customer base while
maintaining profits by selling more units), it is
engaging in __5__. Rising prices are __6__ that draws
producers into markets.

Sometimes government intervenes in the
price system. A __7__ is the legal maximum that
producers may charge for certain goods or
services. A __8__ is the legal minimum amount that
may be paid for a particular good or service.

When certain goods or resources are scarce,
the government may institute a system of __9__,
using some criteria besides price to allocate
resources. An unplanned consequence of this
action by the government is the development of a
__10__, where goods are bought and sold illegally.

CHAPTER **6 Assessment**

REVIEWING KEY CONCEPTS

Seeking Equilibrium: Demand and Supply
(pp. 164–173)

1. How does the concept of market equilibrium reflect
the interaction of producers and consumers in a
market?

2. Why are surpluses and shortages examples of
disequilibrium?

Prices as Signals and Incentives (pp. 174–179)

3. How are producers and consumers equally involved
in the price system?

4. When do prices serve as signals and incentives for
producers to enter a market?

Intervention in the Price System (pp. 180–187)

5. What is the usual result of a price floor?

6. What motivates producers and consumers in the
black market?

APPLYING ECONOMIC CONCEPTS

Look at the table below showing prices and sales
figures for VCRs between 1998 and 2003.

7. Why did dollar sales increase between 1998 and
1999?

8. What is the trend in the average unit price of VCRs
between 1998 and 2003? What does this trend
signal?

FIGURE 6.16 VCR SALES TO DEALERS

	Unit Sales (in thousands)	Sales (in millions $)	Average Unit Price ($)
1998	18,113	2,049	113
1999	22,809	2,333	102
2000	23,072	1,869	81
2001	14,910	1,058	71
2002	13,538	826	61
2003*	11,916	727	61

* projected

Source: *Consumer Electronics Association Market Research,*
January, 2003

9. **Creating Graphs** Suppose that you are the owner of a toy store. Create demand and supply curves for three products that you expect will sell well during the upcoming holiday shopping season. Then consider the following scenarios: one product becomes much more popular than you expected, one is much less popular than you expected, and the third loses half of its production capacity when a factory is leveled by an earthquake. Draw an additional curve on each of your graphs to show the change in demand or supply represented by these scenarios. Under each graph write a caption explaining the change shown and the effect on the equilibrium price.

Use *SMARTGrapher* @ ClassZone.com to complete this activity.

10. **Analyzing Effects** Consumer concerns about nutrition and obesity contribute to a decrease in white bread sales and an increase in sales of whole wheat bread. This change in consumer taste prompts a major manufacturer known for its white bread to enter the market with a whole wheat bread product. What effect will this action have on the supply and equilibrium price of whole wheat bread?

11. **Using Economic Concepts** In 2004, the price of U.S. butter imports increased by more than 30 percent compared to the previous year. In 2003, Canada and New Zealand together supplied more than 80 percent of the butter imported into the United States. In 2004, their combined market share decreased to about 67 percent. What happened in the market to cause this change? How did price serve as a signal and incentive to producers?

12. **Analyzing Effects** How would U.S. government price supports for U.S.-made tennis rackets affect producers and consumers?

13. **Challenge** How would elasticity of demand help producers decide whether competitive pricing is a good strategy for their businesses?

Find the Best Price

Step 1 Form a group with five other students. Imagine that together you are the market for jeans. Three are buyers and three are sellers, according to the following table. Your goal is to bargain with one another for a pair of jeans. Buyers try to get the lowest price possible, without going above their maximum, and sellers try to get the highest price possible, without going below their minimum.

SIX-PERSON JEANS MARKET

		Price ($)	
Buyers	A	20	**Maximum** price you are willing to pay for a pair of jeans
	B	30	
	C	40	
Sellers	D	15	**Minimum** price you are willing to sell a pair of jeans for
	E	25	
	F	35	

Step 2 Choose a letter to determine your role. On a piece of paper write your letter and name, identify yourself as a buyer or seller, and show the dollar amount from the table.

Step 3 Keep track of each proposed transaction in order on a sheet of paper. Recall what you know about demand, supply, and competitive pricing as you bargain to see who will buy and sell jeans and at what price. Bargaining ends when you reach equilibrium. What is quantity and price at equilibrium?

Step 4 Use the information on the chart to create a demand and supply curve for this market. Does the curve reflect your group's bargaining experience?

Step 5 As a class, discuss what you learned from this exercise about how markets reach equilibrium.

Use *SMARTGrapher* @ ClassZone.com to complete this activity.

Market Structures

In markets where businesses offer similar products, sellers compete by trying to make their products stand out from the competition.

Market Structures

CONCEPT REVIEW

Competition involves all the actions that sellers, acting independently, take to get buyers to purchase their products.

CHAPTER 7 KEY CONCEPT

A **market structure** is an economic model that helps economists examine the nature and degree of competition among businesses in the same industry.

WHY THE CONCEPT MATTERS

On trips to the mall, you've probably noticed something about the prices of products you're looking to buy. If there are several different brands of the same kind of product, prices tend to be lower. If there's just one brand, however, prices tend to be higher. The level of competition in a market has a major impact on the prices of products. The more sellers compete for your dollars, the more competitive prices will be.

Online Highlights

More at ClassZone.com

 Economics Update
Go to **ECONOMICS UPDATE** for chapter updates and current news on competition in the cellular telephone industry. (See Case Study, pp. 220–221.) ▶

 SMART Grapher
Go to **SMART GRAPHER** to complete graphing activities in this chapter.

Interactive Review
Go to **INTERACTIVE REVIEW** for concept review and activities.

How do cellular phone makers compete for your business? See the Case Study on pages 220–221.

What Is Perfect Competition?

OBJECTIVES	KEY TERMS	TAKING NOTES
In Section 1, you will • learn that perfect competition is the ideal by which economists measure all market structures • explain the characteristics of perfect competition and why it does not exist in the real world • analyze examples of markets that come close to perfect competition	market structure, *p. 192* perfect competition, *p. 192* standardized product, *p. 192* price taker, *p. 193* imperfect competition, *p. 195*	As you read Section 1, complete a cluster diagram to identify the major characteristics of perfect competition. Use the Graphic Organizer at **Interactive Review @ ClassZone.com**

The Characteristics of Perfect Competition

KEY CONCEPTS

QUICK REFERENCE

A **market structure** is an economic model of competition among businesses in the same industry.

Perfect competition is the ideal model of a market economy.

A **standardized product** is one that consumers see as identical regardless of producer.

When you buy new clothes, you probably shop around for the best deal. But when you buy milk, you know that a gallon will be about the same price no matter where you shop. The market for clothes has a different level of competition than the market for milk. Economists classify markets based on how competitive they are. A **market structure** is an economic model that allows economists to examine competition among businesses in the same industry.

Perfect competition is the ideal model of a market economy. It is useful as a model, but real markets are never perfect. Economists assess how competitive a market is by determining where it falls short of perfect competition. Perfect competition has five characteristics.

1. **Numerous buyers and sellers.** No one seller or buyer has control over price.

2. **Standardized product.** Sellers offer a **standardized product**—a product that consumers consider identical in all essential features to other products in the same market.

3. **Freedom to enter and exit markets.** Buyers and sellers are free to enter and exit the market. No government regulations or other restrictions prevent a business or customer from participating in the market. Nor is a business or customer required to participate in the market.

4. **Independent buyers and sellers.** Buyers cannot join other buyers and sellers cannot join other sellers to influence prices.

5. **Well-informed buyers and sellers.** Both buyers and sellers are well-informed about market conditions. Buyers can do comparison shopping, and sellers can learn what their competitors are charging.

When these five conditions are met, sellers become price takers. A **price taker** is a business that cannot set the prices for its products but, instead, accepts the market price set by the interaction of supply and demand. Only efficient producers make enough money to serve perfectly competitive markets.

QUICK REFERENCE

A **price taker** is a business that accepts the market price determined by supply and demand.

CHARACTERISTIC 1 Many Buyers and Sellers

A large number of buyers and sellers is necessary for perfect competition so that no one buyer or seller has the power to control the price in the market. When there are many sellers, buyers can choose to buy from a different producer if one tries to raise prices above the market level. But because there are many buyers, sellers are able to sell their products at the market price.

Let's consider the Smith family, whom you met in Chapter 5. The Smiths grow raspberries in the summer to sell at the Montclair Farmers' Market. Because many farmers grow and sell raspberries at the same market, all of the farmers charge about the same price. If one farmer tries to charge more than the market price for raspberries, consumers will buy from the other farmers. Because there are many buyers—in other words, sufficient demand—the Smiths and other producers know that they can sell their product at the market price. Lack of demand will not cause them to lower their prices.

Perfect Competition
Farmers' markets exhibit many of the characteristics of perfect competition.

CHARACTERISTIC 2 Standardized Product

In perfect competition, consumers consider one producer's product essentially the same as the product offered by another. The products are perfect substitutes. Agricultural products such as wheat, eggs, and milk, as well as other basic commodities such as notebook paper or gold generally meet this criterion.

Considering the Montclair Farmers' Market, while no two pints of raspberries are exactly alike, they are similar enough that consumers will choose to buy from any producer that offers raspberries at the market price. Price becomes the only basis for a consumer to choose one producer over another.

CHARACTERISTIC 3 Freedom to Enter and Exit Markets

In a perfectly competitive market, producers are able to enter the market when it is profitable and to exit when it becomes unprofitable. They can do this because the investment that a producer makes to enter a market is relatively low. Market forces alone encourage producers to freely enter or leave a given market.

The Smiths and other farmers consider the market price for raspberries when planning their crops. If they believe they can make a profit at that price, they grow raspberries. If not, they try some other crop.

Economics Update

Find an update about perfect competition at **ClassZone.com**

FIGURE 7.1 Characteristics of Perfect Competition

Many Buyers and Sellers A large number of buyers and sellers ensures that no one controls prices.

Standardized Products All products are essentially the same.

Well-informed Buyers and Sellers Both buyers and sellers know the market prices and other conditions.

What Are the Characteristics of Perfect Competition?

Freedom to Enter and Exit Markets Producers can enter or exit the market with no interference.

Independent Buyers and Sellers Buyers and sellers do not band together to influence prices.

ANALYZE CHARTS

Imagine that you own a farm and that you have decided to sell raspberries at the Montclair Farmers' Market. Construct your own diagram to show how the five characteristics of perfect competition will apply to your enterprise.

CHARACTERISTIC 4 Independent Buyers and Sellers

In a perfectly competitive market, neither buyers nor sellers join together to influence price. When buyers and sellers act independently, the interaction of supply and demand sets the equilibrium price. Independent action ensures that the market will remain competitive. At the Montclair Farmers' Market, the farmers do not band together to raise prices, nor do the consumers organize to negotiate lower prices.

CHARACTERISTIC 5 Well-informed Buyers and Sellers

Buyers and sellers in a perfectly competitive market have enough information to make good deals. Buyers can compare prices among different sellers, and sellers know what their competitors are charging and what price consumers are willing to pay. Buyers and sellers at the Montclair Farmers' Market make informed choices about whether to buy or sell raspberries in that market. With all five characteristics met, the Smiths accept the market price for raspberries. All raspberry producers become price takers.

APPLICATION Making Inferences

A. Can you think of another market that comes close to perfect competition? Which of the characteristics does it lack?

Competition in the Real World

In the real world, there are no perfectly competitive markets because real markets do not have all of the characteristics of perfect competition. Market structures that lack one of the conditions needed for perfect competition are examples of **imperfect competition**. (You'll learn more about imperfect competition in Sections 2 and 3.) However, there are some markets—the wholesale markets for farm products such as corn and beef, for example—that come close to perfect competition.

QUICK REFERENCE

Imperfect competition occurs in markets that have few sellers or products that are not standardized.

EXAMPLE 1 Corn

In the United States, there are thousands of farmers who grow corn, and each one contributes only a small percentage of the total crop. Therefore, no one farmer can control the price of corn, and all farmers accept the market price. Individual farmers decide only how much corn to produce to offer for sale at that price. At the same time, there are a large number of buyers, and the price on the wholesale market is easy to determine. Corn is a fairly standardized product, and buyers usually have no reason to prefer one farmer's corn to another's. Buyers will not pay more than the market price.

In reality, there are several reasons that imperfect competition occurs in the corn market. For one thing, the U.S. government pays subsidies to corn farmers to protect them from low corn prices. In addition, sometimes corn farmers band together to try to influence the price of corn in their favor, and corn buyers sometimes pursue the same strategy. Subsidies, group action, and other deviations from perfect competition interfere with the market forces of supply and demand.

Close to Perfect Competition
Wholesale markets for agricultural products, such as corn, come close to perfect competition.

EXAMPLE 2 Beef

The wholesale market for raw beef is another that comes close to perfect competition. There are many cattle producers, and there is little variation in a particular cut of beef from one producer to the next. Because the beef is so similar, the wholesale buyer's primary concern will be price. Both buyers and sellers can easily determine the market price, and producers sell all their beef at that price. Cattle sellers can adjust only their production to reflect the market price.

As in the corn market, there are several reasons that imperfect competition occurs in the beef market. Cattle ranchers, like corn farmers, may try to join together to influence the price of beef in their favor. In addition, many beef producers try to persuade buyers that there are significant differences in their products that warrant higher prices. For example, cattle that eat corn supposedly produce better tasting beef.

APPLICATION Drawing Conclusions

B. Why is the market for corn closer to perfect competition than the market for corn flakes?

For more information on creating and interpreting economic models, see the Skillbuilder Handbook, page R16.

Creating and Interpreting Economic Models

Economic models help solve problems by focusing on a limited set of variables. A production costs and revenue schedule, which you learned about in Chapter 5, is a model that helps businesses decide how much to produce. Creating a graph as part of the model paints a picture of the data that makes it easier to understand.

In this example, imagine you own a business that produces baseballs in a perfectly competitive market. The market price of a baseball is $1, but your costs vary depending on how many you produce. Follow the instructions to create a graph that will help you visualize the way a perfectly competitive market works.

CREATING AN ECONOMIC MODEL OF BASEBALL PRODUCTION

1. Copy the graph below onto your own paper, or use ♪ SMART Grapher @ ClassZone.com.

2. Using data from the table below, plot the curve showing the marginal costs of producing different numbers of baseballs. Label the curve "MC."

3. Using data from the table below, plot the curve showing the marginal revenue of producing different numbers of baseballs. Label the curve "MR."

BASEBALL PRODUCTION COSTS AND REVENUES SCHEDULE					
Total Produced	Total Revenue (in dollars)	Total Cost (in dollars)	Total Profit (in dollars)	Marginal Revenue (in dollars)	Marginal Cost (in dollars)
0	0.00	1.00	−1.00	—	—
1	1.00	2.00	−1.00	1.00	1.00
2	2.00	2.80	−0.80	1.00	0.80
3	3.00	3.50	−0.50	1.00	0.70
4	4.00	4.00	0.00	1.00	0.50
5	5.00	4.50	0.50	1.00	0.50
6	6.00	5.20	0.80	1.00	0.70
7	7.00	6.00	1.00	1.00	0.80
8	8.00	6.86	1.14	1.00	0.86
9	9.00	7.86	1.14	1.00	1.00
10	10.00	9.36	0.64	1.00	1.50
11	11.00	11.50	−0.50	1.00	2.14

BASEBALL PRODUCTION

THINKING ECONOMICALLY Analyzing

1. How many baseballs should you produce each day to maximize profits?

2. Using the same graph, plot the demand curve for this perfectly competitive market. Remember that the market price will not change no matter how many baseballs are demanded.

3. How does the graph help explain the term "price takers"?

REVIEWING KEY CONCEPTS

1. Explain the differences between the terms in each of these pairs:

   a. *market*
   market structure

   b. *perfect competition*
   imperfect competition

2. Why are sellers in a perfectly competitive market known as *price takers*?

3. Why is it necessary to have standardized products in order to have perfect competition?

4. Why is independent action of buyers and sellers important to achieving perfect competition?

5. How is imperfect competition different from perfect competition?

6. **Using Your Notes** What are the five characteristics of perfect competition? Refer to your completed cluster diagram.

   Use the Graphic Organizer at
   Interactive Review @ ClassZone.com

CRITICAL THINKING

7. **Drawing Conclusions** Suppose that you went to a farmers' market and found several different farmers selling cucumbers. Would you be likely to find a wide range of prices for cucumbers? Why or why not?

8. **Analyzing Effects** What would happen to a wheat farmer who tried to sell his wheat for $2.50 per bushel if the market price were $2.00 per bushel? Why?

9. **Making Inferences** Why are brand-name products not found in a perfectly competitive market? You will learn more about this topic in Section 3 of this chapter.

10. **Challenge** At an auction, sellers show their goods before an audience of buyers. The goods for sale may be similar to each other, as in an auction of used cars, or they may be one-of-a-kind, as in an art auction. Buyers usually have an opportunity to inspect items prior to the auction. During the auction, buyers bid against one another to see who is willing to pay the highest price. In what ways is an auction similar to a perfectly competitive market? In what ways is it different?

ECONOMICS IN PRACTICE

How competitive is the market for snowboards?

Identifying Perfect Competition
Perfectly competitive markets can be identified by specific characteristics. The chart below lists these characteristics.

Characteristics of Perfect Competition	Markets				
	Applesauce	Snowboards	Hairbrushes	Computer games	Paper clips
Many buyers and sellers					
Standardized product					
Freedom to enter and leave the market					
Independent action					
Well-informed buyers and sellers					

Complete a Chart Five different markets are shown in the chart. On your own paper, complete the chart by marking which of the characteristics each market has.

Challenge Choose one market from the chart and explain what would need to be done to make it perfectly competitive.

The Impact of Monopoly

OBJECTIVES	KEY TERMS	TAKING NOTES
In Section 2, you will • describe the characteristics of a monopoly • analyze four different types of monopolies and discuss how they come about • explain how a monopoly sets its prices and production goals	monopoly, *p. 198* cartel, *p. 198* price maker, *p. 198* barrier to entry, *p. 198* natural monopoly, *p. 201* government monopoly, *p. 201* technological monopoly, *p. 201* geographic monopoly, *p. 201* economies of scale, *p. 201* patent, *p. 202*	As you read Section 2, complete a chart to show how different types of monopolies exhibit the characteristics of monopoly. Use the Graphic Organizer at **Interactive Review @ ClassZone.com**

	One Seller	Restricted Market	Control of Prices
Natural Monopoly			
Government Monopoly			
Technological Monopoly			
Geographic Monopoly			

Characteristics of a Monopoly

KEY CONCEPTS

QUICK REFERENCE

Monopoly occurs when there is only one seller of a product that has no close substitutes.

A **cartel** is a group that acts together to set prices and limit output.

A **price maker** is a firm that does not have to consider competitors when setting the prices of its products.

A **barrier to entry** makes it hard for a new business to enter a market.

Perfect competition is the most competitive market structure. The least competitive is **monopoly**, a market structure in which only one seller sells a product for which there are no close substitutes. The term *monopoly* may be used for either the market structure or the monopolistic business. Pure monopolies are as rare as perfect competition, but some businesses come close. For example, a **cartel** is a formal organization of sellers or producers that agree to act together to set prices and limit output. In this way, a cartel may function as a monopoly.

Because a monopoly is the only seller of a product with no close substitutes, it becomes a **price maker**, a business that does not have to consider competitors when setting its prices. Consumers either accept the seller's price or choose not to buy the product. Other firms may want to enter the market, but they often face a **barrier to entry**—something that hinders a business from entering a market. Large size, government regulations, or special resources or technology are all barriers to entry.

Let's take a closer look at the three characteristics of monopoly through the De Beers cartel, which held a virtual monopoly on the diamond market for most of the 20th century. At one time it controlled as much as 80 percent of the market in uncut diamonds. De Beers used its monopoly power to control the price of diamonds and created barriers to entry that kept other firms from competing.

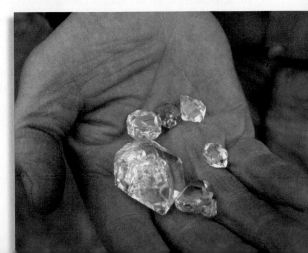

FIGURE 7.2 Characteristics of a Monopoly

What Are the Characteristics of a Monopoly?

Only One Seller
A single business controls the supply of a product that has no close substitutes.

Control of Prices
Monopolies act as price makers because they sell products that have no close substitutes and they face no competition.

Restricted, Regulated Market
Government regulations or other barriers to entry keep other firms out of the market.

ANALYZE CHARTS
Imagine that you are a business person with unlimited funds. Could you gain a monopoly over the market for housing in your neighborhood? Using the chart, explain the steps you would need to take. How might your neighborhood change if one person controlled property prices?

CHARACTERISTIC 1 Only One Seller

In a monopoly, a single business is identified with the industry because it controls the supply of a product that has no close substitutes. For example, De Beers once produced more than half of the world's diamond supply and bought up diamonds from smaller producers to resell. In this way, it controlled the market.

CHARACTERISTIC 2 A Restricted, Regulated Market

In some cases, government regulations allow a single firm to control a market, such as a local electric utility. In the case of De Beers, the company worked with the South African government to ensure that any new diamond mines were required to sell their diamonds through De Beers. The company also restricted access to the market for raw diamonds for producers outside of South Africa. By controlling the supply of diamonds, De Beers made it difficult for other producers to make a profit.

CHARACTERISTIC 3 Control of Prices

Monopolists can control prices because there are no close substitutes for their product and they have no competition. When economic downturns reduced demand for diamonds, De Beers created artificial shortages by withholding diamonds from the market. The reduced supply allowed the cartel to continue charging a higher price.

APPLICATION Analyzing Effects

A. What effect did the De Beers diamond monopoly have on the price of diamonds?

A GLOBAL PERSPECTIVE

OPEC: Controlling the Oil Pipelines

The Organization of the Petroleum Exporting Countries (OPEC) does not have a monopoly on oil reserves or oil production. However, the member nations of the cartel possess more than two-thirds of the world's oil reserves and produce about two-fifths of the world's oil supply. By regulating the amount of oil that flows through its pipelines, OPEC exerts control over the market price for oil.

Market forces often counteract OPEC's supply adjustments. For example, in the early 1980s demand for oil fell as consumers and businesses implemented strategies to reduce energy use. Despite OPEC's efforts to reduce supply and stabilize the price, crude oil prices fell through most of the 1980s. Another factor that limits OPEC's control over oil prices is member unity. Members sometimes choose not to follow OPEC moves to reduce oil output—because that would reduce their revenues. Despite these limitations, OPEC continues to play a major role in the world market for petroleum.

FIGURE 7.3 OPEC MEMBERS

Country	Joined OPEC	Location
Algeria	1969	Africa
Angola	2007	Africa
Ecuador	1973	South America
Iran	1960	Middle East
Iraq	1960	Middle East
Kuwait	1960	Middle East
Libya	1962	Africa
Nigeria	1971	Africa
Qatar	1961	Middle East
Saudi Arabia	1960	Middle East
United Arab Emirates	1967	Middle East
Venezuela	1960	South America

Source: OPEC, 2009

FIGURE 7.4 OPEC Member Nations

OPEC nations

CONNECTING ACROSS THE GLOBE

1. **Applying Economic Concepts** In what ways does OPEC act like a monopoly?

2. **Making Inferences** What will happen to OPEC's monopolistic power as the world discovers new sources of energy? Explain your answer.

Types of Monopolies

There are several reasons why monopolies exist, and not all monopolies are harmful to consumers. A **natural monopoly** is a market situation in which the costs of production are lowest when only one firm provides output. A **government monopoly** is a monopoly that exists because the government either owns and runs the business or authorizes only one producer. A **technological monopoly** is a monopoly that exists because the firm controls a manufacturing method, an invention, or a type of technology. A **geographic monopoly** is a monopoly that exists because there are no other producers or sellers within a certain region.

EXAMPLE 1 Natural Monopoly: A Water Company

In some markets, it would be inefficient to have more than one company competing for consumers' business. Most public utilities fall into this category. Let's look at the water company in your community as an example. It pumps the water from its source through a complex network of pipes to all the homes, businesses, and public facilities in the community. It also monitors water quality for safety and removes and treats wastewater so that it may be recycled.

It would be a waste of community resources to have several companies developing separate, complex systems in order to compete for business. A single supplier is most efficient due to **economies of scale**, a situation in which the average cost of production falls as the producer grows larger. The more customers the water company serves, the more efficient its operation becomes, as its high fixed costs are spread out over a large number of buyers. These economies of scale result in government support for natural monopolies. While supporting natural monopolies, the government also regulates them to ensure that they do not charge excessively high prices for their services.

Natural Monopolies
Most public utilities require complex systems, such as this water treatment facility.

EXAMPLE 2 Government Monopoly: The Postal Service

Government-run businesses provide goods and services that either could not be provided by private firms or that are not attractive to them because of insufficient profit opportunities. One of the oldest government monopolies in the United States is the U.S. Postal Service, which has the exclusive right to deliver first-class mail. Originally, only the government could provide this service in an efficient and cost-effective manner. However, new services and new technologies have been chipping away at this monopoly. Private delivery companies offer services that compete with the U.S. Postal Service. Many people now send information by fax, e-mail, and text messages. In addition, many pay their bills online.

QUICK REFERENCE

A **natural monopoly** occurs when the costs of production are lowest with only one producer.

A **government monopoly** exists when the government either owns and runs the business or authorizes only one producer.

A **technological monopoly** occurs when a firm controls a manufacturing method, invention, or type of technology.

A **geographic monopoly** exists when there are no other producers within a certain region.

Economies of scale occur when the average cost of production falls as the producer grows larger.

▲ E-mail message

▲ Handwritten note

EXAMPLE 3 Technological Monopoly: Polaroid

In 1947, Edwin Land, the founder of the Polaroid Corporation, invented the first instant camera. Land's camera used a special type of film that allowed each picture to develop automatically in about a minute. Through a series of patents, Polaroid created a monopoly in the instant photography market.

A **patent** is a legal registration of an invention or a process that gives the inventor the exclusive property rights to that invention or process for a certain number of years. The government supports technological monopolies through the issuing of patents. Through patents, businesses are able to recover the costs that were involved in developing the invention or technology.

Polaroid's control of instant photography technology through its patents was a barrier to entry for other firms. In 1985, Polaroid won a lawsuit against Eastman Kodak Company for patent infringement. The court ruled that Kodak's instant camera and film had violated Polaroid's property rights, which were protected by several patents. The lawsuit effectively blocked Kodak from the instant photography market.

Technological monopolies last only as long as the patent—generally 20 years—or until a new technology creates close substitutes. Polaroid maintained its monopoly for so long by updating its patents before they expired. But as digital photography spread from cameras to laptops to cell phones, demand for Polaroid's instant camera shrank. Polaroid stopped making instant cameras in 2007.

> **QUICK REFERENCE**
>
> A **patent** gives an inventor the exclusive property rights to that invention or process for a certain number of years.

Technological Monopoly Polaroid instant cameras used patented technology.

EXAMPLE 4 Geographic Monopoly: Professional Sports

One type of geographic monopoly in the United States is the professional sports team. The major sports leagues require that teams be associated with a city or region and limit the number of teams in each league. In other words, the leagues create a restricted market for professional sports. Most cities and towns are not directly represented by a team, so many teams draw their fans from a large surrounding geographic region. Because of their geographic monopolies, the owners of these teams are able to charge higher prices for tickets to games than if they faced competition. They also have a ready market for sports apparel and other merchandise featuring the team logo and colors.

Another type of geographic monopoly is created by physical isolation. For example, Joe operates the only gas station at an

Geographic Monopolies The Boston Red Sox is the only baseball team in New England, so it draws fans from across the six-state region.

interstate exit in the middle of a desert. The next station in either direction is more than 50 miles away. Joe has a geographic monopoly because he is the only supplier of a product with no close substitutes. Drivers on the interstate in that area depend on Joe's gas and have no other choice of supplier. They can either buy gas from Joe or risk running out of gas before they reach the next station. Because of his geographic location as the single supplier of a product that has no close substitutes, Joe is able to control the price that he charges—and gas at Joe's is always very expensive.

Isolated locations or small communities may have other examples of geographic monopolies if the market is too small to support two similar businesses. Geographic monopolies have become less common in the United States. Cars allow people to travel greater distances to shop, and catalog marketers and Internet businesses, combined with efficient delivery companies, offer consumers more alternatives to shopping at local stores.

Economics Update

Find an update on monopolies at **ClassZone.com**

APPLICATION Drawing Conclusions

B. Which type of monopoly do you think is least harmful to consumers? Why?

Profit Maximization by Monopolies

Although a monopoly firm is the only supplier in its market, the firm cannot charge any price it wishes. A monopolist still faces a downward-sloping demand curve. In other words, the monopoly will sell more at lower prices than at higher prices. The monopolist controls price by controlling supply. A monopoly produces less of a product than would be supplied in a competitive market, thereby artificially raising the equilibrium price.

It's difficult to study this process in the real world because most countries have laws to prevent monopolies. We have to look at small instances in which a company has a monopoly over one particular specialized product. Such a limited monopoly lasts only for the life of the patent or until a competitor develops a similar product.

EXAMPLE Drug Manufacturer

Pharmaceutical manufacturers offer an example of how companies with limited monopolies try to maximize their profits. On average, drug patents last for about 11 years in the United States. Drug companies try to maximize their profits during that period because when the patent expires they face competition from other manu-

facturers who begin marketing generic versions of the drug. A generic drug contains the same ingredients and acts in the same way as the patented drug, but it is sold at much lower prices.

"NOW HERE'S MY IDEA... WE COME UP WITH A REALLY HIGH-PRICED DRUG to TREAT DRUG SIDE EFFECTS..."

As an example, consider the Schering-Plough company and its antihistamine Claritin. The drug was originally approved for use as a prescription medication in the United States in 1993, although it had been patented earlier. Unlike many other such drugs, Claritin did not make users drowsy. This advantage, combined with a strong marketing campaign, led Claritin to become a top seller, making as much as $3 billion in annual worldwide sales.

When the patent on Claritin expired in 2002, numerous generic equivalents entered the market. In response, Schering-Plough lowered Claritin's price and gained approval for a nonprescription form of the drug. But sales of Claritin fell to about $1 billion as consumers switched to less costly generic equivalents.

APPLICATION Applying Economic Concepts

C. Using the three characteristics of monopoly, explain what happened to the market for Claritin when its patent expired.

Online Quiz
ClassZone.com

REVIEWING KEY CONCEPTS

1. Explain the differences between the terms in each of these pairs:

   a. *monopoly*   **b.** *natural monopoly*   **c.** *technological monopoly*
   cartel   *geographic monopoly*   *government monopoly*

2. What is the relationship between economies of scale and a natural monopoly?

3. How does a patent awarded to one company act as a barrier to entry to another company wishing to enter the same market?

4. Why is a monopolist a price maker rather than a price taker?

5. Why do technological monopolies exist only for a limited time?

6. **Using Your Notes** Why is a geographic monopoly able to control the price of its product? Refer to your completed chart.

   Use the Graphic Organizer at **Interactive Review @ ClassZone.com**

	One Seller	Restricted Market	Control of Prices
Natural Monopoly			
Government Monopoly			
Technological Monopoly			
Geographic Monopoly			

CRITICAL THINKING

7. **Analyzing Causes and Effects** Companies that produce generic drugs are not required to repeat the clinical tests that the original manufacturer of the drug is required to run before the drug receives its patent. How does this fact affect the prices of generic drugs and why?

8. **Analyzing Effects** A powerful monopoly is broken up into several smaller, competing companies. What are the costs and benefits for the general public?

9. **Drawing Conclusions** In 2003, 95 percent of the households in America had access to only one cable TV company in their area. What kind of monopoly did cable TV companies have? Explain your answer.

10. **Challenge** Among the drugs to fight high cholesterol, the most effective are known as statins. The drugs are similar, but each is different enough to have its own patent. In 2005, there were seven such drugs on the market. In 2006, the patents ended for two of the drugs. What effect did this have on the entire category of statin drugs, including those whose patents were still in effect through 2006? Explain why this might be the case.

ECONOMICS IN PRACTICE

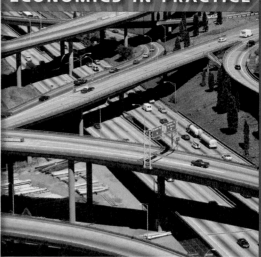

Identifying Types of Monopolies
You learned in this section that there are four types of monopolies: natural, government, technological, and geographical.

What Type? The table below lists examples of several monopolies. For each example, identify the type of monopoly. Some types have more than one example.

Example of Monopoly	Type of Monopoly
U.S. interstate highway system	
Electric utility company	
The only bank in a small town	
The company that received a patent for the Frisbee	
A city's public transportation system	
Natural gas company	

Challenge In which type of monopoly is the government least likely to be involved? Give reasons for your answer.

Other Market Structures

OBJECTIVES

In Section 3, you will
- learn that monopolistic competition and oligopoly are market structures that fall between perfect competition and monopoly
- identify the characteristics of monopolistic competition
- describe the characteristics of oligopoly

KEY TERMS

monopolistic competition, *p. 206*

product differentiation, *p. 206*

nonprice competition, *p. 207*

focus group, *p. 208*

oligopoly, *p. 209*

market share, *p. 209*

start-up costs, *p. 209*

TAKING NOTES

As you read Section 3, complete a chart to compare and contrast monopolistic competition and oligopoly. Use the Graphic Organizer at **Interactive Review @ ClassZone.com**

Monopolistic Competition	Oligopoly

Characteristics of Monopolistic Competition

KEY CONCEPTS

QUICK REFERENCE

Monopolistic competition occurs when many sellers offer similar, but not standardized, products.

Product differentiation is the effort to distinguish a product from similar products.

Most markets in the real world fall somewhere between the models of perfect competition and monopoly. One of the most common market structures is **monopolistic competition,** in which many sellers offer similar, but not standardized, products. The market for T-shirts printed with images or slogans is one example. The market is competitive because there are many buyers (you, your friends, and many other buyers) and many sellers (stores at the mall, online merchants, sports teams, and many other sellers). The market is monopolistic because each seller has influence over a small segment of the market with products that are not exactly like those of their competitors. Someone looking for a pink T-shirt with fuzzy kittens would not accept a black monster-truck rally T-shirt as a close substitute.

Product differentiation and nonprice competition are the distinguishing features of monopolistic competition. **Product differentiation** is the attempt to distinguish a product from similar products. Sometimes, the effort focuses on substantial differences between products, such as vehicle gas mileage ratings.

But companies also try to differentiate their products when there are few real differences between products. For example, a battery company might spend millions of dollars on advertising to convince consumers that their batteries last longer than other batteries—even though the real difference in longevity may be minimal.

Another way companies in monopolistic competitive markets try to gain business is through nonprice competition. **Nonprice competition** means using factors other than low price—such as style, service, advertising, or giveaways—to try to convince customers to buy one product rather than another. If you've ever decided to eat at a particular fast food restaurant just to get the cool gizmo it's giving away, you have participated in nonprice competition.

Monopolistic competition has four major characteristics: many buyers for many sellers, similar but differentiated products, limited lasting control over prices, and freedom to enter or exit the market. Let's take a closer look at each of these characteristics by focusing on the market for hamburgers.

QUICK REFERENCE

Nonprice competition occurs when producers use factors other than low price to try to convince customers to buy their products.

CHARACTERISTIC 1 Many Sellers and Many Buyers

In monopolistic competition there are many sellers and many buyers. The number of sellers is usually smaller than in a perfectly competitive market but sufficient to allow meaningful competition. Sellers act independently in choosing what kind of product to produce, how much to produce, and what price to charge.

When you want a hamburger, you have many different restaurants from which to choose. The number of restaurants assures that you have a variety of kinds of hamburgers to choose from and that prices will be competitive. No single seller has a large enough share of the market to significantly control supply or price.

However, there are probably a few restaurants that make burgers you really like and others with burgers you really don't like. The restaurants that make your favorite burgers have a sort of monopoly on your business.

Economics Update

Find an update about monopolistic competition at **ClassZone.com**

CHARACTERISTIC 2 Similar but Differentiated Products

Sellers in monopolistic competition gain their limited monopoly-like power by making a distinctive product or by convincing consumers that their product is different from the competition. Hamburger restaurants might advertise the quality of their ingredients or the way they cook the burger. They might also use distinctive packaging or some special service—a money-back guarantee if the customer is not satisfied with the meal, for example. One key method of product differentiation is the use of brand names, which

**Hamburger Valhalla
Chili-Cheese Burger**

White bread bun

Cheese and chili

All-beef patty

Standard pickles, onions, tomatoes, lettuce

**Healthy Eats
Veggie Burger**

Whole wheat bun

Organic pickles, onions, tomatoes

Veggie patty

Organic lettuce

encourage consumer loyalty by associating certain desirable qualities with a particular brand of hamburger. Producers use advertising to inform consumers about product differences and to persuade them to choose their offering.

How do hamburger restaurants decide how to differentiate their products? They conduct market research, the gathering and evaluation of information about consumer preferences for goods and services. For local restaurants, market research may be limited to listening to their customers' praise or complaints and paying attention to what competing restaurants offer.

<table>
</table>

QUICK REFERENCE

A **focus group** is a moderated discussion with small groups of consumers.

The large chain restaurants can afford to use more sophisticated research techniques to gain information about consumers' lifestyles and product preferences. One technique is the **focus group**—a moderated discussion with small groups of consumers. Another market research technique is the survey, in which a large number of consumers are polled, one by one, on their opinions. The results of market research help the restaurants differentiate their hamburgers and attract more customers.

CHARACTERISTIC 3 Limited Control of Prices

Product differentiation gives producers limited control of price. Hamburger restaurants charge different prices for their product depending on how they want to appeal to customers. The price of some hamburgers is set as low as possible to appeal to parents of younger eaters or to those on tight budgets. Prices for name-brand hamburgers or burgers with better quality ingredients may be set slightly higher. If consumers perceive that the differences are important enough, they will pay the extra price to get the hamburger they want.

Yet producers in monopolistic competition also know that there are many close substitutes for their product. They understand the factors that affect demand and recognize that consumers will switch to a substitute if the price goes too high.

CHARACTERISTIC 4 Freedom to Enter or Exit Market

There are generally no huge barriers to entry in monopolistically competitive markets. It does not require a large amount of capital for someone to open a hamburger stand, for example. When firms earn a profit in the hamburger market, other firms will enter and increase competition. Increased competition forces firms to continue to find ways to differentiate their products. The competition can be especially intense for small businesses facing much larger competitors.

Some firms will not be able to compete and will start to take losses. This is the signal that it is time for those firms to exit the market. Leaving the restaurant market is relatively easy. The owners sell off the cooking equipment, tables, and other supplies at a discount. If their finances are solid, they may then look for another market where profits might be made.

Ease of Entry and Exit
In monopolistic competition, sellers may enter and exit the market freely.

APPLICATION Applying Economic Concepts

A. Think about an item of clothing that you purchased recently. How did the seller differentiate the product? List several ways, then compare lists with a classmate.

Characteristics of an Oligopoly

Oligopoly (ol-ih-GOP-ah-lee), a market structure in which only a few sellers offer a similar product, is less competitive than monopolistic competition. In an oligopoly, a few large firms have a large **market share**—percent of total sales in a market—and dominate the market. For example, if you want to see a movie in a theater, chances are the movie will have been made by one of just a few major studios. What's more, the theater you go to is probably part of one of just a few major theater chains. Both the market for film production and the market for movie theaters are oligopolies.

There are few firms in an oligopoly because of high **start-up costs**—the expenses that a new business must pay to enter a market and begin selling to consumers. Making a movie can be expensive, especially if you want to make one that can compete with what the major studios produce. And getting it into theaters across the country requires a huge network of promoters and distributors—and even more money.

An oligopoly has four major characteristics. There are few sellers but many buyers. In industrial markets, sellers offer standardized products, but in consumer markets, they offer differentiated products. The few sellers have more power to control prices than in monopolistic competition, but to enter or exit the market is difficult.

QUICK REFERENCE

Oligopoly is a market structure in which only a few sellers offer a similar product.

Market share is a company's percent of total sales in a market.

Start-up costs are the expenses that a new business faces when it enters a market.

CHARACTERISTIC 1 Few Sellers and Many Buyers

In an oligopoly, a few firms dominate an entire market. There is not a single supplier as in a monopoly, but there are fewer firms than in monopolistic competition. These few firms produce a large part of the total product in the market. Economists consider an industry to be an oligopoly if the four largest firms control at least 40 percent of the market. About half of the manufacturing industries in the United States are oligopolistic.

The breakfast cereal industry in the United States is dominated by four large firms that control about 80 percent of the market. Your favorite cereal is probably made by one of the big four manufacturers. Although they offer many varieties of cereals, there is less competition than there would be if each variety were produced by a different, smaller manufacturer.

The Breakfast Cereal Industry
Just a few large companies produce the majority of breakfast cereals available.

CHARACTERISTIC 2 Standardized or Differentiated Products

Depending on the market, an oligopolist may sell either standardized or differentiated products. Many industrial products are standardized, and a few large firms control these markets. Examples include the markets for steel, aluminum, and flat glass. When products are standardized, firms may try to differentiate themselves based on brand name, service, or location.

Breakfast cereals, soft drinks, and many other consumer goods are examples of differentiated products sold by oligopolies. Oligopolists market differentiated products using marketing strategies similar to those used in monopolistic competition. They use surveys, focus groups, and other market research techniques to find out what you like. The companies then create brand-name products that can be marketed across the country or around the world.

CHARACTERISTIC 3 More Control of Prices

Economics Update

Find an update about oligopolies at **ClassZone.com**

Because there are few sellers in an oligopoly, each one has more control over product price than in a monopolistically competitive market. For example, each breakfast cereal manufacturer has a large enough share of the market that decisions it makes about supply and price affect the market as a whole. Because of this, a seller in an oligopoly is not as independent as a seller in monopolistic competition. A decision made by one seller may cause the other sellers to respond in some way.

For example, if one of the leading breakfast cereal manufacturers lowers its prices, the other manufacturers will probably also lower prices rather than lose customers to the competition. Therefore, no firm is likely to gain market share based on price, and all risk losing profits. But if one manufacturer decides to raise prices, the others may not follow suit, in order to take customers and gain market share. Consequently, firms in an oligopoly try to anticipate how their competitors will respond to their actions before they make decisions on price, output, or marketing.

CHARACTERISTIC 4 Little Freedom to Enter or Exit Market

Start-up costs for a new company in an oligopolistic market can be extremely high. Entering the breakfast cereal industry on a small scale is not very expensive—but the profits are low too. The factories, warehouses, and other infrastructure needed to compete against the major manufacturers require large amounts of funds. In addition, existing manufacturers may hold patents that act as further barriers to entry.

High Start-up Costs
New firms may not have the funds to construct large factories.

Firms in an oligopoly have established brands and plentiful resources that make it difficult for new firms to enter the market successfully. For example, breakfast cereal

manufacturers have agreements with grocery stores that guarantee them the best shelf space. Existing manufacturers also have economies of scale that help them to keep their expenses low. Smaller firms, with smaller operations, lack the economies of scale.

However, all of the investments by firms in an oligopoly make it difficult for them to exit the market. When a major breakfast cereal manufacturer begins losing money, its operations are too vast and complex to sell and reinvest easily, as a small business might. It must trim its operations and work to stimulate demand for its product.

APPLICATION Categorizing Information

B. Which of these products produced by oligopolies are standardized and which are differentiated: automobiles, cement, copper, sporting goods, tires?

Comparing Market Structures

Each of the four market structures has different benefits and problems. And each type creates a different balance of power—namely, the power to influence prices—between producers and consumers.

Consumers get the most value in markets that approach perfect competition. No actual markets are perfectly competitive, but in those that come close, prices are set primarily by supply and demand. However, such markets usually deal in a standardized product, so consumers have little choice other than the best price.

In monopolistic competition, consumers continue to benefit from companies competing for their business. But businesses gain some control over prices, so they are more likely to earn a profit. Opening a business in such a market is usually relatively affordable, which is another benefit for businesses.

In markets dominated by oligopolies, consumer choices may be more limited than in more competitive markets. Businesses in such markets gain more control of price, making it easier for them to make a profit. However, the cost of doing business in such a market is high.

A market ruled by a monopoly is very favorable for the business that holds the monopoly. It faces little or no competition from other companies. And monopoly gives consumers the least influence over prices. They decide only whether they are willing to buy the product at the price set by the monopolist.

FIGURE 7.5 Comparing Market Structures

	Number of Sellers	Type of Product	Sellers' Control over Prices	Barriers to Enter or Exit Market
Perfect Competition	Many	Standardized	None	Few
Monopolistic Competition	Many	Similar but differentiated	Limited	Few
Oligopoly	Few	Standardized for industry; differentiated for consumers	Some	Many
Monopoly	One	Standardized, but no close substitutes	Significant	Very many—market restricted or regulated

ANALYZE CHARTS
1. If you were starting a business, which market structures would make it easiest for you to enter the market?
2. Which market structures offer the highest potential profits? Why?

APPLICATION Drawing Conclusions

C. What difference does it make to consumers whether a market is ruled by monopolistic competition or by an oligopoly?

Joan Robinson: Challenging Established Ideas

FAST FACTS

Joan Robinson

Career: Economics professor, Cambridge University

Born: October 31, 1903

Died: August 5, 1983

Major Accomplishment: Developed theory of imperfect competition

Books: *The Economics of Imperfect Competition* (1933), *The Accumulation of Capital* (1956), *Economic Philosophy* (1963), *Introduction to Modern Economics* (1973)

Famous Quotation:
"*It is the business of economists, not to tell us what to do, but show why what we are doing anyway is in accord with proper principles.*"

In this section, you learned about monopolistic competition and oligopoly. British economist Joan Robinson was one of the first to write about these market structures. As strange as it may seem to us now, most economists before 1930 described market competition only in terms of the extremes of perfect competition and monopoly.

Explaining Real-World Competition

In 1933, Joan Robinson challenged the prevailing ideas about competition. Her first major book, *The Economics of Imperfect Competition*, described market structures that existed between monopoly and perfect competition. Robinson's work appeared shortly after Harvard economist Edward Chamberlin published his book *Theory of Monopolistic Competition*. The two economists had developed their ideas independently.

Robinson and Chamberlin described the type of competition that exists among firms with differentiated products. Such firms gain more control over the price of their product, but their control is limited by the amount of competition. They also described the nature of oligopoly and of monopsony, a market structure in which there are many sellers but only one large buyer.

Robinson continued to contribute important ideas throughout her long career in economics. Her theory of imperfect competition remains a key element of the field of microeconomics today. Economists recognized that Robinson's theory more accurately reflected modern market economies in which firms compete through product differentiation and advertising and in which many industries are controlled by oligopolies.

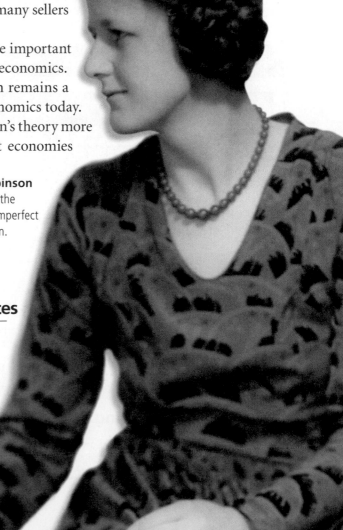

Joan Robinson developed the theory of imperfect competition.

⚡ Economics Update

Learn more about Joan Robinson at **ClassZone.com**

APPLICATION **Making Inferences**

D. Why do you think Joan Robinson chose the term *imperfect competition* to describe the nature of most real-world markets?

SECTION 3 Assessment

Online Quiz
ClassZone.com

REVIEWING KEY CONCEPTS

1. Explain the relationship between the terms in each of these pairs:

   a. *product differentiation* *nonprice competition*

   b. *focus group* *market share*

   c. *oligopoly* *start-up costs*

2. How is monopolistic competition similar to perfect competition and how is it similar to monopoly?

3. Describe some of the techniques sellers use to differentiate their products.

4. Why are standardized products sometimes found in oligopoly but not in monopolistic competition?

5. Is it easier for a new firm to enter the market under monopolistic competition or oligopoly? Why?

6. **Using Your Notes** How does the number of sellers compare in monopolistic competition and oligopoly? Refer to your completed chart.

Monopolistic Competition	Oligopoly

   Use the Graphic Organizer at **Interactive Review @ ClassZone.com**

CRITICAL THINKING

7. **Contrasting Economic Information** What makes the market for wheat different from the markets for products made from wheat, such as bread, cereal, and pasta?

8. **Applying Economic Concepts** In 2005, a major U.S. automaker announced a new discount plan for its cars for the month of June. It offered consumers the same price that its employees paid for new cars. When the automaker announced in early July that it was extending the plan for another month, the other two major U.S. automakers announced similar plans. What market structure is exhibited in this story and what specific characteristics of that market structure does it demonstrate?

9. **Analyzing Effects** Blue jeans are produced under monopolistic competition, so their prices are higher than if they were produced under perfect competition. Do the positive effects for consumers of blue jeans justify the higher prices? Why or why not?

10. **Challenge** Why do manufacturers of athletic shoes spend money to sign up professional athletes to wear and promote their shoes rather than differentiating their products strictly on the basis of physical characteristics such as design and comfort?

ECONOMICS IN PRACTICE

Perfect competition or monopoly?

The Impact of Market Structure Each of the four market structures carries different consequences for businesses and consumers. Imagine what would happen if there were only one type of market structure. Use Figure 7.5 on page 211 as a guide as you do this exercise.

a. What would your town look like if every market was perfectly competitive? What would happen to your consumer choices?

b. What would happen if every market was ruled by monopolistic competition?

c. What would the town look like if oligopolies controlled every market?

d. What if every market in your town was ruled by a monopoly? How could you tell the difference between situation A and D?

Challenge Now think about what your town actually looks like. What types of market structures are most prevalent? Are you satisfied with the mix of market structures, or do you think some markets would be better served by different structures?

Regulation and Deregulation Today

OBJECTIVES	KEY TERMS	TAKING NOTES
In Section 4, you will • explain how government acts to prevent monopolies • analyze the effects of anti-competitive business practices • describe how government acts to protect consumers • discuss why some industries have been deregulated and the results of that deregulation	regulation, *p. 214* antitrust legislation, *p. 214* trust, *p. 214* merger, *p. 214* price fixing, *p. 216* market allocation, *p. 216* predatory pricing, *p. 216* cease and desist order, *p. 217* public disclosure, *p. 217* deregulation, *p. 218*	As you read Section 4, complete a hierarchy diagram to track main ideas and supporting details. Use the Graphic Organizer at **Interactive Review@ ClassZone.com**

Regulation and Deregulation

Promoting Competition

details

Promoting Competition

KEY CONCEPTS

QUICK REFERENCE

Regulation is a set of rules or laws designed to control business behavior.

Antitrust legislation defines monopolies and gives government the power to control them.

A **trust** is a group of firms combined in order to reduce competition in an industry.

A **merger** is the joining of two firms to form a single firm.

The forces of the marketplace generally keep businesses competitive with one another and attentive to consumer welfare. But sometimes the government uses **regulation**—controlling business behavior through a set of rules or laws—to promote competition and protect consumers. The most important laws that promote competition are collectively called **antitrust legislation**, laws that define monopolies and give government the power to control them and break them up. A **trust** is a group of firms combined for the purpose of reducing competition in an industry. (A trust is similar to a cartel, which you learned about in Section 2.) To keep trusts from forming, the government regulates business mergers. A **merger** is when one company combines with or purchases another to form a single firm.

Origins of Antitrust Legislation

During the late 1800s, a few large trusts, such as Standard Oil, dominated the oil, steel, and railroad industries in the United States. The U.S. government became concerned that these combinations would use their power to control prices and output. As a result, in 1890, the government passed the Sherman

Standard Oil Company This cartoon dramatizes how Standard Oil controlled the oil industry.

Antitrust Act. This gave government the power to control monopolies and to regulate business practices that might reduce competition. Over time, other laws strengthened the government's ability to regulate business and to encourage competition.

To understand why government officials pushed for antitrust laws, consider one of the trusts that developed in the late 1800s—the Standard Oil Company. By merging with other companies and eliminating competitors, Standard Oil gained control of about 90 percent of the U.S. oil industry. Such a huge holding, government officials contended, gave Standard Oil the ability to set production levels and prices. In 1911, the U.S. government won a court case under the Sherman Antitrust Act that required the breakup of the trust. In order to increase competition, Standard Oil was forced to relinquish control of 33 companies that had once been part of the trust.

Antitrust Legislation Today

At various times, the U.S. government has used antitrust legislation to break up large companies that attempt to maintain their market power through restraint of competition. The government might allow a large dominant firm to remain intact because it is the most efficient producer. Or it might order that the company change its business practices to allow other firms to compete more easily.

The responsibility for enforcing antitrust legislation is shared by the Federal Trade Commission (FTC) and the Department of Justice. A major focus of their work is the assessment of mergers. The government tends to support mergers that might benefit consumers. For example, larger firms are often able to operate more efficiently, and lower operating costs may lead to lower prices for consumers. On the other hand, the government tends to block mergers that lead to greater market concentration in the hands of a few firms. A merger that makes it more difficult for new firms to enter a market will also be looked upon with concern.

To evaluate a potential merger, the government looks at how a particular market is defined. A company that is proposing a merger would try to define its market as broadly as possible, in order to make its control of the market seem smaller. For example, a soft drink producer might claim that its market competition includes all beverages, such as water, tea, coffee, and juice.

To determine whether the merger will increase the concentration in the market and decrease competition, the government considers the market share of the firms before and after the proposed merger. Government regulators also look at whether the merger allows a firm to eliminate possible competitors. If this analysis shows that a merger will reduce competition and more than likely lead to higher prices for consumers, the regulators will deny the companies' effort to merge.

The Federal Trade Commission (FTC)
In 2004, Deborah Platt Majoras became head of the FTC, an agency that enforces antitrust laws.

APPLICATION Drawing Conclusions

A. Which of these mergers would the government be more likely to approve and why: two airlines that serve different cities or two banks in a small town?

Ensuring a Level Playing Field

In addition to evaluating mergers, the government also tries to make sure that businesses do not engage in practices that would reduce competition. As you have learned, competition enables the market economy to work effectively. When businesses take steps that counteract the effects of competition, prices go up and supplies go down. In the United States, laws prohibit most of these practices. The FTC and the Department of Justice enforce these laws.

Prohibiting Unfair Business Practices

Businesses that seek to counteract market forces can use a variety of methods. One is **price fixing**, which occurs when businesses work together to set the prices of competing products. A related technique is when competing businesses agree to restrict their output, thereby driving up prices.

For example, in the mid-1990s the five major recorded music distributors began enforcing a "minimum advertised price" for compact discs sold in the United States. As a result, CD prices remained artificially high. The FTC estimated that consumers paid about $480 million more for CDs than they would have if prices had been established by market forces. In 2000 the FTC reached an agreement with the distributors to end this anticompetitive practice.

Another way businesses seek to avoid competition is by **market allocation**, which occurs when competing businesses negotiate to divide up a market. By staying out of each other's territory, the businesses develop limited monopoly power in their own territory, allowing them to charge higher prices.

For example, in the early 1990s agribusiness conglomerate Archer Daniels Midland (ADM) conspired with companies in Japan and Korea to divide the worldwide market for lysine, an additive used in livestock feeds. Around the same time, ADM also conspired with European companies to divide the worldwide market for citric acid, an additive used in soft drinks, canned foods, and other consumer products. Both of these illicit agreements also included price fixing. In 1996, the Department of Justice charged ADM with antitrust violations in both the lysine and citric acid markets. ADM pleaded guilty and paid a $100 million fine.

Occasionally, businesses use anticompetitive methods to drive other firms out of a market. One technique used by cartels or large producers is **predatory pricing**, setting prices below cost so that smaller producers cannot afford to participate in a market. Predatory pricing can be difficult to distinguish from competitive pricing. Larger businesses are usually able to offer lower prices because they have economies of scale unavailable to smaller firms.

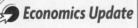
APPLICATION Applying Economic Concepts

B. If you owned an ice cream store, could you negotiate with other ice cream store owners to set a standard price for a scoop of ice cream? Why or why not?

Protecting Consumers

KEY CONCEPTS

When the government becomes aware that a firm is engaged in behavior that is unfair to competitors or consumers, it may issue a **cease and desist order**, a ruling that requires a firm to stop an unfair business practice. The government also enforces a policy of **public disclosure**, which requires businesses to reveal product information to consumers. This protects consumers and promotes competition by giving consumers the information they need to make informed buying decisions.

Consumer Protection Agencies

Besides enforcing laws that ensure competitive markets, the government protects consumers by regulating other aspects of business. Figure 7.6 shows some of the most important federal agencies that protect consumers. The Federal Trade Commission has primary responsibility for promoting competition and preventing unfair business practices. The Federal Communications Commission and Securities and Exchange Commission regulate specific industries. The Food and Drug Administration, Environmental Protection Agency, and Consumer Product Safety Commission protect consumers by regulating multiple industries to ensure the safety and quality of specific products and to protect consumer health.

FIGURE 7.6 Federal Consumer Protection Agencies

Agency	Created	Purpose
Food and Drug Administration (FDA)	1906	Protects consumers from unsafe foods, drugs, or cosmetics; requires truth in labeling of these products
Federal Trade Commission (FTC)	1914	Enforces antitrust laws and monitors unfair business practices, including deceptive advertising
Federal Communications Commission (FCC)	1934	Regulates the communications industry, including radio, television, cable, and telephone services
Securities and Exchange Commission (SEC)	1934	Regulates the market for stocks and bonds to protect investors
Environmental Protection Agency (EPA)	1970	Protects human health by enforcing environmental laws regarding pollution and hazardous materials
Consumer Product Safety Commission (CPSC)	1972	Sets safety standards for thousands of types of consumer products; issues recalls for unsafe products

ANALYZE TABLES
1. What's the difference between the FTC and the SEC?
2. Pick one agency, note the year it was created, and explain what might have led to its creation.

APPLICATION Making Inferences

C. Why do you think the government has decided to set up agencies to protect consumers from unsafe products?

QUICK REFERENCE

A **cease and desist order** requires a firm to stop an unfair business practice.

Public disclosure is a policy that requires businesses to reveal product information.

Deregulating Industries

KEY CONCEPTS

As more industries came under a wider array of government regulations, a counter-movement arose. Businesses and some economists argued that regulations were harming profits, and they lobbied for reduced regulation. In the 1970s, the government began a process of **deregulation**, reducing or removing government oversight and control of business.

The results of deregulation have been mixed. In some cases, removing regulations helped both businesses and consumers. In other cases, lack of regulation led to problems. The example of the airline industry shows some of both the benefits and drawbacks of deregulation. (The role of deregulation in the financial crisis that began in 2007 will be discussed in Chapter 10.)

QUICK REFERENCE

Deregulation reduces or removes government control of business.

Deregulating the Airlines

The Airline Deregulation Act of 1978 removed all government control of airline routes and rates. Only safety regulations remained in place. Prior to 1978, there was limited competition, and airlines differentiated based on service rather than price.

As a result of deregulation, the industry expanded as many new carriers entered the market. Increased competition led to greater efficiency. Economists estimate that prices fell by 10 to 18 percent, falling most sharply on heavily traveled routes where there was the greatest amount of competition. More people than ever before, lured by lower prices, chose to travel by plane.

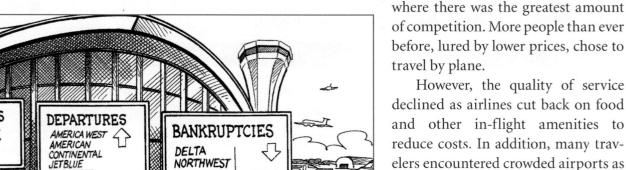

However, the quality of service declined as airlines cut back on food and other in-flight amenities to reduce costs. In addition, many travelers encountered crowded airports as a result of the increase in air travel. It took time for local governments to expand facilities to accommodate the increase in traffic.

The financial pressures led to a large number of bankruptcies among the airline companies. Airline employees faced increased layoffs, lower wages, and loss of pensions.

APPLICATION Analyzing Causes

C. Why did deregulation of the airline industry lead to lower prices for many consumers?

SECTION 4 Assessment

Online Quiz
ClassZone.com

REVIEWING KEY CONCEPTS

1. Explain the differences between the terms in each of these pairs:

   a. *trust* / *merger* **b.** *price fixing* / *predatory pricing* **c.** *regulation* / *deregulation*

2. What is the main purpose of antitrust legislation?

3. How does market allocation lead to reduced competition?

4. When would the government issue a cease and desist order?

5. How do public disclosure requirements protect consumers?

6. **Using Your Notes** Why is it important for the government to evaluate and approve mergers? Refer to your completed hierarchy diagram.

   Use the Graphic Organizer at **Interactive Review @ ClassZone.com**

CRITICAL THINKING

7. **Analyzing Causes and Effects** In 2005, the FTC approved the merger of The Gillette Company with Procter & Gamble. Experts who reviewed the merger said it made sense that it was approved because the two companies had few products in the same market categories. In order to satisfy the government, the companies had to sell only two of their brands to other companies. What factors that affect mergers are illustrated in this story?

8. **Applying Economic Concepts** In the early 2000s, a new form of marketing emerged called word-of-mouth marketing or buzz marketing. Companies hired ordinary people to talk about the benefits of their products to others. Marketing industry lawyers warned their clients that it was important that the hired spokespeople reveal that they were paid for their endorsements. What are the lawyers concerned about? Use the concepts from this section to formulate your answer.

9. **Challenge** The Telecommunications Act of 1996 included provisions to deregulate the cable television industry. In 2003, consumer organizations complained that cable rates had increased by 45 percent since the law was passed. Only 5 percent of American homes had a choice of more than one cable provider in 2003. Those homes paid about 17 percent less than those with no choice of cable provider. How effective had deregulation been in the cable industry by 2003? Cite evidence to support your answer.

ECONOMICS IN PRACTICE

Identifying Regulatory Agencies
Several federal agencies provide protection for consumers. Many of them are listed in Figure 7.6 on page 217. Decide which agency or agencies from Figure 7.6 would best protect consumers in each of the situations below.

a. Children's necklaces sold over the Internet are found to contain high levels of lead. Consumers are concerned about the chance of lead poisoning.

b. Advertising for a skin cream claims that it will eliminate acne problems. Consumers find that the product does not live up to its claim and in fact seems to irritate people's faces and cause rashes.

c. Some apple farmers use a pesticide on their trees that causes illness. More and more of the pesticide has been found in groundwater supplies.

Challenge Find out about a government regulatory agency not listed in Figure 7.6. Discuss the agency's purpose with your class.

⚡ *Economics Update*
Find an update on this Case Study at **ClassZone.com**

Competition in Gadgets and Gizmos

Background Cellular phones are a highly successful telecommunications product. Since they first appeared on the market in the 1980s, cell phone sales have grown steadily. Now, billions of people around the world own cell phones.

As the global market becomes saturated with cell phones, sales growth will slow. To counteract this, cell phone producers rely on product differentiation to increase sales. New gadgets and gizmos aim to make the cell phone both irresistible and indispensable. A director of business development at one cell phone maker summed up his strategy this way: "We are trying to drive the cell phone in[to] every aspect of your life."

What's the issue? What affects your selection of a cell phone? Study these sources to discover how producers use product differentiation to compete for your business.

A. Magazine Article

Nokia Corporation, a maker of phone handsets, developed several add-ons to boost sales. This article describes one of Nokia's plans.

▶ Nokia Hopes to Attract Consumers with Mobile-TV

Web-browsing, picture-messaging, videos, and now TV

Nokia, the world's largest handset-maker, has just released the results of a mobile-TV trial in Helsinki which found that 41% of participants were willing to pay for the service, and thought a monthly fee of €10 [€ is the European Union currency, the euro] ($12.50) was reasonable.

As revenue from voice calls has stopped growing in developed markets, the industry has been searching for new avenues for growth. In recent years, it has championed mobile web-browsing, picture-messaging and video-telephony. . . . But . . . consumers have not taken to these things in large numbers. . . .

Ah, but mobile TV is different from all those other services . . . because there is no need to educate the consumer. "Everyone gets it if you say 'mobile TV'," says Richard Sharp of Nokia.

Source: **"Anyone for Telly?"** *The Economist*, September 10, 2005

Thinking Economically What caused Nokia to develop mobile-TV? Explain, using evidence from the article.

This cartoon makes light of the dozens of features packed into most cellular phones.

Swiss Army Phone

Source: www.CartoonStock.com

Thinking Economically Why do cellular phone makers include so many features in their phones?

C. Online Press Release

Gartner, Inc. provides research and analysis on the information technology industry. This press release presents its projections on mobile phone sales.

Gartner Says Mobile Phone Sales Will Exceed One Billion in 2009

Sales will increase, but so will competition.

Gartner estimates there will be 2.6 billion mobile phones in use by the end of 2009. . . . "The sales volume cannot be attributed to one region in particular. It's a truly global phenomenon," said Carolina Milanesi, principal analyst at Gartner for mobile terminals. "In mature markets like Europe and North America, subscribers are still buying replacement phones. In emerging markets like Brazil and India, new customers are signing up for mobile services at an even faster rate." . . .

Despite spectacular growth on all fronts, not everything is rosy. [Ben] Wood, research vice president for mobile terminals at Gartner, cautioned that "Sales numbers are impressive, but the big names in this industry will have to deliver value as well as volume. We expect the average wholesale price of a mobile phone will decline from US$174 in 2004 to US$161 in 2009. At the same time, phones will keep getting more complex and become ever-more packed with features. Only the sharpest players will survive."

Source: www.gartner.com

Thinking Economically Are manufacturers more likely to offer differentiated products in new markets or in those already established? Explain your answer.

THINKING ECONOMICALLY Synthesizing

1. Compare the product described in document A and the one illustrated in B. Are cell phones likely to become more or less complex? Explain why or why not.

2. Which of the four market structures best fits the market for cellular phones? Use evidence from documents A and C to explain your answer.

3. In documents A and C, compare the role that market research plays in the development of new products. Use evidence from the documents.

Interactive Review

Online Summary

Complete the following activity either on your own paper or online at **ClassZone.com**

Choose the key concept that best completes the sentence. Not all key concepts will be used.

antitrust legislation	monopoly
barrier to entry	natural monopoly
cartel	nonprice competition
cease and desist order	oligopoly
deregulation	patent
economies of scale	perfect competition
geographic monopoly	price fixing
market structure	price taker
merger	standardized product
monopolistic competition	start-up costs

__1__ is an economic model of the nature and degree of competition among businesses in the same industry. In __2__ there are many buyers and sellers of standardized products.

In a __3__ there is a single seller of a product with no close substitutes. The local water company is an example of a __4__ because __5__ make it most efficient for a single company to provide the service.

A __6__ is a group of sellers that acts together to set prices and limit output. A __7__ is anything that makes it difficult for a business to enter a market.

In __8__ there are many buyers and sellers of similar but differentiated products. In such a market the sellers engage in __9__.

In __10__ there are only a few sellers for many buyers. It is hard for new firms to enter such a market due to high __11__. Sellers in such a market engage in __12__ when they all agree to charge the same price for their products.

__13__ gives the government the power to control monopolies and to promote competition.

CHAPTER 7 Assessment

REVIEWING KEY CONCEPTS

What Is Perfect Competition? (pp. 192–197)

1. What determines the difference between one market structure and another?

2. Why is perfect competition not found in real markets?

The Impact of Monopoly (pp. 198–205)

3. How does a monopoly control the price of its product?

4. Name three ways in which a monopoly differs from perfect competition.

Other Market Structures (pp. 206–213)

5. Why is product differentiation necessary for monopolistic competition?

6. Why are firms in an oligopoly less independent in setting prices than firms in monopolistic competition?

Regulation and Deregulation Today (pp. 214–221)

7. What factors does the government consider in deciding whether to approve a merger?

8. Why do economists generally favor deregulation of most industries?

APPLYING ECONOMIC CONCEPTS

Look at the table below showing retail sales.

9. Which retail market is the least concentrated? Which market is most concentrated?

10. Which markets are closer to monopolistic competition and which are closer to oligopoly?

FIGURE 7.7 SALES CONCENTRATION IN RETAIL TRADE

Retail Market	Percent of Total Sales by the Four Largest Firms
Furniture	8
Clothing	29
Supermarkets	33
Music	58
Athletic footwear	71
Books	77
Discount department stores	95

Source: U.S. Census Bureau, 2002 data

11. **Applying Economic Concepts** In 2004, a new trend started in the marketing of music CDs. A variety of retailers, from coffee shop and restaurant chains to large discount stores, began negotiating marketing deals that allowed them to sell a particular recording artist's CDs exclusively for a period of time.

   a. What part of monopolistic competition does this trend reinforce: the monopolistic aspect or the competition aspect?

   b. How is this trend likely to affect prices for these CDs? Give reasons why.

12. **Analyzing Causes and Effects** After deregulation of the airline industry, many of the largest U.S. airlines struggled financially. These airlines then increased their business in the international market in order to boost their profits. What effect of deregulation caused the airlines to make this move?

13. **Making Inferences** The company that invented the first xerographic photocopier initially enjoyed 70 percent profit margins and a 95 percent market share. Several years later a Japanese camera company invented another way to make photocopiers. Over time, the original company's market share fell to 13 percent. What specific kind of market structure is illustrated by this example? When a company invents a new product or process, what concerns might they have, if they studied this example?

14. **Drawing Conclusions** An herbal supplement company claimed that its product would cure serious diseases and promote weight loss. In 2005, the Federal Trade Commission (FTC) required the company to stop making those claims. Why did the FTC rather than the Food and Drug Administration (FDA) handle this case?

15. **Challenge** Why might a local electric company be in favor of regulations that would allow it to remain a natural monopoly? Why might it oppose regulations that would require monitoring the pollution from its generating plants?

Compete for Buyers

Step 1. Choose a partner. Imagine that together you run a company that produces flat-screen televisions under monopolistic competition. Use the criteria in this table to decide how to differentiate your product.

Product and Marketing Considerations
• Physical characteristics
• Where it will be sold
• Packaging or labeling
• Service
• Advertising and promotion
• Price (from $500 to $1,500)

Step 2. Create a poster that outlines your product and marketing decisions. Include a sketch of one of your televisions along with the price.

Step 3. Display all the posters in the classroom. Allow all students to buy a television from the company of their choice. Tally the results and see how many buyers each company attracted.

Step 4. Merge with two or three other companies to form a larger company. There should now be only three or four producers. Discuss how this new situation might affect your marketing decisions.

Step 5. As a class, discuss what would happen if the three or four firms became a cartel and acted like a monopoly.

Challenge Which of these scenarios would you prefer as a producer? Which would you prefer as a consumer?

Types of Businesses

Businesses are organized in different ways. The organization that suits a small business, such as this florist, may not be appropriate for a large manufacturer.

Types of Business Organizations

CONCEPT REVIEW

A **producer** is a maker of goods or provider of services.

CHAPTER 8 KEY CONCEPT

Most of the producers in a market economy are **business organizations**, commercial or industrial enterprises and the people who work in them. The purpose of most business organizations is to earn a profit.

WHY THE CONCEPT MATTERS

Do you have a part-time job after school or on weekends? Perhaps you work behind the counter at the local flower shop or as a server at the juice bar downtown. Or perhaps you work as a stocker at one of the large clothing stores at the shopping mall. These businesses are of varying sizes and are organized differently. The American free enterprise system allows producers to choose the kind of business organization that best suits their purpose.

Online Highlights

More at ClassZone.com

 Economics Update

Go to **ECONOMICS UPDATE** for chapter updates and current news on Apple Inc. (See Case Study, pp. 252–253.) ▶

Animated Economics

Go to **ANIMATED ECONOMICS** for interactive lessons on the graphs and tables in this chapter.

Interactive Review

Go to **INTERACTIVE REVIEW** for concept review and activities.

How did Apple Inc., which began in a garage, grow into a major multinational corporation? See the Case Study on pages 252–253.

Sole Proprietorships

OBJECTIVES	KEY TERMS	TAKING NOTES
In Section 1, you will • identify the characteristics of sole proprietorships • describe how sole proprietorships are established • compare the economic advantages and economic disadvantages of sole proprietorships	business organization, *p. 226* sole proprietorship, *p. 226* limited life, *p. 228* unlimited liability, *p. 228*	As you read Section 1, complete a chart showing the advantages and disadvantages of sole proprietorships. Use the Graphic Organizer at **Interactive Review @ ClassZone.com**

Sole Proprietorships	
Advantages	Disadvantages

The Characteristics of Sole Proprietorships

KEY CONCEPTS

QUICK REFERENCE

A **business organization** is an enterprise that produces goods or provides services, usually in order to make a profit.

A **sole proprietorship** is a business organization owned and controlled by one person.

Every business begins with a person who has an idea about how to earn money and the drive to follow through on the idea and to create a business organization. A **business organization** is an enterprise that produces goods or provides services. Most of the goods and services available in a market economy come from business organizations.

The purpose of most business organizations is to earn a profit. They achieve this purpose by producing the goods and services that best meet consumers' wants and needs. In the course of meeting consumer demand, business organizations provide jobs and income that can be used for spending and saving. Business organizations also pay taxes that help finance government services.

The most common type of business organization in the United States is the **sole proprietorship**, a business owned and managed by a single person. Sole proprietorships include everything from mom-and-pop grocery stores to barbershops to computer repair businesses. They account for more than 70 percent of all businesses in the United States. However, they generate less than 5 percent of all sales by American businesses.

Sole Proprietorships Beauty salons are frequently operated by one owner.

EXAMPLE Bart's Cosmic Comics

To understand how sole proprietorships are set up and run, let's look at the example of Bart's Cosmic Comics. Bart started collecting comic books in grade school. Over the years, he amassed a huge collection of comics as well as other related items—lunch boxes, action figures, and so on. At the same time, he learned a lot about the comic book business. So, few of his friends expressed surprise when Bart announced that he wanted to open a business selling comic books and related merchandise.

Raising Funds Bart needed money to rent and renovate the space he found downtown and to buy new and used comics to stock the store. A hefty withdrawal from his savings account got him started, but he needed to borrow to get the job finished. He tried to get a loan from a local bank. However, because he was not yet an established business owner, bank officers were reluctant to approve the loan. Finally, he turned to his family and friends, who together lent him $15,000.

Preparing to Open After raising the necessary funds, Bart completed the few legal steps required to open his business. These included obtaining a business license and a site permit, a document stating that the local government allowed him to use the space he was renting for business. He also registered the name he had chosen for his business—Bart's Cosmic Comics.

Initial Difficulties At first, business was slow. Bart worried that the store would fail and he would be stuck with no income and no way to repay the loans. He thought the safest course of action might be to hang on to what cash he had so he could keep the store open for as long as possible. After much consideration, however, he decided to take another risk, spending $1,000 on advertisements in local newspapers. He also ran several in-store promotions. His business began to take off.

Economics Update
Find an update on sole proprietorships at **ClassZone.com**

Success Within 18 months, Bart had paid back his loans and was earning a profit. Shortly after, he decided to expand his inventory to include T-shirts and posters and to hire an assistant to help run the store. This time when he asked the bank for a loan to pay for the expansion, bank officers were ready to approve the financing. Bart's success indicated that giving him a loan would be a good business decision.

APPLICATION Applying Economic Concepts

A. Identify two or three examples of businesses you might want to establish as sole proprietorships.

Sole Proprietorships: Advantages and Disadvantages

QUICK REFERENCE

Limited life is a situation where a business closes if the owner dies, retires, or leaves for some other reason.

Unlimited liability means that a business owner is responsible for all the business's losses and debts.

KEY CONCEPTS

The sole proprietorship has certain advantages and disadvantages that set it apart from other kinds of business structures. For example, sole proprietorships are not governed by as many regulations as other types of businesses. Also, sole proprietorships have **limited life**, a situation in which a business ceases to exist if the owner dies, retires, or leaves the business for some other reason. Finally, sole proprietors have **unlimited liability**, a situation in which a business owner is responsible for all the losses, debts, and other claims against the business.

ADVANTAGES Sole Proprietorships

There is a reason that sole proprietorships are by far the most common type of business structure: they have several significant advantages.

Easy to Open or Close Bart's start-up requirements were typical: funding, a license, a site permit, and a legally registered name. If Bart wanted to get out of the business, he would find that process easy as well. As long as he has settled all his bills, Bart may close the business when he sees fit.

Few Regulations Compared with other business organizations, sole proprietorships are lightly regulated. Bart, for example, must locate his store in an area zoned, or officially set aside, for businesses. He also must treat his employees according to various labor laws.

Freedom and Control Bart makes all the decisions and does so quickly without having to check with partners or boards of directors. Having complete control and seeing his ideas come to life gives Bart, like many other sole proprietors, a strong sense of personal satisfaction. In other words, he enjoys being his own boss.

Owner Keeps Profits Bart also enjoys the chief economic advantage of the sole proprietorship. Since he is the sole owner of the business, he gets to keep all the profits the business earns.

Sole Proprietors Are Fully Responsible The owner bears full responsibility for running the business but also keeps all of the profits.

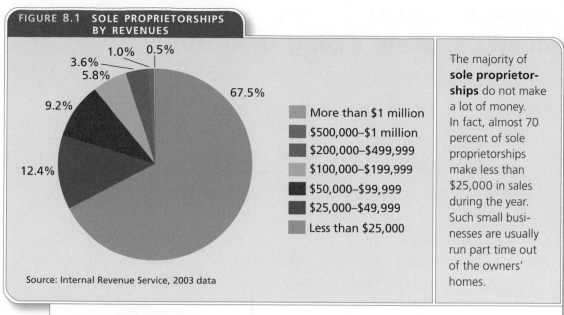

FIGURE 8.1 SOLE PROPRIETORSHIPS BY REVENUES

1.0% 0.5%
3.6%
5.8%
9.2%
67.5%
12.4%

- More than $1 million
- $500,000–$1 million
- $200,000–$499,999
- $100,000–$199,999
- $50,000–$99,999
- $25,000–$49,999
- Less than $25,000

Source: Internal Revenue Service, 2003 data

The majority of **sole proprietorships** do not make a lot of money. In fact, almost 70 percent of sole proprietorships make less than $25,000 in sales during the year. Such small businesses are usually run part time out of the owners' homes.

ANALYZE GRAPHS

1. About what percentage of sole proprietorships make less than $50,000 in annual sales?
2. Make a generalization about sole proprietorships based on information in the graph.

DISADVANTAGES Sole Proprietorships

Bart's story hints at some of the disadvantages of sole proprietorships as well.

Limited Funds Especially at start-up, Bart had very limited funds. This disadvantage is one of the key reasons that sole proprietorships are far more likely to fail than other types of business organizations. Until he had established his business, Bart had trouble securing a bank loan. Without monetary reserves to fall back on, he found it a struggle to stay in business. Even when the business became successful, Bart felt that the lack of funds hurt him. He worried that he would not be able to attract and keep good workers because his limited funds meant he could not pay competitive wages or offer benefits such as health insurance.

Limited Life Bart found that some of the advantages of the sole proprietorship may also prove to be disadvantages. He appreciated the ease with which you can set up or close a sole proprietorship. However, this means that sole proprietorships have limited life. If he leaves the business, Bart's Cosmic Comics ceases to exist.

Unlimited Liability Bart enjoys having total responsibility for running the business, even though that means that he works long hours. Having total responsibility for the business produces perhaps the greatest disadvantage of a sole proprietorship—unlimited liability. Bart is legally responsible for all the financial aspects of the business. If Bart's Cosmic Comics fails, he must still pay all its debts, even without income from the business. If necessary, he may have to sell property and use his personal savings to pay off debts. Sole proprietors, then, may lose their homes, cars, or personal savings if their businesses fail.

APPLICATION Analyzing Cause and Effect

B. Why do you think that sole proprietorships are the most common form of business organization in the United States?

Mary Kay Ash: Going It Alone

Economics Update
Find an update on Mary Kay Inc. at **ClassZone.com**

Do you have what it takes to "go it alone" as an entrepreneur? See how many of these questions you can answer with a "yes."
• Are you willing to take risks?
• Can you live with uncertainty?
• Are you self-confident?
• Are you self-directed, able to set and reach goals for yourself?
• Are you optimistic, energetic, and action-oriented?

Like other entrepreneurs, Mary Kay Ash had all of these qualities. She used them to turn $5,000 in personal savings into Mary Kay Inc., a business that now sells billions of dollars of cosmetics and other merchandise every year.

Building a Business

While raising three children on her own, Ash built a very successful career in direct sales. In 1963, however, Ash suffered a blow when she lost out on a promotion that was given instead to a man she had trained. Feeling she had been treated unfairly, Ash resolved to create an enterprise that would reward women for their hard work. Later that year, she started a cosmetics company with her son Richard and nine sales people—whom Ash referred to as "beauty consultants." In 1964, sales exceeded $198,000. By the end of 1965, sales had skyrocketed to more than $800,000.

Mary Kay Ash
Mary Kay Ash grew her business into a major corporation.

Since its founding, Mary Kay® products have been sold at in-home parties rather than in stores. Mary Kay has always had distinctive programs for recognizing women who reached certain goals. Pink Cadillacs, diamond-studded jewelry, luxury vacations, and other incentives spur the sales representatives to greater and greater efforts.

In 1987, Ash assumed the title of chairman emeritus, though she remained active in the company until her death in 2001. Her company and its culture continued to flourish. In 2005, over 1.6 million Mary Kay beauty consultants operated in more than 30 countries worldwide. As the company expanded globally, China became Mary Kay's largest market outside the United States.

APPLICATION Making Inferences

C. Why do you think Mary Kay Ash proved so successful in her cosmetics venture?

SECTION 1 Assessment

Online Quiz
ClassZone.com

REVIEWING KEY CONCEPTS

1. Explain the relationship between the terms in each of these pairs:

   a. *business organization*
      sole proprietorship

   b. *limited life*
      unlimited liability

2. What are the main advantages of a sole proprietorship?

3. What are the main disadvantages of a sole proprietorship?

4. Who gets the profits from a sole proprietorship? Who has to pay all the debts?

5. What steps do new sole proprietorships usually need to take before they can open?

6. **Using Your Notes** Select one of the businesses you identified in Application A on page 227. If you were starting that business, do you think the advantages of a sole proprietorship would outweigh the disadvantages or vice versa? Why? Refer to your completed chart as you formulate your answer. Use the Graphic Organizer at **Interactive Review @ ClassZone.com**

Sole Proprietorships	
Advantages	Disadvantages

CRITICAL THINKING

7. **Evaluating Economic Decisions** Suppose Cosmic Comics becomes very successful, and Bart decides to try opening a second store. What issues should Bart consider? What challenges will he face?

8. **Making Inferences and Drawing Conclusions** In what ways might limited life be considered an advantage for sole proprietors?

9. **Applying Economic Concepts** Explain how a sole proprietorship rests on the principles of free enterprise.

10. **Writing About Economics** Write a brief paragraph explaining what Bart might learn from Mary Kay Ash.

11. **Challenge** How many "yes" answers did you provide to the questions at the top of page 230? If you had one or more "no" answers, explain how you would change a sole proprietorship in order to suit your skills and abilities. If you answered "yes" to all of the questions, explain what you would like about running your own business.

ECONOMICS IN PRACTICE

Business fairs promote new opportunities.

Starting Your Own Business
Each year, thousands of Americans start businesses as sole proprietorships.

Write a Business Plan Choose a business that you might like to start as a sole proprietorship. Use the following questions to develop a plan that shows how the business will make a profit.

- How much money will it take to start the business? Detail each expense.

- How much money will it take to run the business each month? Detail each expense.

- Who will the customers be and how will you attract them?

- Once the business is established, how much will it earn each month? Detail each source of income.

- How much profit will you earn?

Challenge What challenges do you think you would face in making this business a success? Write a paragraph explaining how you would address these challenges.

Forms of Partnerships

OBJECTIVES	KEY TERMS	TAKING NOTES
In Section 2, you will • identify the characteristics and types of partnerships • compare the economic advantages and disadvantages of partnerships	partnership, *p. 232* general partnership, *p. 233* limited partnership, *p. 233* limited liability partnership, *p. 233*	As you read Section 2, complete a comparison and contrast chart to show similarities and differences between partnerships and sole proprietorships. Use the Graphic Organizer at **Interactive Review @ ClassZone.com**

Sole Proprietorships	Partnerships
One owner	Two or more owners

The Characteristics of Partnerships

KEY CONCEPTS

In Section 1, you read how Bart set up his business as a sole proprietorship. His sister, Mary, who is a whiz at bookkeeping, began helping him with the accounting tasks. As her role in the business expanded, Bart proposed that they join forces in a partnership. A **partnership** is a business co-owned by two or more people, or "partners," who agree on how responsibilities, profits, and losses will be divided. Bart lacks the bookkeeping skills his sister has, and the extra funds she brings could help Cosmic Comics to grow. Forming a partnership might be a good business decision.

Partnerships are found in all kinds of businesses, from construction companies to real estate groups. However, they are especially widespread in the areas of professional and financial services—law firms, accounting firms, doctors' offices, and investment companies. There are several different types of partnerships—general partnerships, limited partnerships, and limited liability partnerships—but they are all run in the same general way.

QUICK REFERENCE

A **partnership** is a business co-owned by two or more partners who agree on how responsibilities, profits, and losses of that business are divided.

TYPE 1 General Partnerships

The most common type of partnership is the **general partnership**, a partnership in which partners share responsibility for managing the business and each one is liable for all business debts and losses. As in a sole proprietorship, that liability could put personal savings at risk. The trade-off for sharing the risky side of the business enterprise is sharing the rewards as well. Partners share responsibility, liability, and profits equally, unless there is a partnership agreement that specifies otherwise. This type of partnership is found in almost all areas of business.

TYPE 2 Limited Partnerships

In a general partnership, each partner is personally liable for the debts of the business, even if another partner caused the debt. There is a way, however, to limit one's liability in this kind of business organization. This is through a **limited partnership**, a partnership in which at least one partner is not involved in the day-to-day running of business and is liable only for the funds he or she has invested.

All limited partnerships must have at least one general partner who runs the business and is liable for all debts, but there can be any number of limited partners. Limited partners act as part owners of the business, and they share in the profits. This form of partnership allows the general partner or partners to raise funds to run the business through the limited partners.

TYPE 3 Limited Liability Partnerships

Another kind of partnership is the **limited liability partnership** (LLP), a partnership in which all partners are limited partners and not responsible for the debts and other liabilities of other partners. If one partner makes a mistake that ends up costing the business a lot of money, the other partners cannot be held liable. In LLPs, partners' personal savings are not at risk unless the debts arise from their own mistakes.

Not all businesses can register as LLPs. Those that can include medical partnerships, law firms, and accounting firms. These are businesses in which malpractice—improper, negligent, or unprincipled behavior—can be an issue. LLPs are a fairly new form of business organization, and the laws governing them vary from state to state.

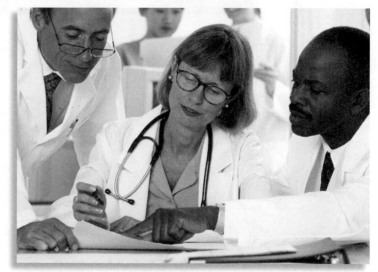

Partnerships Doctors' offices are often run as limited liability partnerships.

APPLICATION Comparing and Contrasting Economic Information

A. What are the differences in liability that distinguish general partnerships, limited partnerships, and limited liability partnerships?

Partnerships: Advantages and Disadvantages

KEY CONCEPTS

Some of the economic advantages of partnerships are similar to those of sole proprietorships. Like sole proprietorships, partnerships are easy to set up and dissolve and have few government regulations. Compared with sole proprietorships, however, partners have greater access to funds. Also, possibilities exist for specialization among partners, which can promote efficiency.

The disadvantages of partnerships are similar to the disadvantages of sole proprietorships. Like the sole proprietor, at least one of the partners, except in LLPs, faces unlimited liability. Partnerships, too, have limited life. However, partnerships have at least one disadvantage that sole proprietorships avoid. Disagreements among partners can lead to serious problems in running the business.

ADVANTAGES Partnerships

Bart and Mary realized that if they formed a partnership they would benefit from some of the same advantages that sole proprietorships have, plus some important additional advantages.

Easy to Open and Close Partnerships, like sole proprietorships, are easy to start up and dissolve. Ending the partnership would be equally straightforward for Bart and

Economics Update

Find an update on partnerships at **ClassZone.com**

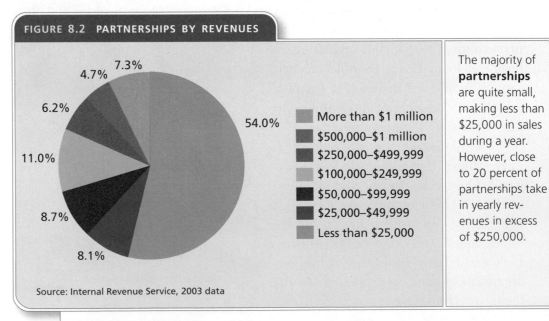

FIGURE 8.2 PARTNERSHIPS BY REVENUES

7.3%
4.7%
6.2%
11.0%
54.0%
8.7%
8.1%

- More than $1 million
- $500,000–$1 million
- $250,000–$499,999
- $100,000–$249,999
- $50,000–$99,999
- $25,000–$49,999
- Less than $25,000

Source: Internal Revenue Service, 2003 data

The majority of **partnerships** are quite small, making less than $25,000 in sales during a year. However, close to 20 percent of partnerships take in yearly revenues in excess of $250,000.

ANALYZE GRAPHS
1. What percentage of partnerships made more than $100,000 in sales?
2. Some 7 percent of partnerships took in more than $1 million in revenues, compared to just 0.5 percent of sole proprietorships. Why do you think partnerships generate more revenues than sole proprietorships?

his sister. As long as they have settled all their bills, Bart and Mary may dissolve the partnership when they see fit.

Few Regulations Bart and Mary would not be burdened with a host of government regulations. They would enter into a legal agreement spelling out their rights and responsibilities as partners. Partners are covered under the Uniform Partnership Act (UPA), a law, adopted by most states, that lays out basic partnership rules.

Access to Resources Mary would bring additional funds to Cosmic Comics. In addition, partnerships generally make it easier to get bank loans for business purposes. A greater pool of funds also makes it easier for partnerships to attract and keep workers.

Joint Decision Making In most partnerships, partners share in the making of business decisions. This may result in better decisions, for each partner brings his or her own particular perspective to the process. The exception is limited partnerships, in which the limited partner does not participate in running the business.

Specialization Also, each partner may bring specific skills to the business. For example, Bart brings knowledge of comic books, while Mary, who studied business accounting in college, brings skills in bookkeeping and finance. Having partners focus on their special skills promotes efficiency.

DISADVANTAGES Partnerships

Bart and Mary also considered the disadvantages of partnerships.

Unlimited Liability The biggest disadvantage of most partnerships is the same as that of sole proprietorships: unlimited liability. Both Bart and Mary are personally responsible for the full extent of the partnership's debts and other liabilities. So they risk having to use their personal savings, and even having to sell their property, to cover their business debts.

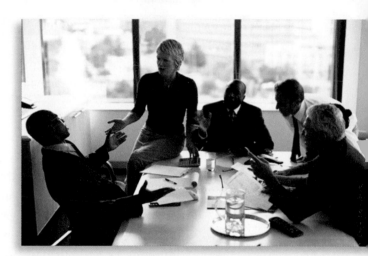

Joint Decision Making Partners benefit by making decisions together. But sometimes disagreements can interfere with running the business.

Potential for Conflict As partners, they may encounter a new disadvantage as well. Having more than one decision maker can often lead to better decisions. However, it can also detract from efficiency if there are many partners and each decision requires the approval of all. Further, disagreements among partners can become so severe that they lead to the closing of the business.

Limited Life Like sole proprietorships, partnerships have limited life. When a partner dies, retires, or leaves for some other reason, or if new partners are added, the business as it was originally formed ceases to exist legally. A new partnership arrangement must be established if the enterprise is to continue.

APPLICATION Applying Economic Concepts

B. Consider the businesses you identified in Application A on page 227 of Section 1. Would these businesses work as partnerships? Why or why not?

ECONOMICS SKILLBUILDER

For more information on distinguishing fact from opinion, see the Skillbuilder Handbook, page R27.

Distinguishing Fact from Opinion

Facts are events, dates, statistics, and statements that can be proved to be true. Facts can be checked for accuracy. Economists use facts to develop **opinions**, which may be expressed as judgments, beliefs, or theories. By learning to distinguish between facts and opinions, you will be able to think critically about the economic theories, interpretations, and conclusions of others.

TIPS FOR ANALYZING TEXT Use the following guidelines to analyze economic information in written works:

FIGURE 8.3 STARTS AND CLOSURES OF SMALL EMPLOYER FIRMS

	2000	2001	2002	2003	2004
New Firms	574,300	585,140	569,750	553,500	580,990
Firm Closures	542,831	553,291	586,890	572,300	576,200
Bankruptcies	35,472	40,099	38,540	35,037	34,317

Sources: U.S. Bureau of the Census; Administrative Office of the U.S. Courts; U.S. Department of Labor, Employment and Training Administration.

> **Facts** used by economists are often in the form of statistics, like the ones in this table.

Many Americans have faith that their ideas will bring them wealth or at least a comfortable living. According to the U.S. government, Americans created more than half a million small firms, or businesses, in the United States each year from 2000 to 2005. While prospective entrepreneurs may interpret these figures as a small business bonanza, overall closures of small businesses also exceeded the half-million mark each year during the same period. And in 2002 and 2003, more small firms closed their doors than opened them, suggesting that market conditions for those two years were particularly unfavorable for the prolonged success of small businesses. Yet bankruptcies among small firms declined in 2002 and 2003. Although such data are likely to be of interest to prospective entrepreneurs, it is limited in nature. Anyone planning to start a business venture would be wise to conduct more extensive research.

> **Opinions.** Look for words, such as *suggest*, *suggesting*, *belief*, and *believe*, which often express assertions, claims, and hypotheses.

> **Facts** include economic data that can be proved. The writer bases this statement on verifiable facts from the table.

> **Judgments**, another form of opinion, often use descriptive words such as *wise*, *foolish*, *sensible*, and *fortunate*, which have an emotional quality.

THINKING ECONOMICALLY Distinguishing Fact from Opinion

1. What facts, if any, does the author use to support the first sentence in the paragraph?

2. Using information from the table and article, write one statement of fact and one statement of opinion. As a class, share your statements and discuss.

REVIEWING KEY CONCEPTS

1. Explain the relationship between the terms in each of these pairs:

   a. *partnership*
   general partnership

   b. *limited partnership*
   limited liability partnership

2. What are the main advantages of a partnership?

3. What are the main disadvantages of a partnership?

4. In what ways do the increased resources of a partnership help a business?

5. What determines how partners will divide responsibilities, profits, and debts?

6. **Using Your Notes** Which type of partnership is most like a sole proprietorship? Explain your answer with specific characteristics. Refer to your completed chart.

Sole Proprietorships	Partnerships
One owner	Two or more owners

   Use the Graphic Organizer at
   Interactive Review @ ClassZone.com

CRITICAL THINKING

7. **Applying Economic Concepts** If you were looking to start a business as a partnership, what traits would you look for in potential partners? Draw up a list of five traits and give a brief explanation for each. Be sure to take the advantages and disadvantages of partnerships into consideration.

8. **Comparing and Contrasting Economic Information** Briefly explore the differences in potential for job satisfaction between sole proprietorships and partnerships. One size does not fit all—try to determine which of these two business organizations would suit you best.

9. **Writing About Economics** American business leader John D. Rockefeller said, "A friendship founded on business is a good deal better than a business founded on friendship." What do you think he had in mind? Write a brief paragraph agreeing or disagreeing, with reference to partnerships.

10. **Challenge** Do you think that major retail or manufacturing businesses would work as partnerships? Why or why not?

ECONOMICS IN PRACTICE

Types of Partnerships
The different types of partnerships suit different types of businesses.

Identify Partnerships Identify the type of partnership represented in each description.

1. Doctors choose this type of partnership because it protects them from malpractice suits brought against other partners.

2. The only role that George plays in the partnership is to collect profits or bear losses based on the amount of funds he contributed.

3. Stephen and Mike start a consulting service to help businesses manage their trademarks and patents. They are the only partners, sharing equally in the work, profits, and losses.

4. Rosa and Serena carefully review expansion plans after new partners provide extra funds. However, they know that they remain fully liable if their decisions are not sound.

Challenge Write a description of three different business partnerships without naming them. Exchange your descriptions with a classmate and identify each other's partnerships.

Corporations, Mergers, and Multinationals

OBJECTIVES	KEY TERMS	TAKING NOTES
In Section 3, you will • identify the characteristics of corporations • compare the advantages and disadvantages of corporations • describe how corporations consolidate to form larger business combinations • explain the role of multinational corporations in the world economy	corporation, *p. 238* stock, *p. 238* dividend, *p. 238* public company, *p. 238* private company, *p. 238* bond, *p. 240* limited liability, *p. 240* unlimited life, *p. 240* horizontal merger, *p. 243* vertical merger, *p. 243* conglomerate, *p. 243* multinational corporation, *p. 243*	As you read Section 3, complete a cluster diagram that categorizes information about corporations. Use the Graphic Organizer at **Interactive Review @ ClassZone.com**

Characteristics of Corporations

KEY CONCEPTS

Corporations are the third main kind of business organization. A **corporation** is a business owned by individuals, called shareholders or stockholders. The shareholders own the rights to the company's profits, but they face limited liability for the company's debts and losses. These individuals acquire ownership rights through the purchase of **stock**, or shares of ownership in the corporation.

For example, suppose a large company sells a million shares in the form of stock. If you bought 10,000 shares, you would own 1 percent of the company. If the company runs into trouble, you would not be responsible for any of its debt. Your only risk is that the value of your stock might decline. If the company does well and earns a profit, you might receive a payment called a **dividend**, part of the profit that the company pays out to stockholders.

A corporation that issues stock that can be freely bought and sold is called a **public company**. One that retains control over who can buy or sell the stock is called a **private company**. Corporations make up about 20 percent of the number of businesses in the United States, but they produce most of the country's goods and services and employ the majority of American workers.

EXAMPLE F & S Publishing, Inc.

To better understand how corporations operate, let's look at F & S Publishing, Inc., a successful publishing business. Frank and Shirley, the founders, decided to turn their business into a corporation because they wished to avoid unlimited liability. A corporation, unlike a partnership or sole proprietorship, is a formal, legal entity separate from the individuals who own and run it. The financial liabilities of F & S

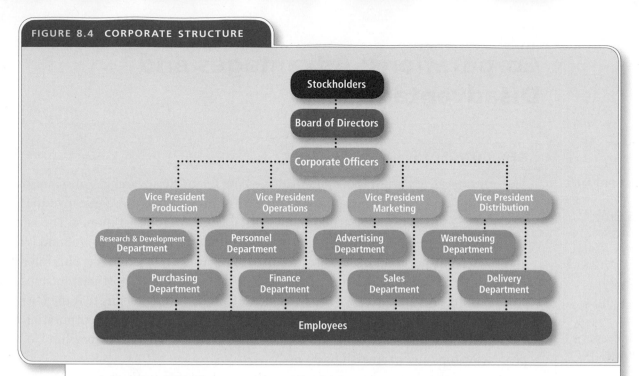

FIGURE 8.4 CORPORATE STRUCTURE

Stockholders

Board of Directors

Corporate Officers

Vice President Production

Vice President Operations

Vice President Marketing

Vice President Distribution

Research & Development Department

Personnel Department

Advertising Department

Warehousing Department

Purchasing Department

Finance Department

Sales Department

Delivery Department

Employees

ANALYZE CHARTS
This chart shows the organization of a typical corporation. Smaller corporations may only have stockholders, corporate officers, and employees. Larger corporations may be much more complex. Imagine you own a company that makes a product you like. Draw an organization chart for your corporation.

Publishing, Inc., are separate from the personal financial liabilities of Frank, Shirley, and other F & S stockholders. If the business fails, only the assets of F & S itself—the office building, equipment, and company bank accounts—are at risk.

Setting up a corporation involves more work and expense than establishing a sole proprietorship or partnership. Frank and Shirley hired a law firm to draw up and file papers requesting permission from the state government to incorporate. The state government agreed to the request and issued a corporate charter. This document named F & S Publishing, Inc., as the business, stated its address and purpose, and specified how much stock Frank and Shirley could sell.

F & S Publishing, Inc., is organized like the majority of corporations. Stockholders—the owners of the corporation—elect a board of directors. The board hires corporate officers, such as the president and the vice-presidents in charge of sales, production, finance, and so on. These officers are responsible for the smooth running of the corporation. In most corporations, the stockholders and the board of directors are not involved in the day-to-day running of the business. F & S Publishing, Inc., however, is a small company, and Frank and Shirley became members of the board of directors as well as managers.

Frank and Shirley decided to make their business a public company. They bought enough of the stock themselves so that they would each have a seat on the board of directors. They sold the rest of the stock to raise money to expand the business.

APPLICATION Applying Economic Concepts

A. Frank and Shirley were worried about unlimited liability. How did incorporating protect them from this problem?

Corporations: Advantages and Disadvantages

QUICK REFERENCE

A **bond** is a contract issued by a corporation that promises to repay borrowed money, plus interest, on a fixed schedule.

Limited liability means that a business owner's liability for debts and losses of the business is limited.

Unlimited life means that a corporation continues to exist even after an owner dies, leaves the business, or transfers his or her ownership.

Economics Update

Find an update on corporations at ClassZone.com

KEY CONCEPTS

The advantages of corporations often address the major disadvantages of sole proprietorships and partnerships. For example, corporations are more effective than either of the other business structures at raising large amounts of money. The key methods of raising money are the sale of stock and the issuing of bonds. A **bond** is a contract the corporation issues that promises to repay borrowed money, plus interest, on a fixed schedule. Also, unlike sole proprietorships and most partnerships, corporations provide their owners with **limited liability**, which means that the business owner's liability for business debts and losses is limited. Further, corporations have **unlimited life**—they continue to exist even after a change in ownership. Sole proprietorships and partnerships do not.

Most of the disadvantages of corporations are related to their size and organizational complexity. Corporations are costly and time-consuming to start up; they are governed by many more rules and regulations; and, because of the organizational structure, the owners may have little control over business decisions. Despite these drawbacks, corporations can be efficient and productive business organizations.

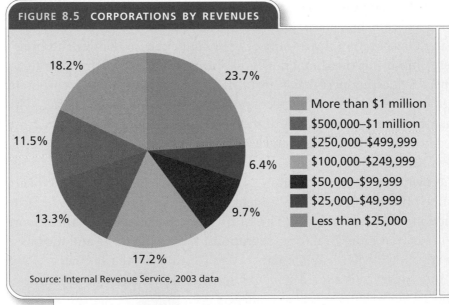

FIGURE 8.5 CORPORATIONS BY REVENUES

- 23.7%
- 18.2%
- 11.5%
- 13.3%
- 17.2%
- 9.7%
- 6.4%

Legend:
- More than $1 million
- $500,000–$1 million
- $250,000–$499,999
- $100,000–$249,999
- $50,000–$99,999
- $25,000–$49,999
- Less than $25,000

Most people think of **corporations** as very large companies with factories and offices that occupy great expanses of land. Actually, more than a third of all corporations in the United States take in less than $100,000 in revenues each year.

Source: Internal Revenue Service, 2003 data

ANALYZE GRAPHS

1. What percentage of corporations made more than $250,000 in sales?
2. Compare Figure 8.5 with Figure 8.1 on p. 229 and Figure 8.2 on p. 234. According to the graphs, which type of business has the highest percentage of firms that earn over $1 million in revenues each year?

ADVANTAGES Corporations

Frank and Shirley had operated F & S as a partnership for several years. They decided to incorporate to gain the advantages of the corporate business structure.

Access to Resources Frank and Shirley have ideas to expand their business, but implementing the ideas may require more money than profits from the business will provide. As a corporation, they have better opportunities for obtaining additional money. Besides borrowing from banks, F & S can raise money by selling more stock or by issuing bonds. This greater access to funds leads to greater potential for growth.

Professional Managers Frank and Shirley are involved in the running of F & S Publishing, Inc. Frank serves as chief executive officer (CEO), while Shirley is chief operations officer (COO). However, they decided to hire managers with strong backgrounds in finance and sales as company treasurer and vice-president for sales. Having professionals in charge of financial and sales matters will probably lead to higher profits.

Limited Liability Because of limited liability, F & S Publishing, Inc., alone is liable for any debts or losses it incurs. Frank, Shirley, and F & S stockholders are liable only for the money they paid for their stock. The board of directors and officers of the corporation, too, are protected from liability.

"Our investors' enthusiasm was gratifying... first time I've ever seen a mosh pit at a stockholders' meeting!"

Source: www.CartoonStock.com

Unlimited Life If any of the owners—the stockholders—of F & S dies or decides to end his or her relationship with the company, the business would continue to operate as before. This even applies to Frank and Shirley. If either or both of them move on to another business, F & S Publishing, Inc., can continue without them for as long as it is a viable business.

DISADVANTAGES Corporations

Frank and Shirley discovered some of the disadvantages to incorporating when they first began the process. They learned about other disadvantages of corporations as they ran their business.

Start-Up Cost and Effort When they first started, Frank and Shirley set up their business as a partnership. Compared to setting up the partnership, Frank and Shirley found the process of setting up a corporation more time-consuming, difficult, and expensive. The paperwork they had to prepare and file with the state government was extensive, and they had to hire a law firm to help with this task.

Heavy Regulation As a public company, F & S Publishing, Inc., must prepare annual reports for the Securities and Exchange Commission (SEC), the government agency

FIGURE 8.6 Business Organizations: Advantages and Disadvantages

Type of Organization	Advantages	Disadvantages
Sole Proprietorship	• Easy to start up, close down • Sole proprietor has satisfaction of running business his or her own way • Few regulations • Sole proprietor keeps all the profits	• Limited funds • Limited life • Unlimited liability
Partnership	• Easy to start up, close down • Few regulations • Greater access to funds • Partners share in decision making • Partners may bring complementary skills to the business	• Unlimited liability • Shared decision making may create conflict among partners • Limited life
Corporation	• Greatest access to funds • Business run by professionals • Limited liability • Unlimited life	• Difficult to start up • More regulations • Double taxation • Owners may have less control of running the business

ANALYZE TABLES

All three forms of business organizations have distinct advantages and disadvantages.
If you were starting a business, which form of business organization would you choose? Why?

that oversees the sale of stocks. It also has to prepare and issue quarterly financial reports for stockholders. Further, the company must hold yearly meetings for its stockholders. All of these regulations help ensure that corporations are run for the benefit of the shareholders. Private companies are subject to fewer regulations related to their ownership.

Double Taxation Frank and Shirley experience an effect known as double taxation. As officers of the company, they are well aware of the taxes on profits that the corporation must pay. As stockholders, they know that their dividend income, paid out of the company profits, is also taxed. Some small corporations qualify for S corporation status, a tax status which avoids double taxation.

Loss of Control Frank and Shirley, as founders, owners, and directors, expect to have a major voice in deciding the direction that F & S Publishing, Inc., will take. However, they experienced some loss of control when the rest of the board of directors voted against them and brought in a new sales manager.

APPLICATION Evaluating Economic Decisions

B. F & S was successful as a partnership. What will Frank and Shirley gain by making their company a corporation?

Business Consolidation

KEY CONCEPTS

You've probably seen news stories about them—business consolidations that merge, or combine, several large companies into one mega-company. These consolidations take place for several possible reasons. These include increasing efficiency, gaining a new identity as a business or losing an old one, keeping rivals out of the marketplace, and diversifying the product line.

There are two main kinds of mergers (see Figure 8.7). A **horizontal merger** describes the joining of companies that offer the same or similar products or services. A **vertical merger** describes the combining of companies involved in different steps of production or marketing of a product or service. An alternative to the two main types is a **conglomerate**, which results from a merger of companies that produce unrelated goods or services. Through growth, consolidations, and other means, an enterprise can grow so big that it becomes a **multinational corporation**, a large corporation with branches in several countries.

QUICK REFERENCE

A **horizontal merger** is the combining of two or more companies that produce the same product or similar products.

A **vertical merger** is the combining of companies involved in different steps of producing or marketing a product.

A **conglomerate** is a business composed of several companies, each one producing unrelated goods or services.

A **multinational corporation** is a large corporation with branches in several countries.

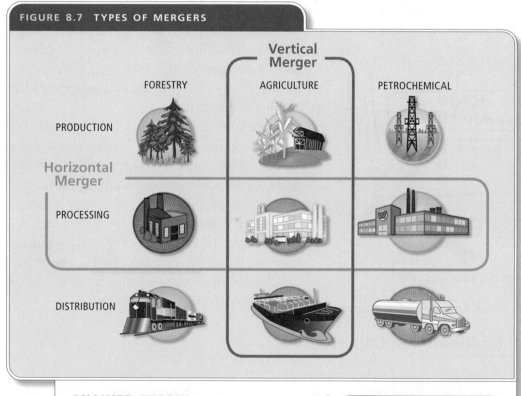

FIGURE 8.7 TYPES OF MERGERS

ANALYZE CHARTS
What kind of mergers took place in each of the following situations?

1. In 1999, Ford Motor Co. purchased Swedish-based car manufacturer Volvo.

2. In 1989, Japanese electronics giant Sony purchased Columbia Pictures Entertainment.

Animated Economics

Use an interactive merger chart at **ClassZone.com**

Mergers

An example of a horizontal merger is the one between Reebok and Adidas in 2005. At the time, they were the second- and third-biggest makers of sports shoes. The subtitle of an article about the merger summed up the potential benefits of all mergers: "Adidas-Reebok merger could trim costs for companies and maybe even some dollars for consumers." The two companies planned to cut production and distribution costs by combining their operations. This, they hoped, would improve their ability to compete against the largest sport-shoe maker, Nike. More efficient production usually leads to lower prices, which would draw consumers away from Nike.

An example of a vertical merger took place in the late 1990s during a period when the oil and gas industry was undergoing major consolidations. Shell Oil, which owned more refineries, joined with Texaco, which owned more gas stations. This type of merger is vertical, since companies involved in different steps of production (refining) or distribution (getting gasoline to customers) combined.

Conglomerates

Another kind of business consolidation, the conglomerate, is formed when two or more companies in different industries come together. In theory, the advantage of this form of consolidation is that, with diversified businesses, the parent company is protected from isolated economic pressures, such as changing demand for a specific product. In practice, it can be difficult to manage companies in unrelated industries.

"I've come up with our new logo, JB."

Source: www.CartoonStock.com

Conglomerates were popular during the 1960s. One conglomerate of the 1960s was Gulf and Western, which included companies in such diverse fields as communications, clothing, mining, and agricultural products. As with many other conglomerates formed in the 1960s, however, Gulf and Western did not produce the desired financial gains. Gulf and Western sold all its companies but the entertainment and publishing endeavors and became known as Viacom.

Multinational Corporations

When you use Google to do an Internet search, you are using the services of a multinational corporation, a large corporation with branches in several countries. Google's headquarters are in Mountain View, California, but it has branch offices in many other countries. Coca-Cola, McDonald's, Nike, and Sony are all examples of multinational, or transnational, corporations.

Multinational corporations like Google are a major force in globalization, commerce conducted without regard to national boundaries. Multinational corporations have many beneficial effects. They provide new jobs, goods, and services around the world and spread technological advances. When such companies open businesses in poorer countries, the jobs and the tax revenues help raise the standard of living.

General Electric: Multinational Corporation

The operations of General Electric (GE), one of the world's largest multinational corporations, span the globe. While its headquarters are located in the United States, GE has manufacturing and production centers located in countries far and near. To supply these centers, GE purchases raw materials from all over the world. Further, the corporation has sales centers on six of the seven continents.

GE is both a multinational and a conglomerate, offering a wide range of services and products. The diagram below portrays GE's major businesses and the units that make up these businesses. GE owns many companies that you know. For example, GE owns NBC Universal, which is made up of the NBC television network, Universal Pictures, and many related businesses. GE's Consumer & Industrial business manufactures such common products as refrigerators, ovens, and light bulbs. But many parts of GE are less well-known because they provide services and products for businesses and governments.

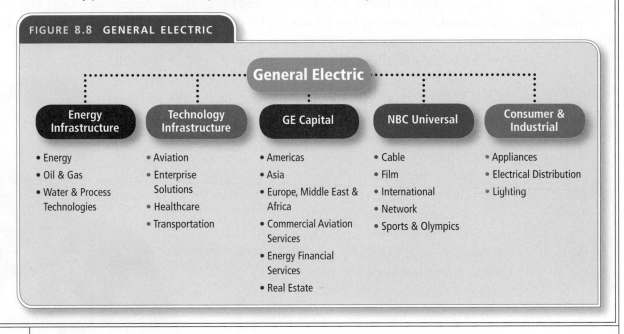

FIGURE 8.8 GENERAL ELECTRIC

General Electric

Energy Infrastructure	Technology Infrastructure	GE Capital	NBC Universal	Consumer & Industrial
• Energy	• Aviation	• Americas	• Cable	• Appliances
• Oil & Gas	• Enterprise Solutions	• Asia	• Film	• Electrical Distribution
• Water & Process Technologies	• Healthcare	• Europe, Middle East & Africa	• International	• Lighting
	• Transportation	• Commercial Aviation Services	• Network	
		• Energy Financial Services	• Sports & Olympics	
		• Real Estate		

CONNECTING ACROSS THE GLOBE

1. **Applying Economic Information** What characteristics of General Electric define it as "multinational"?

2. **Analyzing Charts** General Electric operates in a wide range of industries. Name some industries in which it does not participate. Make sure to check your answer against the chart.

However, multinational corporations can also create problems. Some build factories that emit harmful waste products in countries with lax government regulation. Others operate factories where workers toil for long hours in unsafe working conditions. You will learn more about the impact of multinationals on the world economy in Chapter 17.

APPLICATION Applying Economic Concepts

C. Make up an imaginary conglomerate based on three real companies.

Bill Gates: Entrepreneur and Corporate Leader

Economics Update

Find an update on Bill Gates and Microsoft at **ClassZone.com**

A reporter once asked multibillionaire Bill Gates, founder of Microsoft Corporation, if he thought there was a larger meaning in the universe. Gates joked, "It's possible ... that the universe exists only for me. If so, it's sure going well for me, I must admit." From a small beginning, Bill Gates created the world's largest software company. Microsoft employs more than 95,000 people in more than 100 countries.

Microsoft and Beyond

From an early age, Gates was fascinated with computers and software. He developed software for his high school to schedule classes and for his hometown of Seattle to monitor traffic. At Harvard, he and his friend Paul Allen developed the BASIC language for personal computers. In 1975, during his third year, Gates left college to form a business with Allen to supply BASIC programming for an early brand of personal computers. Gates and Allen called their company Micro-soft (later changed to Microsoft). "I think my most important work was the early work," Gates said in 2005, "conceiving of the idea of the PC and how important that would be, and the role software would play. ..."

Microsoft incorporated in 1981. That same year, it struck a deal to provide the operating system for IBM personal computers, which gave Microsoft a dominant position in the software industry. In 1985, it released what would become the world's most popular operating system, Microsoft Windows. Initially, Microsoft focused on corporate computing. With the release of Windows 95, however, it turned to the consumer market.

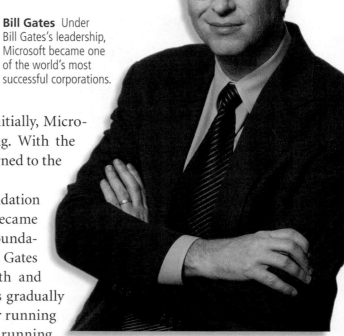

Bill Gates Under Bill Gates's leadership, Microsoft became one of the world's most successful corporations.

In 1994, Gates established a foundation for charitable giving that quickly became one of the largest in the world. The foundation, now called the Bill and Melinda Gates Foundation, focuses on global health and education. From 2006 to 2008, Gates gradually shifted most of his responsibilities for running Microsoft to other executives. Now, running the foundation is his main employment.

APPLICATION Categorizing Economic Information

D. Create a timeline showing the development of Microsoft from its founding to the launch of Windows 95.

SECTION 3 Assessment

Online Quiz
ClassZone.com

REVIEWING KEY CONCEPTS

1. Explain the relationship between the terms in each of these groups.

   a. *stock*   **b.** *public company*   **c.** *merger*
       bond   *private company*   *conglomerate*

2. What are the main advantages of a corporation?

3. What are the main disadvantages of a corporation?

4. How do corporations raise money?

5. What is a multinational corporation?

6. **Using Your Notes** What is the difference between a vertical merger and a horizontal merger? Refer to your completed cluster diagram.

   Use the Graphic Organizer at **Interactive Review @ ClassZone.com**

Characteristics — Advantages — Corporations

CRITICAL THINKING

7. **Analyzing Cause and Effect** Review the table below. If the two largest bottled water manufacturers consolidated in a horizontal merger, what might the effect be on competition?

Company	Annual Sales (in millions of dollars)	Percent of Market
Nature's Springs	1,000	25
Well Water, Inc.	600	15
Best Taste	400	10
Empyrean Isles	400	10
No-Tap Water	200	5

8. **Writing About Economics** In what ways might a vertical merger in the oil industry influence gas prices?

9. **Explaining an Economic Concept** What are the benefits of combining several companies to form a conglomerate? Name an example of a conglomerate.

10. **Challenge** So far in this chapter, you have learned about business enterprises that seek profits. In Section 4, you will learn about nonprofit organizations. How do you think the structure of such organizations might differ from the structure of profit-seeking organizations?

ECONOMICS IN PRACTICE

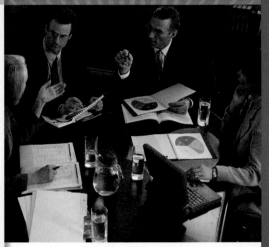

Analyzing Data
When companies decide to merge, they must carefully evaluate how to combine their operations.

Will This Merger Work? Leviathan Motion Pictures wants to purchase Pipsqueak Computer Games.

	Leviathan	Pipsqueak
Head of Company	Ivana Getrich, age 60	Bob L. Head, age 30
Board of Directors	15 business executives	Bob and a couple of his buddies
Publicly Owned Shares	200,000,000	250,000
Market Capitalization	$5,000,000,000	$250,000,000
2008 Sales	$1,000,000,000	$10,000,000
Production Studios	4 in California, 1 in New York	1 in Austin
Employees	15,000 worldwide	150 in Austin

Review the table and imagine what would happen if the companies merge. Write a paragraph describing the challenges and the benefits.

Challenge If you were Bob, would you retire after selling Pipsqueak, or would you want to continue running the company? Explain your answer.

Types of Business Organizations 247

Franchises, Co-ops, and Nonprofits

OBJECTIVES	KEY TERMS	TAKING NOTES
In Section 4, you will • explain how franchises function • identify the characteristics and purpose of cooperatives • describe the types and purposes of nonprofit organizations	franchise, *p. 248* franchisee, *p. 248* cooperative, *p. 250* nonprofit organization, *p. 250*	As you read Section 4, complete a summary chart with information on specialized organizations. Use the Graphic Organizer at **Interactive Review @ ClassZone.com**

Franchises	Co-ops	Nonprofits

Franchises

QUICK REFERENCE

A **franchise** is a business that licenses the right to sell its products in a particular area.

A **franchisee** is a semi-independent business that buys the right to run a franchise.

KEY CONCEPTS

A **franchise** is a business made up of semi-independent businesses that all offer the same products or services. Each **franchisee**, as the individual businesses are known, pays a fee to the parent company in return for the right to sell the company's products or services in a particular area. Fast-food restaurants are the most common franchised business. However, this kind of business organization is also found in many other industries, including hotels, rental cars, and car service.

EXAMPLE An Almost Independent Business

The Mango Grove Juice and Nut Bar in the city center provides an illustration of how a franchise works. Tim, who runs the Mango Grove, had worked as assistant manager at a local restaurant for several years. He really wanted to run his own business, but he didn't think he had the experience or the funds to go it alone. On trips to other cities, he had been impressed by the popularity of the Mango Grove Juice and Nut Bar, an organic juice and sandwich restaurant. So he looked into becoming a franchisee of that business in his home city.

FIGURE 8.9 World's Leading Franchises

Corporation	Franchisees
1. McDonald's	30,300
2. Yum! Brands (KFC, Taco Bell, etc.)	29,300
3. 7-Eleven	28,200
4. Cendent (Howard Johnson, Avis, etc.)	24,600
5. Subway	21,000

Source: International Franchise Association, 2004 data

FRANCHISES

Which franchise would you like to run?

Hundreds of different businesses operate as franchises. Fast-food restaurants and coffee bars are among the most common. Which type of franchise would you like to run? Why?

ADVANTAGES **Franchises**

Becoming a franchisee of Mango Grove Juice and Nut Bar appealed to Tim for several reasons. First, he would have a level of independence he did not have in his job at the restaurant. Second, the franchiser, Mango Grove Fruit and Nut Bar, would provide good training in running the business, since his success affected their own. They would also provide proven products—their famous mango smoothie mixes and nut bread for sandwiches—as well as other materials, such as the décor common to all the Mango Grove juice bars, at a relatively low cost. Further, the franchiser would pay for national or regional advertising that would bring in customers.

DISADVANTAGES **Franchises**

Tim also thought through the disadvantages. He would have to invest most of the money he had saved, with no assurance of success in the business. He would also have to share some of the profits with the franchiser. Further, he would not have control over some aspects of the business. For example, he would have to meet the franchiser's operating rules, such as buying materials only from the franchiser and limiting the products he offered to those from the franchiser.

After considerable thought, Tim decided to apply to become a franchisee. He was accepted, and before long his business became a success. In time, a number of other Mango Grove bars opened in other parts of the city. Since both the franchiser and franchisees had the same incentive—financial reward if the business was successful—they worked well together to make the juice bars succeed.

APPLICATION **Evaluating Economic Decisions**

A. What advantage does the franchiser have over a business that owns and operates all of its own shops?

Cooperatives and Nonprofits

KEY CONCEPTS

The primary purpose of most businesses is to earn money for the owners—in other words, to make a profit. But not all businesses exist solely to make a profit. A **cooperative** is a type of business operated for the shared benefit of the owners, who are also its customers. A **nonprofit organization** is an institution that acts like a business organization, but its purpose is usually to benefit society, not to make a profit.

A Business Organization for Its Members

When people who need the same goods or services band together and act as a business, they can offer low prices by reducing or eliminating profit. Such organizations are called cooperatives, or co-ops. There are three basic types of cooperatives: consumer, service, and producer.

Consumer Consumer, or purchasing, co-ops can be small organizations, like an organic food cooperative, or they can be giant warehouse clubs. Consumer co-ops require some kind of membership payment, either in the form of labor (keeping the books or packaging orders) or monetary fees. They keep prices low by purchasing goods in large volumes at a discount price.

Service Service co-ops are business organizations, such as credit unions, that offer their members a service. Employers often form service cooperatives to reduce the cost of buying health insurance for their employees.

Producer Producer cooperatives are mainly owned and operated by the producers of agricultural products. They join together to ensure cheaper, more efficient processing or better marketing of their products.

A Purpose Other Than Profit

There are several different types of nonprofits. Some, like the American Red Cross, have the purpose of benefiting society. They provide their goods or services for free or for a minimal fee. Other nonprofits, like the American Bar Association, are professional organizations. Such organizations exist to promote the common interests of their members. Business associations, trade associations, labor unions, and museums are all examples of organizations pursuing goals other than profits.

The structure of a nonprofit resembles that of a corporation. A nonprofit must receive a government charter, for example, and has unlimited life. Unlike a corporation, however, many nonprofit organizations are not required to pay taxes because they do not generate profits and they serve society. Nonprofits raise most of their money from donations, grants, or membership fees. Some nonprofits sell products or services, but only as a way of raising funds to support their mission.

APPLICATION Making Inferences

B. The National Association of Home Builders promotes the interests of construction companies. Habitat for Humanity builds homes for the disadvantaged. Which of these nonprofits is the government more likely to excuse from paying taxes? Why?

REVIEWING KEY CONCEPTS

1. Give an example of each of the following terms.

   a. *franchise*   **b.** *cooperative*   **c.** *nonprofit organization*

2. What are the main advantages of a franchise?

3. What are the main disadvantages of a franchise?

4. How do consumer and service cooperatives save their members money?

5. What are some purposes of nonprofit organizations?

6. **Using Your Notes** What are the chief distinctions among franchises, cooperatives, and nonprofits? Refer to your completed summary chart.

   Use the Graphic Organizer at **Interactive Review @ ClassZone.com**

Franchises	Co-ops	Nonprofits

CRITICAL THINKING

7. **Explaining an Economic Concept** Explain how franchisees share the risk of the business venture with the franchiser.

8. **Making Inferences and Drawing Conclusions** How do nonprofits get the money needed to pay the people who work for them and to provide services?

9. **Evaluating Economic Decisions** You're shopping for a new camera. You could buy it from a specialty camera store that offers expert advice or from a discount retail store that carries hundreds of other products. Or you could join a camera club that offers a buying cooperative. What are the advantages and disadvantages of each option?

10. **Challenge** Helping society can be big business. The largest nonprofits generate annual revenues in the billions of dollars. Even small nonprofit organizations can make as much money as many for-profit businesses. Nonprofits employ professional managers, accountants, and marketers, just as any other business would. Should the chief executive officer (CEO) of a nonprofit with $500 million in annual revenue be paid the same salary as the CEO of a for-profit company with the same amount of revenue? Explain your answer.

ECONOMICS IN PRACTICE

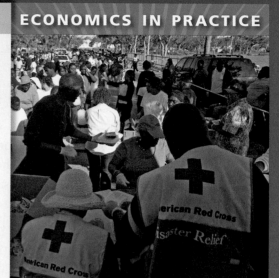

Identifying Business Organizations
Franchises, co-ops, and nonprofits have distinctive features.

What Kind of Organization?
Review the following descriptions of business organizations. Decide what kind of business organization fits each description. Remember that there are three different types of cooperatives.

- Several companies in your city join together to get a better deal on the health insurance they offer to their workers.

- Dan pays a fee for the right to sell Soft Freeze ice cream. Soft Freeze provides all the equipment Dan needs.

- Rachel and Serafina join an association that offers relatively cheap organic products. In return, they pay a small monthly membership fee.

- The Portswood Road Church Club provides a free food service for the poor of the neighborhood.

Challenge Imagine a cooperative you and your friends might form. Describe how it would operate and how it would save you money.

Apple: The Evolution of One Company

Background Steve Jobs and Steve Wozniak joined forces when they were students. Together, they created a personal computer, named it Apple, and in 1976 started a company with the same name. In the years that followed, their company attained worldwide prominence. While the success story of Jobs and Wozniak often sounds like a fairy tale, the evolution of the company was not without its ups and downs. But by 2005, Apple had annual revenues of nearly $14 billion.

What's the issue? How does a company evolve from an idea into a billion-dollar enterprise? Study these sources to discover the factors behind the success of Apple Inc.

A. Online Biography

This article describes how two young men with an interest in computers created the basis for Apple Inc.

Two American Entrepreneurs Start Out in a Garage

Young inventors build their first of many computers.

When the two first met, Wozniak (born 1950) was 18, Jobs (born 1955) only 13. The pair put their electronics and inventing talents to work making unusual devices, and a few years later purchased a $25 microprocessor with the intention of building a computer. Although this first computer was crude and came without memory, a power supply or even a keyboard, it was very reliable. Jobs and Wozniak decided on a name that would convey the simplicity of the product's design and use: the Apple.

Jobs had a passionate belief in bringing computer technology to everyone. So in 1976, Jobs and Wozniak started a company to build and distribute their invention. In true American-dream fashion, their company began in a garage.

To finance their venture, Jobs sold his Volkswagen van and Wozniak sold his programmable calculator to raise $1,300. Weeks later, Jobs secured the company's first sale: 50 Apple I computers at [the retail price of] $666 each.

Source: **Inventor of the Week Archive, MIT**

Steve Wozniak (left) and Steve Jobs (right) founded Apple Computer in 1976.

Thinking Economically According to the document, why were Jobs and Wozniak able to succeed in starting their own company?

In this interview, Evelyn Richards, who covered computers for *Mercury News* in the 1980s, describes Apple's innovative approach to introducing Macintosh, the company's new personal computer.

1984–Apple Launches Macintosh

Marketing plays key role in product's success.

They [Apple] were really more attuned to magazines much more than other tech companies, because magazines can reach a mass market. . . . Steve Jobs got on the cover of *Time* right around then.

The press kit was all really well-packaged. There was the press release for the non-techie people that just talked about how wonderful Macintosh was and how it was going to change the world. Then there were techier press releases, where they talked about the RAM, or the keyboard, or other things. . . .

It was really easily digestible, and easy to use by the press. Lots of great photos, professionally done. Now all that is standard.

Source: **Stanford Library; Interview with Evelyn Richards, 22 June 2000**

Thinking Economically How did Apple's marketing of Macintosh contribute to its success?

This timeline shows some of the highlights and challenges that Apple Inc. has experienced.

Highlights in Apple Company History

1976–Jobs and Wozniak incorporate Apple Computer
1977–Apple II computer, the first PC with color graphics, introduced
1980–Apple becomes public company, offering 4.6 million shares for sale
1984–Commercial during Super Bowl XVIII introduces the first Macintosh
1985–Both Jobs and Wozniak leave Apple
1988–Apple sues Microsoft when Windows begins using features similar to those developed by Apple
1989–First portable Macintosh introduced
1993–Debut of Newton, an early personal digital assistant
1995–Apple loses its case against Microsoft
1997–Jobs returns to Apple as chief executive officer
1998–Newton discontinued
2001–Portable digital music player iPod introduced
2003–Safari browser introduced; iTunes Music Store debuts
2006–Apple computers begin using Intel Core Duo processors

Sources: **Macworld March 30, 2006; Apple Inc.**

Thinking Economically How might Apple's history have been different if it had become a partnership instead of a corporation? Explain your answer.

THINKING ECONOMICALLY **Synthesizing**

1. Based on information in the documents, how would you describe the evolution of Apple Inc.?

2. How did Apple's advertising and marketing affect its success or failure? Use examples from the documents in your answer.

3. What single overriding concern has defined the evolution of Apple and determined its success? Use information from the documents to support your answer.

Interactive Review

Review this chapter using interactive
activities at **ClassZone.com**
- Online Summary
- Quizzes
- Vocabulary Flip Cards
- Graphic Organizers
- Review and Study Notes

 Online Summary

Complete the following activity either on your
own paper or online at **ClassZone.com**

**Choose the key concept that best completes
the sentence. Not all key concepts will be used.**

bond	limited partnership
conglomerate	merger
cooperative	multinational corporation
corporation	nonprofit organization
dividend	partnership
franchise	regulation
general partnership	sole proprietorship
horizontal merger	stock
limited liability	unlimited liability
limited liability partnership	unlimited life
limited life	vertical merger

In a __1__ , the business is owned and managed by
a single person. One key drawback of this is that
the owner has __2__ , putting even personal savings
at risk. A __3__ is a business structure in which two
or more owners share the management of the
business, profits, and full liability. The __4__ and
__5__ provide ways for some partners to risk only
the amount of their investment.

A __6__ is a business that can raise money by
selling __7__ and allows for limited liability of its
owners and __8__ of the enterprise. Two or more
businesses can consolidate through a __9__ . If they
provide the same kinds of goods or services,
their consolidation is known as a __10__ . When
a business has branches in other countries, it is
known as a __11__ .

If someone pays for the right to sell a
company's goods or services in a certain area,
that person is operating a __12__ . A business whose
owners are also its customers is known as a __13__ .
A __14__ is structured like a business but pursues
goals other than profits.

CHAPTER 8 Assessment

REVIEWING KEY CONCEPTS

Sole Proprietorships (pp. 226–231)

1. What are the advantages of a sole proprietorship?

2. What are the disadvantages?

Forms of Partnerships (pp. 232–237)

3. What are three different kinds of partnerships, and
how do they differ?

4. What are the advantages and disadvantages of a
partnership?

**Corporations, Mergers, and Multinationals
(pp. 238–247)**

5. What are the advantages and disadvantages of
a corporation?

6. In what three ways can companies consolidate?

Franchises, Co-ops, and Nonprofits (pp. 248–253)

7. How is a franchise "an almost independent"
business?

8. What is the difference between a cooperative and a
nonprofit organization?

APPLYING ECONOMIC CONCEPTS

9. What might be the outcome of raising the fees
and requiring more paperwork in order to start
a corporation? What would happen if fees were
lowered and the application process was simplified?

10. Do you think the number of multinationals will
continue to increase? Give reasons for your
answer.

11. As you have read, sometimes merged companies
are not more efficient than they were separately.
In some cases, the chief executive officers (CEOs)
who arranged the deal make an enormous
amount of money from the merger even though
the deal itself does not improve profits. What
incentives might a board of directors offer to
CEOs to make sure they make deals that pay off in
profits?

Use the following graph showing the number of mergers in the years from 1970 to 2000 to answer questions 12–14.

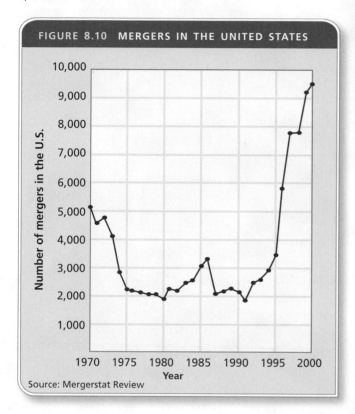

FIGURE 8.10   MERGERS IN THE UNITED STATES

Number of mergers in the U.S.

Year

Source: Mergerstat Review

Design a New Business Structure

Each business structure you have read about in this chapter has both advantages and disadvantages. Follow the steps below to design a new business structure that attempts to avoid the worst disadvantages and to capitalize on the most important advantages of the other structures. You can imagine changing laws to accommodate your new structure, but try to make sure your creation makes economic sense.

Step 1. Break into small groups. In your group, draw up a list of advantages and disadvantages of all the business structures. The table on page 242 will help you begin the list.

Step 2. Discuss how the advantages and disadvantages would affect the ability of a business to earn a profit. Choose the three advantages and three disadvantages that your group feels have the most impact.

Step 3. Brainstorm possible ways to avoid the disadvantages and make the most of the advantages. Remember that in brainstorming any idea is allowed, no matter how crazy or simple it might sound.

Step 4. Sort through your brainstorming ideas. Use them to develop a new "ideal" business structure.

Step 5. Share your business structure with the rest of the class, and compare your efforts to those of your classmates.

12. **Analyzing Graphs** Which of the following can you determine from the information about mergers in the graph?

   a. how many companies merged in any given year from 1970 to 2000

   b. how many more mergers took place in 2000 than in 1990

   c. how long each of the new companies lasted after the merger

13. **Predicting Economic Trends** Which decade saw the greatest increase in the number of mergers? What probably happened after that decade?

14. **Challenge** The number of mergers can reflect the economic times, which in turn are often affected by national and world events. What events may have contributed to tighter economic times—and therefore a decrease in mergers—in the 1970s?

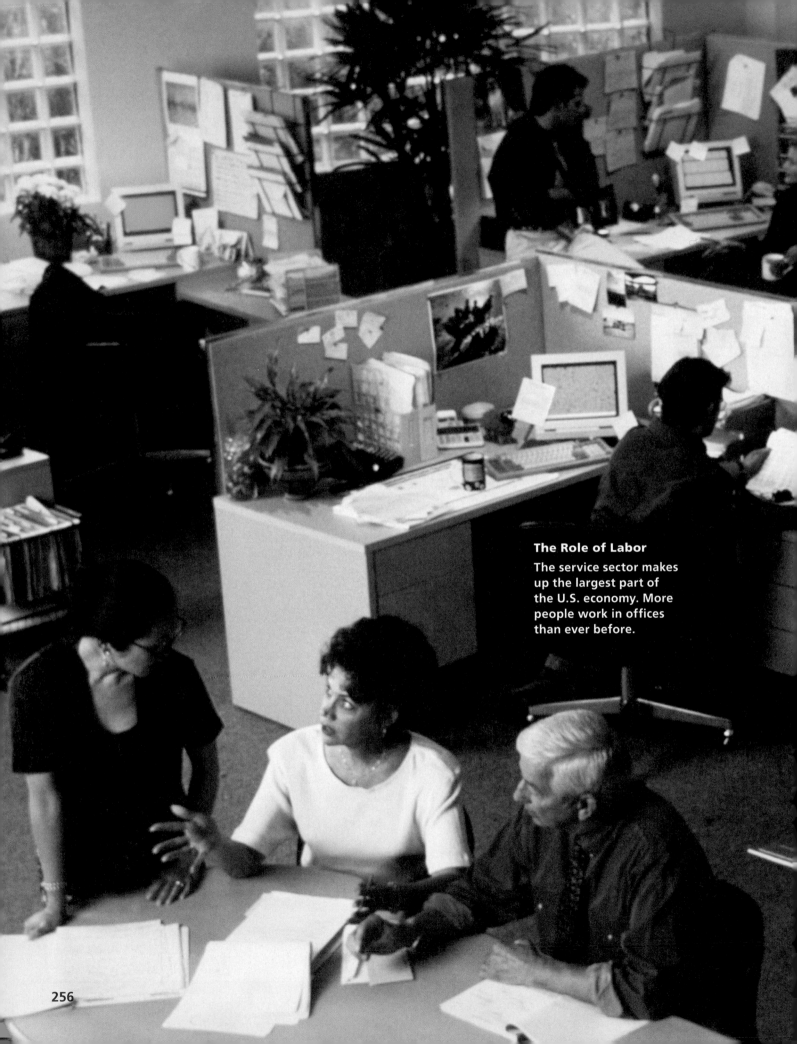

The Role of Labor
The service sector makes up the largest part of the U.S. economy. More people work in offices than ever before.

256

The Role of Labor

CONCEPT REVIEW

Labor productivity is the value of the goods or services a worker can produce in a set amount of time.

CHAPTER 9 KEY CONCEPT

Labor, the human effort used to produce goods and services, is subject to the same forces of demand and supply that govern the rest of the economy.

WHY THE CONCEPT MATTERS

The value of your labor depends on the demand for what you do and the supply of other people able to do the same thing. It's up to you to figure out what you do best and to distinguish yourself from other workers. Maybe what you really want to do will require special training or years of experience. Think of your dream job, and write a plan for how you will get that job. Evaluate the demand for the job and the supply of people capable of performing it.

Online Highlights
More at ClassZone.com

Economics Update
Go to **ECONOMICS UPDATE** for chapter updates and current news on managing change in your worklife. (See Case Study, pp. 282–283.) ▶

Animated Economics
Go to **ANIMATED ECONOMICS** for interactive lessons on the graphs and tables in this chapter.

Interactive ◀◀Review
Go to **INTERACTIVE REVIEW** for concept review and activities.

The world of work is changing. Will you be able to keep pace? See the Case Study on pages 282–283.

How Are Wages Determined?

OBJECTIVES	KEY TERMS	TAKING NOTES
In Section 1, you will • identify what wages are • describe how the interaction of supply and demand determines wages • explain why wage rates differ	wages, *p. 258* equilibrium wage, *p. 258* derived demand, *p. 259* wage rate, *p. 261* human capital, *p. 261* glass ceiling, *p. 262* minimum wage, *p. 262*	As you read Section 1, complete a cluster diagram like the one below to record what you learn about wages. Use the Graphic Organizer at **Interactive Review @ ClassZone.com**

Labor: Demand and Supply

KEY CONCEPTS

QUICK REFERENCE

Wages are payments received in return for work.

Equilibrium wage is the wage at which the quantity of workers demanded equals the quantity of workers supplied; the market price for labor.

Have you ever wondered why working at a fast food restaurant pays so little? This section will help answer that question. In Chapter 1 you learned about the four factors of production: land, labor, capital, and entrepreneurship. Each of those has a price that must be figured into production costs. The price of labor is **wages**, the payments workers receive in return for work.

Wages, just like the other factors of production, are governed by the forces of supply and demand. The interaction of these two economic forces produces an equi-

librium, or balance. An **equilibrium wage** is the wage at which the number of workers needed equals the number of workers available. In other words, an equilibrium wage produces neither a surplus nor a shortage of workers. Let's look at demand and supply separately and see how they affect wages at fast food restaurants.

Demand for Labor

In a competitive labor market, wages reflect a worker's labor productivity—the value of the goods or services a worker produces in a set amount of time. A business hires workers to help it produce goods or provide

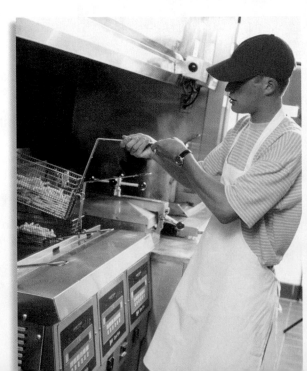

services. A producer's demand for labor is therefore a **derived demand**, a demand for a product or resource because of its contribution to the final product.

Workers with higher productivity tend to earn higher wages. In one hour, a fast food chef might be able to produce $50 worth of food that customers want. An attorney, by contrast, might be able to provide services worth $300 in the same hour's time. Employers, then, are willing to pay attorneys higher wages than fast food chefs.

The demand for labor depends in part on its price. As with anything else, when the price goes down, the quantity demanded goes up; and when the price goes up, the quantity demanded goes down. For example, suppose that fast food chefs are paid $12 per hour. If the wage should fall to $10 per hour, many restaurants would hire additional chefs. On the other hand, if the wage rose to $14 per hour, some restaurants would stop hiring and others would have to lay off some chefs. This is illustrated in Figure 9.1. The demand curve for labor, then, is a downward slope—the lower the price of labor, the greater the quantity of labor employers would demand.

FIGURES 9.1 AND 9.2 DEMAND AND SUPPLY CURVES FOR LABOR

FIGURE 9.1 **DEMAND CURVE**

FIGURE 9.2 **SUPPLY CURVE**

These graphs show demand and supply curves for fast food chefs.

ⓐ The restaurant is willing to hire more chefs if the hourly wage is lower.

ⓑ As the wage increases, so does the number of workers willing to work as fast food chefs.

ANALYZE GRAPHS

1. How many fast food chefs would the restaurant hire at the wage $10 per hour?

2. How many workers would be willing to be fast food chefs at the wage of $10 per hour?

3. What would happen if the restaurant tried to hire chefs at $10 per hour?

Animated Economics

Use interactive demand and supply curves for labor at **ClassZone.com**

Supply of Labor

Now let's consider the situation from the worker's point of view, to see how the supply of labor works. Suppose a new fast food restaurant opens and wants to hire chefs. If it puts an ad in the newspaper for chefs who would be paid $10 per hour, fewer people will respond—and probably none of the chefs currently employed at $12 per hour. Workers who are earning less than $10 per hour in some other kind of job might leave their jobs and become fast food chefs because the wages are higher than their current wages.

Economics Update

Find an update on demand and supply of labor at **ClassZone.com**

But suppose the new restaurant offers fast food chefs $15 per hour. Any worker earning less than that will be interested—including experienced chefs currently employed at $12 per hour. More workers will be willing to work at higher wages than at lower wages. For this reason, the supply curve for labor is upward sloping, as illustrated in Figure 9.2 on page 259.

Equilibrium Wage

You learned in Chapter 6 that the equilibrium price for goods or services is the price at which there is neither a surplus nor a shortage—in other words, the point at which the supply curve and the demand curve intersect. Since wages are the price of labor, they too gravitate toward equilibrium.

For example, fast food restaurants might offer higher wages to attract chefs. Given the upward-sloping supply curve, before long there would be more people wanting to be chefs than there are jobs, resulting in a labor surplus. With so many chefs to choose from, restaurants could lower the wage and still attract workers. If they offered a wage that was too low, however, people would have less incentive to work as fast food chefs. A shortage would eventually result, so restaurants would need to raise the wages to attract more. The downward and upward forces push until an equilibrium wage is reached, as illustrated in Figure 9.3.

FIGURE 9.3 EQUILIBRIUM WAGE

This graph shows how demand and supply interact to determine the **equilibrium wage** for fast food chefs.

a In this case, five workers are demanded and five are available at the wage of $12 per hour. The equilibrium wage for fast food chefs is $12 per hour.

ANALYZE GRAPHS

1. How many fast food chefs would the restaurant hire at the wage of $15 per hour?

2. How many workers would be willing to be fast food chefs if the wage rose to $15 per hour?

3. What would result if the wage rose to $15 per hour?

APPLICATION Applying Economic Concepts

A. Suppose that a new high school opens next to a popular fast food restaurant. Explain what will happen to the derived demand for chefs at the restaurant.

Why Do Wage Rates Differ?

KEY CONCEPTS

Different jobs have different **wage rates**, the rates of pay for specific jobs or work performed. Wage rates are determined by supply and demand, which in turn are influenced by four key factors: (1) **human capital**, which is the knowledge and skills that enable workers to be productive, (2) working conditions, (3) discrimination in the workplace, and (4) government actions.

FACTOR 1 Human Capital

Economists group workers according to the amount of human capital they have. *Unskilled workers,* such as house cleaners and sanitation workers, have a low level of human capital. *Semiskilled workers*—construction and clerical workers, for example—have received some training, so their human capital is higher. *Skilled workers,* such as plumbers and electricians, have made a significant investment in human capital in the form of specialized training. *Professional workers*—doctors, lawyers, and others with intensive specialized training—have the highest human capital.

The demand for skilled and professional workers is high, but the supply of these workers is relatively low. For this reason and because training increases their productivity, highly skilled workers tend to receive higher wages. The prospect of higher wages leads many people to invest in their human capital and enroll in vocational school, specialist training programs, and higher education.

QUICK REFERENCE

Wage rate is the established rate of pay for a specific job or work performed.

Human capital is the knowledge and skills that enable workers to be productive.

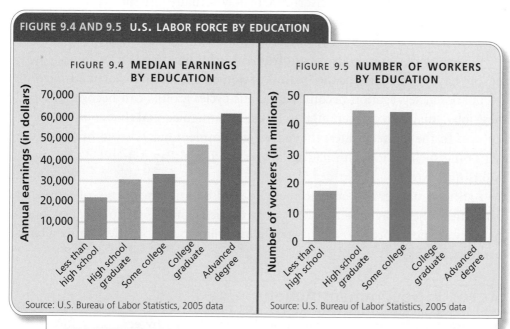

FIGURE 9.4 AND 9.5 U.S. LABOR FORCE BY EDUCATION

FIGURE 9.4 MEDIAN EARNINGS BY EDUCATION

Source: U.S. Bureau of Labor Statistics, 2005 data

FIGURE 9.5 NUMBER OF WORKERS BY EDUCATION

Source: U.S. Bureau of Labor Statistics, 2005 data

ANALYZE GRAPHS

1. In terms of average annual salary, about how much is graduating from high school worth?

2. There are almost as few people without a high school diploma as with an advanced degree. Why doesn't the reduced supply make their salaries as high as the salaries for people with an advanced degree?

Working Conditions
Painters who work at high altitudes receive higher wages.

FACTOR 2 Working Conditions

"It's a tough job, but someone has to do it." That statement is often used humorously by people who have dream jobs, such as vacation planners who get to go on fabulous trips as "research" or taste testers who sample chocolate or other goodies. However, some jobs really are tougher than others. Some jobs, such as washing windows on a skyscraper, are very dangerous. Other jobs can be very unpleasant, such as collecting garbage. Higher wages are often paid to workers in dangerous and unpleasant occupations in order to attract qualified people to those jobs.

While the disadvantages of some jobs may be offset by higher wages, the advantages of other jobs may make up for low wages. These advantages vary widely, depending on the worker. For example, a student who loves movies might take a job as a clerk at a video store. Although the pay is low, the student might get to borrow movies free of charge. Someone tired of a long commute in rush hour traffic might welcome a lower-paying job that is only minutes away from home.

FACTOR 3 Discrimination

Another factor affecting differences in wage rates is discrimination. Wage discrimination may be based on race, ethnicity, gender, or other factors. For example, the average pay of women tends to be lower than that of men doing the same job. Racial prejudices sometimes lead to discrimination in wages. A prejudiced employer might be unwilling to hire a minority candidate except at a lower wage.

However, employers who discriminate may actually lose money. By eliminating qualified candidates because of their gender, ethnic group, or other trait irrelevant to performance, employers may miss out on the best worker for the job.

Wage differences may also result from occupational segregation. Some low-paying jobs have been viewed as the "realm" of women or certain racial or ethnic groups. Occupational segregation becomes a vicious cycle: groups can become trapped in these jobs, unable to earn enough to invest in human capital that could move them upward. In the United States, the federal government has tried to break this cycle by passing such antidiscrimination laws as the Equal Pay Act (1963) and the Civil Rights Act (1964).

Artificial barriers to advancement may also limit the wages of women and minorities. They may have the skills and experience necessary to advance, but find that they are never promoted. The term **glass ceiling** describes these unseen barriers to advancement.

FACTOR 4 Government Actions

In a pure market economy, wages would be set strictly by economic forces. However, in many countries, including the United States, the government steps in when market forces produce results that people disagree with. The **minimum wage**, the lowest wage legally allowed for one hour of work, is one example. As you read in Chapter 6, the minimum wage acts as a price floor designed to boost wages for low-income workers. The forces of supply and demand might set the equilibrium wage

QUICK REFERENCE

Glass ceiling is an artificial barrier to advancement faced by women and minorities.

The **minimum wage** is the legal minimum amount that an employer must pay for one hour of work.

Suppose you are offered two jobs, one that pays $12.50 per hour or another that pays $30,000 per year. In both jobs, you will work 40 hours per week and get two weeks off per year. Assuming both offer the same benefits, which job pays better?

You could either figure out how much you would make in a year at the hourly job or you could convert the annual salary into an hourly wage. In this exercise, we will calculate how much a wage of $12.50 per hour pays for a year's worth of work.

Step 1: Multiply to determine the number of hours worked per year. Assume the job includes two weeks of unpaid vacation.

Example Calculations

Hours per week	×	Weeks per year	=	Total hours per year		40	×	50	=	2,000

Step 2: Then, multiply to find the amount of pay annually.

Total hours per year	×	Hourly wage	=	Annual wages		2,000	×	$12.50	=	$25,000

The job that pays a salary of $30,000 per year pays better than the one that pays a wage of $12.50 per hour.

Comparing Earnings Use the calculations to determine the annual wages of a job that pays $15 per hour for 40 hours per week. What about one that pays $20 per hour but only offers 20 hours of work each week? What other factors do you need to consider when comparing pay between jobs?

for certain jobs so low that no one could reasonably make a living at these jobs. The minimum wage attempts to help the people who hold these jobs to make ends meet. However, businesses point out that they might hire more workers if they were allowed to pay a lower wage.

The first national minimum wage law in the United States was passed in 1933 during the Great Depression. In part, it was intended to raise wages so that workers could consume products and help the economy recover. In 1938, the minimum wage became part of the Fair Labor Standards Act, which included other protections for workers. The U.S. Congress has increased the minimum wage several times, but the increases have not kept up with the general rise in prices. In response, some state and local governments have passed their own laws requiring minimum wages higher than the federal standard.

APPLICATION Applying Economic Concepts

B. Explain how each of the four factors influences wages at fast food restaurants.

Gary Becker: The Importance of Human Capital

FAST FACTS

Gary S. Becker

Born: December 2, 1930, Pottsville, Pennsylvania

Major Accomplishment: Applying economic analysis to social issues

Honors: Nobel Prize in Economics (1992), National Medal of Science (2000), Presidential Medal of Freedom (2007)

Notable Quotation: *"No discussion of human capital can omit the influence of families on the knowledge, skills, values, and habits of their children."*

Gary Becker demonstrated that economic principles could be used to analyze other spheres of life. For example, when he arrived late one day at Columbia University, Becker decided to save time by parking illegally, even though he knew he might get fined. This incident led him to wonder if people committing other crimes also considered the consequences of their decisions rationally. Becker extended an economic way of thinking into new areas, including crime and punishment, family relations, and human competence.

Investing in Yourself

When Gary Becker graduated from high school, he was torn between following a career in mathematics and doing something to help solve social problems. He studied economics at Princeton University and the University of Chicago, and he went on to teach at Chicago and at Columbia University. In 1957, Becker published *The Economics of Discrimination*, which examined the "effects of prejudice on the earnings, employment, and occupations of minorities." However, most economists did not pay much attention, feeling that such a study belonged in the fields of sociology or psychology. Today, though, Becker's approach is widely appreciated and has led economists to explore new areas.

Becker is best known for his contributions to the idea of human capital and for formulating the economic theory that explains differences in wages in terms of investments in human capital. To Becker, human capital is more than education and training: it is all the investments people make in themselves to improve their output, including the development of good work habits and receiving good medical treatment. The more abundant the capital, the more productive the labor. Becker helped to quantify the importance of education and on-the-job training and, by doing so, broadened the reach of economics.

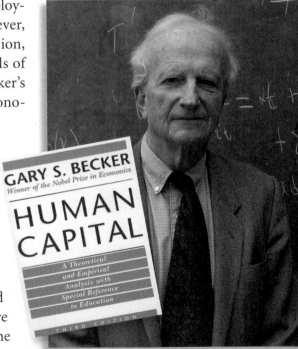

Gary Becker pioneered the use of economic analysis to explain social behavior.

Economics Update

Find an update on Gary Becker at **ClassZone.com**

APPLICATION Conducting Cost-Benefit Analysis

C. Becker debated with himself about whether to park illegally, weighing the possible costs against the advantages. Explain a decision you made using cost-benefit analysis. Is that always the best way to make a decision? Why or why not?

SECTION 1 Assessment

Online Quiz
ClassZone.com

REVIEWING KEY CONCEPTS

1. Explain the relationship between the terms in each of these pairs.

   a. *wages*
      derived demand

   b. *equilibrium wage*
      minimum wage

   c. *wage rate*
      human capital

2. What market forces influence wages?

3. What nonmarket forces influence wages?

4. Why are education and training considered a kind of capital?

5. Why would a star athlete receive wages so much higher than an insurance sales representative?

6. **Using Your Notes** Suppose you are the owner of a video store. Explain how you would decide what to pay your workers, making reference to the terms in your completed cluster diagram.

   Use the Graphic Organizer at **Interactive Review @ ClassZone.com**

CRITICAL THINKING

7. **Analyzing Cause and Effect** If the equilibrium wage for bowling alley managers is $16 per hour, why would a wage of $20 per hour result in a labor surplus? Why would a wage of $12 per hour lead to a labor shortage?

8. **Solving Economic Problems** What economic problem does the minimum wage try to address?

9. **Applying Economic Concepts** Explain why working conditions can either justify higher wages or make up for lower wages.

10. **Making Inferences and Drawing Conclusions** Despite efforts to close the wage gap between men and women, the gap has actually been widening. Using what you have learned in this section, write a paragraph discussing what could be done to close the gap.

11. **Challenge** Gary Becker said that economics "is easy in the sense that there are only a few principles that really guide most economic analysis." Identify the basic principles behind how wages operate.

ECONOMICS IN PRACTICE

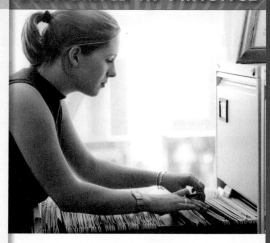

Graphing Equilibrium Wages
Read each job description below. Then make a graph showing a hypothetical equilibrium wage for each job using the same values for both axes in each graph.

Job Description #1	Job Description #2
Structural metal worker for high-rise construction project. Must have at least 2 years of experience.	Filing clerk, small accounting office. No experience necessary, but must have a high school diploma or GED.

Apply Economic Concepts
Using the economic knowledge you gained in this section, briefly explain why each graph appears as it does.

Challenge In many dangerous industries, including mining, safety laws establish standards that protect workers. Explain what effect these laws might have on wages.

Use *SMART Grapher* @ ClassZone.com to complete this activity.

Trends in Today's Labor Market

OBJECTIVES	KEY TERMS	TAKING NOTES
In Section 2, you will • identify the changes that have taken place in the labor force • explain how occupations have changed • explain how the way people work has changed	civilian labor force, *p. 266* outsourcing, *p. 269* insourcing, *p. 269* telecommuting, *p. 270* contingent employment, *p. 270* independent contractor, *p. 270*	As you read Section 2, complete a hierarchy chart like the one below. In each box write the main ideas. Use the Graphic Organizer at **Interactive Review @ ClassZone.com**

A Changing Labor Force

KEY CONCEPTS

The labor market in the United States has changed dramatically since the 1950s, and it continues to change. For example, in the 1950s, many companies hired workers with the expectation that they would stay with the company for most of their working lives. After a lifetime of service, workers could count on company pension plans to help fund their retirement. Today, few workers stay with the same company their entire career, and workers take more responsibility for funding their retirement.

Those are only some of the profound changes that affect the **civilian labor force**, people who are 16 or older who are employed or actively looking for and available to do work. The civilian labor force excludes people in the military, in prison, or in other institutions. In 2005, about 150 million Americans made up the civilian labor force. That figure was up from 126 million workers in 1990 and is expected to rise to almost 165 million workers by 2020.

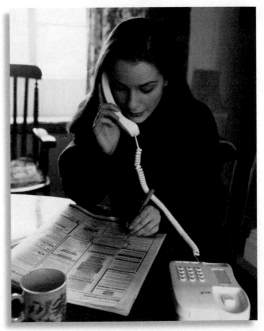

Labor Force
The civilian labor force is composed of people age 16 or older who are working or looking for work.

QUICK REFERENCE

The **civilian labor force** is made up of people age 16 or older who are employed or actively looking for and available to do work.

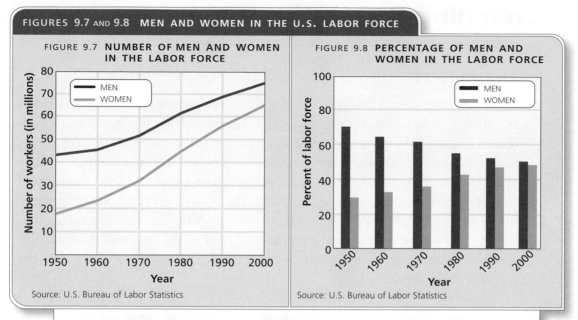

FIGURES 9.7 AND 9.8   MEN AND WOMEN IN THE U.S. LABOR FORCE

FIGURE 9.7 **NUMBER OF MEN AND WOMEN IN THE LABOR FORCE**

Source: U.S. Bureau of Labor Statistics

FIGURE 9.8 **PERCENTAGE OF MEN AND WOMEN IN THE LABOR FORCE**

Source: U.S. Bureau of Labor Statistics

ANALYZE GRAPHS

1. About how many more men were in the labor force than women in 1950? in 2000?
2. What percentage of the labor force did women account for in 1950? in 2000?

Changes in the U.S. Labor Force

To understand some of the changes in the U.S. labor force, consider these two scenes. In the first scene, the year is 1955. A young woman pulls into a gas station, and the attendant fills up her car with gas. Then she picks up her children at school and heads home to get dinner ready in time for her husband's arrival from work. The second scene is set in today's world. A young mother pulls into a gas station, swipes her credit card, and fills up her tank. Her business meeting ran long, and she is late getting to the daycare center. Her husband will pick up dinner for the family on his way home from work.

One obvious change these scenes demonstrate is the addition of many more women to the work force. As shown in Figures 9.7 and 9.8, women have been a significant factor in the growth of the labor market in the United States. Since the 1950s, the kinds of jobs open to women have expanded. As job opportunities have improved, wages for women have risen, and many more women have been drawn into the work force.

The U.S. work force has also become better educated. About 30 percent of people in the labor force have a college degree, and an additional 30 percent of workers have some college credits. In a work force with such a high degree of human capital, productivity and wages are also high compared with many other nations.

Economics Update

Find an update on the U.S. work force at **ClassZone.com**

APPLICATION Evaluating Economic Decisions

A. Explain how rising opportunity costs have led more women into the workplace.

Changing Occupations

Economists group occupations into three economic sectors. The *primary sector* is made up of jobs related directly to natural resources, such as farming, forestry, fishing, and mining. Jobs in the *secondary sector* are related to the production of goods, including the materials and energy needed to produce them. Examples include welders, truck drivers, and construction workers. The *tertiary sector* is made up of service-related jobs in such industries as banking, insurance, retail, education, and communications. As you can see in Figures 9.9 and 9.10, U.S. manufacturing jobs have declined since the 1950s, while service-sector jobs have increased dramatically. All of the ten fastest-growing occupations are service related, most of them in the area of medical services.

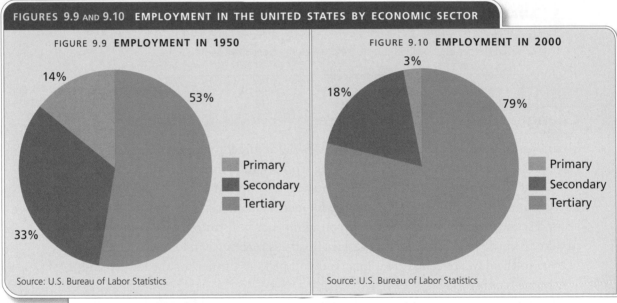

FIGURES 9.9 AND 9.10 EMPLOYMENT IN THE UNITED STATES BY ECONOMIC SECTOR

FIGURE 9.9 EMPLOYMENT IN 1950

14%
53%
33%

Primary
Secondary
Tertiary

Source: U.S. Bureau of Labor Statistics

FIGURE 9.10 EMPLOYMENT IN 2000

3%
18%
79%

Primary
Secondary
Tertiary

Source: U.S. Bureau of Labor Statistics

ANALYZE GRAPHS

1. Which sector grew the most from 1950 to 2000? By how much did it grow?
2. How much of the civilian labor force was employed in the combined primary and secondary sectors in 1950? How much in 2000?

Technology and Change

Think back for a moment to the young mother at the gas station. In the years between 1955 and today, the job of gas station attendant has been mainly replaced by the computerized, credit-card operated gasoline pump. In the same way, ATMs have greatly affected the occupation of bank teller. Technological changes have eliminated or redefined many other jobs in all three sectors.

The personal computer and the Internet have drastically changed the way on-the-job information is stored, transferred, and used. About half of all American workers use a computer on the job. As a result, those occupations that support the

1950s gas station   **2000s gas station**

use of computers—software engineers and network and data communications analysts, for example—have been among the fastest growing in the United States.

More than 80 percent of managers and professionals use a computer at work. However, even in less skilled jobs, more and more workers are using computers. About 20 percent of machine operators, laborers, and farmers use a computer on the job. Basic computer skills have become necessary for many different types of jobs.

Globalization and Jobs

Today's labor market is global. Technology allows companies to employ people not just all over the country, but all over the world. Many companies have sought to cut their costs by **outsourcing**, the practice of contracting with an outside company to provide goods or services.

Most outsourcing by U.S. companies goes to other U.S. companies. For example, many American businesses hire other American firms to handle their accounting. However, the term outsourcing has become connected with the practice of moving jobs from the United States to foreign countries where wages are lower. As this happens more frequently, it would seem that their American operations would lose jobs. But many companies actually add more jobs in the United States than they outsource abroad, just in different parts of their businesses. In 2004, IBM decided to send about 3,000 jobs overseas. But at the same time, it created about 4,500 jobs in the United States.

The American economy has also benefited from **insourcing**, the practice of foreign companies establishing operations in, and therefore bringing jobs to, the United States. Both outsourcing and insourcing are tied to the trends toward more service-related jobs and more technology-related work.

> **QUICK REFERENCE**
>
> **Outsourcing** is the practice of contracting with an outside company, often in a foreign country, to provide goods or services.
>
> **Insourcing** is the practice of foreign companies establishing operations in, and therefore bringing jobs to, the United States.

APPLICATION Predicting Economic Trends

B. Think of an example of an occupation that is likely to be eliminated or substantially redefined as a result of technology.

Changes in the Way People Work

KEY CONCEPTS

The way people work has been transformed by technology. In the past, many workers needed to physically commute to and from an office in order to accomplish their work. The Internet and laptop computers have allowed some of these workers to engage in **telecommuting**, the practice of doing office work in a location other than the traditional office.

But the job market has also changed. In the past, companies offered most workers permanent positions. Today, companies offer fewer permanent positions and more **contingent employment**, work that is temporary or part-time. Similarly, more people work as **independent contractors**, selling their services to businesses on a contract basis. People used to enter a field and stay in more or less the same line of work for most of their work life. Now, most people will change careers several times as the world of work continues to evolve.

Working at the Office from Home

Many telecommuters enjoy the reduced stress, flexibility in work time, and increased free time they have by avoiding a commute to work. Employers benefit from an expanded labor pool, increased productivity, and lower real estate costs. Society benefits, too, from fewer drivers on crowded freeways and lower pollution.

However, there are also costs. People who work at home may feel that their work too often spills over into their personal time. Some miss the social life of the office and the chance to network. Some at-home workers also fear that on-site workers might be more likely to get promoted. Still, experts estimate that the number of telecommuting workers grew by about 20 percent each year from 2000 to 2005.

YOUR ECONOMIC CHOICES

TELECOMMUTING

Where would you want to work?

Technology allows people to work in many different places. Alternative work places have different benefits—and drawbacks—than the traditional office.

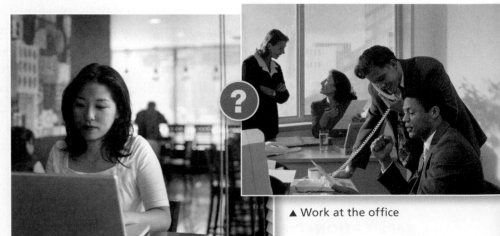

▲ Work at the office

▲ Work at the coffee shop

Alternatives to Permanent Employment

Through much of the 1900s, U.S. companies would hire workers for permanent, full-time jobs. Employees would work 40 hours per week in exchange for both wages and benefits. In the 1990s, companies began to hire fewer full-time employees and more contingent employees and contract workers. Contingent workers, sometimes called temps, make up over 5 percent of the total work force. Independent contractors make up over 7 percent of the work force.

Hiring contingent employees and contract workers makes it easier for businesses to adjust their work force to suit production demands. Discharging temporary workers is easier and less costly than discharging permanent employees. Since most temporary workers do not receive benefits, labor costs are also lower.

Most contingent workers would prefer to have the steady income and benefits that come with permanent, full-time employment. But many independent contractors prefer the flexibility of being their own boss to working in a permanent position. They are willing to take the risk of not having enough work to support themselves, and they find alternative ways to pay for health insurance and retirement. Businesses sometimes offer permanent positions to contingent and contract workers who have done a good job.

Changing Careers More Often

As technology has advanced, jobs have changed, too. Much of the work done today in the United States and other advanced countries did not exist 100 years ago. Some of the work did not exist even ten years ago. With every new technology, new types of jobs are created. But as technology advances, many older professions become less in demand or even obsolete. To fill the new jobs, workers must learn and adapt to the new technologies. Someone who started out as a radio repair technician might need to learn how to work with cellular phone technology.

In a similar way, the economy changes more quickly than it did in the past. Companies have become more flexible, changing their business plans constantly to maximize profits. Globalization allows companies to move jobs across national boundaries. As the economy changes, workers must change and adapt. The technician who adapted to cellular phone technology might need to change yet again in a few years.

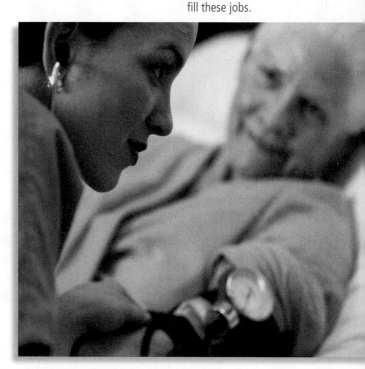

Changing Careers
As the demand for healthcare workers increases, some people will change careers to fill these jobs.

APPLICATION Analyzing Cause and Effect

C. A 2003 report concluded that telecommuters can save their employers $5,000 a year. Explain how that savings may come about.

For more on interpreting graphs, see the Skillbuilder Handbook, page R29.

Drawing Conclusions from Graphs

Drawing conclusions means analyzing a source of information and forming an opinion. You have already had some practice analyzing line and pie graphs in Chapters 6 and 8. These graphs are bar graphs.

PRACTICING THE SKILL Begin by using the following strategies to analyze the graphs. They are similar to the strategies you used in Chapter 6 to analyze a line graph. Your analysis will enable you to draw conclusions about the information shown on the graphs.

Read the title to identify the main idea of the graphs.

Check the vertical axes. Note that the axes use different scales.

Check the horizontal axes. Both axes list a variety of occupations.

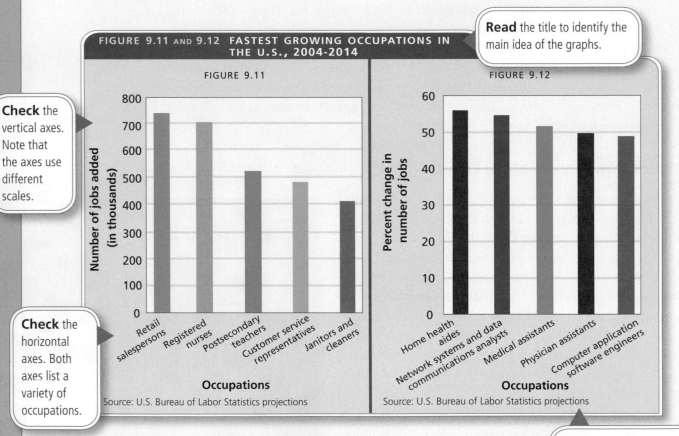

FIGURE 9.11 AND 9.12 FASTEST GROWING OCCUPATIONS IN THE U.S., 2004-2014

Read the source lines to confirm that the data come from a reliable source.

NOW PUT IT ALL TOGETHER Both graphs claim to present the same information. Compare the two graphs, and consider their differences.

THINKING ECONOMICALLY Drawing Conclusions

1. What is the main difference between the two graphs?
2. Which graph really shows the fastest growing occupations? Explain your answer.
3. What would be a better title for each graph?
4. Which of these jobs are most likely to have higher than average wages? Why?

REVIEWING KEY CONCEPTS

1. Explain the differences between the terms in each of these pairs.

    a. *outsourcing*   **b.** *contingent employment*
        insourcing   *independent contractor*

2. Name three of the fastest growing occupations. What do they have in common?

3. What are the economic reasons that explain why so many women joined the labor force in the late 1900s?

4. Name two ways technology has altered the U.S. labor market.

5. For an employee, what are the advantages and disadvantages of telecommuting?

6. Using Your Notes Write a paragraph explaining how you can use the information in this section to prepare for your future career. Refer to your completed hierarchy chart to help you anticipate the employment trends you will be facing.

Use the Graphic Organizer at **Interactive Review @ ClassZone.com**

CRITICAL THINKING

7. Making Inferences and Drawing Conclusions Given the trends in the labor market, do you think today's employees will need to be more independent than the last generation's or less independent? Why?

8. Analyzing Cause and Effect Explain how changing technologies have led to workers changing careers more often.

9. Evaluating Economic Decisions The United States has shifted to an economy driven by service industries. The primary sector, which deals in natural resources, and the secondary sector, which produces goods, are both shrinking. Do you think the shift toward a service economy is helping American workers or hurting them? Give reasons for your answer.

10. Challenge Adam Smith explained that countries maximize their wealth when they concentrate on producing the goods that they produce most efficiently and rely on international trade for goods they don't produce efficiently. Explain how outsourcing is an example of this concept.

ECONOMICS IN PRACTICE

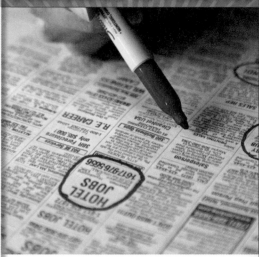

Examining Labor Market Trends
Make a copy of the table below. On your copy, list the reasons for the trend toward contingent labor in the left column. In the right column, describe its impact on the labor force.

Move to Contingent Labor	
Why?	Impact on Labor Force

Analyze Cause and Effect
In what ways have women in the work force influenced the growth of contingent labor? In what ways has the growth of contingent labor influenced women?

Challenge What personal issues might lead a worker to seek part-time employment?

Organized Labor in the United States

OBJECTIVES	KEY TERMS	TAKING NOTES
In Section 3, you will • describe how the labor movement developed in the United States • discuss why organized labor has declined in the United States • explain how labor unions affect wage rates and employment	labor union, *p. 274* strike, *p. 274* closed shop, *p. 279* union shop, *p. 279* right-to-work law, *p. 279* collective bargaining, *p. 280* binding arbitration, *p. 280*	As you read Section 3, complete a summary chart like the one below. In each box, write the main ideas for each topic. Use the Graphic Organizer at **Interactive Review @ ClassZone.com**

Topic	Main Ideas	Related Facts
Labor movement's rise to power		

The Labor Movement's Rise to Power

KEY CONCEPTS

Organized labor helped to shape the modern workplace. Most of the benefits that workers in the United States take for granted today did not exist 200 years ago. The eight-hour workday, the five-day work week, vacations, even sick leave—none of these basic amenities would have existed without the efforts of organized labor.

In the industries of the 1800s, workers put in long hours—often 60 hours per week or more—for low pay. Factory laborers often worked in dangerous conditions. Individual workers had little power to demand improvements from a business owner. If a worker complained too much, they would be fired. Workers in industrialized nations around the world faced similar problems, but this section will focus on the labor movement in the United States.

To improve their bargaining power, factory workers in the 1800s began to join together and act as a group. A **labor union** is an organization of workers who collectively seek to improve wages, working conditions, benefits, job security, and other work-related matters. Unions attempted to negotiate with businesses to achieve their goals, but businesses often resisted. As unions sought ways to gain negotiating power, they turned to the **strike**, or work stoppage. The threat of shutting down production demonstrated the power of organized labor.

Different types of unions addressed different needs. Some workers joined a craft union, a union of workers with similar skills who work in different industries for different employers. Examples include typesetters or, more recently, electricians. Others joined an industrial union, a union for workers with different skills who work in the same industry. For example, workers in the textile industry formed some of the earliest industrial unions.

QUICK REFERENCE

A **labor union** is an organization of workers that seeks to improve wages, working conditions, fringe benefits, job security, and other work-related matters for its members.

A **strike** is a work stoppage used to convince an employer to meet union demands.

Early Developments

Local craft unions were the main kind of worker association during the early years of the United States. By the 1830s, local unions began joining together into federations to advance their common cause. The first national federation was the National Trades Union (NTU), founded in 1834. A financial crisis that gripped the country in 1837 brought an end to the NTU and temporarily subdued union activity.

In 1869, organized labor took a huge step forward when Uriah Stephens founded the Knights of Labor. Unlike other unions, it organized workers by industry, not by trade or skill level. The Knights of Labor became a nationwide union and adopted political goals including an eight-hour workday for all workers and the end of child labor. Its membership grew quickly, especially after the union helped workers win concessions from the big railroad companies in the 1880s.

During the explosion of industrialism in the late 1800s, employers strongly resisted the efforts of workers to organize, and many labor protests turned violent.

- In 1886, one person was killed and several others were seriously wounded when police attacked workers protesting for an eight-hour workday outside the McCormick Harvester Company in Chicago. The next day, people gathered at Haymarket Square to protest the deaths, and police troops arrived to disperse the crowd. Someone threw a bomb into the police, killing seven officers, and the riot that followed left dozens of other people dead and hundreds injured.

- In 1892, ten workers were killed in a strike against Carnegie Steel in Homestead, Pennsylvania, and the union was broken up.

- In 1894, a strike in Illinois against the Pullman Palace Car Company won the support of railway workers across the country, who collectively brought the nation's railroads to a halt. The dispute turned violent when National Guard troops were brought in to keep the nation's railroads running. A federal court ruled that the American Railway Union could not interfere with the trains, and the strike was broken.

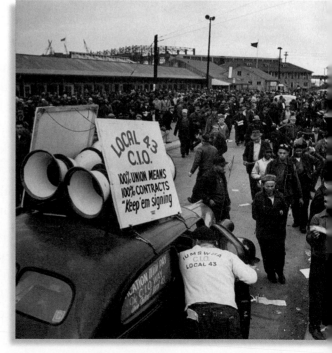

Union Organizing
A union rally takes place at a shipyard in 1943.

A New Model for Unions

The violence associated with organized labor, as well as its often controversial political agenda, led to a decline in union membership. But Samuel Gompers offered a different model for union organization. In 1886, he founded the American Federation of Labor (AFL), an organization of craft unions that focused on the interests of skilled labor. The AFL continued to seek improvements in wages, benefits, and working conditions, but it focused on achieving these goals through the economic power of workers, instead of through legislation. By the early 1900s, the AFL had a membership of about 1.7 million workers. Legal action against organized labor forced Gompers to modify his stance against political activity, and the AFL began supporting pro-union candidates.

The International Ladies' Garment Workers Union was founded in 1900. The union gained strength following successful strikes in 1909 and 1910. Perhaps the most famous

FIGURE 9.13 **History of the American Labor Movement**

1893
▼ Eugene V. Debs founds the American Railway Union.

1869
◀ Uriah Stephens founds the Knights of Labor.

1900
▲ International Ladies' Garment Workers' Union founded.

1825   **1850**   **1875**   **1900**

1834
National Trades Union formed.

Attention Workingmen!
MASS-MEETING
TO-NIGHT, at 7.30 o'clock.

1886
◀ Protest in Chicago, advertised by this flyer, turns into the Haymarket Riot.

1894
Labor Day becomes a national holiday.

1886
American Federation of Labor (AFL) founded by Samuel Gompers.

woman to participate in the U.S. labor movement was Mary Harris Jones, known as Mother Jones. In 1903, she led 80 children, many of whom had been injured while working, on a march to the home of President Theodore Roosevelt. The march helped to emphasize the need for child labor laws.

Unions Gain Power

During the Great Depression of the 1930s, union membership in the United States declined as millions of people lost their jobs. Yet unions gained power through laws passed as part of the New Deal, a series of reforms that attempted to revive the country's economy.

- The Norris-LaGuardia Act (1932) outlawed the practice of hiring only workers who agreed not to join a union. It also required employers to allow workers to organize without interference from their employer.

- The National Labor Relations Act (1935), also known as the Wagner Act, protected the rights of workers in the private sector to form unions and to use strikes and other job actions.

- The Fair Labor Standards Act (1938) set a minimum wage, required extra pay for overtime work, and made most child labor illegal.

During this period, the Congress of Industrial Organizations (CIO) organized unions for industrial workers. Originally part of the AFL, which favored skilled workers in craft unions, the CIO broke away in 1938. The two organizations came together again in 1955 as the AFL-CIO.

The AFL succeeded in organizing the United Auto Workers (UAW) union in 1935. After a tense sit-down strike in Flint, Michigan, in 1937, General Motors

1962
◄ Cesar Chavez founds National Farm Workers Association (NFWA), which later becomes United Farm Workers.

2005
Service Employees International Union breaks away from AFL-CIO.

| 1925 | 1950 | 1975 | 2000 |

1935
Congress passes the National Labor Relations Act, also called the Wagner Act.

1959
Congress passes Landrum-Griffin Act.

1981
► Air traffic controllers' strike is unsuccessful.

1935
United Auto Workers organized.

became the first automaker to recognize the union. Chrysler and Ford soon followed. In the 1940s, Walter Philip Reuther, as president of the UAW, helped auto workers become some of the nation's highest paid industrial workers. Also in the 1940s, John L. Lewis, the tough-talking, cigar-smoking leader of the CIO, brought his own United Mine Workers back from near failure and waged a fierce and successful fight to organize the nation's steelworkers.

Backlash Against Unions Following World War II

The end of World War II ushered in a period of anti-union legislation. In 1947, over the veto of President Harry S. Truman, the Taft-Hartley Act was passed. It amended the Wagner Act and limited union activities, increasing the government's power to intervene if a strike might threaten national security.

America's fear of Communism, the political and economic system of the Soviet Union, led to further restrictions on unions. The Landrum-Griffin Act (1959) forbade communists from holding union offices and required tighter financial and electoral accounting. George Meany, president of the AFL-CIO from 1955 to 1979, was a strong anti-communist and worked to get rid of unions that he considered sympathetic to communist ideas.

APPLICATION Comparing and Contrasting Economic Information

A. What motivated workers in the 1800s to form unions? Why did they continue to form unions in the early- to mid-1900s?

The Labor Movement's Steady Decline

KEY CONCEPTS

For 30 years following World War II, labor unions represented about 30 percent of the U.S. work force. Since the mid-1970s, membership in unions has declined steadily, falling to about 12.5 percent in 2005. The decline in unions can be traced to three causes: unions' tarnished reputations, changes in the labor force, and laws restricting union influence.

Loss of Reputation and Labor Force Changes

In the late 1900s, labor unions began to lose their luster in the eyes of many Americans. Prolonged strikes both disrupted the public and placed a burden on the striking families. Some unions began requiring companies to employ more workers than necessary, a tactic known as featherbedding. Featherbedding, especially in the railroad industry, raised criticisms of wastefulness. Investigators discovered that a few labor unions had ties to organized crime, which reflected badly on all unions.

The changing nature of the U.S. work force also led to reduced union membership. Union membership was traditionally rooted in manufacturing industries. But the number of manufacturing jobs in the United States fell sharply in the second half of the 20th century as the economy shifted toward service industries. The increase in the number of contingent and contract workers also led to lower union membership because such workers are less likely to pursue union representation.

As manufacturing declined, unions shifted their organizing efforts toward service workers. The American Federation of State, County, and Municipal Employees

Economics Update

Find an update on labor unions at **ClassZone.com**

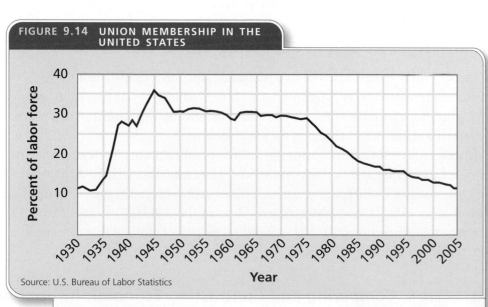

FIGURE 9.14 UNION MEMBERSHIP IN THE UNITED STATES

Source: U.S. Bureau of Labor Statistics

ANALYZE GRAPHS

1. During this time period, when was union membership highest? What percent of the labor force belonged to a union that year?

2. Which year was union membership lowest, and what percent of the labor force belonged to a union then?

had about 1.4 million members in 2005. The Service Employees International Union (SEIU), which organizes such service workers as caregivers and janitors, had a membership of 1.8 million in 2005. The SEIU was the largest union in the AFL-CIO, but in 2005 it left the group. Several other smaller unions also left the AFL-CIO and joined SEIU to form a new coalition with different priorities.

Right-to-Work Laws

Another factor in the steady decline of union membership in the United States is legislation that tries to limit union influence. Unions had developed the **closed shop**, a business required to hire only union members. The closed shop was intended to maintain union standards for workers who only work at a business briefly, such as musicians or restaurant employees. Unions also developed the **union shop**, a business where workers are required to join a union within a set time period after being hired. Union shops allowed businesses to hire nonunion workers without diluting the strength of the union.

The Taft-Hartley Act outlawed the closed shop and weakened possibilities for a union shop. It also gave states the power to make it illegal to require workers to join unions. Such laws became known as **right-to-work laws**, a name meant to emphasize that workers are free not to join a union. However, the effect of right-to-work laws and similar legislation is to weaken unions and to help businesses operate without unions. Most right-to-work states are in the Southeast and the central West, and union membership in these areas is low.

QUICK REFERENCE

A **closed shop** is a business where an employer can hire only union members.

A **union shop** is a business where workers are required to join a union within a set time period after being hired.

Right-to-work laws make it illegal to require workers to join unions.

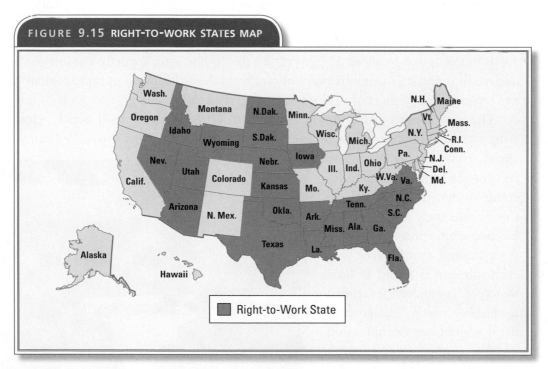

FIGURE 9.15 RIGHT-TO-WORK STATES MAP

Right-to-Work State

APPLICATION Predicting Economic Trends

B. Consider the trends in today's labor force that you learned about in Section 2. As more service industries unionize, is union membership, as a percent of the labor force, likely to return to the levels of the mid-1900s? Why or why not?

Union Negotiating Methods

QUICK REFERENCE

Collective bargaining is the way businesses and unions negotiate wages and working conditions.

KEY CONCEPTS

Despite the decline in membership, organized labor still wields power in the American economy. Unions continue to use **collective bargaining**, the process of negotiation between businesses and their organized employees to establish wages and to improve working conditions. Since it represents many employees together, a union can arrive at a better deal for workers than if each employee bargained with the employer separately. As a result, unionized companies tend to pay higher wages than companies without unions.

Collective Bargaining

In the 1930s and 1940s, unions negotiated for higher wages, better working conditions, and fair grievance procedures for workers who felt that they had been treated unjustly. As these demands were increasingly met, unions negotiated for job security and such fringe benefits as health insurance. Benefits and job security are important issues in today's negotiations as well, but in many cases today's workers are not pressing for higher wages. Instead they are trying to hold the line against pay cuts and reductions in benefits, including pensions.

Unions have the threat of a strike to provide a motivation for management to come to terms, but strikes occur much less frequently than in the past. Large-scale work stoppages in the United States occurred hundreds of times a year before the 1980s but dropped to about 20 per year by the 2000s. This is partly a result of the decline in union membership, but it also reflects the willingness of management to use replacement workers or to close a plant permanently.

The vast majority of union contracts are settled without such action. However, some negotiations require additional interventions if the two sides cannot agree. First, a mediator may be brought in to help the sides come to terms. If that fails, the dispute may be settled by **binding arbitration**—a decision by a neutral third party that each side agrees ahead of time to accept. For industries related to public safety, the government might issue an injunction to force workers back to work after a stoppage, or to stop protest activities that may interfere with public safety.

QUICK REFERENCE

Binding arbitration is a process in which an impartial third party resolves disputes between management and unions.

Collective Bargaining
Union leaders meet with business management to negotiate the details of union contracts.

APPLICATION Analyzing Cause and Effect

C. Explain why high wages and high employment do not necessarily go hand in hand.

REVIEWING KEY CONCEPTS

1. Explain the differences between the terms in each of these pairs.

   a. *closed shop*   **b.** *strike*
   union shop   *collective bargaining*

2. Why was the formation of the Knights of Labor a key event for organized labor in the United States?

3. Name two laws that supported labor's rights and two laws that restricted them.

4. Opponents of right-to-work laws sometimes call them "work-for-less" laws. Why do you think they use that name?

5. Why would a business care if its workers went on strike?

6. **Using Your Notes** Write a paragraph explaining why unions grew in the 1800s and the first half of the 1900s. Refer to your completed summary chart to help you develop your argument with strong supporting detail.

Topic	Main Ideas	Related Facts
Labor movement's rise to power		

   Use the Graphic Organizer at **Interactive Review @ ClassZone.com**

CRITICAL THINKING

7. **Analyzing Cause and Effect** What effect might outsourcing have on union membership?

8. **Evaluating Economic Decisions** In 1981, a group of air traffic controllers, employees of the Federal Aviation Administration, went on strike. They wanted to reduce their workweek to 32 hours instead of the usual 40 because of the high stress of their jobs. President Ronald Reagan broke the strike and disbanded the union of air traffic controllers, claiming that they were striking illegally. About 100 strikers were arrested, and all of them were banned for life from jobs in air traffic control. Did Reagan do the right thing by firing the striking workers? Explain your answer.

9. **Challenge** The firing of the air traffic controllers and the breaking of their union was one of the key events for labor in the United States. What trends in organized labor are evident in that event?

ECONOMICS IN PRACTICE

Automated factories reduced the need for assembly line workers.

Analyzing Economic Data
Look at Figure 9.14 on page 278, which shows changes in union membership in the United States.

Analyze Union Membership
Compare the upward and downward movements of the graph to the events going on in the United States and world.

1930s—The Great Depression

1940s—World War II; postwar recovery

1950s—Korean War; economy thrives

1960s—Civil Rights movement; Vietnam War; steady economy

1970s—End of Vietnam War; oil embargo; inflation

1980s—Recession and recovery

1990s—Fall of Communism in Europe and Russia; Internet boom

2000s—September 11; Iraq War; recession and recovery

Challenge Does there seem to be a relationship between how well the economy is doing and union membership? Explain.

Managing Change in Your Work Life

Background The United States economy has shifted from manufacturing to service and knowledge-based industries. New technologies offer increasingly sophisticated tools. Telecommuting provides businesses the option of having employees work effectively from outside the office.

Globalization has revolutionized the way companies do business. Companies are no longer tied to a specific location. Instead, they establish offices around the globe. The outsourcing and insourcing of jobs result both in benefits and challenges. The dynamics of the workplace are defined by a single factor—change.

What's the issue? How will you respond to the changing dynamics of the work environment? Study these sources to discover how change affects the type of work we do, as well as where and how we do it.

A. Online Magazine Article

Call centers in India help businesses reduce costs because local wages are low. But some Westerners accept the low wages for a chance to live in India.

Subcontinental Drift

More Westerners are beefing up their resumés with a stint in India

After a year answering phones for Swiss International Air Lines Ltd. in a Geneva call center, Myriam Vock was eager to see something of the world. So she packed her bags and hopped a plane to India. Two and a half years later she's still there, sharing a five-bedroom apartment in an upscale New Delhi suburb with four other foreigners.

And how does she pay the bills? She works in a call center, getting paid a fraction of what she did back home. "I'm not earning much, but there is enough to live well and travel," says Vock, 21. . . . "I don't pay taxes here, and life is so much cheaper," she says.

Worried about your job fleeing to India? One strategy is to chase it—an option a growing number of twentysomething Westerners are choosing. Sure, the trend will never make up for the thousands of positions lost back home, but for adventurous young people, a spell in a call center in Bangalore or Bombay can help defray the costs of a grand tour of the subcontinent and beyond.

Source: **BusinessWeek.com, January 16, 2006**

Call centers in India serve customers of companies all over the world.

Thinking Economically Explain Myriam's decision to work in a call center in India using cost-benefit analysis.

B. Business Cartoon

Canadian cartoonist Andrew Toos drew this cartoon about working in an increasingly technological society.

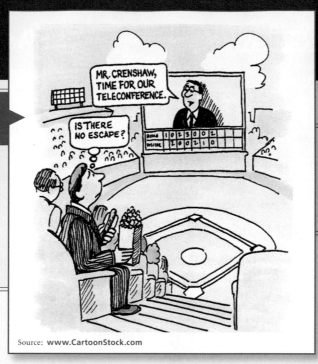

Source: www.CartoonStock.com

Thinking Economically
What does the cartoon suggest about new technological developments in the world of work? Explain your answer.

C. Online Newspaper Article

Many worry that outsourcing may reduce the number of jobs in the United States. This article presents a different perspective.

Outsourcing Benefits Permac Employees

Permac creates a win-win situation.

Permac Industries in Burnsville [Minnesota] fashions parts ranging from rings that tie parachutes to small planes to parts for soda fountain machines and construction trucks. President and CEO Darlene Miller plans to send some work to China, but she said it's to the benefit of her 27 Minnesota employees.

"No one here will lose a job. We're not planning to let anybody go—in fact, we're hiring," she said.

Miller is investing in a $700,000 piece of equipment to give workers in Burnsville better tools for specialized work that demands higher skills than the work she plans to send to China. A side benefit for the company's Burnsville workers is that the work going to China will reduce the need for what at times has seemed relentless overtime.

"The simple parts eat up a lot of machine time," said John Keith, a Permac team leader. "If we farm that out we have time to look at getting new business, more complicated business."

Source: www.startribune.com, September 5, 2004

Thinking Economically How will Permac employees benefit from outsourcing? Identify others who also will benefit and explain why.

THINKING ECONOMICALLY Synthesizing

1. What skills are you likely to need in order to manage change successfully in your work life? Support your answer with examples from the documents.

2. In documents A and B, are the types of change similar or different? Are their effects on workers positive or negative? Explain your answer.

3. Compare the opportunities afforded by change in documents A and C. How are they similar? How are they different?

Interactive Review

Review this chapter using interactive activities at ClassZone.com
- Online Summary
- Quizzes
- Vocabulary Flip Cards
- Graphic Organizers
- Review and Study Notes

Online Summary

Complete the following activity either on your own paper or online at **ClassZone.com**

Choose the key concept that best completes the sentence. Not all key concepts will be used.

civilian labor force	insourcing
closed shop	labor union
collective bargaining	minimum wage
contingent employment	outsourcing
craft union	productivity
derived demand	right-to-work law
equilibrium wage	strike
glass ceiling	telecommuting
human capital	union shop
industrial union	wages

__1__ are the cost of labor. The demand for labor is a __2__, growing out of the demand for the goods or services workers can produce. The forces of supply and demand determine the __3__, at which there is neither a surplus nor a shortage of workers. Wages are directly correlated to a worker's __4__. Workers with the lowest level often earn only the __5__.

Since the 1950s, many women have entered the __6__. They are sometimes limited by the __7__, which keeps them from reaching the highest levels of management. Other trends in the labor market include __8__, working away from a central office, and __9__, working part-time or temporary jobs. U.S. firms sometimes use __10__ to hire workers in other countries. When foreign companies open plants in the United States, it is called __11__.

Changes in the work force have reduced the number of workers who belong to a __12__. Such organizations press for higher pay and better working conditions through __13__. If talks fail, union workers might __14__, putting pressure on employers to meet their demands.

CHAPTER 9 Assessment

REVIEWING KEY CONCEPTS

How Are Wages Determined? (pp. 258–265)

1. What forces determine the equilibrium wage?

2. What four factors contribute to differences in wages?

Trends in Today's Labor Market (pp. 266–273)

3. How has the labor market in the United States changed since the 1950s?

4. Name two new developments in the way Americans work.

Organized Labor in the United States (pp. 274–283)

5. Name an important U.S. labor leader and describe what he or she contributed to the labor movement.

6. What are some of the reasons membership in unions has declined since the 1950s?

APPLYING ECONOMIC CONCEPTS

The table below shows the median weekly earnings of full-time wage and salary workers by union affiliation and selected characteristics.

FIGURE 9.16 UNION AND NONUNION WAGES

Median Weekly Earnings of Full-Time Workers in the United States (in dollars)				
Race or Ethnicity	Union Men	Women	Nonunion Men	Women
African-American	689	632	523	478
Asian	819	789	827	643
Hispanic	713	609	473	414
White	884	749	714	576

Source: U.S. Bureau of Labor Statistics, 2005 data

7. What is the only group for which union affiliation does not yield higher pay?

8. Calculate the percentage difference between each group's union and nonunion wages. Which group gains the most in wages from union membership?

9. **Creating Graphs** Create a bar graph using the following information about alternative work arrangements in the United States. Include an appropriate title and a source line showing that the data, which are for 2005, come from the Bureau of Labor Statistics.

Independent contractors (Self-employed workers, such as independent sales consultants or freelance writers): 10.3 million

On-call workers (Workers called as needed, sometimes working several days or weeks in a row, such as substitute teachers): 2.5 million

Temporary workers (Workers paid by the hour, such as file clerks, hired through a temporary employment agency): 1.2 million

Contract workers (Workers paid a salary, such as training specialists, provided by contract firms and hired for a limited contract): 0.8 million

Use 🖊 *SMART Grapher* @ ClassZone.com to complete this activity.

10. **Synthesizing Economic Data** Explain the differences in median weekly earnings in Figure 9.16 in terms of this chapter's key concepts.

11. **Explaining an Economic Concept** Have you ever been paid to work? If so, explain how the rate you were paid was determined. If not, think of someone you know who has earned money and explain how that person's wages were determined.

12. **Applying Economic Concepts** Think back to a time when you negotiated with someone in a position of authority for something you strongly wanted. Briefly describe the tactics you used and look for similarities or differences between those and the tactics unions use with employers.

13. **Challenge** In 2003, the Fair Labor Standards Act was amended to clarify who was entitled to overtime pay. At the center of the issue were computer programmers, who lost entitlement to overtime if their regular pay is $65,000 per year or more. What impact might this have had on the workers and the economy?

Collective Bargaining

It's time to renegotiate the union contract at the Acme auto parts factory in Springfield. Read these descriptions of the two sides, then follow the instructions to experience what union negotiations are like.

Union workers currently earn $25 per hour, plus overtime pay if they have to work more than 35 hours per week. Benefits include health-care insurance paid for by the company, plus vision and dental coverage, also funded by the company. The workers' pension fund is handled through the union.

The Acme company is a conglomerate based in the United States. Its auto parts business has been struggling to make a profit, so it is considering outsourcing the work to a factory in China. It would then like to turn the Springfield factory into a computer manufacturing facility.

Step 1 Divide the class evenly into union members and the Acme management team.

Step 2 Separately and privately, each group discusses its objectives and negotiating strategies. Try to keep the conversation quiet so that the other side does not gain an advantage by learning your bargaining points.

Step 3 Each group chooses three representatives to conduct the negotiations.

Step 4 The representatives from both sides meet and negotiate the new contract. The rest of the two groups may listen to the negotiations, but they may not participate. If the two sides still disagree on an issue after several minutes of negotiations, put that issue aside for the moment. Keep a list showing the status of each issue.

Step 5 If time permits, repeat steps 2–4 to address the unresolved issues.

Discuss what happened. Did one side have more bargaining power? How did the two sides resolve their differences? Why were some issues more difficult to resolve than others?

U.S. TREASURY

What constitutes money?

Money isn't born, it's made. Each society decides what it will accept as money, but effective moneys all share certain attributes and perform certain functions.

CHAPTER 10

Money and Banking

SECTION 1
Money: Its Functions and Properties

SECTION 2
The Development of U.S. Banking

SECTION 3
Innovations in Modern Banking

CASE STUDY
Housing Boom and Bust

CONCEPT REVIEW

Macroeconomics is the study of the behavior of the economy as a whole and how major economic sectors, such as industry and government, interact.

CHAPTER 10 KEY CONCEPT

Money provides a low-cost method of trading one good or service for another. It makes the system of voluntary exchange efficient.

WHY THE CONCEPT MATTERS

What were the last three economic transactions you completed using money? Perhaps you put four quarters in the fare machine on the bus to school or bought a slice of pizza and a drink in the cafeteria at lunch. Or maybe you caught an early movie after school yesterday. To gauge the importance of money to the economy, imagine trying to make such transactions without bills, coins, or cards.

Online Highlights

More at ClassZone.com

 Economics Update

Go to **ECONOMICS UPDATE** for chapter updates and current news on the housing price bubble. (See Case Study, pp. 312–313.) ▶

Animated Economics

Go to **ANIMATED ECONOMICS** for interactive lessons on the graphs and tables in this chapter.

Interactive ◀◀Review

Go to **INTERACTIVE REVIEW** for concept review and activities.

Source: www.CartoonStock.com

How did lax lending policies contribute to the housing price bubble? See the Case Study on pages 312–313.

How Much Money?

How much money is in supply in the United States? Economists use various instruments to measure the money supply, but the most often cited are M1 and M2. M1 is the narrowest measure of the money supply, consisting of currency, demand deposits, and other checkable deposits. It is synonymous with transactions money. The elements of M1 are referred to as liquid assets, which means that they are or can easily become currency.

M2 is a broader measure of the money supply, consisting of M1 plus various kinds of near money. M2 includes savings accounts, other small-denomination time deposits (CDs of less than $100,000), and money market mutual funds. You will learn about these financial instruments in Chapter 11.

Figure 10.2 shows the amounts of the different forms of money that make up M1 and M2. You can see that M1 is almost evenly split between currency and checkable deposits. Notice that more of M2 comes from savings than from M1. You will learn the importance of the money supply in the economy and how the government manages it in Chapter 16.

Economics Update

Find an update on measures of the money supply at **ClassZone.com**

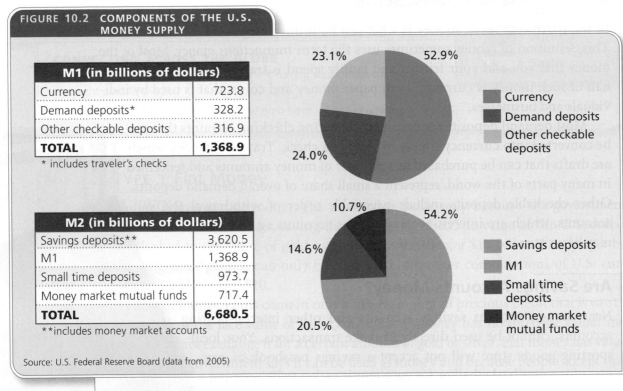

FIGURE 10.2 COMPONENTS OF THE U.S. MONEY SUPPLY

M1 (in billions of dollars)	
Currency	723.8
Demand deposits*	328.2
Other checkable deposits	316.9
TOTAL	**1,368.9**

* includes traveler's checks

M2 (in billions of dollars)	
Savings deposits**	3,620.5
M1	1,368.9
Small time deposits	973.7
Money market mutual funds	717.4
TOTAL	**6,680.5**

**includes money market accounts

Source: U.S. Federal Reserve Board (data from 2005)

ANALYZE TABLES

1. What amount of M2 does not come from currency and checkable deposits?
2. If currency is 52.9 percent of M1, and M1 is 20.5 percent of M2, what percentage of M2 is currency?

APPLICATION Applying Economic Concepts

D. Classify each of the following as M1 and M2: **a.** dollar bill; **b.** savings account; **c.** money market account; **d.** traveler's check; **e.** $50,000 CD.

REVIEWING KEY CONCEPTS

1. Explain the difference between the terms in each of these pairs.

   a. *standard of value*   b. *commodity money*   c. *demand deposits*
        store of value   *representative money*   *near money*

2. Why are economic transactions easier with money than with barter?

3. Why is it important that money be divisible?

4. Why are checking accounts called demand deposits?

5. What aspect of fiat money allows it to have more stability than representative money?

6. **Using Your Notes** How are the economic properties of money related to its functions? Refer to your completed cluster diagram.

   Use the Graphic Organizer at **Interactive Review @ ClassZone.com**

Money

CRITICAL THINKING

7. **Categorizing Economic Information** Which of these forms of money are included in M1:
   - checking accounts
   - coins
   - money market accounts
   - paper money
   - savings accounts
   - time deposits
   - traveler's checks
   - NOW accounts

8. **Making Inferences** The U.S. government has tried to get people to use dollar coins rather than dollar bills. Most consumers prefer to use dollar bills. Which physical properties of money are involved in these different preferences?

9. **Applying Economic Concepts** Maria's parents told her that for the ten years prior to her high school graduation, they saved $200 per month for her college education—$24,000 (plus interest). Which function of money does this example best illustrate? Why?

10. **Challenge** Why is there more near money than transactions money in the U.S. money supply?

ECONOMICS IN PRACTICE

Evaluating Economic Decisions
In the past, indigenous people of Central and South America used cacao beans (the source of chocolate) as currency.

Evaluate Money In Section 1, you learned that money should function as a medium of exchange, a standard of value, and a store of value. Use what you've learned about these functions to evaluate how useful cacao beans might be as money today. Show your answer by filling in the table below.

Function	Possible Problems
Medium of exchange	
Standard of value	
Store of value	

Challenge How well do cacao beans exhibit each of the physical and economic properties of money?

The Development of U.S. Banking

OBJECTIVES	KEY TERMS	TAKING NOTES
In Section 2, you will • describe how banking developed in the United States • identify the banking institutions that operate in the United States	state bank, *p. 296* national bank, *p. 299* gold standard, *p. 299*	As you read Section 2, complete a chart using the key concepts and other helpful words and phrases. Use the Graphic Organizer at **Interactive Review @ ClassZone.com**

Development of U.S. Banking		
Origins	19th Century	20th Century

The Origins of Banking

KEY CONCEPTS

Modern banking arose in Italy in the late Middle Ages. Italian merchants stored money or valuables for wealthy people and issued receipts that promised to return the property on demand. They realized that they did not have to hold all the deposits, since all depositors did not reclaim their property at the same time, but could lend some of the deposits and earn interest on those loans. This was the beginning of fractional reserve banking (see Section 3), the practice of holding only a fraction of the money deposited in a bank and lending the rest.

Early "Bankers" The Italian word *banco*, means "bench." From benches in the street, Italian merchants used some practices that are part of banking today.

In colonial America, many merchants followed the same practice. However, these banks were far from secure. If a merchant's business failed, depositors lost all of their savings. After the Revolutionary War, many **state banks**—banks chartered, or licensed, by state governments—were established. Some of these banks, however, followed practices that tended to create instability and disorder. Many issued their own currency that was not linked to reserves of gold or silver held by the bank.

QUICK REFERENCE

A **state bank** is a bank chartered by a state government.

Alexander Hamilton: Shaping a Banking System

Imagine what it would be like if every bank issued its own currency. How would buyers know if sellers would accept their money? How would sellers know if the money they received was worth anything? That was the confusing situation that Alexander Hamilton faced when he became Secretary of the Treasury in 1789. He immediately set to work to bring stability to U. S. banking.

The First Bank of the United States

Hamilton was a leading Federalist who believed in a strong central government. He proposed chartering a privately owned national bank to put the government on a sound financial footing. This bank would issue a national currency and help control the money supply by refusing to accept currency from state banks that was not backed by gold or silver. It also would lend money to the federal government, state banks, and businesses.

The Constitution did not specifically authorize Congress to charter a national bank. The Anti-federalists, led by Thomas Jefferson and James Madison, interpreted the Constitution strictly and feared putting too much power in the hands of the central government. Hamilton argued that the Constitution implied that the federal government had the authority to create a national bank to carry out its duty to regulate the currency.

Hamilton won the fight, and the First Bank of the United States was chartered in 1791. Over time, it achieved the financial goals that Hamilton had set. However, opponents argued that the bank's policies restrained economic growth, and Congress refused to renew the charter in 1811.

The fact that Hamilton was the architect of the bank was always a strike against it, as he had made many enemies during his career. (One, Aaron Burr, killed him in a duel.)

Alexander Hamilton (above) and the First Bank of the United States (right)

Maybe Hamilton was right when he said, "Men often oppose a thing merely because they have had no agency in planning it, or because it may have been planned by those whom they dislike."

FAST FACTS

Alexander Hamilton

Position: First Secretary of the Treasury (1789–1795)

Born: January 11, 1755 in Nevis, British West Indies

Died: July 12, 1804

Writings: *The Federalist Papers* (1787), with James Madison and John Jay; *Report on a National Bank* (1790)

Major Accomplishment: Strengthened the national government and established the First Bank of the United States

Hamilton's Visible Legacy: Portrait on the $10 bill

Economics Update

Learn more about Alexander Hamilton at **ClassZone.com**

APPLICATION Making Inferences

A. How did the First National Bank force state banks to become more stable?

FIGURE 10.3 **Major Developments in American Banking**

1816
◄ Congress charters Second Bank of the United States.

1863
◄ Congress creates national banks and currency.

| 1775 | 1800 | 1825 | 1850 | 1875 |

1791
Congress charters First Bank of the United States.

1837–1865
Wildcat banking leads to unstable currency. ▶

19th-Century Developments

KEY CONCEPTS

Without a central bank, the government had difficulty financing the War of 1812 against Britain. Furthermore, state banks soon returned to the unrestrained issuing of currency that was not linked to reserves of gold or silver held by the banks. The resulting increase in the money supply led to inflation during the war.

The Second Bank of the United States

Congress finally agreed to charter the Second Bank of the United States in 1816. The new bank had greater financial resources than the First Bank and succeeded in making the money supply more stable. Opponents continued to see the central bank as too powerful and too closely aligned with the wealthy. President Andrew Jackson was an outspoken critic who mistrusted banks and paper money He vetoed the renewal of its charter in 1832.

Wildcat Banking

After the Second Bank's charter lapsed in 1836, there was no federal oversight of the banking industry. During this period, all banks were state banks, each of which issued its own paper currency, called bank notes. States passed free banking laws that allowed individuals or groups that met its requirements to open banks.

Jackson and the Second Bank This 1828 cartoon lampoons Jackson's battle against the bank.

1913
President Wilson establishes Federal Reserve System. ▶

1950
Banks issue first credit cards.

1980s
Savings and Loan crisis rocks U.S. banking industry.

2007
Credit crunch leads to worldwide financial crisis.

1900 **1925** **1950** **1975** **2000**

1900
◀ United States adopts gold standard.

1933
Banking Act creates Federal Deposit Insurance Corporation.

1971
◀ President Nixon ends the dollar's link to gold.

1990s
Deregulation opens up bank competition.

Some of these banks were located in remote areas to discourage people from redeeming their bank notes, which were often worth less outside the region where they had been issued. It was this practice, along with the questionable quality of many bank notes, that resulted in the term *wildcat bank*. In addition, such banks were susceptible to bank runs when depositors demanded gold or silver for their currency. Since the banks often did not have sufficient reserves of these precious metals, financial panics and economic instability were common results.

The Struggle for Stability

During the Civil War, it was particularly difficult for the government to finance its operations without a national currency and a federal bank. The government's first solution to this problem was to issue a new currency backed by government bonds. These U.S. bank notes, called greenbacks, were printed with green ink.

In 1863, Congress passed the National Banking Act, which led to the creation of a system of **national banks**, banks chartered by the national government. The act provided for a national currency backed by U.S. Treasury bonds and regulated the minimum amount of capital required for national banks as well as the amount of reserves necessary to back the currency. Congress taxed state bank notes issued after 1865, effectively eliminating these notes from circulation.

In 1900, the government officially adopted the **gold standard**, a system in which the basic monetary unit—for example, one dollar—is equal to a set amount of gold. The national currency and gold standard helped to bring some stability to the banking system. Money was now uniform throughout the country, backed by something of intrinsic value, and limited by the supply of gold.

QUICK REFERENCE

National banks are banks chartered by the national government.

The **gold standard** is a system that backs the basic monetary unit with a set amount of gold.

APPLICATION Analyzing Effects

B. How did the National Banking Act of 1863 attempt to eliminate the problems caused by wildcat banking?

20th-Century Developments

The system of national banks and a national currency linked to the gold standard initially brought stability to U.S. banking. Yet the economy still experienced periods of inflation and recession and financial panics. This economic instability was largely due to the lack of a central decision-making institution that could manage the money supply in a flexible way to meet the economy's changing needs.

The Struggle for Stability

In 1913, Congress passed the Federal Reserve Act, which established the Federal Reserve System (commonly known as the Fed)—a true central bank. It consists of 12 regional banks with a central decision-making board. The Fed provides financial services to the federal government, makes loans to banks that serve the public, issues Federal Reserve notes as the national currency, and regulates the money supply to ensure that money retains its purchasing power. You'll learn more about the structure and functions of the Federal Reserve in Chapter 16.

The Great Depression and the New Deal

At the start of the Great Depression in 1929, many banks failed due to bank runs, as consumers panicked and withdrew all of their money. When the banks failed, many more depositors lost their money. Part of President Franklin Roosevelt's New Deal program was the Banking Act of 1933, which instituted reforms such as regulating interest rates that banks could pay and prohibiting banks from selling stocks. The Federal Deposit Insurance Corporation (FDIC) provided federal insurance so that if a bank failed, people would no longer lose their money. This legislation set the tone for almost 50 years by increasing the regulation of banking in the United States.

Deregulation and the Savings and Loan Crisis

The profitability of savings and loan associations (S&Ls) was constrained by the limits placed on interest rates. Owners of S&Ls petitioned Congress for reduced regulation, and in 1980 and 1982, Congress passed laws that lifted the limits on interest rates. Deregulation allowed the S&Ls to take more risks in the types of loans they made. As a result of investment mistakes, combined with other factors, many S&Ls failed and lost their depositors' money. To protect consumers, Congress agreed to fund the S&L industry's restructuring, which cost taxpayers hundreds of billions of dollars.

Despite the S&L crisis, the deregulation of banking continued. For more on the effects of deregulation and to learn what happened to U.S. banking in the 21st century, see Section 3.

APPLICATION Comparing and Contrasting

C. How are the First Bank of the United States and the Federal Reserve different?

Financial Institutions in the United States

KEY CONCEPTS

The term *bank* is used to refer to almost any kind of financial institution that takes in deposits and makes loans, helping individuals, businesses, and governments to manage their money. In the end, though, the goal of a bank is to earn a profit.

All financial institutions receive a charter from the government, either state or federal. Government regulations set the amount of money the owners of a bank must invest in it, the size of the reserves a bank must hold, and the ways that loans may be made. The term may refer to commercial banks, savings and loan associations, or credit unions.

Economics Update

Find an update on U.S. financial institutions at **ClassZone.com**

In the past, these institutions provided very different and distinct services. Today, however, because of the deregulation of banking, these distinctions are much less apparent. The distinctive characteristics of each type of financial institution are described in more detail below. Figure 10.4 compares the three types of banks.

TYPE 1 Commercial Banks

Privately owned commercial banks are the oldest form of banking and are the financial institutions most commonly thought of as banks. As their name implies, commercial banks were initially established to provide loans to businesses. The Banking Act of 1933 created a distinction between commercial banks and investment banks. Commercial banks provided basic banking services; investment banks bought and sold assets through the financial markets. Deregulation did away with that distinction. Now commercial banks provide a wide range of services, including checking and savings accounts, loans, investment assistance, and credit cards to both businesses and individual consumers. You will learn more about these services in Section 3.

FDIC Insurance Deposit insurance helps to stabilize the banking system.

Deregulation led to a wave of mergers and consolidations, reducing the number of commercial banks from over 12,000 in 1990 to about 7,500 in 2005. The FDIC insures all commercial banks based in the United States. All national commercial banks belong to the Federal Reserve System, but only about 15 percent of state-chartered banks choose to join the Fed.

TYPE 2 Savings and Loans

Savings and loan associations (S&Ls) began in the United States in the 1830s. They were originally chartered by individual states as mutual societies for two purposes—to take savings deposits and provide home mortgage loans. In other words, groups of people pooled their savings in a safe place to earn interest and have a source of financing for families who wanted to buy homes.

In 1933, the federal government began chartering S&Ls, and in 1934 the government established the Federal Savings and Loan Insurance Corporation (FSLIC). In 1989, following the S&L crisis, the FSLIC was abolished, and the FDIC began insuring S&Ls.

The S&Ls continue to fulfill their original purpose, but they also offer many services provided by commercial banks. Many savings institutions raise financing through the sale of stock, just as commercial banks do.

TYPE 3 Credit Unions

The idea for credit unions began in Europe in the mid-1800s. The first credit unions in the United States began in 1909 as state-chartered institutions. The Federal Credit Union Act of 1934 created a system of federally chartered credit unions.

Credit unions are cooperative savings and lending institutions, rather like the early S&Ls. They offer services similar to those of commercial banks and S&Ls, including savings and checking accounts. But most credit unions specialize in mortgages and auto loans. Most credit unions have deposit insurance through the National Credit Union Association (NCUA), an organization similar to the FDIC.

The major difference between credit unions and other financial institutions is that credit unions have membership requirements. To become a member, a person must work for a particular company, belong to a particular organization, or be part of a particular community affiliated with the credit union. Credit unions are cooperatives—nonprofit organizations owned by and operated for members.

FIGURE 10.4 BANKING INSTITUTIONS IN THE UNITED STATES

	Total Number of Institutions	Total Assets (billions of dollars)	Average Assets per Institution (billions of dollars)	Number of Large Institutions (assets of $3 billion or more)	Assets Controlled by Large Institutions (billions of dollars)
Commercial Banks	7,282	11,176.5	1.535	204	9,445.0
Savings and Loans	1,251	1,862.6	1.489	64	1,448.0
Credit Unions	8,101	753.4	0.093	22	144.8

Sources: FDIC, NCUA, 2007 data

ANALYZE TABLES
1. Which type of bank has the largest number of institutions? Why?
2. How do the assets held in savings and loans compare to the assets held in commercial banks?

APPLICATION Categorizing Economic Information

D. What type of bank would a chain of shoe stores be most likely to use? Why?

REVIEWING KEY CONCEPTS

1. Use each of the three terms below in a sentence that illustrates the meaning of the term.

   a. *state bank*   **b.** *national bank*   **c.** *gold standard*

2. Explain the relationship between the gold standard and the concept of representative money.

3. How does the Federal Reserve System serve as a central bank?

4. What is the difference between a national bank and a state bank?

5. How did the FDIC make fractional reserve banking less risky for consumers?

6. **Using Your Notes** What role did state banks play in the era of wildcat banking? Refer to your completed chart.

   Use the Graphic Organizer at **Interactive Review @ ClassZone.com**

Development of U.S. Banking		
Origins	19th Century	20th Century

CRITICAL THINKING

7. **Creating Graphs** Use the information in Figure 10.4 to create two pie graphs, one showing the percentage that each type of bank contributes to the total number of financial institutions and another showing the percentage that each type of bank contributes to total bank assets. State one conclusion that you can draw from the two graphs.

   Use **SMARTGrapher @ ClassZone.com** to complete this activity.

8. **Synthesizing Economic Information** On the basis of what you learned about the history of U.S. banking in the 19th and 20th centuries, were Alexander Hamilton's ideas about the need for a central bank and a national currency shown to be mostly accurate? Cite specific examples to support your answer.

9. **Applying Economic Concepts** Suppose that Mariel deposits $100 in her local bank. If the Fed's reserve requirement is 15 percent, how much can the bank loan out on the basis of Mariel's deposit? What concept does this scenario illustrate?

10. **Challenge** How do banks facilitate saving and borrowing in the same way that money facilitates buying and selling?

ECONOMICS IN PRACTICE

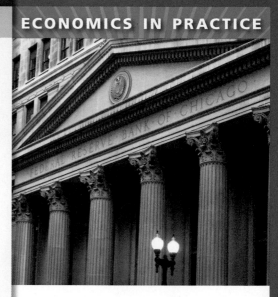

Constructing Graphs
Consider what you have learned about different types of financial institutions. The table below shows how the numbers of commercial banks and savings institutions have changed over time.

Year	Commercial Banks	Savings Institutions
1985	14,417	3,626
1990	12,347	2,815
1995	9,942	2,030
2000	8,315	1,589
2005	7,526	1,307

Create Line Graphs Use the information in the table to create two line graphs that show the changes in the numbers of each type of bank.

Use **SMARTGrapher @ ClassZone.com** to complete this activity.

Challenge On the basis of this information, what trends can you identify? Which type of financial institution experienced a greater percentage loss from 1985 to 2005?

Innovations in Modern Banking

OBJECTIVES	KEY TERMS	TAKING NOTES
In Section 3, you will • describe the services that banks provide • discuss the changes that deregulation has brought to banking • explain how technology has changed banking in the United States	automated teller machine, *p. 308* debit card, *p. 308* stored-value card, *p. 308*	As you read Section 3, complete a hierarchy diagram to track main ideas and supporting details. Use the Graphic Organizer at **Interactive Review @ ClassZone.com**

What Services Do Banks Provide?

KEY CONCEPTS

Banks offer a number of services that allow them to act like "money stores." In other words, just as stores are places where goods are bought and sold, banks are places where money can be bought (borrowed) and sold (lent). By using these services, customers are able to do three things—store money, earn money, and borrow money. Banks are businesses that earn money by charging interest or fees on these services.

SERVICE 1 Customers Can Store Money

As you read in Section 2, banks began as safe places to store money and other valuables. They still serve the same purpose today. Customers deposit money in the bank, and the bank stores currency in vaults and is also insured against theft and other loss. Customers' bank accounts are also insured in case the bank fails. Banks are also a safe place to store important papers and valuables—through the use of safe deposit boxes.

SERVICE 2 Customers Can Earn Money

When customers deposit their money in bank accounts, they can earn money on their deposits. Savings accounts and some checking accounts pay some level of interest. Banks offer other accounts, such as money market accounts and certificates of deposits (CDs), that pay a higher rate of interest. You will learn more about saving and investing in Chapter 11 and in Consumer and Personal Finance, which begins on page 574.

SERVICE 3 Customers Can Borrow Money

Banks also allow customers to borrow money through the practice of fractional reserve banking. (See Figure 10.5.) The percent of deposits that banks must keep in reserve is set by the Fed.

Banks provide customers, each of whom must be approved by the bank, with different loans for different circumstances. One common loan is a mortgage. A mortgage loan allows a buyer to purchase a real estate property, such as a house, without paying the entire value of the property up front. The lender and the borrower agree on a time period for the loan (often up to 30 years) and an interest rate to be paid to the lender. From this, a monthly mortgage payment amount is settled. In this arrangement, the real estate property acts as collateral. So if the borrower defaults on the loan (stops making the payments), the lender takes control of the property. It can then be sold by the bank to cover the balance of the mortgage.

It may not seem so, but a purchase made on a credit card is a loan too. Credit cards are issued by banks to users who are, in effect, borrowers. When you use a credit card to buy a new skateboard or a tank of gasoline, the issuing bank pays the seller and lends you the money. When you pay the bank back, you're repaying a loan. And if you don't pay it back within a month, you'll owe the bank extra in interest.

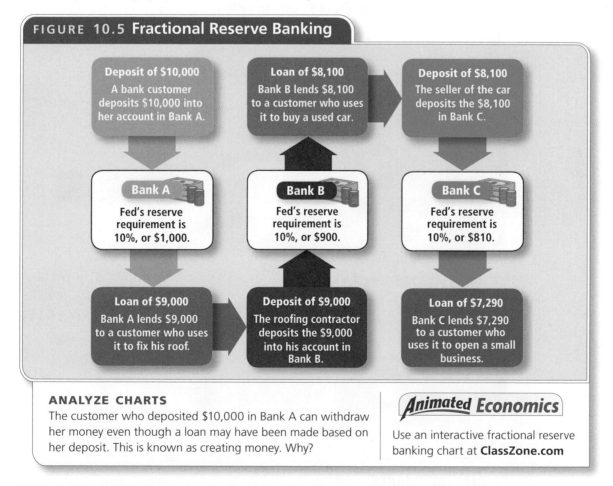

FIGURE 10.5 Fractional Reserve Banking

Deposit of $10,000
A bank customer deposits $10,000 into her account in Bank A.

Loan of $8,100
Bank B lends $8,100 to a customer who uses it to buy a used car.

Deposit of $8,100
The seller of the car deposits the $8,100 in Bank C.

Bank A
Fed's reserve requirement is 10%, or $1,000.

Bank B
Fed's reserve requirement is 10%, or $900.

Bank C
Fed's reserve requirement is 10%, or $810.

Loan of $9,000
Bank A lends $9,000 to a customer who uses it to fix his roof.

Deposit of $9,000
The roofing contractor deposits the $9,000 into his account in Bank B.

Loan of $7,290
Bank C lends $7,290 to a customer who uses it to open a small business.

ANALYZE CHARTS
The customer who deposited $10,000 in Bank A can withdraw her money even though a loan may have been made based on her deposit. This is known as creating money. Why?

Animated Economics
Use an interactive fractional reserve banking chart at **ClassZone.com**

APPLICATION Applying Economic Concepts

A. Explain the ways in which bank transactions are beneficial to customers and banks.

Banking Deregulation

The Banking Act of 1933 tightly regulated the amount of interest that banks could pay on deposits and could charge on loans. Regulations also prevented banks from operating in more than one state. Several states also had limitations on the number of branches that a bank could have within a state. Deregulation in the 1980s and 1990s ended these restrictions and brought major changes to the banking industry.

Bank Mergers

The end of restrictions on interstate banking led to a large number of mergers. Larger banks expanded by acquiring smaller banks. Some groups of smaller banks joined together to form larger, interstate operations. Mergers created a few very large banks with national operations. Figure 10.6 shows two examples of this trend. By 2004, Bank of America and JPMorgan Chase & Co. had become two of the largest banks in the United States, with assets of around $1 trillion each. In contrast, some 95 percent of commercial banks had assets of $1 billion or less.

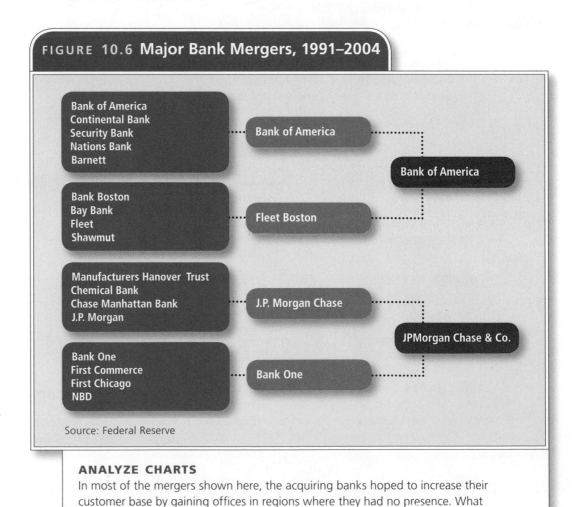

FIGURE 10.6 Major Bank Mergers, 1991–2004

Bank of America Continental Bank Security Bank Nations Bank Barnett	Bank of America	
Bank Boston Bay Bank Fleet Shawmut	Fleet Boston	Bank of America
Manufacturers Hanover Trust Chemical Bank Chase Manhattan Bank J.P. Morgan	J.P. Morgan Chase	
Bank One First Commerce First Chicago NBD	Bank One	JPMorgan Chase & Co.

Source: Federal Reserve

ANALYZE CHARTS

In most of the mergers shown here, the acquiring banks hoped to increase their customer base by gaining offices in regions where they had no presence. What reasons might target banks (the banks acquired) have for entering into a merger?

One benefit of the mergers was an increase in the number of bank branches. While the number of bank companies declined, the major banks could afford to open more small branches in shopping centers and grocery stores. However, by the 2000s, banking had become an oligopoly, and it began to exhibit those characteristics. Banks offered standardized products at prices that were generally not as good as they had been prior to the wave of mergers.

Banking Services

The Financial Services Act of 1999 lifted the last restrictions from the Banking Act of 1933 that had prevented banks, insurance companies, and investment companies from selling the same products and competing with one another. This change allowed banks to sell stocks, bonds, and insurance. At the same time, some investment companies and insurance companies began offering traditional banking services.

The change in banking services was based on the idea that consumers would prefer to have a single source for all their financial services needs—something that might function as a kind of "financial supermarket." However, banks have not always been able to effectively realize the benefits they had envisioned from offering this array of services. While banks establish relationships with customers through deposit accounts and loans for homes and autos, they have not been as successful in selling insurance or in helping customers to buy and sell stocks and bonds. Most bank customers continue to look to traditional insurance companies for their insurance needs and investment brokers and mutual fund companies to meet investment desires.

Deregulation and the Financial Crisis

The financial crisis that gripped the United States and the world beginning around 2007 was very complex. Real estate prices ballooned, in part because of lax lending standards. Banks had lowered their standards because they stopped holding mortgages for the life of the loan and began selling them. The banks and other financial companies would bundle the mortgages and sell them as mortgage-backed securities, an investment similar to a bond. The market for such securities was hot: investors plowed billions of dollars into mortgage-backed securities. The easy profits encouraged banks to generate more mortgages by lowering their lending standards further, which drove house prices even higher.

When the real estate bubble finally burst, falling home prices led to a rise in foreclosures. Suddenly, mortgage-backed securities changed from "hot investment" to "toxic asset." Credit markets around the world seized up as banks lost faith that their loans would be repaid.

The role of banking deregulation in the financial crisis is a matter of debate. Some claim that deregulation allowed banks to take risks that led to the crisis. Others say that getting rid of Depression-era laws had little to do with the root causes of the crisis. Still others blame the trend away from government supervision; they say the crisis could have been avoided if government watchdogs had done their job properly.

APPLICATION Analyzing Effects

B. How did deregulation change the ways that banks competed?

Technology and Banking

QUICK REFERENCE

An **automated teller machine** (ATM) is an electronic device that allows bank customers to make transactions without seeing a bank officer.

A **debit card** can be used like an ATM card or like a check.

A **stored-value card** represents money that the holder has on deposit with the issuer.

Deregulation is not the only thing that has changed the nature of banking. Technology—particularly computer technology—has changed the way customers use banks, producing a system generally referred to as electronic banking. For example, banks have begun using **automated teller machines** (ATMs), electronic devices that allow bank customers to make deposits, withdrawals, and transfers and check their account balances at any time without seeing a bank officer. Other innovations include **debit cards**, cards that can be used like an ATM card to withdraw cash or like a check to make purchases, and **stored-value cards**—cards that represent money that the holder has on deposit with the issuer, such as a department store. These cards give customers the ability to use the money in their accounts in more convenient ways. (You'll learn more about ATM and debit cards in Consumer and Personal Finance.)

Automated Teller Machines

Between school, sports practice, and a part-time job, you might find it difficult to get to the bank while it is open to deposit your paycheck and to withdraw spending money. The ATM solves that problem. ATMs are the oldest and most familiar of the developments in electronic banking. They began to be used widely in the 1970s and are now located not just at banks but also at retail stores, workplaces, airports, and entertainment venues, such as movie theaters and sports stadiums.

ATM Boom Between 1998 and 2003, the number of ATMs in the United States nearly doubled, from 187,00 to 371,000. By 2007, there were over 1.5 million ATMs worldwide.

ATMs are basically data terminals that are linked to a central computer that is in turn linked to individual banks' computers. The bank provides you with a plastic ATM card with a magnetic strip on the back that contains your account information. You insert your card into the ATM, enter your personal identification number (PIN), and follow the instructions on the screen. You may check your account balance, make deposits, withdraw cash, transfer money between accounts, and make loan payments through the ATM.

All ATM networks are connected so that consumers can use their ATM cards at any machine, no matter what bank owns it. Some banks charge fees for ATM use, especially to consumers who do not have an account at the bank that owns the particular ATM. ATMs allow people to bank even when the bank is closed and to avoid waiting in line for simple transactions. Many drive-through ATMs allow customers to bank from their cars. ATMs save banks money because it is much less expensive to process ATM transactions than transactions that involve a teller. They also allow banks to provide services at more locations without constructing complete bank branch offices.

Debit Cards

Debit cards are similar to ATM cards but offer additional benefits. Like ATM cards, debit cards can be used to withdraw cash and make other transactions at ATM machines. Debit cards are sometimes called check cards because they are linked to bank accounts and can be used like checks to make purchases at many retail outlets. Retailers often prefer debit cards because they avoid the problem of people writing checks with insufficient funds in their accounts.

Debit cards often look like credit cards, and they are similar in that they can be used to make purchases at stores. An important difference is that credit card purchases involve getting a loan. Your money stays in your account until you pay your credit card bill. With a debit card you make an immediate payment, since the price of your purchase is deducted from the account that is linked to your card. Therefore, it is important to keep track of debit card purchases along with checks so that you know how much money is available in your account at any given time.

Because of the way debit cards work, they are often seen as safer ways to manage your money than with credit cards. With credit cards, if you do not pay your balance in full each month, you pay interest on the outstanding balance and can build up considerable debt. With debit cards, you can only spend money that you actually have in a bank account.

YOUR ECONOMIC CHOICES

CREDIT CARD VS. DEBIT CARD

Which one should you use?

You have $250 in your checking account, and you don't get your next paycheck for a week. You want to buy a $75 birthday gift for a friend, and you have to pay $225 for a car repair. With your classmates, talk through each of the ways to handle the situation to find out what works best.

Entering a PIN for a debit card

Signing for a credit card

Stored-Value Cards

Stored-value cards, which represent money that the holder has on deposit with the card issuer, give consumers another convenient way to use electronic banking. These cards are sometimes called prepaid cards because customers have paid a certain amount of money for the card and can then use it to make payments for various goods and services. Some examples of stored-value cards include transit fare cards, gift cards from retail stores, and telephone cards. Consumers benefit from using transit fare cards and telephone cards because they do not have to worry about having the exact change needed each time they ride the bus or use a pay phone.

In 2004, there were more than 2,000 different stored-value card programs in the United States with about 20 million users. The number of users was expected to be 49 million by 2008. The $42 billion in transactions in 2003 was expected to grow to more than $72 billion by 2006.

Multipurpose stored-value cards—cards that can be used like debit cards—are becoming more popular. This type of card may take the place of a checking account, especially for people who have not traditionally used banks. While stored-value cards are a convenient way for people to make purchases and pay bills, consumers need to evaluate the fees involved in using such cards to determine whether they are less expensive than having a checking account or using a check-cashing service. In addition, the money paid into such cards is not always covered by FDIC insurance to protect customer deposits in case of a bank's failure.

Electronic Banking

Electronic banking allows customers who have set up accounts with a bank to perform practically every transaction without setting foot in a bank. Indeed, some banks are virtual banks with no physical buildings at all. Through the use of the Internet, customers can arrange for direct deposit of their paychecks, transfer funds from account to account, and pay their bills.

Most bank Web sites allow customers to review the most recent transactions on their accounts, view images of canceled checks, and download or print their periodic statements. Through electronic fund transfers, consumers can pay a credit card bill at one bank with funds from a checking account at another bank. Recurring bills, such as mortgage payments, may be paid automatically from a customer's checking account each month or through their bank's bill paying service.

However, electronic banking presents several challenges. Information security and identity theft are related, high-profile issues for the industry. Electronic banking allows banks to amass large amounts of information about their customers. Banks contend that this allows them to provide customers with better service. New laws require that banks make customers aware of privacy policies and offer them the opportunity to decide what information may be shared with others. Consumer concerns have led banks to developing increasingly sophisticated information security systems. (For information on identity theft, see Consumer and Personal Finance, which begins on p. 574.)

Online Convenience Online bill paying cuts time and expense by eliminating the need to mail checks.

APPLICATION Contrasting Economic Information

C. How are debit cards different from most stored-value cards?

SECTION 3 Assessment

Online Quiz
ClassZone.com

REVIEWING KEY CONCEPTS

1. How are these three terms related? How are they different?

   a. *automated teller*   **b.** *debit card*   **c.** *stored-value card* *machine*

2. What are two reasons that people deposit money in banks?

3. It is said that fractional reserve banking allows banks to create money? What is meant by this?

4. How did deregulation lead to a decrease in the number of banks between 1980 and the present?

5. How are debit cards related to automated teller machines?

6. **Using Your Notes** How does computer technology support home banking? Refer to your completed hierarchy diagram.

   Use the Graphic Organizer at **Interactive Review @ ClassZone.com**

CRITICAL THINKING

7. **Analyzing Data** Over the course of one year, Hometown Bank paid Mary Lee 3 percent interest on a $1,000 deposit and charged Owen's Bakery 8 percent interest on a $900 loan. How much net income did Hometown bank make? Show your calculations.

8. **Applying Economic Concepts** Suppose that Liz inherits $2,000 from her grandmother and deposits it into her college savings account at Hamilton Savings Bank. Assume that the reserve requirement is 20 percent. Create a chart showing five successive loans that could be made from this initial deposit.

9. **Making Inferences** Some parents think that allowing teenagers to use a debit card prepares them for using a credit card. What are the possible reasons behind this thinking? Do you think this reasoning is sound? Why or why not?

10. **Challenge** Look again at Figure 10.5, Fractional Reserve Banking, on page 305. Suppose that when Bank A made the $9,000 loan to the man with the leaky roof, it turned out the job cost only $7,000. The contractor deposited that money into Bank B. How much could Bank B then lend to the used-car buyer? If she bought a car for that amount, and the seller of the car deposited the money in Bank C, what size small-business loan could Bank C then turn around and make?

ECONOMICS IN PRACTICE

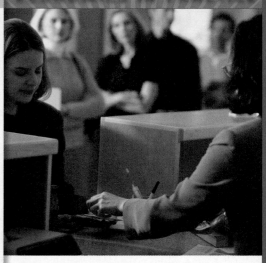

Starting a Bank
Think about what you have learned about the services that banks provide and how banks make money. Imagine that you are starting a bank for the other members of the class. Consider the following questions:

- What services would you provide? Why?
- How would your bank make a profit?
- What challenges might you face in making your bank profitable?

Write a Proposal Answer the above questions in a one-page proposal outlining what your bank would be like. Share your proposal with a classmate.

Challenge Include a section in your proposal about what you would do to make your bank more attractive to customers than the other banks run by your classmates.

Case Study

Economics Update
Find an update on this Case
Study at **ClassZone.com**

Housing Boom and Bust

Background From 2000 to 2006, house prices in the United States skyrocketed. Many factors contributed to the boom, but bank lending practices played a major role.

Deregulation changed banks from local institutions into national megabanks. Instead of collecting payments on a mortgage for 30 years, banks began to sell those loans to other financial institutions for a quick profit. Banks became less interested in verifying that clients could repay a mortgage and more interested in making as many mortgage loans as possible. The easy money fueled the housing price bubble.

What's the issue? How did bank lending practices contribute to the real estate boom? Study these sources to learn more about the bubble in house prices.

A. Online News Story

Huge gains in house prices led to speculative purchases—until the market failed.

Las Vegas House Flipping Boom Goes Bust

Home speculators hurting across country, especially in desert boomtown

In the rampant real estate speculation of the Las Vegas valley three years ago, people lined up outside Pulte Homes sales offices overnight as if they were waiting for the release of the latest video game console or hot new movie.

Having seen his house in an upscale part of suburban Henderson, Nev. jump $200,000 in value in 18 months, Sam Schwartz felt he couldn't miss any part of the boom.

He spent the night in the parking lot with TV, snacks and drinks, along with about a hundred other people.

Schwartz intended to buy a new home and then quickly sell it within the year — for a huge profit. Most people waiting were flippers just like him, he said.

"We had seen real evidence of what was possible in this crazy, inflated market, and we just wanted to get a piece of that investment equity," Schwartz said.

But when home prices unexpectedly took a backward step, many investors seeking to cash in quickly were left "upside-down," or owing more on their mortgages than what their homes were worth.

The result was a glut of homes in the marketplace, communities spotted with empty houses and for sale signs — and a foreclosure rate in Nevada that leads the nation as owners unable to sell became saddled with unbearable debt payments.

Source: **Associated Press, April 27, 2007**

Thinking Economically How did rising prices and speculators form a vicious cycle?

B. Cartoon

Cartoonist Grizelda imagined this mortgage loan scenario.

Source: www.CartoonStock.com

Thinking Economically
What does the cartoon imply about bank lending practices during the housing boom?

C. Online Editorial

Everyone from Main Street to Wall Street contributed to the housing price bubble.

From Subprime to the Ridiculous

How did mortgage financing turn into a house of cards?

The bottom line is that far too many Americans, not simply those with low credit scores, have borrowed more money than they are realistically capable of repaying. The credit boom was created by initially low adjustable rate mortgages, interest-only or negative amortization loans, and an appreciating real estate market that allowed homeowners to extract equity to help make mortgage payments. Now that real estate prices have stopped rising, and mortgage payments are resetting higher, borrowers can no longer afford to make these payments. . . .

Of course, the vast majority of home loans in the last few years, subprime or otherwise, should never have been made in the first place. However, when real estate prices were rising, no one cared about the wildly optimistic assumptions or the out-and-out fraud inherent in the loan process. Everyone was making money. Borrowers, regardless of their ability to pay off their loans, thought they were getting rich as real estate prices rose. On the other side, home builders, real estate agents, appraisers, mortgage brokers, mortgage originators, Wall Street brokerages that securitized the loans and the hedge fund clients who bought them were all getting rich as a result of booming credit. For the charade to continue, borrowers pretended they could pay and lenders pretended that they would be paid.

Source: **Forbes.com, March 15, 2007**

Thinking Economically According to this editorial, can the blame for the real estate bubble be assigned to any one party? Why or why not?

THINKING ECONOMICALLY Synthesizing

1. How might the bank lending practices parodied in Document B lead to the speculation described in Document A?

2. Document B humorously characterizes the low standards banks used when granting mortgage loans. What parts of Document C support this characterization?

3. According to Documents A and C, what inspired everyone from borrowers to builders to brokers to participate in the real estate boom?

Interactive ⏴⏵ Review

Review this chapter using interactive activities at **ClassZone.com**

- Online Summary
- Graphic Organizers
- Quizzes
- Review and Study Notes
- Vocabulary Flip Cards

○○○   ◯

 Online Summary

Complete the following activity either on your own paper or online at **ClassZone.com**

Choose the key concept that best completes the sentence. Not all key concepts will be used.

automated teller machine	M2
barter	medium of exchange
commodity money	money
currency	national bank
debit card	near money
demand deposits	representative money
fiat money	standard of value
fractional reserve banking	state bank
gold standard	store of value
M1	stored-value card

__1__ is anything that people will accept as payment for goods and services. Money makes trade easier by serving as a __2__. As a __3__, money allows people to compare the prices of goods and services. Money must be a __4__, or something that holds its value over time.

Gold coins and salt are both examples of __5__. Most money in the world today is __6__, which has no tangible value but is declared by the government to have worth.

__7__ consists of __8__, which includes paper money and coins and __9__, which is another name for checking accounts. Savings accounts and time deposits are called __10__ because they can be converted into cash easily.

__11__ allows banks to hold only part of their deposits and make loans based on the rest. The Federal Reserve Bank is the central __12__ in the nation.

The __13__ is the oldest form of electronic banking. A __14__ can be used like an ATM card or like a check.

CHAPTER 10 Assessment

REVIEWING KEY CONCEPTS

Money: Its Functions and Properties (pp. 288–295)

1. What three functions does money serve in the economy?

2. Why do economists make a distinction between M1 and M2?

The Development of U.S. Banking (pp. 296–303)

3. Why does fractional reserve banking leave banks vulnerable to failure if too many consumers demand their money at the same time?

4. How is the Federal Reserve System different from the system of national banks created in the 1860s?

Innovations in Modern Banking (pp. 304–313)

5. How did the automated teller machine change the nature of banking?

6. Which type of stored-value card is most like a debit card?

APPLYING ECONOMIC CONCEPTS

Look at the table below showing changes in use of electronic payments between 1995 and 2001.

7. Which type of electronic banking increased the most among all households between 1995 and 2001?

8. How did education generally affect the use of electronic payments?

FIGURE 10.8	PERCENTAGE OF HOUSEHOLDS USING ELECTRONIC BANKING					
Education of head of household	**ATM**		**Debit card**		**Automatic bill paying**	
	1995	2001	1995	2001	1995	2001
All households	61.2	69.8	17.6	47.0	21.8	40.3
No college degree	52.8	63.7	14.3	42.3	18.2	33.7
College degree	80.1	81.6	25.2	56.2	30.1	53.2

Source: *Statistical Abstract of the United States, 2006*

9. **Analyzing Effects** Suppose that the government changes the tax policy so that people pay lower taxes if they save more money. The benefits are significant enough that people shift about 10 percent of their money from their checking accounts into certificates of deposit. How would this change affect the amount of money in M1 and M2?

10. **Drawing Conclusions** Today, there are about three times as many state chartered commercial banks as there are nationally chartered commercial banks. How does the current U.S. economy avoid the kinds of problems caused by state banks in the 19th century?

11. **Applying Economic Concepts** One Saturday, four friends go shopping at the local mall. Catherine uses her ATM card to withdraw some cash. Tara has a gift card that she received for her birthday. It is worth $50 at her favorite clothing store. Charlotte uses a credit card, and Alyssa pays with a debit card.

    a. Which of the shoppers has a stored-value card? Why does she have less flexibility in her shopping than the other shoppers?

    b. If Catherine, Charlotte, and Alyssa each spend $50, which one has not reduced the amount of money in her checking account at the end of the day? Why?

    c. Which shopper may end up paying more than face value for her purchases?

12. **Analyzing Causes** What are the different motives behind these two mergers: a stock brokerage firm buys a bank; a California bank buys a Florida bank?

13. **Challenge** Why are credit cards and debit cards not considered to be money?

Promote Electronic Banking

Step 1 Choose a partner. Imagine that you work for a bank in the late 1990s. Your bank intends to be a pioneer in Internet banking and asks you to design its first Web page. Your boss gives you the following criteria for the Web page:

- Allow existing customers to access account balances and transfer funds between accounts.

- Promote traditional bank products, including checking, savings, CDs, credit cards, mortgages, and auto loans.

- Allow customers to find the most convenient branch or ATM location.

Step 2 Sketch out a design for the Web page to meet your boss's criteria, showing appropriate links.

Step 3 Two years later, deregulation has led to significant changes in the banking industry. In addition, more consumers are interested in Internet banking. Your boss asks you to redesign the Web page with these additional criteria:

- Allow customers to pay bills, apply for loans, buy stocks, and shop for insurance through the bank's Web site.

- Allow customers to view transactions on all their accounts, including credit and debit card transactions, and receive statements and other bank communications electronically.

- Reassure customers that online banking is secure and that their privacy will be protected.

Step 4 Sketch out a new Web page that shows the complete range of services the bank now offers and that meets all six criteria.

Step 5 Share your Web page designs with another pair of students and discuss what aspects would be most important and effective for you as a customer.

Stock Market
The stock market, which consists of institutions such as the NASDAQ, is where stocks and bonds are traded.

CHAPTER

11

Financial Markets

CONCEPT REVIEW

Voluntary exchange is a trade in which both parties involved believe that what they are getting is worth more than what they are giving up.

CHAPTER 11 KEY CONCEPT

The **financial system** consists of institutions, such as banks, insurance markets, bond markets, and stock markets, that help transfer funds between savers and investors.

WHY THE CONCEPT MATTERS

Do you have a savings account? If so, you play a very important role in our economy. Your savings—what you gave up to get those assets—will be borrowed and invested by businesses and the government to build factories, offices, roads, and so on. The jobs and new products and services created by these investments, in turn, further help to fuel the nation's economy.

Online Highlights
More at ClassZone.com

 Economics Update
Go to **ECONOMICS UPDATE** for chapter updates and current news on the financial crisis. (See Case Study, pp. 344–345.) ▶

 SMART Grapher
Go to **SMART GRAPHER** to complete graphing activities in this chapter.

Interactive ⟨↔⟩ Review
Go to **INTERACTIVE REVIEW** for concept review and activities.

How did advanced financial tools contribute to the financial crisis? See the Case Study on pages 344–345.

Savings and Investment

| OBJECTIVES | KEY TERMS | TAKING NOTES |

OBJECTIVES

In Section 1, you will
- identify what constitutes the financial system
- describe the various financial intermediaries
- explain how economists categorize the various markets where financial assets are sold

KEY TERMS

savings, *p. 318*
investment, *p. 318*
financial system, *p. 318*
financial asset, *p. 319*
financial market, *p. 319*
financial intermediary, *p. 319*
mutual fund, *p. 320*
capital market, *p. 322*
money market, *p. 322*
primary market, *p. 322*
secondary market, *p. 322*

TAKING NOTES

As you read Section 1, complete a hierarchy diagram to track main ideas and supporting details. Use the Graphic Organizer at **Interactive Review @ ClassZone.com**

The Financial System

KEY CONCEPTS

QUICK REFERENCE

Savings is income not used for consumption.

Investment is the use of income today that allows for a future benefit.

The **financial system** is all the institutions that help transfer funds between savers and investors.

There are two things you can do with your money—spend it or save it. **Savings** is income not used for consumption, in other words not spent on immediate wants. Savings that are put to use are investments. In general, **investment** is the use of income today in a way that allows for a future benefit. More specifically, *economic investment* refers to money lent to businesses—to finance the construction of a new factory, for example. *Personal investment* refers to the act of individuals putting their savings into financial assets, such as CDs, stocks, bonds, or mutual funds.

Consider what happens when you put money in a savings account. Through this act, you benefit—your savings account earns interest—but others do too. By saving, you make funds available for the bank to lend. Borrowers use these funds for many purposes, such as investing in new businesses or in new equipment for established businesses. The **financial system**, which consists of institutions such as banks, insurance markets, bond markets, and stock markets, allows for this transfer of funds between savers and investors.

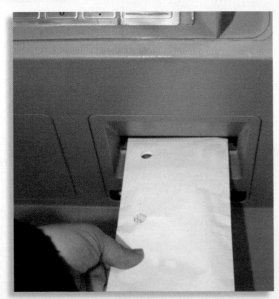

ATM Deposits Using an ATM to make deposits makes saving easy and convenient.

Economics Update

Find an update on saving at **ClassZone.com**

FIGURE 11.1 The Financial System

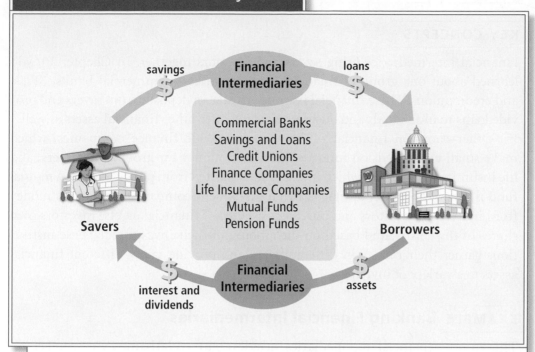

savings
Financial
Intermediaries
loans

Commercial Banks
Savings and Loans
Credit Unions
Finance Companies
Life Insurance Companies
Mutual Funds
Pension Funds

Savers

Borrowers

Financial
Intermediaries

interest and
dividends

assets

ANALYZE CHARTS

1. What do savers get in exchange for the funds they deposit with financial intermediaries?

2. Why do you think that financial intermediaries perform their vital function? Think back to Chapter 10 if you need help.

Bringing Savings and Investment Together

Individuals and businesses can save surplus funds in many ways, including savings accounts at commercial banks or S&Ls, certificates of deposit (CDs), corporate or government bonds, and stocks. The agent receiving these funds is a borrower, who issues savers written confirmation of the transaction. This written confirmation is called a **financial asset**, or a claim on the property of the borrower.

Sometimes savers and borrowers come together directly in a **financial market**, a situation in which buyers and sellers exchange particular types of financial assets. For example, an individual or business might buy corporate bonds or shares of stock. More often, however, financial intermediaries bring savers, borrowers, and financial assets together. A **financial intermediary** is a financial institution that collects funds from savers and then invests these funds in loans and other financial assets. Figure 11.1 shows how funds flow from savers to investors through the financial markets and financial intermediaries that make up the financial system.

QUICK REFERENCE

A **financial asset** is a claim on the property of the borrower.

A **financial market** is where buyers and sellers exchange financial assets.

A **financial intermediary** is an institution that collects funds from savers and invests the funds in financial assets.

APPLICATION Applying Economic Concepts

A. Look again at the example opposite of a person depositing money into a savings account. How is this an example of Adam Smith's "invisible hand"?

Financial Intermediaries

Financial intermediaries bring savers and investors together. In Chapter 10, you learned about one group of financial intermediaries—commercial banks, S&Ls, and credit unions. These financial institutions take in deposits from savers and provide loans to individuals and businesses. Many offer other financial assets as well.

Other common financial intermediaries include finance companies, which make small loans; pension funds, which invest money for groups of workers; and life insurance companies, which invest funds collected from policyholders. A **mutual fund** is a pool of money managed by an investment company that gathers money from individual investors and purchases a range of financial assets. Investors own shares of the entire fund based on the amount of their investment. These institutions gather their money in different ways and provide many different financial assets to a variety of investors.

QUICK REFERENCE

A **mutual fund** is an investment company that gathers money from individual investors and purchases a range of financial assets.

The New York Stock Exchange Stocks are an important element of the assets that make up a mutual fund.

EXAMPLE Banking Financial Intermediaries

This group of financial intermediaries includes commercial banks, S&Ls, and credit unions. All of these institutions provide checking and savings accounts. Depositors earn interest on their savings deposits and some checking deposits. Most also offer CDs and money market deposit accounts that pay slightly higher rates of interest. (Figure 11.2 explains how savers earn money from interest.) The federal government insures deposits, including CDs and money market accounts, up to $100,000 per depositor in any given bank.

These institutions lend a portion of their deposits to borrowers. Banks charge borrowers a higher rate of interest than they pay to savers and hope to earn a profit. The loans are financial assets to the bank. If a borrower does not pay back the loan on time, the bank may repossess the property, such as a home or a car.

Deregulation has allowed banks to offer other financial assets, such as money market mutual funds, stocks, bonds, and insurance. The federal government does not insure funds invested in these financial assets.

EXAMPLE Nonbank Financial Intermediaries

This group of financial intermediaries includes finance companies, mutual funds, pension funds, and life insurance companies. Finance companies make loans to households and small businesses. Generally, the loans are under $2,000 and are paid back in monthly installments, including interest, over a few years.

A mutual fund pools money from many personal investors. In return, each investor receives shares in a fund that is made up of a large number and variety of stocks, bonds, or other financial assets. Mutual funds make it easier and more affordable for individual investors to own a wide variety of financial assets. Once investors purchase shares of a fund, they allow its managers to make investment decisions.

Pension funds allow employees to save money for retirement and sometimes include contributions from employers. The pension fund then invests these pooled contributions in various financial assets that will increase in value and provide workers with more money when they retire.

Life insurance companies allow individuals to accumulate savings by building cash values and protect against losses from death or disability. Just as banks lend some of their deposits, insurance companies lend or invest some of the income earned from policyholders in a variety of financial assets.

MATH CHALLENGE

FIGURE 11.2 Calculating Interest

Banks pay savers interest in order to use their money. A saver's initial deposit is called the principal. Simple interest is the interest paid on the principal alone. Compound interest is paid on the principal plus any earned interest. The following steps show how an annual rate of 5 percent interest is paid on the principal ($1,000) over three years.

Year 1 Simple interest is calculated using the following formula:

| Principal | × | Interest rate | = | Interest earned | $1,000 | × | .05 | = | $50.00 |

Year 2 The amount in this account is now $1,050.00. Compound interest, which is paid on the principal plus the earned interest, is calculated as follows:

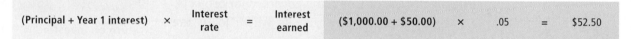

| (Principal + Year 1 interest) | × | Interest rate | = | Interest earned | ($1,000.00 + $50.00) | × | .05 | = | $52.50 |

Year 3 There is now $1,102.50 in the account. Interest continues to compound.

| (Principal + Year 1 interest + Year 2 interest) | × | Interest rate | = | Interest earned | ($1,000.00 + $50.00 + 52.50) | × | .05 | = | $55.13 |

After three years, the total in the account is $1,157.63.

Using a Formula Instead of using the multiple steps shown above, you can calculate the total value of an account using the following formula (wherein P=principal, r=interest rate, and t=number of years):

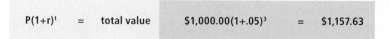

| $P(1+r)^t$ | = | total value | $1,000.00(1+.05)^3$ | = | $1,157.63 |

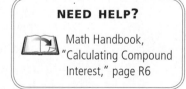

NEED HELP?

Math Handbook, "Calculating Compound Interest," page R6

APPLICATION Comparing and Contrasting

B. How is a pension fund like a savings account? How is it different?

Financial Asset Markets

QUICK REFERENCE

The **capital market** is where long-term financial assets are bought and sold.

The **money market** is where short-term financial assets are bought and sold.

The **primary market** is for buying financial assets directly from the issuer.

The **secondary market** is where financial assets are resold.

KEY CONCEPTS

The different financial assets discussed in this section are bought and sold on various financial markets. Economists tend to categorize these markets based on two factors—time (how long the loan is for) and whether the financial assets can be resold. Based on time, economists distinguish between the **capital market**, the market for buying and selling long-term financial assets, and the **money market**, the market for buying and selling short-term financial assets. In regard to resalability, economists distinguish between the **primary market**, which is the market for buying newly created financial assets directly from the issuing entity, and the **secondary market**, which is the market where financial assets are resold.

FACTOR 1 Time

There are two time-sensitive markets. Capital markets are markets where assets are held for longer than a year. Some examples of assets sold on the capital market include certain kinds of securities, namely stocks and bonds, mortgages, and long-term CDs. Because these loans are for longer periods of time, the money may be invested in projects that require large amounts of capital, such as buying homes, building new factories, retooling established factories, or financing government projects.

Money markets are markets where loans are made for less than a year. Examples of assets traded in these markets include short-term CDs that depositors can redeem in a few months and Treasury bills, which allow the U.S. government to borrow money for short periods of time.

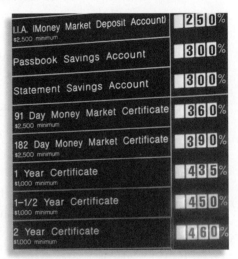

Return on Investment Time is an important factor in the level of return for many investments.

FACTOR 2 Resalability

There also are two kinds of markets based on whether the financial assets can be resold. Primary markets are markets for financial assets that can be redeemed only by the original buyer. Examples include savings bonds and small denomination CDs. The term *primary market* also refers to the market where the first issue of a stock is sold to the public through investment bankers.

Secondary markets are resale markets for financial assets. These markets offer liquidity to personal investors. So, investors are able to turn their assets into cash relatively quickly. Stocks and bonds, which you'll learn more about later in this chapter, are two of the most prominent financial assets sold on the secondary market.

APPLICATION Analyzing Effects

C. Why are stocks and bonds part of the capital market and the secondary market?

Online Quiz
ClassZone.com

REVIEWING KEY CONCEPTS

1. Explain the difference between the terms in each of these pairs.

   a. *savings* *investment*

   b. *capital market* *money market*

   c. *primary market* *secondary market*

2. What is the purpose of the financial system?

3. Why do banks receive financial assets when they make loans?

4. How does a mutual fund serve as a financial intermediary?

5. What determines whether a loan is part of the capital market or the money market?

6. **Using Your Notes** What is the relationship between financial intermediaries and the financial system? Refer to your completed hierarchy diagram.

   Use the Graphic Organizer at **Interactive Review @ ClassZone.com**

CRITICAL THINKING

7. **Categorizing Information** Which of the following are banking financial intermediaries and which are nonbanking financial intermediaries?
   • Consumer Finance Company
   • Family Life Insurance Company
   • First National Bank
   • Home Savings and Loan
   • Investors' Mutual Fund
   • Employee Credit Union
   • Employee Pension Fund

8. **Making Inferences** A local bank offers savings accounts that have no minimum balance requirement and pay 3 percent interest per year. Account holders can withdraw any amount of money from their accounts at any time. The bank also offers money market accounts that require a $500 minimum balance and pay 4 percent interest each year. Account holders are allowed two withdrawals per month, but each must be for at least $100. Why does the money market account pay a higher interest rate?

9. **Applying Economic Concepts** Suppose that you deposit $100 into your savings account, which earns 3 percent interest per year. Use what you've learned about calculating interest to determine how much money you'll have in your account at the end of one year and at the end of six years.

10. **Challenge** Why might a decrease in household savings have an adverse effect on small businesses in a local community?

ECONOMICS IN PRACTICE

Stock certificates

Identifying Markets

Consider how economists categorize financial markets. Copy the table shown below. Review the bulleted list of financial assets and place each one in the correct location(s) in the table. Assets may be placed in more than one category.

- 15-year mortgage
- 6-month CD for $1,000
- 2-year CD for $25,000
- 5-year corporate bond
- 10-year savings bond
- Shares of stock
- 26-week Treasury bill
- 30-year Treasury bond

Capital Market	Money Market
Primary Market	**Secondary Market**

Challenge Why do savings bonds and small certificates of deposit have less liquidity than shares of stock?

Investing in a Market Economy

OBJECTIVES	KEY TERMS	TAKING NOTES
In Section 2, you will • discuss the issues that should be considered when making investment decisions • explain how risk and return are related	investment objective, *p. 324* risk, *p. 327* return, *p. 327* diversification, *p. 327*	As you read Section 2, complete a chart like the one shown using the key concepts and other helpful words and phrases. Use the Graphic Organizer at **Interactive Review @ ClassZone.com**

Investing in a Market Economy	
objectives	risk vs. return

Why Are You Investing?

KEY CONCEPTS

In Section 1, you saw that there are two types of investing: personal and economic. Note that for the remainder of the chapter, we'll be using all forms of the word *invest* as a quick way to refer to personal investing—which is, in effect, saving.

You've now learned that there are a number of assets you can own. But how do you determine which is, or are, right for you? The first thing that you might do is to decide why you are investing. This reason is your **investment objective**, a financial goal that an investor uses to determine if an investment is appropriate. Some possible financial goals are saving money for retirement, for a down payment on a house or an automobile, for college tuition, or for a vacation. Your goal helps you to determine the right investments.

QUICK REFERENCE

An **investment objective** is a financial goal used to determine if an investment is appropriate.

Investment Objectives

Two issues play a major role in determining which investments work best to achieve different investment objectives. The first issue is time. For example, is this a short-term financial goal, such as saving for a vacation, or a long-term financial goal, such as saving for

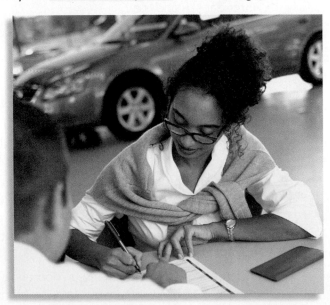

Savings Goals Saving for a car down payment suggests certain kinds of longer-term investments.

What reasons do you have for investing?

Do you have any investment objectives? Maybe you have a short-term objective, such as saving money to go on spring break. Or your objective is more long term, such as saving for college. What kinds of investments might be appropriate for your objective?

Saving for vacation

Saving for college

retirement? The amount of time you have to build your savings influences the kinds of investments that would be most appropriate.

The second issue is income. How much money do you have available to save after meeting current expenses? The answer to this question is influenced by a series of other questions: Will your income change in the future? Is there money available for emergencies? To respond to all these questions, having a savings plan that is realistic and that is flexible enough to adjust to changing circumstances can be a big help.

Other important questions are: Do you have any outstanding debts? Are you paying taxes on time? Paying off debts is an important first step to investing. Generally, the interest you pay on debts, such as credit card balances, is higher than what you can earn through most investments. Tax considerations are most important for investors with higher incomes who are subject to higher tax rates.

Different types of investments are suitable to various investment objectives. For example, savings for emergencies should be in highly liquid investments, such as savings accounts or money market accounts. With these investments, the risk of loss is low and money can be withdrawn at any time. Saving for a vacation would also require investments that are short-term and liquid. Investors who are saving for longer-term goals may be less concerned with immediate liquidity and may want to invest in stocks that increase in value over a longer period of time. CDs that commit funds for a certain length of time may be chosen to coincide with the timing of certain savings goals, such as making a major purchase or starting college. Many bonds offered by state and local governments offer tax-free earnings.

Economics Update

Find an update on investing at **ClassZone.com**

APPLICATION Drawing Conclusions

A. Would a CD be a more appropriate way to save for a down payment on a car or for emergencies? Why?

Mellody Hobson: Investing in the Future

Economics Update

Find an update on Mellody Hobson at **ClassZone.com**

What do the Chicago Bulls, hip-hop stars, and inner-city elementary school students have to do with personal finance? All are part of Mellody Hobson's efforts to get more households interested in investing. Hobson believes that many people lack the necessary knowledge to determine their investment objectives and manage their money to create wealth. How is she trying to change this situation?

Creating Educated Investors

Mellody Hobson began as a college intern at Ariel Investments, a small mutual fund company in Chicago. After Hobson graduated in 1991, Ariel hired her to work in its marketing department. Her hard work, determination, and bright ideas led to a series of promotions, and in 2000 Hobson became president of Ariel.

One of Hobson's bright ideas was to incorporate financial education in the school curriculum from the early grades. Working with the Chicago Public Schools, Hobson helped to start the Ariel Community Academy in 1996. The academy teaches students about investing, beginning in first grade. Hobson also developed the first ongoing study of investing by African Americans and looked for ways to increase their participation in the stock market. "The stock market represents a major source of wealth creation in this country," Hobson has stated, "but . . . African Americans have been largely left out." Ariel's marketing efforts to the black community included cosponsoring events with the Chicago Bulls and creating a stock-picking contest involving well-known hip-hop stars.

When Hobson became the financial contributor to the *Good Morning America* television program in 2000, she began to reach millions of people with easy-to-understand information about economic matters. Hobson believes that more knowledge about how to invest and greater diversity in the investment industry will help bring the benefits of investing to people of all racial and economic backgrounds.

Mellody Hobson explains the benefits of investing to a wide audience.

APPLICATION Making Inferences

B. Why does Mellody Hobson want to make more people aware of investing?

Risk and Return

KEY CONCEPTS

Once investors have decided their financial objectives, there are two other related issues they might consider—risk and return. **Risk** is the possibility for loss on an investment, and **return** is the profit or loss made on an investment.

While savings deposits in banks are insured against loss, most investments carry some possibility of losing part of the money invested. Return may refer to the interest paid on a savings account or CD or the increase in value of a stock over time. Most investors try to balance risk and return through **diversification**, the practice of distributing investments among different financial assets to maximize return and limit risk.

What Kind of Risk Are You Willing to Take?

When most investors think about risk, they think about the possibility of losing some of their initial investment, often referred to as their principal. Even if they don't earn a lot of money on the investment, they want to get back at least what they put in. Investments that guarantee no loss of principal include insured savings deposits and CDs. Bonds that are backed by the U.S. government are also considered to be almost risk-free because it is highly unlikely that the government would not pay back its loans. Almost all other investments carry some risk.

One of the biggest risks investors face, even with safe investments like those described above, is loss of the purchasing power of the money invested due to inflation. (Remember that inflation is a general rise in the level of prices.) That is why many financial advisers warn against investing everything in safe investments that pay a guaranteed rate of interest that may not keep up with inflation.

Other investments, such as stocks and corporate bonds, carry a higher degree of risk because the return depends on how profitable the company is. Investors who purchase stock with the expectation that it will appreciate in value over time may lose some of their money if the company runs into problems or other economic factors affect the value of the stock. In that case, investors may find that they cannot sell the stock for as much as they paid for it, and they suffer a loss. Investors in corporate bonds face similar risks, although bonds are considered less risky than stocks because creditors such as bondholders are paid off before stockholders if a company has financial problems.

FIGURE 11.3 THE RELATIONSHIP OF RISK AND RETURN

Risk

Return

Risk and Return
Risk and return have a direct relationship—the higher the risk of the investment, the greater the possible return.

How can you balance risk and return?

When you consider what financial assets further your investment objective, you must address both risk and return. A high-risk investment may bring large returns, but can you absorb the potential losses? A low-risk investment may provide a steady return, but because of inflation you may be losing money. How would you decide which type of investment to make?

▲ Return

▲ Risk

What Kind of Return Do You Want?

When making investment decisions, investors estimate what kind of return they expect to earn. The safest investments, such as Treasury bills, interest-bearing savings accounts, and shorter-term CDs, generally offer the lowest return in the form of fixed rates of interest. The returns on stocks and bonds are not guaranteed and may vary considerably at different times, depending on how the company you invest in performs and the state of the economy as a whole. Generally, stocks provide a higher return over time than do other investments.

As Figure 11.3 on page 327 shows, risk and return are directly related—the greater the possible return, the higher the risk that the investment will lose value. Investors always want the highest return possible, but they must balance that desire with a realistic understanding about the level of risk they can tolerate. The factors of time and income come into play here. People who are investing for retirement over a period of 20 to 30 years may be willing to take more risk by investing in stocks because their investments are likely to increase over that period, even though they might have losses in some years. People with less time and less income to invest might not be willing to risk possible losses.

Diversification is the most common way for investors to maximize their returns and limit their risks. For example, you might put 70 percent of your investments for retirement in a variety of stocks, 20 percent in bonds, and 10 percent in CDs. By spreading out your money in a variety of assets, you have a better chance of offsetting losses from one investment with gains from another. Mutual funds, which invest in a large number of stocks or bonds, help small investors diversify their investments.

APPLICATION Drawing Conclusions

C. Is it possible to have a low-risk, high-return investment? Why or why not?

SECTION 2 Assessment

Online Quiz
ClassZone.com

REVIEWING KEY CONCEPTS

1. Use each of the three terms below in a sentence that illustrates the meaning of the term:

   a. *investment objective*   b. *return*   c. *diversification*

2. What is the relationship between risk and return?

3. How would the risk of investing in a single stock compare with the risk of investing in a mutual fund? Why?

4. How is diversification related to risk and return?

5. How are risk and return related to investment objectives?

6. **Using Your Notes** How do time and income influence investment objectives? Refer to your completed chart.

   Use the Graphic Organizer at **Interactive Review @ ClassZone.com**

Investing in a Market Economy	
objectives	risk vs. return

CRITICAL THINKING

7. **Comparing and Contrasting** Matthew's parents started saving for his college education when he was born. When Matthew turned 16, he got a part-time job and saved part of his earnings for his college expenses. Compare and contrast the investment objectives of Matthew and his parents and describe the factors that influenced their investment decisions.

8. **Drawing Conclusions** Ryan owns shares in a single mutual fund that includes stocks and bonds. Maggie invests her money in Treasury bonds, state bonds, and corporate bonds. Joshua invests in shares of stock in five different high-tech companies. Which of these investors best understands the concept of diversification? Give reasons for your answer.

9. **Applying Economic Concepts** Inez bought 100 shares of a mutual fund for $10 each and sold them five years later for $15 each. Ethan put $1,000 in a 5-year CD and received a total of $235 in interest. Which investment provided the better return? How does this illustrate the relationship between risk and return?

10. **Challenge** Stocks that are sold on the secondary market and savings accounts both provide liquidity. For each of these investments, what kinds of risks does this liquidity entail?

ECONOMICS IN PRACTICE

Evaluating Investments
Consider what you have learned about risk and return as they relate to various investments, then study the table below and evaluate each investment.

Identify Risk and Return Place a check mark in the appropriate columns for each investment.

Investment	Risk		Return	
	Low	High	Low	High
$1,000 CD				
100 shares of a mutual fund				
100 shares of stock				
Corporate bond				
Government bond				
Regular savings account				

Challenge Rank the investments in order from the lowest risk to the highest risk and from the lowest return to the highest return. Make a generalization about risk and return based on your rankings.

Buying and Selling Stocks

OBJECTIVES	KEY TERMS	TAKING NOTES
In Section 3, you will • discuss why people buy stocks • describe how stocks are traded • explain how the performance of stocks is measured	stock exchange, *p. 330* capital gain, *p. 330* common stock, *p. 331* preferred stock, *p. 331* stockbroker, *p. 332* future, *p. 333* option, *p. 333* stock index, *p. 334* bull market, *p. 335* bear market, *p. 335*	As you read Section 3, complete a cluster diagram using the key concepts and other helpful words and phrases. Use the Graphic Organizer at **Interactive Review @ ClassZone.com**

The Stock Market

KEY CONCEPTS

Recall that in Chapter 8 you learned that corporations raise money through stock and bond issues. You will learn more about the sale—and resale—of stocks in this section. When a company first issues stock, it is sold to investment bankers in the primary market. Known as an initial public offering, or IPO, this is the stock sale that raises money for the corporation.

However, most stock is then resold to investors through a **stock exchange**, a secondary market where securities (stocks and bonds) are bought and sold. Most people buy stocks as a financial investment, with the expectation that the stock price will rise and that they can resell the stock for a profit. Gains made from the sale of securities are called **capital gains**.

Why Buy Stock?

Investors buy stock for two reasons. The first is to earn dividend payments, which are a share of the corporation's profits that are paid back to the corporation's stockholders. The second reason is to earn capital gains by selling the stock at a price greater than the purchase price. If stock is sold below the buying price, the seller makes a capital loss. Investors who want to earn income

QUICK REFERENCE

A **stock exchange** is a market where securities are bought and sold.

Capital gain is profit made from the sale of securities.

from their investment will be most interested in dividends. Those who want to see their investment grow over time will be most interested in potential for capital gain.

As you learned in the previous section, investing in stocks carries a higher risk than most other investments but provides the opportunity for higher returns over time. Corporations are not required to pay dividends, so an investor has no guarantee that they will earn income from stocks. Similarly, there is no guarantee that the stock price will be higher when the investor wants to sell the stock.

"IN LIEU OF A DIVIDEND, YOU'LL BE E-MAILED A 'STOCK TIP DU JOUR'."

Source: www.CartoonStock.com

No Guarantees Dividend payments are a possibility, not a certainty; stocks come with risk.

Types of Stock

There are essentially two types of stock—common stock and preferred stock. **Common stock** is share of ownership in a corporation, giving holders voting rights and a share of profits. **Preferred stock** is share of ownership in a corporation giving holders a share of profits (paid before common stockholders) but no voting rights. Most people who buy stock choose to buy common stock.

Figure 11.4 shows the similarities and differences between the two types of stock. Notice that both types of stock give a share of ownership in the corporation that entitles a shareholder to receive dividends. The difference is that holders of preferred stock receive guaranteed dividends and will be paid before common stockholders if the company is liquidated. As a tradeoff for this preference, holders of preferred stock generally have no voting rights in the corporation, and their dividends do not increase if the company's stock increases in value. Each holder of common stock generally gets one vote per share owned to elect the board of directors, which makes important decisions about how the company conducts business.

QUICK REFERENCE

Common stock gives shareholders voting rights and a share of profits.

Preferred stock gives shareholders a share of profits but, in general, no voting rights.

FIGURE 11.4 Common Stock and Preferred Stock

Characteristic	Preferred Stock	Common Stock
Share of ownership	Yes	Yes
Eligible for dividends	Yes	Yes
Guaranteed dividends	Yes	No
Voting rights	No	Yes

ANALYZE CHARTS
1. What preference do holders of preferred stock have?
2. What do holders of common stock have that holders of preferred stock do not have?

APPLICATION Drawing Conclusions

A. What kind of stock do you think investors who wanted a steady income from their investment would buy? Why?

Trading Stock

Most people who invest in stock do so with the hope of earning capital gains when they sell it. Like anything else sold in a free market, stock prices are determined by demand and supply. Some factors that affect stock prices include company profits or losses, technological advances that may affect a company's business or a whole industry, and the overall state of the economy. When investors perceive that a company's value is likely to increase, the demand for the stock will increase and its price will rise. As the price rises, more people will want to sell the stock for a profit.

Few investors buy stock directly from companies. Most investors use a **stockbroker**, an agent who is paid a commission for buying and selling securities on behalf of customers. Stockbrokers, sometimes just called brokers, generally work for brokerage firms. Investors may interact with brokers in person, by phone, or online. The broker's primary job is to carry out the investor's instructions to make trades. Some brokers also provide investment advice. Brokers buy and sell stocks for their customers on a variety of stock exchanges.

Organized Stock Exchanges

The New York Stock Exchange (NYSE) is the oldest and largest of the organized stock exchanges in the United States. It is located in New York City on Wall Street, a name that has become synonymous with the U.S. stock market. Most of the largest and most successful U.S. corporations list their stock with the NYSE. Brokerage firms pay to become members of the exchange.

Many trades on the NYSE continue to take place in the traditional, organized auction format. Each stock has a specified location or trading post on the floor of the exchange. A specialist representing that stock runs the auction that matches buyers and sellers through open bidding to determine the price of shares. Prices for a stock often vary from minute to minute as the auction process continues throughout the day.

Technological advances have brought changes to the NYSE. Since 1996, floor traders have used small hand-held computers to execute many trades, and more than half of the orders to buy and sell are now sent electronically. In 2006, the NYSE merged with Archipelago Exchange, an electronic stock-trading company. The merger created a second stock exchange called NYSE Arca. Unlike the more traditional NYSE, NYSE Arca is an all-electronic exchange.

In 2007, the NYSE merged with Euronext, a group of European stock exchanges. Euronext includes stock exchanges in Paris, London, Brussels, Amsterdam, and Lisbon. In 2008, NYSE Euronext acquired the American Stock Exchange (AMEX). Most of the companies traded on AMEX, which is also located in New York City, are smaller than those traded on the NYSE.

Controlled Chaos Don't be fooled by the seeming disorder of the exchange floor. It is a secure and organized trading system.

Over-the-Counter Stock Exchanges

The term *over-the-counter* (OTC) is used to describe the market for stocks that are not traded on a formal stock exchange. In 1970, the National Association of Securities Dealers (NASD) introduced a centralized computer system that allows OTC traders around the country to make trades at the best prices possible. This automated quotation system became the market known as NASDAQ.

In terms of number of companies listed and number of shares traded, the NASDAQ is one of the world's largest stock exchanges. The majority of stocks listed on the NASDAQ are those of technology companies, but many other sectors of the economy are also represented.

In 1990, the NASD began operating another electronic market called the OTC Bulletin Board (OTCBB). This market deals in the stocks of smaller companies and lacks some of the regulations of the NASDAQ.

FIGURE 11.5 SOME NASDAQ STOCKS

Amgen Inc.	eBay Inc.
Apple, Inc.	Intel Corporation
Comcast Corporation	Microsoft Corporation
Cisco Systems, Inc.	Oracle Corporation
Dell Inc.	Qualcomm Incorporated

Futures and Options Markets

Businesses involved in agriculture developed ways to protect themselves from the price fluctuations typical of that market. A **future** is a contract to buy or sell a commodity at a specified future date and price. An **option** is a similar contract that gives the right, but not the obligation, to buy or sell. For example, a farmer might use a futures contract on a crop of tomatoes to lock in a price high enough to ensure a profit. Or a corn processing plant might sign an options contract for corn, giving it the right to buy if prices don't rise too high.

The futures and options contracts developed for agriculture can now be used for stocks and other financial instruments. Institutional investors use these and similar tools to reduce the risk of their investments. Some speculators attempt to use such tools to earn large profits, but their use can also lead to large losses.

QUICK REFERENCE

A **future** is a contract to buy or sell a stock on a specific future date at a preset price.

An **option** gives an investor the right to buy or sell stock at a future date at a preset price.

Recent Developments

Revised stock market regulations and advances in computer technology have changed the way stocks are traded. Stocks listed on any exchange are now available to any trading firm. The growth of electronic communication networks increased electronic stock trading, especially on the NASDAQ market. Trades now take place 24 hours a day, not just when the stock exchanges are open.

Many individual investors have access to the Internet and have become more knowledgeable about investing. These investors wanted to trade stocks without relying on traditional stockbrokers. The result has been huge growth in online brokerage companies. Investors now have the ability to make trades at any time and generally pay lower commissions than those charged by traditional brokers. Computer technology matches buyers and sellers automatically, providing rapid trades at the best possible prices.

APPLICATION Drawing Conclusions

B. How is the NASDAQ similar to the NYSE? How are they different?

Measuring How Stocks Perform

KEY CONCEPTS

QUICK REFERENCE

A **stock index** measures and reports the change in prices of a set of stocks.

About half of all U.S. households now own stocks, and the stock market's performance is followed closely on the nightly news, not just in specialized business media. Perhaps you have heard a statement like this one: "Wall Street responded positively to the latest employment figures, with the Dow making robust gains for the first time in several weeks." The Dow is a **stock index**, a measure of the change in prices for a specific set of stocks.

Stock Indexes

Stock indexes provide a snapshot of how a stock market, or a segment of a stock market, is performing. The Dow Jones Industrial Average (DJIA) is a well-known index that tracks the stocks of 30 of the largest companies traded on the NYSE. Figure 11.6 shows the performance of the DJIA from 1988 to 2008, and Figure 11.7 shows when the index experienced its largest gains or losses. (For help reading Figure 11.6, turn to the Skillbuilder on page 342.) Other U.S. indexes often cited include the Standard & Poor's 500 (S&P 500) and the NASDAQ Composite. Global stock indexes include the Hang Seng Index (Hong Kong), the DAX (Germany), the Nikkei 225 (Japan), the TSE 300 (Canada), and the FTSE 100 (United Kingdom). Each index measures the performance of a different group of stocks.

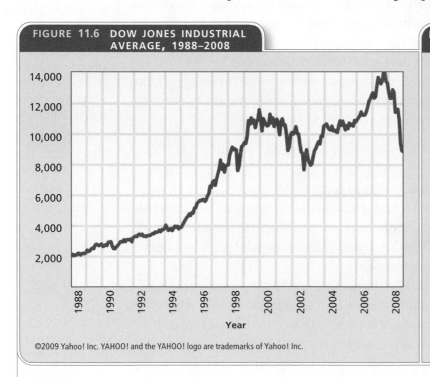

FIGURE 11.6 DOW JONES INDUSTRIAL AVERAGE, 1988–2008

©2009 Yahoo! Inc. YAHOO! and the YAHOO! logo are trademarks of Yahoo! Inc.

FIGURE 11.7 THE DOW'S BEST AND WORST YEARS

The Dow's Best Years		
Rank	Year	% Change
1	1915	81.66
2	1933	66.69
3	1928	48.22
4	1908	46.64
5	1954	43.96

The Dow's Worst Years		
Rank	Year	% Change
1	1931	−52.67
2	1907	−37.73
3	2008	−33.84
4	1930	−33.77
5	1920	−32.90

ANALYZE CHARTS

1. Imagine that in 1988 you had invested $1,000 in a fund that tracked the performance of the DJIA. About how much would your investment have been worth in 2007?

2. What were the most recent best and worst years for the Dow?

FIGURE 11.8 THE 30 STOCKS IN THE DJIA

Alcoa Inc.	Exxon Mobil Corp.	McDonald's Corp.
American Express Co.	General Electric Co.	Merck & Co.
AT&T Inc.	General Motors Corp.	Microsoft Corp.
Bank of America Corp.	Hewlett-Packard Co.	3M
Boeing Co.	The Home Depot Inc.	Pfizer Inc.
Caterpillar Inc.	Intel Corp.	The Procter & Gamble Co.
Chevron Corp.	International Business Machines Corp.	United Technologies Corp.
Citigroup Inc.	JPMorgan Chase & Co.	Verizon Communications Inc.
The Coca-Cola Co.	Johnson & Johnson.	Wal-Mart Stores Inc.
E.I. DuPont de Nemours & Co.	Kraft Foods Inc.	Walt Disney Co.

Source: Dow Jones Indexes, 2009

The Dow Jones Company, publisher of the *Wall Street Journal* newspaper, first published the DJIA in 1896. The index included the stocks of 12 companies that reflected the economy of the time, which was focused heavily on agriculture and mining. In 1928, Dow Jones expanded the index to 30 companies. As the strength of the U.S. economy shifted from agriculture to industry to services, Dow Jones changed the companies in the index accordingly. The original DJIA was the actual average of the prices of the 12 stocks. Now the average is weighted so that higher-priced stocks have more influence on the average than lower-priced stocks do. The number that is quoted is not a price but an average measured in points, not dollars.

Although the Dow is the best-known index, some analysts contend that it does not reflect the national economy as well as the S&P 500 index does. The Dow includes only 30 "blue chip" stocks—stocks of the largest, most successful companies. The S&P 500 includes 500 companies, so the index represents a broader swath of the economy. In addition, the DJIA is based on share price, so the high-priced stock of a smaller company changes the Dow more than the low-priced stock of a larger company does. By contrast, the S&P 500 is based on market capitalization—the total value of all of a company's stock. The larger the company, the more it influences the S&P 500 index.

Bulls and Bears

You may have seen the bronze statue of a bull in New York City's financial district. Or you may have heard pessimistic investors described as "bears." What do these animals have to do with the stock market? When stock prices rise steadily, it is described as a **bull market**. When the trend in stock prices is a steady decline, it is described as a **bear market**. Generally, a 20 percent increase over at least two months is considered a bull market. Likewise, a 20 percent decline over two months or more is considered a bear market.

Most bull or bear markets last only a year or so. But there have been some remarkably long upward and downward trends. In the 1990s, the U.S. stock market experienced its longest bull market. Both the Dow and the S&P 500 more than quadrupled, and many individual stocks saw much larger gains. However, this record bull market was immediately followed by a long bear market from 2000 to 2002. One contributor to the bull market was a bubble in share prices for technology stocks. Investors drove up prices through what has been described as "irrational exuberance," losing sight of the true value of the tech companies. When the bubble burst, the market experienced a correction—share prices fell back to more rational levels during the bear market.

Economics Update

Find an update on stocks in the Dow Jones Industrial Average at **ClassZone.com**

QUICK REFERENCE

A **bull market** occurs when stock market prices rise steadily over time.

A **bear market** occurs when stock market prices decline steadily over time.

A GLOBAL PERSPECTIVE

Stock Exchanges Around the World

Stock exchanges began in Europe in the 1600s, and now they have spread around the world. They fulfill a fundamental need in market economies—helping businesses to raise capital. Almost every country has at least one stock exchange. Generally, the largest economies have the largest and most active stock exchanges.

Many investors look outside their own countries for investment opportunities. Financial companies often advise clients to diversify by holding some international stocks. The theory is that a downturn that reduces stock prices in one country might not affect investments in a different part of the world. In practice, the global economy has become so intertwined that stock markets around the world frequently rise and fall together.

FIGURE 11.9 World Markets

Market	Country or Region	Companies Listed	Value of Stocks (trillions of U.S. dollars)	Leading Index
NYSE	United States	3,330	9.363	DJIA
Tokyo SE	Japan	2,389	2.923	Nikkei 225
NASDAQ	United States	2,919	2.204	NASDAQ Composite
Euronext	European Union	1,013	1.863	Euronext 100
London SE	United Kingdom	3,072	1.758	FTSE 100
Shanghai SE	China	864	1.557	SSE Composite
Hong Kong Exchanges	China	1,262	1.238	Hang Seng

Source: World Federation of Exchanges, January 2009

CONNECTING ACROSS THE GLOBE

1. **Synthesizing Economic Information** Besides avoiding downturns, what are some other reasons someone in the U.S. might invest in stocks in a foreign country?

2. **Drawing Conclusions** What does the listing of world markets in Figure 11.9 show about the nature of overseas investment? Explain your answer using information from both the chart and the article.

The most severe bear market began with a stock market crash in 1929. From 1929 to 1932, the DJIA fell from a high of 341 to a low of 41—and it did not reach 341 again until 1954. The bear market that began at the end of 2007 was also severe. After reaching highs above 14,000, the Dow lost over half of its value by early 2009. Likewise, the S&P 500 fell from highs above 1,500 in 2007 to below 700 in early 2009. No one was sure how long this bear market might last.

APPLICATION Drawing Conclusions

C. Why have the stocks in the DJIA changed over time?

REVIEWING KEY CONCEPTS

1. Explain the relationship between the terms in each of these pairs:

   a. *stock exchange*   **b.** *future*   **c.** *bear market*
      stockbroker   *option*   *bull market*

2. Are owners of common stock generally more interested in dividends or capital gains? Why?

3. Why do most people who buy stock choose common stock over preferred stock?

4. What is the difference between a bear market and a bull market?

5. How has the growth of individual online trading affected stockbrokers?

6. **Using Your Notes** What are the four different ways that stocks are traded? Refer to your completed cluster diagram.

   Use the Graphic Organizer at **Interactive Review @ ClassZone.com**

CRITICAL THINKING

7. **Applying Economic Concepts** Rachel paid $10 per share for 100 shares of common stock in her favorite clothing store.

   a. If she receives 10 cents per share in dividends each year, about how many years would it take her to earn $100 on her investment?

   b. If the share price increases to $11 in two years and she chooses to sell the stock, how much capital gain would she make?

8. **Analyzing and Interpreting Data** Rearrange the data in Figure 11.7 into one table in chronological order. Use a plus sign to indicate a best year and a minus sign to indicate a worst year.

   a. What relationship, if any, do you see between best years and worst years?

   b. What does the data reveal about the stock market in the 1930s?

9. **Challenge** The Standard and Poor's 500 (S&P 500) is an index composed of 500 stocks, while the Dow Jones Industrial Average is composed of 30 stocks. Many analysts feel the S&P 500 is a better representation of the U.S. stock market. Do you agree? Why?

ECONOMICS IN PRACTICE

Analyzing Demand for Stock
The graph below shows the combined market demand and supply curve for the stock of a company that makes mp3 players.

Draw New Demand Curves Copy the graph above on your own paper and draw new demand curves to reflect each of the following scenarios:

a. A competitor announces a technological breakthrough that will dramatically cut its production costs.

b. The company announces a new product that offers features that consumers have been asking for.

Challenge How does the change in demand in each scenario affect the price of the stock?

Bonds and Other Financial Instruments

OBJECTIVES	KEY TERMS	TAKING NOTES
In Section 4, you will • discuss why people buy bonds • describe the different kinds of bonds • explain the factors that affect bond trading • outline investment options other than stocks and bonds	par value, *p. 338* maturity, *p. 338* coupon rate, *p. 338* yield, *p. 338* junk bond, *p. 339*	As you read Section 4, summarize what you learn by completing a chart using the key concepts and other helpful words and phrases. Use the Graphic Organizer at **Interactive Review @ ClassZone.com** Bonds | Other Financial Instruments

Why Buy Bonds?

QUICK REFERENCE

Par value is the amount a bond issuer must pay the buyer at maturity.

Maturity is the date when a bond is due to be repaid.

The **coupon rate** is the interest rate a bondholder receives every year until maturity.

Yield is the annual rate of return on a bond.

KEY CONCEPTS

You learned in Chapter 8 that a bond is a contract issued by a corporation promising to repay borrowed money, plus interest, on a fixed schedule. Governments also issue bonds. The amount that the bond issuer promises to pay the buyer at maturity is its **par value**. **Maturity** is the date when the bond is due to be repaid. The **coupon rate** is the interest rate a bondholder receives every year until a bond matures.

There are two reasons to invest in bonds—the interest paid on bonds and the gains made by selling bonds. Most people buy bonds for the interest. Generally, bonds are considered less risky than stocks because bondholders are paid before stockholders. It is important to determine the **yield**—the annual rate of return—for a bond when deciding to buy and sell bonds. If a bond is sold at par value, the yield is the same as the coupon rate. If a bond is sold for less than par value, the yield will be higher than the coupon rate. On the other hand, if demand is strong and the price of a bond is higher than the par value, the yield will be lower than the coupon rate.

Generally speaking, bonds with longer maturity dates have higher yields than those with shorter dates. This is because there is more uncertainty and risk involved with repayment dates that are farther in the future.

Types of Bonds

Investors may choose to invest in many different kinds of bonds. The yields and risks associated with these bonds vary considerably. As is the case with stocks, the higher the risk the greater the potential yield of a bond. Figure 11.10 shows the yields for different types of bonds. Bonds are classified based on who issues the bonds.

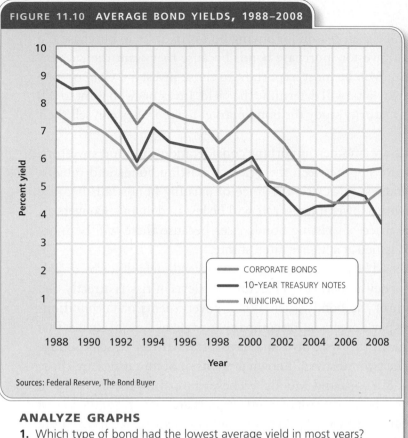

FIGURE 11.10 AVERAGE BOND YIELDS, 1988–2008

Percent yield / Year

CORPORATE BONDS
10-YEAR TREASURY NOTES
MUNICIPAL BONDS

Sources: Federal Reserve, The Bond Buyer

ANALYZE GRAPHS

1. Which type of bond had the lowest average yield in most years?
2. Which type of bond carries the highest risk? How do you know?

Corporate bonds
help businesses expand.

Treasury bonds
help keep the federal
government operating.

Municipal bonds
make state and local
projects possible.

The U.S. government issues securities called Treasury bonds, notes, or bills. The different terms denote loans with different maturity dates, with Treasury bonds having the longest maturity (more than ten years) and Treasury bills having the shortest (one year or less). The money borrowed through the sale of these securities helps keep the government running. Because they are backed by the "full faith and credit" of the federal government, these securities are considered to be virtually risk free. Governments all over the world issue bonds for the same reasons as the U.S. government. The risk level of international bonds depends on the financial strength of the particular government.

Bonds issued by state and local governments are called municipal bonds. Funds raised by these bonds finance government projects such as construction of roads, bridges, schools, and other public facilities. The interest earned on many municipal bonds is not subject to federal income tax. Generally, municipal bonds are considered low-risk investments. A major reason for this is that state and local governments collect taxes, so it is assumed that they'll be able to make interest payments and repay the buyer upon maturity. However, there have been instances of governments being unable to repay bondholders the full amount of their loans.

One way that companies finance expansion is by issuing corporate bonds. These bonds generally pay a higher coupon rate than government bonds because the risk is higher. One kind of corporate bond, a **junk bond**, is considered high risk but has the potential for high yields. The risk involved with investing in junk bonds is similar to that of investing in stocks.

QUICK REFERENCE

Junk bonds are high-risk, high-yield corporate bonds.

Financial Markets 339

Buying Bonds

Investors need to determine their reason for buying bonds in order to purchase the right type of bond. Most investors purchase bonds because they want the guaranteed interest income. Yield will be most important to those investors. Coupon rate and price relative to the par value will determine the yield. Investors who want to sell bonds before they reach maturity study the bond market to see if they can sell their investment at a profit.

Market interest rates are another important consideration for bond investors. There is an inverse relationship between the price of existing bonds and interest rates. For example, as interest rates rise, the price of existing bonds falls because bonds that were issued with a lower interest rate will be less in demand. Conversely, if interest rates fall, the price of existing bonds rises because there will be more demand for those bonds issued at a higher interest rate.

The main risk that bond buyers face is that the issuer will default, or be unable to repay the borrowed money at maturity. Therefore, the level of risk is directly tied to the financial strength of the bond issuer. When governments or corporations want to issue bonds, they pay a credit-rating company to evaluate how likely it is that they will repay the loans. In this way, investors have a standard by which to judge the risk of the bonds. The two most well-known systems of bond ratings are those established by Standard & Poor's and Moody's. These companies use a system of letters to designate the relative credit risk of bonds. Bonds are rated from the lowest risk of U.S. Treasury securities (Aaa or AAA) to the higher risks associated with junk bonds. (See Figure 11.11.)

FIGURE 11.11 Bond Ratings

Bond Rating		Grade	Risk
Moody's	Standard & Poor's		
Aaa	AAA	Investment	Lowest risk
Aa	AA	Investment	Low risk
A	A	Investment	Low risk
Baa	BBB	Investment	Medium risk
Ba, B	BB, B	Junk	High risk
Caa, Ca	CCC, CC, C	Junk	Highest risk
C	D	Junk	In default

ANALYZE TABLES
1. What are the lowest-rated investment grade bonds in each system?
2. Why do junk bonds have lower ratings than investment grade bonds?

APPLICATION Drawing Conclusions

A. Why is bond yield not always the same as the coupon rate?

Other Financial Instruments

Investors have investment options other than bonds and stocks. The most common of these are certificates of deposit (CDs) and money market mutual funds. Both of these investments have very low risk and provide income in the form of interest. Individual investors do not generally sell these financial instruments for profit.

Certificates of Deposit

As you learned earlier, CDs are a form of time deposit offered primarily by banks, savings and loans, and credit unions. Like bonds, CDs have a maturity date (usually 6 months to 5 years), when the investor receives the principal back with interest.

The issuer of the CD pays the investor a rate of either fixed or variable interest during the period that the CD is held. Usually the interest is reinvested in the CD so that the investor enjoys the benefits of compound interest. In general, CDs with longer maturity dates pay higher rates of interest. For example, a 6-month CD might pay 3.4 percent interest while a 5-year CD might pay 4.4 percent.

The federal government insures funds deposited in CDs at most banks and credit unions up to $100,000 per depositor in any given institution. The main risk that investors in CDs face is the loss of interest or possibly some principal if funds are withdrawn before the maturity date. In addition, investors might face interest-rate risk if rates rise and funds are locked in for a length of time at a lower rate.

Money Market Mutual Funds

Recall from Section 1 that the money market involves financial assets with maturities of one year or less. Also, remember that mutual funds allow investors to buy shares that represent an investment in all the financial assets held by the fund. Money market mutual funds (MMMF) allow investors to own a variety of short-term financial assets, such as Treasury bills, municipal bonds, large-denomination CDs, and corporate bonds.

These mutual funds give investors a higher yield than bank savings accounts, but provide a similar level of liquidity. Investors can redeem their shares by check, by phone, or by electronic transfer to a separate checking account.

Although the federal government does not insure MMMFs, the funds are tightly regulated, and these investments are considered to be quite safe with regard to loss of principal. There is less interest-rate risk than with CDs because the money is not committed for a specified length of time. The yield of the MMMF varies based on the yield of the assets in the fund.

"'Oh, no,' said Goldilocks, 'don't tell me that the return on invested capital is only *three* percent—less than you can earn on a money-market account!'"

Source: www.CartoonStock.com

APPLICATION Making Inferences

B. Why do longer-term CDs pay higher interest rates than shorter-term CDs?

For more information on evaluating online sources, see the Skillbuilder Handbook, page R29.

Interpreting Graphs: Online Financial Information

Evaluating means making a judgment about information. Investors make judgments about stocks based on their analysis of financial information. Many use the Internet to acquire up-to-the-minute information about stock market trading. The graphs on this page provide information about Apple Computer, Inc. (In 2007, Apple dropped the word *Computer* from its name.) These graphs offer an example of the type of online information investors use to evaluate stocks.

TIPS FOR EVALUATING ONLINE INFORMATION Use the following guidelines to evaluate economic information online:

Read the title to identify the company for which stock information is shown. Here it is Apple Computer (AAPL), traded on the NASDAQ (Q).

Read the vertical axis. This graph has two parts. The upper part shows the stock's price; the lower part shows the volume of shares traded.

Read the horizontal axis. This graph shows stock prices and volume traded from May 2005 through April 2006.

Look for other information. This statement indicates that there is a 15-minute lag time in updating the graphs.

Source: TheGlobeandMail.com

THINKING ECONOMICALLY Evaluating

1. As an investor, which month would have been best for you to acquire Apple stock? Why?

2. How does the price per share at the beginning of June 2005 compare with the price in mid-January 2006? Use information from the graph in your answer.

3. From January through April of 2006, the price of Apple shares fluctuated greatly. Volume of trading was also very heavy. Are these two facts related? Why?

REVIEWING KEY CONCEPTS

1. Use each of the three terms below in a sentence that illustrates the meaning of the term:

   a. *coupon rate*   **b.** *maturity*   **c.** *yield*

2. What does par value represent to the issuer of a bond?

3. What is the relationship between par value and maturity?

4. When does yield equal the coupon rate?

5. Why do junk bonds offer a higher yield than other types of bonds?

6. **Using Your Notes** Compare the risk of investing in a CD with the risk of investing in a money market mutual fund. Refer to your completed chart.

Bonds	Other Financial Instruments

   Use the Graphic Organizer at **Interactive Review @ ClassZone.com**

CRITICAL THINKING

7. **Comparing and Contrasting** Dmitri bought a $1,000 bond at par value with a coupon rate of 5 percent. He determines the yield by dividing the amount of interest he earns by the price.

   a. How much interest would he earn in the first year and what would be the yield?

   b. How much interest would he earn in the first year and what would be the yield if he had paid $950 for the bond? What would be the interest and yield if he paid $1,050?

8. **Making Inferences** In 2003, Molly bought a 10-year Treasury note for $1,000. The market interest rate was 3.5 percent. In 2005, Molly wanted to sell the note to pay for college expenses. Interest rates had risen to 4.5 percent. How would the change in interest rates affect the price that Molly was likely to receive for her note? Give reasons for your answer.

9. **Applying Economic Concepts** Julie has accumulated $1,000 in a bank savings account, which pays 2.7 percent interest. She investigates several options and finds that she can invest her money in a 1-year Treasury note paying 4.4 percent interest, a 1-year CD paying 3.9 percent interest, or a money market mutual fund with an average yield of 3.7 percent. What are the pros and cons of each of these investment options?

10. **Challenge** How would a lower bond rating by Moody's or Standard & Poor's affect the coupon rate that a corporation has to offer when it issues its bonds? Give reasons for your answer.

ECONOMICS IN PRACTICE

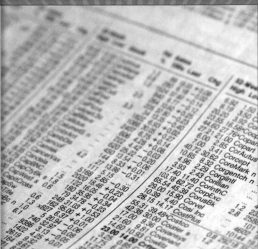

Making Investment Decisions
Suppose that you have been advised to invest in bonds. Recall what you have learned about the factors to consider when buying and selling bonds and then complete the following activities.

Ask Investment Questions Fill in the chart by developing a series of questions you might ask to help you decide which type of bond to buy.

Categories of Questions to Ask About Bonds	My Questions
Investment objectives	
Tolerance for risk	
Desired return	
Resalability of bonds	

Challenge How might you apply the concept of diversification to a portfolio of bond investments?

High Finance Goes Awry

Background The global financial crisis that began in 2007 had many causes. Among the key factors were complicated financial tools such as mortgage-backed securities and credit-default swaps. Banks and investment firms designed such tools to maximize profits, and under normal circumstances the tools performed as intended. But when the bubble in housing prices burst, many of the tools backfired, maximizing losses instead of profits.

What's the issue? How did new financial tools contribute to the financial crisis? Study these sources to learn more about high finance.

A. Congressional Report

The crisis stemmed in part from banks bundling mortgages and selling them through financial markets.

▶ The Securitization of Loans

How mortgages became investment vehicles

Over the past decade, credit was increasingly "securitized". Banks would pool together many different loans, and then sell securities . . . to outside investors. The sales of these securities provided banks with immediate cash, which they could then use to make more mortgages. And investors liked these securities, because they were considered safe investments—frequently, nearly as safe as U.S. Treasury bills. . . .

The most common and well-known of these securitized loans is the "mortgage-backed security" (MBS), based on pools of residential mortgages. . . . Over the past decade, this type of securitized credit saw explosive growth, because of the superior returns and perception of safety. By the first quarter of 2006, the total value of all outstanding U.S. MBS totaled approximately $6.1 trillion. . . .

The deflation of the housing bubble has brought increased mortgage defaults which, coupled with concerns about poor mortgage underwriting standards, and the widespread belief that US housing prices are still overvalued, have led to tremendous declines in the values of MBS. And because MBS—and other forms of securitized debt—were so widely held, some major financial institutions have been forced to take huge writedowns in recent months.

As these writedowns have become recognized, these financial institutions have been forced to raise capital to cover the losses incurred. Those which have been able to raise sufficient capital have so far been able to survive, while those which have been unable to raise sufficient capital have failed, sometimes suddenly and unexpectedly.

Source: *From Wall Street to Main Street: Understanding How the Credit Crisis Affects You,* The Joint Economic Committee Majority Staff, October 3, 2008

Thinking Economically What does it mean to "securitize" a group of loans?

B. Cartoon

This cartoon by Piero Tonin takes a dim view of high finance.

Thinking Economically

What does the cartoon say about the financial maneuvers of some companies?

C. Newspaper Article

This article suggests that credit-default swaps deserve part of the blame for the crisis.

Time to Unravel the Knot of Credit-Default Swaps

Any honest assessment [of the financial crisis] must include the role that credit-default swaps have played in this mess: it's the elephant in the room, the $30 trillion market that people do not want to talk about.

Credit-default swaps are insurancelike contracts that Wall Street created in the early 1990s. They allow bondholders to protect themselves against losses if a company or a debt issuer defaults. There is a viable and legitimate use for C.D.S.'s, especially when they allow bondholders and corporations to limit their risks. But in recent years, these contracts became a haven for speculators who were doing nothing more than betting on whether a debt issuer would survive.

Buyers of C.D.S.'s pay premiums to companies issuing the contract. If a debt default occurs, the party providing the credit protection has to make the buyer whole on the amount of insurance bought. It is similar to payments that insurers pay to homeowners if their houses burn down.

These arrangements, struck privately by parties on both sides of a C.D.S. contract, have been extremely profitable to the Wall Street banks and insurers that traded in them. Sellers of C.D.S.'s spent years raking in premiums while underestimating or simply ignoring the possibility of rising defaults. Regulators let the market grow unchecked. In the end, far too much of this insurance was written at way too cheap a cost. Now, with Wall Street and the economy in tatters, the fear that already-hobbled financial companies may have to pay off huge amounts on C.D.S. arrangements hangs like a cloud over the markets.

Source: *The New York Times*, **January 25, 2009**

Thinking Economically How is a credit-default swap like insurance?

THINKING ECONOMICALLY Synthesizing

1. Imagine a conversation between the characters portrayed in Document B. What would the financial director say about creating the mortgage-backed securities described in Document A?

2. If Company X invests in the mortgage-backed securities described in Document A, how might it use the credit-default swaps described in Document C?

3. Company Y issues credit-default swaps to hundreds of companies that invest in mortgage-backed securities. What will happen if the value of mortgage-backed securities plummets?

Interactive ◄◄Review

Review this chapter using interactive activities at **ClassZone.com**
- **Online Summary**
- **Graphic Organizers**
- **Quizzes**
- **Review and Study Notes**
- **Vocabulary Flip Cards**

Online Summary

Complete the following activity either on your own paper or online at **ClassZone.com**

Choose the key concept that best completes the sentence. Not all key concepts will be used.

capital gain	money market
capital market	par value
common stock	preferred stock
coupon rate	primary market
diversification	return
financial asset	risk
financial intermediary	savings
investment	secondary market
investment objective	stock index
maturity	yield

__1__ is income not used for consumption. __2__ is the use of income today that allows for greater production in the future.

A __3__ is a claim on the property of a borrower. A __4__ collects funds from savers and invests the funds in loans and other financial assets. Examples include banks and mutual funds. The __5__ is the market for buying and selling short-term financial assets. The __6__ is the market where financial assets are resold.

The two issues that play a major role in setting an __7__ are time and income. Investors try to maximize __8__ and limit __9__ through __10__, the practice of distributing investments among different financial assets.

__11__ is profit made from the sale of securities. __12__ is share of ownership in a corporation that gives holders voting rights and a share of the profit. The Dow Jones Industrial Average is a __13__ that measures the performance of a group of 30 stocks. __14__ is the interest rate paid on a bond. The __15__ is the amount that a bond issuer promises to pay the buyer at maturity.

REVIEWING KEY CONCEPTS

Savings and Investment (pp. 318–323)

1. How are savings and investment related?

2. What is the role of financial intermediaries in the circular flow of the financial system?

Investing in a Market Economy (pp. 324–329)

3. Why do investors need to determine their investment objective before they invest?

4. Explain the relationship between risk and return.

Buying and Selling Stocks (pp. 330–337)

5. How do people earn money by investing in stocks?

6. How does the Dow Jones Industrial Average reflect trends in the stock market?

Bonds and Other Financial Instruments (pp. 338–345)

7. What are two reasons people buy bonds?

8. How are interest rates and bond prices related?

APPLYING ECONOMIC CONCEPTS

Look at the graph below showing savings as a percentage of after-tax income in various countries.

9. Which country had the lowest rate of savings?

10. What was the overall trend from 1980 to 2000?

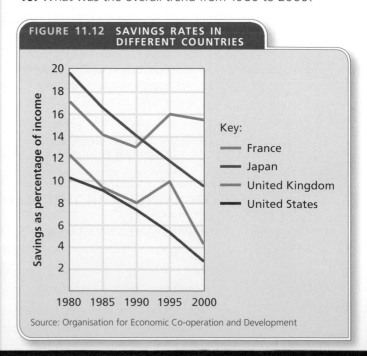

FIGURE 11.12 SAVINGS RATES IN DIFFERENT COUNTRIES

Key:
- France
- Japan
- United Kingdom
- United States

Source: Organisation for Economic Co-operation and Development

11. **Analyzing Causes and Effects** In 2005, many leading advertisers announced plans to increase use of online advertising and to decrease the amount of advertising dollars spent in traditional print media, such as newspapers. In addition, newspaper circulation figures declined steadily as more people read news on the Internet.

   a. How was this situation likely to affect the stock prices of online search-engine companies that featured banner ads and sponsored links on their Web pages?

   b. How would it affect the stock prices of newspapers? Explain your answers.

12. **Comparing and Contrasting** What are the similarities and differences between stock dividends, a bond coupon rate, and interest on a CD?

13. **Drawing Conclusions** Alex, Kate, and Rashid all invested money in a software company. Alex bought a corporate bond, Kate bought shares of common stock, and Rashid bought shares of preferred stock. Which of these investors would be least at risk of losing money if the company became unprofitable?

14. **Making Inferences** Suppose that you heard the following statement on the financial news: "Bonds fell as the yield on 10-year Treasury notes rose to 4.56 percent, the highest in two years." What does "bonds fell" mean and how is it related to the increase in yield?

15. **Challenge** Steve purchases an option contract to buy 100 shares of stock in a big high-tech company for $50 per share in six months. The stock is currently selling for $40 per share. Steve pays $5 per share for the option contract. If the share price rises to $60, Steve exercises his option to buy the shares at $50 and then resells the stock on the market for $60 per share. How much profit does Steve make per share? If the price never rises to $50 before the option expires, how much money does Steve lose?

Advise Your Clients

Choose a partner. Imagine that you are financial planners whose job is to help clients meet their investment objectives and use diversification to maximize return and limit risk.

Step 1 Make a list of several possible financial instruments that you might recommend and rate them for risk and return.

Step 2 Review each client's objectives and risk tolerance to consider what investments to recommend.

   a. Carlos and Juanita Diaz want to invest for their two young children's college education. They would like a return of 7 to 10 percent a year and have a moderate tolerance for risk.

   b. Patrick Hurd is 30 years old and wants to begin saving for his retirement. He wants the highest return possible and is willing to take risks.

   c. Alison Leveridge has recently retired. She wants to invest the money from her pension fund so that she can have a guaranteed amount of income and little risk of losing her capital.

Step 3 Decide what percentage of each client's money to invest in different types of financial instruments. Create pie graphs to show your recommendations for each client.

Step 4 Present your recommendations to another pair of students. Discuss the choices that each of you made.

Step 5 As a class, discuss how changes in your clients' financial circumstances or changes in the stock market might affect your recommendations.

Use **SMARTGrapher** @ ClassZone.com to complete this activity.

Measuring the Economy
Millions of workers and businesses participate in the U.S. economy. Measuring the country's economy requires special economic tools.

Bourses up but volatility remains
WORLD OVERVIEW

There was a bounce in European shares following Monday's rout, while US markets opened firmer after consumer confidence figures turned out less gloomy than feared.

The meeting of the Federal Open Market Committee, which concludes today, is not expected to alter the 1.75 per cent interest rate. Markets will be looking for any change in the Fed's opinion on whether the dangers of increasing were the stocks that led of the lessening of inflation are European session, such as telecoms and US com-

FTSE Eurotop 300
Indices rebased

Eurotop 300
Automobile

Source: Thomson Datastream

BMW
Share price (€)

SAP
Share price (€)

WORLD STOCK MARKETS

Techs and telecoms lead gains

EUROPE
European indices

Technology and telecommunication companies, closely followed by car companies, led the way back yesterday...

Economic Indicators and Measurements

CONCEPT REVIEW

Macroeconomics is the study of the economy as a whole and how major sectors of the economy interact.

CHAPTER 12 KEY CONCEPT

National income accounting uses statistical measures of income, spending, and output to help people understand what is happening to a country's economy.

WHY THE CONCEPT MATTERS

Your economic decisions—combined with those of millions of other people—determine the fate of the nation's economy. Can you afford to buy a new car? Is now a good time to change jobs? Should you take a risk in the stock market or keep your money safe in the bank? Understanding what is happening to the country's economy will help you make better economic decisions.

Online Highlights
More at ClassZone.com

 Economics Update
Go to **ECONOMICS UPDATE** for chapter updates and current news on the economy of Poland. (See Case Study, pp. 376–377.) ▶

Animated Economics
Go to **ANIMATED ECONOMICS** for interactive lessons on the graphs and tables in this chapter.

Interactive ◀◀Review
Go to **INTERACTIVE REVIEW** for concept review and activities.

How has free enterprise transformed Poland's economy? See the Case Study on pages 376–377.

Gross Domestic Product and Other Indicators

OBJECTIVES	KEY TERMS	TAKING NOTES
In Section 1, you will • define GDP and describe how it is measured • explain how GDP has certain limitations • identify other national income accounting measures	national income accounting, *p. 350* gross domestic product (GDP), *p. 350* nominal GDP, *p. 352* real GDP, *p. 352* nonmarket activities, *p. 354* underground economy, *p. 354* gross national product (GNP), *p. 355* net national product (NNP), *p. 355* national income (NI), *p. 355* personal income (PI), *p. 355* disposable personal income (DPI), *p. 355*	As you read Section 1, complete a hierarchy chart like the one below to record what you learn about national income accounting. Use the Graphic Organizer at **Interactive Review @ ClassZone.com**

What Is GDP?

QUICK REFERENCE

National income accounting is a way of evaluating a country's economy using statistical measures of its income, spending, and output.

Gross domestic product (GDP) is the market value of all final goods and services produced within a nation in a given time period.

KEY CONCEPTS

As you have read, microeconomics and macroeconomics look at the economy through different lenses. While microeconomics examines the actions of individuals and single markets, macroeconomics examines the economy as a whole. Macroeconomists analyze the economy using **national income accounting**, statistical measures that track the income, spending, and output of a nation. The most important of those measures is **gross domestic product (GDP)**, the market value of all final goods and services produced within a nation in a given time period.

The Components of GDP

To be included in GDP, a good or service has to fulfill three requirements. First, it has to be final rather than intermediate. For example, the fabric used to make a shirt is an intermediate good; the shirt itself is a final good. Second, the good or service must be produced during the time period, regardless of when it is sold. For example, cars made this year but sold next year would be counted in this year's GDP. Finally, the good or service must be produced within the nation's borders. Products made in foreign countries by U.S. companies are not included in the U.S. GDP.

Products Included in GDP
Cars made in the United States are an example of goods counted toward U.S. gross domestic product (GDP).

Calculating GDP

Although there are several different ways to calculate GDP, economists often use the expenditures approach. With this method, they group national spending on final goods and services according to the four sectors of the economy: spending by households, or consumption; spending by businesses, or investment; government spending; and total exports minus total imports, or net exports. Economists identify consumption with the letter C; investment with the letter I; government spending with the letter G; and net exports with the letter X. To calculate GDP, economists add the expenditures from all sectors together: $C+I+G+X=GDP$.

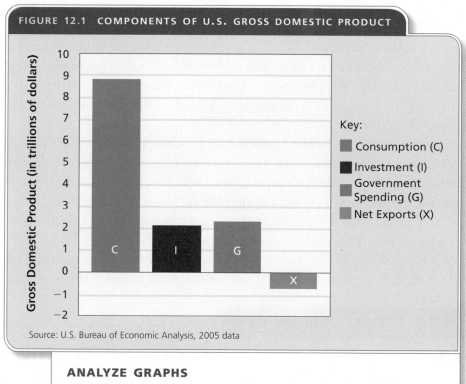

FIGURE 12.1 COMPONENTS OF U.S. GROSS DOMESTIC PRODUCT

Key:
- Consumption (C)
- Investment (I)
- Government Spending (G)
- Net Exports (X)

Source: U.S. Bureau of Economic Analysis, 2005 data

ANALYZE GRAPHS

1. In 2005, net exports was a negative number. What does this say about the relative amounts of exports and imports?
2. Did households, businesses, or the government contribute the most to U.S. GDP in 2005?

Economics Update

Find an update on the U.S. GDP at **ClassZone.com**

Consumption includes all spending by households on durable goods, nondurable goods, and services. You drive to the movies in a durable good (an item that does not wear out quickly). You purchase a service when you pay for the movie (since you are not buying to own something). And you obtain a nondurable good (a good that is used up relatively soon after purchase) when you buy popcorn.

Investment, which measures what businesses spend, has two categories. One is fixed investment, which includes new construction and purchases of such capital goods as equipment, machinery, and tools. The other is inventory investment. This category, also called unconsumed output, is made up of the unsold goods that businesses keep on hand.

Government spending includes all the expenditures of federal, state, and local governments on goods and services. Examples include spending for defense, highways, and public education. However, government spending on transfer payments, such as social security and unemployment benefits, is not included. These payments allow the recipients to buy goods and services, and these are counted as consumption.

Net exports, the final component of GDP, represents foreign trade. This component takes into account the goods and services produced in the United States but sold in foreign countries—in other words, exports. However, U.S. consumers and businesses also buy, or import, goods made in foreign countries. Cars, car parts, and crude oil are the largest imports in dollar value. The GDP counts only net exports—the value of U.S. exports minus the value of U.S. imports.

Two Types of GDP

Economists use GDP to gauge how well a country's economy is doing. When GDP is growing, an economy creates more jobs and more business opportunities. When GDP declines, jobs and more business opportunities become less plentiful. To get a clearer picture of a country's economic health, economists calculate two forms of GDP—nominal and real.

The most basic form is **nominal GDP**, which is stated in the price levels for the year in which the GDP was measured. If prices never changed, nominal GDP would be sufficient. But prices tend to increase over time. In Figure 12.2, find the line that represents nominal GDP. If you estimate the difference from 1990 to 2005, the nominal GDP of the United States about doubled. However, during this time prices went up, adding dollars to GDP without adding value to the nation's output.

To factor out rising prices, economists use **real GDP**, which is nominal GDP adjusted for changes in prices. Real GDP is an estimate of the GDP if prices were to

QUICK REFERENCE

Nominal GDP states GDP in terms of the current value of goods and services.

Real GDP states GDP corrected for changes in prices from year to year.

FIGURE 12.2   U.S. NOMINAL AND REAL GROSS DOMESTIC PRODUCT

Source: U.S. Bureau of Economic Analysis

ANALYZE GRAPHS

1. About how much did nominal GDP increase from 1990 to 2000?

2. About how much did real GDP increase over the same period?

3. Why do the two lines cross at the year 2000?

To better understand nominal and real GDP, imagine a country that produces only one good: TVs. If you know the price of TVs and the number produced, you can calculate that country's nominal and real GDP. Use the table to find the data for these calculations.

	2004	2005	2006
TVs Produced	500	600	600
TV Price	$100	$100	$120
Nominal GDP	$50,000	$60,000	$72,000
Real GDP, base: 2004	$50,000	$60,000	$60,000

Step 1: Calculate nominal GDP for 2004. Nominal GDP is the product of the number of TVs produced and the price of TVs that year.

Number produced	×	Price in that year	=	Nominal GDP	500 × $100 = $50,000

The table shows that nominal GDP grew each year. If you judged only by nominal GDP, the economy of this country would seem to be growing.

Step 2: Analyze the nominal GDP figures. Why did nominal GDP increase from 2004 to 2005? The number of TVs produced increased. Why did nominal GDP increase from 2005 to 2006? The price of TVs increased.

The output of the country's economy grew from 2004 to 2005, but it stayed the same from 2005 to 2006, despite the increase in prices. Calculating real GDP produces a better estimate of how much a country's economy is growing.

Step 3: Calculate real GDP for 2006. Real GDP is the product of the number of TVs produced in the current year and the price of TVs in the base year. In this case, use 2004 as the base year.

Number produced	×	Price in the base year	=	Real GDP	600 × $100 = $60,000

Since 2004 is the base year, nominal and real GDP are the same for 2004. Real GDP allows you to compare the output of the country's economy in different years.

remain constant from year to year. To find real GDP, economists compare nominal GDP to a base year. Look again at Figure 12.2, which uses 2000 as a base year. Since real GDP eliminates price differences, the line for real GDP rises more gradually than the line for nominal GDP. Real GDP provides a more accurate measure of economic performance.

APPLICATION Applying Economic Concepts

A. If output remained the same, how would a year of falling prices affect nominal GDP? How would it affect real GDP?

What GDP Does Not Measure

KEY CONCEPTS

Although GDP provides an important estimate of how well the economy is performing, it does not measure all output. It does not measure **nonmarket activities**, such as home childcare or performing one's own home repairs. GDP also does not measure output from the **underground economy**, market activities that go unreported because they are illegal or because those involved want to avoid taxation. Further, GDP does not measure "quality of life" issues related to economic output.

Nonmarket Activities

Some productive activities do not take place in economic markets. For example, there is no effective way to measure the output of plumbers who install or repair plumbing systems in their own homes or people who do volunteer work for schools or hospitals. By far the biggest nonmarket activity, also left out of GDP, consists of the many services—cooking, cleaning, childcare—provided by homemakers.

Nonmarket Activities Housework is an example of a productive activity not measured by GDP.

Underground Economy

Also missing from GDP is the underground sector of the economy. Some activities are kept underground because they are illegal—drug dealing, smuggling, gambling, and selling stolen goods, for example. When goods are rationed or otherwise restricted, illegal trading occurs on what is called the black market. Other underground activities are themselves legal, but the way the payment is handled is not. For example, a plumber who does repairs for a neighbor might receive payment in cash and not declare it as taxable income. Estimates suggest that the underground economy would make up 8 to 10 percent of the U.S. GDP.

Quality of Life

Countries with high GDPs have high living standards. But GDP does not show how the goods and services are distributed. The United States has the largest GDP of any country, but more than 10 percent of its people still live in poverty. GDP also does not express what products are being built and services offered: for example, are there more jails being built than schools?

APPLICATION Explaining an Economic Concept

B. If you get paid in cash to baby-sit, mow lawns, or do other chores for neighbors, are you part of the underground economy? Why or why not?

Other Economic Performance Measures

KEY CONCEPTS

GDP is not the only measure that economists use to gauge economic performance. Several other measures are derived by making adjustments to GDP.

- **Gross national product (GNP)** is the market value of all final goods and services a country produces in a given time period. GNP equals GDP plus the income from goods and services produced by U.S. companies and citizens in foreign countries but minus the income foreign companies and citizens earn here.

- **Net national product (NNP)** is GNP minus depreciation of capital stock—in other words, the value of final goods and services less the value of capital goods that became worn out during the time period.

- **National income (NI)** is the total income earned in a nation from the production of goods and services in a given time period. It is calculated by subtracting indirect business taxes, such as property and sales taxes, from NNP.

- **Personal income (PI)** is the income received by a country's people from all sources in a given time period. It can be calculated from NI by subtracting social security taxes, corporate profit taxes, and corporate profits not paid to stockholders and by adding social security, unemployment, and welfare payments.

- **Disposable personal income (DPI)** is personal income minus personal income taxes. It shows how much money is actually available for consumer spending.

QUICK REFERENCE

Gross national product (GNP) is the market value of all final goods and services produced by a country.

Net national product (NNP) is the value of final goods and services less the value of capital goods that have become worn out.

National income (NI) is the total income earned in a nation from the production of goods and services.

Personal income (PI) is the income received by a country's people from all sources.

Disposable personal income (DPI) is personal income minus taxes.

FIGURE 12.4 National Income Accounting

GDP + income earned abroad by U.S. businesses and citizens
    − income earned in U.S. by foreign businesses and citizens

= GNP − depreciation of capital stock

= NNP − indirect business taxes

= NI − income earned but not received
    + income received but not earned

= PI − personal taxes

= DPI

ANALYZE CHARTS
What three figures do you need in order to calculate personal income (PI)?

APPLICATION Making Inferences

C. Under what circumstances might a country's GNP be greater than its GDP?

ECONOMICS
SKILLBUILDER

For more on synthesizing economic data,
see the Skillbuilder Handbook, page R23.

Synthesizing Economic Data

Synthesizing is a skill used by economists to interpret economic trends. Synthesizing involves interpreting various data to form an overview of economic performance. A synthesis is often stated as a broad summary statement.

PRACTICING THE SKILL National income accounting involves the collection and analysis of data on key economic variables. Economists synthesize the data to arrive at an overview of national economic performance. The table below presents data for variables used to determine gross domestic product (GDP), a key factor in national income accounting.

> **Read** the title to learn the main idea of the table. This table shows the components of U.S. GDP for selected years.

> **Read** the column heads carefully. The four types of expenditures are used to determine GDP.

> **Determine** how the types of data relate to one another. For 1990, calculating the sum of the four expenditures yields $5,803 billion, the nominal GDP for 1990.

FIGURE 12.5 COMPONENTS OF U.S. GDP (IN BILLIONS OF DOLLARS)

Year	Consumption Expenditure	Investment Expenditure	Government Expenditure	Net Export Expenditure	Nominal GDP
1980	1,757	479	566	−13	2,789
1985	2,720	736	879	−115	4,220
1990	3,840	861	1,180	−78	5,803
1995	4,976	1,144	1,369	−91	7,398
2000	6,739	1,736	1,722	−380	9,817
2005	8,746	2,105	2,363	−727	12,487

Source: U.S. Bureau of Economic Analysis

> **Check** the source of the data to evaluate its reliability.

> **Look** for patterns in the data. For example, notice that net exports have been negative.

THINKING ECONOMICALLY Synthesizing

1. What trend can be seen in U.S. nominal GDP? What can you tell from this about the growth of the U.S. economy? Do you need more information?

2. Which expenditure accounts for most of GDP?

3. Does the proportion of this expenditure to the other two positive expenditures remain about the same in the six years shown here? Briefly explain how you estimated this.

SECTION 1 Assessment

Online Quiz
ClassZone.com

REVIEWING KEY CONCEPTS

1. Explain the relationship between the terms in each of these pairs.

   a. *nominal GDP*   **b.** *gross national product*   **c.** *personal income*
   real GDP   *net national product*   *disposable personal income*

2. What are the four components of GDP?

3. What is an example of a durable good? a nondurable good?

4. Name two economic activities that GDP does not measure.

5. Why are transfer payments not included as a government expenditure when calculating GDP?

6. **Using Your Notes** Write a brief summary of the methods used to calculate national income and the purposes of each accounting method. Refer to your completed hierarchy chart.

National Income Accounting
GDP

   Use the Graphic Organizer at **Interactive Review @ ClassZone.com**

CRITICAL THINKING

7. **Drawing Conclusions** List some things that have become more expensive during your lifetime. Explain how a rise in price level affects nominal GDP and real GDP.

8. **Making Inferences** If consumption is especially high compared with other years, what might you generalize about the health of the economy?

9. **Explaining an Economic Concept** What is the underground economy? What impact does it have on a nation's GDP?

10. **Drawing Conclusions** Imagine that a new country is discovered on an island in the middle of the Pacific Ocean. The country's people have never left the island, and no foreigners have ever been there. What would the relationship be between the country's GDP and its GNP? Why?

11. **Challenge** How would the following affect GDP?
    a. Government transfer payments increase.
    b. Student sells used CD to record store.
    c. Car owner pays auto repair shop $500 to fix his car.

ECONOMICS IN PRACTICE

Identifying Intermediate and Final Goods
Look at the following list of goods and who purchased them.

Goods	Purchaser
copier paper	accounting firm
refrigerator	home consumer
stainless steel	manufacturer
eggs	home consumer
eggs	factory that makes frozen baked goods
battery	car owner
paint	furniture maker

Categorize Economic Information Decide whether each good is an intermediate good or a final good.

Challenge Why is it important to make a distinction in national income accounting between intermediate and final goods?

357

Productivity and Economic Growth

KEY CONCEPTS

Productivity refers to the amount of output produced from a set amount of inputs. When the same amount of inputs produces more output, productivity has increased. In Chapter 9, you learned about labor productivity—the amount of goods or services produced by a worker in an hour. But the broader sense of productivity includes the productivity of both labor and capital.

For example, imagine that you begin building bookshelves. The inputs would include your labor plus capital, in the form of the workshop, hammers, glue, and other supplies. At first, it may take you a week to complete one bookshelf. In the process, you may waste materials as you make mistakes, and you may find that some of your tools are not ideal for the task. But after you have built several bookshelves and acquired the right tools for the job, your productivity increases. Using the same amount of input, you might now be able to produce two bookshelves per week.

This section concerns the productivity of a country's entire economy. As a country becomes more productive, its economy is likely to grow.

How Is Productivity Measured?

To measure the productivity of a single business, you would compare the inputs to the outputs. Using the bookshelf example, you would compare the amount of capital and number of hours worked to the number of bookshelves produced. But how can we measure the productivity of a nation's economy, which is made up of millions of different people and businesses? Economists use a measurement called **multifactor productivity**, the ratio between an industry's economic output and its labor and capital inputs. By collecting multifactor productivity data on a country's major industries and business sectors, economists can estimate the productivity of the entire economy.

What Contributes to Productivity?

Several factors contribute to changes in productivity.

Quality of Labor A better educated, healthier workforce tends to be more productive. Using the bookshelf example, if you were to take classes in woodworking, your enhanced knowledge would enable you to produce more and better shelves. In general, the more educated the workforce, the more productive it is. As for health, people are usually more productive when they feel well than when they feel sluggish or ill.

Technological Innovation Historically, as during the Industrial Revolution, new machines and technologies helped countries produce more output from the same amount of inputs. In recent times, the desktop computer and computer technology generally have generated productivity gains.

Energy Costs Gas, electricity, and other fuels power the technologies that increase productivity. When energy costs rise, those tools become more expensive to use and productivity declines. By the same token, when energy costs fall, using advanced tools becomes less expensive and productivity rises.

Financial Markets The easier it is for funds to flow to where they are needed, the more productive the economy becomes. Banks, stock markets, and similar institutions allow a country's funds to be put to their best use. When such institutions do not exist or when they do not function efficiently, productivity is reduced.

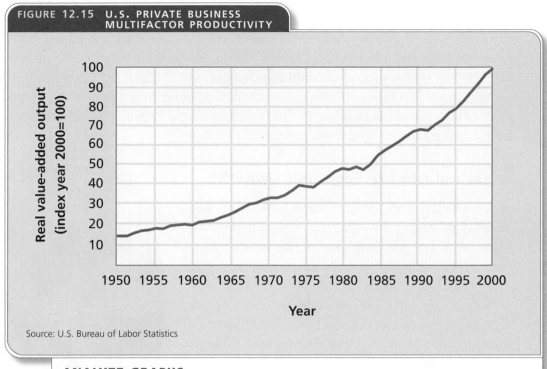

FIGURE 12.15 U.S. PRIVATE BUSINESS MULTIFACTOR PRODUCTIVITY

Source: U.S. Bureau of Labor Statistics

ANALYZE GRAPHS

1. What happened to productivity in the three years after the 1973 oil embargo? Why?

2. Compare this graph with Figure 12.13 on page 369, which shows real per capita GDP. How closely is economic growth related to productivity?

How Are Productivity and Growth Related?

Economic growth is a measure of change in production. It does not consider how much effort or how many resources it took to produce that quantity of production. Productivity, on the other hand, is a measure of efficiency. It reflects the amount of effort and resources it took to produce a certain quantity.

A country could experience economic growth—as measured by real GDP—without increasing its productivity. Such growth would be tied to an increase in the quantity of natural resources, labor, capital, or technology. If the productivity of a country increases, its real GDP can grow without increasing the quantity of inputs.

As shown in Figure 12.15, productivity in the United States grew at a steady pace from 1950 to 2000. Among other things, a better educated labor force and advances in information technology contributed to the increase. The dips in the graph represent productivity setbacks, such as tighter financial markets during recessions.

APPLICATION Drawing Conclusions

C. Some countries have limited natural resources but high economic growth. Does this prove that worldwide economic growth is unlimited by natural resources? Why or why not?

Thomas Robert Malthus: The Population Problem

Economics Update

Find an update on Thomas Robert Malthus at **ClassZone.com**

In the late 1700s, many European thinkers and writers predicted a future of peace and harmony in which poverty and hunger would be eliminated. Discussing humanity's future with his father led Thomas Robert Malthus to question whether the prevailing view was perhaps too rosy. Malthus saw a problem that others had overlooked, namely, that the world's population seemed likely to outgrow the available supply of food. He published his ideas in 1798 in "An Essay on the Principle of Population as It Affects the Future Improvement of Society."

A Natural Limit to Economic Growth?

Malthus's essay argued that human population would increase geometrically—that is, it would double—every 25 years. Malthus also estimated that food production would only increase arithmetically—that is, by the same amount each time—over that time period. Figure 12.16 uses hypothetical numbers to illustrate the problem. As time went on, agriculture would produce less food per person, and millions would be thrown into poverty and starvation.

"An Essay on the Principle of Population" caused a tremendous backlash. People could not accept that the rosy future they had imagined might not come to pass. Malthus and his essay were widely attacked and criticized—but no one could ignore his argument.

Malthus's estimates turned out to be flawed. Human population increased at a slower pace than he predicted. World population was about 1 billion in 1800, but it took until 1930 to reach 2 billion. Agricultural productivity rose dramatically with the introduction of mechanized farming and advances in fertilization and pest control. Although world population accelerated around 1950, reaching about 6.5 billion by 2005, agricultural production kept pace with the growing population.

Thomas Robert Malthus
Malthus predicted a population explosion that would result in poverty and famine.

FIGURE 12.16 MALTHUS'S POPULATION PROBLEM

Elapsed Years	Bushels of Wheat (in millions)	Population (in millions)	Bushels per Person
0	10	10	1.00
25	20	20	1.00
50	30	40	0.75
75	40	80	0.50
100	50	160	0.31

APPLICATION Applying Economic Concepts

D. How is Malthus's population problem an example of the problem of scarcity?

REVIEWING KEY CONCEPTS

1. Explain the differences between the terms in each of these pairs.

   a. *economic growth*   **b.** *capital deepening*
   real GDP per capita   *labor input*

2. Name the key measurement of economic growth.

3. What four factors drive economic growth?

4. How are productivity and growth related?

5. Briefly explain the problem Malthus identified.

6. **Using Your Notes** Write a persuasive paragraph arguing one side or the other of economic growth possibilities. Refer to your completed summary chart.

What Is Economic Growth?		

   Use the Graphic Organizer at **Interactive Review @ ClassZone.com**

CRITICAL THINKING

7. **Solving Economic Problems** In 2000, the world's population was about 6 billion, and about 800 million of those people did not have enough to eat. By 2050, the world's population is expected to grow to about 9 billion. What steps should we take now to avoid having more than 1 billion people without enough to eat by 2050? Employ the ideas you learned about in this section in formulating your solution.

8. **Explaining an Economic Concept** Why is real GDP per capita a useful measure? Why couldn't real GDP or GDP per capita be used for the same purpose?

9. **Analyzing Cause and Effect** Globalization opens international boundaries to companies, creating markets that stretch around the world. What role might global competition play in the development of innovations?

10. **Challenge** Going to school is your job. Your product is increasing your knowledge, and your grades are the main measure of this. Increasing your productivity would result in better grades—and more free time. Adapt the factors that contribute to economic productivity to explain how you might increase your productivity as a student.

ECONOMICS IN PRACTICE

A busy factory is one route to economic growth.

Stimulating Economic Growth

Government policies affect economic growth. Some policies have immediate effects that last for a short time. Other policies take longer to show results but have lasting impact.

Create a Healthy Economy

Reflecting on what you learned in this section, consider the following possible government actions.

- open a protected wilderness area for coal mining
- increase funding for scholarships for low-income students
- provide tax breaks for companies purchasing new equipment
- strengthen laws protecting the rights of inventors

Explain how each potential action might lead to economic growth.

Challenge Estimate the costs and the benefits of each action. Which actions would have the most lasting positive effect on the economy?

Case Study

Economics Update
Find an update on this Case
Study at **ClassZone.com**

Poland: Economic Freedom and Economic Growth

Background Communists ruled Poland and controlled its economy from 1948 to 1989. After holding its first free elections in 1990, Poland made rapid progress toward full democracy and a free market economy. Economic reforms included ending government price controls, privatizing industries formerly controlled by the government, and entering the international marketplace. As Poland moved away from government control of the economy, it experienced a surge in economic growth—outdistancing many other former Communist countries in eastern and central Europe. In 2004, Poland became a member of the European Union, further increasing its economic potential.

What's the issue? How successful is Poland's economy? Read these documents to learn about the challenges and rewards of the country's economic transition.

A. Online News Article

Wroclaw, a city in southwest Poland, offers one example of the country's success through embracing global capitalism. This article describes that phenomenon.

Wroclaw, Poland: Europe's Next Appliance Capital?

Appliance Manufacturers Pour into Southwest Poland

Money and companies are pouring in—not just the prestige nameplates like Bombardier, Siemens, Whirlpool, Toyota, and Volvo, but also the network of suppliers that inevitably follows them. At first, most of the new jobs were of the semi-skilled variety. Now they have been followed by design and engineering work that aims to tap into the largest concentration of university students in Eastern Europe.

"Everyone is coming, and they are coming very fast," reports Josu Ugarte . . . who heads the appliance manufacturing operations here of Mondragon, the giant Spanish industrial cooperative. He predicts, confidently, that the region around Wroclaw will soon surpass Northern Italy as Europe's appliance capital. . . .

The secret isn't just lower wages. It's also the attitude of workers who take pride and are willing to do what is necessary to succeed, even if it means outsourcing parts production or working on weekends or altering vacation schedules. . . .

Source: **"Europe's Capitalism Curtain" WashingtonPost.com July 23, 2004**

Many manufacturers have opened factories in Wroclaw, Poland. This Volvo factory produces buses.

Thinking Economically How has Poland's human capital contributed to the country's economic growth?

B. Political Cartoon

Poland's farmers were sceptical about the benefits of European Union membership. This cartoon reflects their change of heart as agricultural exports increased and they received new subsidies from the European Union.

Thinking Economically Does the cartoon emphasize the free market benefits of the European Union or other benefits?

C. Magazine Article

Joining the European Union brought tremendous growth to Poland's economy. This article explains some of the elements that led to the success.

Reaping the European Union Harvest

How the new central European members learnt to stop worrying and love the European Union

After grumbling furiously about dangers to their sovereignty and their social values when they joined the European Union in May, Poles are discovering themselves now to be among the Union's most loyal citizens. Some three-quarters say they are happy with EU membership—and no wonder. In its first eight months of membership Poland got some €2.5 billion [€ is the euro, the currency of the European Union] ($3.4 billion) from the EU budget, or roughly twice what it paid in, according to the newspaper Rzeczpospolita. Rural incomes have risen by one-third for small farmers and two-thirds for big ones, reversing eight years of stagnation and decline, thanks to munificent EU subsidies and an influx of foreign buyers offering high prices for Polish meat and fruit.

Poland's total exports rose by more than 30% in the first nine months of 2004, helped by the abolition of customs formalities. EU rules have opened the skies to budget airlines, boosting tourist numbers by 20% last year. Higher-than-expected tax revenues have meant lower-than-expected budget deficits. . . .

Source: *The Economist*, January 8, 2005

Thinking Economically According to the document, how has membership in the EU helped Poland's economic growth?

THINKING ECONOMICALLY   Synthesizing

1. Which economic measurements and indicators are evident in documents A and C? Explain what they convey about the strengths and weaknesses of Poland's economy.

2. What factors have driven Poland's economic growth?

3. Compare documents A and C, written about six months apart. What continued economic trends and new economic strengths do they describe?

Interactive Review

Review this chapter using interactive activities at ClassZone.com

- Online Summary
- Graphic Organizers
- Quizzes
- Review and Study Notes
- Vocabulary Flip Cards

Online Summary

Complete the following activity either on your own paper or online at **ClassZone.com**

Choose the key concept that best completes the sentence. Not all key concepts will be used.

aggregate demand	macroeconomic equilibrium
aggregate supply	national income (NI)
business cycle	national income accounting
capital deepening	net national product (NNP)
coincident indicators	nominal GDP
depression	nonmarket activities
disposable personal income (DPI)	per capita real GDP
economic growth	personal income (PI)
gross domestic product (GDP)	real GDP
gross national product (GNP)	recession
lagging indicators	stagflation
leading indicators	underground economy

__1__, the market value of all goods and services produced in a nation, is one of the key measurements used in __2__. __3__ is especially useful because it gives the market value of all goods and services corrected for price level changes. Another very useful measurement is __4__, which shows the actual amount of money people have to spend.

The economy goes through regular changes called the __5__. Economists watch __6__, such as building permits issued and stock prices, to predict changes in the economy. Low points in the economy are usually self-correcting, but in times of a __7__, such as the one that happened in the 1930s, government intervention may be needed.

Several factors influence __8__, including an increase in capital. __9__, an increase in the ratio between capital and labor, increases productivity, helping the economy grow. Economists use __10__, real GDP divided by whole population, to distinguish an increase in population from a higher level of economic output.

CHAPTER **12 Assessment**

REVIEWING KEY CONCEPTS

Gross Domestic Product and Other Indicators (pp. 350–357)

1. What is the purpose of national income accounting?

2. In what way is GDP a baseline for other economic indicators?

Business Cycles (pp. 358–367)

3. What do leading indicators say about the economy?

4. Explain how a business decision might have a ripple effect that would tilt the economy on a new phase of the business cycle.

Stimulating Economic Growth (pp. 368–377)

5. Explain how a country with few natural resources can still have economic growth.

6. What are the four key factors that influence economic growth?

APPLYING ECONOMIC CONCEPTS

The table below shows the size of the underground economies of selected countries.

FIGURE 12.17 UNDERGROUND ECONOMIES IN SELECTED COUNTRIES

Country	GDP Per Capita (in U.S. dollars)	Underground Economy as Percent of GDP
Egypt	3,900	69
Thailand	8,300	70
Russia	11,100	44
Chile	11,300	19
Singapore	28,100	14
Italy	29,200	27
Switzerland	32,300	9
United States	41,800	10

Sources: International Monetary Fund, U.S. Central Intelligence Agency, 1998-2005 data

7. Is there a relationship between GDP per capita and the size of a country's underground economy?

8. If a country incorporated its underground economy into the main economy, what would happen to its GDP per capita? Why?

CRITICAL THINKING

9. **Creating Graphs** Copy the blank graph onto your own paper. Then use the data in the table to create a line graph showing the percent change in U.S. real gross domestic product from 1999 through 2003.

Use **SMARTGrapher @ ClassZone.com** to complete this activity.

FIGURE 12.18 PERCENT CHANGE IN REAL GDP FROM PRECEDING PERIOD

Year	Quarter 1	Quarter 2	Quarter 3	Quarter 4
1999	3.4	3.4	4.8	7.3
2000	1.0	6.4	−0.5	2.1
2001	−0.5	1.2	−1.4	1.6
2002	2.7	2.2	2.4	0.2
2003	1.7	3.7	7.2	3.6

Source: U.S. Bureau of Economic Analysis

10. **Analyzing and Interpreting Data** Which year had the highest growth? The lowest?

11. **Analyzing Cause and Effect** The government enacted tax cuts and issued child tax credit refunds in 2003. What component of GDP would likely have increased because of these?

12. **Distinguishing Fact from Opinion** Does the graph support or counter the idea that the September 11, 2001 terrorist attacks caused a recession?

13. **Challenge** How could GDP grow by 5 percent a year but leave the economy no better off—or even worse off? Give two different explanations.

SIMULATION

Surveying Consumer Confidence

The Consumer Confidence Survey is one poll used to determine consumer expectations. Another is the ABC/Washington Post Consumer Comfort Index, which makes 1,000 phone calls to adults each month and asks the following questions:

• National Economy: "Would you describe the state of the nation's economy these days as excellent, good, not so good, or poor?"

• Personal Finances: "Would you describe the state of your own personal finances these days as excellent, good, not so good, or poor?"

• Buying Climate: "Considering the cost of things today and your own personal finances, would you say now is an excellent time, a good time, a not so good time, or a poor time to buy the things you want and need?"

To understand the consumer comfort index better, take a survey of your class.

Step 1. Break into five small groups and discuss each of the questions. The point is to share your thoughts, not to debate who is right or wrong.

Step 2. Return to your desk and write down your answers to each of the questions anonymously.

Step 3. Collect the anonymous answers from the whole class. Have one person tabulate the answers to each question on the board.

Step 4. Now calculate the consumer confidence of your class. For each question, add up the number of positive responses (either "excellent" or "good"). Then subtract the number of negative responses (either "not so good" or "poor"). Divide by the total number of students and multiply by 100.

Add the result from all three questions together, and then divide by three. That will yield an overall comfort level. A level of 100 would mean everyone is satisfied with everything. A level of −100 would mean that everyone felt negatively about everything.

Step 5. Discuss the result. Does it seem to accurately reflect the mood of the class? What would happen to the nation's GDP if all consumers felt as you do?

Economic Challenges
The national economy faces many challenges. Economics can help us understand and cope with these challenges.

Facing Economic Challenges

CONCEPT REVIEW

Business cycle is the series of growing and shrinking periods of economic activity, measured by increases or decreases in real gross domestic product.

CHAPTER 13 KEY CONCEPT

Unemployment has a variety of causes. Some level of unemployment is expected, even when an economy is healthy.

WHY THE CONCEPT MATTERS

As the nation's economy goes through business cycles, it will face the twin problems of unemployment and inflation. You may find yourself unemployed at some point during your working years, if only for a short period. For some people, persistent unemployment leads to poverty. During periods of inflation, you may have a job but your wages may buy less.

Online Highlights

More at ClassZone.com

 Economics Update

Go to **ECONOMICS UPDATE** for chapter updates and further information on inflation in the 1970s. (See Case Study, pp. 404–405.) ▶

 SMART Grapher

Go to **SMART GRAPHER** to complete graphing activities in this chapter.

Interactive ◀◀Review

Go to **INTERACTIVE REVIEW** for concept review and activities.

How did inflation in the 1970s affect people and businesses? See the Case Study on pages 404–405.

Unemployment in Today's Economy

OBJECTIVES	KEY TERMS	TAKING NOTES
In Section 1, you will • explain how economists measure unemployment • identify the different types of unemployment • discuss the impact that unemployment has on the economy and on individuals	unemployment rate, *p. 382* underemployed, *p. 383* full employment, *p. 383* frictional unemployment, *p. 384* seasonal unemployment, *p. 384* structural unemployment, *p. 384* cyclical unemployment, *p. 384*	As you read Section 1, complete a cluster diagram like the one below to record and organize what you learn about unemployment. Use the Graphic Organizer at **Interactive Review @ ClassZone.com**

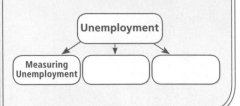

Measuring Unemployment

KEY CONCEPTS

During the economic downturn that started in 2007, companies in the United States laid off millions of workers. The impact of such decisions is far-reaching. Because the unemployed cannot buy as many goods and services as they did when they had a paycheck, other companies lose business. Some of those companies might lose so much revenue that they might also need to lay off workers. If businesses across the country decide to stop hiring or to cut back, the unemployment rate rises. The **unemployment rate** is the percentage of the labor force that is jobless and actively looking for work.

Unemployment Job fairs allow people looking for work to meet with many potential employers.

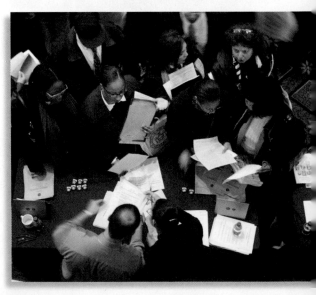

The Unemployment Rate

The civilian labor force, as you learned in Chapter 9, is made up of people over the age of 16 who are employed or actively looking and available for work. It does not include people in the military or those in schools, prisons, or other institutions. To determine the unemployment rate, the U.S. Bureau of Labor Statistics (BLS) surveys the labor

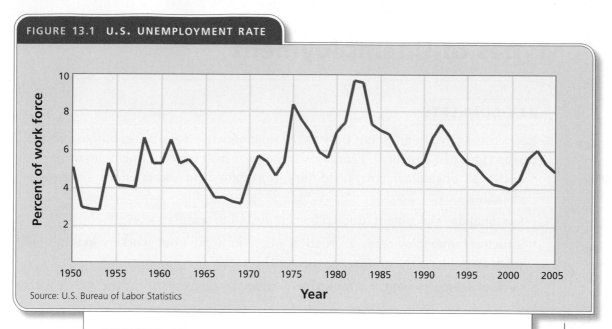

FIGURE 13.1 U.S. UNEMPLOYMENT RATE

Percent of work force (y-axis: 2, 4, 6, 8, 10)

Year (x-axis: 1950, 1955, 1960, 1965, 1970, 1975, 1980, 1985, 1990, 1995, 2000, 2005)

Source: U.S. Bureau of Labor Statistics

ANALYZE GRAPHS
1. From 1950 to 2005, when was the unemployment rate the highest?
2. From 1950 to 2005, when was the unemployment rate the lowest?

Economics Update

Find an update on the U.S. unemployment rate at **ClassZone.com**

force in 60,000 households each month. Workers over the age of 16 who are not working but are able to work and who have looked for work sometime during the previous four weeks are considered unemployed. The BLS then divides the number of unemployed persons by the total number of workers in the civilian labor force to arrive at the unemployment rate. While very useful, the unemployment rate does not account for discouraged workers who have stopped looking for work. Nor does it count the **underemployed**, those who work part-time when they want full-time employment or those who work at a job below their skill level. These include recently laid-off workers who may be in a temporary, lower-paying job.

Full Employment

Despite its name, **full employment** does not mean a zero unemployment rate. Instead, it means a level of unemployment in which none of the unemployment is caused by decreased economic activity. Even in a healthy economy there is always some level of unemployment. Sometimes people become unemployed when they relocate or when they leave one job to try to find another job that suits them better. Sometimes the available jobs do not match up with the skills of the available workers. In other words, some amount of unemployment is inevitable.

Economists generally agree that an unemployment rate of four to six percent indicates full employment in the United States. In other countries, with different labor markets and economic policies, full employment may occur at higher or lower rates of unemployment.

QUICK REFERENCE

The **underemployed** are part-time workers who want to work full-time or people working below their skill level.

Full employment means no unemployment caused by decreased economic activity.

APPLICATION Explaining an Economic Concept

A. Explain why the unemployment rate is based on a country's civilian labor force, not its entire population.

Facing Economic Challenges 383

Types of Unemployment

KEY CONCEPTS

Economists pay attention not only to the unemployment statistics, but also to the reasons for unemployment. Economists recognize four types of unemployment:

- **Frictional unemployment**, temporary unemployment experienced by people changing jobs
- **Seasonal unemployment**, unemployment linked to seasonal work
- **Structural unemployment**, a situation where jobs exist but workers looking for work do not have the necessary skills for these jobs
- **Cyclical unemployment**, unemployment caused by a part of the business cycle with decreased economic activity

TYPE 1 Frictional Unemployment

Frictional unemployment refers to the temporary unemployment of workers moving from one job to another. The frictionally unemployed might include a parent who has spent time at home raising children and decides to move back into the work force; a magazine designer who leaves his job to seek work as a designer at a book publisher; or a recent college graduate who is looking for her first full-time job. Frictional unemployment is a reflection of workers' freedom to find the work best suited for them at the highest possible wage. Economists consider frictional unemployment normal and not a threat to economic stability.

TYPE 2 Seasonal Unemployment

Demand for some jobs changes dramatically from season to season, resulting in seasonal unemployment. Demand for construction workers, for example, typically falls in the winter months when construction activities are more difficult. Tourism peaks at certain times of the year, and different regions have different tourist seasons. Migrant farm workers, who move from one area to another following the growing schedules of the crops, are hard hit by seasonal unemployment. The winter months are especially slow, resulting in economic hardship for many migrant families.

TYPE 3 Structural Unemployment

Structural unemployment results when the available jobs do not match up well with the skills and experience of the available workers. A dynamic economy will often create structural unemployment as businesses become more efficient and require fewer workers to create the same amount of output. There are a number of possible triggers for structural unemployment. New technology can replace human workers or require workers to retrain. New industries requiring specialized education can leave less well-educated workers

Seasonal Unemployment
Demand for lifeguards is high during the warmer months.

A GLOBAL PERSPECTIVE

Offshore Outsourcing: Scourge or Boon?

Many American workers fear losing their jobs to offshore outsourcing—the contracting of work to suppliers in other countries. But the likelihood of offshore outsourcing varies widely from one occupation to the next. According to a report issued by the McKinsey Global Institute in 2005, about 11 percent of all service jobs in the United States have the potential to be outsourced to another country. Jobs in information technology, engineering, and accounting are much more likely to be outsourced than jobs in health care, retail sales, and other fields that require direct personal interaction.

Office worker in India

The offshore outsourcing trend has created some structural unemployment, as laid-off workers seek new jobs. But ultimately, it should make the U.S. economy more efficient. The firms that save money by outsourcing will be more competitive. As these businesses grow, they will hire more U.S. workers.

For some U.S. workers, outsourcing may offer unique opportunities. India has been so successful in securing business outsourced by other countries that it has a shortage of qualified labor. Because many jobs outsourced to India require workers to be fluent in English or European languages, one study predicts that 120,000 Europeans, Americans, and Australians will be working in India by 2010.

CONNECTING ACROSS THE GLOBE

1. **Synthesizing Economic Information** Explain how outsourcing might change the American economy.
2. **Evaluating** What career do you want to pursue? Explain whether it has the potential to be outsourced.

out of work. A change in consumer demand—from compact discs to computer music files, for example—can shift the type of workers needed. Offshore outsourcing, when jobs once held by Americans are staffed overseas, is another cause of structural unemployment.

TYPE 4 Cyclical Unemployment

Cyclical unemployment results when the economy hits a low point in the business cycle and employers decide to lay off workers. Workers who lose their jobs during a recession can have trouble finding new jobs because the economy as a whole is scaling back, and the demand for labor declines. When the economy picks up again, many workers are again able to find jobs.

The duration of unemployment in these four types ranges widely, but the average duration of unemployment is relatively short. More than a third of the unemployed are out of work for five weeks or less.

APPLICATION Making Inferences

B. If you owned a clothing factory, how would a high rate of unemployment affect your business?

The Impact of Unemployment

KEY CONCEPTS

Although some unemployment is unavoidable, excessive or persistent unemployment hurts the economy in several ways. It reduces efficiency; it hurts the least economically secure; and it damages workers' self-confidence.

Efficiency Unemployment is inefficient. It wastes human resources, one of the key factors of economic growth.

Inequality Unemployment does not follow equal opportunity rules. In an economic slowdown, those with the least experience lose their jobs first—usually minorities and the young (see the graphs below). Also, with fewer jobs available, people on the lower rungs of the employment ladder have less opportunity to advance.

Discouraged Workers People who are unemployed—or underemployed—for long periods of time may begin to lose faith in their abilities to get a job that suits their skills. Potentially productive workers may give up their search for work. If they are underemployed, they may not be motivated to do their best work.

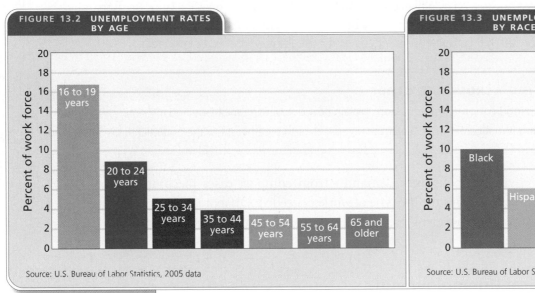

FIGURE 13.2 UNEMPLOYMENT RATES BY AGE

Source: U.S. Bureau of Labor Statistics, 2005 data

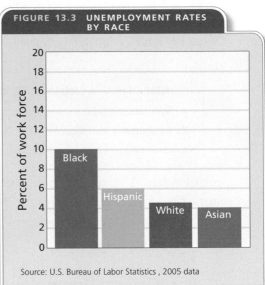

FIGURE 13.3 UNEMPLOYMENT RATES BY RACE

Source: U.S. Bureau of Labor Statistics , 2005 data

ANALYZE GRAPHS

1. Which group, either age or race, has the highest rate of unemployment?
2. What happens to the unemployment rate as people get older?
3. If the majority of people aged 65 and older are retired, why is the unemployment rate for that group so low?

APPLICATION Writing About Economics

C. In 1889, Jane Addams founded the Hull House Association in Chicago to help newly arrived immigrants adjust to the challenges of city life. In 1910, she wrote that "of all the aspects of social misery nothing is so heartbreaking as unemployment." Write a paragraph explaining the impact of unemployment on immigrants.

REVIEWING KEY CONCEPTS

1. Explain the relationship between the terms in each of these pairs.

   a. *frictional unemployment* **b.** *seasonal unemployment*
   structural unemployment   *cyclical unemployment*

2. Explain how the unemployment rate is calculated.

3. Why are economists interested in the unemployment rate?

4. Name a job that might be affected by structural unemployment. Explain why it might be affected.

5. What is full employment?

6. **Using Your Notes** Write a brief summary of this section, covering measuring unemployment, types of unemployment, and the impact of unemployment. Refer to your completed cluster diagram.

   Use the Graphic Organizer at **Interactive Review @ ClassZone.com**

CRITICAL THINKING

7. **Solving Economic Problems** Unemployment insurance provides money to workers who have lost their jobs through no fault of their own. In most states, the insurance is funded entirely by employers. What else might business and government do to help unemployed workers?

8. **Analyzing Cause and Effect** In June 2005, claims for unemployment insurance in Illinois from construction workers made up about 14 percent of all claims. In December 2005, they made up about 21 percent. Why might more construction workers file for unemployment benefits in December than in June? What type of unemployment best explains the difference?

9. **Applying Economic Concepts** Give specific examples from the Great Depression of the 1930s of ways in which the widespread unemployment (1) affected efficiency, (2) was distributed unequally, and (3) eroded self-esteem.

10. **Challenge** Think about the type of career you hope to have when you are finished with your education. Do you think it is more likely or less likely than others to be affected by each of the various types of unemployment? Explain each of your answers.

ECONOMICS IN PRACTICE

Identifying Types of Unemployment
Read the following descriptions of unemployment scenarios.

Categorize Economic Information Decide which of the four types of unemployment each scenario describes.

- Because of reduced demand, an appliance company temporarily closes one of its factories and lays off workers.

- In September, a part-time student at the University of Central Florida in Orlando loses his job at a theme park.

- A newspaper journalist leaves her job to make a switch into television journalism. She has been looking for a new job for several months.

- A local travel agency has to close down because of the widespread availability of direct online booking options.

Challenge Young people are two to three times more likely than older people to be unemployed. Why is this?

Poverty and Income Distribution

OBJECTIVES	KEY TERMS	TAKING NOTES
In Section 2, you will • explain how economists measure poverty • discuss the causes of poverty • describe how economists measure income inequality • identify what antipoverty programs are available	poverty, *p. 388* poverty threshold, *p. 388* poverty rate, *p. 389* income distribution, *p. 390* income inequality, *p. 390* Lorenz curve, *p. 391* welfare, *p. 392* workfare, *p. 393*	As you read Section 2, complete a summary chart like the one below to pull together the most important ideas about poverty and income distribution. Use the Graphic Organizer at **Interactive Review @ ClassZone.com**

What Is Poverty?			

What Is Poverty?

KEY CONCEPTS

Persistent unemployment sometimes leads to **poverty**, a situation in which a person lacks the income and resources to achieve a minimum standard of living. This minimum standard varies from country to country because different countries have different ways of life. Someone who herds sheep and lives in a hut would probably be considered poor in the United States. But such a person might be thought to have a comfortable life in some other countries. Because of such disparities, there is no universal standard for what constitutes poverty.

The U.S. government has established its own standard for poverty based on income levels. This **poverty threshold** is the official minimum income needed for the basic necessities of life in the United States.

The Poverty Threshold

The poverty threshold, also called the poverty line, is the amount of income the government has determined to be necessary for meeting basic expenses. People with incomes below that threshold are considered to live in poverty. The threshold, first formulated in the early 1960s, was calculated by finding the cost of nutritionally sound food and then multiplying by three, on the assumption that food costs are about a third of a person's expenses.

The threshold differs according to the size of the household and is adjusted annually to reflect changing prices. In 2005, the poverty threshold for a family of four in the United States was about $20,000. That same year, the median income for a family of four was over $65,000.

The Poverty Rate

The **poverty rate** is the percentage of people living in households that have incomes below the poverty threshold. Unlike the unemployment rate, the poverty rate is based on the population as a whole. Through census information, the poverty rate can be estimated for individuals, households, or specific segments of the population, such as African-American children or single-parent households.

The overall poverty rate in the United States declined between 1993 and 2000 to a low of 11.3 percent. It began to rise in 2000 and by 2004 had climbed to 12.7 percent, with 37 million people living below the poverty line. (See Figure 13.4.)

Poverty, like unemployment, does not hit all sectors of society equally. Children are especially at risk. Children made up more than half of the 1.3 million increase in the number of people living in poverty between 2002 and 2003. The number of families below the poverty line that are headed by a single mother also rose. Minorities and families that live in either an inner city or a rural area tend to have higher than average poverty rates. While the numbers tell the statistical story of poverty, only personal voices can convey the toll of being poor. James Baldwin, an African-American writer born in poverty, wrote that "anyone who has ever struggled with poverty knows how extremely expensive it is to be poor."

QUICK REFERENCE

The **poverty rate** is the percentage of people living in households that have incomes below the poverty threshold.

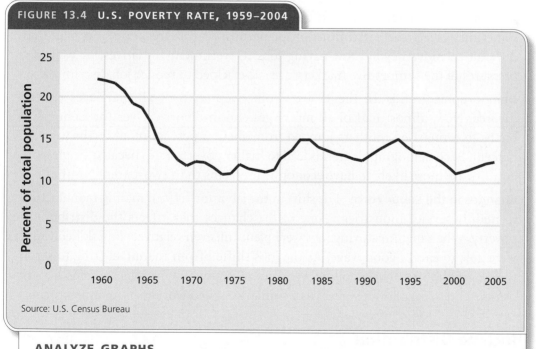

FIGURE 13.4 U.S. POVERTY RATE, 1959–2004

Source: U.S. Census Bureau

Economics Update

Find an update on the U.S. poverty rate at **ClassZone.com**

ANALYZE GRAPHS

1. From 1959 to 2004, when was the poverty rate the highest? When was it lowest?
2. What decade saw the largest drop in the rate of poverty?

APPLICATION Drawing Conclusions

A. Why is the poverty rate based on the entire population, while the unemployment rate is based on the civilian work force?

The Problem of Poverty

Across the globe, about half of the world's 6 billion people live in poverty. In the United States, one of the world's wealthiest countries, almost 40 million people live below the poverty level. Even good economic times, such as the boom that the United States experienced in the 1990s, do little to move large numbers of people out of poverty. Why is an adequate income out of reach for so many people?

Factors Affecting Poverty

Four major factors have the strongest influence on who lives in poverty in the United States: education, discrimination, demography, and changes in the labor force.

Education As you learned in Chapter 9, usually there is a direct relationship between level of education and income: the higher the level of education, the higher the income. In the United States, the poverty rate of people who did not complete high school is 12 times higher than that of people with a college education.

Discrimination White males tend to have higher incomes than racial minorities and women, even when there are no differences in education or experience. Certain groups sometimes face wage discrimination or occupational segregation and may find it difficult to move beyond low-paying jobs. Government initiatives, as well as the pressures of the competitive marketplace, have helped to reduce job discrimination.

Demographic Trends In the 1950s, about one-fourth of all marriages ended in divorce. Now, almost half of all marriages end in divorce. Over the same period, births to unmarried mothers jumped from about 5 percent of all births to over 30 percent. Such demographic trends lead to higher poverty rates because single-parent families are more likely to have economic problems than two-parent families.

Changes in the Labor Force The shift in the labor force from mainly manufacturing to mainly service industries is one of the changes that affects the distribution of poverty. When manufacturing jobs were plentiful, even relatively low-skilled workers were able to earn a good wage. As the jobs shifted from manufacturing to service, the wages did not always follow. Workers in many service jobs, such as fast-food clerks, tend to earn lower wages than similarly skilled workers in manufacturing.

Income Distribution

The United States has one of the highest median family incomes in the world, yet millions of Americans live below the poverty line. This disparity is reflected in the country's **income distribution**, the way income is divided among people in a nation.

All countries have some degree of **income inequality**, an unequal distribution of income. Unless everyone earns the same amount, there will always be a difference between the incomes of the wealthiest citizens and those of the poorest. Compared to other advanced nations, the United States has relatively high income inequality. However, less advanced countries tend to have the most extreme differences between what the rich earn and what the poor earn.

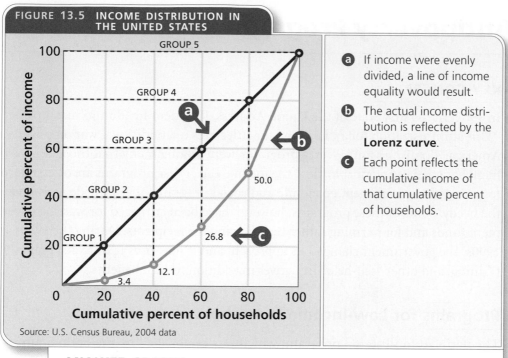

FIGURE 13.5 INCOME DISTRIBUTION IN THE UNITED STATES

Cumulative percent of income (y-axis)
Cumulative percent of households (x-axis)

GROUP 5, GROUP 4, GROUP 3, GROUP 2, GROUP 1

50.0
26.8
12.1
3.4

a If income were evenly divided, a line of income equality would result.

b The actual income distribution is reflected by the **Lorenz curve**.

c Each point reflects the cumulative income of that cumulative percent of households.

Source: U.S. Census Bureau, 2004 data

ANALYZE GRAPHS

1. According to the graph, about how much of the total income in the United States is earned by the lowest 60 percent of households?

2. How would the graph change if the lower groups earned a greater percent of the nation's total income?

A **Lorenz curve** graphically illustrates the degree of income inequality in a nation. The Lorenz curve in Figure 13.5, for example, plots income distribution in the United States. If income were distributed equally, then 20 percent of the population would receive 20 percent of the income, 40 percent would receive 40 percent, and so on. That distribution would be represented with a diagonal line.

However, income is not equally divided. The Lorenz curve in Figure 13.5 shows that the lowest 20 percent of the population (Group 1) receives only about 3.4 percent of the nation's total income. The lowest 40 percent (Group 2)—which includes the lowest 20 percent plus the next 20 percent—receive about 12.1 percent of the nation's total income. The more the Lorenz curve dips away from the diagonal line of equality, the greater the level of income inequality.

In the United States, the income gap between the lower 80 percent of the population and the top 20 percent grew steadily throughout the late 1900s. In 1970, the richest 20 percent of Americans earned on average 9 times more than the poorest. By 1997, they were earning 15 times more. Households are not stuck in one group. When people gain experience and education, their incomes tend to increase. When they retire or make poor economic decisions, their incomes decrease.

QUICK REFERENCE

Lorenz curve is a curve that shows the degree of income inequality in a nation.

APPLICATION Applying Economic Concepts

B. In 2004, the richest 20 percent of households in the United States received about 50 percent of the nation's income. Based on that proportion, if $100 was shared among five people, how much would the richest one receive? How much would each of the other four get if they shared the rest equally?

Antipoverty Programs

KEY CONCEPTS

QUICK REFERENCE

Welfare is government economic and social programs that provide assistance to the needy.

In 1964, in his first State of the Union Address, President Lyndon Johnson pledged: "This administration today, here and now, declares unconditional war on poverty in America." Johnson's antipoverty programs were among many that the U.S. government has tried in an effort to close the income gap. These programs are often referred to as **welfare**, government economic and social programs that provide assistance to the needy. Some of these programs, however, have been criticized for wasting government funds and for harming rather than helping the recipients. During the 1980s and 1990s, the government changed its approach, and it now uses tax breaks, grants, job training, and other "self-help" initiatives in addition to cash benefits.

Programs for Low-Income Households

The national food stamp program, which was established by the Food Stamp Act of 1964, helps ensure that no one will go hungry. Qualifying individuals and families receive electronic benefit transfers, which have replaced the paper food stamps that had been used originally. Recipients are given a card tied to an account into which the government makes monthly deposits of food benefits. The card can be used only to purchase food at grocery stores. Since 1975, the number of food stamp recipients has fluctuated from year to year from about 16 million to about 27 million. In 2005, almost 26 million people participated in the program.

Food Stamps The food stamp program helps those with low incomes to buy groceries.

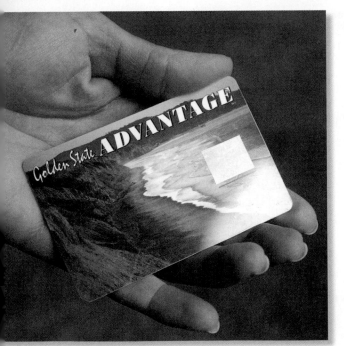

The Medicaid program is another antipoverty measure for low-income households. Medicaid offers health care for the poor and is funded by both the federal and state governments. The expense to each state is often as much as 25 percent of the state budget. Medicaid is the only health care coverage for about 40 million Americans, nearly half of them children.

Another antipoverty program is the earned-income tax credit. This program provides the working poor a refund of payroll taxes and other taxes deducted from their paychecks. About 21 million people received these credits in 2004. One benefit of the program is that the money refunded to the recipients generally gets spent in their own communities. This spending helps to boost the economies of poor neighborhoods.

General Programs

The U.S. government's Social Security program—which pays benefits to retirees, survivors, and the disabled—is the largest government program in the world. In the year 2004 alone, it paid out $500 billion, and that amount is expected to increase as people born during the baby boom after World War II reach retirement age. It was established in 1935 by the Social Security Act.

The Social Security program is funded through a special payroll tax. At retirement, all workers—rich and poor alike—are entitled to monthly checks to help with living expenses. Another payroll tax helps to fund Medicare, a government health insurance program for seniors. Medicare became part of the Social Security program in 1965. These benefits have been key in reducing the number of older Americans in poverty. From 1960 to 1995, the poverty rate of those aged 65 and over fell from about 35 percent to about 10 percent.

The Social Security Act also established a system of unemployment insurance administered through state governments. People who lose their jobs through no fault of their own are eligible to receive income while they look for work. Each state administers its own unemployment insurance program. Most of the programs are funded by taxes paid by employers, but in a few states employees contribute too. These benefits, which usually last no more than 26 weeks, help people avoid financial problems while they seek new employment.

Other Programs

Other antipoverty programs supplement the largest programs. One is the Community Services Block Grant program, which provides blocks of federal money to local communities to address such issues as employment, education, and housing. Job training is another. One such program provides grants to community colleges to develop training for high-tech, high-growth jobs. Another way to provide jobs for the unemployed and at the same time boost the economy of a struggling neighborhood is through Empowerment Zones. The government tries to attract businesses to these specially designated neighborhoods by not charging them certain taxes. Businesses that operate in Empowerment Zones provide needed services and offer employment opportunities to area residents.

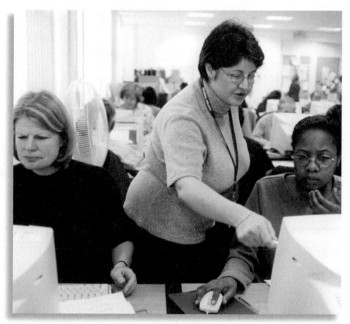

Job Training Job training helps unemployed people to learn new skills.

In 1996, the federal welfare program underwent substantial revision in a series of changes often referred to as welfare-to-work. These changes included new incentives for working, which older welfare programs often did not provide. **Workfare**, for example, is a program that requires welfare recipients to do some kind of work in return for their benefits. Their work provides a useful service and also helps prepare the workers for future jobs. Direct financial aid, now called Temporary Assistance for Needy Families (TANF), now has a limit of five years.

APPLICATION Explaining an Economic Concept

C. In terms of government spending, what is a fundamental difference between the food stamp program and the Empowerment Zone initiative?

Hernando de Soto: Another Path out of Poverty

Economics Update

Find an update on Hernando de Soto at **ClassZone.com**

Peruvian economist Hernando de Soto has attacked the problem of poverty by redefining it: "The poor . . . are essentially the biggest source of wealth within [a] country." According to de Soto, the poor have numerous assets—but in most countries they lack the basic property rights they need to grow economically. "They have houses but not titles; crops, but not deeds; businesses, but not statutes of incorporation." In short, their wealth is not protected by the rule of law.

Prosperity Through Property Rights

As a young man, de Soto was struck by the sharp contrast between the poverty in Peru's shantytowns and the energetic industry of the people who lived there. These thoughts led him, in time, to establish the Institute for Liberty and Democracy (ILD), which addresses this contrast in Peru and throughout the world.

De Soto estimates that 4 billion of the world's 6 billion people are shut out of the formal economy. Antiquated and needlessly complex laws make it difficult for these people to gain legal ownership of their homes and businesses, assets that are recognized as theirs in the informal economy.

De Soto estimates that the assets of the world's poor add up to about $10 *trillion*. He argues that until legal systems change to accommodate the poor, they will continue to prefer to operate in the informal economy—at the cost of lost economic opportunity for everyone. If the resources of the poor could be brought into the formal economy and developed, the wealth they would create could lift struggling nations from poverty into prosperity.

Hernando de Soto developed innovative ideas about the origins of poverty.

De Soto's critics point to his non-scholarly approach, but he says that he purposely "closed the books and opened his ears" as he traveled throughout the world listening to the voices of the poor. Former U.S. President Bill Clinton echoed the sentiments of many world leaders when he described de Soto's ILD as "the most promising antipoverty initiative in the world."

APPLICATION Writing About Economics

D. De Soto said: "Capitalism . . . allowed the people that came from humble origins of the world to have economic rights the way only nobility . . . had it before. So capitalism is essentially a tool for poor people to prosper." Do you agree with that explanation? Write a paragraph to explain your answer.

REVIEWING KEY CONCEPTS

1. Explain the relationship between the terms in each of these pairs.

   a. *poverty threshold*
   poverty rate

   b. *income distribution*
   income inequality

   c. *welfare*
   workfare

2. Why is it difficult to determine a universal poverty threshold?

3. What groups are especially hard hit by poverty?

4. What four factors help explain the distribution of poverty?

5. What does the Lorenz curve show?

6. **Using Your Notes** Describe five different antipoverty programs and the problems each combats. Refer to your completed summary chart.

What Is Poverty?			

   Use the Graphic Organizer at **Interactive Review @ ClassZone.com**

CRITICAL THINKING

7. **Making Inferences and Drawing Conclusions** A number of antipoverty programs are targeted specifically at children:

   • State Children's Health Insurance Program (SCHIP) provides health insurance to low income children who do not qualify for Medicaid and have no health insurance

   • National School Lunch Program provides free or reduced price lunches to eligible children

   • School Breakfast Program provides cash to schools for offering breakfasts to more than 8 million children nationally

   What are the economic benefits of antipoverty programs aimed at children?

8. **Solving Economic Problems** Antipoverty programs in the United States are least effective for immigrant families and for non-elderly people without children. Why might this be so?

9. **Analyzing Cause and Effect** How does the earned income tax credit aid both the working poor and their communities?

10. **Challenge** In 2005, the poverty threshold for a family of four was an annual income of just over $19,800. Based on this income, devise a monthly budget for a family of four. Assume that no taxes or payroll deductions will reduce the family's income. Also assume that the family lives in an apartment that costs $700 per month. Provide a detailed account of your estimated allowances for food, clothing, and other expenses.

ECONOMICS IN PRACTICE

Food aid from the United States and other nations assists those in extreme poverty.

Understanding World Poverty
Different parts of the world have different levels of poverty.

FIGURE 13.6 PERCENT OF POPULATION IN POVERTY	
Region	**Percent**
Sub-Saharan Africa	75
South-Central Asia	75
World	53
China	47
North Africa	29
Latin America / Caribbean	26
Eastern Europe	14

Source: World Bank, 2004 data

Analyze and Interpret Data Use the information in the table to answer these questions.

1. The table uses a poverty threshold of living on less than $2 a day. Why doesn't North America appear?

2. China has a population of about 1.3 billion people. About how many of them, in millions, live in poverty?

Challenge Do the same factors that affect poverty in the United States apply to the rest of the world?

Causes and Consequences of Inflation

OBJECTIVES	KEY TERMS	TAKING NOTES
In Section 3, you will • explain how economists measure inflation • identify what causes inflation • describe how inflation affects the economy	inflation, *p. 396* consumer price index (CPI), *p. 396* producer price index (PPI), *p. 397* inflation rate, *p. 397* hyperinflation, *p. 398* deflation, *p. 398* demand-pull inflation, *p. 399* cost-push inflation, *p. 399* wage-price spiral, *p. 400*	As you read Section 3, complete a cluster diagram like the one below to record what you learn about inflation. Use the Graphic Organizer at **Interactive Review @ ClassZone.com**

What Is Inflation and How Is It Measured?

KEY CONCEPTS

In 2006, militants attacked many of Nigeria's oil installations, demanding that more of the country's oil wealth be shared with the Nigerian people. Before the attacks, Nigeria produced about 2.5 million barrels of oil a day, and the country was the fifth largest source of oil imported by the United States. On news of the attacks, the price of oil rose by almost 20 percent. Some economists predicted that if oil stayed at those price levels, manufacturers might raise the prices of their products to compensate for higher fuel costs. They suggested that the high oil prices might ultimately lead to **inflation**, a sustained rise in the level of prices generally or a sustained fall in the purchasing power of money. Economists have several instruments for measuring inflation.

Consumer Price Index

One tool for gauging inflation is the **consumer price index (CPI)**, a measure of changes in the prices of goods and services commonly purchased by consumers. Creating the index requires many different steps, but the following describes the basic process. The U.S. government surveys thousands of people across the country to find out what goods and services they buy on a regular basis. The government then creates a "market basket" of about 400 different goods and services purchased by a typical household. The basket is adjusted to account for how much of a household's budget goes to purchase each type of item. For example, families tend to spend more on food than on lawn care, so the market basket is balanced to reflect this.

Each month, government workers research the current prices of the items in the market basket. What consumers spend to fill the basket can then be compared to prices in the reference base, which reflects the level of prices in the three years 1982 to 1984. Those numbers are given the value of 100. See the Connect to Math sidebar for more information.

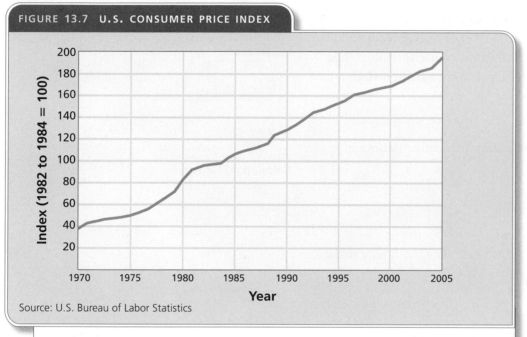

Economics Update

Find an update about the U.S. consumer price index at **ClassZone.com**

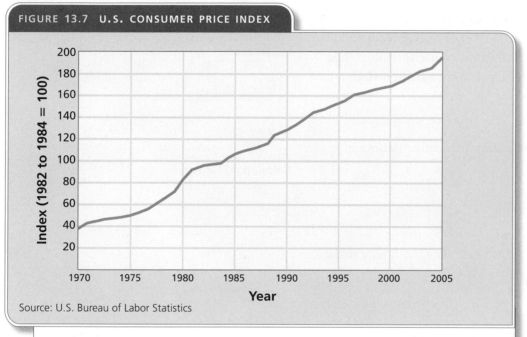

FIGURE 13.7 U.S. CONSUMER PRICE INDEX

Index (1982 to 1984 = 100) vs. Year

Source: U.S. Bureau of Labor Statistics

CONNECT TO MATH

Suppose the original value of the market basket was $500 and the current year's value is $550. To determine CPI, you divide the new value by the original value and multiply by 100. The current CPI, then, is 110.

$550 / $500 x 100 = 110

ANALYZE CHARTS

1. If you paid $500 to fill the market basket in 1984, about how much would you pay to fill the basket in 2005?

2. Prices doubled from 1971 to 1980. How long did it take them to double again after 1980?

Producer Price Index

The CPI shows the level of inflation experienced by consumers, but producers also experience inflation. The tool that gauges that kind of inflation is the **producer price index (PPI)**, a measure of changes in wholesale prices. The PPI is constructed in roughly the same way as the CPI, but it reflects the prices producers receive for their goods rather than the prices consumers pay. The difference between consumer prices and producer prices lies in all the additional fees consumers pay, such as sales taxes or shipping charges. Like the CPI, the PPI is tied to a reference base of producer prices. More than 10,000 PPIs for individual products and groups of products are available. The indices are grouped either by stage of production (finished goods, intermediate goods, and raw materials, for example) or by industry. Index changes from period to period are calculated in the same general way as the CPI.

Because producers tend to encounter inflation before consumers, PPI tends to lead CPI as an indicator of inflation. Economists use CPI and PPI to calculate the **inflation rate**, the rate of change in prices over a set period of time.

QUICK REFERENCE

Producer price index (PPI) is a measure of changes in wholesale prices.

Inflation rate is the rate of change in prices over a set period of time.

FIGURE 13.8 Calculating the Rate of Inflation

To calculate the rate of inflation, economists evaluate the prices of many different goods. This hypothetical example uses a simplified market basket consisting of prices for milk, bread, and juice. The table shows that the prices of milk and bread increased from Year B to Year C, but the price of juice decreased. To see the general trend in prices, you must look at the total price of the market basket of milk, bread, and juice. The steps below show how to use this simplified market basket to calculate the rate of inflation for Year C. The base year is Year A.

Price of a Market Basket			
	Year A	Year B	Year C
1 gallon milk	$2.50	$2.40	$2.60
1 loaf bread	$1.00	$1.35	$1.53
1 gallon juice	$2.00	$2.30	$2.20
Price of basket	$5.50	$6.05	$6.33
CPI, base: Year A	100	110	115

Step 1: Calculate each year's consumer price index (CPI).

Calculations for Year C

$$\frac{\text{Price of market basket}}{\text{Price of basket in base year}} \times 100 = CPI$$

$$\frac{\$6.33}{\$5.50} \times 100 = 115$$

Step 2: Use the CPI to calculate the rate of inflation.

$$\frac{\text{CPI} - \text{CPI for preceding year}}{\text{CPI for preceding year}} \times 100 = \text{Rate of Inflation}$$

$$\frac{115 - 110}{110} \times 100 = 4.5$$

The rate of inflation in Year C was about 4.5 percent.

Choosing a market basket To calculate the rate of inflation, economists use a complicated market basket of hundreds of goods. The market basket is intended to represent the goods that are purchased by a typical urban consumer.

Types of Inflation

The different types of inflation are defined according to the degree or level of the inflation rate. Rates below 1 percent are negligible, and those between 1 and 3 percent are moderate. If a moderate rate continues over a period of time, the result is *creeping inflation*. A rapid increase in price level is known as *galloping inflation*. If galloping inflation gets out of hand, the result is **hyperinflation**—a rapid, uncontrolled rate of inflation in excess of 50 percent per month. One of the most dramatic episodes of hyperinflation happened in Germany in 1922 and 1923. At the height of the crisis, prices rose at a rate of about 322 percent per month. **Deflation**, a decrease in the general price level, happens more rarely. The Great Depression of the 1930s in the United States was marked by deflation.

APPLICATION Applying Economic Concepts

A. If the price of milk goes up, is that inflation? Why or why not?

What Causes Inflation?

Economists generally distinguish between two kinds of inflation, each with a different cause. When the inflationary forces are on the demand side of the economy, the result is **demand-pull inflation**, a situation where total demand is rising faster than the production of goods and services. When the forces that lead to inflation originate on the supply side of the economy, the result is **cost-push inflation**, a situation where increases in production costs push up prices.

Demand-Pull Inflation

In demand-pull inflation, total demand rises faster than the production of goods and services, creating a scarcity that then drives up prices. Suppose, for example, that consumers gain confidence in the economy and decide they want to buy more durable goods—new refrigerators, stoves, second cars, and so on. It takes producers some time to recognize this rise in demand and to gear up for higher production. During this lag period, consumer demand pushes up prices on the currently available goods. Figure 13.9 illustrates how demand-pull inflation happens.

As you will learn in Chapter 16, the U.S. government creates and controls money through the Federal Reserve Bank. If the government creates too much money during the lag period before an increase in production makes more goods available, there will be too much money chasing too few goods, and prices will rise. The creation of excess money is the main reason for demand-pull inflation.

FIGURE 13.9 Demand-Pull Inflation

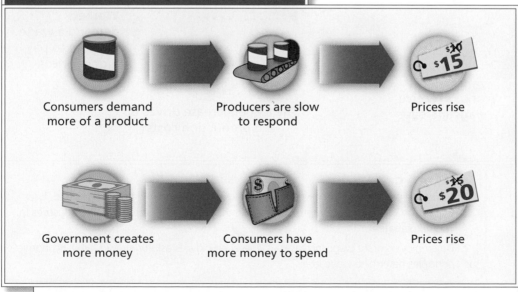

Consumers demand more of a product	Producers are slow to respond	Prices rise
Government creates more money	Consumers have more money to spend	Prices rise

ANALYZE CHARTS

1. In the first scenario, did the demand curve shift or the supply curve?

2. In the second scenario, which curve shifts when the supply of money increases?

Cost-Push Inflation

In cost-push inflation, prices are pushed upward by rising production costs. When production costs increase, producers make less of a profit. If consumer demand is strong, producers may raise their prices in order to maintain their profits. A general trend of rising prices leads to inflation.

Cost-push inflation is often the result of supply shocks—sharp increases in prices of raw materials or energy. For example, in 1973 and 1974, many members of the Organization of Petroleum Exporting Countries (OPEC)

SORRY

TEMPORARILY OUT OF ALL GRADES OF GASOLINES

Cost-Push Inflation Shortages of raw materials or energy can lead to cost-push inflation.

limited the amount of oil they sold to the United States and other Western countries. The resulting rapid rise in the price of oil led to cost-push inflation.

Wages are a large part of the production costs for many goods, so rising wages can lead to cost-push inflation. A **wage-price spiral** is a cycle in which increased wages lead to higher production costs, which in turn result in higher prices, which then lead to demands for higher wages. You can see the wage-price spiral in motion in Figure 13.10.

QUICK REFERENCE

A **wage-price spiral** is a cycle that begins with increased wages, which lead to higher production costs, which in turn result in higher prices, which result in demands for even higher wages.

FIGURE 13.10 Wage-Price Spiral

Producers raise prices to pay for higher production costs

~~$7.89~~ $9.99

Workers demand a wage increase to pay higher prices

Workers receive a wage increase

The wage increase drives up the production costs

ANALYZE CHARTS

1. Using the cotton industry as an example, explain how the cycle might proceed. Use the cotton workers, cotton growers, textile mills, and other intermediate industries in your explanation.

2. Do employers grant wage increases whenever employees ask for a raise? What economic principles determine wage levels?

APPLICATION Categorizing Economic Information

B. What type of inflation would result if bad weather hit farmers hard over a long stretch of time?

What Is the Impact of Inflation?

KEY CONCEPTS

Since the 1960s, the impact of inflation on the United States economy has been significant. Inflation has raised interest rates, limited the growth of the stock market, forced agricultural bankruptcies, and slowed production. It has also had a huge impact on politics. More than half of those who voted for Ronald Reagan in 1980 said that his promise to stop the long-running inflation of the 1970s was the decisive factor. Inflation is a major challenge to economic stability. For the economy as a whole and for individual consumers, inflation has an especially strong impact on the purchasing power of the dollar and on interest rates.

EFFECT 1 Decreasing Value of the Dollar

With inflation, today's dollar buys less than last year's. The consumer price index, illustrated in Figure 13.7, shows that the real value of a dollar has declined steadily. The rising index represents the declining value of the dollar.

Consider how this declining value affects people who are on a fixed income. Suppose, for example, that your cousin started college with a savings of $10,000 to see him through. He planned to spend $2,500 a year on carefully budgeted expenses. However, because of inflation, each of those dollars bought less each year. To pay for exactly the same things he bought in his freshman year for $2,500, by the time he was a senior he needed $2,750. Inflation had pushed prices up by 10 percent over the four-year period. Senior citizens living on a fixed retirement income—as well as anyone else with a fixed income—are especially vulnerable to the decreasing value of the dollar through inflation.

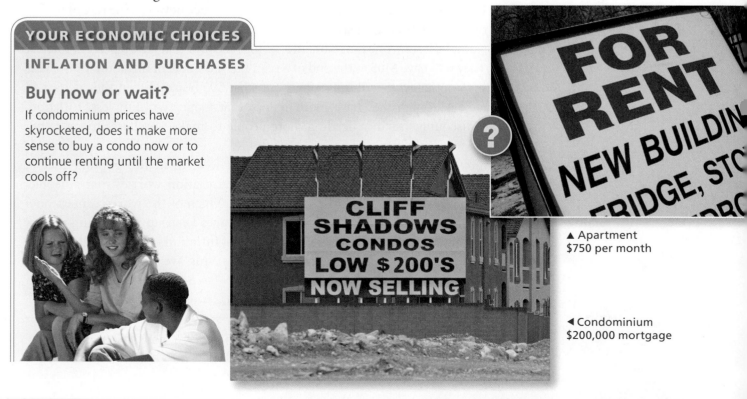

YOUR ECONOMIC CHOICES

INFLATION AND PURCHASES

Buy now or wait?

If condominium prices have skyrocketed, does it make more sense to buy a condo now or to continue renting until the market cools off?

CLIFF SHADOWS CONDOS LOW $200'S NOW SELLING

FOR RENT NEW BUILDIN FRIDGE, STC

▲ Apartment
$750 per month

◄ Condominium
$200,000 mortgage

Conversely, inflation can help borrowers. With inflation, those who borrow at a fixed rate of interest can repay their debts with dollars that are worth less, making their repayments smaller than they would have been without inflation. Suppose someone borrows $100 at 5 percent interest, promising to pay the lender $105 after a year. If inflation rises at 5 percent, the $105 the borrower pays the lender will have the same purchasing power as the $100 of the original loan. The borrower essentially paid no real interest on the money he borrowed.

EFFECT 2 Increasing Interest Rates

As prices increase, interest rates also tend to increase. Lenders raise their interest rates to ensure they earn money on their loans despite inflation. Higher interest rates mean that borrowing money becomes more expensive. For example, a $10,000 loan at 10 percent interest to be repaid over the course of five years would have a monthly payment of $212.47. At 5 percent interest, the monthly payment would be only $188.71. At the end of five years, you would have paid over $1,425 more for the loan at the higher rate. When interest rates are high, businesses are less likely to borrow to expand or to make capital improvements. Consumers are less likely to make purchases of high-priced items that they would need to finance. People carrying debt on credit cards have to make higher monthly payments as their rates rise.

EFFECT 3 Decreasing Real Returns on Savings

Inflation also has a significant effect on savings. People who save at a fixed interest rate get a lower rate of return on their savings. While the interest paid on savings tends to increase during inflationary times, the difference between the rate of return and the rate of inflation still leaves them at a disadvantage.

For example, if someone puts $100 in a savings account that pays 5 percent interest per year, they will have $105 at the end of a year. But if the rate of inflation for the year was 10 percent, that $105 will buy only about what $95 bought when they deposited their money. Although they have more dollars, that money will buy less. Inflation, then, can discourage savings, leading more people to make purchases today rather than saving for tomorrow.

Inflation is the most commonly used economic term in the popular media, far outpacing the distant second, *unemployment*. Inflation worries many people, especially those who remember the volatile 1970s. Much of the worry centers on a person's individual standard of living: Will my wages keep up with rising prices? Will my savings see me through retirement? Fear of inflation has contributed to the shift away from the traditional American belief in saving over consumption.

APPLICATION Writing About Economics

C. According to opinion polls, most Americans feel inflation is a more serious problem than unemployment. Write a paragraph stating your view on which is more serious. Use convincing reasons and examples.

SECTION 3 Assessment

Online Quiz
ClassZone.com

REVIEWING KEY CONCEPTS

1. Explain the relationship between the terms in each of these pairs.

   a. *consumer price index* **b.** *hyperinflation* **c.** *demand-pull inflation*
   producer price index   *deflation*   *cost-push inflation*

2. What are the stages in a wage-price spiral?

3. Use a specific example to explain cost-push inflation.

4. Use a specific example to explain demand-pull inflation.

5. What are three effects of inflation?

6. **Using Your Notes** If you were a business owner, what decisions might you make on news of a steady rise in inflation? Refer to your completed cluster diagram and provide specific examples.

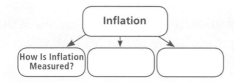

   Use the Graphic Organizer at **Interactive Review @ ClassZone.com**

CRITICAL THINKING

7. **Analyzing Cause and Effect** Why would producers tend to experience inflation before consumers? What type of inflation would the producers experience?

8. **Explaining an Economic Concept** How does the creation of excess money cause a demand-pull inflation? Refer to Figure 13.9 to help you answer this question.

9. **Applying an Economic Concept** Imagine that union leaders are meeting with the owners of a steel manufacturer to negotiate a new five-year contract for union employees. Explain how both sides of the union-management negotiation team must take the unpredictability of future inflation into account.

10. **Challenge** The cost of attending college has been rising faster than the inflation rate, at times twice as fast. For proof, ask your school guidance counselor for a catalog from a private college that shows prices from several years ago. Compare the old prices to the current prices shown on the college website. Calculate the percentage increase for this school.

ECONOMICS IN PRACTICE

MACROECONOMIC EQUILIBRIUM

Estimating the Effects of Inflation
Suppose that a natural disaster disrupts the production of oil so dramatically that prices for oil and related products double in a short period of time. In this graph of macroeconomic equilibrium, P1 shows the price level before the natural disaster.

Draw Aggregate Supply and Demand Curves On your own paper, recreate the graph of macroeconomic equilibrium. Then draw the new aggregate supply curve that would result from the natural disaster scenario, and indicate where P2 would fall.

Challenge Explain what will happen to total economic output because of the change in prices. How does the new graph show this?

Use *SMARTGrapher* @ **ClassZone.com** to complete this activity.

Case Study

Economics Update
Find an update on this Case
Study at **ClassZone.com**

The Effects of Inflation in the 1970s

Background Periods of high inflation can wreak havoc with a country's economy. In the 1970s, for example, the United States experienced the biggest and most sustained period of inflation in the country's history. By 1979, inflation had risen into the "double digits," that is, to 10 percent per year or higher. The prices of consumer goods—everything from food and gas to cars and houses—rose dramatically. Those on fixed incomes were particularly hard-hit, because as prices rose their limited budgets bought less.

What's the issue? How did inflation affect people and businesses in the 1970s? Study these sources to discover what it was like to live with a high rate of inflation.

A. Economic Analysis

In the late 1960s, the rate of inflation began rising in many countries. This article explains inflation's effects on the U.S. economy.

The Industrialized World and Inflation

How inflation affected the U.S. economy

For the years 1967 through 1978, the U.S. inflation rate averaged 6.1 per cent a year, compared with an average of 2 per cent for the years 1952 through 1967. Even during the 1973–74 recession, unlike most previous recessions, the inflation rate continued at a relatively high rate. In the late 1970s inflation speeded up again, reaching unprecedented levels.

Inflation would not be so bad, in the opinion of some economists, if it were accompanied by substantial increases in output and employment. But economic growth in the United States slowed during the high-inflation 1970s, bringing on a condition that economists describe as "stagflation." Another measure of economic health—productivity, or output per worker—also slowed dramatically in [those] years throughout the industrialized world, and in the United States and Great Britain for a time failed to increase at all. For the United States, a country long accustomed to ever-increasing material wealth, the fall-off in economic growth and the constantly eroding value of the dollar were traumatic developments. If the trends continued, the average American could no longer anticipate a constantly rising standard of living.

Source: *The Search for a New Economic Order*, The Ford Foundation, 1982

Thinking Economically Explain how the effects of inflation might be offset by increases in output and employment.

In this cartoon by Larry Katzman, a father offers an early lesson in economics.

Source: www.CartoonStock.com

"... but if daddy raised your allowance he'd be hurting the economy by stimulating inflation. You wouldn't want him to do that, would you?"

Thinking Economically Which type of inflation does the cartoon reflect? Explain your answer.

C. Newspaper Editorial

Prices rose dramatically during the 1970s. This editorial reflects the anger many consumers felt about the situation.

Protesting Inflation

Consumers grew impatient with the government's inability to control inflation.

Here we are, spending more and getting less, but the [government] economists are optimistic. What makes them so happy? The rate of inflation may have dropped 1 per cent. Just suppose the rate of inflation had gone down from 5 per cent to 4 per cent. . . . To me this is another increase of four cents, and a further shrinkage of my dollar.

Obviously this type of economics is good for someone. It certainly isn't good for me, or my friends, or my relatives. Everyone is complaining, but the experts are satisfied.

I have a family of meat eaters. . . . Long ago I discovered a marvelous cut of meat called skirt steak. It used to cost 89 cents a pound. It has inched its way up and has recently taken a leap to $1.59 and overtaken sirloin steak. Chopped meat is now where my skirt steak used to be. . . . Even the lowly onion is no longer cheap. A weekly trip to the supermarket, which in 1969 cost $50, now costs $70.

Source: *The New York Times*, September 29, 1972

Thinking Economically Why might a small decrease in a large rate of inflation satisfy government economists but frustrate consumers?

THINKING ECONOMICALLY   Synthesizing

1. Name one example from each document that shows how inflation has a negative impact on the economy.

2. Inflation is a general rise in price levels. Are the examples of price increases in documents B and C symptoms of inflation or isolated price increases?

3. Compare the tone of documents A and C. Do economists care as much about inflation as consumers? Explain your answer.

Interactive Review

Review this chapter using interactive activities at ClassZone.com
- Online Summary
- Quizzes
- Vocabulary Flip Cards
- Graphic Organizers
- Review and Study Notes

Online Summary

Complete the following activity either on your own paper or online at **ClassZone.com**

Choose the key concept that best completes the sentence. Not all key concepts will be used.

consumer price index (CPI)	Lorenz curve
cost-push inflation	poverty
cyclical unemployment	poverty rate
deflation	poverty threshold
demand-pull inflation	producer price index (PPI)
frictional unemployment	seasonal unemployment
full employment	structural unemployment
hyperinflation	underemployed
income distribution	unemployment rate
income inequality	wage-price spiral
inflation	welfare
inflation rate	workfare

There are different types of unemployment. __1__ represents workers changing jobs to increase their working satisfaction or to accommodate a move to another region. __2__ results from significant changes in the economy and in the way work is done. Even during periods of __3__ about 4 to 6 percent of the work force is still unemployed.

Nearly 40 million people in the United States have incomes below the __4__, even though the nation has one of the highest median incomes in the world. The poorest receive assistance through __5__. In recent years __6__, which requires an exchange of labor for government benefits, has replaced some direct cash payments.

__7__, a rise in the general level of prices, is another economic challenge. To monitor it, government economists developed the __8__, which tracks what consumers pay for a market basket of items, and the __9__, which tracks prices from the producers' point of view. They monitor the __10__ using these indices.

CHAPTER **13 Assessment**

REVIEWING KEY CONCEPTS

Unemployment in Today's Economy (pp. 382–387)

1. What are the four main kinds of unemployment and how do they differ from one another?

2. What are three negative impacts of unemployment?

Poverty and Income Distribution (pp. 388–395)

3. Which of the following persons is most likely to live in poverty: a senior citizen, a disabled adult, a college graduate, or a child? Explain your answer with specific facts and reasons.

4. Describe three antipoverty programs you feel are most useful and give reasons for your position.

Causes and Consequences of Inflation (pp. 396–405)

5. Describe two causes of inflation.

6. Which consequence of inflation would be the most troublesome to you personally? Explain your answer.

APPLYING ECONOMIC CONCEPTS

The table below shows employees laid off from selected industries in 2004. It also shows how many of these jobs were replaced by outsourcing.

7. What type of unemployment is it when an industry lays off workers but outsources their jobs? Name an example from the table.

8. Which industries' job cuts are probably due to changes in the business cycle?

FIGURE 13.11 LAYOFFS AND OUTSOURCING

Industry	Employees Laid Off	Replaced by Outsourcing
Mining	6,123	0
Apparel Manufacturing	11,583	4,102
Computer and Electronic Products	14,979	6,481
Transportation Equipment	40,634	6,223
Retail Trade	143,660	5,298
Transportation and Warehousing	59,098	2,090
Educational Services	1,429	0
Health Care and Social Assistance	44,212	621

Source: U.S. Census Bureau, 2004 data

9. **Creating Graphs** The population can be divided into five equal groups—or quintiles—according to income. Income mobility means moving from one quintile to another. A study done by the U.S. Treasury Department between 1979 and 1988 showed the following about taxpayers who started out in the lowest quintile:

   • 14.2 percent of the taxpayers in the bottom quintile in 1979 were still there in 1988

   • 20.7 percent had moved to the next higher quintile

   • 25 percent had moved to the middle quintile

   • 25.3 percent had moved to the second highest quintile

   • 14.4 percent of those who started in the lowest quintile had moved into the highest quintile

   Create a bar graph that illustrates these facts about income mobility in the United States.
   Use **⚡SMARTGrapher @ ClassZone.com** to complete this activity.

10. **Analyzing and Interpreting Data** What conclusions can you draw about income mobility based on the above data?

11. **Analyzing Cause and Effect** Think of three possible reasons a person might be able to move from one level of income to another.

12. **Explaining an Economic Concept** Which antipoverty programs use market forces to achieve their goals? Explain your answer.

13. **Analyzing and Interpreting Data** Consider the following data:

Consumer Price Index:	up by 6 percent
Unemployment Rate:	up to 7 percent
Gross Domestic Product:	up by 1 percent

    What's the economic problem? To correct the problem, which of these measures would you address first and why?

14. **Challenge** Which economic challenge— unemployment, poverty, or inflation—represents the greatest threat to social stability, in your opinion? Explain your answer with reasons and examples.

The Pursuit of Happiness

Do you need money to be happy? Since income alone does not tell the whole story of someone's quality of life, some people think other measures besides income should be used to determine a household's well-being. Many elements beyond material possessions also affect a person's quality of life.

To better understand the relationship between wealth and happiness, create a quality-of-life threshold by following the steps below.

Step 1. As a whole class, discuss the differences between income and quality of life.

Step 2. Break into five small groups and devise a quality-of-life threshold, a standard below which a person would be considered seriously impoverished.

Step 3. Try to find a measure for each of your criteria. For example, if one standard is "lives in warm climate," define the temperature range that qualifies as warm.

Step 4. Report your criteria to the rest of the class and explain how you would measure each.

Step 5. With the whole class, debate the relative merits of each quality-of-life threshold and its measurement.

Challenge Write a paragraph explaining how the quality-of-life threshold you developed relates to Hernando de Soto's ideas about property and prosperity (see page 394).

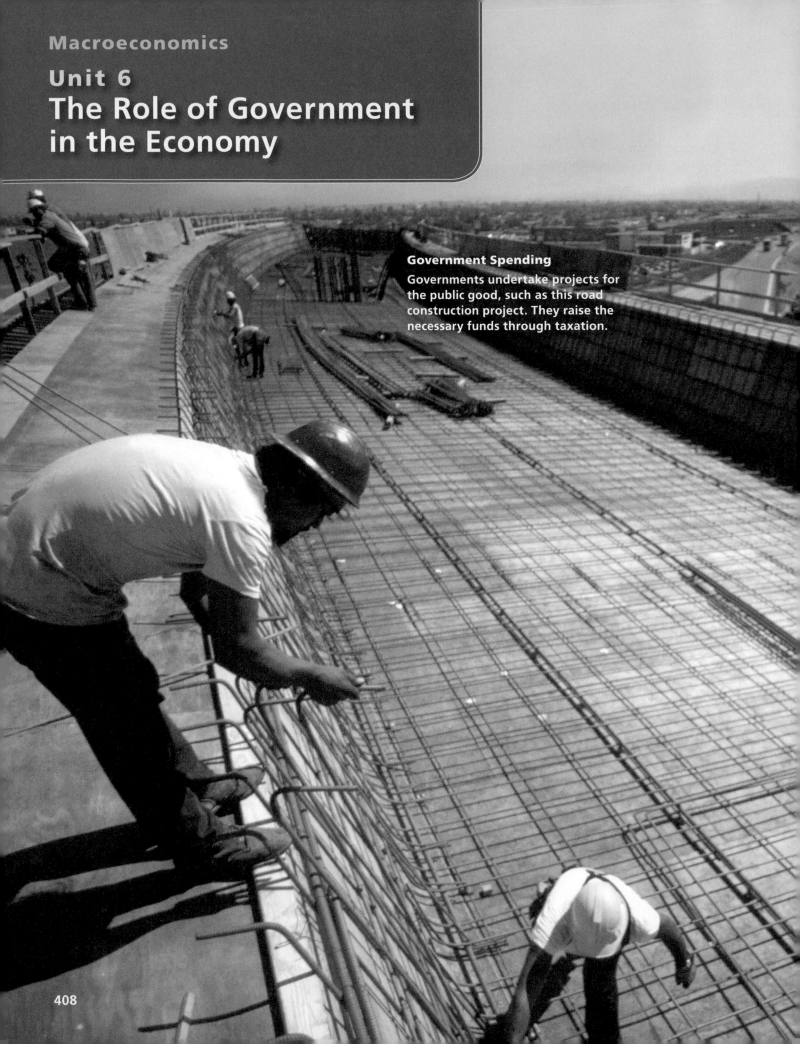

Macroeconomics

Unit 6
The Role of Government in the Economy

Government Spending
Governments undertake projects for the public good, such as this road construction project. They raise the necessary funds through taxation.

Government Revenue and Spending

CONCEPT REVIEW

A **modified free enterprise economy** is an economic system, like that of the United States, that includes some government involvement that influences the free enterprise system.

CHAPTER 14 KEY CONCEPT

A **tax** is a mandatory payment to a local, state, or national government, while **revenue** is government income from taxes and other nontax sources.

WHY THE CONCEPT MATTERS

Taxes are a part of your everyday life—from the income tax withheld from your paycheck to the sales tax you pay on the snack you bought at the sandwich shop. The revenues raised from these taxes fund programs that are familiar to you. For example, the highways you drive on, the police that protect you, and the parks that you use are all paid for by government revenues.

Online Highlights

More at ClassZone.com

Economics Update

Go to **ECONOMICS UPDATE** for chapter updates and current news on sales taxes on Internet purchases. (See Case Study, pages 440–441.)

Animated Economics

Go to **ANIMATED ECONOMICS** for interactive lessons on the graphs and tables in this chapter. ▶

Interactive Review

Go to **INTERACTIVE REVIEW** for concept review and activities.

FIGURE 14.3 SHIFTING TAX INCIDENCE

Who pays more of a tax—the consumer or the producer? See Figures 14.3 and 14.4 on page 415.

How Taxes Work

OBJECTIVES	KEY TERMS	TAKING NOTES
In Section 1, you will • explain why the government establishes taxes • identify the principles and structure of taxes • examine the incidence of taxes • describe how taxes affect the economy	tax, *p. 410* revenue, *p. 410* tax base, *p. 412* individual income tax, *p. 412* corporate income tax, *p. 412* sales tax, *p. 412* property tax, *p. 412* proportional tax, *p. 412* progressive tax, *p. 412* regressive tax, *p. 412* incidence of a tax, *p. 415* tax incentive, *p. 417*	As you read Section 1, complete a cluster diagram, using the key concepts and other helpful words and phrases. Use the Graphic Organizer at **Interactive Review @ ClassZone.com** Taxes

Government Revenue

KEY CONCEPTS

Governments provide certain public goods that generally are not provided by the market, such as street lighting, highways, law enforcement, and the court system. Government also provides aid for people in need. Where does the money come from to pay for such goods and services? The most important source is taxes. A **tax** is a mandatory payment to a local, state, or national government. **Revenue** is government income from taxes and nontax sources. Nontax sources include borrowing and lotteries. The rights of government to tax are set down in the U.S. Constitution and in state constitutions.

Principles of Taxation

When Chelsea started her 12-hour-per-week job at the local library, she expected to receive $120 in her weekly paycheck. However, she was surprised to see that some money was deducted from her pay for various taxes. She wondered why she had to pay these taxes.

Economists use certain principles and criteria to evaluate whether or not taxes should be paid and who should pay them. These principles most often are based on the benefits taxpayers receive from taxes and their ability to pay.

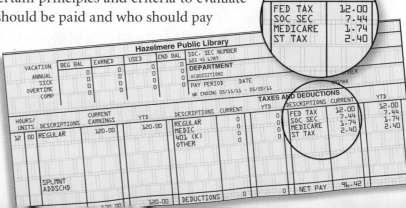

Benefits-Received Principle The benefits-received principle of taxation holds that people who benefit directly from public goods should pay for them in proportion to the amount of benefits received. One example of this principle is the financing of road construction and maintenance through taxes on gasoline. However, it is difficult for governments to assess exactly how much different taxpayers benefit from services like national defense, national parks, local police and fire protection, and public education.

Ability-to-Pay Principle The ability-to-pay principle of taxation holds that people should be taxed on their ability to pay, no matter the level of benefits they receive. According to this principle, people with higher incomes will pay more than people with lower incomes. The level of benefits received is not a consideration. Yet, income alone might not completely determine someone's ability to pay taxes. Other questions also arise. For example, should everyone pay the same percentage of income, which still results in wealthier people paying more in taxes, or should those with higher incomes pay a higher percentage of their income in taxes?

Criteria for Taxation

Tax systems attempt to meet three criteria: equity, simplicity, and efficiency. However, the criteria are sometimes in conflict, and a given tax may not meet all of the criteria equally well.

Equity The equity, or fairness, of a tax is established by how uniformly the tax is applied. Equity requires that people in similar situations pay a similar amount of taxes. For example, everyone who buys gasoline pays the same tax, or all people with the same level of income pay the same amount in taxes. In addition, some believe that equity requires that people with higher incomes pay more than people with lower incomes.

Simplicity One criticism of the U. S. tax code is that it is too complicated.

Simplicity The simplicity of a tax is determined by how easy it is for the taxpayer to understand and how easy it is for the government to collect. In addition, there should be no confusion about the time the tax is due and the amount to be paid. The sales tax, which you'll read about on the next page, meets the criterion of simplicity. A set percentage of the price of a taxed item is collected every time that item is purchased.

Efficiency The efficiency of a tax can be judged by how well the tax achieves the goal of raising revenue for the government with the least cost in terms of administration. From the taxpayers' viewpoint, tax efficiency can be judged by the amount of effort and expense it takes to pay the tax. Of all the types of taxes levied, the individual income tax—which you'll learn more about on the next page—best meets the criterion of efficiency.

Economics Update

Find an update on taxation at **ClassZone.com**

APPLICATION Drawing Conclusions

A. Businesses and homeowners both benefit from police protection. How does this statement show the limitations of the benefits-received principle of taxation?

Tax Bases and Structures

Government imposes taxes on various forms of income and wealth in order to raise the revenue to provide public goods and various other services. Each type of wealth subject to taxes is called a **tax base**. The four most common tax bases are individual income, corporate income, sales, and property.

Tax Bases

Individual income tax is a tax based on an individual's income from all sources: wages, interest, dividends, and tips. All taxes are ultimately paid from income, but using income as a tax base means that the amount of tax is directly linked to a person's earnings. For most individuals, income is earned mainly from work in the form of wages or tips. It may also come from savings and investment in the form of interest and dividends. Corporations pay income tax too. **Corporate income tax** is a tax based on a corporation's profits.

Sales tax is a tax based on the value of designated goods or services at the time of sale. Generally, sales taxes are imposed on a wide range of goods and services. The tax usually is a percentage of the posted price of the good or service and is included in the final price that the buyer pays. The seller then passes the tax revenue collected from customers on to the government that has imposed the tax.

Property tax is a tax based on the value of an individual's or business's assets, generally real estate. Homeowners and business owners pay property taxes based on the value of their buildings and the land on which the buildings stand. Property tax is generally included in the rents charged by property owners to individuals or businesses that rent the property, whether it is an apartment, an office, a factory, or a retail store. Property tax may also be imposed on other assets such as automobiles.

You may have heard references to a particular government's tax base growing or shrinking. Such statements refer to the amount of wealth that is available to be taxed. If overall personal income rises, the individual income tax base grows. If there are fewer homes or businesses in a certain locality or if their value declines, the property tax base shrinks because there is less wealth for the government to tax.

Tax Structures

The way in which taxes are imposed on the different tax bases gives rise to three different tax structures. These tax structures are distinguished from one another based on the percentage of income that a particular tax takes. A **proportional tax** takes the same percentage of income from all taxpayers regardless of income level. A **progressive tax** places a higher percentage rate of taxation on high-income earners than on low-income earners. A **regressive tax** takes a larger percentage of income from people with low incomes than from people with high incomes.

Proportional Tax A proportional tax is sometimes called a flat tax, because the rate of tax is the same for all taxpayers. For example, all taxpayers in a given country or state might be charged a flat 15 percent tax on their income, no matter how much

QUICK REFERENCE

A **tax base** is a form of wealth—such as income, property, goods, or services—that is subject to taxes.

Individual income tax is based on an individual's income from all sources.

Corporate income tax is based on a corporation's profits.

Sales tax is based on the value of goods or services at the time of sale.

Property tax is based on the value of an individual's or a business's assets.

A **proportional tax** takes the same percentage of income from all taxpayers.

A **progressive tax** places a higher percentage rate of taxation on high-income people.

A **regressive tax** takes a larger percentage of income from low-income people.

Step 1: Study the table to the right, which shows income tax brackets for a progressive tax. Each marginal tax rate is applied only to the income in that tax bracket. For example, for a taxable income of $12,000, $10,000 is taxed at 10 percent and the remaining $2,000 is taxed at 15 percent.

Income Bracket	Marginal Tax Rate
$0–$10,000	10%
$10,001–$30,000	15%
$30,001–$50,000	25%

Step 2: Assume you have a taxable income of $40,000. The table to the right shows how much of that income is in each tax bracket.

Income in Each Bracket	Tax Bracket
$10,000	10%
$20,000	15%
$10,000	25%

Step 3: Calculate the marginal tax for the income in each bracket. Add these figures to get the total tax for a taxable of income of $40,000. The total tax on $40,000 of taxable income is $6,500.

Income in bracket	×	Marginal tax rate	=	Marginal tax
$10,000	×	10%	=	$1,000
$20,000	×	15%	=	$3,000
$10,000	×	25%	=	$2,500

Total tax: $6,500

More Calculations Repeat calculations for taxable incomes of $25,000 and $45,000.

NEED HELP?

Math Handbook, "Understanding Progressive Taxes," page R7

their income is. An individual who earns $20,000 would pay $3,000 in taxes, and an individual who earns $50,000 would pay $7,500 in taxes. In the United States, some state and local governments have proportional taxes on individual income. States with flat taxes generally charge rates from three to five percent of income. Cities and counties with proportional taxes charge about one to three percent of income.

Progressive Tax As you saw above, even with a proportional tax, the amount of tax increases as income increases. A progressive tax is one in which the tax rate also increases as a person's income increases. In other words, under a progressive tax structure, a high-income person not only pays more in the amount of taxes but also pays a higher percentage of income in taxes. Figure 14.1 shows how a progressive income tax works. You can see that a progressive tax is most closely linked to the ability-to-pay principle.

In the United States, the federal income tax is a progressive tax, because the tax rate increases as income increases. (You'll learn more about the federal income tax in Section 2.) Most states have progressive income taxes. State tax rates range from under one percent to over ten percent.

FIGURE 14.2 Three Types of Tax Structures

What is the impact of each of the tax structures?

Proportional Tax
A proportional tax takes the same percentage of income from all taxpayers, regardless of income level.

Progressive Tax A progressive tax is based on income level. It takes a larger percentage of income from high-income earners and a smaller percentage of income from low-income earners.

Regressive Tax
A regressive tax hits low-income earners harder than it hits high-income earners. This is because the proportion of income that goes to taxes falls as income rises.

ANALYZE CHARTS
Look again at the description of the various tax bases on page 412. Consider which kind of tax structure applies to each of these tax bases. Write a brief paragraph explaining your choices.

Regressive Tax With a regressive tax, the percentage of income paid in taxes decreases as income increases. Some taxes are regressive because they are applied to sales, not income. For example, although a sales-tax rate is applied equally to all items subject to the tax, the tax as a percentage of income is regressive. This is because low-income earners tend to spend a higher proportion of income than do high-income earners. Suppose that a state charges 5 percent sales tax on certain goods sold in the state. If the Jones family earns $20,000 and spends $15,000 on taxable goods, they pay $750 in sales taxes (5 percent of $15,000), or 3.75 percent of their income. If the Smith family earns $50,000 and spends $25,000 on taxable goods, they pay $1,250 in sales tax (5 percent of $25,000), or 2.5 percent of their income.

For similar reasons, property taxes on homes are also considered regressive. Low-income homeowners usually spend a higher percentage of their income on housing than do high-income homeowners. Therefore, property taxes take a higher percentage of their income. In addition, poorer communities often charge a higher tax rate, because the property has a lower value and therefore the property tax base is smaller. Even those who do not own homes are subject to the regressive property tax, because property taxes are generally passed on to renters. Figure 14.2 above shows the impact of each type of tax structure on low-income earners and high-income earners.

APPLICATION Comparing and Contrasting

B. How do proportional, progressive, and regressive taxes meet the criteria of simplicity and equity?

Who Pays the Tax?

KEY CONCEPTS

The impact of a tax can also be measured by who actually pays it. The **incidence of a tax** is the final burden of that tax. In other words, it is the impact of the tax on a taxpayer. For example, taxes imposed on businesses may get passed on to the consumer in the form of higher prices or rents. To understand this, you need to apply the concepts of supply and demand.

QUICK REFERENCE

The **incidence of a tax** is the final burden of the tax.

Effect of Elasticity on Taxes

Suppose that the government imposes a $1 tax on a product. Demand elasticity influences the incidence of this tax. If a product has elastic demand, the seller pays more of the tax, because the seller faces decreased quantity demanded if prices rise. If the product has inelastic demand, the consumer pays more of the tax in the form of higher prices. The seller recognizes that quantity demanded will go down only slightly for goods or services that have inelastic demand, because they are less price-sensitive. Figures 14.3 and 14.4 illustrate the difference in tax incidence between products with elastic and inelastic demand.

FIGURES 14.3 AND 14.4 SHIFTING TAX INCIDENCE

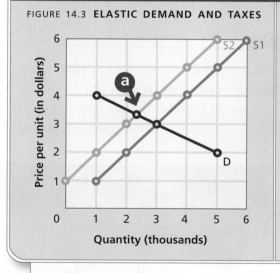

FIGURE 14.3 **ELASTIC DEMAND AND TAXES**

FIGURE 14.4 **INELASTIC DEMAND AND TAXES**

When a $1 tax is imposed, the supply curve (S1) shifts to the left (S2) by the amount of the tax.

a In Figure 14.3, the equilibrium price increases to $3.40, and the seller pays more of the tax.

b In Figure 14.4, the equilibrium price rises to $3.80, and the consumer pays more of the tax.

ANALYZE GRAPHS

1. In Figure 14.3, how does quantity demanded at equilibrium change?
2. Which producer's revenues would be least affected by the $1 tax?

Animated Economics

Use interactive demand elasticity curves at **ClassZone.com**

APPLICATION Applying Economic Concepts

C. Who would bear the greater incidence of these taxes: a. $1 tax on movie tickets? b. $1 tax on gasoline? Give reasons for your answers.

Impact of Taxes on the Economy

KEY CONCEPTS

Taxes do more than provide government with the revenue that allows it to provide public goods and other programs. Taxes have an economic impact on resource allocation, productivity and growth, and the economic behavior of individuals and businesses. Government chooses what to tax and how to tax based on the amount of income it wants to raise and the other economic effects it wants to achieve.

IMPACT 1 Resource Allocation

A tax placed on a good or service will increase the costs of production and therefore shift the supply curve to the left. If the demand remains the same, the price of the good or service will go up. This shift will likely result in a shift in resources. Recall what you learned about tax incidence earlier. If a supplier is not able to pass increased costs along to the consumer in the form of higher prices, the supplier may choose to shift production to another good that will be more profitable.

For example, if the government imposed a 10 percent tax on luxury yachts, which have elastic demand, the producer of the yachts would not be able to raise prices enough to cover the full cost of the tax. If it were no longer profitable to sell the yachts because of the extra cost of the tax, the producer might decide to shift resources to producing small fishing boats or go into a different business.

IMPACT 2 Productivity and Growth

When taxes on interest and dividends are high, people tend to save less than when taxes on this source of income are low. Therefore, taxes also have an impact on the amount of money available to producers to invest in their businesses. Some economists also believe that high taxes reduce incentives to work. They suggest that people may spend more time on activities other than work if a large percentage of their income goes to taxes.

Other economists suggest that the underground economy is a result of high taxes. The underground economy refers to jobs, services, and business transactions conducted by word of mouth and, for the most part, paid for in cash to avoid paying taxes. For example, Bob has a part-time landscaping business. He works on the weekends, charges lower prices than larger landscaping companies, and insists that his customers pay him in cash. Since there are no records of Bob's business transactions, it is difficult for the government to tax his income.

Underground Economy Bob avoids paying taxes on his landscaping business by working on a cash-only basis.

IMPACT 3 Economic Behavior

A **tax incentive** is the use of taxes to encourage or discourage certain economic behaviors. By providing tax credits or rebates, the government may encourage behavior that it believes is good for the economy and for society. For example, it may give tax rebates to businesses for opening new factories, offices, and stores in economically depressed areas. Or government may give tax credits to consumers for activities such as recycling or using energy more efficiently. The positive tax incentive with the widest impact is perhaps the home mortgage interest deduction, which is designed to encourage home ownership. (You'll learn more about tax deductions later in this chapter.)

QUICK REFERENCE

A **tax incentive** is the use of taxes to influence economic behavior.

So-called sin taxes are often imposed on products or activities considered to be unhealthful or damaging to society, such as gambling, alcohol, and cigarettes. These taxes are generally levied on products or activities for which there is relatively inelastic demand, so that the incidence of the tax will fall on the consumer. Yet because demand for such products is relatively inelastic, the government knows that decline in quantity demanded will not cause tax revenues to decrease dramatically. (Figure 14.5 shows how the quantity demanded of cigarettes changes when states enact higher cigarette taxes.) Demand for sin-tax products becomes somewhat more elastic as tax increases get steeper. For example, cigarette sales in Washington fell by nearly 19 percent in the year after the state imposed a 60-cents-per-pack tax increase in 2002. Even so, since the tax increase was so large, cigarette tax revenues went up by more than 40 percent.

FIGURE 14.5 THE EFFECT OF CIGARETTE TAXES ON QUANTITY DEMANDED

When a tax is imposed on cigarettes, the supply curve shifts to the left by the amount of the tax. On this graph, a 75-cent tax shifts the supply curve from $3.40 per pack to $4.15 per pack. The increased price results in less demand.

ANALYZE GRAPHS

1. How does the quantity demanded of cigarettes change when the price rises from $3.40 to $4.15 per pack?
2. How does this graph illustrate the concept of tax incentives?

APPLICATION Analyzing Effects

D. What effect does the underground economy have on government revenue?

For more information on evaluating sources, see the Skillbuilder Handbook, page R28.

Using the Internet for Research

The Internet is a powerful tool for researching information. The Web site of the U.S. Treasury Department, for example, provides information on government revenue and spending.

RESEARCHING ON THE INTERNET Below is an example of FAQs, or "frequently asked questions." Use the following tips to help you navigate this and similar Internet Web sites that you might use for research.

Source: U.S. Department of the Treasury

THINKING ECONOMICALLY Using the Internet

1. Why do you think the student used the phrase "taxation without representation"? (If you are unfamiliar with the phrase, use a search engine to research its origin.)

2. How might you navigate this page of the U. S. Department of the Treasury Web site to locate a press release on new tax legislation?

3. Access this Web site and use the FAQs to discover how the Treasury Department answers the question: Why do I have to pay taxes?

Online Quiz
ClassZone.com

REVIEWING KEY CONCEPTS

1. Explain the difference between the terms in each of these pairs.

   a. *tax*
   revenue

   b. *sales tax*
   property tax

   c. *progressive tax*
   regressive tax

2. Why do governments collect taxes?

3. What are the four most used tax bases?

4. How does demand elasticity influence the incidence of a tax?

5. What is the purpose of a tax incentive?

6. **Using Your Notes** What are the major criteria for a good tax system? Refer to your completed cluster diagram.

   Use the Graphic Organizer at **Interactive Review @ ClassZone.com**

Taxes

CRITICAL THINKING

7. **Categorizing Economic Information** Colorado has a state income tax of 4.63 percent on all income and a sales tax of 2.9 percent. Are these taxes proportional, progressive, or regressive? Give reasons for your answers.

8. **Drawing Conclusions** In 2005, Hurricane Katrina destroyed many homes and businesses along the Gulf Coast of the United States. How did this natural disaster affect the tax bases in communities in that region?

9. **Analyzing Effects** Where does the burden of an increase in a sin tax usually fall? Illustrate your answer with supply and demand curves.

   Use **SMART Grapher @ ClassZone.com** to complete this activity.

10. **Applying Economic Concepts** Demand for insulin is highly inelastic. Would the government be likely to use a tax on insulin as a tax incentive? Why or why not?

11. **Challenge** Pennsylvania and Illinois each have state income taxes of about 3 percent of income. In Illinois, the first $2,000 of individual income is exempt from taxation. Pennsylvania has no similar individual tax exemptions. Is one state's tax more progressive than the other? Why or why not? (You'll learn more about tax exemptions in Section 2.)

ECONOMICS IN PRACTICE

Driver's license

Evaluating Taxes
Review what you have learned about the principles and criteria used to evaluate the effectiveness of a tax, and then complete the following activities.

Draw Conclusions Evaluate the effectiveness of each tax listed in the chart below by indicating with a checkmark whether it meets each principle and criterion.

Tax	Principles		Criteria		
	Benefits received	Ability to pay	Equity	Simplicity	Efficiency
Fee for driver's license					
Sales tax					
Flat rate income tax					
Progressive income tax					
Highway tolls					
Property tax					
Corporate income tax					

Challenge How would you evaluate a tax to support public education that was imposed only on families with children?

Federal Taxes

OBJECTIVES	KEY TERMS	TAKING NOTES
In Section 2, you will • describe the process of paying individual income taxes • explain taxes for Social Security, Medicare, and unemployment • identify other taxes that are collected by the federal government	withholding, *p. 421* taxable income, *p. 421* tax return, *p. 421* FICA, *p. 423* Social Security, *p. 423* Medicare, *p. 423* estate tax, *p. 425* gift tax, *p. 425* excise tax, *p. 425* customs duty, *p. 425* user fee, *p. 425*	As you read Section 2, complete a cluster diagram using the key concepts and other helpful words and phrases. Use the Graphic Organizer at **Interactive Review @ ClassZone.com**

Individual Income Tax

KEY CONCEPTS

The federal government takes in around $2.5 trillion in revenue each year. This money comes from several sources, including individual income tax, social insurance taxes, corporate income taxes, estate taxes, gift taxes, excise taxes, and customs taxes. The largest source of taxes for the federal government is the individual income tax. (You can see the contribution of the various taxes to total revenue in Figure 14.8 on page 425.) The government began using the income tax after the Sixteenth Amendment to the U.S. Constitution, which recognized this type of direct taxation on individuals, was ratified in 1913. Prior to that time, excise taxes and customs duties were the main sources of federal revenue. (Figure 14.8 shows that today only a very small portion of federal tax revenue comes from excise taxes and customs duties.) Social insurance taxes are the second largest source of federal tax revenue. Workers and employers share the burden of these taxes.

EXAMPLE Paying Your Taxes

If taxpayers had to pay their income taxes in one lump sum at the end of each year, some people would have difficulty coming up with all the money at once. Also, receiving revenue just once a year would create problems for the government. Drawing up a budget for the year would be very difficult, and developing sound economic plans for the future would be almost

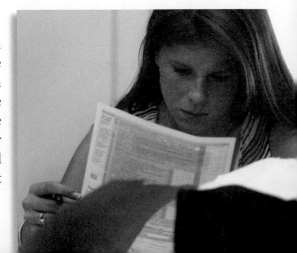

impossible. Therefore, to make it easier for taxpayers and the government, a payroll tax—a tax that is taken from a worker's paycheck—is collected. The payroll tax is deducted from a paycheck as **withholding**, or money taken from a worker's pay before the worker receives it.

To see how this works, let's look at the example of Scott, who works part-time during the school year and full-time during the summer at the Main Street Grocery Store. For every hour Scott works, he earns $6. Because of withholding for taxes, the amount he receives in his paycheck is less than the total amount he earns. In this way, he pays his taxes as he earns income, and the government receives a steady stream of revenue. The Main Street Grocery Store forwards the money withheld from Scott's paycheck to the Internal Revenue Service (IRS). The IRS is the government agency that collects the money for the federal government and administers the federal tax system.

The federal income tax is a progressive tax based on the ability-to-pay principle of taxation. This means that people with higher incomes not only pay more in total taxes but also pay a higher percentage of their income in taxes. The amount owed is based on **taxable income**, the portion of income subject to taxation. Under federal income tax laws, taxpayers may take certain exemptions and deductions from their total earned income to reduce the amount of their taxable income. Exemptions are allowed for each individual adult and child, so larger families reduce their taxable income by a greater amount than do smaller families. In addition, taxpayers may take a standard deduction or itemize deductions, such as interest paid on a home mortgage, state and local taxes, charitable contributions, and a certain portion of medical expenses. Figure 14.6 below provides information on some of the itemized deductions taken by taxpayers in 2004.

Each year, taxpayers must complete a **tax return**, a form used to report income and taxes owed to various levels of government. The federal tax return shows how much income has been earned, the exemptions being claimed, and how much tax has been paid through withholding. State and local tax returns show similar, but less detailed, information. Taxpayers who have too much tax withheld receive a refund for overpayment. Taxpayers who have not had enough withheld must then pay any additional taxes owed directly to the IRS or to state or local revenue departments.

FIGURE 14.6 SELECTED ITEMIZED DEDUCTIONS ON INDIVIDUAL INCOME TAX RETURNS

Deduction	Number of Returns	Amount Claimed (in $)
Interest Paid	37,961,584	346.0 billion
State and Local Sales and Income Taxes	44,685,865	217.2 billion
Charitable Contributions	40,594,576	156.2 billion
Medical and Dental Expenses	9,458,443	61.3 billion

Source: Internal Revenue Service, 2004 figures

About 132.4 million individual income tax returns were filed in 2004. Some 46.2 million—or 35 percent—of these returns claimed itemized deductions to taxable income. Total itemized deductions equaled close to $972 billion, or just over $21,000 for each return.

ANALYZE GRAPHS

1. Which was the largest deduction taken in terms of the dollar amount claimed?

2. What percentage of total deductions taken in 2004 did state and local sales and income taxes represent?

EXAMPLE Indexing

Because the federal income tax is a progressive tax, the tax rate increases as taxable income increases. The level of income that causes someone to pay a higher rate of tax is the dividing point between tax brackets. The tax bracket is identified by the tax rate for that income span. For example, the tax schedule at the bottom of this page shows that in 2006 a single taxpayer with $7,550 or less in taxable income is in the 10 percent tax bracket. Someone with taxable income between $7,550 and $30,650 is in the 15 percent tax bracket, someone with taxable income between $30,650 and $74,200 would be in the 25 percent bracket, and so on.

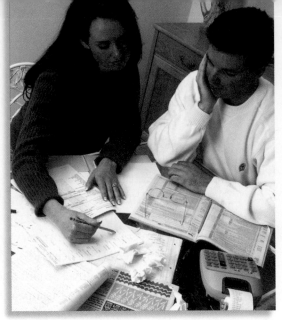

Tax Return Checking your taxable income against the various tax brackets is an important step in completing your tax return.

Look again at the tax schedule below. Suppose that Scott has $7,000 in taxable income. He is in the 10 percent bracket and pays 10 percent, or $700, in taxes. If, however, he had $8,000 in taxable income, he would be in the 15 percent tax bracket. He would pay 10 percent on the first $7,550 of his earnings and 15 percent on the remaining $450. His total taxes would be $822.50 ($755 + $67.50) or about 10.3 percent of his income.

Indexing is a revision of tax brackets to prevent workers from paying more taxes due to inflation. For example, suppose Scott's taxable income rises from $8,000 to $8,320—a 4 percent increase—due to inflation. Without indexing, $770 of his income is taxed at the 15 percent rate and he pays $870.50 in taxes, or about 10.5 percent of his income. With indexing, the beginning level of the 15 percent bracket is adjusted by 4 percent to $7, 852. So Scott continues to pay 10.3 percent of his income in taxes. Indexing, therefore, combats the effect of inflation and keeps the rate of taxation relatively constant.

Economics Update

Find an update on tax schedules at **ClassZone.com**

2006 Tax Rates: Schedule X—Single

If your taxable income is:		The tax is:
Over—	But not over—	
$0	$7,550	**10% of the amount over $0**
7,550	30,650	**$755 plus 15% of the amount over $7,550**
30,650	74,200	**$4,220 plus 25% of the amount over $30,650**
74,200	154,800	**$15,108 plus 28% of the amount over $74,200**
154,800	336,550	**$37,676 plus 33% of the amount over $154,800**
336,550	No limit	**$97,653 plus 35% of the amount over $336,550**

APPLICATION Analyzing Effects

A. How much of Scott's income of $8,320 would be taxed at 15 percent if the 10 percent tax bracket were indexed and increased to $7,780? What effect would this have on his overall tax rate?

FICA: Taxes to Ease Hardships

FICA is the Federal Insurance Contributions Act, a payroll tax that provides coverage for the elderly, the unemployed due to disability, and surviving family members of wage earners who have died. Also known as social insurance, FICA encompasses Social Security and Medicare. Both employees and employers make payments into FICA accounts.

Social Security Social Security is a federal program to aid older citizens who have retired, children who have lost a parent or both parents, and people with disabilities. The program began during the Great Depression of the 1930s as a way to help people who were in desperate need of economic assistance. The employer and employee each pay 6.2 percent of the employee's income up to an annual maximum. In 2006, Social Security tax was applied to $94,200 of earned income. The limit generally rises each year.

Medicare Introduced in 1966, **Medicare** is a national health insurance program for citizens over 65 and certain other groups of people. Employers and employees each pay 1.45 percent of employee income. There is no limit on the amount of income subject to the tax for Medicare.

Unemployment Taxes Unemployment compensation is a program funded by federal and state taxes and administered by the states. It provides benefits for a certain period of time to employees who lose their jobs through no fault of their own. Unemployment tax applies to the first $7,000 earned by an employee and, for the most part, is paid only by employers.

"SURELY YOU CAN EARN MORE THAN THIS! SOMEONE HAS to SUPPORT MEDICARE AND SOCIAL SECURITY."

Source: www.CartoonStock.com

FICA Accounts As the American population ages, fears are growing that there will not be enough workers to fund FICA.

APPLICATION Applying Economic Concepts

B. How would the employee portion of total FICA taxes for an individual earning $100,000 be split between Social Security and Medicare? Show your calculations.

Corporate Income and Other Taxes

KEY CONCEPTS

The federal government collects more than individual income and FICA taxes. It also uses corporate income, estate, gift, and excise taxes, as well as customs duties and user fees, to finance its operations.

Corporate Income Taxes

As you recall from earlier in this chapter, corporate income tax is tax on corporate profits. This tax is the third largest source of tax revenue for the federal government. Between 1941 and 1968, corporate income tax was the second largest source of revenue. Since that time, however, it has been surpassed by social insurance taxes. As Figure 14.7 shows, corporate income tax receipts have increased in total dollars since the mid-1900s, but have decreased relative both to total federal tax revenues and to the overall size of the economy.

Only certain types of corporations are subject to corporate income tax. These corporations are about 8 percent of all businesses that file tax returns. While the tax rate for most corporations is 35 percent of profits, most pay only about 26 percent of their profits in taxes. Like individuals, corporations can deduct certain expenses from their profits to reduce their taxable income. Some of the most important tax breaks for corporations include deductions for investment in buildings, equipment, and research, and rules that benefit multinational corporations.

A common criticism of the corporate income tax is that corporate profits are subject to double taxation. Profits are taxed at the corporate level and again at the individual level, since shareholders pay taxes on the income they receive in the form of dividends or capital gains. In recent years, the tax rate on capital gains has decreased in answer to this criticism.

FIGURE 14.7 CORPORATE INCOME TAX RECEIPTS, 1950–2009

	Receipts (in millions of $)	As Percentage of Total Federal Tax Revenue	As Percentage of GDP
1950–59	185,406	27.5	4.8
1960–69	262,891	21.3	3.8
1970–79	437,564	15.0	2.7
1980–89	675,358	9.3	1.7
1990–99	1,434,246	10.5	1.9
2000–09*	2,189,162	10.0	1.8

Source: The Budget of the United States, FY 2007

*Reflects government budget estimates for 2006–2009

ANALYZE GRAPHS
1. What overall trend is shown in the chart?
2. Which decade diverges from this overall trend? How does it differ from the overall trend?

Other Taxes

Several miscellaneous taxes provide a small part of total federal revenue, as you can see in Figure 14.8 below. The **estate tax** is a tax on property that is transferred to others on the death of the owner. Most estates are not subject to this tax, because the government only taxes large estates. In 2006, estates valued at less than $2 million were not subject to this tax. The **gift tax** is a tax on money or property given by one living person to another. As with the estate tax, there are exemptions to the gifts that are subject to the tax. For the most part, these exemptions allow family members to give money to other family members tax-free.

The **excise tax** is a tax on the production or sale of a specific product, such as gasoline or telephone service. The sin taxes discussed earlier in this chapter are other examples of excise taxes. In general, the government places excise taxes on goods or services for which there is relatively inelastic demand in order to maintain a steady stream of revenue. The **customs duty** is a tax on goods imported into the United States from another country. Customs duties are basically excise taxes on imports and are also known as tariffs. (You'll read more about tariffs in Chapter 17.)

The **user fee** is money charged for the use of a good or service. These fees are based on the benefits-received principle of taxation. For example, the federal government charges entrance, parking, and camping fees to visitors to national parks. So the people enjoying the parks the most pay for the benefits provided by the parks.

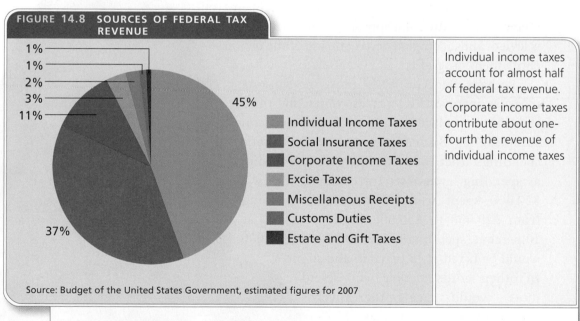

FIGURE 14.8 SOURCES OF FEDERAL TAX REVENUE

- 1%
- 1%
- 2%
- 3%
- 11%
- 45%
- 37%

- Individual Income Taxes
- Social Insurance Taxes
- Corporate Income Taxes
- Excise Taxes
- Miscellaneous Receipts
- Customs Duties
- Estate and Gift Taxes

Individual income taxes account for almost half of federal tax revenue. Corporate income taxes contribute about one-fourth the revenue of individual income taxes

Source: Budget of the United States Government, estimated figures for 2007

ANALYZE GRAPHS

1. What percentage of federal tax revenue comes from individual income taxes and social insurance taxes combined?

2. If total tax revenue for 2007 is estimated to be about $2.35 trillion, about how much revenue will come from individual income taxes?

APPLICATION Drawing Conclusions

C. There are plans to eliminate the estate tax. Who will benefit most from this?

Maya MacGuineas: Reforming the Tax System

Most tax reform measures involve tinkering with tax rates, exemptions, deductions, and the like. Maya MacGuineas believes it is time for far more dramatic change—a complete overhaul of the U.S. tax system. As one of the nation's leading tax policy analysts, she has built a career arguing for change.

A Tax Revolution?

Why does MacGuineas think that drastic action is needed? The present tax system, she says, is complicated, inefficient, and unfair, and it does not raise enough revenue to fund all of the government's programs. The new tax system, she argues, ought to be based on simplicity, efficiency, equity, and responsible budgeting.

To this end, MacGuineas suggests that the income tax should be simplified by ending most tax deductions and exemptions. This, she says, would also make the system more equitable, since taxpayers in higher marginal tax brackets gain the greatest benefit from these measures. In part for reasons of efficiency, MacGuineas believes that the corporate income tax should be phased out. She also supports new environmental taxes, a different approach to how the estate tax is levied, and a complete restructuring of the nation's entitlement programs.

Perhaps MacGuineas's most revolutionary measure involves FICA taxes, which she thinks should be replaced with a progressive consumption tax. Such a tax would be tied to total spending rather than income, with rates rising as spending levels rise. For example, the first $20,000 spent would be tax-free, spending from $20,000 to $50,000 would be taxed at 10 percent, spending from $50,000 to $175,000 would be taxed at 15 percent, and so on. In other words, people who spend more would face progressively higher marginal tax rates. MacGuineas argues that in addition to being simpler and fairer, a progressive consumption tax would provide a tremendous incentive to save.

Maya MacGuineas wants to make taxes more equitable and less complex.

APPLICATION Making Inferences

D. Should spending on education and housing be exempt from MacGuineas's consumption tax? Why or why not?

REVIEWING KEY CONCEPTS

1. Explain the relationship between the terms in each of these pairs.

   a. *taxable income*
      tax return

   b. *FICA*
      Social Security

   c. *estate tax*
      gift tax

2. Why is indexing important to taxpayers?

3. What is the role of the IRS in relationship to federal taxes?

4. How are excise taxes and customs duties similar? How are they different?

5. How are payroll taxes and user fees different?

6. **Using Your Notes** What two programs are financed by FICA? Refer to your completed cluster diagram. Use the Graphic Organizer at **Interactive Review @ ClassZone.com**

Federal Taxes

CRITICAL THINKING

7. **Analyzing and Interpreting Data** In 2005, the 10 percent tax bracket limit was $7,300. In 2006, it increased to $7,550. By what percentage did the tax bracket limit increase? How does this example illustrate the concept of indexing?

8. **Applying Economic Concepts** The Social Security tax rate for employees is 6.2 percent, and the Medicare tax rate is 1.45 percent. Are both parts of the FICA tax proportional? Give reasons for your answer.

9. **Drawing Conclusions** Study these two statements about tax payments for the 2005 tax year:

   • On average, an individual with $100,000 in taxable income paid about 29.5 percent in combined income and FICA taxes.

   • On average, an individual with $150,000 in taxable income also paid about 29.5 percent in combined taxes.

   Why were the combined tax rates the same for these two taxpayers?

10. **Challenge** Review the data in Figure 14.7. As a share of federal tax revenue and as a share of GDP, by what percentage have corporate income taxes declined between the 1950s and the first decade of the 21st century?

ECONOMICS IN PRACTICE

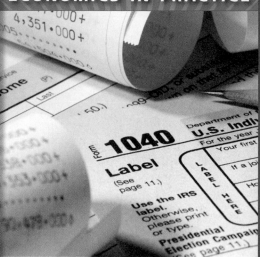

Analyzing Tax Schedules
The IRS provides tax schedules, or tables, to help taxpayers calculate their taxes.

Calculate Taxes Suppose that you work for a tax preparation company. Use the tax schedule on page 422 to answer the questions about the taxpayers described below.

a. Chris has $8,500 in taxable income. What is her tax bracket, how much tax does she pay, and what is her actual tax rate?

b. Miguel earned $35,000 in taxable income this year. How much more does he pay in taxes than if he had earned $30,000?

c. Meredith had $125,000 in taxable income and had $30,000 in taxes withheld. Will she receive a refund or owe money? How much?

Challenge Calculate the FICA taxes and tax rates for each of the above taxpayers.

427

Federal Government Spending

OBJECTIVES

In Section 3, you will
- compare the two types of government expenditures
- explain how the federal budget is developed
- describe how government payments are made
- identify the impact that federal spending has on the economy

KEY TERMS

mandatory spending, *p. 428*
discretionary spending, *p. 428*
entitlements, *p. 428*
Medicaid, *p. 429*
federal budget, *p. 431*
fiscal year, *p. 431*
appropriations, *p. 431*
transfer payments, *p. 432*
grant-in-aid, *p. 432*
private sector, *p. 432*

TAKING NOTES

As you read Section 3, complete a hierarchy diagram to track main ideas and details. Use the Graphic Organizer at **Interactive Review** @ ClassZone.com

Federal Spending

main idea — main idea

details — details

Federal Expenditures

KEY CONCEPTS

As you have seen, the federal government takes in a huge amount of money in taxes. The programs and services the federal government funds with this revenue are divided into two categories. These are **mandatory spending**, or spending that is required by current law, and **discretionary spending**, or spending that the government must authorize each year. For example, the law requires that the government spend money to fund the Social Security and Medicare programs. However, the federal government can decide to fund or not fund highway construction or maintenance of national parks. The federal government, then, has certain expenses that must be paid under current law, while other expenses are covered with what is left after those required expenses have been met.

TYPE 1 Mandatory Spending

Mandatory spending makes up well over half of all federal spending. Most of this spending is in the form of **entitlements**, which are social welfare programs with specific requirements. Social Security and Medicare are entitlement programs that provide payments to anyone who is eligible based on age or disability. Many

Medicare About 42 million Americans are enrolled in the Medicare program.

of these programs are not "means tested." In other words, anyone who meets the eligibility requirements receives the benefits, regardless of income level. For some other programs, however, income level is part of the requirement.

Social Security The Social Security program takes the largest amount of federal spending. It provides benefits to older retired workers, disabled workers with limited incomes, and survivors of workers who have died. Social Security is financed through a payroll tax. Therefore, workers must have worked for a certain period of time before they are eligible to receive full benefits under the program.

As the population of the United States has gotten older and more people have retired, costs for Social Security have increased. To help control costs, the government has gradually raised the age of full retirement—the point at which a worker is eligible to receive maximum benefits. Full retirement age ranges from 65 to 67, depending on the person's year of birth. Retirement benefits are not means tested. However, if retirees have additional income, benefits may be subject to withholding. For example, in 2006 retirees could earn $1,040 a month and still receive full Social Security benefits. However, retirees who earned more than this amount had their benefits reduced by $1 for every $3 over the income limit.

Economics Update

Find an update on Social Security at **ClassZone.com**

Medicare The Medicare program was introduced in 1966 as an additional old-age benefit under Social Security. Originally, Medicare provided hospital insurance, funded by a payroll tax, for people over 65, as well as optional medical coverage for items such as doctor bills. This part of Medicare is funded by premiums paid by those choosing the coverage and by general tax revenues.

Because of increasing numbers of retirees and increasing health care costs, Medicare costs have risen dramatically since the program began. Beginning in 2006, reforms to the program required Medicare to compete with private health insurance providers. Means testing was added for all but the lowest-income group of senior citizens. In addition, some coverage was added for prescription drugs.

QUICK REFERENCE

Medicaid is a government medical insurance program for low-income people.

Medicaid Established at the same time as Medicare, **Medicaid** is a joint federal-state medical insurance program for low-income people. The federal government funds about 63 percent of the costs of the program, and the states pay about 37 percent. In recent years, states have tightened their eligibility requirements for Medicaid in an effort to control costs.

Other Mandatory Spending Programs There are a variety of other mandatory spending programs that define eligibility requirements and are then funded based on an estimate of how many people meet those requirements. The Food Stamp program provides funds for about 26 million low-income people to purchase food. Veterans' benefits include health care coverage and disability payments for service-related illness or injury. People who have served in the military are also eligible for education assistance. The federal government spends about $50 billion a year on veterans' benefits.

Payments for the federal portion of unemployment insurance are also part of mandatory spending. In addition, the federal government pays its workers some retirement benefits. Federal employees hired after 1983 are also eligible for some Social Security retirement benefits.

Services for Veterans The Veterans Administration serves the needs and represents the interests of some 26 million veterans and their dependents.

TYPE 2 Discretionary Spending

More than one-third of federal revenue is devoted to discretionary spending. The programs covered by discretionary spending fall into several different categories. These categories include

• interstate highway system and transportation programs, such as Amtrak;

• natural resources and the environment, including conservation programs, pollution clean-up, and national parks;

• education, most notably college tuition assistance;

• science, space, technology, and other research programs;

• justice administration, including enforcement agencies, such as the Federal Bureau of Investigation (FBI), and the federal court system.

The largest discretionary expenditure category, however, is national defense, which takes up about 50 percent of the total discretionary budget. National defense includes a large amount of the nation's military spending, including the salaries of military personnel, weapons, and the construction and maintenance of military bases. Not all national defense spending is discretionary. Some spending on homeland security—border protection and the enforcement of some immigration laws, for example—falls in the mandatory expenditures category. In addition, certain military spending, such as additional funding requests for the wars in Iraq and Afghanistan, is outside the basic federal budget.

YOUR ECONOMIC CHOICES

DISCRETIONARY SPENDING

How will you assign discretionary spending funds?

Two programs are competing for $100 million in discretionary funds—an initiative to improve math and science education in high schools and a research project to test new developments in toy safety. How will you advise officials to assign the funds and why?

Math class

Safer toys

APPLICATION Categorizing Economic Information

A. Categorize the following items as either mandatory spending or discretionary spending: AIDS prevention programs, air traffic regulation, medical coverage for low-income people, pollution control, retirement benefits for older workers.

The Federal Budget and Spending

Each year the President and Congress work together to establish the **federal budget**, a plan for spending federal tax money. The budget is prepared for a **fiscal year**, a 12-month period for which an organization plans its expenditures. The federal government's fiscal year runs from October 1 through September 30. The President's budget is prepared by the Office of Management and Budget (OMB) and takes into account estimated tax receipts and requests by all federal departments and agencies. Figure 14.9 shows the OMB budget estimate for fiscal year 2007.

Congress Acts on the Budget

The Congressional Budget Office helps the House and Senate develop guidelines for different **appropriations**, which are set amounts of money set aside for specific purposes. Members of Congress often make deals to gain votes for appropriations that they support. Congress votes on the final budget and sends it to the president for approval. If the budget is not approved by the beginning of the new fiscal year, Congress passes resolutions to keep the government running on a day-to-day basis.

Methods of Federal Spending

After budget approval, the funds are spent in several ways. One way is direct spending, by which the government buys goods and services that it needs to operate, such as military equipment and office supplies. Paying the salaries of government

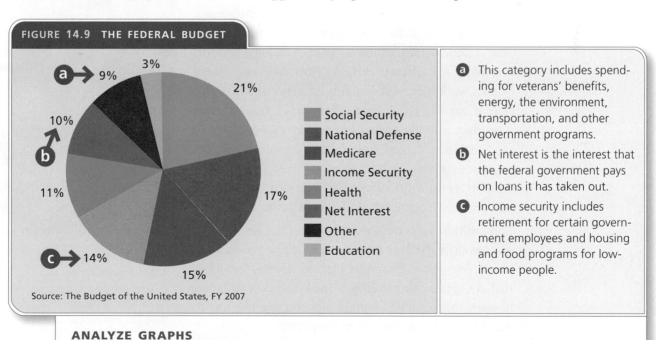

FIGURE 14.9 THE FEDERAL BUDGET

- Social Security
- National Defense
- Medicare
- Income Security
- Health
- Net Interest
- Other
- Education

3%
9% **a**
21%
10% **b**
11%
17%
14% **c**
15%

Source: The Budget of the United States, FY 2007

a This category includes spending for veterans' benefits, energy, the environment, transportation, and other government programs.

b Net interest is the interest that the federal government pays on loans it has taken out.

c Income security includes retirement for certain government employees and housing and food programs for low-income people.

ANALYZE GRAPHS
1. What is the largest category of spending in the federal budget?
2. Approximately how much of the federal budget goes to health and education?

QUICK REFERENCE

Transfer payments are money distributed to individuals who do not provide anything in return.

A **grant-in-aid** is a transfer payment from the federal government to state or local governments.

The **private sector** is the part of the economy owned by individuals or businesses.

employees is another type of direct spending. A second way the government spends the money is through **transfer payments**—money distributed to individuals who do not provide goods or services in return. A **grant-in-aid** is a transfer payment from the federal government to state or local governments.

Transfer Payments These payments are generally part of the mandatory spending you learned about earlier. For example, Social Security retirement or disability benefits and health care benefits from Medicare or veterans' programs are transfer payments from the government to individuals. The individuals do not provide specific goods or services in exchange for these government funds.

Grants-in–aid These grants are transfer payments between levels of government. The federal government makes grants to states, local governments, and regions. The grants are designated for specific categories of activities such as highway construction, certain school services, or Medicaid funding.

The Impact of Federal Spending

Because the federal government spends trillions of dollars, it is a big factor in the economy. The federal government influences the economy in three ways: resource allocation, income redistribution, and competition with the **private sector**, which is that part of the economy owned by individuals or businesses.

Resource Allocation The federal government makes choices concerning where to spend money and on what to spend it, and that influences how resources are allocated. For example, if money goes to urban transit, it cannot go to fix rural roads. Similarly, money spent on weapons systems for the military cannot be spent on some other program, such as environmental protection.

Income Redistribution Government spending affects the incomes of families, individuals, and businesses. Transfer payments for health care, retirement, and Food Stamp benefits, for example, provide income support for many low-income earners. How the government awards work contracts can also influence the distribution of income. For example, if the government awards a contract to build several submarines to a shipyard in the Northeast, workers there will be assured work and an income. However, workers at a California shipyard that failed to get the contract may lose their jobs. In turn, they will not have income to spend at local businesses.

Government Contracts
A government contract, such as one to build submarines, has a huge impact on local, state, and regional economies.

Competition with the Private Sector The government may produce goods or services that are also produced in the private sector. Examples include veterans' hospitals that compete with privately owned hospitals, or federal housing that competes with homes and apartments provided by private developers and landlords.

APPLICATION Drawing Conclusions

B. How are transfer payments related to income redistribution?

REVIEWING KEY CONCEPTS

1. Explain the relationship between the terms in each of these pairs.

a. *mandatory spending*   **b.** *federal budget*   **c.** *transfer payment*
    entitlement   *fiscal year*   *grant-in-aid*

2. What is the difference between mandatory spending and discretionary spending?

3. Why is Medicaid an example of an entitlement program?

4. What does Congress do when it decides on appropriations?

5. How does the government compete with the private sector?

6. Using Your Notes How is the federal budget established? Refer to your completed hierarchy diagram. Use the Graphic Organizer at **Interactive Review @ ClassZone.com**

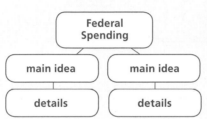

CRITICAL THINKING

7. Making Inferences From 2005 to 2009, spending on Social Security rose from 21.2 percent of the federal budget to 22.4 percent. Over the same period, spending on education declined from 2.8 percent to 2.0 percent of the budget. How does this show the difference between mandatory and discretionary spending?

8. Categorizing Economic Information Categorize each of these examples of federal spending as direct spending, transfer payment, or grant-in-aid:

- computers for IRS
- disability benefits
- flood control in Gulf Coast region
- highway funds for states
- medical care for elderly
- money for urban housing
- price supports for farmers
- repair of space shuttle
- salaries for national park rangers

9. Challenge Molly's grandmother was born in 1953. If she retires in 2015, she'll receive $750 per month in Social Security benefits. If she waits until 2019, she will receive $1,000, and if she waits until 2020, her monthly benefit increases to $1,080. Why do you think Congress structured the Social Security benefit payments program in this way?

ECONOMICS IN PRACTICE

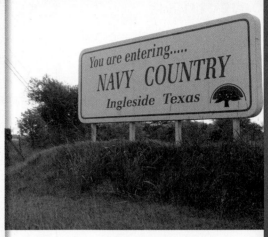

This town's economy depended on a naval base.

Studying Economic Impact Consider what you have learned about the impact of federal spending on the economy. The chart below shows information on the impact of a hypothetical military base on an area's economy.

Direct military base employment	27,400 jobs, $1 billion payroll
Additional related jobs	19,500 jobs, $800 million payroll
Payments to private health care providers	$19 million
Contracts for goods and services	$115 million
State and local taxes	$102.8 million

Analyze Data Study the chart to answer these questions:

- What is the total number of jobs attributable to the military base?
- How much does the base spend on health care?

Challenge Write a summary of the economic impact of the military base.

<table>
<tr><td>SECTION</td><td rowspan="2"># State and Local Taxes and Spending</td></tr>
<tr><td>4</td></tr>
</table>

OBJECTIVES	KEY TERMS	TAKING NOTES
In Section 4, you will • identify the major sources of revenue for both state and local governments • examine the concept of a balanced budget • describe the major categories of state and local expenditures	balanced budget, *p. 436* operating budget, *p. 436* capital budget, *p. 436* tax assessor, *p. 437*	As you read Section 4, complete a chart using the key concepts and other helpful words and phrases. Use the Graphic Organizer at **Interactive Review @ ClassZone.com**

State Government		Local Government	
Revenue	Spending	Revenue	Spending

State Revenues

KEY CONCEPTS

As you recall from earlier in this chapter, all levels of government may impose taxes to raise revenue to support their activities. The federal government has the broadest tax base, while the smallest tax base is at the local level. There are thousands of local governmental units, from towns, cities, and counties to districts set up to handle a specific problem such as mosquito control or sewage treatment.

State revenues come from a variety of sources, the largest of which is intergovernmental revenue, mostly grants-in-aid from the federal government. States also raise funds from state sales taxes and from state income tax, both on individuals and on corporations. (See Figure 14.11 on page 437.)

TYPE 1 Sales and Excise Taxes

> **Economics Update**
>
> Find an update on state sales taxes at **ClassZone.com**

All states except Alaska, Delaware, New Hampshire, Montana, and Oregon levy a state sales tax. Rates range from 2.9 percent in Colorado to 7.25 percent in California. These taxes generally are applied to most goods and services sold within the state. However, many states exempt food and prescription drugs from sales tax. Some other states tax these goods, over-the-counter drugs, and certain other medical supplies at a lower rate. In addition, charitable, religious, and educational organizations are often exempt from paying sales taxes.

All states also have excise taxes on cigarettes, alcohol, gasoline, and diesel fuel. Certain government organizations, volunteer fire-fighting companies, and farmers may be exempt from fuel taxes. Many states also have special sales taxes that mostly affect tourists, such as taxes on car rentals and hotel and motel room rates.

TYPE 2 Income Tax and Other Revenue Sources

Most states levy taxes on both individual and corporate income. However, Alaska, Florida, South Dakota, Texas, and Washington have no individual income tax. Nevada and Wyoming levy neither individual nor corporate income taxes. Most states have progressive tax rates on individual income. Individual income tax rates range from under one percent to over nine percent. Figure 14.10 below shows the states with the highest corporate and individual income tax rates.

FIGURE 14.10 COMPARING STATE TAXES

Highest Corporate Income Taxes			Highest Individual Income Taxes		
State	Highest Rate (percent)	On Income Above (in dollars)	State	Highest Rate (percent)	On Income Above (in dollars)
Iowa	12.00	249,999	Vermont	9.50	357,699
Pennsylvania	9.99	0	California	9.30	44,814
Minnesota	9.80	0	Oregon	9.00	7,299
Massachusetts	9.50	0	Iowa	8.98	62,054
Alaska	9.40	89,999	New Jersey	8.97	499,999

Source: Federation of Tax Administrators, 2008 data

ANALYZE TABLES

1. What is the only state that appears in both tables?
2. Why might states with high corporate taxes have lower individual taxes?

Most states charge a flat tax rate on corporate income. Corporate income tax rates range from one percent to twelve percent. Many state governments structure their corporate tax rates to attract businesses to the state. These governments give up billions of dollars in tax revenues by providing tax cuts and other incentives to promote economic development. However, the states hope to receive benefits from these tax practices in the increased economic activity that development brings.

States also raise revenue from several other sources. Many of these sources, including estate taxes and user fees, are the same as those used by the federal government. (See Figure 14.8 on page 425.) Most states also levy property taxes. In addition, most states charge several fees related to business operations. These include registration fees for certain types of businesses and license fees for doctors, dentists, lawyers, and accountants.

APPLICATION Comparing Economic Information

A. How do state income tax rates compare to federal income tax rates?

State Budgets and Spending

KEY CONCEPTS

QUICK REFERENCE

A **balanced budget** requires that total government revenue is equal to total government spending.

An **operating budget** is a plan for day-to-day expenses.

A **capital budget** is a plan for major expenses or investments.

All states except Vermont are required to have a **balanced budget**, in which total government revenue from all sources is equal to total government spending. However, balanced-budget requirements usually apply only to certain kinds of spending. Further, nearly every state has a reserve fund or may run a surplus, both of which can be used to balance the budget in subsequent years.

State Budgets

States actually work with two types of budgets—an **operating budget,** a plan for day-to-day expenses, and a **capital budget**, a plan for major expenses or investments. The operating budget generally covers expenses that occur each year, such as salaries for state government employees, payments for health and welfare benefits, and funds for education systems. Capital budgets provide funds for large construction and maintenance projects on state buildings, roads, and bridges, as well as for land acquisition for state construction needs or state parks. Usually, operating budgets are subject to balanced-budget requirements. Capital budgets are not, because they are usually funded through borrowing. In fact, capital budgets often are run at a deficit, meaning that more is spent than is collected in revenues.

Deficit Spending Both federal and state governments practice deficit spending—spending more than they collect in revenues—to cover their expenses.

State Expenses

Education is a major expense for the states, which not only support community colleges and state university systems but also provide assistance to local school districts. For example, state assistance accounted for about 49 percent of public school funding in 2002. Public safety, too, is a significant state expense. Spending on public safety includes state police, crime labs, and prisons and other correctional facilities. States also support a court system.

Public welfare expenses involve funds for state-run hospitals as well as cash assistance and medical care payments to the needy. States also fund programs that help citizens with problems related to housing, disability, unemployment, and job training. Other expenses include state government administration, retirement funds for state employees, natural resources, and economic development.

APPLICATION Categorizing

> **B.** Would a grant to a city to build a new sewage treatment plant be part of the city's operating budget or capital budget?

Local Revenue and Spending

Local government units include counties, cities, towns, villages, townships, school districts, and other special districts. They have fewer options for raising revenue than do other levels of government. Their major revenue sources are intergovernmental revenue—or transfers—from state and federal governments and property taxes. Local governments also tap other sources, many of which are similar to the state tax base. Figure 14.11 shows revenue sources for state and local governments.

Property Tax

Recall that you read about property tax in the first section of the chapter. This tax can be levied on real estate and on personal property such as motor vehicles, boats, expensive jewelry, or computers. Local governments rely on a **tax assessor**, a government official who determines the value of the property. They then enact a tax based on a percentage of the property's value.

Other Taxes

Local governments also use sales taxes, sin taxes on activities such as gambling, hospitality taxes on hotels and restaurants, entertainment taxes on tickets or entrance fees, and payroll taxes. The local payroll tax is a tax on people who work in a city but live outside the city. Such a tax is often used in large metropolitan areas where workers from the suburbs benefit from city services such as police and fire protection.

> **QUICK REFERENCE**
>
> A **tax assessor** determines the value of property.

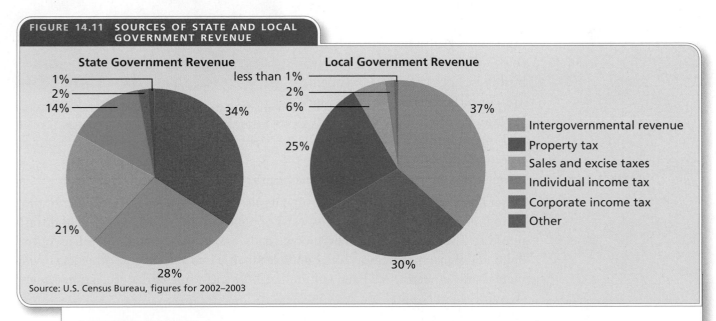

FIGURE 14.11 SOURCES OF STATE AND LOCAL GOVERNMENT REVENUE

State Government Revenue
1%
2%
14%
34%
21%
28%

Local Government Revenue
less than 1%
2%
6%
37%
25%
30%

- Intergovernmental revenue
- Property tax
- Sales and excise taxes
- Individual income tax
- Corporate income tax
- Other

Source: U.S. Census Bureau, figures for 2002–2003

ANALYZE GRAPHS
1. What are the two largest sources of revenue for both state and local governments?
2. Which type of government gets a larger percentage of its revenue from sales and excise taxes?

Local Spending

Local governments provide most of the direct services that citizens receive. To deliver these services, local governments employ almost three times the number of workers as state governments do. Some of the most important areas of local spending are described below.

Public Schools Local governments have the main responsibility for elementary and secondary schools. About 46 percent of local government spending goes to education. Government funds pay for construction and maintenance of school buildings, salaries for teachers, administrators, and other personnel, as well as for items such as textbooks and computers. Reliance on the property tax has led to difficulties for many local governments, since communities with lower property values have smaller tax bases to finance education.

Public Safety Local governments provide police and fire protection to secure lives and property in their communities. They are also responsible for emergency medical equipment and personnel to provide on-site treatment and transportation to medical facilities. Local governments maintain the 911 emergency telephone number system. Other expenditures in this category include animal control, consumer protection, and preparation for and response to natural disasters.

Public Welfare Local governments spend less than state governments on direct payments for medical care and assistance to the needy. However, many local governments maintain public health departments, and some own and operate their own hospitals. Local health departments are concerned with immunization programs, environmental health, and maintaining birth and death records. They also are responsible for making sure that restaurants meet health standards.

Public Safety Ensuring the safety of life and property in the community—by providing fire protection, for example—is the responsibility of local government.

Other Responsibilities Local governments also have primary responsibility for providing most public utilities such as water, public transit, sewage systems, and trash removal. They maintain local highways, roads, and streets, including traffic control lights and signs, snow removal, and pothole repair. Finally, local governments provide many kinds of recreational and cultural facilities including parks, recreation centers, swimming pools, and libraries.

APPLICATION Drawing Conclusions

B. Why do local governments rely more on property taxes as a source of revenue than do state governments?

SECTION 4 Assessment

REVIEWING KEY CONCEPTS

1. Use each of the three terms below in a sentence that illustrates the meaning of the term.

    a. *balanced budget*   **b.** *capital budget*   **c.** *tax assessor*

2. What is the difference between an operating budget and a capital budget?

3. How is an operating budget related to a balanced budget?

4. What is the largest revenue source for state governments? What is the largest source for local governments?

5. Why do local governments need tax assessors?

6. **Using Your Notes** What kinds of education do state and local governments spend money on? Refer to your completed chart. Use the Graphic Organizer at **Interactive Review @ ClassZone.com**

State Government		Local Government	
Revenue	Spending	Revenue	Spending

CRITICAL THINKING

7. **Comparing and Contrasting** What are the similarities and differences in the sources of revenue for state and local governments?

8. **Analyzing Effects** Which level of government would be most affected if the federal government decided to limit the amount of money that it spent on the Medicaid program? Give reasons for your answer.

9. **Making Inferences** Voters in your city must decide whether to raise revenue by increasing the rate of property tax for owners of homes and businesses or by placing a new tax on motel and hotel room rates and car rentals. Which tax are voters more likely to choose? Give reasons for your answer.

10. **Challenge** Between 1992 and 2002, average state funding for public schools increased from 46 percent of all state expenditures to 49 percent of all state expenditures. At the same time, local government funding of public schools decreased from 47 percent to 43 percent. Why do you think the source of school funding has changed in this way?

ECONOMICS IN PRACTICE

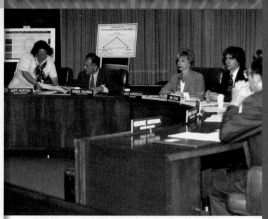

School board meeting

Using a Decision Making Process
Suppose that you are on a local school board. Total budget for the school district is $25,000,000. The chart below lists the items to be funded out of this budget.

Spending Category	Priority
Administrative salaries	
Classroom computers	
School lunch program	
Special education programs	
Teacher salaries	
Textbooks and other instructional materials	
Utilities	

Decide on Funding Priorities Use a decision-making process to decide how to allocate the budget. Complete the chart by ranking the items from 1 to 7, from most important to least important.

Challenge Based on your priorities, allocate a percentage of the budget to each category.

Should Online Sales Be Taxed?

Background In 1992 the Supreme Court upheld a law making Internet retailers exempt from collecting most sales taxes. The ruling was based on the fact that, at the time, the various state and local rules for tax collection varied widely. The differing rules would have placed a heavy burden on Internet retailers charged with having to collect taxes on what they sold.

Today, however, tax collection is becoming simpler and more streamlined. In addition, Internet purchases have become commonplace, with shoppers buying everything from computers to airplane tickets. Many online shoppers fail to realize that they are required to pay sales tax for Internet purchases at their home state's rate. To date, most states have tried to collect Internet sales tax on a voluntary basis. Needless to say, results have been poor. Given this and other considerations, Internet sales tax once again is a subject for debate.

What's the issue? Should there be sales tax on Internet purchases? Study these sources to discover arguments for and against taxing purchases online.

A. Online News Story

This news story on whether to impose the "iPod tax"—a tax on digital products—illustrates the differences of opinion on online sales tax.

Entertainment Lovers May Soon Pay Tax on Downloads

Wisconsin governor and legislators disagree over "iPod" tax.

Wisconsin Gov. Jim Doyle now wants his state to start collecting taxes on digital music, videos and software. Key Republicans in the GOP-dominated legislature say they will block the proposal, but administration officials say they're just trying to make things fair.

"It's an issue of tax equity," said Jessica Iverson, a spokeswoman for the Wisconsin Department of Revenue. "If you go into a Main Street business and purchase a CD, you are paying tax. . . ."

Economists are split . . . as to whether adding these kinds of taxes is a good idea. Some say that taxes on digital goods will hamper the growth of a potentially vibrant new marketplace, while others say that having taxes only on offline versions of the same goods distorts the operation of free markets.

Source: **News.com, March 10, 2005**

Thinking Economically What do you think economists mean when they say that taxing only offline versions of the same goods "distorts the operation of free markets"?

FIGURE 14.12 U.S. ONLINE PURCHASES

B. Graph

This graph shows the growth of online purchases during the 2000s.

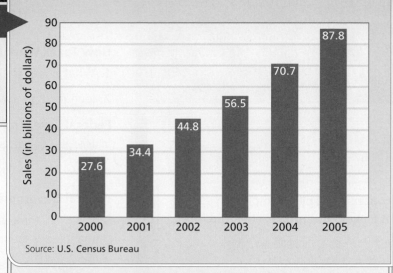

Thinking Economically How might state and local governments use the information in the graph to support their demand to levy sales taxes on online purchases?

C. Newspaper Editorial

Some states are becoming pro-active in their efforts to promote Internet sales tax. This newspaper editorial describes one multistate project to facilitate the collection of the tax.

Internet Sales Tax

Eighteen states agree to establish uniform sales tax rules.

Last week, 18 state tax collectors met in Chicago to announce an interstate agreement establishing uniform sales tax rules. Starting in October, the group will offer free software that will allow any business to easily collect the required taxes online.

   The states' demonstration project will drive home the point that online sales-tax collection can be done nationwide. Many retailers already collect the taxes. Now Congress should step up and pass a law overturning the court's exemption in states that have streamlined their tax systems. That would allow hard-pressed states to take in roughly $20 billion a year in annual sales tax revenue that is rightfully theirs, and perhaps much more, depending on the growth in online shopping. It would also help level the playing field between local and online retailers.

Source: "Internet Sales Tax," *New York Times*, July 5, 2005

Thinking Economically What impact has Internet shopping had on state and local revenues? Explain your answer.

THINKING ECONOMICALLY **Synthesizing**

1. Summarize the arguments for and against an Internet sales tax as presented in the documents.
2. Who is most likely to benefit from Internet sales tax revenue? Explain your answer, using information from the documents.
3. How has government responded to e-commerce—the selling of goods and services online? Use information from the documents in your answer.

Review this chapter using interactive activities at **ClassZone.com**
- Online Summary
- Quizzes
- Vocabulary Flip Cards
- Graphic Organizers
- Review and Study Notes

 Online Summary

Complete the following activity either on your own paper or online at **ClassZone.com**

Choose the key concept that best completes the sentence. Not all key concepts will be used.

ability-to-pay principle of taxation
balanced budget
benefit principle of taxation
capital budget
discretionary spending
entitlement
incidence of tax
indexing
mandatory spending
progressive tax

proportional tax
regressive tax
revenue
tax
tax base
tax incentive
tax return
taxable income
transfer payment
withholding

__1__ is a mandatory payment to a government. __2__ is government income. The __3__ holds that people should be taxed on their ability to pay, no matter the level of benefits they receive.

A __4__ is the income, property, goods or services subject to taxes. A __5__ takes the same percentage of income from all taxpayers. A __6__ places a higher rate of taxation on high-income people, and a __7__ takes a larger percentage of income from low-income people. The __8__ is the final burden of tax.

__9__ is money taken from a worker's pay before the worker receives it. __10__ is a revision of tax brackets to prevent workers from paying more taxes due to inflation. Social Security is an example of an __11__, a social welfare program with specific requirements. Such programs make up most of federal __12__, which is spending that is required by law.

States are required to have a __13__, in which government revenue and spending are equal.

CHAPTER 14 Assessment

REVIEWING KEY CONCEPTS

How Taxes Work (pp. 410–419)

1. What is the relationship between tax and revenue?

2. Identify three ways that taxes affect the economy.

Federal Taxes (pp. 420–427)

3. What is the largest source of federal revenue?

4. Which tax pays for Social Security and Medicare?

Federal Government Spending (pp. 428–433)

5. What are three programs that make up most mandatory spending?

6. How does federal spending affect the economy?

State and Local Taxes and Spending (pp. 434–441)

7. What are the two types of state budgets?

8. What tax base are tax assessors concerned with?

APPLYING ECONOMIC CONCEPTS

Look at the chart below showing average combined city and state tax rates for families with different incomes in several cities.

FIGURE 14.13 STATE AND LOCAL TAXES FOR A FAMILY OF FOUR

City	Total taxes paid as a percent of income				
	$25,000	$50,000	$75,000	$100,000	$150,000
Atlanta	8.1	10.3	11.4	11.5	11.7
Chicago	9.3	9.5	10.0	9.7	9.3
Houston	6.2	6.0	6.3	5.9	5.5
Jacksonville	4.3	4.6	5.0	4.8	4.6
Los Angeles	8.6	8.7	10.3	11.2	12.3
New York	5.6	10.8	12.7	13.4	14.1
Philadelphia	11.0	13.2	13.0	12.6	12.2

Source: *Statistical Abstract of the United States, 2002 figures*

9. Which city has the lowest tax rate for the lowest-income families? Which has the lowest tax rate for the highest-income families?

10. Which combined city and state tax structures are progressive and which are regressive?

11. Creating Graphs The state legislature proposes new 10 percent excise taxes on the following goods and services: gasoline, ice cream, local telephone service, and sports cars. For each good or service create supply and demand curves showing the supply curve before the tax and how the supply curve shifts after the tax. Under each graph, write a caption explaining who will pay more of the tax—the consumer or the producer—and why.

Use 🖉*SMARTGrapher* @ ClassZone.com to complete this activity.

12. Analyzing Data Shandra earns $30,000 per year from her job as a radiology technician. She takes a personal exemption of $3,200 and the standard deduction of $5,000 to reduce her taxable income.

a. If she pays 10 percent tax on the first $7,300 of taxable income and 15 percent on the rest, how much does she pay in income tax?

b. Shandra's FICA tax rate is 7.65 percent. What are her FICA taxes?

c. How much total tax does Shandra pay? What is her effective tax rate as a percentage of her taxable income and of her total income?

13. Making Inferences When Rajiv goes shopping for a new MP3 player, he notices that he pays 7.35 percent sales tax on the purchase. He knows that the state sales tax rate is 4.22 percent. What accounts for the difference?

14. Comparing and Contrasting All states have excise taxes on cigarettes and gasoline. What are the similarities and differences in the reasons why states tax these two items?

15. Challenge In 2003, Congress reduced the tax rate paid by individual investors on dividends and capital gains to 15 percent. Previously the rate for dividends had been as high as 38.6 percent, and capital gains had been taxed at 20 percent. Which of these changes addressed the charge that corporate income is subject to double taxation? Give reasons for your answer.

Develop a Federal Budget

Step 1 Choose a partner. Imagine that you are members of Congress who must determine the discretionary spending portion of the federal budget. The table below shows the categories of spending. You have a total of $960 billion to spend. Determine your spending priorities by deciding what percent of the budget to allocate to each category.

FEDERAL DISCRETIONARY SPENDING CATEGORIES

Administration of justice	Health (non-Medicaid)
Agriculture	International affairs
Community & regional development	National defense
Education	Natural resources & environment
Energy	Science, space & technology
General government	Transportation

Step 2 Form a group with two or three other pairs of students so that there are now a total of four groups in the class. Compare your budgets, noting areas of agreement and disagreement. Negotiate to develop a single budget proposal for your group.

Step 3 Present your group's budget proposal to the class. Include a list of reasons to support your budget choices.

Step 4 As a class, decide on a final recommendation that resolves any differences among the four budget proposals.

Step 5 Present your final budget to your teacher, who is acting as the President. Make necessary changes to the budget to resolve any differences between the Congress and the President.

Government
Federal government actions in the areas of taxing and spending are designed to enhance the nation's economic stability.

444

Using Fiscal Policy

CONCEPT REVIEW

The **business cycle** is the series of growing and shrinking periods of economic activity.

CHAPTER 15 KEY CONCEPT

Fiscal policy uses taxes and government spending in an effort to smooth out the peaks and troughs of the business cycle.

WHY THE CONCEPT MATTERS

In history classes, you've probably read about instances of rampant inflation when people needed bags and bags of cash to pay for their groceries. Or you might have read about periods of economic depression when millions of workers lost their jobs. By using a combination of spending and taxation, the federal government tries to reduce the impact of such economic extremes.

Online Highlights

More at ClassZone.com

Economics Update

Go to **ECONOMICS UPDATE** for chapter updates and current news on the federal deficit. (See Case Study, pp. 468–469.) ▶

Animated Economics

Go to **ANIMATED ECONOMICS** for interactive lessons on the graphs and tables in this chapter.

Interactive ◀◀ Review

Go to **INTERACTIVE REVIEW** for concept review and activities.

BUREAU OF SPENDING INCREASES AND DEFICIT REDUCTION

SCHWADRON

"WAIT A MINUTE! HOW CAN THAT BE?"

Source: www.CartoonStock.com

How big a problem is the federal deficit? See the Case Study on pages 468–469.

What Is Fiscal Policy?

OBJECTIVES	KEY TERMS	TAKING NOTES
In Section 1, you will • examine the tools used in fiscal policy • determine how fiscal policy affects the economy • identify the problems and limitations of fiscal policy	fiscal, *p. 446* fiscal policy, *p. 446* expansionary fiscal policy, *p. 446* contractionary fiscal policy, *p. 446* discretionary fiscal policy, *p. 446* automatic stabilizers, *p. 447* rational expectations theory, *p. 452* Council of Economic Advisers, *p. 452*	As you read Section 1, complete a cluster diagram that organizes the main ideas about fiscal policy. Use the Graphic Organizer at **Interactive Review @ ClassZone.com**

Fiscal Policy Tools

KEY CONCEPTS

In Chapter 14, you learned that the government puts the tax dollars it collects to a variety of uses. The term **fiscal** refers to anything related to government revenue, spending, and debt. **Fiscal policy** is the federal government's use of taxes and government spending to affect the economy. Fiscal policy has one of two goals: to increase aggregate demand or to fight inflation.

To stabilize or strengthen the economy, the government may use one of two basic policies. When the economy slows, the government may use **expansionary fiscal policy**, a plan to increase aggregate demand and stimulate a weak economy. When the economy is in an inflationary period, the government may use a **contractionary fiscal policy**, a plan to reduce aggregate demand and slow the economy in a period of too-rapid expansion. The federal government has two basic fiscal tools to influence the economy: taxation and government spending.

Discretionary Fiscal Policy

As you learned in Chapter 14, discretionary spending is spending that the government must authorize each year. In other words, the government must make a choice about this type of spending. Similarly, **discretionary fiscal policy** involves actions taken by the government by choice to correct economic instability. This type of policy involves an active government response, through choices about taxes or government spending, to help stabilize the economy. Congress must enact legislation for these policies to be implemented. This type of fiscal policy is discussed in more depth later in this section and in Section 2.

Automatic Stabilizers

Unlike discretionary fiscal policy, **automatic stabilizers** are features of fiscal policy that work automatically to steady the economy. Both of these approaches use taxes and government spending to influence the economy. Discretionary fiscal policy involves government choices about whether an expansionary or contractionary policy is needed and how the chosen policy should be put into action. Automatic stabilizers, such as public transfer payments and progressive income taxes, may work in an expansionary or contractionary manner, but they work automatically rather than through active policy choices.

QUICK REFERENCE

Policy features called **automatic stabilizers** work automatically to steady the economy.

Public Transfer Payments As you recall from Chapter 14, public transfer payments include programs such as unemployment compensation, food stamps, and other entitlements. These payments automatically set up a flow of money into the economy. Therefore, this form of government spending helps stabilize the economy automatically.

For example, during a recession more people are unemployed and qualify to receive unemployment compensation and other government benefits, such as food stamps or welfare payments. When people receive these benefits, they gain a certain amount of income to spend, and the effects of the recession are less severe than they would be without the transfer payments.

Automatic Stabilizers
Unemployed workers wait to register for unemployment compensation, a program designed to stabilize the economy by providing temporary replacement wages.

When the economy improves, fewer people qualify for food stamps, unemployment compensation, and other entitlements, and government spending automatically decreases. This automatic decrease keeps the economy from growing too fast. By helping to control aggregate demand, this automatic stabilizer keeps prices from rising too quickly and leading to inflation.

Progressive Income Taxes The individual income tax is progressive. As income increases, so do the tax rate and the amount of taxes paid. The progressive nature of the income tax allows it to act as an automatic stabilizer to the economy without additional government action.

For example, during prosperous times, individual incomes rise, and some individuals move into higher tax brackets. These taxpayers pay more in taxes and do not have all of their increased income to spend or save. By preventing some of the increased income from entering the economy, this automatically higher taxation keeps the economy from growing too quickly and helps keep inflation in check. On the other hand, during a recession, individuals earn less income and may move into lower tax brackets. Therefore, lower incomes result in lower taxes, which automatically reduce the impact of the recession.

🚀 *Economics Update*

Find an update on automatic stabilizers at **ClassZone.com**

APPLICATION Applying Economic Concepts

A. Programs such as unemployment insurance ensure that people experiencing economic hardship have a basic level of income. How does this help to stabilize the economy?

The Purpose of Fiscal Policy

KEY CONCEPTS

Fiscal policy can be used for expansionary or contractionary purposes. The choice of policy depends on whether the economy is weak or strong. Expansionary fiscal policy is designed to stimulate a weak economy to grow. Contractionary fiscal policy is used to slow the economy down in order to control inflation.

POLICY 1 Expansionary Fiscal Policy

Government may use expansionary policy to increase the level of aggregate demand so that growth occurs in the economy. As you recall from Chapter 13, increased aggregate demand causes prices to rise, providing incentives for businesses to expand and causing GDP to increase. Expansionary fiscal policy also reduces the rate of unemployment, as there are more jobs available when businesses are expanding. Expansionary fiscal policy may involve increased government spending, decreased taxes, or both.

For example, suppose the economy is in recession and, in response, the government decides to increase spending for highways. The government spends the money by contracting with private firms in many cities to build new roads. This spending creates additional jobs as the contractors hire more and more construction workers to complete the projects. If employment increases, more people will have income to spend, and aggregate demand increases for all goods and services in the economy.

The government may also choose to cut taxes to stimulate the economy. By lowering individual and corporate income tax rates, the government allows individuals and businesses to have more income left after taxes. Individuals may spend their increased income and thereby increase demand for numerous goods and services. Increased income may allow them to increase their savings, which makes more money available to businesses to invest. Lower taxes also leave businesses with more money to invest in new equipment or plants, or in additional workers to produce more goods and services to meet increased demand.

Whether the government increases spending, decreases taxes, or uses some combination of the two, the result is somewhat similar. As Figure 15.1 on the opposite page shows, expansionary fiscal policy leads to an increase in aggregate demand (the curve shifts to the right) and, therefore, economic growth.

Expansion Increased construction of new housing is an indication that the economy is expanding.

POLICY 2 Contractionary Fiscal Policy

The federal government may use contractionary policy to decrease the level of aggregate demand so that inflation is reduced. When the economy is growing too rapidly, aggregate demand may increase faster than aggregate supply, leading to demand-pull inflation. This type of inflation, which you read about in Chapter 13, is characterized by a steadily rising price level and a decrease in the purchasing power of people's incomes.

When the government faces such an economy, it may employ contractionary fiscal policy and use spending and taxes in ways opposite to expansionary fiscal policy. In other words, it may choose to decrease government spending or increase taxes in order to control inflation.

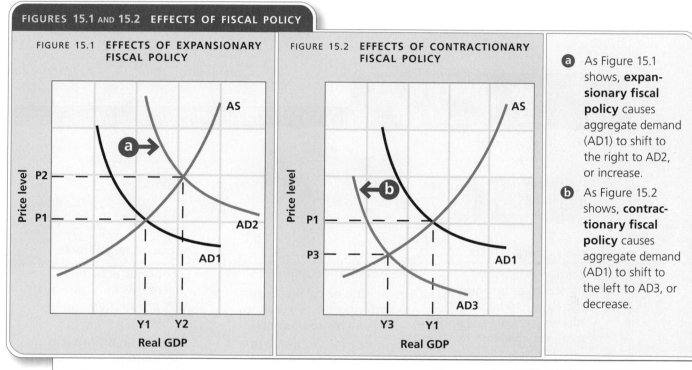

FIGURES 15.1 AND 15.2 EFFECTS OF FISCAL POLICY

FIGURE 15.1 **EFFECTS OF EXPANSIONARY FISCAL POLICY**

FIGURE 15.2 **EFFECTS OF CONTRACTIONARY FISCAL POLICY**

a As Figure 15.1 shows, **expansionary fiscal policy** causes aggregate demand (AD1) to shift to the right to AD2, or increase.

b As Figure 15.2 shows, **contractionary fiscal policy** causes aggregate demand (AD1) to shift to the left to AD3, or decrease.

ANALYZE GRAPHS
1. In Figure 15.1, what happens to real GDP as a result of expansionary fiscal policy?
2. In Figure 15.2, what happens to the price level as a result of contractionary fiscal policy?

Animated **Economics**

Use interactive aggregate demand and aggregate supply curves at **ClassZone.com**

For example, if the economy is growing too rapidly, the government may cut its spending on a variety of programs such as highway construction, education, and health care. By cutting spending, the government takes money out of the economy. This decreased government spending results in less income for individuals or businesses that are directly affected by the cuts in government programs. So these individuals have less money to spend on goods and services, and aggregate demand decreases. Businesses may cut production in response to decreased aggregate demand. As aggregate demand decreases, the rise in the price level is stopped, and inflation is brought under control.

Rather than cut spending, the government may choose to increase taxes. This leads to a decrease in consumer spending and, therefore, a slowdown in the rate of inflation. In other words, when individuals and businesses have to pay higher taxes, they have less income left over to spend or invest. As a result, aggregate demand will decrease. As aggregate demand decreases, businesses may cut back production and lay off workers. This will cause a further decrease in aggregate demand, because workers will have less to spend on goods and services. And as aggregate demand falls, so will the price level.

Whether the government decreases spending or increases taxes or uses some combination of the two, the impact of contractionary fiscal policy on aggregate demand and inflation is somewhat similar. Turn back to Figure 15.2 on page 449. Notice that contractionary fiscal policy results in the aggregate demand curve shifting to the left. This indicates that aggregate demand is decreasing. This decline in aggregate demand, in turn, helps control inflation. (The major fiscal policy tools, and their impact on the economy, are reviewed in Figure 15.3.)

ECONOMICS ESSENTIALS

FIGURE 15.3 Effects of Fiscal Policy on the Economy

Fiscal Policy Tools

Expansionary Effects

- Economic activity increases as businesses increase production, hire more workers, and increase investment
- More workers have more income to spend on goods and services
- Aggregate demand increases, resulting in economic growth

- Automatic stabilizers
- Raising or cutting taxes; offering tax breaks and incentives to businesses
- Increasing or decreasing government spending

Contractionary Effects

- Economic activity decreases as businesses cut production and lay off workers
- Workers have less income to spend on goods and services
- Aggregate demand decreases, bring inflation under control

ANALYZE CHARTS

The government can use a combination of taxing and spending policies to stimulate a sluggish economy or to slow down an overheated economy. At what point in the business cycle do you think the economy is today? What type of fiscal policy do you think the government should apply at this time?

APPLICATION Analyzing Cause and Effect

B. What effect does expansionary fiscal policy have on consumer spending? Explain your answer.

Limitations of Fiscal Policy

KEY CONCEPTS

The purpose of fiscal policy is to reduce economic slowdowns, which result in unemployment, and to curb inflation. The success of fiscal policy, however, is limited by a number of issues, including policy lags and timing.

LIMITATION 1 Policy Lags

Fiscal policy lags behind the economic conditions it is designed to address. This situation is often related to identifying the problem and getting Congress to move on the issue. Months of debate may precede policy change. The lag also may be related to how quickly the change in policy takes effect. For example, the time for tax changes to take effect is shorter than that for government spending. In particular, it may take a long time for public spending programs to get started and money to begin flowing into the economy. Therefore, tax changes may be more effective than policy changes in dealing with short-term recessions.

LIMITATION 2 Timing Issues

The goal of fiscal policy is to provide a stable economic environment. This means that it should coordinate with the business cycle. Fiscal policy is described as countercyclical because the goal is to smooth out the peaks and troughs of the business cycle. If the timing of the policy is good, fluctuations in the business cycle will be less severe, as Figure 15.4 illustrates. If the timing is bad, however, it could make matters worse. For example, if the economy is already moving out of a recession when an expansionary fiscal policy takes effect, the result could be inflation.

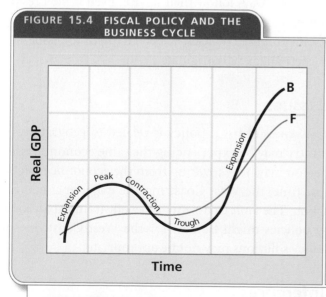

FIGURE 15.4   FISCAL POLICY AND THE BUSINESS CYCLE

Real GDP

Time

Expansion   Peak   Contraction   Trough   Expansion   B   F

Line B shows how the economy fluctuates during the normal business cycle if fiscal policy actions are not used. Line F shows economic fluctuations if fiscal policy actions are effective.

ANALYZE GRAPHS
1. What kind of fiscal policy might be used to address rapid movement toward a trough?
2. How does this diagram illustrate that fiscal policy is countercyclical?

LIMITATION 3 Rational Expectations Theory

QUICK REFERENCE

The **rational expectations theory** states that people anticipate that changes in fiscal policy will affect the economy in a particular way and that, as a result, people will take steps to protect their interests.

A second phenomenon affecting timing is explained by the **rational expectations theory**, which states that individuals and business firms expect that changes in fiscal policy will have particular outcomes, and they take actions to protect their interests against those outcomes. These actions may limit the effectiveness of fiscal policy. For example, expansionary fiscal policy attempts to stimulate aggregate demand to increase employment. An increase in aggregate demand might also pull up the price level, causing inflation. In anticipation of rising inflation, people spend more to keep their buying power from decreasing. However, this increased spending causes more inflation and defeats the aims of the expansionary policy.

LIMITATION 4 Political Issues

Fiscal policy decisions are not always based on economic considerations. Sometimes, political considerations, most notably enhancing the chances of reelection, may influence the kind of fiscal policy that a government follows. The **Council of Economic Advisers** is a three-member group that advises the President on fiscal policy and other economic issues. Because of political pres-

QUICK REFERENCE

The **Council of Economic Advisers** is a group of economic advisors to the president.

Fiscal Policy and Politics Decisions on economic policy often are influenced by politics.

sures, however, the President may not always follow their advice. Even if the President does accept the council's guidance, members of Congress—again because of political considerations—may not agree with proposed policies. This is an important issue, since the House of Representatives is where all tax bills originate.

LIMITATION 5 Regional Issues

Another limitation of the effectiveness of fiscal policy is related to geography. Not every state or region of the country may be experiencing the same economic issues. For example, the Gulf Coast region may be recovering from the economic effects of hurricane damage. At the same time, the West Coast may be experiencing a high tech boom that is causing inflation. The Gulf Coast might benefit from expansionary policies, while contractionary policies might be best for the West Coast. In such circumstances, broad fiscal-policy solutions may not be appropriate.

APPLICATION Making Inferences

C. How do policy lags and timing issues work together to limit the effectiveness of fiscal policy?

REVIEWING KEY CONCEPTS

1. Use each of the three terms below in a sentence that illustrates the meaning of the term.

   a. *expansionary fiscal policy*   **b.** *discretionary fiscal policy*   **c.** *rational expectations theory*

2. What are the two basic goals of fiscal policy?

3. How do expansionary fiscal policy and contractionary fiscal policy use the same fiscal policy tools in different ways?

4. What is the difference between discretionary fiscal policy and automatic stabilizers?

5. What is the role of the Council of Economic Advisers?

6. **Using Your Notes** What are the limitations of fiscal policy? Refer to your completed cluster diagram.

   Use the Graphic Organizer at **Interactive Review @ ClassZone.com**

   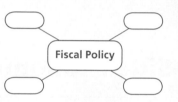
   Fiscal Policy

CRITICAL THINKING

7. **Making Inferences** Between 2001 and 2004, Congress passed a series of tax cuts and increased government spending. Do these actions reflect expansionary or contractionary fiscal policy? Explain your answer.

8. **Applying Economic Concepts** Agricultural price supports provide farmers with government subsidies when market prices of certain crops are low. What kind of fiscal policy is at work in this situation and how does it work?

9. **Drawing Conclusions** Federal government officials want to prevent a slowing economy from going into recession. They debate whether to increase spending on new public transit systems or decrease individual and corporate income tax rates.

   a. How would an understanding of policy lags help them decide which government action would be most effective?

   b. What other issues might affect their decision?

10. **Challenge** Make a copy of Figure 15.4 on page 451 and label the part of line F that might represent expansionary fiscal policy and the part that might represent contractionary fiscal policy.

ECONOMICS IN PRACTICE

Analyzing Economic Conditions Consider what you've learned about economic instability and fiscal policy. Then complete the following activities.

Propose Fiscal Policies For each situation listed in the chart, identify the problem and decide whether the fiscal policy should be expansionary or contractionary.

Economic Situation	Problem/Fiscal Policy Needed
Business investment spending declines for six straight months	
Consumer Price Index rises for four straight months	
Unemployment rate increases from 4% to 6.5% over six months	
Consumer confidence falls for five straight months	

Challenge Choose one situation and give examples of how fiscal policy might be applied to it.

Demand-Side and Supply-Side Policies

OBJECTIVES	KEY TERMS	TAKING NOTES
In Section 2, you will • describe how demand-side fiscal policy can be used to stimulate the economy • describe how supply-side fiscal policy can be used to stimulate the economy • identify the role that fiscal policy has in changing the economy	Keynesian economics, *p. 454* demand-side fiscal policy, *p. 454* spending multiplier effect, *p. 455* supply-side fiscal policy, *p. 458* Laffer Curve, *p. 459*	As you read Section 2, complete a chart to show the major features of demand-side and supply-side policies. Use the Graphic Organizer at **Interactive Review @ ClassZone.com**

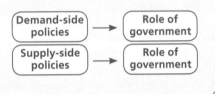

Demand-side policies → Role of government

Supply-side policies → Role of government

Demand-Side Economics

KEY CONCEPTS

Economists have not always supported the idea of discretionary fiscal policy. Historically, most think that the national government should have a limited role in the economy. When the country experienced financial panics and depressions, the government did little to help the economy get back on track.

The Great Depression of the 1930s changed many people's minds about the role of the government. High unemployment and low production persisted for several years. Many economists concluded that the old ways were ineffective in this situation. One economist, John Maynard Keynes, proposed a new way to address the problem.

The theories that Keynes put forward are called **Keynesian economics**, the idea that in times of recession aggregate demand needs to be stimulated by government action. Keynes believed that such an approach would lower unemployment. Keynesian economics forms the basis of **demand-side fiscal policy**, fiscal policy to stimulate aggregate demand.

QUICK REFERENCE

Keynesian economics states that aggregate demand needs to be stimulated by government action.

Demand-side fiscal policy is a plan to stimulate aggregate demand.

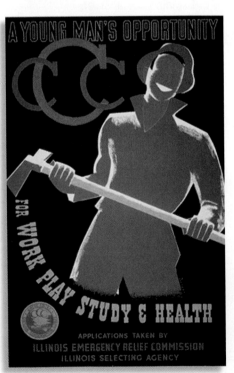

Demand-Side Policies The Civilian Conservation Corps (CCC), an employment program for young men, was one government action aimed at stimulating the economy during the Great Depression.

Keynesian Theory

Keynes argued that changes in aggregate demand influence the business cycle, and he expressed this idea in an equation. His equation states that the GDP equals the total market value of all consumer goods (C), investment goods (I), government goods (G), and net exports (F). The equation looks like this: $GDP = C + I + G + F$.

Keynes believed that net exports played only a small role in the economy and that government and consumer expenditures were fairly stable. He reasoned that it was investment that caused the economy to fluctuate and that investment creates a greater than one-for-one change in national income. That is, one dollar spent in investment has a **spending multiplier effect**, meaning that a change in spending is multiplied into a larger change in GDP. (See Figure 15.5.)

QUICK REFERENCE

The **spending multiplier effect** states that a small change in spending causes a much larger change in GDP.

MATH CHALLENGE
FIGURE 15.5 Spending Multiplier Effect

If Zain receives a $100 raise and spends $60 of it to buy products from Joan, Joan's income increases too. Similarly, if Joan uses $36 of her increased income to buy products from Ravi, Ravi's income increases. Ravi then buys from Sarah, and so on. Each increase in income contributes to the GDP, so the total effect of Zain's spending is multiplied. To quantify how spending increases GDP, economists use the spending multiplier.

NEED HELP?

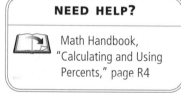

Math Handbook, "Calculating and Using Percents," page R4

Step 1: Determine the percentage of the money that is spent on domestic goods and services each time the money is reused. In the example, this is 60 percent.

Step 2: Use this equation, where A is the percentage, to calculate the spending multiplier.

Sample Calculations

$$\frac{1}{1-A} = \text{Spending multiplier} \qquad \frac{1}{1-60\%} = \frac{1}{1-0.60} = 2.5$$

Step 3: Use the spending multiplier to calculate the total increase in GDP.

Initial investment	×	Spending multiplier	=	Total increase in GDP		$100	×	2.5	=	$250

If businesses invest less, the spending multiplier effect means that the decrease in overall spending is greater than the initial decrease in business investment. Because this effect touches the entire economy, the government may need to step in to offset changes in investment. This idea became the basis of demand-side fiscal economics, which favors the use of fiscal policy to stimulate aggregate demand.

APPLICATION Making Inferences

A. How did Keynes's equation help him conclude that if investment declined, government needed to increase spending or cut taxes to stimulate aggregate demand?

John Maynard Keynes: Architect of Demand-Side Policy

FAST FACTS

John Maynard Keynes

Career: British academic and government economist

Born: June 5, 1883, in Cambridge, England

Died: April 21, 1946

Major Accomplishment: Introduced the idea of using government action to stimulate aggregate demand

Books: *A Treatise on Money* (1930); *The General Theory of Employment, Interest, and Money* (1936)

Famous Quotation: *The difficulty lies, not in the new ideas, but in escaping from the old ones.*

Jobs: Lecturer in economics, Cambridge University; editor of the *Economics Journal*; positions with the British Treasury office during World Wars I and II

Economics Update

Learn more about John Maynard Keynes at **ClassZone.com**

Many Americans are accustomed to the idea that the government plays an active role in the market economy. However, when John Maynard Keynes proposed his ideas in the 1930s, they were considered revolutionary. He questioned the principles of economics that had been accepted since the time of Adam Smith. How did Keynes's work change the way that people viewed the role of government in the economy?

Using Government Action to Stimulate Demand

The economic situation of the 1920s led John Maynard Keynes to question the classical economic theories of supply and demand. Classical economists believed that a free market would eventually correct any imbalances. However, as aggregate demand fell, businesses invested and produced less, which led to layoffs. As a result, consumers had even less money to spend, and businesses cut back production even further.

As early as 1929, Keynes proposed that the British government spend money on public works projects to help ease unemployment. However, he had no theoretical backing for his proposal until he read an article in 1931 about the spending multiplier. This concept proved to be the key to his new economic theory, which he published in *The General Theory of Employment, Interest, and Money* (1936). This ground-breaking book marked the beginning of the field of macroeconomics.

Keynes's first revolutionary idea was to define aggregate demand as the sum of investment, consumer spending, government spending and net exports. He further stated that only government intervention could break the business cycle patterns that caused so much economic suffering. Even more revolutionary, however, was his argument that it was better for the government to spend money to help stabilize the economy than to have a balanced budget.

A Continuing Influence
Keynes's ideas continue to influence the way some governments deal with economic depressions.

APPLICATION Contrasting Economic Information

B. What made Keynes's ideas different from those of classical economists?

Government and Demand-Side Policies

KEY CONCEPTS

Discretionary fiscal policy involves choices about how to use government spending and taxation to increase aggregate demand or control inflation. Demand-side policies advocate use of these fiscal policy tools to control aggregate demand and stabilize the economy.

The Role of Government

Keynes proposed an active role for government in the economy. He argued that the federal government ought to step into the economy using expansionary fiscal policy to promote full employment. The Great Depression had shown that the economy could reach equilibrium with less than full employment and that business was unable to break out of this cycle because of insufficient aggregate demand. Therefore, Keynes advocated increased government spending and decreased taxation to end recessions. Increased government spending helps create jobs and increases income, and decreased taxation encourages consumers to spend more, which prompts businesses to invest more. Such actions help increase aggregate demand.

Wartime Spending
Massive government spending on wartime industries brought the United States out of economic depression.

On the other hand, Keynes thought that when inflation was high the government should use contractionary fiscal policy to keep prices from rising. The government would take an active role through decreasing government spending or increasing taxes. Both of these actions help decrease aggregate demand and control inflation.

Demand-Side Policies—Analysis

In some circumstances, an increase in government spending may lead to economic recovery. For example, government spending on public works programs and on production related to World War II brought the United States out of the Great Depression. However, it is not easy to limit such spending to times of recession, because federal programs seem to take on a life of their own and are difficult to terminate. Politicians are often reluctant to discontinue programs that are popular.

Excessive aggregate demand due to government or consumer spending can lead to inflation. Contractionary fiscal policy requires decreases in government spending or increases in taxation. Just as it is difficult to decrease government spending, it is difficult to enact the tax increases. Politicians must often choose between doing what is best for the economy and doing what is most likely to ensure their reelection. Furthermore, when the economy experiences stagflation—slow economic growth with high unemployment and inflation—as it did in the 1970s, demand-side policies seem to be ineffective.

APPLICATION Drawing Conclusions

C. Why are demand-side policies more effective against recession than against inflation?

Supply-Side Economics

KEY CONCEPTS

QUICK REFERENCE

Supply-side fiscal policy provides incentives to producers to increase aggregate supply.

Some economists believe that the best way to influence the economy is through the supply side rather than through the demand side. **Supply-side fiscal policy** is designed to provide incentives to producers to increase aggregate supply. In other words, demand-side economics uses fiscal policy to encourage consumers to spend more, while supply-side economics focuses on cutting the cost of production to encourage producers to supply more. Figure 15.6 compares supply-side economics to demand-side economics.

The Role of Government

As you have learned, the role of the government in the economy falls into three categories: taxation, spending, and regulation. For the most part, supply-side economists favor less government involvement in these three areas.

Supply-side economists favor cutting the tax rates on individual and corporate income because they believe that high tax rates slow economic growth by discouraging working, saving, and investing. Lower tax rates, on the other hand, encourage individuals and businesses to work, save, and invest more. Specifically, reducing the highest tax brackets provides more available income to the people most likely to invest in new business activities. Spending cuts are another way that supply-side economics seeks to stimulate aggregate supply. Cuts in spending are related to tax cuts. If the government spends less, it needs to take in less in revenue and, therefore, is able to lower taxes. Finally, decreased government regulation can also stimulate business production. Government regulations add to the costs of production and make it harder for businesses to grow. Deregulation, however, cuts costs and leads to increases in aggregate supply.

FIGURE 15.6 Supply-Side and Demand-Side Economics

Supply-Side Economics	Demand-Side Economics
• Focuses on stimulating production (supply) to increase business output	• Focuses on stimulating consumption (demand) to increase business output
• Lower taxes + decreased government spending + deregulation = greater incentives for business investment	• Increased government spending results in more money in people's hands
• Businesses expand and create jobs; people work, save, and invest more	• People spend more
• Greater investment and productivity cause businesses to increase output	• Increased demand causes business to increase output

ANALYZE CHARTS

1. What is similar about supply-side and demand-side tax policies?

2. Which system favors less government involvement in the economy?

The Laffer Curve

Supply-side economists refer to the **Laffer Curve**, a graph developed by economist Arthur Laffer, to illustrate how tax cuts affect tax revenues and economic growth. As Figure 15.7 shows, Laffer theorized that tax revenues increase as tax rates increase up to a certain point. After that point, higher tax rates actually lead to decreased tax revenues. The reasoning behind the curve is that higher taxes discourage people from working, saving, and investing. So, at a tax rate of 100 percent, the government would theoretically collect no tax revenues, because people would have no incentive to earn income if it all went to the government for taxes.

In other words, the higher the tax rate, the likelier it is that people will take some type of action to avoid paying more taxes. When people find alternatives to income-producing activity, total taxable income declines, tax revenues decrease, aggregate supply falls, and economic growth slows. Conversely, as tax rates fall, people are more inclined to undertake income-producing activity because less of their income will go to taxes. Further, they are more likely to save and invest this extra income, which will lead to increasing aggregate supply and greater economic growth.

QUICK REFERENCE

The **Laffer Curve** is a graph that illustrates the economist Arthur Laffer's theory of how tax cuts affect tax revenues.

FIGURE 15.7 THE LAFFER CURVE

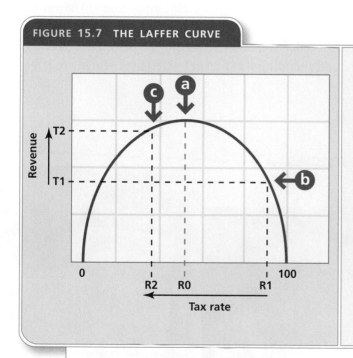

a There is a tax rate between 0 and 100 percent (point R0) at which maximum revenue is collected.

b Tax rates higher than R0, such as R1, will not bring in more revenue (T1), because higher taxes discourage productive activity and shrink the tax base.

c When tax rates are higher than R0, lowering the tax rate (R2) will lead to higher tax revenue (T2). Lower tax rates tend to encourage productive activity and increase the tax base.

ANALYZE GRAPHS

1. There is no tax revenue at two points on the graph—when the tax rate is 0 percent and when it is 100 percent. Why is this so?
2. How does this graph support the ideas of supply-side economists?

Supply-Side Policies—Analysis

When the principles of the Laffer Curve were applied in the United States in the 1980s, the results were much as Laffer had predicted. Legislation passed in that decade reduced federal income tax rates substantially. For example, the top bracket went from 70 percent to around 30 percent. At the same time, federal government receipts from income taxes over the whole decade were about 13 percent higher than they had been in the 1970s. Inflation and unemployment rates both fell during the decade. Further, the economy grew steadily in the 1980s, with real GDP increasing by about 3 percent each year.

Even so, some of Laffer's predictions did not hold true. The supply-side approach suggests that with lower tax rates, people will work more. However, while some people did choose to work more, others chose to work less, since they could earn the same amount of after-tax income by working fewer hours. In addition, supply-side theory states that lower tax rates encourage people to save and invest. In fact, the savings rate declined during the 1980s.

Some economists have suggested that the success of supply-side policies depends on where the economy is located on the Laffer Curve. Look again at Figure 15.7 on page 459. Find the tax rate R0 on the horizontal axis and trace the broken line from that point to where the line intersects the curve. Tax revenue is maximized at this point. If the economy is not at this point on the curve, then tax rate cuts will decrease tax revenue rather than increase it. Supply-side theory offers no measures for establishing where on the curve an economy might be. Other economists have argued that it is difficult to isolate the effects of supply-side incentives from demand-side results to determine what caused unemployment and inflation rates to fall and the economy to grow during the 1980s. They suggest that tax cuts and increased government spending on defense drove up aggregate demand, resulting in economic growth. This increased spending was fueled by deficits, which you'll learn more about in Section 3.

APPLICATION Analyzing Causes

D. What fiscal policy techniques do supply-side economists advocate to reduce unemployment and fight inflation at the same time?

SECTION 2 Assessment

Online Quiz
ClassZone.com

REVIEWING KEY CONCEPTS

1. Explain the relationship between the terms in each of these pairs.

   a. *Keynesian economics*
   demand-side fiscal policy

   b. *supply-side fiscal policy*
   Laffer Curve

2. How did the Great Depression influence Keynesian economics?

3. How is the spending multiplier effect related to demand-side economics?

4. How are supply-side and demand-side economics different?

5. Which fiscal policy tool does the Laffer Curve address?

6. **Using Your Notes** How does the role of government differ in demand-side and supply-side economics? Refer to your completed flow chart.

   Use the Graphic Organizer at **Interactive Review @ ClassZone.com**

CRITICAL THINKING

7. **Creating Graphs** Create a graph showing aggregate demand and aggregate supply in the economy. Then add new curves to show the expected shifts based on expansionary demand-side policies and supply-side policies. What happens to price level and GDP as a result of each type of policy?

   Use *SMART Grapher* @ **ClassZone.com** to complete this activity.

8. **Applying Economic Concepts** Suppose that the federal government decides to increase its spending on highway construction by $5 billion to keep the economy from falling into a recession. Explain the real impact on GDP of this spending.

9. **Analyzing Effects** Tom, Cia, and Julie were all in the 50 percent tax bracket. When a tax cut program reduced their tax bracket to 28 percent, they all made changes in their lives. Tom decided to work fewer hours so he could begin training to run in a marathon. Cia bought the new sports car she'd been wanting. Julie chose to work more hours so she could save extra money for her daughter's college education. Explain the effects of the tax cut for each individual. Use supply-side or demand-side economics reasoning in your answer.

10. **Challenge** Why is it difficult for demand-side economics to solve the problems of high unemployment and high inflation when they occur at the same time?

ECONOMICS IN PRACTICE

Space research center

Categorizing Economic Information Consider what you've learned about demand-side or supply-side fiscal policy. Then complete the following activities.

Identify Policies Complete the chart by indicating whether each action reflects a demand-side or a supply-side policy.

Government Action	Demand-Side or Supply-Side
Cut capital gains tax rates to encourage investment	
Expand government spending on space exploration	
Increase federal grants for education	
Reduce safety rules that businesses must follow	

Challenge Why is it difficult to tell if a cut in individual income tax rates is the result of a demand-side or a supply-side policy?

Deficits and the National Debt

OBJECTIVES

In Section 3, you will
- examine the difference between the deficit and the debt
- explain why national deficits occur
- describe how deficits are financed
- identify the impact of the national debt on the economy

KEY TERMS

budget surplus, *p. 462*
budget deficit, *p. 462*
deficit spending, *p. 462*
national debt, *p. 462*
Treasury bills, *p. 464*
Treasury notes, *p. 464*
Treasury bonds, *p. 464*
trust funds, *p. 465*
crowding-out effect, *p. 466*

TAKING NOTES

As you read Section 3, complete a comparison chart to show the similarities and differences between federal deficits and the national debt. Use the Graphic Organizer at **Interactive Review @ ClassZone.com**

Federal Deficits	National Debt

The Federal Deficit and Debt

KEY CONCEPTS

Governments have frequently made efforts to balance their budgets so that spending equals the revenues collected. In reality, however, all levels of government often struggle to achieve a balanced budget. As you recall, Congress and state legislatures make budget decisions with both economic and political considerations in mind.

Federal government spending falls into one of three categories: a balanced budget; a **budget surplus**, when the government takes in more than it spends; or a **budget deficit**, when government spends more than it takes in. In recent years, the federal government has rarely achieved a budget surplus. Since 1970, a surplus was recorded only between 1998 and 2001. Figure 15.8 on the opposite page shows the pattern of budget deficits and surpluses since 1980.

It is important to note that a budget surplus or budget deficit refers to only one year. **Deficit spending** occurs when a government spends more than it collects in revenue for a specific budget year. Annual deficits contribute to the **national debt**, which is the total amount of money that the government owes. In effect, the national debt is equal to the sum of annual budget deficits minus any budget surpluses or other payments against the debt.

Source: www.CartoonStock.com

Controlling the Deficit This cartoon suggests one way to deal with a budget deficit.

Causes of the Deficit

There are four main causes of deficit spending: national emergencies, a desire for more public goods, stabilization of the economy, and the role of government in society. Many times a budget deficit may be the result of more than one of these causes.

National Emergencies Generally speaking, national emergencies are wars in which the United States is involved. Deficit spending has been used in wartime from the Revolutionary War to the war in Iraq that began in 2003. The terrorist attacks of September 11, 2001, and catastrophic weather events are other examples of national emergencies. All may require massive spending beyond the normal outlay of funds.

Need for Public Goods and Services Public goods and services benefit many different people and groups. The interstate highway system, dams, flood-control projects, and airports are examples of public goods. Building such infrastructure is expensive and lasts many years. The public expects the government to provide these goods to facilitate commerce, agriculture, and transportation.

Stabilization of the Economy As you learned earlier in this chapter, fiscal policy can include government spending to stimulate the economy. The classic example of this occurred during the Great Depression. The government spent money on a variety of public works projects to build roads, bridges, schools, and parks, putting millions of unemployed people to work. This government spending led to budget deficits.

Role of Government in Society As you have seen, people have also come to depend on government programs such as Social Security, Medicare, Medicaid, and unemployment insurance to provide help for those in need. These programs are expensive, and because they are entitlement programs, they require funding each year.

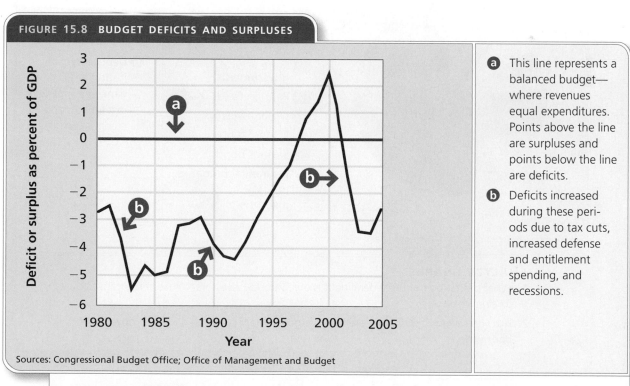

FIGURE 15.8 BUDGET DEFICITS AND SURPLUSES

ⓐ This line represents a balanced budget—where revenues equal expenditures. Points above the line are surpluses and points below the line are deficits.

ⓑ Deficits increased during these periods due to tax cuts, increased defense and entitlement spending, and recessions.

Sources: Congressional Budget Office; Office of Management and Budget

ANALYZE GRAPHS

1. When did the largest deficit occur and about how much was it? The largest surplus?

2. How would the trends shown on this graph affect the national debt?

Raising Money for Deficit Spending

When the federal government does not receive enough revenue from taxes to finance its spending, it can borrow money to expand the economy. In effect, the government pays for its present needs by borrowing money that it will have to repay at some future date. It does this by issuing government bonds, through the Department of the Treasury.

Perhaps the best known type of bond issued by the government is the savings bond. Savings bonds mature in 20 years and are available in both small and large denominations—from $25 up to $10,000. The Department of the Treasury issues three other types of bonds. **Treasury bills** (T bills) are short-term bonds that mature in less than one year. **Treasury notes** are bonds that mature between two and ten years. And finally, **Treasury bonds** are issued for 30 years. Interest is paid on all these bonds, with higher interest rates sometimes being paid on instruments with longer maturity dates.

Individuals, state and local governments, insurance companies, pension funds, financial institutions, the Federal Reserve banks, and foreign investors hold these bonds. Figure 15.9 shows the percentage of federal debt held by different types of investors. A trend in recent years has been an increase in the percentage of the federal debt owned by foreign investors. Most foreign investors in U.S. Treasury bonds are the central banks of other countries. Japan and China hold the largest amount of foreign investors' share of the debt.

QUICK REFERENCE

Treasury bills mature in less than one year.

Treasury notes mature between two and ten years.

Treasury bonds mature in 30 years.

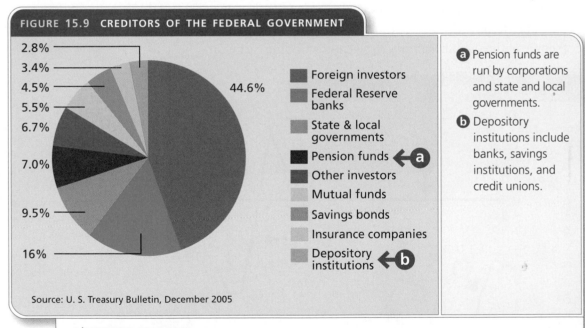

FIGURE 15.9 CREDITORS OF THE FEDERAL GOVERNMENT

2.8%
3.4%
4.5%
5.5%
6.7%
7.0%
9.5%
16%
44.6%

- Foreign investors
- Federal Reserve banks
- State & local governments
- Pension funds ← a
- Other investors
- Mutual funds
- Savings bonds
- Insurance companies
- Depository institutions ← b

a Pension funds are run by corporations and state and local governments.

b Depository institutions include banks, savings institutions, and credit unions.

Source: U. S. Treasury Bulletin, December 2005

ANALYZE GRAPHS

1. What percentage of the federal debt is owed to U.S. investors? What percentage is owed to foreign investors?

2. How do savings bonds compare to other government bonds as a form of government borrowing?

APPLICATION Drawing Conclusions

A. Why do all levels of government often struggle to achieve balanced budgets or budget surpluses?

The National Debt

KEY CONCEPTS

As you have seen, the national debt consists of the total accumulation of government deficits and surpluses over time. The money is owed to savers for the bonds they purchase and the interest paid on them. However, the actual debt situation is somewhat more complicated. The government also borrows from **trust funds**, which are funds being held for specific purposes to be expended at a future date. Examples of government trust funds include Social Security, Medicare, Medicaid, and government pension funds. When the trust funds accumulate surpluses by taking in more tax revenue than is needed for annual benefit payments, the surplus is invested in government bonds until the specific programs need the funds. In essence, therefore, the government borrows from itself to cover some deficit spending.

Some economists do not consider this to truly be debt. The money is transferred from one part of the government to another. This borrowing does not place a burden on the current economy because the current budget is not used to pay for it.

QUICK REFERENCE

Trust funds are held for specific purposes to be expended at a future date.

The Size of the National Debt

In August 2006, the total national debt was about $8.4 trillion. About $4.8 trillion was privately owned by the creditors shown in Figure 15.9, and about $3.6 trillion was in government trust funds.

There were only five years from 1962 to 2005 in which the federal government had a surplus of funds. In all the other years of that period, the government borrowed money to cover its deficits. Each time it borrowed money, it increased the size of the national debt. From 1980 to 1994 alone, the national debt grew by more than five times, from about $930 billion in 1980 to about $4.7 trillion in 1994.

Economists often look at the country's debt as a percentage of GDP. That perspective allows them to see how the burden of borrowing compares to the strength of the overall economy. The national debt was 33 percent of GDP in 1981. By 2006, it had doubled to nearly 68 percent of GDP. However, in 1981 about 80 percent of the debt was privately owned. In 2006, less than 60 percent was privately owned.

Economics Update

Find an update about the national debt at **ClassZone.com**

More About the National Debt

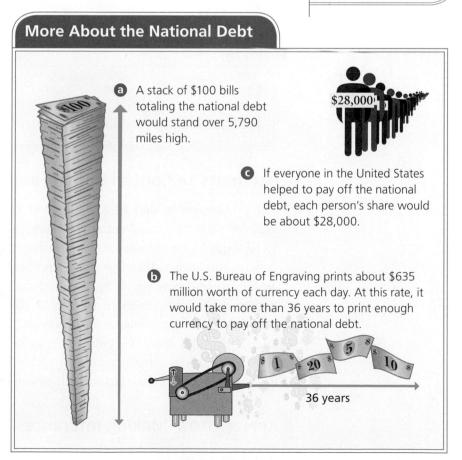

a A stack of $100 bills totaling the national debt would stand over 5,790 miles high.

c If everyone in the United States helped to pay off the national debt, each person's share would be about $28,000.

b The U.S. Bureau of Engraving prints about $635 million worth of currency each day. At this rate, it would take more than 36 years to print enough currency to pay off the national debt.

$28,000

36 years

The Effect of the Debt on the Economy

The national debt can have positive or negative effects on the economy. When government spending stimulates the economy, jobs are created and public goods such as the infrastructure may be improved. These improvements benefit everyone. However, when the government competes with the private sector to raise money by paying higher interest rates to get the savers' dollars, the results often are negative. The **crowding-out effect** is what happens when the government outbids private bond interest rates to gain loanable funds. Money leaves the private sector, and interest rates increase.

Repaying the interest on government bonds, or servicing the debt, also can have a negative impact on the economy. The 2007 federal budget estimate showed interest payments to be nearly 10 percent of all federal spending. Constant borrowing raises the amount of interest to be paid. This, in turn, increases the need for taxes to service the debt. Higher taxes mean less spending by consumers and less investment by businesses, both of which may hurt the economy.

QUICK REFERENCE

The **crowding-out effect** is the result of the government's outbidding private bond interest rates.

FIGURE 15.10 Actions to Control Deficits and Debt

Budget Action	Goal	Key Points	Analysis
Gramm-Rudman Hollings (1985)	Eliminate the deficit by 1991	Set annual deficit targets; automatic spending cuts	Unrealistic goals; deficits increased
Budget Enforcement Act (1990)	Ensure new laws do not increase deficits	Caps on discretionary spending; "pay-as-you-go" financing	Deficits declined after 1992
Omnibus Budget Reconciliation Act (1993)	Cut deficit by $500 billion over 5 years	Make income tax more progressive; some spending cuts	Deficits declined significantly; strong economy
Balanced Budget Agreement (1997)	Balance the budget by 2002	Cut some entitlement spending; increase education spending; targeted tax cuts	Budget surpluses 1998–2001

Attempts To Control Deficits and Debt

Sharp increases in deficits and the debt in the 1980s led government officials to look for ways to control deficit spending. (These efforts are summarized in Figure 15.10 above.) One measure set annual deficit targets with the goal of eliminating the deficit completely within five years. Another set limits on discretionary spending and mandated that new spending required cuts elsewhere in the budget, an approach known as "pay-as-you-go" financing. A third attempted to trim the deficit with a combination of tax increases and spending cuts. Still another sought to balance the budget through spending cuts in entitlement programs. Some of these measures failed, and deficits actually increased. Others enjoyed only limited success. As a result, the government continues to struggle to control the national debt.

APPLICATION Making Inferences

B. Why is paying interest on the national debt considered mandatory spending?

SECTION 3 Assessment

REVIEWING KEY CONCEPTS

1. Explain the difference between the terms in each of these pairs.

   a. *budget surplus*   **b.** *national debt*   **c.** *Treasury bills*
   budget deficit   *deficit spending*   *Treasury bonds*

2. How do budget deficits affect the national debt? Why?

3. What do Treasury bills, Treasury notes, and Treasury bonds have in common?

4. Why is government borrowing from trust funds different from privately-owned debt?

5. How is the crowding-out effect related to the national debt?

6. **Using Your Notes** What are the four causes of budget deficits? Refer to your completed chart.

Federal Deficits	National Debt

   Use the Graphic Organizer at **Interactive Review @ ClassZone.com**

CRITICAL THINKING

7. **Applying Economic Concepts** In 2007, the federal government was expected to have tax revenue of $2,350.8 billion. Total federal spending was estimated at $2,592.1 billion. Would the government have a budget deficit or a budget surplus that year? How much would it be?

8. **Analyzing Causes** Each of the following headlines reflects an example of deficit spending. Which of the causes of budget deficits is suggested by each headline?

   a. President Proposes Tax Cut Extensions to Keep Economy on Track

   b. Baby Boomers' Retirement Will Strain Social Security and Medicare

   c. Hurricane Recovery Effort to Require Massive Federal Aid

9. **Analyzing Data** Assume that the privately-owned part of the debt is $4,900 billion and the amount held by government trust funds is $3,500 billion. Use the percentages shown in Figure 15.9 to calculate the dollar amounts held by different creditors.

10. **Challenge** The Social Security Administration estimates that annual revenue from payroll taxes will be insufficient to meet annual benefit payments beginning in 2018. The Social Security trust fund will be used to make up the difference. How will this change affect the nature of the national debt?

ECONOMICS IN PRACTICE

Government bonds

Applying Economic Concepts
Recall what you learned about the crowding-out effect and then complete the following activities.

Analyze the Crowding-Out Effect The graph below shows the crowding-out effect in terms of supply and demand. Why would some private bond issuers be crowded out as a result of government borrowing?

Challenge What part of the national debt might cause the crowding-out effect, the public-owned portion, the portion in government trust funds, or both? Explain your answer.

Case Study

Economics Update
Find an update on this Case
Study at **ClassZone.com**

Is the Federal Deficit Too Large?

Background The federal deficit is a matter of interest not only to economists but also to the average American, because it is the taxpayer who ultimately pays the interest on the country's debt. This debt was created by pursuing a policy of deficit spending that requires the government to borrow money to make up the difference between how much it takes in and the amount it spends.

There are several reasons for using deficit spending. One major reason is the need to deal with national emergencies, such as the September 11 terrorist attacks or natural disasters like Hurricane Katrina. Another is to implement expansionary fiscal policies during periods of recession. Regardless of the reasons for deficit spending, the larger the deficit grows, the more controversial it becomes.

What's the issue? Is the federal deficit too large? Study these sources offering various opinions regarding what is a manageable federal deficit.

A. Online News Story

This article discusses a major problem that could arise from the government's continued deficit spending.

Federal Budget Deficit Sparks Worries

Higher Borrowing Costs Could Slow Economic Activity

. . . Here's the worry: Persistent deficits will lead to higher borrowing costs for consumers and companies, slowing economic activity. As Uncle Sam seeks to borrow . . . to finance those deficits, rates on Treasury securities would rise to entice investors. That would push up other interest rates, such as home mortgages, many auto loans, some home equity lines of credit and some credit cards. . . . For businesses, rates on corporate bonds would climb. It would become more expensive to borrow to pay for new plants and equipment and other capital investments.

Economists are troubled by the prospects of budget deficits as far as the eye can see and want to see them trimmed. But the size of the current budget deficits, while unwelcome, do not signal that a crisis is imminent. . . .

[But] there is more concern about higher borrowing costs over time crimping business investment and ultimately the production of goods and services. . . .

Source: "Federal Budget Deficit Sparks Worries," Associated Press, January 15, 2006.

Yearly deficits add to the country's growing national debt.

Thinking Economically What negative impact of deficit spending is discussed in this article?

B. Political Cartoon

Cartoonist Harley Schwadron made this comment about government spending.

BUREAU OF SPENDING INCREASES AND DEFICIT REDUCTION

"WAIT A MINUTE! HOW CAN THAT BE?"

Source: www.CartoonStock.com

Thinking Economically In what way is the statement on the bureau door contrary to valid economic principles?

C. Online News Story

In this article, former Secretary of the Treasury John Snow outlines the Bush administration's fiscal policy designed to reduce the federal deficit.

Setting Sights on the Deficit

Reducing the Deficit by Controlling Spending

The Bush administration's highest economic priority for its remaining three years is to control the growth of federal spending and bring down the U.S. budget deficit, John Snow, [former] U.S. Treasury secretary, said.

"The clear priority of the administration right now is the deficit, making sure that we achieve the president's objective of cutting the deficit in half by the time he leaves office," he said . . . This would put the deficit below 2 per cent of gross domestic product, low by historical standards. . . .

When he came to office in 2001, the president inherited a projected 10-year surplus of $5,600 billion. But tax cuts and growing spending for the military and homeland security have contributed to a sharp reversal, with the Congressional Budget Office now predicting a $2,100 billion deficit over the next decade. The annual deficit has been falling, however, from $413 billion in the 2004 fiscal year to $316 billion this year, according to CBO figures . . .

Mr. Snow made it clear that, in spite of the focus on the deficit, the administration would not reconsider its low tax policies.

Source: **"U.S. Sets its Sights on Deficit,"** by Edward Alden, Andrew Balls and Holly Yeager. *Financial Times*, November 4, 2005.

Thinking Economically How does the Bush administration plan to cut the deficit by half in three years? What other steps might it take to control the deficit?

THINKING ECONOMICALLY Synthesizing

1. Identify the economic cause-and-effect relationships described in Documents A and C.

2. How does Document B illustrate the challenge facing the Bush administration in its efforts to carry out the plan discussed in Document C?

3. Do you think the Bush administration shares the concerns about the deficit expressed in Document A? Use information from the documents to explain your answer.

Interactive ◀▶ Review

Review this chapter using interactive
activities at ClassZone.com

- Online Summary
- Graphic Organizers
- Quizzes
- Review and Study Notes
- Vocabulary Flip Cards

○ ○ ○

 Online Summary

Complete the following activity either on your
own paper or online at **ClassZone.com**

**Choose the key concept that best completes
the sentence. Not all key concepts will be used.**

automatic stabilizers	fiscal policy
budget deficit	Keynesian economics
budget surplus	Laffer Curve
contractionary fiscal policy	national debt
Council of Economic Advisers	spending multiplier effect
crowding-out effect	supply-side fiscal policy
deficit spending	Treasury bills
demand-side fiscal policy	Treasury bonds
discretionary fiscal policy	Treasury notes
expansionary fiscal policy	trust funds

__1__ is the government's use of taxes and
government spending to affect the economy. __2__
is a plan to stimulate a weak economy. __3__ is a
plan to slow the economy when it is expanding
too rapidly. __4__ refers to actions chosen by the
government to stabilize the economy. Public
transfer payments and progressive income taxes
are examples of __5__.

   __6__ is the idea that aggregate demand needed
to be stimulated by government action. It forms
the basis of __7__. The __8__ means that small changes
in income cause a larger change in spending.

   __9__ is fiscal policy that provides incentives to
producers to increase aggregate supply. The __10__
illustrates how tax cuts affect tax revenues and
economic growth.

   A __11__ occurs when the government takes in
more than it spends. When it spends more than it
takes in __12__ occurs. The __13__ is the total amount
of money owed to federal bondholders. The __14__
results when the government outbids private bond
interest rates.

◀◀ ◀ ▶

CHAPTER **15 Assessment**

REVIEWING KEY CONCEPTS

What Is Fiscal Policy? (pp. 446–453)

1. What is the difference between expansionary fiscal
policy and contractionary fiscal policy?

2. How do automatic stabilizers avoid the limitations
that affect discretionary fiscal policy?

**Demand-Side and Supply-Side Policies
(pp. 454–461)**

3. Why does Keynesian economics advocate
government spending during a recession?

4. What economic problems does supply-side
economics try to address simultaneously?

Deficits and the National Debt (pp. 462–469)

5. How does government finance deficit spending?

6. How does deficit spending contribute to the
national debt?

APPLYING ECONOMIC CONCEPTS

Look at the bar graph below showing national debt as
a percentage of GDP in several countries.

7. Which European countries on this graph have lower
ratios of debt to GDP than the United States?

8. How does U.S. debt compare to Japan's debt as a
percentage of GDP?

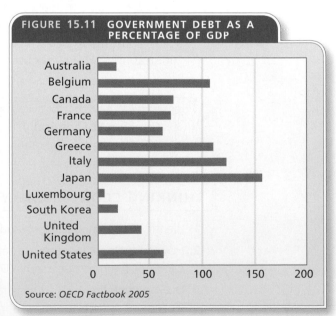

FIGURE 15.11 GOVERNMENT DEBT AS A
PERCENTAGE OF GDP

Source: *OECD Factbook 2005*

CRITICAL THINKING

9. Analyzing Cause and Effect In early 2001, the federal budget had shown surpluses for the previous three fiscal years and was predicted to continue to do so. The President and Congress thought the best thing to do was to return some of the surplus to taxpayers through tax cuts. How would supply-side economics describe the expected outcome of these tax cuts?

10. Applying Economic Concepts Suppose that you got a better job that increased your take-home pay each week from $250 to $300. Assume that you spent 80 percent of that increase. Give specific examples to show how your spending would create a multiplier effect.

11. Drawing Conclusions Recessions in 1990–1991 and in 2001 lasted about eight months each and were relatively mild in their effects on the overall economy. Why would policy lags limit the effectiveness of discretionary fiscal policy in bringing the country out of such recessions?

12. Making Inferences Between 1998 and 2001, the annual federal budgets showed surpluses, and the amount of national debt held by the public decreased by about $450 billion, yet the total federal debt grew by about $400 billion during that same time period. What do you think accounts for this difference?

13. Challenge In 1997, some members of Congress proposed a constitutional amendment that would require the federal budget to be balanced each year. Opponents argued that such an amendment would make recessions worse by requiring the government to use contractionary fiscal policy during such times. Why would a balanced budget require that kind of fiscal policy?

SIMULATION

Advise the President

Step 1 Form a team with two other students. Imagine that you are the Council of Economic Advisers whose job is to advise the president on the best fiscal policy to use in different economic situations. The current state of the economy is indicated by the following facts:

a. The unemployment rate has risen from 4.5 percent to 6 percent.

b. Automobile dealers, home improvement stores, and computer retailers have noted that their sales have dropped off sharply from the previous year.

c. Fewer houses and commercial buildings are being built.

Decide whether an expansionary or contractionary fiscal policy is needed.

Step 2 Develop some specific government spending and taxation recommendations to follow through with your decision in Step 1. Think about what kinds of federal spending you would increase or decrease and what kinds of taxes you would cut or increase to achieve your objectives.

Step 3 Some economic indicators have improved. However, the unemployment rate has not changed, and high energy costs have led to rapid increases in the Consumer Price Index. In light of this new information, recommend changes in fiscal policy to solve these problems.

Step 4 The economy seems to be back on track. However, annual budget deficits are getting larger each year, and there is concern about the growing national debt. Recommend some ways to control deficit spending without harming the economy.

Step 5 Present your policy suggestions to the rest of the class. As a class, discuss the differences and similarities among the plans offered by various groups.

The Money Supply
Paper currency—an important part of the money supply—is distributed by the Federal Reserve.

The Federal Reserve and Monetary Policy

CONCEPT REVIEW

Fiscal policy is the federal government's use of taxes and government spending to affect the economy. It has one of two goals: to decrease unemployment or to fight inflation.

CHAPTER 16 KEY CONCEPT

Monetary policy includes all the Federal Reserve actions that change the money supply in order to influence the economy. Its purpose is to curb inflation or to reduce economic stagnation or recession.

WHY THE CONCEPT MATTERS

All economies experience the business cycle, a series of periods of growing and shrinking economic activity. Sometimes, these ups and downs become extreme, and the government takes action to even out the business cycle. The government has many tools available to do this—monetary policy is one of the most important.

Online Highlights

More at ClassZone.com

 Economics Update

Go to **ECONOMICS UPDATE** for chapter updates and current news on monetary policy. (See Case Study, pp. 504–505).

Animated Economics

Go to **ANIMATED ECONOMICS** for interactive lessons on the graphs and tables in this chapter. ▶

Interactive ◀▶ Review

Go to **INTERACTIVE REVIEW** for concept review and activities.

FIGURES 16.10 AND 16.11 SHORT-TERM EFFECTS OF MONETARY POLICY

FIGURE 16.10 MONETARY EXPANSION

FIGURE 16.11 MONETARY CONTRACTION

How do interest rates affect the demand for money? See Figures 16.10 and 16.11 on page 495.

The Federal Reserve System

OBJECTIVES	KEY TERMS	TAKING NOTES
In Section 1, you will • examine the purpose and duties of a central bank • identify the distinctive features of the Federal Reserve System • explain the structure of the Federal Reserve System	central bank, *p. 474* monetary, *p. 474* Federal Reserve System, *p. 474* currency, *p. 475* Board of Governors, *p. 476* Federal Open Market Committee, *p. 477* thrift institution, *p. 478*	As you read Section 1, complete a cluster diagram to identify the major characteristics of the Federal Reserve System. Use the Graphic Organizer at **Interactive Review @ ClassZone.com**

Creating the Fed

KEY CONCEPTS

As you recall from Chapter 10, there were times when the U.S. economy suffered from panics and banking was very unstable. The government made many efforts to address this problem, but had only limited success. Perhaps the most far-reaching of these efforts to stabilize the American financial system was the passage of the Federal Reserve Act in 1913. This act created a central bank for the United States. A **central bank** is a nation's main monetary authority, which is able to conduct certain monetary practices. (**Monetary** means "relating to money.") The **Federal Reserve System** is the central bank of the United States and is commonly called the Fed. The Fed is an independent organization within the government, which has both public and private characteristics.

The Duties of a Central Bank

Most countries have a central bank to oversee their banking system. The central bank may be owned and controlled by the government or it may have considerable political independence. There are three common duties that all central banks perform: holding reserves, assuring stability of the banking and monetary systems, and lending money to banks and the government.

Holding Reserves Central banks are sometimes called reserve banks. You learned in Chapter 10 that banks lend only a part of their funds to individuals and businesses and keep the rest in reserve. The central bank holds these reserves to influence the amount of loanable funds banks have available. This allows the central bank to control the money supply.

Assuring Stability The central bank also acts to assure stability in the national banking and monetary systems. For example, it is one of the banking regulatory agencies that regulate and supervise banks to make sure that they act in ways that serve the interests of depositors and of the economy. Also, by controlling the way money is issued and circulated, the central bank attempts to avoid the confusion that might result when individual banks issue their own bank notes.

Lending Money The final duty of the central bank involves one of the primary functions of all banks—it lends money. Its lending practices are unlike those other banks, however. It does not seek to make a profit through lending, and it serves private banks and the government rather than individual customers and businesses.

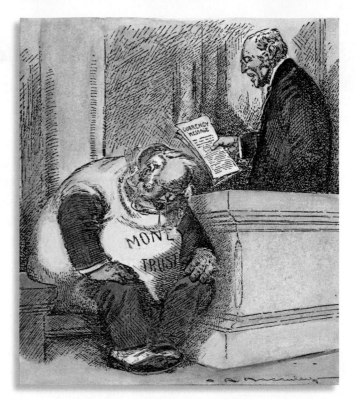

Creating the Fed
President Woodrow Wilson proposed the Federal Reserve Act, in part, to break the power of the nation's biggest banks.

The Duties of the Fed

With the passage of the Federal Reserve Act of 1913, Congress created the first national bank in the United States that could truly fulfill the duties of a central bank. The Fed supervises banking in the United States by providing regulation and oversight to make sure that banks follow sound practices in their operations. The Fed also takes steps to ensure that banks do not defraud customers and works to protect consumers' rights as they relate to borrowing money.

Like all central banks, the Fed provides banking services for both private banks and the national government. It accepts and holds deposits in the form of cash reserves, transfers funds between banks or between banks and the government, and makes loans to these institutions. Because it performs such functions, the Fed is sometimes referred to as the bankers' bank.

This responsibility of the Fed is especially important in times of emergency. Shortly after the Fed was created, it played a major role in financing U.S. involvement in World War I by purchasing government war bonds. The Fed also took emergency action after the terrorist attacks on New York City and Washington, D.C. in 2001. It issued $45 billion in loans to banks throughout the United States in order to ensure that there would be as little disruption to the banking system as possible in light of the destruction in these cities.

The Fed also distributes **currency**, which is coins and paper money, and regulates the supply of money. The supply of money does not mean actual cash but all available sources of money. Specifically, the amount of money that banks have available to lend has important effects on the whole economy. You will learn more about these functions of the Fed in Section 2.

Economics Update

Find an update on the duties of the Fed at **ClassZone.com**

QUICK REFERENCE

Currency is coins and paper money.

APPLICATION Comparing and Contrasting

A. Recall what you learned about the structure and functions of commercial banks in Chapter 10. What are the similarities and differences between the Federal Reserve and a commercial bank?

The Structure of the Fed

The Fed is different from most countries' central banks because it is not a single national bank but has both a national and a regional structure. This structure represents a compromise between power resting at the regional level and at the national level. As you may recall from Chapter 10, many U.S. citizens were hesitant to give too much power to a national bank. In addition, the United States is a large and economically diverse country with a complex banking system.

Elements of the Fed

The elements that make up the Fed reflect this balance between national and regional authority. An appointed board sets national Fed policy, and a regional system of district banks carries out this policy and performs the duties of the central bank. This approach gives the Fed some independence from political influence. Even so, the Fed is ultimately accountable to Congress. Figure 16.1 shows how the Fed is organized.

Board of Governors The **Board of Governors** is a board of seven appointed members who supervise the operations of the Fed and set policy. The president appoints members for a single 14-year term, with the approval of the Senate. One board member's term expires every two years, and the president may also appoint replacements to fill vacancies created by members who leave before the end of their terms. The president chooses the chairman and vice-chairman, who serve four-year terms, from among

QUICK REFERENCE

The **Board of Governors** supervises the operations of the Fed.

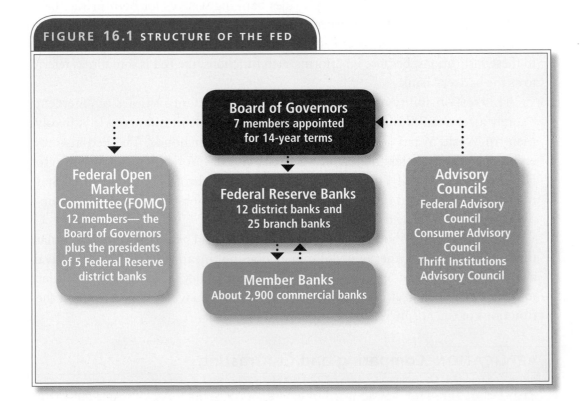

FIGURE **16.1** STRUCTURE OF THE FED

Board of Governors
7 members appointed
for 14-year terms

Federal Open Market Committee (FOMC)
12 members— the Board of Governors plus the presidents of 5 Federal Reserve district banks

Federal Reserve Banks
12 district banks and 25 branch banks

Advisory Councils
Federal Advisory Council
Consumer Advisory Council
Thrift Institutions Advisory Council

Member Banks
About 2,900 commercial banks

the seven members. The chairman is considered the most influential member and is the spokesperson for the board. Alan Greenspan, who held the position for nearly 20 years, was so influential as Fed chairman that he almost came to personify the institution. (You can read more about Alan Greenspan on page 494.)

Twelve District Banks The Federal Reserve System is organized into 12 districts. Figure 16.2 shows these districts and the cities where the Federal Reserve district banks and the offices of the Board of Governors are located. While the district banks are responsible for carrying out the national policy set forth by the Board of Governors, each one also serves the needs of its particular region.

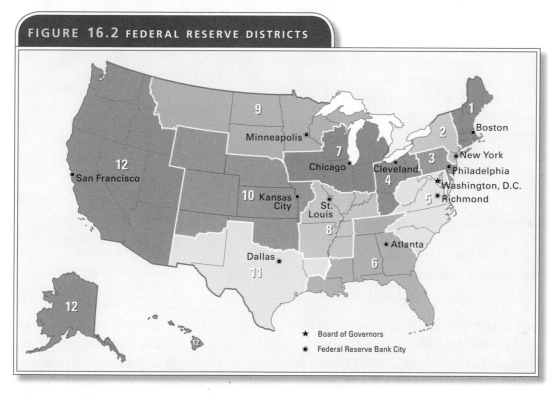

FIGURE 16.2 FEDERAL RESERVE DISTRICTS

★ Board of Governors
◉ Federal Reserve Bank City

Member Banks All nationally chartered banks automatically are members of the Federal Reserve System. State-chartered banks, if they wish, may apply to join the Fed. In 2004, there were about 2,000 national bank members and 900 state bank members, about 37 percent of all commercial banks.

Each member bank must purchase stock in its Federal Reserve district bank. However, this stock ownership is not the same as ownership of stock in a private corporation or a commercial bank. It may not be bought or sold on the open market. Member banks earn a set dividend rate on the stock they hold. This helps to make up for the interest they do not earn on the reserves that the Fed requires them to hold. (See the information on reserve requirements on page 484.)

Federal Open Market Committee The **Federal Open Market Committee (FOMC)** is a board of the Fed that supervises the sale and purchase of federal government securities. The term *open market* refers to the way that government securities are bought and sold. The FOMC consists of 12 voting members, including the Board of Governors, the president of the Federal Reserve Bank of New York, and four other Fed district bank presidents who take turns serving one-year terms. All Fed bank presidents attend the meetings and provide input even when they have no vote.

QUICK REFERENCE

The **Federal Open Market Committee (FOMC)** supervises the sales and purchase of government securities.

Comparing Central Banks

Chinese bank note

Today, more than 160 nations have central banks. These banks function as the main monetary authority for their respective nations. They also serve the same purpose—maintaining economic stability. Further, they use similar tools to fulfill this purpose. Even so, these central banks do have several differences. One difference is historical. The Federal Reserve, for example, was established by an act of Congress in 1913. The Bank of England, Great Britain's central bank, claims a royal pedigree, having been established in 1694 during the reign of William and Mary. In China, the People's Bank of China (PBC) began as a commercial bank in 1948. It functioned as a central bank and a commercial bank until 1983, when it was reorganized solely as a central bank.

British bank note

Another difference lies in the production of money. The central banks of Great Britain and China both produce and distribute currency. In the United States, the Treasury produces currency and the Federal Reserve distributes it.

CONNECTING ACROSS THE GLOBE

1. Why do you think central banks are common to countries that have very different forms of government, such as the United States and China?

2. In terms of money production, how does the Bank of England differ from the Federal Reserve?

The sale and purchases of federal government bonds on the open market are the principal tools used by the Fed to promote a stable, growing economy. At the end of each of its meetings, the FOMC issues a public statement to explain its assessment of the economy and its latest actions. You will learn more about the functions of the FOMC in Section 3.

Advisory Councils Three committees provide advice directly to the Board of Governors. The 12 members of the Federal Advisory Council, one from each Fed district, represent the commercial banking industry. The Consumer Advisory Council advises the board on matters concerning the Fed's responsibilities in enforcing consumer protection laws related to borrowing. Its 30 members, for the most part, are drawn from consumer groups and the financial services industry.

The Federal Reserve Board created the Thrift Institutions Advisory Council in 1980 to provide advice about the needs of this important segment of the financial services industry. **Thrift institutions** are savings and loan institutions, savings banks, or other institutions that serve savers. While the Fed does not regulate thrift institutions, the thrifts must conform to the Fed's reserve requirements and may borrow from the Fed.

QUICK REFERENCE

A **thrift institution** is a financial institution that serves savers.

APPLICATION Making Inferences

B. How does the 14-year term of members of the Board of Governors help make the Fed an independent government agency?

Online Quiz
ClassZone.com

REVIEWING KEY CONCEPTS

1. Explain the relationship between the terms in each of these pairs.

   a. *central bank*
   Federal Reserve System

   c. *Board of Governors*
   Federal Open Market Committee

   b. *monetary*
   currency

2. What are the three duties of a central bank?

3. How is the Fed different from other central banks?

4. How does the composition of the Federal Open Market Committee reflect the blend of national and regional power in the Fed?

5. What do all thrift institutions have in common?

6. **Using Your Notes** What are the five elements of the Fed? Refer to your completed cluster diagram.

   Use the Graphic Organizer at **Interactive Review @ ClassZone.com**

   > Federal Reserve System

CRITICAL THINKING

7. **Analyzing Causes and Effects** If all members of the Board of Governors served 14-year terms, no president would appoint more than four members during two terms in office. However, many board members do not serve full terms, and vacancies occur on average more than once every two years. How does this situation affect a president's influence on the Board?

8. **Drawing Conclusions** The four rotating members on the Federal Open Market Committee are chosen from these groups:
   • Boston, Philadelphia, and Richmond
   • Cleveland and Chicago
   • Atlanta, St. Louis, and Dallas
   • Minneapolis, Kansas City, and San Francisco
   Why does the Fed mandate that one of the rotating members must come from each of these four groups?

9. **Challenge** The Federal Reserve Act of 1913 created the Federal Advisory Council. The Consumer Advisory Council was not created until 1976. How does this difference reflect changes in the duties of the Fed?

ECONOMICS IN PRACTICE

Analyzing Information

Refer to Figure 16.2 on page 477 to answer the following questions about the creation and present alignment of the Fed.

Analyze Maps Complete the chart below by indicating your answer to each question in the space provided.

Question	Response
Which region of the country has the most Fed district banks?	
How does the size of Fed districts 1–5 compare with districts 9–12?	
Where is the Board of Governors located?	
In which Fed district is your community located?	
How do the Federal Reserve Districts reflect U.S. geographic and economic diversity?	

Challenge How might the Federal Reserve districts be different if they were created today?

Functions of the Federal Reserve

OBJECTIVES	KEY TERMS	TAKING NOTES
In Section 2, you will • identify the services the Fed provides for the banking system • explain how the Fed acts as a banker for the federal government • describe the creation of money • discuss what factors influence the money supply	check clearing, *p. 480* bank holding company, *p. 481* bank exams, *p. 481* required reserve ratio, *p. 484* deposit multiplier formula, *p. 485*	As you read Section 2, complete a chart to identify the major functions of the Federal Reserve. Use the Graphic Organizer at **Interactive Review @ ClassZone.com** **Functions of the Federal Reserve** <table><tr><td>Serving the banking system</td><td>Serving the federal government</td><td>Creating money</td></tr><tr><td></td><td></td><td></td></tr></table>

Serving the Banking System

KEY CONCEPTS

As the banker's bank, the Fed has the responsibility of helping banks do their jobs. The Fed serves the banking system in a variety of ways, including providing check clearing and other services that facilitate the transfer of funds, lending money, and regulating and supervising banking activity.

QUICK REFERENCE

Check clearing is a service offered by the Fed to record receipts and expenditures of bank clients.

SERVICE 1 Check Clearing

One of the services that the Fed offers to banks is **check clearing**, a process in which banks record the receipts and expenditures of their clients. Each Fed district processes millions of checks every day, but most checks clear in two days or less. Figure 16.3 on the next page shows how a check is cleared by following its path from the time it is written until the money is taken from the check writer's account. Electronic-payment methods, such as credit and debit cards, have begun to replace checks. Further, more private companies are involved in the check-clearing process. As a result, check clearing has become a less important function of the Fed.

SERVICE 2 Lending Money

Banks often loan each other money on a short-term basis. Sometimes all the banks in a region are faced with short-term cash flow issues, usually during natural disasters. At such times, the Fed will provide

FIGURE 16.3 The Federal Reserve and Check Clearing

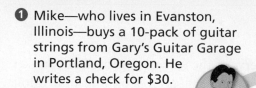

① Mike—who lives in Evanston, Illinois—buys a 10-pack of guitar strings from Gary's Guitar Garage in Portland, Oregon. He writes a check for $30.

② Gary, the store owner, deposits the check at his bank.

③ Gary's bank credits his account with $30 and then sends Mike's check to the Federal Reserve Bank of San Francisco—the Fed district bank that serves Portland.

④ The Federal Reserve Bank of San Francisco credits $30 to Gary's bank's reserve account and then sends Mike's check to the Federal Reserve Bank of Chicago—the Fed district bank that serves Evanston.

⑤ The Federal Reserve Bank of Chicago transfers $30 from its reserves to the San Francisco Fed district bank and then sends Mike's check to his bank in Evanston.

⑥ Mike's bank transfers $30 from its reserve to the Federal Reserve Bank of Chicago and deducts $30 from Mike's account. This transaction is reflected on Mike's next bank statement.

ANALYZE CHARTS

This diagram illustrates the steps in the check-clearing process for a typical check transaction. Note how many banks handle Mike's check during the process. What is the importance of the Fed's role in clearing Mike's check?

loans to banks and may charge reduced interest rates. Banks must have sufficient assets and capital to qualify for Fed loans. In addition, smaller banks that have seasonal cash flow needs due to the nature of their local economy may borrow from the Fed. The Fed also acts as the lender of last resort to prevent a banking crisis.

SERVICE 3 Regulating and Supervising Banks

Each Federal Reserve Bank supervises the practices of state-chartered member banks and bank holding companies in its district. A **bank holding company** is a company that owns, or has a controlling interest in, more than one bank. This supervision includes **bank exams**, which are audits of the bank's financial practices. These exams make sure that banks are not engaged in risky or fraudulent practices, especially in lending. The Fed monitors bank mergers to ensure that competition is maintained and enforces truth-in-lending laws to protect consumers in such areas as home mortgages, auto loans, and retail credit.

QUICK REFERENCE

A **bank holding company** owns, or has a controlling interest in, more than one bank.

A **bank exam** is an audit of the bank's financial practices.

APPLICATION Making Inferences

A. Why might the Fed help a small bank in an agricultural region stabilize its cash flow?

Serving the Federal Government

A second function of the Fed is to serve as the federal government's banker. As you learned in Chapter 14, the federal government receives billions of tax dollars each year and uses this money on a variety of programs through direct spending and transfer payments. In its role as the federal government's banker, the Fed also fulfills certain fiscal responsibilities by helping the government to carry out its taxation and spending activities.

SERVICE 1 Paying Government Bills

When the IRS collects tax revenues, the funds are deposited with the Fed. The Fed then issues checks or makes electronic payments, via the U.S. Treasury, for such programs as Social Security, Medicare, and IRS tax refunds. When these funds are deposited in the recipient's bank account or the check is cashed, the Fed deducts that amount from the government's account.

Including military personnel, the federal government employs about 4.6 million people, and their wages and benefits are processed through the Fed. Direct government spending also comes from accounts at the Fed. Whether the government is buying office supplies or military equipment or paying contractors to maintain federal highways, the money is funneled through the Fed. The Fed also processes food stamps, which are issued by the Department of Agriculture, and postal money orders, which are issued by the U.S. Postal Service. The Fed, therefore, facilitates government payments in a way that is similar to the way it clears checks and processes electronic payments in the private sector.

Economics Update

Find an update on the Fed's role in the sale of government securities at **ClassZone.com**

SERVICE 2 Selling Government Securities

As you learned in Chapter 15, the federal government has different kinds of securities that it sells when it wants to borrow money. (Remember that securities are another name for bonds and stocks.) The Fed processes U.S. savings bonds and auctions other kinds of securities for the U.S. Treasury to provide funds for various government activities.

The Fed has many roles in this process. It provides information about the securities to potential buyers, receives orders from customers, collects payments from buyers, credits the funds to the Treasury's account, and delivers the bonds to their owners. It also pays the interest on these bonds on a regular basis or at maturity. Many of these transactions are now handled electronically. Even when individuals purchase government securities on the Treasury Department's Web site, the Fed transfers funds between the purchaser and the Treasury and pays the interest when it is due. The Fed does not charge fees for these services.

In addition to selling government securities to raise money to fund government activities, the Federal Open Market Committee supervises the sales and purchases of government securities as a way to stabilize the economy. You'll learn more about this aspect of the Fed's work in Section 3.

SERVICE 3 Distributing Currency

One of the important functions of a central bank is to issue a standard currency that is used throughout the economy. In the United States, Federal Reserve notes are the official paper currency. These notes are fiat money backed by the confidence of the federal government and managed by the Federal Reserve. The government's backing is made plain by the statement on each note: "This note is legal tender for all debts, public and private." Figure 16.4 highlights several important features of Federal Reserve notes.

The Department of the Treasury's Bureau of Engraving and Printing prints Federal Reserve notes, which are distributed by the Fed to its district banks. The notes are then moved on to depository institutions and finally into the hands of individuals and businesses. The Fed makes sure that bills are distributed to banks in the amounts that they need. Paper money has a life span of between two and five years. Smaller denomination bills tend to have a shorter life span. Larger denomination bills stay in circulation longer. When bills get worn out, they are taken out of circulation, destroyed, and replaced with new ones. In a similar way, the Fed distributes coins that are produced by the U.S. Mint.

FIGURE 16.4 A FEDERAL RESERVE NOTE

a Federal Reserve Notes are the official U.S. paper **currency**.

b Code indicates to which Federal Reserve Bank the Treasury issued the note. For example, B2 is New York, E5 is Richmond, and K11 is Dallas.

c Each note has a unique serial number. The second letter identifies the Fed district to which the note was issued.

d The Federal Reserve seal is on the left, the Treasury Department seal on the right.

e The signature of the Treasurer is on the left, the signature of the Secretary of the Treasury on the right.

f In 1955, Congress required that the phrase "In God We Trust" be used on all currency and coins.

ANALYZE
1. To which Federal Reserve Bank was this bill issued?
2. How might serial numbers help the authorities detect counterfeit bills?

APPLICATION Comparing Economic Information

B. How are the banking services the Fed provides to the government similar to the services it provides to banks?

Creating Money

Creating money does not mean printing paper currency and minting coins. It refers to the way money gets into circulation through deposits and loans at banks. (You learned briefly about this process in Chapter 10.) Because the United States has a fractional reserve banking system, banks are not allowed to loan out all the money they have in deposits. The Fed establishes a **required reserve ratio (RRR)**, which is the fraction of the bank's deposits that must be kept in reserve by the bank, to control the amount a bank can loan. Money on deposit in excess of the required reserve amount can be loaned out. The money in reserve may be stored as cash in the bank's vault or deposited with the Fed.

EXAMPLE Money Creation

The banking system creates money whenever banks receive deposits and make loans. The level of the RRR determines how much money may be loaned and, therefore, how much money gets created. Let's see how this works by studying Figure 16.5. At the top of the chart, the RRR is set at 20 percent. If Bank A has $10,000 in deposits, it must keep 20 percent, or $2,000, on reserve. It lends the remaining $8,000 to Kecia's Fitness Studio, which Kecia deposits in Bank B. Bank B keeps 20 percent of the $8,000, or $1,600, on reserve as required. Bank B lends the remaining $6,400 to Juan's Computer Repair, and Juan deposits it in Bank C. At this point, the money supply has increased by $14,400, the total of the loans made. The process could continue until there was nothing left to lend.

FIGURE 16.5 The Fed Creates Money

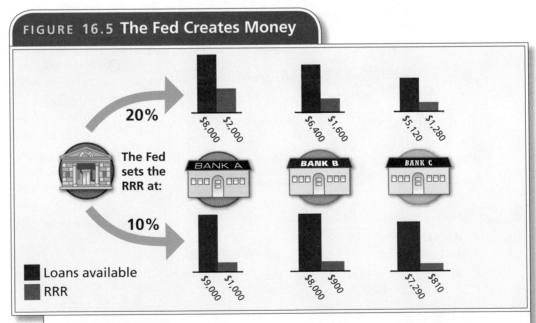

ANALYZE CHARTS
Remember that the amount of money that each bank can loan is limited by the RRR. Suppose that Bank C loaned its available funds to Miles and Miles deposited the money in Bank D. How much money would Bank D have to hold in reserve and how much would it have available for loans if the RRR is set at 20 percent? What would these figures be if the RRR were set at 10 percent?

Now look at what happens if the Fed reduces the RRR to 10 percent. The change is shown at the bottom of Figure 16.5. Bank A can now lend $9,000 to Kecia and Bank B can lend $8,100 to Juan. In this scenario, the money supply would increase by $17,100. The decrease in the RRR allowed the money supply to increase by an additional $2,700.

How do you figure out how much the money supply will increase after all possible loans have been made? The **deposit multiplier formula** is a mathematical formula that tells how much the money supply will increase after an initial cash deposit in a bank. The formula is 1/RRR. For example, if the RRR is 10 percent the deposit multiplier equals 10. Figure 16.6 illustrates how the deposit multiplier formula is used to determine the amount of increase in the money supply from an initial deposit of $100 and a reserve requirement of 10 percent.

QUICK REFERENCE

Deposit multiplier formula tells how much the money supply will increase after an initial cash deposit.

MATH CHALLENGE

FIGURE 16.6 Deposit Expansion Multiplier

Step 1: Study the table below, which shows how an initial deposit of $100 can increase the money supply. To quantify the total amount of money that can be created from this initial deposit, economists use the deposit expansion multiplier.

	Money deposited	=	10% held as reserves	+	90% loaned out
Bank A	$100.00	=	$10.00	+	$90.00
Bank B	$90.00	=	$ 9.00	+	$81.00
Bank C	$81.00	=	$ 8.10	+	$72.90
Bank D	$72.90	=	$ 7.29	+	$65.61
---	---		---		---
Total			$100.00		$900.00

Step 2: Calculate the deposit expansion multiplier.

Sample Calculations

$$\frac{1}{\text{Required reserve ratio}} = \text{Deposit expansion multiplier}$$

$$\frac{1}{10\%} = \frac{1}{0.10} = 10$$

Step 3: Use the deposit expansion multiplier to calculate the total money that can be loaned.

$$\text{Initial deposit} \times \left[\text{Deposit expansion multiplier} - 1 \right] = \text{Total available for loans}$$

$$\$100 \times [10-1] = \$100 \times 9 = \$900$$

APPLICATION Analyzing Effects

C. If the Fed raised the RRR from 10 percent to 12 percent, how would it affect the money supply and by approximately how much, if the initial deposit was $5,000? Show your calculations.

Factors Affecting Demand for Money

KEY CONCEPTS

The Fed monitors two major indicators of the money supply, namely M1 and M2. Recall that you learned in Chapter 10 that M1 includes cash and checkable deposits, while M2 includes M1 plus savings deposits and certain time deposits. The Fed needs to know how large each type of money is in order to act appropriately to manage the supply of money. Four factors influence how much money individuals and businesses need—cash on hand, interest rates, the cost of consumer goods and services, and the level of income.

FACTOR 1 Cash on Hand

Individuals and businesses need cash to complete certain financial transactions. Recall that M1, which includes cash and checkable deposits, is also called transactions money. Consumers use this money to pay for things such as food, clothing, transportation costs such as gasoline and bus or train fares, and entertainment. Businesses also use cash and checks for many day-to-day expenses. The fastest growing form of payment is the debit card, which was used for more than 23 billion transactions in 2005. While a debit card is not money, it is linked to a checking account, and the funds in the account are considered money.

The Fed understands that there are certain times when people need more cash. It routinely increases the amount of cash at banks during the holiday season because people want more money to buy gifts. Similarly, during the summer months the Fed ensures that banks in areas popular with tourists have more cash. Natural disasters also influence the amount of cash the Fed puts into circulation. In response to Hurricane Katrina's devastation of the Gulf Coast in 2005, the Fed shipped large amounts of currency to banks in several nearby districts because of the immediate demand for more cash by residents. Since many parts of the Gulf Coast were without electricity, people were not able to use debit cards and credit cards as they ordinarily would.

Cash on Hand Portable ATMs dispensed much-needed cash to evacuees from the Gulf Coast after Hurricane Katrina.

FACTOR 2 Interest Rates

When interest rates are high, individuals and businesses may place excess cash in savings instruments, such as bonds, stocks, or savings accounts. This of course pulls cash out of circulation. The money then exists as a part of M2. Figure 16.7 shows how the demand for money is affected by interest rates. When interest rates are high, the demand for money is lower because there is less incentive for individuals and businesses to spend and more incentive to save and earn interest. When interest rates are lower, however, more money is demanded because people have less incentive to save and more incentive to spend.

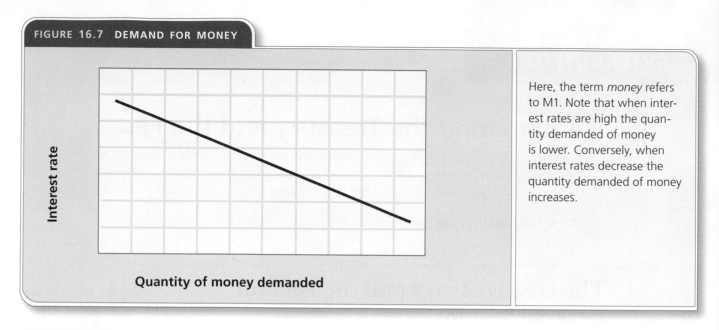

FIGURE 16.7 DEMAND FOR MONEY

Interest rate

Quantity of money demanded

Here, the term *money* refers to M1. Note that when interest rates are high the quantity demanded of money is lower. Conversely, when interest rates decrease the quantity demanded of money increases.

FACTOR 3 Cost of Consumer Goods and Services

As the cost of consumer goods or services increases, buyers may wish to have more money available. Suppose that adverse weather conditions and higher energy prices have driven up the prices of fresh fruits and vegetables. People may need to have more cash when they buy groceries at the supermarket than they did before the prices increased. They might also find that it takes more cash to buy gasoline than it used to.

Businesses face the same challenges. They would also wish to have more cash to purchase the goods and services they need for their operations. Of course, when businesses pay more for goods and services, production costs increase and the higher costs are often passed on to consumers. This, in turn, may lead consumers to want to have more money available.

FACTOR 4 Level of Income

As income increases, individuals and companies have a tendency to hold more cash. Recall that level of income is one of the factors that affect demand. Suppose that Bob has a part-time job cooking at a restaurant. When he gets a raise, he notices that he keeps more money in his wallet because he feels he can afford to spend more on clothes and DVDs. The same holds true for businesses. When their income increases, they will keep more cash because they are able to spend more on the goods and services that they need to pay for operations. In general, when income levels rise, so will the demand for money.

The Fed can take several actions to change the money supply in response to changes in demand for money. More important, the Fed can use these methods of increasing or decreasing the money supply to stabilize the economy. In the next section, you'll learn about the nature of these methods and how they are used to establish economy stability.

APPLICATION Analyzing Effects

D. Which factor is likely to increase the size of M2? Why?

Comparing the Treasury and the Fed

The following passage provides information about the U.S. Treasury and the Federal Reserve System. Compare the two by looking for similarities and differences between them. This will help you understand the role that each plays in the nation's economy.

TIPS FOR COMPARING Use the following tips to help you compare economic information.

The U.S. Treasury and the Federal Reserve System

Although the U.S. Treasury and the Federal Reserve are both essential to the functioning of the nation's economy, they differ in many ways. The U.S. Treasury Department was established by an act of Congress in 1789. It is the primary federal agency responsible for the economic prosperity of the United States. As such, it is responsible for managing federal finances, including the collection of taxes, duties, and other monies due to the United States; the paying of the nation's bills; and the management of government accounts and the public debt. In addition, the Treasury Department produces stamps, currency, and coinage.

The Federal Reserve System similarly was established by an act of Congress but much later, in 1913. Unlike the U.S. Treasury, which is a department of the federal government, the Fed is the nation's central bank. According to its mission statement, the purpose of the Federal Reserve is "to provide the nation with a safer, more flexible, and more stable monetary and financial system."

The duties of the Federal Reserve fall into four general areas: conducting the nation's monetary policy in pursuit of maximum employment and economic stability; supervising and regulating the nation's banking institutions; maintaining the stability of the financial system; and providing financial services such as check clearing and short-term loans to member banks. The Fed consists of a board of governors and 12 regional banks, a structure that varies considerably from that of the Treasury.

> **Look** for words that signal similarities, such as *both*, *similarly*, and *also*.

> **Look** for words that signal differences, or contrasts, such as *unlike*, *differ*, and *varies*.

THINKING ECONOMICALLY Analyzing

1. In what ways are the Treasury and the Fed similar?
2. What are some important differences between the Fed and the Treasury?
3. Which do you think is more policy oriented, the Fed or the Treasury? Explain why you think so.

Online Quiz
ClassZone.com

REVIEWING KEY CONCEPTS

1. Use each of the three terms below in a sentence that illustrates the meaning of the term.

   a. *check clearing*   **b.** *bank holding company*   **c.** *required reserve ratio*

2. Why are bank exams an important way for the Fed to help create a sound banking system?

3. What is the relationship between the required reserve ratio and the deposit multiplier formula?

4. How does the Fed's check-clearing service help the banking system?

5. How does the deposit multiplier formula allow the Fed to create money through the banking system?

6. **Using Your Notes** What are the three services that the Fed provides to the federal government? Refer to your completed chart.

   Use the Graphic Organizer at **Interactive Review @ ClassZone.com**

Functions of the Federal Reserve		
Serving the banking system	Serving the federal government	Creating money

CRITICAL THINKING

7. **Applying Economic Concepts** Daniel is a high school senior living in California. He receives a check from his grandmother in Florida as a graduation gift. How is the Federal Reserve involved in transferring the money from Daniel's grandmother's bank account to his account? Illustrate your answer with a flow chart.

8. **Applying Economic Concepts** You've been planning your college finances and you know that you'll have to take a bank loan to cover tuition costs. You read that the Fed intends to raise the RRR from 10 percent to 20 percent. How will this change affect the money supply and your ability to borrow money for college tuition?

9. **Analyzing Data** The Fed sets the required reserve ratio at 10 percent. What is the initial deposit if the money supply increases by $40,000? Use the deposit multiplier formula to determine your answer and show your calculations.

10. **Challenge** Banks do not earn interest on the funds they hold as reserves. How does this provide an incentive to banks to create money by making loans rather than to deposit excess funds in a Fed bank?

ECONOMICS IN PRACTICE

Buying school supplies

Evaluating Demand for Money
Consider the factors that affect the demand for money and then complete the following activities.

Identify Changes in Demand The chart below shows some scenarios that would cause demand for money to change. For each example, note if demand is increasing or decreasing.

Factor Affecting Demand for Money	Increasing or Decreasing?
Back-to-school shopping begins	
Banks lower the interest rate on CDs from 6% to 3%	
Energy costs for home heating are up by 20%	
Interest rates on savings deposits increase from 1% to 4.5%	

Challenge What type of potential economic instability is suggested by rising prices? How might the Fed adjust the money supply in such a situation? You will learn more about this topic in Section 3.

Monetary Policy

OBJECTIVES

In Section 3, you will
- examine the Fed's tools for monetary policy
- explain how the Fed's monetary policy promotes growth and stability
- analyze the challenges the Fed faces in implementing its policy

OBJECTIVES

In Section 3, you will
- examine the Fed's tools for monetary policy
- explain how the Fed's monetary policy promotes growth and stability
- analyze the challenges the Fed faces in implementing its policy

KEY TERMS

monetary policy, *p. 490*
open market operations, *p. 490*
federal funds rate, *p. 490*
discount rate, *p. 491*
prime rate, *p. 491*
expansionary monetary policy, *p. 492*
contractionary monetary policy, *p. 492*
easy-money policy, *p. 492*
tight-money policy, *p. 493*
monetarism, *p. 496*

TAKING NOTES

As you read Section 3, complete a hierarchy diagram to track main ideas and supporting details about monetary policy. Use the Graphic Organizer at **Interactive Review @ ClassZone.com**

The Fed's Monetary Tools

KEY CONCEPTS

QUICK REFERENCE

Monetary policy includes the Fed's actions that change the money supply in order to influence the economy.

Open market operations are the sales and purchase of federal government securities.

The **federal funds rate (FFR)** is the interest rate that banks charge one another to borrow money.

Monetary policy involves Federal Reserve actions that change the money supply in order to influence the economy. There are three actions the Fed can take to manage the supply of money: open market operations, adjusting the reserve requirement, and adjusting the discount rate. They may be taken individually or in combination with one another. The impact of these actions is shown in Figure 16.8.

ACTION 1 Open Market Operations

Open market operations are the sales and purchase of marketable federal government securities. This is the monetary policy tool most used by the Fed to adjust the money supply. When the Fed wants to expand the money supply, it buys government securities. The Fed pays for the bonds it buys from commercial banks or the public by writing checks on itself. When sellers receive the funds from the Fed, they deposit them in banks. The banks can then lend their new excess reserves. When the Fed wants to contract the money supply, it sells government bonds on the open market. The purchasers of the bonds transfer funds to the Fed to pay for the bonds. These funds are taken out of circulation, and the reserves available for loans decrease.

The Fed communicates its intention to buy or sell bonds by announcing a target for the federal funds rate. The **federal funds rate (FFR)** is the interest rate at which a depository institution lends immediately available funds (balances at the Federal Reserve) to another depository institution overnight. When the Fed lowers the target for the FFR, it buys bonds. When it raises the target, it sells bonds. The Fed does not set the rate directly but influences it through its actions.

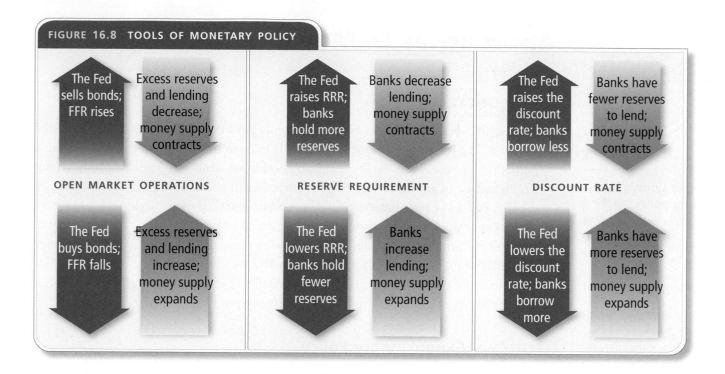

FIGURE 16.8 TOOLS OF MONETARY POLICY

OPEN MARKET OPERATIONS

The Fed sells bonds; FFR rises → Excess reserves and lending decrease; money supply contracts

The Fed buys bonds; FFR falls → Excess reserves and lending increase; money supply expands

RESERVE REQUIREMENT

The Fed raises RRR; banks hold more reserves → Banks decrease lending; money supply contracts

The Fed lowers RRR; banks hold fewer reserves → Banks increase lending; money supply expands

DISCOUNT RATE

The Fed raises the discount rate; banks borrow less → Banks have fewer reserves to lend; money supply contracts

The Fed lowers the discount rate; banks borrow more → Banks have more reserves to lend; money supply expands

ACTION 2 Adjusting the Reserve Requirement

As you recall from Section 2, the Fed sets the required reserve ratio (RRR) for all depository institutions. The RRR affects the money supply through the deposit multiplier formula. Increasing the RRR can reduce the money supply; decreasing the RRR can expand the money supply. Since the early 1990s, the RRR has been between 10 and 12 percent for transaction deposits and between 0 and 3 percent for time deposits.

ACTION 3 Adjusting the Discount Rate

The **discount rate** is the interest rate that the Fed charges when it lends money to other banks. The discount rate affects the money supply because it sets the reserves that banks have available to lend. When the Fed increases the discount rate, banks tend to borrow less money from the Fed. They must then use their existing funds to meet reserve requirements and have less excess reserves to lend. Therefore, the money supply decreases. The opposite happens when the discount rate is lowered. Banks borrow more money from the Fed and increase their reserves. When this happens, they have more money to lend, and the money supply increases.

The Fed's actions also impact businesses and individuals who borrow. The **prime rate** is the interest rate that banks charge their best customers. Interest rates for other borrowers tend to be two or three percentage points above prime. To make a profit on the loans they make, banks need to charge higher rates than they pay to borrow. So when the discount rate increases, so does the prime rate and, therefore, the cost of business and consumer credit.

APPLICATION Analyzing Causes

A. Which open market operation causes the money supply to expand? Why?

Approaches to Monetary Policy

The most important job of the Fed is to promote growth and stability in the American economy. The purpose of monetary policy is to curb inflation and reduce economic stagnation or recession. By focusing on these goals, the Fed tries to promote full employment and growth without rapid increases in prices or high interest rates.

The Fed uses two basic policies—expansionary or contractionary monetary policy. **Expansionary monetary policy** is a plan to increase the amount of money in circulation. **Contractionary monetary policy** is a plan to reduce the amount of money in circulation. When the economy slows, the Fed uses expansionary monetary policy to pump more money into the economy. When the economy is overheated, the Fed uses a contractionary policy to reduce the amount of money in the economy.

QUICK REFERENCE

Expansionary monetary policy is a plan to increase the money supply.

Contractionary monetary policy is a plan to reduce the money supply.

Easy-money policy is another name for expansionary monetary policy.

POLICY 1 Expansionary Policy

In Chapter 15 you studied expansionary policy as it related to the federal government's fiscal-policy actions. This type of fiscal policy is used during a slowdown in economic activity. The Fed's expansionary monetary policy is used at the same point in the business cycle. It is sometimes called the **easy-money policy** because it puts more money into circulation by making it easier for borrowers to secure a loan.

During a recession, when unemployment is high, the Fed wants to have more money circulating in the economy to stimulate aggregate demand. When it is easier to borrow money, consumers will take out more loans to buy homes, automobiles, and other goods and services. In response, businesses then produce more, which creates jobs and decreases unemployment. An easy-money policy allows businesses to borrow funds to help them expand. When more loans are made, more money is created in the banking system.

The Fed enacts an easy-money policy by buying bonds on the open market, by decreasing reserve requirements, by decreasing the discount rate, or by some combination of these tools. The Fed's most common action in this situation is to buy bonds on the open market. When the Fed decides to buy more bonds, it increases the demand for them, which raises their price. Recall that bond prices have an inverse, or opposite, relationship to interest rates. When bond prices rise, interest rates fall. Lower interest rates will encourage more lending. More lending increases consumer spending and investment. This, in turn, increases aggregate demand, resulting in the growth of GDP and lower unemployment. If the Fed expands the money supply too much, however, aggregate demand may increase to a level that causes inflation.

Monetary Policy The Fed's monetary policy must be well-timed and well-balanced to have the required effect.

Frank and Ernest

©1998 Thaves. Reprinted with permission. Newspaper dist. by NEA, Inc.

POLICY 2 Contractionary Policy

In Chapter 15, you also studied the federal government's contractionary fiscal policy, used during an expansionary period. The Fed's contractionary monetary policy also is used when economic activity is rapidly increasing. It is sometimes called a **tight-money policy** because it is designed to reduce inflation by making it more difficult for businesses and individuals to get loans.

Suppose that aggregate demand is increasing faster than aggregate supply, leading to higher prices and concerns about inflation. The Fed would want to have less money circulating because more money fuels demand and may lead to inflation in wages and prices. In other words, the Fed would want to make it harder for businesses and individuals to borrow money. Therefore, it would decrease the money supply by decreasing reserves available for loans.

The Fed enacts a tight-money policy by selling bonds on the open market, increasing reserve requirements, or increasing the discount rate. As with easy-money policy, the Fed's most likely action involves open market operations. Selling bonds causes bond prices to fall and interest rates to increase. Higher interest rates discourage lending. Less lending decreases aggregate demand, which decreases growth in GDP, and lowers the general price level. If the Fed contracts the money supply too much, however, aggregate demand may decrease to a level where unemployment increases. Figure 16.9 summarizes how the Fed uses expansionary and contractionary monetary policies.

QUICK REFERENCE

Tight-money policy is another name for contractionary monetary policy.

ECONOMICS ESSENTIALS

FIGURE 16.9 Approaches to Monetary Policy

How does the Fed use its monetary policy tools?

Expansionary Policy

- Buy bonds on the open market
- Lower the reserve requirement
- Reduce the discount rate

Contractionary Policy

- Sell bonds on the open market
- Raise the reserve requirement
- Increase the discount rate

ANALYZE CHARTS
Monetary policy is designed to even out the extremes of the business cycle by expanding or contracting the money supply. Explain how the actions listed under Expansionary Policy increase the supply of money and those under Contractionary Policy decrease the supply of money.

APPLICATION Comparing and Contrasting

B. What are the similarities and differences between expansionary fiscal policy and expansionary monetary policy?

Alan Greenspan: The Oracle of the Fed

FAST FACTS

Alan Greenspan

Title: Chairman of the Federal Reserve Board (1987–2006)

Born: March 6, 1926, New York City

Major Accomplishment: Controlled inflation while supporting unprecedented economic growth

Presidents Served Under: Ronald Reagan, George H. W. Bush, Bill Clinton, George W. Bush

Notable Quotation:
"But how do we know when irrational exuberance has unduly escalated asset values, which then become subject to unexpected and prolonged contractions. . . ?"

During his 18-plus years as chairman of the Federal Reserve, Alan Greenspan came to personify the institution. The worldwide financial community and the media waited eagerly to hear what he would say after each meeting of the Federal Open Market Committee (FOMC). Why did so many people come to believe that one man's decisions could have such a profound effect on the economy?

Managing Monetary Policy

President Ronald Reagan appointed Alan Greenspan chairman of the Federal Reserve Board of Governors in 1987. Greenspan had a reputation as a committed inflation fighter and fulfilled that role with great success. During his tenure, the core inflation rate fell to historically low levels at the same time that the economy expanded.

Greenspan's success was due to his clear understanding of the tools of monetary policy and how to apply them, as well as in-depth knowledge of a wide range of economic indicators. Also, throughout his years as chairman, he demonstrated a keen sense of timing, knowing the most effective time at which to order an expansion or contraction of the money supply.

Although the chairman has only one vote on the FOMC, Greenspan's economic insight and persuasiveness gave him great power. His authoritative but difficult-to-understand pronouncements led some to nickname him the Oracle. As his time as chairman drew to a close, many praised Greenspan for bringing years of steady growth and low inflation to the U.S. economy.

However, the financial crisis that began soon after Greenspan left office led to a reassessment of his contributions. He had supported the use of derivatives and opposed tighter regulation of financial markets. Some now speculate that if Greenspan had taken a more skeptical view of derivatives and other new financial tools, the financial crisis might have been averted.

Alan Greenspan achieved celebrity status as chairman of the Federal Reserve.

Economics Update

Find an update about Alan Greenspan at **ClassZone.com**

APPLICATION Making Inferences

C. Why did Alan Greenspan's opinions matter so much to investors?

Impacts and Limitation of Monetary Policy

As you recall, the purpose of monetary policy is to curb inflation and to halt recessions, which result in unemployment. But what impact does monetary policy have on the economy, and how successful is it in fulfilling its purpose?

IMPACT 1 Short-Term Effects

Adjustments to monetary policy have both short-term and long-term effects. The short-term effect is change in the price of credit—in other words, the interest rates on loans. The Fed's open market operations influence the FFR fairly quickly by increasing or decreasing the level of reserves that banks have available to lend. Figure 16.10 shows that when the Fed uses an easy-money policy to expand the money supply, interest rates decline. When the Fed uses a tight-money policy, as shown in Figure 16.11, interest rates rise.

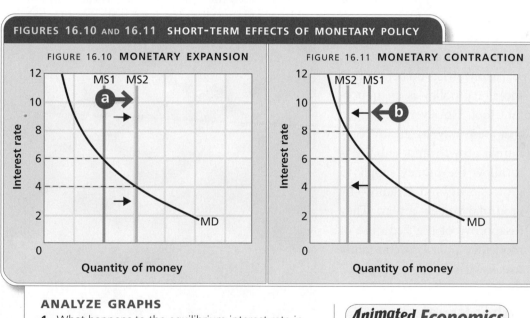

FIGURES 16.10 AND 16.11 SHORT-TERM EFFECTS OF MONETARY POLICY

FIGURE 16.10 **MONETARY EXPANSION**

FIGURE 16.11 **MONETARY CONTRACTION**

The money supply (MS1, MS2) is a vertical line because it represents the fixed amount of money available as determined by the Fed.

Demand for money (MD) is the same as demand for any product. As prices (interest rates) fall, demand increases. As prices rise, demand falls.

a The supply curve shifts to the right when the money supply expands.

b The supply curve shifts to the left when the money supply contracts.

ANALYZE GRAPHS

1. What happens to the equilibrium interest rate in Figure 16.10? What happens to it in Figure 16.11?

2. How do these graphs show the effects of easy-money and tight-money policy?

Animated Economics

Use an interactive money supply curve at **ClassZone.com**

IMPACT 2 Policy Lags

Some lags, or delays, that affect monetary policy are related to identifying the problem. The Fed needs specific information and statistics in order to identify the problem and take action. Other lags have to do with how quickly the change in policy takes effect. Many economists suggest that it may take as long as two years for adjustments in monetary policy to take full effect. This may have long-term effects on the economy. For example, businesses often delay plans for expansion if interest rates are too high. Because policies designed to lower rates may take some time to take effect, actual investment in expansion may lag months or years behind the plans.

IMPACT 3 Timing Issues

As with fiscal policy, monetary policy must be coordinated with the business cycle in order to provide a stable economic environment. If the policy is correct and the timing is good, extremes in the business cycle will be evened out. If the timing is bad, a business cycle phase may be exaggerated. For example, high interest rates in 1990 that were intended to help fight inflation actually took effect as the economy was going into a recession, worsening the effects of that recession.

Supporters of monetarism cite such situations to show that using monetary policy to influence short-term changes in the business cycle can create major problems. **Monetarism** is a theory that suggests that rapid changes in the money supply are the main cause of economic instability. Milton Friedman is the most prominent monetarist. (You can read more about Friedman on page 76.) He studied how changes in the growth rate of the money supply affected prices and concluded that inflation is always accompanied by rapid monetary growth. Conversely, he noted that there has been little or no inflation when the money supply has grown slowly and steadily.

QUICK REFERENCE

Monetarism is a theory that holds that rapid changes in the money supply cause economic instability.

Monetarists do believe that monetary policy is an important tool. However, they argue that best way to ensure economic growth and stability is to allow the money supply to grow slowly and steadily—by around 3 percent a year. They disapprove of the Fed's use of monetary policy to constantly tinker with the money supply.

Other Issues

The use of the monetary policy tools is just one way the economy can be corrected. It is

Monetarism According to monetarists, a slow, steady growth in the amount of money in circulation is the best monetary policy.

more effective if it is coordinated with fiscal policy. In addition, the goals of the Fed may clash with those of Congress or the president. Since members of the Fed's Board of Governors serve for 14-year terms, they are not as susceptible to political pressure as are politicians, who are elected every two to six years.

APPLICATION Analyzing Causes

D. What will happen to interest rates when the Fed sells bonds in open market operations? Why?

REVIEWING KEY CONCEPTS

1. Explain the difference between the terms in each of these pairs.

   a. *monetary policy*
   monetarism

   b. *easy-money policy*
   tight-money policy

   c. *discount rate*
   prime rate

2. How should a contractionary monetary policy affect interest rates and the rate of inflation? Why?

3. How should an expansionary monetary policy affect interest rates and the unemployment rate? Why?

4. How does the Fed use open market operations as a monetary policy tool?

5. What is the main short-term effect of monetary policy?

6. **Using Your Notes** Which monetary policy tool does the Fed use least often? Refer to your completed hierarchy diagram.

   Use the Graphic Organizer at **Interactive Review @ ClassZone.com**

   ```
              Monetary
               Policy
         ┌────────┼────────┐
   (main ideas)(main ideas)(main ideas)
      │          │          │
   (details)  (details)  (details)
   ```

CRITICAL THINKING

7. **Analyzing Causes** To curb inflation, why is it easier for the Fed to use monetary policy to raise interest rates than it is for Congress to implement contractionary fiscal policy?

8. **Making Inferences** What are the Fed's underlying assumptions about the state of the economy, based on these Fed actions?

   a. The Fed's open market operations caused the FFR to drop from 6.25 percent to 1 percent.

   b. The FFR rose from 1 percent to 4.25 percent.

9. **Applying Economic Concepts** In 2005, the Fed set the discount rate for banks in good financial condition at 1 percent above the targeted FFR.

   a. Would these banks be more likely to borrow short-term funds from another bank or from the Fed? Why?

   b. How does this policy help keep the federal funds rate close to the target set by the Fed?

10. **Challenge** Explain how the Fed buying bonds affects interest rates, aggregate demand, price level, and GDP. Illustrate your answer using two graphs, one showing the money market and one showing aggregate supply and aggregate demand.

ECONOMICS IN PRACTICE

Durable goods—washing machines

Applying Economic Concepts
Think about the ways monetary policy is used to address economic problems. Then complete the following activities.

Determine Monetary Policy The chart below lists several economic situations. For each one, decide whether an easy-money or tight-money policy is needed.

Economic Situation	Monetary Policy Needed
Consumer spending on durable goods rises faster than production	
Rising energy prices are pushing prices of many products higher	
Unemployment rate increases from 5.4% to 6.8% over six months	

Challenge Choose one example that requires an easy-money policy and one that requires a tight-money policy and explain how open market operations would be used in each case.

Applying Monetary and Fiscal Policy

OBJECTIVES	KEY TERMS	TAKING NOTES
In Section 4, you will • describe how monetary and fiscal policy can coordinate to improve the economy • understand how monetary and fiscal policy can work against each other • identify other measures that can be used to manage the economy	wage and price controls, *p. 501*	As you read Section 4, complete a cause-and-effect chart using the key concepts and other helpful words and phrases. Use the Graphic Organizer at **Interactive Review @ ClassZone.com**

Expansionary Policies → results

Contractionary Policies → results

Conflicting Policies → results

Policies to Expand the Economy

KEY CONCEPTS

The goals of both fiscal and monetary policy are to stabilize the economy by easing the effects of recession and controlling inflation. Fiscal policy relies on government spending and taxation to achieve its goals. Monetary policy uses open market operations, the discount rate, and reserve requirements as its tools.

These policies, as well as affecting the economy, also have an impact on each other. As you recall, both monetary and fiscal policy have limitations. These include policy lags, political constraints, and timing issues. Policy lags relate to the time it takes to identify the problem and for policy actions to take effect. Political considerations may limit government's ability to do what is best for the economy. Timing, too, is important because to be effective government actions must counteract the negative effects of the business cycle. Intervention at the wrong time may skew the cycle and make the problem worse.

A second phenomenon affecting timing is explained by the rational expectations theory. As you recall from Chapter 15, this states that individuals and business firms learn, through experience, to anticipate changes in monetary and fiscal policy and take steps to protect their interests. For example, if there is debate in Congress about tax cuts, individuals and businesses may take actions before the legislation is even passed, based on their expectations that tax cuts will increase their income. Individuals may decide to purchase durable goods, such as automobiles, refrigerators, and washing machines. Similarly, businesses may decide to expand their operations by building new factories and hiring more workers. On the other hand, if individuals and businesses think the tax cuts will be temporary, they may choose not to spend as the policy intended.

Rational Expectations
Expectations that tax cuts will increase their incomes may cause people to buy "big-ticket" items such as refrigerators.

People who disagree with the use of most discretionary policy often support their argument with the rational expectations theory. They suggest that rather than fiddling with fiscal and monetary policy, the government should aim for a stable monetary policy so that business decisions are made for economic reasons and not in anticipation of new policies.

EXAMPLE Expansionary Monetary and Fiscal Policy

The goal of expansionary policy is to stimulate the economy by reducing unemployment and increasing investment. As you recall, expansionary fiscal policy involves increased government spending or tax cuts. Also, to enact expansionary monetary policy, the Fed buys government bonds or reduces the discount rate or the reserve requirement.

For example, suppose that the unemployment rate is 9.5 percent and the Consumer Price Index (CPI) is at 2 percent. The economy is in recession and inflation is a minimal concern. In order to increase the money supply, the Fed buys bonds on the open market and lowers the discount rate. The federal government also cuts personal income taxes and increases government spending. These expansionary policies are designed to increase aggregate demand and decrease unemployment. Real GDP will expand and prices will rise as aggregate demand increases. Figure 16.12 shows how expansionary policies affect these key economic indicators.

Expansionary fiscal policy is likely to raise interest rates, while expansionary monetary policy should decrease interest rates. Therefore, the actual change in interest rates will depend on the relative strength of the two policies. The amount of investment spending will depend on what happens with interest rates.

FIGURE 16.12 Effects of Expansionary Policies

Policies

a

Monetary Policy The Fed buys bonds and lowers the discount rate to increase money supply

Fiscal Policy Increased spending/ tax cuts to increase aggregate demand

Effects

b

Real GDP increases and **prices** rise

Unemployment falls

a Here, fiscal and monetary policies work together to expand the economy.

b These policies tend to increase aggregate demand, increase real GDP, and lower unemployment.

ANALYZE CHARTS

1. According to the chart, what are the goals of expansionary policies?
2. Which indicator in the chart suggests that expansionary policy might lead toward inflation?

APPLICATION Analyzing Effects

A. What effect would government borrowing to finance increased spending have on interest rates and why?

Policies to Control Inflation

The goal of contractionary monetary policy is to tighten up the economy by decreasing inflation and increasing interest rates. Contractionary fiscal policy tools include decreased government spending or tax increases. The Fed will sell bonds on the open market or raise the discount rate or the reserve requirement as contractionary monetary policy tools.

EXAMPLE Contractionary Monetary and Fiscal Policy

Suppose that the unemployment rate is 4.5 percent and the CPI is running in excess of 10 percent. The economy is operating at or above a sustainable level of output, and inflation is very high. In order to decrease the money supply, the Fed sells bonds on the open market and raises the discount rate. The federal government cuts spending on government programs. It also may raise taxes. These contractionary policies are designed to decrease aggregate demand and bring inflation under control. Real GDP will decrease, and prices will fall as aggregate demand decreases. Further, unemployment tends to rise as real GDP decreases. Figure 16.13 shows how contractionary monetary and fiscal policies affect the key economic indicators of unemployment and real GDP.

Contractionary fiscal policy is likely to lower interest rates because decreased government spending will decrease demand for loans. Contractionary monetary policy should raise interest rates. Therefore, the actual change in interest rates will depend on the relative strength of the two policies. The amount of investment spending depends on what happens with interest rates.

FIGURE 16.13 Effects of Contractionary Policies

Policies

a

Monetary Policy
The Fed sells bonds and raises the discount rate to cut money supply

Fiscal Policy
Decreased spending/ tax increases to decrease aggregate demand

Effects

b

Real GDP and **prices** fall

Unemployment increases

a Here, fiscal and monetary policies work together to contract the economy.

b These policies decrease aggregate demand, control inflation, and raise unemployment.

ANALYZE CHARTS

1. According to the chart, what are the goals of contractionary policies?

2. In what way might the fiscal policy shown here not help to control inflation?

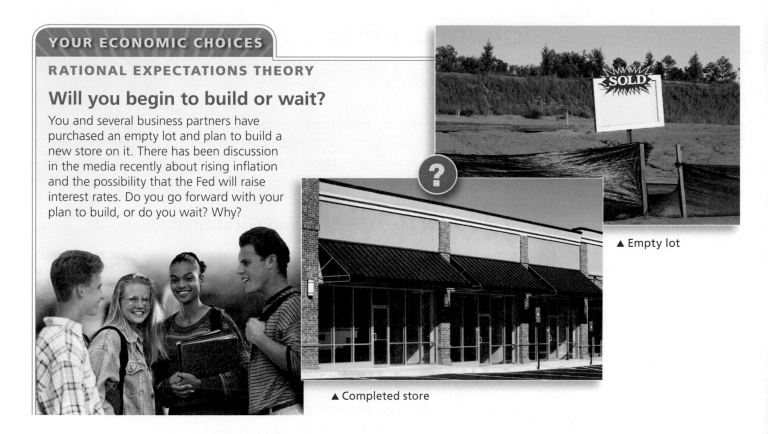

RATIONAL EXPECTATIONS THEORY

Will you begin to build or wait?

You and several business partners have purchased an empty lot and plan to build a new store on it. There has been discussion in the media recently about rising inflation and the possibility that the Fed will raise interest rates. Do you go forward with your plan to build, or do you wait? Why?

▲ Empty lot

▲ Completed store

EXAMPLE Wage and Price Controls

At times in the past, the government has taken extreme measures to control the economy, especially during wartime. For example, the government may establish a set of wage and price guidelines that are not mandatory. **Wage and price controls** are limits, established by the government, on increases in certain wages and prices. These controls, unlike wage and price guidelines, are mandatory and enforced by the government.

World War II led to increased production of goods needed by the military. This situation created shortages of many consumer goods as well as a labor shortage, which tended to drive up prices and wages. In an effort to control inflation, President Franklin D. Roosevelt established the Office of Price Administration (OPA) in 1942. This agency set strict wage and price controls on all sectors of the economy. These measures had some, but not total, success. They were phased out almost immediately after the end of the war.

In 1971, President Richard M. Nixon was faced with stagflation, a situation in which rising unemployment is accompanied by rising inflation rates. In August of that year, Nixon announced a 90-day freeze on wages and prices to try to control inflation. The program was renewed several times and lasted until April 1974. Even so, it had little impact. From late 1971 to early 1974, the inflation rate actually rose from about 4 percent to 11 percent.

> **QUICK REFERENCE**
>
> **Wage and price controls** are government limits on increases in wages and prices.

APPLICATION Comparing and Contrasting

B. What are the similarities and differences between contractionary monetary policy and wage and price controls?

Policies in Conflict

KEY CONCEPTS

As you have seen, coordinated policies are, for the most part, effective in reaching a mutually agreed upon goal—that is, a stable but growing economy with little inflation. When fiscal and monetary policies are not coordinated, however, one policy can counter the effect of the other and thwart this goal, creating economic instability instead.

EXAMPLE Conflicting Monetary and Fiscal Policies

Suppose that the unemployment rate is 7 percent and the CPI stands at 6 percent and is steadily rising. The Fed may decide that the most pressing problem for the economy is rising inflation. So, to cool down the economy it follows a contractionary monetary policy, selling bonds on the open market and raising the discount rate. At the same time, the federal government may decide that rising unemployment needs is a bigger problem. To stimulate aggregate demand, it follows an expansionary fiscal policy, cutting personal taxes and increasing spending on public works programs.

The only clear result of these conflicting policies is that interest rates will increase. Because the policies are in conflict, the effects on GDP, prices, and unemployment cannot be predicted. This is illustrated in Figure 16.14.

FIGURE 16.14 Effects of Conflicting Policies

Policies

(a)

Monetary Policy
The Fed sells bonds and raises the discount rate to cut money supply

Fiscal Policy
Tax cuts/ increased spending to increase aggregate demand

Effects

(b)

Real GDP and prices
may rise or fall

Unemployment
may rise or fall

(a) This shows that the policies are working against each other in efforts to stabilize the economy.

(b) Here, conflicting policies make it impossible to predict the effects on GDP, prices, and unemployment.

ANALYZE GRAPHS

1. According to the chart, which policy is designed to increase GDP?

2. How do you think conflicting monetary and fiscal policies, like those described above, will affect consumer spending? Why?

APPLICATION Analyzing Causes

C. Why do tax cuts and increased government spending result in a rise in interest rates?

Online Quiz
ClassZone.com

REVIEWING KEY CONCEPTS

1. Use the term below in a sentence that illustrates the meaning of the term.

   wage and price controls

2. How is rational expectations theory related to the limitations of fiscal and monetary policy?

3. Why does rational expectations theory oppose most discretionary fiscal and monetary policy?

4. Does monetary policy or fiscal policy most directly affect the economy? Why?

5. Why might an expansionary fiscal policy and a contractionary monetary policy work against each other?

6. **Using Your Notes** What are the effects of expansionary fiscal and monetary policies? Refer to your completed diagram.

   Use the Graphic Organizer at **Interactive Review @ ClassZone.com**

Expansionary Policies	→	results
Contractionary Policies	→	results
Conflicting Policies	→	results

CRITICAL THINKING

7. **Drawing Conclusions** What happens to interest rates if the Fed implements a contractionary monetary policy when Congress and the president cut taxes and increase government spending? What effect do you think this would have on the economy? Why?

8. **Applying Economic Concepts** When President Nixon imposed wage and price controls in the 1970s in an attempt to control inflation, he felt he could then use expansionary fiscal policy to decrease unemployment. These policies helped him win reelection in 1972, but inflation rose sharply over the next three years. Use the economic concepts you have learned in this section to explain what happened.

9. **Challenge** Many economists argue that the economy is better off when monetary policy is used most often to stabilize the economy, with fiscal policy being used primarily as a backup to bring the economy out of longer recessions. Do you agree or disagree with this assessment? Why or why not?

ECONOMICS IN PRACTICE

Applying Economic Concepts
Recall what you have learned about the effectiveness of monetary policy, then complete the activities below.

Interpreting Economic Models
Which graph shows poor timing of monetary policy in relation to the business cycle? What is the effect of monetary policy on the business cycle shown on each graph?

Challenge How do these graphs reflect rational expectations theory?

Case Study

Economics Update
Find an update on this Case
Study at **ClassZone.com**

Interpreting Signals from the Fed

Background The Federal Reserve is a powerful institution, so people pay attention to the Fed chairman's comments. A hint that the Fed might raise the discount rate can lead to a great deal of activity in the stock market. Some people might buy stock because they are confident that the Fed will keep inflation low. Others might sell stock because they are worried that the economy is slowing down. Over the 18 years that Alan Greenspan was Fed chairman, economists and financial observers scrutinized his every word in an attempt to predict how his statements would affect the economy. When Ben Bernanke was appointed as Fed chairman in 2006, observers had to learn a new language.

What's the issue? How much does the market rely on signals from the Fed to make economic decisions? Read the following to see what happened when the status quo changed and the signals were different.

A. Internet Article

This article demonstrates how Fed Chairman Ben Bernanke had to carefully review his public comments.

Crossed Economic Signals

Fed Expected to Boost Key Interest Rates

After nearly two decades of decoding Alan Greenspan's famously opaque speaking style, financial markets are having to learn to interpret his successor Ben Bernanke. So far, the results have been a little rocky. . . .

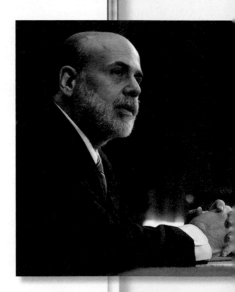

Some economists believe the Fed will stop with the funds rate at 5 percent, up significantly from the 46-year low of 1 percent in effect before the rate increases began. Others think the Fed will only pause for a meeting or two and then raise rates one or two more times. And still a third group thinks there won't be any pause as the Fed continues a steady march toward higher rates.

Part of the blame for the confusion is being assigned to Bernanke, who took over as Fed chairman on Feb. 1. He roiled markets over the past two weeks, first with testimony before the Joint Economic Committee on April 27 that the markets read as a strong signal that the Fed was going to pause in its string of rate increases, and then the next week when he told a reporter that the markets had misinterpreted his comments.

Economists said that the incident showed that there is a new Fed chairman with a different speaking style. . . . In any event, forecasters predicted Bernanke will be brushing up on his communication techniques.

Source: **"Fed Expected to Boost Key Interest Rates," by Martin Crutsinger. Associated Press, May 10, 2006.**

Thinking Economically Why does the Fed chairman need to develop strong communication techniques?

B. Political Cartoon

Harley Schwadron drew this cartoon about the new Fed chairman following in his predecessor's footsteps.

Source: www.CartoonStock.com

I THINK IT WAS A SUCCESSFUL MEETING. THEY DIDN'T UNDERSTAND A WORD I SAID.

ECONOMIC HEARING TODAY

SCHWADRON

BERNANKE FOLLOWS IN GREENSPAN'S FOOTSTEPS.

Thinking Economically What message does this cartoon convey about how the Fed has been known to give information?

C. Newspaper Article

This article reports on a speech Chairman Bernanke made at an international financial conference and the reaction that followed.

Open to Analysis

Bernanke Talks Tough on Inflation

Ben S. Bernanke, chairman of the Federal Reserve, warned Monday that recent inflation trends were "unwelcome developments," indicating that he was far less worried about signs of weaker economic growth than about the danger of higher prices.

In his toughest comments yet about the risks of inflation, Mr. Bernanke said consumer prices were rising faster than he would like. . . . Investors, increasingly convinced that the central bank will raise rates . . . immediately began selling stocks.

The Dow industrials and the broader Standard & Poor's 500-stock index each fell about 1.75 percent, and the Nasdaq index tumbled more than 2 percent. . . .

Speaking to a conference . . . on international monetary issues with other central bankers, Mr. Bernanke said inflation had climbed to the upper limits of his acceptability.

"Core inflation, measured over the past three to six months, has reached a level that, if sustained, would be at or above the upper range that many economists, including myself, would consider consistent with price stability," Mr. Bernanke said. . . .

Mr. Bernanke made clear that he thought the economy was now in a "transition" to slower economic growth. . . . Instead of highlighting signs of a cooling economy, which would ease inflationary pressures, Mr. Bernanke placed top emphasis on the need for vigilance against rising prices.

Source: **"Bernanke Talks Tough on Inflation,"** by Edmund L. Andrews. *New York Times,* June 6, 2006

Thinking Economically What kind of monetary policy did investors expect Bernanke to follow—expansionary or contractionary policy? Explain your answer.

THINKING ECONOMICALLY Synthesizing

1. How do articles A and C illustrate the rational expectations theory?
2. Based on these three sources and your own knowledge, how would you describe the differences and similarities between Greenspan and Bernanke and their impact on the market?

Interactive ◄◄ Review

Review this chapter using interactive activities at ClassZone.com

- **Online Summary**
- **Quizzes**
- **Vocabulary Flip Cards**
- **Graphic Organizers**
- **Review and Study Notes**

○○○   ◯

 Online Summary

Complete the following activity either on your own paper or online at **ClassZone.com**

Choose the key concept that best completes the sentence. Not all key concepts will be used.

bank holding company	Federal Reserve System
Board of Governors	monetarism
central bank	monetary policy
contractionary monetary policy	open market operations
deposit multiplier formula	prime rate
discount rate	required reserve ratio
easy-money policy	thrift institution
expansionary monetary policy	tight-money policy
federal funds rate	wage and price controls
Federal Open Market Committee	

The __1__ is the __2__ of the United States and is commonly known as the Fed. The __3__ supervises the operations of the Fed. The __4__ supervises the sales and purchase of federal government securities.

The Fed controls the amount of money a bank can loan through the __5__. The __6__ tells how much the money supply will increase after an initial cash deposit.

__7__ is actions by the Fed that change the money supply in order to influence the economy. The three tools used by the Fed to change the money supply are reserve requirements, the __8__, which is the rate the Fed charges when it lends money to banks, and __9__. The last tool allows the Fed to influence the __10__, the rate banks charge one another to borrow funds overnight.

__11__ seeks to increase the amount of money in circulation and is also known as __12__. __13__ seeks to decrease the amount of money in circulation and is also known as __14__.

CHAPTER 16 Assessment

REVIEWING KEY CONCEPTS

The Federal Reserve System (pp. 474–479)

1. What are the three duties of the Federal Reserve?

2. What are the different responsibilities of the Board of Governors and the Federal Open Market Committee?

Functions of the Federal Reserve (pp. 480–489)

3. What are the three functions of the Federal Reserve?

4. How does the size of the RRR affect the banking system's ability to create money?

Monetary Policy (pp. 490–497)

5. What is the Fed's most frequently used monetary policy tool?

6. What is the purpose of monetary policy?

Applying Monetary and Fiscal Policy (pp. 498–505)

7. What tools would be used to implement contractionary monetary and fiscal policy?

8. Why might it be important to coordinate monetary and fiscal policy?

APPLYING ECONOMIC CONCEPTS

Look at the line graph below showing the FFR and the prime rate over several years.

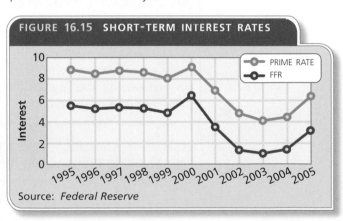

FIGURE 16.15 SHORT-TERM INTEREST RATES

Source: *Federal Reserve*

9. What is the relationship of the prime rate to the FFR as shown on this graph?

10. What conclusion can you draw about the U.S. economy based on interest rates in 2002–2004?

11. **Making Inferences** Eight times per year the Fed collects economic information from each of its districts and compiles a report to help the FOMC make its decisions. How does this practice reflect the benefits of the Fed's structure?

12. **Applying Economic Concepts** In response to the terrorist attacks of September 11, 2001, the Fed started lowering the FFR target the following week. Congress was unable to agree on a program to help stimulate the economy until March 2002. How does this situation illustrate the effects of policy lags on monetary and fiscal policy?

13. **Analyzing Causes and Effects** Suppose that the Fed buys a $10,000 T-bond from the First National Bank. What effect will this have on First National's reserves and on the FFR? Why?

14. **Drawing Conclusions** In 2001, Congress approved a major tax cut package, while the Fed lowered the FFR target. In January 2006, the president asked Congress to make the tax cuts permanent, and the Fed raised the FFR target. When were fiscal and monetary policies working together, and when were they in conflict?

15. **Challenge** The FOMC issued the following statement after one of its meetings:

> *Although recent economic data have been uneven, the expansion in economic activity appears solid. Core inflation has stayed relatively low in recent months, and longer-term inflation expectations remain contained. Nevertheless, possible increases in resource utilization as well as elevated energy prices have the potential to add to inflation pressures.*
>
> *The Committee judges that some further policy firming may be needed to keep the risks to the attainment of both sustainable economic growth and price stability roughly in balance.*

Did the committee raise, lower, or maintain the target for the FFR? Cite evidence from the statement to support your answer.

Stabilize the Economy

Step 1 Choose a partner. Imagine that you are advisers to the president of your Federal Reserve District bank. Your job is to prepare the president for the next FOMC meeting. The current state of the economy is shown in column A of the Key Economic Indicators table below. Decide whether an expansionary or contractionary monetary policy is needed. Recommend the type of open market operations needed as well as a target for the FFR. Give reasons for your recommendation and outline what you expect to happen to the other indicators as a result of this policy.

KEY ECONOMIC INDICATORS (IN PERCENT)			
Indicator	A	B	C
GDP	+3.00	+2.00	+6.50
CPI	+6.25	+3.00	+1.50
Unemployment Rate	5.60	7.50	4.50
Federal Funds Rate	7.75	4.75	5.25

Step 2 The state of the economy two years later is shown in column B. Develop a new recommendation based on this data, with the same kind of details you included in Step 1.

Step 3 The economy has experienced several years of growth as indicated by the information in column C. Develop a new recommendation based on your evaluation of this situation.

Step 4 Share your three recommendations with the class. As a class, decide on a final monetary policy recommendation for each scenario.

Step 5 Consider what would happen if the government used a coordinated fiscal policy for the data in columns A and B and a conflicting fiscal policy with the data in column C. Discuss as a class what would happen to the three key indicators when fiscal policy effects are considered.

A Global Marketplace

International trade allows nations to produce some items and trade them for other items. How do they decide what to produce and what to trade for?

International Trade

CONCEPT REVIEW

The **global economy** is the sum of all economic interactions that cross international boundaries.

CHAPTER 17 KEY CONCEPT

Economic interdependence involves producers in one nation that depend on producers in other nations to supply them with certain goods and services.

WHY THE CONCEPT MATTERS

Japan is a world-class producer of automobiles, in spite of the fact that it has few mineral resources. How can this be? The answer lies in the realm of international trade, where nations choose to produce some things and trade for others. In the case of Japan, it must trade for the raw materials it uses in order to produce automobiles. It then turns around and trades the automobiles for other goods.

Online Highlights
More at ClassZone.com

 Economics Update

Go to **ECONOMICS UPDATE** for chapter updates and current news on how tariffs and subsidies affect the sugar market. (See Case Study, pp. 538–539). ▶

Animated Economics

Go to **ANIMATED ECONOMICS** for interactive lessons on the graphs and tables in this chapter.

Interactive ◀◀Review

Go to **INTERACTIVE REVIEW** for concept review and activities.

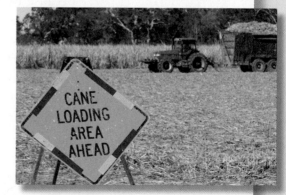

Are U.S. government subsidies to sugar producers a problem? See the Case Study on pages 538–539.

Benefits and Issues of International Trade

OBJECTIVES	KEY TERMS	TAKING NOTES
In Section 1, you will • determine why nations choose to specialize their economies • examine the difference between absolute and comparative advantage • explain how international trade impacts prices and quantity	specialization, *p. 510* economic interdependence, *p. 510* absolute advantage, *p. 513* comparative advantage, *p. 513* law of comparative advantage, *p. 514* exports, *p. 516* imports, *p. 516*	As you read Section 1, complete a diagram that shows how the concepts in the section relate to international trade. Use the Graphic Organizer at **Interactive Review @ ClassZone.com**

Resource Distribution and Specialization

KEY CONCEPTS

A nation's economic patterns are based on its unique combination of factors of production: natural resources, human capital, physical capital, and entrepreneurship. For example, a nation rich in arable land but lacking well-educated workers is less likely to develop a strong technology sector than a country with better-educated citizens and diverse natural resources. Economic patterns may also change over time. The United States, for example, once relied heavily on its agricultural sector, but the U.S. economy is now also extremely high-tech and highly skilled.

Because each nation has certain resources and cannot produce everything it wants, individuals and businesses must decide what goods and services to focus on. The result is **specialization**, a situation that occurs when individuals or businesses produce a narrow range of products. Through specialization, businesses can increase productivity and profit—the driving force of world trade. Specialization also leads to **economic interdependence**, a situation in which producers in one nation depend on others to provide goods and services they do not produce.

QUICK REFERENCE

Specialization is a situation that occurs when individuals or businesses produce a narrow range of products.

Economic interdependence is a situation in which producers in one nation depend on others to provide goods and services they do not produce.

Specialization A coal-rich nation that lacks advanced technology can trade its coal for manufactured goods, such as automobiles, from nations with higher levels of technology.

Will you specialize in lawn mowing or babysitting?

Do you have a lawn mower? Do you know children that need to be watched? What other questions might you ask yourself before deciding what you will specialize in?

Mow lawns

Babysit

EXAMPLE Specialization

The concept of specialization can be illustrated by looking at the agricultural production of two nations: Costa Rica and New Zealand. The climate, the labor conditions, and the level of technology of each nation have made some agricultural products more important than others. In other words, each nation has decided to specialize in certain agricultural areas because they have an advantage in doing so.

For Costa Rica, the product of choice is bananas. It is the world's seventh-largest producer and second-largest exporter of bananas. For New Zealand, the product of choice is sheep. It is the world's third-largest producer and second-largest exporter of wool and is responsible for about 50 percent of the world's lamb and mutton exports. What explains each nation's specialization?

Costa Rica has the necessary climate for bananas—warm and wet. In addition, agricultural wages are relatively low, an important point as banana production is quite labor intensive.

On the other hand, New Zealand has the temperate climate, water resources, and vast expanses of open grasslands to support the grazing of millions of sheep. (Today, there are about 10 sheep for every person in New Zealand.) Raising sheep is not nearly as labor intensive as banana production, and this suits the fairly low population density of this remote island nation. Also, scientific breeding practices and mechanized wool- and meat-processing operations are available to a developed nation such as New Zealand.

It makes sense for each nation to specialize as it does and to trade for the things it cannot produce as efficiently.

Economics Update

Find an update on Costa Rica's economy at **ClassZone.com**

APPLICATION Drawing Conclusions

A. Why should nations specialize in what they produce most efficiently and trade for the rest?

David Ricardo: The Theory of Comparative Advantage

FAST FACTS

David Ricardo
British political economist and stockbroker

Born: April 18 or 19, 1772

Died: September 11, 1823

Major Accomplishment: Explaining the economic principles behind free trade

Major Work: *On the Principles of Political Economy and Taxation* (1817)

Notable Quotation:
"*The labor of 100 Englishmen cannot be given for that of 80 Englishmen, but the produce of the labor of 100 Englishmen may be given for the produce of the labor of 80 Portuguese, 60 Russians, or 120 East Indians.*"

Unlike Adam Smith and many other important economists, David Ricardo was hardly an academic. He was a stockbroker, and he earned a fortune at that business—worth over $100 million in today's dollars. Ricardo became interested in economics when he read Smith's *The Wealth of Nations* while on vacation in 1799. As his interest grew, Ricardo deepened his studies and began writing economic commentaries for newspapers and other publications.

Perhaps his greatest contribution to economics was an idea that became the backbone of free trade—comparative advantage. Ricardo asserted that a trading nation should produce a certain product if it can do so at an opportunity cost lower than that of another trading nation.

Trading in Opportunity

Before Ricardo's influence, the prevailing view on international trade was based on the idea of absolute advantage, the ability of one nation to make a product more efficiently than another. For example, if Portugal could make grape juice more efficiently than England, and if England could make cloth more efficiently than Portugal, then trade would be beneficial to both.

Ricardo challenged this viewpoint. What if, he suggested, Portugal makes both products more efficiently than England? Would trade, at least for Portugal, no longer be beneficial? His surprising answer was that trade would still be beneficial. He based his conclusion on the opportunity costs each nation spends to make its products.

Suppose that in Portugal it takes two hours of labor to produce a jug of grape juice, while in England it takes four hours. Suppose also that in Portugal a yard of cloth takes six hours to make; in England it takes eight hours. Ricardo reasoned that in Portugal, every yard of cloth costs three jugs of grape juice in lost opportunity. In England, however, every yard of cloth costs only two jugs of grape juice. Portugal, then, would be wise to buy cloth from England and to specialize in grape juice. This understanding has become known as the law of comparative advantage: countries gain when they produce items they are most efficient at producing and that have the lowest opportunity cost.

David Ricardo argued in favor of free trade.

Economics Update

Learn more about David Ricardo at **ClassZone.com**

APPLICATION Applying Economic Concepts

B. Does the law of comparative advantage apply only to nations, or does it apply to individuals as well? Explain your answer.

Absolute and Comparative Advantage

KEY CONCEPTS

Absolute advantage is the ability of one trading nation to make a product more efficiently than another trading nation. Some regions or nations have absolute advantage in producing certain products or services because of the uneven distribution of production factors.

Comparative advantage, in contrast, is the idea that a nation will specialize in what it can produce at a lower opportunity cost than any other nation. When determining comparative advantage, you look not for the absolute cost of a product, but for its opportunity cost.

EXAMPLE Absolute Advantage

Consider the trade relations between two countries on the Pacific Rim today, China and Australia. Both countries produce iron ore; both also produce steel. Suppose that every week, Australia produces 5,000 tons of iron ore and 1,000 tons of steel. In the same period of time, and with the same amount of labor, China produces 2,700 tons of iron ore and 900 tons of steel. In this case, Australia has an absolute advantage over China in both areas.

Before Ricardo, the standard logic held that, in this situation, the nation that held the absolute advantage for both commodities would trade for neither. But, as you've read, when the important factor of opportunity cost is considered, this logic doesn't stand up. Why would it benefit Australia to import steel from China, in spite of its absolute advantage? The answer is comparative advantage.

> ### QUICK REFERENCE
>
> **Absolute advantage** is the ability of one trading nation to make a product more efficiently than another trading nation.
>
> **Comparative advantage** is a trading nation's ability to produce something at a lower opportunity cost than that of another trading nation.

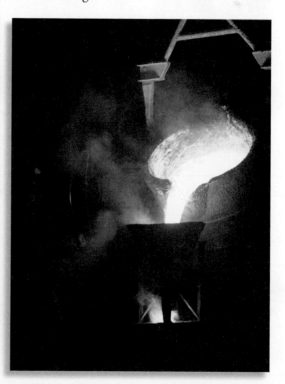

What Does Opportunity Cost? Should Australia specialize in mining iron ore (left) and leave the steel production (right) to China? Where does the comparative advantage lie?

| EXAMPLE | **Comparative Advantage** |

Let's start with a simple example of comparative advantage. After years as an office manager at a law firm by day and a law student by night, Ellen becomes a lawyer and starts her own practice. She charges $150 per hour for her legal services. She hires Miguel to run her office, and she pays him $25 per hour. Although Miguel works hard and is good at his job, Ellen soon realizes that, due to her years of experience, she could run her own office better than Miguel. Should she take over these duties? The answer lies in opportunity cost. Every hour that Ellen spends engaged in the duties that are worth $25 per hour costs her an hour that could be spent doing work that is worth $150 per hour. Clearly it makes sense for her to employ an office manager and concentrate on the legal end of her practice.

Back to our previous example of Australia and China, we see that Australia's production ratio of steel to iron ore is 1:5. In other words, Australia's opportunity cost for one ton of steel is five tons of iron ore. Applying the same logic to China, we find that its production ratio of steel to iron ore is 1:3. Its opportunity cost for one ton of steel is three tons of iron ore. So, in the production of steel, China has a comparative advantage. Australia would benefit by trading for Chinese steel. This is the **law of comparative advantage**: countries gain when they produce items that they are most efficient at producing and that are at the lowest opportunity cost.

QUICK REFERENCE

The **law of comparative advantage** states that countries gain when they produce items they are most efficient at producing and are at the lowest opportunity cost.

FIGURE 17.1 Specialization and Trade

No Specialization

One day's labor in France results in **40** tons of cheese and **80** tons of fish.

One day's labor in Japan results in **50** tons of cheese and **200** tons of fish.

France's opportunity cost for **1** ton of cheese is **2** tons of fish.

Japan's opportunity cost for **1** ton of cheese is **4** tons of fish.

Specialization and Trade

France trades 1 ton of cheese.

Japan trades 3 tons of fish.

It used to cost France **1** ton of cheese to get **2** tons of fish; now it trades **1** ton of cheese for **3** tons of fish.

It used to cost Japan **4** tons of fish for **1** ton of cheese; now it trades only **3** tons of fish for **1** ton of cheese.

Economic Success with Few Natural Resources

Some economies thrive as a direct result of natural resources—Saudi Arabia and its oil, for instance. But, many nations, such as the Republic of Ireland, thrive economically in spite of a relative lack of natural resources.

It is not rich in mineral resources and relies on imports for the majority of its energy supply. However, it has formulated and carried out certain policies that have helped to produce today's dynamic economy.

The headquarters of the Industrial Development Agency of Ireland, in Dublin

In the mid-1950s, Ireland began a continuing process of reversing protectionist tariff and quota policies. The Programmes for Economic Expansion (1958 and 1963) attracted large amounts of foreign direct investment through financial grants and tax concessions. Levels of human capital were increased through educational reforms in the 1960s. It was also an original member of the EU and took advantage of EU funds to shore up its infrastructure. These and other policies set the stage for Ireland's economic boom of the 1990s. During this decade, it became a major manufacturer of high-tech electronics, computer products, chemicals, and pharmaceuticals. It has also become an important center for banking and finance.

CONNECTING ACROSS THE GLOBE

1. **Drawing Conclusions** What specialization has, for the most part, driven Ireland's economic boom?
2. **Applying Economic Concepts** Why might an economy like Ireland's be more desirable than one that relies solely on natural resources?

EXAMPLE Advantages of Free Trade

If China and Australia decide to specialize and trade, they can improve their ratio of return. Previously, China's ratio of steel production to iron ore production was 1:3 and Australia's was 1:5. If the two nations establish a trade ratio of 1:4 (China trades one ton of its steel for four tons of Australian iron ore), both countries win. China now gets four tons of iron ore for a ton of steel; it got three before. Also, one ton of steel now costs Australia only four tons of iron ore; it previously cost five.

When countries specialize and trade, they not only improve their production ratios but they also increase world output. If China specializes in steel and Australia in iron ore, each can make more of their products than the two nations could have made together if they had not specialized. Increased output is a mark of economic growth, which is a factor in raising standards of living.

APPLICATION Interpreting Tables

C. Use the example in Figure 17.1 to explain how output for both nations increases through specialization and trade.

International Trade Affects the National Economy

KEY CONCEPTS

QUICK REFERENCE

Exports are goods and services produced in one country and sold to other countries.

Imports are goods and services produced in one country and purchased by another.

Because of the law of comparative advantage, nations gain through trading goods and services. Goods and services produced in one country and sold to other countries are called **exports**. Goods and services produced in one country and purchased by another are called **imports**.

The costs and benefits of international trade vary by nation. To understand how trade affects a nation's economy, economists use supply and demand analysis. They look at the impact of exports and imports on prices and quantity.

IMPACT 1 Exports on Prices and Quantity

Suppose that a county called Plecona existed and that it did not trade with other countries. Figure 17.2 shows the equilibrium price for Plecona's motorbikes.

What would happen to prices and demand if Plecona decided to become a trading nation and export its motorbikes? In some countries, such as Nepocal, people would give up their bicycles and begin to buy Pleconese motorbikes. This results in an increase in demand for Pleconese motorbikes, shifting the demand curve to the right and establishing a new equilibrium price. Motorbikes will now cost more in Plecona too. However, the greater demand resulting from exporting offsets this by creating more jobs and more income in Plecona, as the motorbike producer invests its profits to expand production and hire more workers.

IMPACT 2 Imports on Prices and Quantity

Now suppose that Nepocal and Plecona agree that Nepocal may sell its major product, microwave ovens, in Plecona. Instead of having only Pleconese-made microwaves, consumers in Plecona may now purchase ovens imported from Nepocal. This change adds to the number of microwave oven producers in the Pleconese market. Adding producers shifts the supply curve of microwave ovens to the right and thereby establishes a new, lower equilibrium price. (See Figure 17.3.)

In other words, there are now more microwave ovens in Plecona, and the consumers are paying a lower price for them. However, because of the lower price, Pleconese producers of microwave ovens will choose to offer fewer microwaves for sale. So imports have the effect of initially increasing supply and of providing consumers with greater selection and lower prices. The competition also establishes incentives for domestic producers to become more efficient in production, improve worker productivity, and enhance customer service.

Both consumers and producers, then, benefit from international trade. Consumers benefit from imports because the selection of goods increases and prices decrease. Producers benefit from exports by gaining a new market for their products, and thereby giving them the opportunity to increase revenues and earn a profit.

17.2 PLECONA'S MOTORBIKE EXPORT MARKET

Price (in thousands of dollars) — vertical axis: $12, 10, 8, 6, 4, 2

Quantity supplied and demanded of motorbikes (in thousands) — horizontal axis: 0, 5, 10, 15, 20, 25, 30

Labels: a→, S, D2, D1

17.3 PLECONA'S MICROWAVE OVEN IMPORT MARKET

Price (in dollars) — vertical axis: $120, 100, 80, 60, 40, 20

Quantity supplied and demanded of microwave ovens (in thousands) — horizontal axis: 0, 5, 10, 15, 20, 25, 30

Labels: S1, b→, S2, D

a Increased demand causes the demand curve to shift to the right.

b Increased supply causes the supply curve to shift to the right.

ANALYZE GRAPHS

What are the initial and then post-shift equilibrium prices for motorbikes in Figure 17.2? for microwaves in Figure 17.3?

Animated **Economics**

Use an interactive supply and demand graph at **ClassZone.com**

IMPACT 3 Trade Affects Employment

As nations specialize in their changing areas of strength, the availability of certain jobs can undergo dramatic changes. For example, if Australia specializes in producing iron ore or providing educational services (another area of strength for that nation) at the expense of making steel, then some Australian steelworkers may lose their jobs. At the same time, however, the overall number of Australian jobs may increase significantly. The Australian Trade Commission estimates that a ten percent increase in exports results in 70,000 new jobs for workers in Australia.

In the United States, manufacturing output increased 600 percent between 1950 and 2000. During the same period, however, employment in manufacturing, as a share of total employment, declined by nearly two-thirds. The United States was shifting its specialization from manufacturing to technology. In the process, it became a world leader in technology exports. So, while many manufacturing jobs in some sectors were lost, the shift in specialization and the resulting trade had positive effects on U.S. employment in general. During the 1990s, for example, U.S. exports were responsible for about 25 percent of the nation's economic growth, supporting about 12 million jobs. About 20 percent of all U.S. factory jobs depend on trade. Also, jobs in plants that export their products pay an average of 18 percent higher wages than jobs in non-exporting plants.

Biotech Jobs The U.S. economy's move to the technology sector has meant a sharp rise in biotechnology employment.

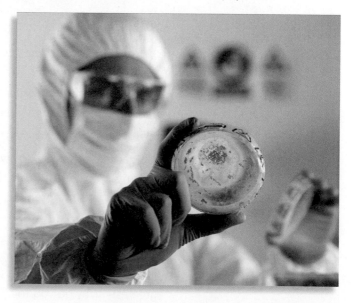

The United States in the World Economy

The United States is a leading nation in a number of aspects of the world economy. It is the largest exporter in the world, selling more than $900 billion in goods and services in 2005. The United States mostly exports capital goods (computers, machinery, civilian aircraft, and so on), automobiles, industrial supplies, consumer goods, and agricultural products. It is also the world's largest importer, buying nearly $1.7 trillion worth of goods and services from all over the world. It imports mainly crude oil and refined petroleum products, machinery, automobiles, consumer goods, and industrial raw materials.

Economics Update

Find an update on U.S. imports at **ClassZone.com**

While the United States imports more goods than it exports, it exports more services than it imports. Such services as travel and tourism, transportation, architecture and construction, and information systems find ready customers in Europe, Japan, Canada, and Mexico. The four most important trading partners for the United States in goods and services are Canada, accounting for 20 percent of trade, China (12 percent), Mexico (11 percent), and Japan (7 percent). Trade with these four partners accounts for half of U.S. foreign trade.

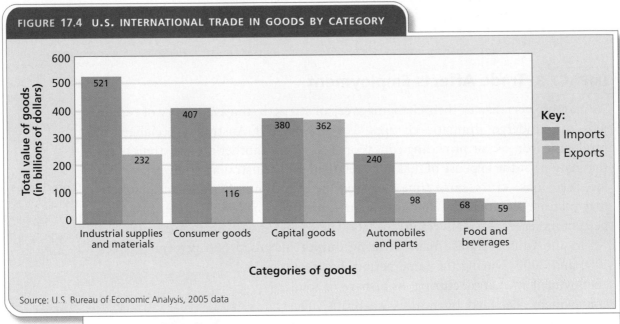

FIGURE 17.4 U.S. INTERNATIONAL TRADE IN GOODS BY CATEGORY

Source: U.S. Bureau of Economic Analysis, 2005 data

ANALYZE GRAPHS

1. In what two areas do U.S. export totals approach import totals?
2. What do these graphs show about the United States and specialization?

In recent years, as shown in Figure 17.4, the United States has imported an increasingly larger amount than it has exported. You will learn more about this in Section 4 of this chapter.

APPLICATION Interpreting Graphs

D. In what category of goods is the difference between imports and exports the greatest? Why do you think this is so?

Online Quiz
ClassZone.com

REVIEWING KEY CONCEPTS

1. Explain the difference between the terms in the following pairs:

    a. *specialization* and *economic interdependence*

    b. *absolute advantage* and *comparative advantage*

    c. *export* and *import*

2. What principle explains why nations specialize and trade?

3. Explain why trade is good for nations that produce exports as well as buy imports.

4. What effect do imports have on price and supply? Why?

5. What effect do exports have on price and demand? Why?

6. **Using Your Notes** Write a speech for the president of Australia, explaining why your nation should specialize in the production of iron ore and trade for steel. Use the Graphic Organizer at **Interactive Review @ ClassZone.com**

International Trade

CRITICAL THINKING

7. **Analyzing Cause and Effect** You have just learned that high-quality electric guitars made in South Korea will soon be exported to the United States. Should you buy a new guitar now or wait until after the imports begin arriving? Explain your answer.

8. **Making Inferences and Drawing Conclusions** Why does the law of comparative advantage explain that all people and nations can trade?

9. **Explaining an Economic Concept** How does international trade help create jobs? How does it shift jobs?

10. **Challenge** Shelley started her own comedy improvisation club right after college, and at first she did everything: developed new material, starred in the show, handled publicity, and sold tickets. As the enterprise grew, however, she hired an assistant to handle publicity and sell tickets, even though she was better at doing those things than he was. Explain why that was a good idea, using terms from this lesson.

ECONOMICS IN PRACTICE

Figuring Absolute and Comparative Advantage

Review the following scenario that describes cordless drill and drill bit production in the fictional nations of Freedonia and Sylvania.

Freedonia and Sylvania both produce cordless drills and drill bits. Over the span of a month, Freedonia can produce 3,000 cordless drills and 21,000 drill bits. During this same period, Sylvania can produce 2,000 cordless drills and 10,000 drill bits.

Drawing Conclusions Use what you've learned in this section to answer the following questions:

1. For each product, which nation has the absolute advantage?

2. What are the production ratios for each nation? What is each nation's opportunity cost for each cordless drill produced?

3. Which country has the comparative advantage in cordless drill production?

Challenge Draw up and explain a scenario whereby Freedonia and Sylvania agree to trade, and each gets a better deal by adjusting its trade ratio.

Trade Barriers

OBJECTIVES	KEY TERMS	TAKING NOTES
In Section 2, you will • identify barriers to trade • examine the economic consequences of trade barriers • describe protectionism and the arguments for it	trade barrier, *p. 520* quota, *p. 520* dumping, *p. 521* tariff, *p. 521* revenue tariff, *p. 521* protective tariff, *p. 521* voluntary export restraint, *p. 521* embargo, *p. 521* trade war, *p. 522* protectionism, *p. 523* infant industries, *p. 523*	As you read Section 2, complete a chart that shows the causes and effects of trade barriers. Use the Graphic Organizer at **Interactive Review @ ClassZone.com**

Cause	Effect
quota	higher prices

Barriers to Trade

KEY CONCEPTS

In order to offer some short-term protection to jobs and industries located within their borders, almost all nations pass some sort of laws that limit trade. These laws lead to higher prices on the restricted items or to economic retaliation by other nations. In the end, these industries and the jobs they provide can only be saved by becoming more competitive. The issue of trade restrictions is basically political in nature, and governments struggle to find the best policies to enact.

Types of Trade Barriers

A **trade barrier** is any law passed to limit free trade among nations. There are five basic types of trade barriers. Most are mandatory, but some are voluntary.

Quotas Nations often impose **quotas**, limits on the amount of a product that can be imported. For example, the United States had quotas on the amount of textiles allowed to be imported. These quotas limited supply and kept textile prices relatively high.

Quota Lifted Chinese textiles cross the Great Wall on their way to markets in the United States and the EU.

These quotas expired on January 1, 2005. Chinese producers then flooded the United States (and the European Union) with low-priced textiles. Prices for Chinese textiles increased, however, in other nations. This practice of **dumping**, the sale of a product in another country at a price lower than that charged in the home market, hurts domestic producers but provides consumers a lower price.

Tariffs Another trade barrier is the **tariff**, a fee charged for goods brought into a country from another country. There are two types of tariffs: revenue and protective. **Revenue tariffs**, taxes on imports specifically to raise money, are rarely used today. In the past, however, nations regularly used them as a source of income. Today nations use **protective tariffs**, taxes on imported goods, to protect domestic goods. Protective tariffs raise prices on goods produced more cheaply elsewhere, thereby minimizing the price advantage the imports have over domestic goods. Tariff rates have fallen worldwide since the late 1980s. (See Figure 17.5.)

Voluntary Export Restraint Sometimes, to avoid a quota or a tariff, a country may choose to limit an export. This is called a **voluntary export restraint (VER)**. It usually comes about when a trade ambassador from one nation makes appeals to a counterpart, warning of possible consequences without the VER.

Embargoes An **embargo** is a law that cuts off most or all trade with a specific country. It is often used for political purposes. Since the early 1960s, for example, the United States has had an embargo on trade with Communist Cuba.

Informal Trade Barriers Other trade restrictions are indirect. Licenses, environmental regulations, and health and safety measures (such as a ban on the use of certain herbicides) are, in effect, trade barriers.

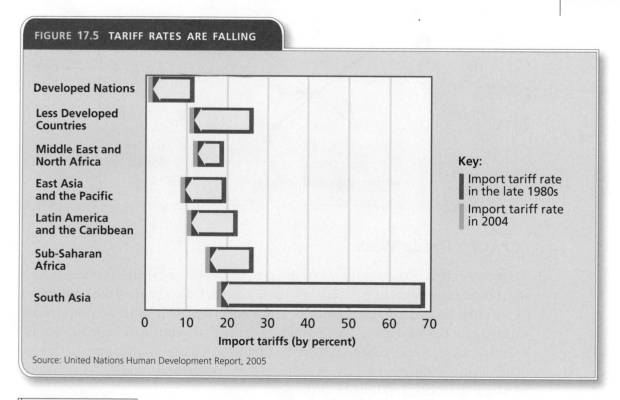

FIGURE 17.5 TARIFF RATES ARE FALLING

Key:
■ Import tariff rate in the late 1980s
■ Import tariff rate in 2004

Import tariffs (by percent)

Source: United Nations Human Development Report, 2005

APPLICATION Categorizing Economic Information

A. Aside from imposing an embargo, how might one nation limit the import of a product from another nation?

The Impact of Trade Barriers

QUICK REFERENCE

trade war succession of increasing trade barriers between nations

KEY CONCEPTS

Trade barriers have numerous effects. They may temporarily save domestic jobs in certain industries, but without competition, those industries might continue to operate inefficiently. In the end, consumers pay higher prices. Further, limits on trade sometimes lead to a **trade war**, a succession of trade barriers between nations.

IMPACT 1 Higher Prices

Trade barriers raise prices or keep them high. For example, in the early 2000s, the United States and Japan, who both produce semiconductor chips, imposed tariffs on chips from South Korea. The reason for the tariff was that the Korean government had subsidized the chip maker, allowing the chips to be sold at a very low price. The result was a higher price in U.S. and Japanese markets for both the Korean chips (up 27 to 44 percent) as well as for those produced domestically. (See Figure 17.6.)

FIGURE 17.6 THE EFFECT OF AN IMPORT TARIFF ON PRICE

a This is the pre-tariff price of an imported good.

b A tariff increases the price, moving the supply curve up the demand curve by the amount of the tariff.

c There is less demand at the new, higher price, so the supply of imported goods is reduced.

IMPACT 2 Trade Wars

Trade wars often occur when nations disagree on quotas or tariffs. One recent trade war, however, came about in 1999 when the European Union banned the importation of hormone-treated U.S. beef. Many U.S. ranchers treat their cattle with hormones, which cause the animals to develop muscle faster than untreated animals. But EU scientists, citing health concerns, helped push through a ban. In response, the United States levied 100 percent tariffs on a range of EU products, including ham, onions, mustard, chocolate, and Roquefort cheese.

APPLICATION Applying an Economic Concept

B. Boeing, a U.S. airplane producer, and Airbus, its European competitor, each claim the other receives unfair governmental support. Why does each object to the alleged unfair support?

Arguments for Protectionism

KEY CONCEPTS

Considering all the disadvantages of trade barriers, why would a country enact such laws? The answer lies in the concept of **protectionism**, the use of trade barriers between nations to protect domestic industries. Protectionists argue that trade barriers protect domestic jobs, promote **infant industries** (new industries that are often unable to compete against larger, more established competitors), and protect national security.

QUICK REFERENCE

Protectionism is the use of trade barriers between nations to protect domestic industries.

Infant industries are new industries that are often unable to compete against larger, more established competitors.

ARGUMENT 1 Protecting Domestic Jobs

Between 2000 and 2003, Stark County, Ohio, lost ten percent of its manufacturing jobs, including hundreds at a plant that makes Hoover vacuum cleaners. Imports from Asia and Mexico forced a ten percent drop in the price of vacuum cleaners. The U.S. workers, many of whom earned high wages to do their skilled work, were understandably upset by the shift of their jobs to overseas facilities.

In Ohio and elsewhere, people argue that trade barriers are needed to protect domestic jobs, even though, in reality, these actions generally protect inefficient production and result in higher prices for everyone. Voters in industrial areas bring their voices to the national debate about foreign trade. By doing so, they have helped bring about federal job training programs for workers who find themselves unemployed as a result of the movement of jobs to places where the per unit cost of labor is lower.

Irish Success Bono suggested that Ireland's ability to protect its industries helped the Irish economy become stronger.

ARGUMENT 2 Protecting Infant Industries

What was an Irish rock star, Bono, doing at the 2006 World Economic Conference in Davos, Switzerland? For one thing, this performer, known for his commitment to Africa, was arguing that African infant industries should be protected. Referring to the history of his own country, he said that Irish infant industries were protected in their day but that such protection is "denied . . . to the poorest countries in the world."

The idea behind protecting infant industries is to assist newly developing industries in their growth process until they are able to compete with better-developed foreign rivals. This argument is often used by newly developing nations to keep out goods from economically well developed nations. In Africa, for example, Uganda has received protection for its infant industries in the form of tariffs on exports from neighboring Kenya. However, even with these protective tariffs, Ugandan industry has not yet found a way to become competitive on its own and continues to request extensions of the tariff.

This example points to a potential problem. Critics say that, provided with a sheltered existence that is free from the need to compete on equal terms, these industries settle into perpetual infancy. And a perpetual infant needs perpetual support.

Non-Economic Trade Barriers

French movie poster

Some nations impose trade barriers for religious reasons. Iran, for instance, has banned any Western movies that portray secularism, feminism, and other activities deemed unethical. Western popular music has also been deemed indecent and "un-Islamic" and, therefore, banned. These barriers have driven demand for Western movies and music underground, where they can be found on the black market.

Some nations enact trade barriers based on more general notions of culture. During the 1994 round of negotiations related to the Global Agreement on Tariffs and Trade (GATT), the French movie industry won a victory on a principal close to its heart.

It's known as the cultural exception, and it basically states that cultural goods are different from other goods and should not be covered by trade agreements. The cultural exception has been used, notably by France and Canada, to boost domestic television and film industries (through subsidies and quotas) and limit foreign competition, mostly from the United States.

Without these protections, the exception's proponents say, a handful of U.S. media multinationals would be able to dominate the area of audiovisual entertainment, thereby overwhelming the traditional cultures of other nations.

CONNECTING ACROSS THE GLOBE

1. **Explaining an Economic Concept** Some would argue that all trade barriers lack sound, economic reasoning. Do you agree? Why?

2. **Making Inferences and Drawing Conclusions** Which one of the three arguments for protectionism most resembles the actions taken by France and Canada? Explain.

ARGUMENT 3 Protecting National Security

National security affects the trade of industries that nations consider to be vital to their safety. The energy industry is considered vital by most. In 2005, a government-run Chinese company bid on U.S. oil company UNOCAL. Many in Congress and elsewhere in the United States warned against allowing a foreign government to take over an important U.S. energy supplier. After the House of Representatives voted 398 to 15 to ask President Bush to step in, the Chinese company withdrew its bid.

But sharp political differences exist over what industries are truly vital to national security. In 2006, a company from Dubai, which had purchased the rights to operate port facilities in New York, Miami, New Orleans, and elsewhere, was forced to abandon the deal in light of political pressure over port security. Many analysts were skeptical of the security concerns, however, and worried more about the implications of interference in free international trade for purely political reasons.

APPLICATION Making Inferences and Drawing Conclusions

C. Do you think that political pressure for protectionist trade barriers rises or falls during a recession? Explain your answer.

REVIEWING KEY CONCEPTS

1. Explain the relationship between the terms in the following pairs:

   a. *trade barrier* **b.** *tariff*   **c.** *trade war*   **d.** *infant*
   quota   *voluntary export*   *protective tariff*   *industries*
                    restraint   *protectionism*

2. Why would a country engage in dumping?

3. How does a trade war get started? What effects does it have?

4. Why do some people feel that barriers to free trade are essential for national security?

5. Who benefits from trade barriers, inefficient or efficient producers?

6. **Using Your Notes** Take a position on free trade vs. protectionism and explain your position in a brief essay. Refer to your completed cause-and-effect chart. Use the Graphic Organizer at **Interactive Review @ ClassZone.com**

Cause	Effect
quota	higher prices

CRITICAL THINKING

7. **Analyzing Cause and Effect** In 1996, the United States expanded the embargo against Cuba, declaring that any foreign corporation that engaged in trade with Cuba would lose its privilege of trading with the United States. Give two possible effects of this embargo expansion.

8. **Solving Economic Problems** If you were the CEO of a manufacturing company facing stiff foreign competition, what are some ways you could adjust your business to stay competitive? What are the advantages and disadvantages of these changes?

9. **Applying Economic Concepts** Give three examples of U.S. citizens earning an income by selling products domestically that were made in other countries. Give three examples of U.S. citizens earning an income by selling products or services that are ultimately purchased by people in other countries.

10. **Challenge** A trade agreement between Kenya and some nations in Europe requires Kenyan farmers, most of whom have small peasant farms, to comply with 400 conditions before they can export their produce to European countries. They must be able to document the fertilizers, pesticides, and other additives used in the growing of their crops. How would you categorize this trade restriction? What impact do you think it will have on Kenyan exports and prices in the European nations?

ECONOMICS IN PRACTICE

Analyzing Tariff Rates
Look at the graph below showing selected U.S. tariff rates for nations with which it has "Normal Trade Relations" (NTR), also known as the "most-favored nation" (MFN) status.

Item	NTR/MFN Tariff (%)
Ceramic tableware	4.5
Cars	2.5
Trucks	25.0
Most bicycles	11.0
Sports footwear	10.5

Analyzing and Interpreting Data How much does the cost of a $32,000 truck increase because of the tariffs? If you pay $245.31 for a bicycle, what amount is the tariff?

Challenge Suppose a pair of imported running shoes costs $10. With the tariff added, the importer has to pay $11.50. The importer, however, has to raise the price of the shoes to cover the expense of selling and shipping them to retailers, and retailers have to raise the price to cover their expenses in selling the shoes. Assuming the price increases by 50 percent at each stage of the process, what amount does the initial $1.50 tariff grow into?

Measuring the Value of Trade

OBJECTIVES	KEY TERMS	TAKING NOTES
In Section 3, you will • describe how nations determine the value of their currency in a world market • explain why nations want a favorable balance of trade	foreign exchange market, *p. 526* foreign exchange rate, *p. 526* fixed rate of exchange, *p. 526* flexible rate of exchange, *p. 527* trade weighted value of the dollar, *p. 528* balance of trade, *p. 529* balance of payments, *p. 529* trade surplus, *p. 529* trade deficit, *p. 529*	As you read Section 3, complete a cluster diagram summarizing key information about measuring trade. Use the Graphic Organizer at **Interactive Review @ ClassZone.com** Measuring Trade

Foreign Exchange

KEY CONCEPTS

If a certain good costs $100, how many euros does it cost? How many Mexican pesos? Or Russian rubles? International trade requires some way to establish the relative value of the different currencies of the nations doing the trading. So nations have worked out systems that facilitate the exchange of currencies between buyers and sellers. One key element is the **foreign exchange market**, a market in which currencies of different countries are bought and sold. This market is a network of major commercial and investment banks that link the economies of the world. Another key element in facilitating international trade is the **foreign exchange rate**, the price of one currency in the currencies of other nations.

Rates of Exchange

During the 1800s and early 1900s, gold was the standard against which the value of a nation's currency was determined. Nations traded on the basis of a **fixed rate of exchange**, a system in which the currency of one nation

Currency Exchange The Mexican peso, the Australian dollar, and the Chinese yuan are all bought and sold on the foreign exchange market.

is fixed, or constant, in relation to other currencies—in this case to gold. After the profound economic disruption of World War II, other currencies were "pegged" to the stable U.S. dollar. That is, their currency was valued according to its relation to the U.S. dollar. The price of an ounce of gold was fixed at $35.

The volatile 1970s brought another change. As the United States ran up a trade deficit and the dollar declined in value, the standard of $35 per ounce of gold was no longer sustainable, and the **flexible rate of exchange**, also called the floating rate, became predominant. This is a system in which the exchange rates for currencies change as the supply of and demand for the currencies change. For example, suppose that one British pound (GBP) is worth two U.S. dollars (USD). If an American importer wants to buy 100 British-made watches valued at 100 GBP each, then the importer would sell 20,000 USD in the foreign exchange market to obtain the necessary 10,000 GBPs. As the supply of dollars increases, their relative value drops. So the next time the importer wants to buy watches, the exchange rate might be 1 GPB:2.5 USD, and the watches would cost 25,000 U.S. dollars, making them less attractive as imports. Over time, the flexible exchange rate acts as a regulator on foreign exchange, balancing imports and exports.

QUICK REFERENCE

The **flexible rate of exchange** is a system in which the exchange rate for currency changes as supply and demand for the currency changes.

MATH CHALLENGE

FIGURE 17.7 Calculating Exchange Rates

Suppose you want to buy a book in Germany, where the currency is the euro (€). The book costs €25, and the seller wants you to pay in euros, but you have U.S. dollars. To buy the book you must first buy euros.

To find out how much €25 costs in U.S. dollars, you must know the exchange rate. In this case, let's say the exchange rate is 1.25, which means that one euro costs $1.25. Now use the following formula.

Example Calculation

Amount of currency you want to buy	×	Exchange rate	=	Cost in currency you have	€25 × 1.25 $/€ = $31.25

To buy €25, you must pay $31.25.

Reciprocal exchange rate The exchange rate 1.25 can be written as a fraction: $1.25/€1. You can use this fraction to find the exchange rate a German must use to buy U.S. dollars with euros. First take the reciprocal of the fraction by swapping the numerator and the denominator; then use a calculator to write the fraction as a decimal.

The reciprocal of	$\frac{\$1.25}{€1}$	is	$\frac{€1}{\$1.25}$,	which is 0.80 €/$

So to convert from U.S. dollars to euros, multiply by the exchange rate 0.80.

Strong and Weak Currencies

QUICK REFERENCE

The **trade-weighted value of the dollar** is a measure of the international value of the dollar.

The Federal Reserve keeps a measure of the international value of the dollar called the **trade-weighted value of the dollar**. It determines if the dollar is strong or weak as measured against another currency. Because of the flexible exchange rate, as currencies are traded, some increase or decrease in value when measured against another currency.

For example, if the U.S. dollar becomes stronger in comparison to the Mexican peso, then the U.S. dollar buys more Mexican pesos than it could previously. What this means is that imports from Mexico now cost less. As you can see in Figure 17.8, importers in the United States benefit because they are able to buy foreign goods and services relatively cheaply.

At the same time, however, goods made in the United States may have a hard time competing with these inexpensive imports in the U.S. domestic market. Also, the strong dollar has a negative effect on U.S. exporters, since goods made here would be more costly to purchase abroad at the strong dollar rate. The weak dollar has the same effects but in reverse, as imported goods become more expensive and exporters are able to sell relatively cheaply.

FIGURE 17.8 THE STRONG DOLLAR AND U.S. TRADE

As the **value of the dollar** increases → **imports** to the U.S. become less expensive and increase → but **exports** from the U.S. become more expensive and decrease

YOUR ECONOMIC CHOICES

STRONG DOLLAR AND WEAK DOLLAR

Which sweater will you buy?

The U.S. dollar is very weak versus the Hong Kong dollar (HKD). How might this influence your decision to buy a new sweater made in the United States, or one imported from Hong Kong?

Domestically produced

Imported from overseas

100% MERINO EXTRA FINE WOOL MADE IN HONG KONG RN 77219 SEE REVERSE FOR CARE

APPLICATION Applying Economic Concepts

A. If you are an American exporter, does a strong dollar help your business? Explain.

Balance of Trade

KEY CONCEPTS

In Chapter 12, you read about net exports as an economic measure. Another name for the difference between the value of a country's imports and exports is its **balance of trade**. It is tallied through the **balance of payments**, a record of all the transactions that occurred between the individuals, businesses, and government units of one nation and those of the rest of the world. The U.S. balance of payments includes the goods and services traded between it and other nations, as well as the investments foreign interests make in the United States and those made by Americans in a foreign country. A nation is said to have a favorable balance of trade if it has a **trade surplus**—that is, it exports more than it imports. If a nation imports more than it exports it has a **trade deficit**, also known as an unfavorable balance of trade.

EXAMPLE U.S.-China Trade

In recent years, China has undergone one of the most rapid industrializations in history. In addition to its fast-growing output of manufactured goods, the Chinese currency, the RenMinBi (RMB), or yuan, has also been weak compared to the U.S. dollar. The yuan's weakness versus the dollar resulted from China's decision to peg its value at a fixed rate versus the dollar, beginning in 1994. This artificially weak position helped make the United States the number-one destination for Chinese exports. By 2005, China had a record trade surplus of just over $200 billion with the United States. The surplus helps China fuel its continued manufacturing growth.

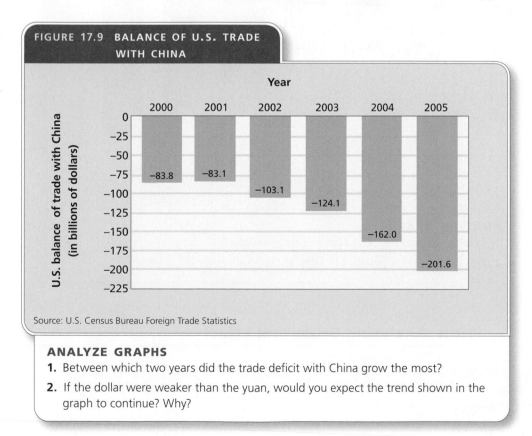

FIGURE 17.9 BALANCE OF U.S. TRADE WITH CHINA

Source: U.S. Census Bureau Foreign Trade Statistics

ANALYZE GRAPHS

1. Between which two years did the trade deficit with China grow the most?

2. If the dollar were weaker than the yuan, would you expect the trend shown in the graph to continue? Why?

EXAMPLE The U.S. Trade Balance

The balance of trade in the United States has gone through roughly five phases. From about 1770 to 1870, the young nation had a deficit in goods and services but a surplus in capital investment from foreign countries that recognized the nation's potential for growth. Between 1870 and 1920, the nation was paying back foreign debts from the previous phase, but it was also exporting more goods and services than it was importing. In the years between 1920 and 1945, the United States had a surplus in exports but a deficit in foreign investments, as the nation sought to help rebuild Europe after World War I. From 1945 to 1980, the nation had a deficit in merchandise and continued its deficit in foreign investments as large amounts of money went to post–World War II reconstruction.

In the current phase, the United States has a large surplus of foreign investment, which is attracted by a relatively low inflation rate and a generally stable economy. However, high rates of consumer spending (versus low rates of saving), as well as high oil prices (which significantly increased the dollar value of U.S. imports) have helped create a very large merchandise deficit. An advantage of this deficit is that it allows U.S. consumers to buy low-priced imports. A disadvantage is that financing the deficit may require borrowing money from the rest of the world, selling off assets, or tapping into foreign currency reserves.

Economics Update

For an update on the U.S. balance of trade go to **ClassZone.com**

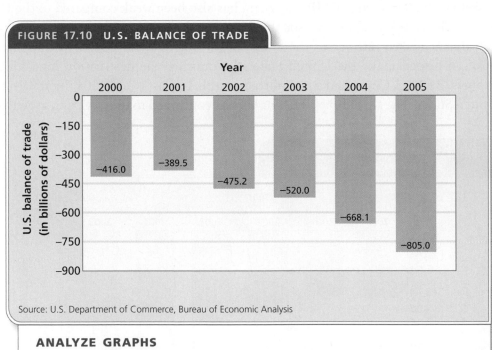

FIGURE 17.10 U.S. BALANCE OF TRADE

Source: U.S. Department of Commerce, Bureau of Economic Analysis

ANALYZE GRAPHS

1. In what year did the U.S. balance of trade improve?
2. Does this overall trend point to rising or falling prices for U.S. consumers?

APPLICATION Analyzing Cause and Effect

B. Between 1870 and 1920, the United States was exporting more goods and services than it imported. What does this say about the relative strength of the dollar during this period?

REVIEWING KEY CONCEPTS

1. Explain the differences between the terms in each of these pairs:

   a. *foreign exchange market*   b. *fixed rate of exchange*   c. *trade surplus*
   foreign exchange rate   *flexible rate of*   *trade deficit*
                                 exchange

2. What is an advantage of a trade surplus? A disadvantage?

3. What is an advantage of a trade deficit? A disadvantage?

4. How does the value of the U.S. dollar affect the U.S. trade surplus or deficit?

5. How does a flexible exchange rate help to stabilize trade balances?

6. **Using Your Notes** Write a brief essay arguing for or against a single world currency. Refer to your completed cluster and use the section's key words.

   Use the Graphic Organizer at **Interactive Review @ ClassZone.com**

CRITICAL THINKING

7. **Analyzing Cause and Effect** In July 2005, the Chinese RMB became fixed to a "market-basket" of currencies, including the U.S. dollar and the Japanese yen, removing a decade-long peg to the U.S. dollar alone. The new formula slightly raised the value of the RMB. If China's trade surpluses continue, what will happen to the value of the RMB?

8. **Applying an Economic Concept** While you are in France on a business trip, you find out that the euro has gained strength against the U.S. dollar. Will your hotel room and food now be more or less expensive? Why? What about the goods you're trying to sell on your trip; will they be more or less expensive to your customers in France? Why?

9. **Making Inferences and Drawing Conclusions** Japan has the world's largest foreign currency reserves, followed by China. State two conclusions you can draw about the economies of these two nations based on their foreign currency reserves.

10. **Challenge** What are the advantages of a large supply of foreign investment in a domestic economy? What are the disadvantages?

ECONOMICS IN PRACTICE

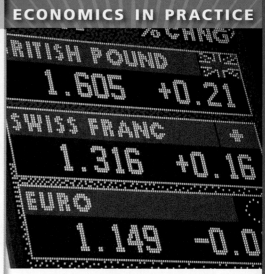

Understanding Exchange Rates
Just as there are stock markets for trading company shares, there are currency markets for trading currencies. The picture shows the prices of three currencies in dollars and how the prices have changed.

Buys	One			
	U.S. Dollar	Euro	Chinese Yuan	Indian Rupee
U.S. Dollar	1.00	1.32	0.13	0.02
Euro	0.76	1.00	0.10	0.02
Chinese Yuan	7.82	10.33	1.00	0.18
Indian Rupee	44.48	58.72	5.69	1.00

Average rates, December 2006

Analyze Data Use this exchange rate table to answer the following questions.

- How much of each of the other currencies will $5 U.S. purchase?

- If the exchange rate from euros to dollars changed from 1.32 to 1.40, which currency has gotten weaker?

- How would that affect EU businesses that export to the United States?

Challenge Why might businesses need to buy foreign currencies?

Modern International Institutions

OBJECTIVES	KEY TERMS	TAKING NOTES
In Section 4, you will • describe what agreements were made to start the free-trade movement • identify international and regional trade groups • explain what role multinationals play in world trade	free-trade zone, *p. 532* customs union, *p. 532* European Union, *p. 532* euro, *p. 533* NAFTA, *p. 533* OPEC, *p. 535* cartel, *p. 535* WTO, *p. 535*	As you read Section 4, complete a summary chart like the one shown, using the key concepts and other helpful words and phrases. Use the Graphic Organizer at **Interactive Review @ ClassZone.com** | Regional	International
---	---

Regional and World Trade Organizations

QUICK REFERENCE

A **free-trade zone** is a specific region in which trade between nations takes place without protective tariffs.

A **customs union** is an agreement that abolishes trade barriers among its members and establishes uniform tariffs for non-members.

The **European Union**, the EU, is an economic and political union of European nations established in 1993.

KEY CONCEPTS

Following the failed protectionist policies of the 1930s, nations have sought to expand trade and reduce or eliminate trade barriers. They have organized regional trading groups to create **free-trade zones**, specific regions in which trade between nations takes place without protective tariffs. Some have created **customs unions**, agreements that abolish trade barriers among the members and establish uniform tariffs for non-members. Some of these organizations are called common markets. As a result of these efforts, global tariffs have dropped by about one-third.

GROUP 1 The European Union

In 1957, six European nations recognized the benefits of abolishing trade barriers and formed a customs union called the European Economic Community. It was widely known as the Common Market. In 1993 the Common Market evolved into the **European Union**, or EU , which tightly bound its member nations to one another both economically and politically. The political nature of the EU, the fact that its members surrender some sovereignty in specified areas, makes it unique among

EU Expansion Lithuanians celebrate their nation's admission to the EU in 2004.

trading groups. The Treaty on European Union had monetary union and a common foreign policy as key goals. Monetary union was established in 2002, as 12 member states adopted the **euro**. (See "The Euro as Common Currency" on p. 292.)

The six original members were Belgium, France, Germany, Italy, Luxembourg, and the Netherlands. In 1973, Denmark, Ireland, and the United Kingdom became members. Greece joined in 1981, and Portugal and Spain in 1986. In 1995, after the Common Market became the European Union, Austria, Finland, and Sweden joined. In 2004, ten nations became members: Cyprus, the Czech Republic, Estonia, Hungary, Latvia, Lithuania, Malta, Poland, Slovakia, and Slovenia. In 2007, Bulgaria and Romania joined, raising the total number of members to 27.

The EU accounts for about 20 percent of global exports and imports, making it the world's biggest trader. It has removed barriers to free trade among member nations, with the ultimate goal that Europe's national borders will be no more a barrier to free trade than are the borders of U.S. states.

QUICK REFERENCE

The **euro** is the currency of the European Union.

GROUP 2 NAFTA

In 1990, negotiations began on a free-trade agreement among the United States, Canada, and Mexico. The result of these negotiations, the North American Free Trade Agreement, or **NAFTA**, created the largest free-trade zone in the world. When it went into effect on January 1, 1994, it immediately eliminated tariffs on half of the goods exported to Mexico from the United States. The agreement called for an eventual phase-out of all trade barriers on goods and services. It also called for improved protection of intellectual property rights, stronger environmental and worker protections, and standardized investment policies.

Many groups have raised objections to NAFTA, especially on political and environmental grounds. However, economically, NAFTA appears to have achieved its intended result. The graphs in Figure 17.11 show how U.S. trade with Canada and Mexico changed over the treaty's first ten years. In particular, two-way agricultural

QUICK REFERENCE

NAFTA, the North America Free Trade Agreement, is designed to ensure trade without barriers between Canada, Mexico, and the United States.

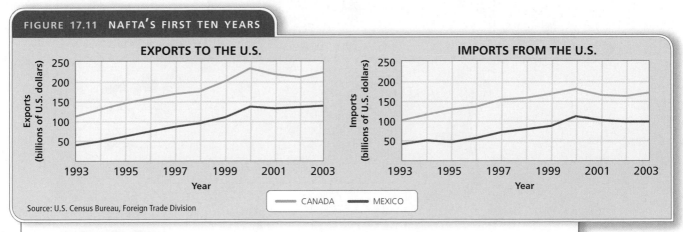

FIGURE 17.11 NAFTA'S FIRST TEN YEARS

EXPORTS TO THE U.S.

IMPORTS FROM THE U.S.

Source: U.S. Census Bureau, Foreign Trade Division

CANADA   MEXICO

ANALYZE GRAPHS

1. Which nation, Canada or Mexico, increased its trade with the United States by a larger percentage?

2. Is an increase in trade typically beneficial for nations? Explain.

trade between Mexico and the United States increased 125 percent—from $6.2 billion in 1993 to $14.2 billion in 2003. Productivity in Mexico increased a remarkable 55 percent. Canada's exports to its NAFTA partners increased by 104 percent, and its overall economy grew by over 30 percent. Overall trade between the three partners more than doubled during this period, from $289.3 billion in 1993 to $623.1 billion in 2003.

GROUP 3 Other Regional Trade Groups

Throughout the world, nations are forming trade organizations to specialize, promote free trade, and stay competitive with other trade groups. Descriptions of a number of these agreements from all parts of the world follow:

Mercosur (*Mercado Comun del Cono Sur*) This group promotes the movement of goods and people in South America. Formed in 1995, Mercosur eliminated tariffs on 90 percent of goods traded between the group's full members (Argentina, Brazil, Paraguay, and Uruguay). Venezuela became a full member in July of 2006. Counting associate members Mexico, Chile, Bolivia, and Peru, Mercosur has become the world's fourth-largest trade association.

ASEAN The Association of Southest Asian Nations was formed in 1967 to accelerate economic growth, social progress, and cultural development in the region, and to promote regional peace and stability. Its members include Indonesia, the Philippines, Singapore, Thailand, Vietnam, Laos, Cambodia, and others.

FIGURE 17.12 Some Regional Trade Groups

Andean Community	Commonwealth of Independent States (CIS)	Organization of Petroleum Exporting Countries (OPEC)
Asia-Pacific Economic Cooperation (APEC)	European Union (EU)	Southern Common Market (MERCOSUR)
Association of Southeast Asian Nations (ASEAN)	Group of Eight (G8)	Southern African Development Community (SADC)
Common Market for Eastern & Southern Africa (COMESA)	North American Free Trade Agreement (NAFTA)	

ANALYZE MAPS

How many trading groups do the United States and Canada belong to? Why does it make sense for such developed nations to be part of multiple trading groups?

APEC The Asia-Pacific Economic Cooperation group is a trade organization of nations on the Pacific Rim—those that are adjacent to or within the Pacific Ocean. It includes developed nations such as Australia, Japan, and the United States, transitional economies such as Russia and China, as well as less developed countries such as Thailand, Papua New Guinea, and Chile. The group has set ambitious goals for trade liberalization throughout the region by 2020. However, since all APEC decisions require a unanimous vote, progress toward its goals has been slow.

OPEC The Organization of Petroleum Exporting Countries is a **cartel**—a group of producers who regulate the production, pricing, and marketing of a particular product. In OPEC's case, that product is petroleum, or oil. It has had mixed results in controlling the oil market since its formation in 1960. However, surging demand, from nations such as China and the United States, and periods of regional political instability have strengthened OPEC's position in recent years.

SADC Founded in 1979, the South African Development Community's original goal was to act as a counterbalance to the region's main economic power—South Africa. After South Africa finally abandoned minority white rule—the apartheid system—it also became a member in 1994. A regional free-trade zone was established in 2000.

Dedication to free trade is a key element in boosting the region's economies. However, corruption, political instability, various health issues (most importantly, AIDS), substandard education, and poor infrastructure consistently hamper development. (You'll learn about these and other development issues in Chapter 18.)

QUICK REFERENCE

OPEC is the Organization of Petroleum Exporting Countries.

A **cartel** is a group of producers that regulates the production, pricing, and marketing of a product.

GROUP 4 World Trade Organization

In 1944, the Allied nations met to plan for recovery after World War II. Among other important outcomes, they produced the General Agreement on Tariffs and Trade (GATT), which laid out rules and policies for international trade. In 1995, the GATT principles were incorporated into a new organization, the **World Trade Organization**, or WTO. The WTO has over 150 member nations.

The purposes of the WTO include negotiating and administering trade agreements, resolving trade disputes, monitoring the trading policies of member nations, and providing support for developing countries. The principles underlying these purposes include that trade rules should apply equally to domestic and imported products. To that end, all member nations should offer one another most favored nation (MFN) status, sometimes called normal trade relation (NTR) status. This means that no nation should extend more favorable trade terms to one WTO member than it does to another. Members should also work toward lowering trade barriers of all kinds and support fair trade as well as free trade.

To varying degrees, the WTO has been successful. It has helped reduce tariffs on manufactured goods, lower trade barriers in agriculture, and promote intellectual property rights. It has also resolved disputes among members while maintaining each nation's sovereignty, and promoted stability among member nations.

QUICK REFERENCE

The **World Trade Organization**, or **WTO**, is a group of nations that adhere to the policies of the General Agreement on Tariffs and Trade.

APPLICATION Making Inferences and Drawing Conclusions

A. What is the purpose of most of the regional and world trade organizations?

Multinationals Bring Changes to International Trade

Multinational corporations (see Chapter 8) cross many borders and must deal with tariffs, labor restrictions, and taxes in different nations. They often bring jobs and technology to developing nations, while boosting overall levels of international trade—something that benefits everyone involved.

International Trade Within Multinationals

As multinationals have become more prevalent, trade between the various divisions of multinationals has become an area of increasing interest. Intrafirm trade, as it is known, can simply be the exchange of goods between two parts of a multinational. But international intrafirm trade also covers the coordination of production between parts of a multinational. This means, for instance, that when a U.S. parent company sends parts to an overseas affiliate to assemble, that is counted in the export column for U.S. statistics on trade. Likewise, when the assembled goods are shipped back to the U.S. parent from its overseas affiliate, that is counted in the import column. In general, intrafirm imports account for about 40 percent of total U.S. imports. Intrafirm exports account for about one-third of total U.S. exports.

EXAMPLE A Multinational Telecom Corporation

Consider the case of Worldwide Cellular, a U.S.-based multinational that makes, markets, and services cellular phones. It imports an essential raw material from its mining arm in Australia, manufactures the phones at its facility in South Korea, markets the phones in Europe, and then directs customers who have questions or complaints to technical support and customer service representatives in India. Throughout the process, the people and the economies of each nation benefit.

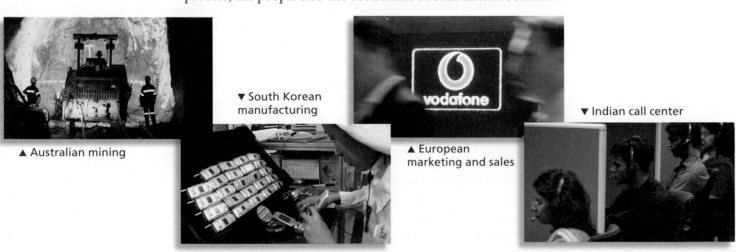

▲ Australian mining

▼ South Korean manufacturing

▲ European marketing and sales

▼ Indian call center

APPLICATION to come

B. In 1969, there were about 7,200 known multinationals. By 2000, that number had grown to more than 63,000. Give three possible contributing reasons for that growth.

REVIEWING KEY CONCEPTS

1. Explain the relationship between the terms in each of these pairs:

   a. *free-trade zone*
   customs union

   b. *EU*
   NAFTA

   c. *OPEC*
   cartel

2. What circumstances led to a liberalization in global trading?

3. How do customs unions help member nations?

4. How is the EU different from other regional trading groups?

5. What are some advantages of NAFTA?

6. **Using Your Notes** Write a brief summary of the major regional and international trade organizations. Refer to your completed summary chart and use the section's key words. Use the Graphic Organizer at **Interactive Review @ ClassZone.com**

Regional	International

CRITICAL THINKING

7. **Making Inferences and Drawing Conclusions** Some regional trade associations are viewed as an attempt by less developed countries to protect themselves and their regions from globalization's aggressive momentum. Explain how regional groups might have that effect.

8. **Analyzing Cause and Effect** Many multinationals grew out of exporting businesses. How might the exporting business prepare a company to become a multinational?

9. **Predicting Economic Trends** Before NAFTA was passed, some experts predicted a reduction in illegal immigration from Mexico to the United States. In fact, in the first few years after NAFTA went into effect, illegal immigration increased. What reasoning might have explained the prediction that illegal immigration would decline? What reasons might explain the increase?

10. **Challenge** At the Hong Kong gathering of the World Trade Organization in 2005, Supachai Panitchpakdi, secretary general of the United Nations Conference on Trade and Development (UNCTAD) said: "Rich countries will have to reject not just protectionism, but populism, too. They will have to speak honestly to their people about the changing economies of the 21st century, and about global interdependence and the fact that prosperity elsewhere means prosperity and jobs at home." Write a brief essay that "speaks honestly" to the rich countries about the changing economies of the 21st century.

ECONOMICS IN PRACTICE

The Effects of NAFTA
Between 1993 and 2002, the total trade among Canada, the United States, and Mexico more than doubled. The table below shows export figures for NAFTA members Canada and Mexico in each of those years.

Nation	Exports (in billions of dollars)	
	1993	2002
Canada		
to United States	113.6	213.9
to Mexico	.9	1.6
Mexico		
to United States	31.8	136.1
to Canada	2.9	8.8

Analyzing and Interpreting Data Canada has a higher export amount than Mexico, but did its level of trade increase more than Mexico's in the interval? Explain.

Challenge Can Canadian companies produce, package, and market products for both of its NAFTA partners in the same way? Explain why or why not.

Case Study

⟡ **Economics Update**
Find an update on this Case
Study at **ClassZone.com**

Analyzing Tariffs—Who Wins and Who Loses?

Background Tariffs on foreign sugar have been around almost as long as the United States itself. Although early tariffs were a form of revenue, their purpose expanded in the 19th century to provide protection for the domestic sugar industry. That protection continues to this day.

Globalization, however, is having a direct impact on the way nations trade. Agricultural subsidies and tariffs have become a point of contention in recent WTO talks, with less-developed countries unhappy about the lack of market access for their goods and about their price disadvantage.

What's the issue? How do the trade barriers set up by the U.S. government affect producers (both foreign and domestic) and consumers?

A. Online Article

This article describes how the U.S. government supports sugar prices. Note that sugar subsidies are paid to the processor, rather than the farmer. The farmer receives a share once the sugar is processed.

Sugar Interests Harm the National Interest

USDA loan rates set floor on price of sugar.

The [government] program allows sugar processors to take out loans from the USDA [U.S. Department of Agriculture] by pledging sugar as collateral. The loan rates—18 cents per pound for cane sugar, 22.9 cents per pound for beet sugar—are significantly higher than average world sugar prices. These loans must be repaid within nine months, but processors also have the option of forfeiting their sugar to the government in lieu of repaying their debt.

This arrangement effectively guarantees that the processors receive a price for their sugar that is no lower than the loan value: If prices fell below that level, they would simply forfeit their sugar and keep the government's money.

In order to avoid that scenario, the USDA must prop up the domestic price of sugar. It does this by controlling supply through two mechanisms. First, it sets quotas on how much foreign sugar can be imported without facing prohibitive tariffs; second, it regulates the amount of sugar that domestic processors can sell.

Source: Jason Lee Steorts, *National Review*, July 18, 2005

Thinking Economically In your own words, describe the mechanisms by which the U.S. government props up domestic sugar prices.

FIGURE 17.13 U.S. AND WORLD RAW SUGAR PRICES

B. Government Report

This information from the U.S. Department of Agriculture charts U.S. raw sugar prices versus raw sugar prices for the rest of the world.

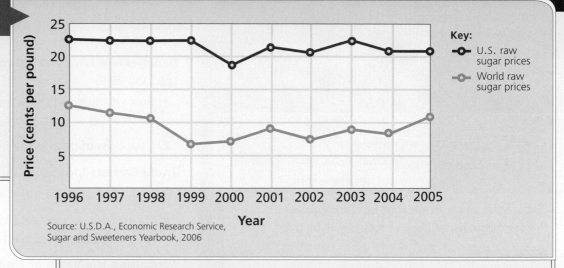

Key:
- ●—○ U.S. raw sugar prices
- ○—○ World raw sugar prices

Source: U.S.D.A., Economic Research Service, Sugar and Sweeteners Yearbook, 2006

Thinking Economically On average, how much greater are U.S. raw sugar prices than those for the rest of the world?

C. Trade Association Web Page

The American Sugar Alliance's Web site makes the case that the U.S. sugar industry is an important part of the overall U.S. economy.

Sweetener's Impact on the U.S. Economy

The American sweetener industry has a significant impact on the nation's economy.

- Economic impact: $21.1 billion of economic activity in 42 states is generated in the U.S. each year by the sugar and corn sweetener industries.
- Beet sugar industry: Over 1,400,000 acres of sugarbeets are grown in 12 states and are processed in 25 sugarbeet factories. The industry creates 88,200 full time direct and indirect jobs for people across the nation.
- Cane sugar industry: Seven cane refineries and 22 mills process sugar cane raised in four states: Florida, Hawaii, Louisiana and Texas. The production and processing of sugarcane creates 71,900 full time direct and indirect jobs.
- Jobs: 372,000 jobs in the U.S. rely on a strong U.S. sweetener industry.

Source: www.sugaralliance.org

Thinking Economically Why does the American Sugar Alliance want to emphasize the economic impact of the sugar industry?

THINKING ECONOMICALLY Synthesizing

1. Which argument for protection does document C seem to make? Use the document and pages 523 and 524 to formulate your answer. Is this argument economically valid? Explain.

2. Is the difference in price shown in document B an unavoidable outcome of the program outlined in document A? Explain your answer.

3. How does U.S. government intervention in the sugar industry limit the functioning of the economy as a free market? Use examples from the documents in your answer.

Interactive ◄◄Review

Review this chapter using interactive
activities at **ClassZone.com**

- Online Summary
- Quizzes
- Vocabulary Flip Cards
- Graphic Organizers
- Review and Study Notes

⟶ Online Summary

Complete the following activity either on your
own paper or online at **ClassZone.com**

**Choose the key concept that best completes
the sentence. Not all key concepts will be used.**

absolute advantage	NAFTA
balance of trade	protectionism
comparative advantage	quota
economic interdependence	revenue tariffs
embargo	tariff
exports	trade barrier
foreign exchange market	trade deficit
foreign exchange rate	trade surplus
free trade zone	trade war
imports	WTO

When nations can produce something at a lower
cost than other nations, they are said to have a(n)
__1__. This is different from a(n) __2__, which means
that goods or services are produced at a lower
opportunity cost. Through trade, nations develop
__3__, relying on one another.

Policies of __4__ have created __5__ between
nations, including __6__—limits on imports—and
__7__—fees charged on goods brought into a country.

International trade would not be possible
without the __8__, where currencies of different
countries are bought and sold. Nations keep track
of their __9__, the difference between their exports
and their imports. With a __10__, large reserves
of foreign currency accumulate. With a __11__,
domestic consumers enjoy lower prices.

The trend since the end of World War II has
been toward free trade. Nations have formed
regional __12__ that abolish trade barriers among
members. In 1994 the United States became part
of a trading organization with Mexico and Canada
known as __13__.

CHAPTER 17 Assessment

REVIEWING KEY CONCEPTS

**Benefits and Issues of International Trade
(pp. 510–519)**

1. How do nations gain by specializing in products
for which they have a comparative advantage?

2. How does trade affect a national economy?

Trade Barriers (pp. 520–525)

3. Name and describe four trade barriers.

4. What three reasons are protectionists likely to
offer to support their position?

Measuring the Value of Trade (pp. 526–531)

5. Explain how an importer purchases a foreign
product and what effect those actions would have
on the value of each currency.

6. What does the term *strong dollar* mean?

Modern International Institutions (pp. 532–539)

7. What agreements helped launch the free trade
movement?

8. Create a fictional multinational and explain how
it might operate from raw materials all the way
through marketing the finished product.

APPLYING ECONOMIC CONCEPTS

Look at the graph below showing U.S. imports and
exports to and from various trading regions.

9. To which group does the United States export the
lowest dollar value of goods and services?

10. With which group does the United States have the
largest trade deficit? the smallest trade deficit?

FIGURE 17.14 U.S. TRADE WITH REGIONAL GROUPS

Key:
- Imports from
- Exports to

Source: www.eurunion.org

11. **Creating Graphs** Create a bar graph to illustrate the following trade data for China, the European Union, and the United States.

FIGURE 17.15 IMPORTS AND EXPORTS FOR SELECTED REGIONS

Country or Region	Total Imports (trillions of U.S. dollars)	Total Exports (trillions of U.S. dollars)
China	1.156	1.465
European Union	1.690	1.952
United States	2.190	1.377

Source: CIA World Factbook, 2007 and 2008 data

Use *SMARTGrapher* @ ClassZone.com to complete this activity.

12. **Analyzing and Interpreting Data** Which two of the three trading entities in the table above are likely to have good reserves of foreign currency?

13. **Synthesizing Economic Data** In which trading entity in the table above are imports the highest percent of total trade value? The lowest?

14. **Comparing and Contrasting Economic Information** What are developed nations hoping to gain through reduced global trade barriers? What are developing nations hoping to gain?

15. **Challenge** The World Trade Organization, unlike GATT, has an organizational structure to implement its principles. However, it has no authority to force a nation to do something against its own laws. How is it able, then, to resolve disputes among members?

The Advantages of International Trade

The concept of comparative advantage explains why specialization and international trade are so important to economic success. Complete this exercise with a partner to help further your understanding.

Each of you will represent a trading nation. One of you will be El Estado, and the other will be Lichtenbourg. Both countries produce lemons and televisions. The following table shows monthly production by each nation.

	El Estado	Lichtenbourg
Lemons (in pounds)	20,000	9,000
Televisions	4,000	3,000

Step 1 Decide whether El Estado or Lichtenbourg has the absolute advantage for each product. Explain why this is so.

Step 2 Each student should calculate what his or her nation's production ratio is. Express your ratio in terms of opportunity cost. How many pounds of lemons does it cost to make one TV?

Step 3 With your ratios calculated, decide which nation has the comparative advantage in the production of TVs. On this basis, decide which nation should specialize in the production of each product.

Step 4 Now that you've decided to specialize and trade, calculate a trade ratio that makes trade between your two nations even more advantageous. Explain how the new ratio achieves this goal.

Economic Development

Issues of economic development are as much about the basic building blocks of societies as they are about money. When governments are stable and help to provide their people with resources and opportunities, economic development can become a reality.

18 Issues of Economic Development

CONCEPT REVIEW

Free enterprise system is another name for capitalism, an economic system based on private ownership of productive resources.

CHAPTER 18 KEY CONCEPT

A **transitional economy** is a country that has moved (or is moving) from a command economy, such as communism, to a market economy.

WHY THE CONCEPT MATTERS

The development of the world's less developed countries has grown increasingly important as globalization has taken hold. Promoting development also promotes good government and economic opportunity in less developed countries. When a nation's government is democratic and stable and its citizens are prosperous, the benefits reach beyond that emerging economy to the world community, which gains a new economic and political partner.

Online Highlights
More at ClassZone.com

 Economics Update
Go to **ECONOMICS UPDATE** for chapter updates and current news on trade and China's transition to a market economy. (See Case Study, pp. 570–571.) ▶

 SMART Grapher
Go to **SMART GRAPHER** to complete graphing activities in this chapter.

Interactive ⟨⟨⟩Review
Go to **INTERACTIVE REVIEW** for concept review and activities.

How has international trade helped China make the transition to a market economy? See the Case Study on pages 570–571.

Definitions of Development

OBJECTIVES	KEY TERMS	TAKING NOTES
In Section 1 you will • determine how economic development is defined • explain how certain indicators can illustrate the level of economic development of a nation	developed nations, *p. 544* transitional economies, *p. 545* less developed countries (LDC), *p. 545* infrastructure, *p. 545* per capita GDP, *p. 546* infant mortality rate, *p. 547* life expectancy, *p. 547* literacy rate, *p. 547* human development index (HDI), *p. 547*	As you read Section 1, complete a summary table like the one shown. Use the Graphic Organizer at **Interactive Review @ ClassZone.com** **Definitions of Development** | Levels of Development	Standards of Economic Development
---	---	

Levels of Development

KEY CONCEPTS

Do you have at least $1 in your pocket at the moment? If so, you have more money than over a billion of the world's people have for food, shelter, and clothing for today. Economists gather this type of data to compare the economies of nations and the impact of those economies on people's standard of living. They use the data to measure the nations' level of economic development.

Developed Nations

Economists have defined three major levels of economic development. The nations with the highest standards of living are known as **developed nations**. In addition to a relatively high standard of living, these nations have a market economy, a high GDP, industrialization, widespread private ownership of property, and stable and effective governments. The nations of Western Europe, the United States, Canada, Australia, New Zealand, Japan, and South Korea are all developed nations.

You can identify some of the features of a developed nation by looking around you. Most people live fairly comfortable lives and enjoy such consumer goods as television sets, washing machines, and cars. You will also see that most people live in urban areas, where they have jobs in service and industrial enterprises: banks, insurance companies, auto parts manufacturing, and so on. Even though few people work in agriculture, the nation produces a surplus of agricultural products using advanced science and technology and highly efficient farming methods. You will also see that, on the whole, people are generally healthy and well-educated. They have political and economic freedom, and they exercise those freedoms in pursuit of well-being. You will see exceptions to all of these features—poverty, unemployment, poor living conditions—but they are not the prevailing features of the society.

QUICK REFERENCE

Developed nations have a market economy, a relatively high standard of living, a high GDP, industrialization, widespread private ownership of property, and stable and effective governments.

Transitional Economies

Economists have also defined the development that occurs in **transitional economies**. These are countries that have moved (or are moving) from a command economy to a market economy. China, Russia, and a number of Eastern European countries are considered to be transitional economies.

Poland, in Eastern Europe, is in transition and categorized as a less developed country. Like other transitional economies, however, it is on a clear path toward improving standards of living. As democracy and economic freedom begin to take hold, Poland's economy and its citizens' quality of life have steadily improved.

QUICK REFERENCE

A **transitional economy** is a country that has moved (or is moving) from a command economy to a market economy.

In Transition A developed economy, such as the United States (left), generally has greater access to technology than a transitional economy, such as China (right).

Less Developed Countries

Less developed countries (LDCs), such as many African, South American, and Eastern European countries, have a lower GDP, less well developed industry, and a lower standard of living. Often, these nations have ineffective or even outright corrupt governments that fail to protect private property rights. LDCs are sometimes called emerging economies, but some have emerged, so to speak, more than others. As a result, they can be divided into middle-income nations, such as Brazil and Thailand, and low-income nations, such as Mozambique and Cambodia.

The picture in the low-income nations is starkly different from what you see when you look around the United States. A high percentage of people live in substandard housing. Few families own televisions or washing machines. Even if they owned cars, there are few good roads to drive them on, since developing nations often lack infrastructure. **Infrastructure** is the basic set of support systems needed to keep an economy going. It includes such things as power, communications, transportation, water, sanitation, and education systems.

In these economies, a relatively high percentage of the people work at subsistence farming and have little savings. Often, even children toil with the rest of the family. Some go to school for only three or four years; some children receive no schooling. Health conditions are substandard, as medical care is hard to come by in rural areas. In many developing nations, political freedom is still a dream.

QUICK REFERENCE

A **less developed country** (LDC) has a lower GDP, less well developed industry, and a lower standard of living.

Infrastructure is the basic support systems needed to keep an economy going, including power, communications, transportation, water, sanitation, and education systems.

Economics Update

Find an update on health statistics in LDCs at **ClassZone.com**

APPLICATION **Economies**

A. What role does technology play in economic development?

Standards of Economic Development

KEY CONCEPTS

How is it possible to compare economies when each country may have its own ideas of what is valuable? For example, the number of television sets per thousand households yields valid information about the economic conditions in most nations. However, not every culture values television ownership to the same extent. Such statistics need to be used in conjunction with others, so that a more nuanced image of a nation's overall level of development can be obtained. Economists use the following standards of development to bring this detailed image into focus.

Per Capita Gross Domestic Product

QUICK REFERENCE

Per capita gross domestic product is a nation's GDP divided by its total population.

The most popular measure of economic development is **per capita gross domestic product**, a nation's overall GDP divided by its total population. This statistic is informative because it estimates the amount of goods and services produced per person in a given year. These figures can be used to compare one country to another. (See Figure 18.1.) For example, the per capita GDP of the United States is among the world's highest—over $40,000. In Tanzania, in east Africa, it is $700—among the lowest. Often these figures are adjusted to take into account the idea that a dollar may go further in some less developed countries where goods and services are less costly.

FIGURE 18.1 World Per Capita GDPs

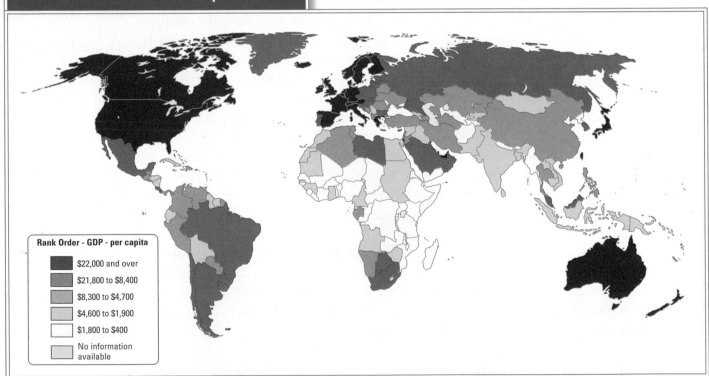

Rank Order - GDP - per capita

- $22,000 and over
- $21,800 to $8,400
- $8,300 to $4,700
- $4,600 to $1,900
- $1,800 to $400
- No information available

ANALYZE MAPS

1. Which continent is the least developed?

2. Which continents have no countries in the top per capita GDP bracket?

Health

Statistics showing various aspects of health and health care are also useful in determining economic development. Especially indicative are statistics on the survival rate of babies. This measure is called the **infant mortality rate**, the number of children who die within the first year of life per 1,000 live births.

The infant mortality rate in Japan is 3. In China it is 23. In Angola it is 185. What can economists learn from these figures? The answer lies in understanding the conditions in which infants thrive. These conditions include a safe and sanitary birth environment with access to needed emergency care, adequate nutrition, an adequately fed mother who has access to clean drinking water and acceptable shelter, and protection from disease in the form of early-childhood vaccinations. A subsistence society, or one in extreme poverty, is unlikely to be able to provide these conditions. Less developed economies may be able to provide them to some degree, but in developed economies, these conditions are the norm.

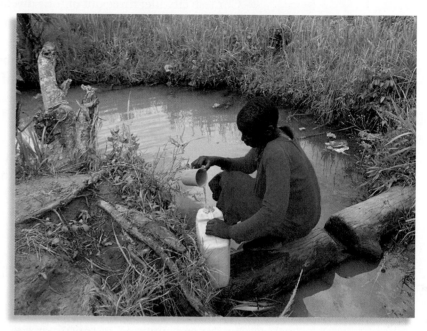

Dangerous Water More than a billion people worldwide use unsafe drinking water sources. Disease and death can be real consequences of this fact.

Another useful standard is **life expectancy**, the average number of years a person could expect to live if current mortality trends were to continue for the rest of that person's life. For example, people born today in Japan can expect to live to age 82, in China, to age 72, while in Angola, only to age 39.

Education

The World Education Forum declares in its Framework for Action that "education is . . . the key to sustainable development and peace and stability within and among countries, and thus an indispensable means for effective participation in the societies and economies of the twenty-first century. . . ." Since education is so clearly tied into the economy, education statistics are tracked as useful indicators of the development level of a nation. One key education figure is the **literacy rate**, the percentage of people older than 15 who can read and write. Japan's literacy rate is 99 percent; Somalia's is 38 percent. Another useful statistic is student enrollment at all levels. This figure tells the percentage of school-age individuals who are actually going to school. In Belgium and Japan, for example, primary-school enrollment is 100 percent. In Niger, it is about 40 percent.

In 1990, another standard was introduced that combines some of these other statistics. It is the **human development index** (HDI)—the brainchild of Pakistani economist Mahbub ul Haq. A nation's HDI is a combination of its real GDP per capita, life expectancy, adult literacy rate, and student enrollment figures. Its measures are an important indicator of what life is like in a specific country.

QUICK REFERENCE

Infant mortality rate is the number of children who die within the first year of life per 1,000 live births.

Life expectancy is the average number of years a person can expect to live if current mortality trends were to continue for the rest of that person's life.

Literacy rate is the percentage of people older than 15 who can read and write.

The **human development index** (HDI) uses targeted economic, education, and health statistics to assess a nation's level of development.

Consumption of Goods and Services

In the mid-1990s, home appliances were still relatively rare in less developed countries like China. By the year 2000, however, the refrigerator had become a familiar part of Chinese city life; three out of four dwellings in major urban areas had one. Refrigerators have even begun to reach the secondary cities and rural areas, though they are still so rare there that they are sometimes displayed proudly in the living room rather than hidden away in the kitchen. Washing machines are also becoming increasingly commonplace. China's consumption of cell phones has risen rapidly in recent years too. At the beginning of 2001, there were approximately 65 million cell phones in use in China; by 2004, there were about 335 million—more than in any other country. The number of personal computers owned in China is doubling every 28 months.

What do these statistics say about China's economic development? These data show how people choose to spend their income after they have food and shelter. When consumption of such big-ticket items as refrigerators, automobiles, and washing machines increases, an economy is growing and developing. This indicates that people's living standards are rising. Goods that once were available only to the rich are now purchased by middle- and even low-income families.

In the less developed nations of China and India, 16 percent of the population is following this consumption pattern, compared with 89 percent of the population in Europe. The less developed nations therefore have the greatest room for growth in the consumption of consumer goods and services. For now, however, consumers in North America and Western Europe, whose population is about 12 percent of the global total, are responsible for 60 percent of the global total of consumption of goods and services. The 30 percent of the world population that lives in South Asia and sub-Saharan Africa, on the other hand, spends only 3.2 percent. Comparisons like the one below in Figure 18.2 offer another way to measure relative growth.

FIGURE 18.2 Ownership of Typical Consumer Goods

(per thousand residents)

Country	Television Sets	Telephone Mainlines
United States	835	659
Ukraine	456	212
India	83	40

Source: The State of the World, 2004

Energy Use

Of the roughly 6.5 billion people in the world, as many as 2 billion are without electricity. Since electricity and other forms of energy contribute to economic development, statistics on energy use can reveal an aspect of a nation's economic development. Energy use is not spread evenly throughout the population. Asia, with 50 percent of the world's people, accounts for just over 21 percent of annual energy consumption. For another example, the average global consumption of electricity is 2,744 kilowatt hours (KWh) per capita. Japan's annual per capita consumption of electricity, like that of other industrialized nations, is well over 7,000 KWhs. Colombia's annual rate of about 820 KWh per capita is typical of LDCs, which average about 750 KWh per capita each year.

How the energy is put to use is another revealing statistic, especially the amount used for commercial purposes. The United States, for example, uses the equivalent energy of 8,148 kilograms of oil per person in commercial enterprises. India uses the equivalent of about 494 kilograms of oil per person for commercial activities. The amount of energy used for commercial purposes correlates to a nation's level of technological achievement and other economic measures.

Projected energy use to the year 2025 follows the same pattern as the projected consumption of consumer goods and services, with LDCs outpacing developed nations. The LDCs are expected to increase their energy use by about 3.2 percent per year. In Asia, including China and India, the demand for energy is expected to double between 2002 and 2025. The relatively rapid increase in energy use coincides with the move toward industrialization and technological advances. In fact, transportation and industry account for nearly all of the projected increase in the use of fossil fuels.

Wind Power Wind farms contribute a small but growing part of the world's electricity.

Personal Computers	Cellular Telephones
625	451
18	44
6	6

In contrast, the developed nations are projected to increase their energy use by only 1.1 percent a year. Developed economies use fuel more efficiently, which accounts in part for their slower rate of increase in energy use. Transitional economies are expected to increase their energy use by 1.6 percent each year as they face the challenges of moving to a market economy.

Labor Force

In what kind of job do most of a nation's workers find themselves employed? The answer to this question reveals one aspect of a nation's level of development. According to the World Bank, this measure includes all the economically active people between the ages of 15 and 65 in a country—including the employed, the unemployed, and soldiers, but excluding students and unpaid caregivers. The fewer workers there are engaged in agriculture, and the greater the number of workers in manufacturing and service industries, the more developed the nation.

A GLOBAL PERSPECTIVE

Botswana's Growing Economy

Since it became independent in 1966, Botswana's per capita income growth has been among the fastest of any nation in the world. This small African country transformed itself from one of the world's poorest countries to a middle-income nation in under 50 years. In 2004, Botswana received an A credit rating from Moody's and from Standard and Poor's.

Botswana has succeeded largely by maintaining a stable and responsible governmental system. The government has managed the income from large-scale mining operations wisely, reinvesting it in the nation's physical and human infrastructure. In recent years, the development of the financial services and tourism industries has been stressed. Together, they now represent about one-quarter of the nation's GDP.

Botswana still faces a number of social and economic challenges, including high unemployment, low manufacturing output, and one of the world's highest rates of HIV/AIDS infection. But through its moves to diversify the economy, the government has put the nation on a solid development track.

CONNECTING ACROSS THE GLOBE
1. How has the government of Botswana helped keep the nation's economy growing?
2. In the article, what tells investors that Botswana is a relatively safe place to invest?

APPLICATION Drawing Conclusions

B. Would you expect a positive or negative correlation between literacy rates and infant mortality rates? Explain.

SECTION 1 Assessment

REVIEWING KEY CONCEPTS

1. Explain the relationship between the terms in each of these pairs:

   a. *developed nations*
      less developed countries

   b. *human development index*
      infant mortality rate

2. What does the state of a nation's infrastructure say about the country's level of economic development?

3. Why is per capita GDP a more useful statistic than overall GDP when comparing nations?

4. What does an analysis of the labor force and energy usage tell economists about a nation?

5. Why are health and longevity statistics useful in determining a nation's level of development?

6. **Using Your Notes** Pick one example of a developed nation, one of a transitional economy, and one of a less developed nation. Use your notes to explain why you chose each.

   Use the Graphic Organizer at **Interactive Review @ ClassZone.com**

Definitions of Development	
Levels of Development	Standards of Economic Development

CRITICAL THINKING

7. **Comparing and Contrasting** Compare and contrast three characteristics of a developed nation and a less developed nation.

8. **Making Inferences and Drawing Conclusions** One measure of economic development is the extent to which a nation buys big-ticket consumer goods. Does the production of those goods also indicate a level of economic development? Explain your answer.

9. **Writing About Economics** Some economists argue that GDP does not give an accurate picture of a nation's well-being. They point out that GDP reflects economic activity that pollutes the environment and depletes resources as well as economic activity that counteracts the pollution. In other words, it shows both the polluting enterprises and the cost of cleaning up the pollution on the plus side of the balance sheet. Write a paragraph speculating on how to revise GDP figures to reflect this concern.

10. **Challenge** In poorer countries, where does the money for development initiatives come from?

ECONOMICS IN PRACTICE

Health care in Bangladesh

Understanding Levels of Development

The chart below shows life expectancy, infant mortality rates, and literacy rates for five countries.

Country	Life Expectancy (years)	Infant Mortality (per 1,000 live births)	Literacy Rate (%)
Bolivia	65.8	51.8	87.2
Germany	78.8	4.1	99.0
Moldova	65.7	38.4	99.1
Philippines	70.2	22.8	92.6
Bangladesh	62.5	60.8	43.1

Source: *CIA World Factbook, 2006*

Drawing Conclusions Which nation is probably the most developed? Which nation is probably the least developed? Which nation is more developed, Bolivia or the Philippines? Explain your answers.

Challenge If you were "weighting" the various measures used to show economic development, which would you consider most meaningful: life expectancy, infant mortality, or literacy rate? Explain your answer.

A Framework for Economic Development Objectives

OBJECTIVES	KEY TERMS	TAKING NOTES
In Section 2 you will • evaluate the importance of developing human and physical capital • examine the importance of stability and opportunity in economic development • describe how developing nations raise money for development programs	capital flight, *p. 558* default, *p. 559* World Bank, *p. 559* International Monetary Fund (IMF), *p. 559* debt restructuring, *p. 559* stabilization program, *p. 559*	As you read Section 2, complete a cluster diagram like the one shown for each major concept. Include key concepts and other helpful words and phrases. Use the Graphic Organizer at **Interactive Review @ ClassZone.com** Development Framework stability stable prices

Resources

KEY CONCEPTS

What does a nation need to develop economically? Natural resources such as minerals and fossil fuels play a role in economic development. A nation's climate and the amount of land suited for agriculture are also factors. Each nation uses the resources it has. However, natural resources are not enough. Investing in human capital and physical capital, for example, are ways that many nations promote economic expansion.

High Levels of Human Capital

People are the most valuable resources in a market economy. One element of a healthy and growing market economy is a commitment to make the most of its human resources through education and training. Education and training help people develop the skills to enter into and function productively in the economy.

Human Capital Societies benefit in many ways when their citizens are well educated.

Investing in education also affects other aspects of a society. Educated citizens are able to make informed decisions about health matters. Educated parents are likely to vaccinate their children and invest in their children's education. Furthermore, educated citizens are likely to vote, participate in civic affairs, rise above poverty, and avoid criminal activity.

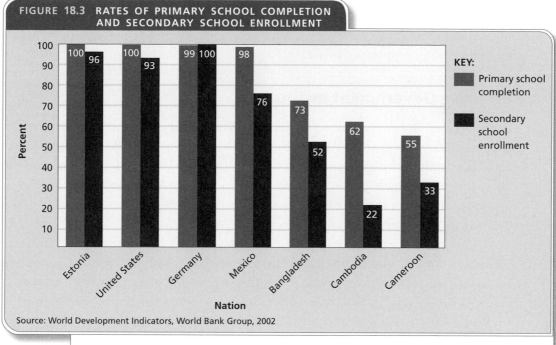

FIGURE 18.3 RATES OF PRIMARY SCHOOL COMPLETION AND SECONDARY SCHOOL ENROLLMENT

KEY:
- Primary school completion
- Secondary school enrollment

Source: World Development Indicators, World Bank Group, 2002

ANALYZE GRAPHS

1. What nation shows the largest drop-off between the percentage of students that complete primary school and the percentage who go on to secondary school?

2. Do you think the amount of drop-off between education levels is a clue to a nation's level of development? Explain your answer.

High Levels of Physical Capital

Physical capital is also an important factor contributing to economic growth. As you read in Chapter 1, physical capital consists of the human-made goods—machines— that are used in the production of other goods and services. Investments in physical capital make people more productive.

Fortunately, LDCs do not have to reinvent the wheel. Technology and other innovative capital resources are always being refined in developed nations. LDCs need only copy or import the technology. The desire to copy or import technologies points to the link between human and physical capital. Copying technology requires educated and well-trained people. Importing technology requires money, which is generally in short supply in LDCs, so these nations look to foreign investment. However, a country that lacks human capital is less attractive to investors that might supply this money.

APPLICATION Explaining an Economic Concept

A. Think of your own examples to explain the ripple effect that education has on a society and economy.

Stability

KEY CONCEPTS

While such inputs as human capital and physical capital are necessary for increased output, they are only part of the framework for economic growth. The overall governmental and economic environments must be stable enough to support growth before those inputs can best be put to use.

Effective Government Institutions

In the United States, the rule of law is so fundamentally a part of the culture that it may be taken for granted. We are used to laws made by a legislature that we elect according to the principles laid out in the Constitution. We take for granted that the laws will then be made public for all to know and follow. We expect those laws to be applied fairly. When there are disputes, we trust that our legal system will sort out the differences according to the law, not by bribery or intimidation.

In many countries, however, the rule of law is still out of reach, and in those places, economic growth suffers. Business investment always carries risk, even in a nation with effective government institutions. That risk rises sharply in countries where the enforcement of laws is unpredictable, where private property rights are unprotected, where a bureaucracy is corrupt or bloated or both, and where judges can be bought and sold. The rule of law provides a foundation of predictability and certainty that reduces economic risk.

Democracy itself is a key factor of economic growth. Democratic nations have a higher rate of economic growth than nations with a different form of government. In nations where people can choose their representatives in free and open elections, they can promote their economic self-interest with the same degree of power as other citizens. When the press is uncensored, views that oppose government policy can be aired and debated. In a famous study, one Nobel Prize–winning economist, Amartya Sen, concluded that crop failures are not the chief cause of famines: political systems are. He points out that no widespread famine has ever occurred in a democratic nation. India has had famines, but none since it became a democracy in 1947. The democratic process reduces the likelihood that the government will interfere with the self-correcting market forces that could prevent widespread famine.

Law Enforcement A fair and transparent court system is key to the kind of governmental stability that promotes development.

Stable Prices

In areas where prices are stable and where the governments' fiscal and monetary policies are sound, economic growth can take root. Investors in such an environment know what to expect. They do not see volatile changes in interest rates, prices, or the level of the government debt.

With price stability, businesses can make long-term plans with some assurance that conditions will not change too dramatically and that the government will not go bankrupt. In contrast, in nations with a high inflation rate or with unstable interest rates, investors run a high risk. Many will choose to avoid investing in such an environment in the first place. And even if they do take a chance, they are likely to withdraw their investment at the first sign of trouble. That leaves the unstable country further behind, since the funds it could use for economic expansion are placed in more stable nations.

Monetary Stability Runaway prices in post–World War I Germany made money into children's toys (left). A stable currency and stable prices create real purchasing power (right).

Protected Property Rights

Guaranteed protection of private property provides an incentive for economies to grow. If businesses have no way to assert ownership of their enterprises, they will have little incentive to take economic risks, since they will have no guarantee of reaping the rewards if they succeed. Assured property rights give investors confidence and stimulate entrepreneurship.

Business owners also need private property rights to prevent the government from interfering with or restricting their operations. In such unstable nations as Haiti, Kazakhstan, and Indonesia, where corruption and favoritism are widespread, private property rights are insecure. This lack of stability is more than enough to cause investors to look elsewhere to locate their enterprises.

In some LDCs, especially former colonies of Western nations, land ownership is in the hands of a very small percentage of the population—usually the descendants of the colonists. In some cases, this land is seized by the government for redistribution to the majority population. Foreign investors are wary of locating businesses in countries that threaten private property.

APPLICATION Drawing Conclusions

B. Why is the rule of law a stabilizing force that promotes development?

Opportunity

KEY CONCEPTS

Economic opportunity depends on a number of functions that fall to the government. These include opening international trade, helping people move up the income ladder, controlling corruption, and limiting regulations.

Open International Trade

The government can also create opportunities for economic growth by lowering restrictions on international trade. As you read in Chapter 17, trade benefits the trading nations by allowing them to produce what they are most efficient at producing and trading for the rest. Partners in a trading relationship produce more than they would without trade, leading to economic growth.

However, in less developed countries, governments have imposed high tariffs on imports and instituted other protectionist measures in an effort to give local producers an advantage. Governments often justify these protections as a short-term effort to help local industries until they grow strong enough to compete with foreign competitors. Protectionist measures come with costs, though. Consumers have to pay more for goods than they would in a market open to imports. Also, government protections may reduce incentives for producers to become more efficient. Industries may become dependent on tariffs and other trade barriers.

Increase Social and Economic Mobility

Economic opportunity leads to the most vigorous economic growth when that opportunity is open to the entire population. If all citizens have an equal opportunity under the law to engage in economic enterprise, many will be motivated to lift themselves into a higher income bracket. A number of studies have found that in the United States, for example, about 25 to 33 percent of the population moves into a new income quintile each year. Over a ten-year period, that number rises to 60 percent. In the process of seeking personal economic reward, these people are also helping the economy to grow.

In some traditional cultures, however, social conditions do not promote equal opportunity. For example, in some LDCs with a traditional culture, the lower status of women keeps half the labor force from developing its full potential. Further, an entrenched class structure in some nations hampers growth, since the rich do not want changes that could deprive them of their wealth. Governmental changes that promote equal opportunity will help create a successful framework for economic growth.

Economic Potential In many traditional societies, women are an untapped resource that could give development a boost.

Economics Update

Find an update on women in the workplace in LDCs at **ClassZone.com**

Control Corruption

Corruption, the abuse of public office for private gain, is an especially urgent problem that helps explain why some nations are able to develop and others are not. When government officials are at liberty to enrich themselves and others—by taking bribes and kickbacks, funneling lucrative government jobs and contracts to relatives and allies, skimming aid and loan money, and so on—the rest of the nation, especially the poor, pays the price. (See Figure 18.4.) Although there is not an exact correlation between corruption and per capita GDP, much more often than not, countries with less corruption have higher per capita GDPs.

Limit Regulation

Governments with reasonable tax levels and business regulations help to create economic opportunity. Businesses and other investors are more likely to be attracted to nations with relatively little "red tape."

Even in the United States, which has relatively few regulations on business, it is estimated that companies with 20 or fewer employees have to pay over $7,500 per employee each year to comply with government regulations. In many LDCs, the number of regulations is significantly higher. In a climate of instability, the high number of regulations can lead to corruption. Rather than comply with all the regulations, businesses are tempted to bypass them through payoffs. As you have read, a corrupt environment removes economic incentive and slows economic growth.

FIGURE 18.4 Corruption and Per Capita GDP

Country	Corruption Index*	Per Capita GDP (in U.S. dollars)
Finland	9.6	31,000
Australia	8.7	31,600
Chile	7.3	11,900
United States	7.3	41,600
Slovenia	6.4	21,500
Bhutan	6.0	1,400
South Korea	5.1	22,600
South Africa	4.6	12,200
Turkey	3.8	8,400
Bolivia	2.7	2,900
Uganda	2.7	1,800
Albania	2.6	5,300
Russia	2.5	11,000
Kyrgyzstan	2.2	2,000
Cambodia	2.1	2,500

*10=least corrupt; 0=most corrupt
Sources: Transparency International; CIA World Factbook; 2006 and earlier data

APPLICATION Applying Economic Concepts

C. Nations with the highest corruption index tend to have their wealth distributed less evenly, with a large percentage of people living in poverty. Why might this be so?

Financing Development

Nations seeking to finance economic development can look to four main sources: internal investment, foreign investment, aid from foreign governments, or investments from international agencies. A developing nation must consider both the positive and negative aspects of each source.

Internal Investment

Investment funds for economic development can come from both public and private internal investment. Banks within the nation invest in economic enterprises, such as roads, bridges, and other infrastructure. Egypt, for example, set a goal to make domestic savings the key force in development and worked toward increasing the savings rate to 25 percent of GDP. To reach this goal, Egypt bolstered the insurance industry, which works to pool and channel savings.

In poorer nations, personal savings are very low, so banks have little to invest. Compounding the problem, the wealthy citizens of these countries sometimes invest their funds in developed countries rather than their own country, a problem known as **capital flight**. If private banks lack the funds to invest, the country's government may provide funds. It might also seek foreign investment from multinational corporations or through sales of government bonds.

Foreign Investment

There are several ways in which foreign interests can invest in an economy. One is foreign direct investment (FDI), the establishment of a business enterprise in a foreign country. A second is foreign portfolio investment, through which foreign investors take part in a nation's stock and other financial markets. Foreign investment in less developed countries increased from $44 billion in 1990 to $226 billion in 2000. One reason for the increase is that less developed nations had created a more attractive business climate for investors. Multinationals that open manufacturing plants in foreign nations provide jobs and training to the local population and reap the benefits of cheaper labor.

Foreign Direct Investment Multinational corporations bring employment, training, and new technology to less developed countries. This automotive factory in Beijing was a joint venture between a Chinese company and Chrysler.

Loans and Aid

Developing nations have also turned to loans to help finance their economic development. External debt, money borrowed from foreign banks or governments, has become an issue of great concern in some LDCs. Some countries, especially in South America and Africa, have more debt than they can pay back. When a nation cannot pay interest or principle on a loan, it is said to be in **default**.

Nations may also seek foreign aid—money from other nations. (See Figure 18.5 for aid figures from the U.S. Agency for International Development [USAID]).

FIGURE 18.5 USAID ALLOCATIONS BY REGION

6%
7.7%
30.8%
13.2%
18.8%
23.5%

- Africa ($2,050)
- East and South Asia ($1,559)
- Middle East ($1,251)
- Latin America / Caribbean ($877)
- Central Asia ($512)
- Europe ($402)

All figures are in millions of dollars.

Source: U.S. Agency for International Development, 2006

International Help Agencies

LDCs also receive aid from several important international organizations. The World Bank, the International Monetary Fund, and the United Nations Development Program are the main international organizations devoted to economic development.

- **World Bank** is a financial institution that provides loans, policy advice, and technical assistance to low- and middle-income countries to reduce poverty.

- **International Monetary Fund (IMF)** is an international organization established to promote international monetary cooperation, foster economic growth, and provide temporary financial assistance to countries to help ease balance of payments adjustment. The IMF helps nations overloaded with debt to develop **debt restructuring**, a method used by countries with outstanding debt obligations to alter the terms of the debt agreements in order to achieve some advantage. It often oversees **stabilization programs**, in which it requires these troubled nations to carry out reforms—reducing foreign trade deficits and external debt, eliminating price controls, closing inefficient public enterprises, and slashing budget deficits.

- **United Nations Development Program** (UNDP) is a United Nations agency working to fight poverty. In 2006 it had active programs in 174 nations.

APPLICATION Making Inferences and Drawing Conclusions

D. Why would Kuwait, a developing nation, offer aid to countries in its region?

QUICK REFERENCE

Default is when a nation cannot pay interest or principle on a loan

The **World Bank** is a financial institution that provides loans, policy advice, and technical assistance to low- and middle-income countries to reduce poverty.

The **International Monetary Fund (IMF)** promotes international monetary cooperation, fosters economic growth, and provides temporary financial assistance to countries to help ease balance of payments adjustment.

Debt restructuring is a method used by countries to alter the terms of their debt agreements in order to achieve some advantage.

A **stabilization program** is a required program of reforms imposed by the IMF to steady the economy of a debtor nation in danger of default.

Anne Krueger: Reforming Development Policies

On September 1, 2001, Anne Krueger became First Deputy Director of the International Monetary Fund. Ten days later, the terrorist attacks on the United States sent shockwaves through the global economy. Three months later, Argentina suspended payments on its $132 billion foreign debt—the biggest default ever, at that time. In addition, international protests over the burden of debt in developing nations were on the rise. Clearly, she didn't have the luxury of easing into her new position.

A New Role for the IMF

Luckily, Krueger came very well prepared for her new job. In addition to her professorships at Stanford University, Duke University, and the University of Minnesota, Krueger had also been Director of the Center for Research on Economic Development and Policy Reform at Stanford, and the Vice President for Economics and Research at the World Bank.

In November 2001, anticipating Argentina's default, Krueger put forward a proposal for the role of the IMF in debt restructuring and dispute resolution. In her proposal, the IMF would oversee the restructuring of the debt rather than simply providing bailout funds. The reform effort also called for collective action clauses, measures that let a supermajority of creditors overrule a creditor who is holding out for more repayment than may be possible. Thanks to Krueger's efforts, in early 2005 most of Argentina's creditors accepted 35 cents on the dollar and Argentina's credit rating climbed once again.

However, even 35 cents on the dollar seems too high to many critics, who believe that 100 percent of the debt of most developing nations should be forgiven. These critics argue that the money used to service the debt should be put to use providing important services such as health care and education. Krueger has disagreed: "Unless there is radical change from past behavior on the part of the debtors, their priorities for the use of released resources are not likely to be on education, health, or other expenditures that will enable the poor to improve their lot." Nonetheless, the IMF has considered plans to forgive debt completely in the most heavily indebted poor nations in exchange for economic policies that favor trade liberalization and other development goals.

Anne Krueger helped to reform policies on development.

APPLICATION Solving Economic Problems

C. Krueger believes that direct aid to nongovernmental organizations working in health or education are more effective than debt cancellation. Critics argue that grants with conditions show that the IMF desires to control national economies. Which viewpoint do you agree with? Why?

FAST FACTS

Anne O. Krueger

Title: Professor of International Economics, Johns Hopkins School of Advanced International Studies

Born: February 12, 1934, New York City

Major Accomplishments: First Deputy Managing Director, International Monetary Fund (2001–2006); Vice President for Economics and Research, World Bank (1982–1986)

Selected Awards:
- Distinguished Fellow and past President of the American Economic Association
- Frank E. Seidman Distinguished Award in Political Economy (1993)
- Bernard Harms Prize awarded by the Kiel Institute of World Economics (1990)

Economics Update

Find an update on Anne Krueger at **ClassZone.com**

SECTION 2 Assessment

Online Quiz
ClassZone.com

REVIEWING KEY CONCEPTS

1. Explain the relationship between this pair of terms:

   a. *International Monetary Fund*   **b.** *stabilization program*

2. What are four key sources of funding for development?

3. How can a nation develop its human capital?

4. How can a nation improve its business climate?

5. What roles do foreign nations play in a country's development?

6. **Using Your Notes** Use your completed cluster diagram to help you explain how the economic development of one nation might be an opportunity for growth for another nation. Use the Graphic Organizer at **Interactive Review @ ClassZone.com**

CRITICAL THINKING

7. **Analyzing Cause and Effect** How might the bailout by an international agency of a nation that has defaulted on foreign debt lead to more corruption in the future?

8. **Writing About Economics** Many economists believe that a country that is rich in a particular natural resource may actually be at a developmental disadvantage. They point out that nations such as these tend to put all of their resources into this one industry. Write a paragraph about how you, as leader of a nation, would use the large income from your nation's natural resource to take other avenues to developing your economy.

9. **Applying Economic Concepts** Look again at Figure 18.5. The United States grants aid money each year to nations in the developing world. Do you think Anne Krueger would think this aid money should come with certain terms or conditions? Explain.

10. **Challenge** If you were in charge of development efforts for a poor nation, which source of development funds would you focus on? Why?

ECONOMICS IN PRACTICE

Understanding the Path to Development
Read the following scenarios of fictional less developed countries:

- In nation A, there is a democratically elected government, but a corrupt law enforcement system has made property rights shaky. There is little foreign trade, and few foreign firms have set up manufacturing facilities. However, a foreign nation gives nation A hundreds of millions of dollars in aid each year.

- In nation B, the move toward democracy has begun. A system of fair and transparent law enforcement is in place, and international trade and foreign direct investment are on the rise. High levels of foreign debt, however, could pose a problem in the future.

Categorizing Economic Information Is nation A or nation B more likely on a path to successful development? Explain why you think so.

Challenge What's more beneficial to development— a connection to a large amount of foreign aid money or a plan to increase social, political, and economic stability? Why?

SECTION 3

Transition to a Market Economy

OBJECTIVES	KEY TERMS	TAKING NOTES
In Section 3 you will <ul><li>identify problems that emerge when an economy goes from command to market</li><li>describe the transitions to a market economy in the former Soviet Union and nations it dominated</li><li>discuss the transitions to a market economy in China</li></ul>	privatization, *p. 563* shock therapy, *p. 563* perestroika, *p. 564* special economic zone (SEZ), *p. 567*	As you read Section 3, complete a cluster diagram like the one shown, using the key concepts and other helpful words and phrases. Use the Graphic Organizer at **Interactive Review @ ClassZone.com**

New Challenges

KEY CONCEPTS

In Chapter 2, you read about different economic systems, including a command, or centrally planned, economy in which all economic decisions are made by the society's leaders, usually government officials acting in a central location. For a while, much of the world's population lived in a command economy. However, China, the nations that formerly made up the Soviet Union, and many Eastern European countries have taken steps toward a market economy. The transition requires new answers to the basic economic questions that central planners used to answer. Both the government and private individuals and companies face a number of challenges.

CHALLENGE 1 **Poor Infrastructure**

A market economy needs a solid infrastructure to facilitate the production and distribution of goods and services. In a command economy, transportation, communications, banking, and education—the infrastructure of an industrialized nation—are as inefficient as other industries tend to be. With no competition there

is little incentive to create a more robust physical and institutional infrastructure. Modernized airports, phone systems, roads, harbors, bridges, and computer connections help a transitional economy support and spread the goods and services it produces.

Bridging the Gap Transportation infrastructure is vital to develop a successful market economy.

CHALLENGE 2 Privatization

Under communism, the government owns all property. As transitional nations move toward a market economy, they have all undertaken the challenges of **privatization**, the process of transferring state owned-property and businesses to individuals. A major problem with privatization is how to sell the property. It can, for example, be auctioned off, but command economies have little private savings, and few people have the needed finances. Also, as you'll read later, these auctions can sometimes be rigged to benefit those close to the ruling elites. A second method is to sell shares of businesses through a vehicle like the stock market. A third way is to give vouchers to people to purchase shares of a business, making cash unnecessary.

CHALLENGE 3 Rise in Prices

In a command economy, some goods may have artificially low prices. Part of the switch to a market economy is the removal of price controls, allowing the market to operate. On January 1, 1990, Poland's government gave the go-ahead for an economic program referred to as **shock therapy,** involving the abrupt shift from a command to a free-market economy. The initial result indeed shocked consumers; the inflation rate that first month was 78 percent. However, this inflationary "correction" eased as the free-market policies were allowed to take hold. (See Figure 18.6.)

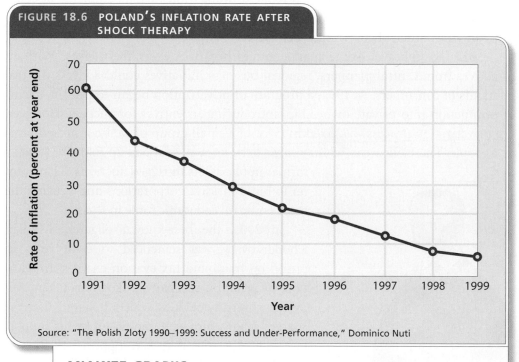

FIGURE 18.6 POLAND'S INFLATION RATE AFTER SHOCK THERAPY

Source: "The Polish Zloty 1990–1999: Success and Under-Performance," Dominico Nuti

ANALYZE GRAPHS
1. After 1991, how many years did it take Poland to cut its inflation rate in half?
2. Why did the inflation rate consistently decrease after the initial "shock" of 1991?

APPLICATION Making Inferences and Drawing Conclusions

A. Which of the challenges above do you think is the most serious? Give reasons for your answer.

Economic Change in the Former Soviet Bloc

QUICK REFERENCE

Perestroika was a gradual plan to incorporate markets into the Soviet Union's command economy.

KEY CONCEPTS

In the 1980s, Soviet leader Mikhail Gorbachev introduced **perestroika**, a plan to gradually incorporate markets into the Soviet Union's command economy. People began to push for political freedom as well, and in 1991 the Soviet Union dissolved. The collapse of the Soviet Union caused a period of dramatic transition throughout Eastern Europe and Central Asia.

EXAMPLE 1 Russia

The transition was a turbulent time for Russia. Like Poland and several other Eastern European nations, Russia pursued a program of economic "shock therapy." The resulting inflation was devastating. Supplies of goods were very low, and many industries were forced into bankruptcy when faced with the need to become "self-financing." Further, the state was poorly equipped to carry out even the most basic functions of government, such as tax collection. Having little revenue to work with, Russia's government could offer few welfare services to citizens whose lives had been disrupted by the economic shift, and the burden of government debt began to rise.

Amid the upheaval, some market forces began to exert themselves. Without directives from central planners, regional business initiatives could address the real demands of consumers. In 1992, a program of privatization began to put the means of production into private ownership, introducing incentives for success. However, the privatization process was fixed in favor of a small group of well-connected businesspeople. These oligarchs, as they came to be known, snapped up many of Russia's former public assets in rigged auctions. They went on to build massive corporations and became the most powerful economic force in Russia.

In 2005, the best-known oligarch, Mikhail Khodorkovsky, was sentenced to eight years in prison on fraud and tax evasion charges. In addition, his giant oil company, Yukos, was taken over by the government. It is widely believed that the charges against him were motivated by his support for political parties that were opposed to Russia's president, Vladimir Putin. Many saw this case and others as symptoms of Putin's reluctance to truly adopt democratic reforms and a market economy. Taken together, Putin's actions, the power of Russian organized crime, and the persistence of widespread corruption threatened to undermine Russia's successful development.

Putin and the Oligarchs The prosecution of Mikhail Khodorkovsky served as a warning to Russia's oligarchs: the price of opposition to Putin's government may be your freedom.

EXAMPLE 2 Former Soviet Republics

The transition of the former Soviet Republics has been varied. The Baltic Republics—Latvia, Lithuania, and Estonia—have fared better than others, experiencing a 45 percent inflation rate while Ukraine had a 400 percent rate and Kazakhstan in Central Asia had a rate higher than 1,000 percent. Of all the former republics, only the Baltic Republics, Armenia, Belarus, and Kazakhstan have a higher output now than they did before the collapse of the Soviet Union. Nevertheless, many economists believe the quality of goods and services produced is higher. In the other republics, poor infrastructure, complicated bureaucracies, undeveloped property laws, and corruption have interfered with economic growth.

Vilnius Since independence, the capital of Lithuania has thrived. It accounts for one-third of the nation's GDP and attracted 2.815 billion euros in FDI in 2005.

EXAMPLE 3 Eastern Europe

The formerly Communist nations of Eastern European have faced some of the same challenges as their neighbors and had similarly varying degrees of success. The largest nations, the Czech Republic, Hungary, and Poland, are now much like Western countries. They are members of the European Union, but some experts believe they will need until 2035 to catch up economically with other member nations. Nonetheless, progress is apparent. Since the transition, Poland's economy has been growing at an average rate of 6 percent annually, industrial productivity has increased by more than 20 percent, and the private sector is responsible for more than 70 percent of the national income. There are more than 2.5 million small- or medium-sized businesses operating today, and Western franchises, such as the McDonald Corporation and the IKEA Group, have become entrenched.

However, Poland also has problems that are common across the nations of Eastern Europe. Its infrastructure is out of date, and telephone and internet services are very costly. The laws for registering to do business in the Polish market are confusing, and the patent process that protects property rights is slow. The health care and pension systems have weakened, and unemployment is high. Averaged throughout the country, the unemployment rate is about 18 percent, but in some regions it is as high as 40 percent, and workers are discouraged. In Hungary, the illegal "hidden economy" may account for up to 30 percent of GDP.

APPLICATION Comparing and Contrasting Economic Information

B. Which of the three regions—Russia, the former Soviet Republics, or Eastern European nations—has had the hardest transition? Explain your answer.

China Moves Toward a Market Economy

KEY CONCEPTS

China became a Communist country in 1949, but it began a transition to a free market economy in 1978. At that time, its leader, Deng Xiaoping, introduced free market economic principles to stimulate China's economy. The result was a vastly changed and rapidly growing economy.

EXAMPLE Rapid but Uneven Growth

In the early years of China's Communist economy, central planners focused on redistributing land, developing heavy industry, and improving China's transportation system. In 1958, the government introduced the Great Leap Forward. This plan focused on the building of huge collective farms and the development of the steel industry. For a while, both agricultural and steel output increased. However, the gains were short-lived. Poor economic planning and a series of natural disasters led to stark times. Millions of people died in famines.

When Deng Xiaoping came to power in the late 1970s, hundreds of millions of Chinese villagers lived in poverty, sometimes sharing one pair of trousers among a whole family. Deng brought hope and practical programs to the people. "It is time to prosper. . . . To get rich is glorious," he said. Deng began a far-reaching but gradual program to relax government control over the economy and let market forces drive economic growth.

In agriculture, farmland that had been confiscated was returned to the farmers in household units. Under this "household responsibility system," farms still had to supply a quota of staple goods to the government at set prices, but beyond that the farmers could grow what they wanted and sell any surplus on the open market. China reported a ten percent annual growth in agricultural output between 1979 and 1984. Brick homes began to replace thatched huts as farmers' income soared.

A Growing Divide
Modernization has come at breakneck speed in many of China's urban centers, while life in rural China can seem to be in a different century.

In the mid-1980s, Deng focused his reform effort on industry, where two-thirds of the manufacturing plants were still state-owned. Deng moved slowly and cautiously. Instead of privatizing suddenly or making drastic, uniform changes, he scattered the reforms among different industries. In one industry, local managers might have more decision-making power. In another, workers might get raises based on the profits of the factory. Deng's reforms also called for localities to invest in the industries they thought would thrive. In this process, resources were re-allocated from heavy to light industry, a key factor in China's rapid growth.

Deng also created **special economic zones (SEZs)**, regions that have economic laws that are different from a country's usual economic laws, with the goal of increasing foreign investment. The first four were begun in 1979 as an experiment. In 1984, fourteen more were created in cities along the coast, including Shanghai; now there are hundreds. The SEZs have tax incentives for foreign investment, and the economic activities are driven entirely by market forces. Further, when capitalist Hong Kong was returned to China in 1997 after a 99-year lease by the United Kingdom, it was reunified under the "one country, two systems" framework. The government did not interfere with its economy; in fact, it became a model for the nation.

Areas with high foreign investment have raced ahead of other parts of the country economically, contributing to China's annual growth in GDP of between 5 and 15 percent since the reforms began. Some people, encouraged by Deng's proclamation, have become very rich. However, in 2003, the number of people living in extreme poverty (on less than $77 a year) rose for the first time in 25 years, to about 3 percent of the population. In some villages of western China, 90 percent of the people live on government welfare and do not have indoor plumbing or telephones.

QUICK REFERENCE

A **special economic zone (SEZ)** is a geographical region that has economic laws that are different from a country's usual economic laws, with the goal of increasing foreign investment.

Economics Update

Find an update on China's special economic zones at **ClassZone.com**

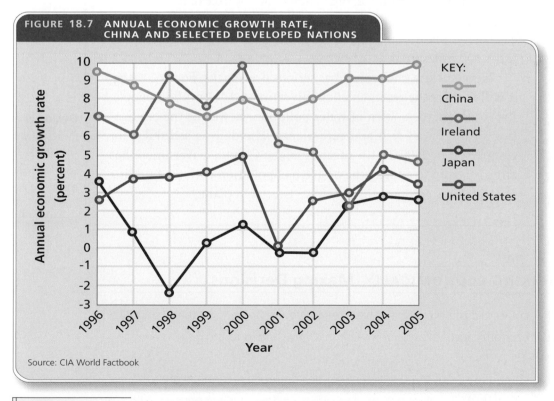

FIGURE 18.7 ANNUAL ECONOMIC GROWTH RATE, CHINA AND SELECTED DEVELOPED NATIONS

KEY:
China
Ireland
Japan
United States

Source: CIA World Factbook

APPLICATION **Explaining an Economic Concept**

C. What role do the SEZs play in China's transition to a market economy?

For more on using a decision-making process, see the Skillbuilder Handbook, page R17.

Using a Decision-Making Process

Making decisions in complicated situations can be extremely difficult. Having a plan, or process, in place can be quite helpful.

TECHNIQUES USED IN MAKING DECISIONS Making decisions involves (1) gathering information to identify the situation in question, (2) identifying options, (3) predicting consequences, and (4) implementing a decision. The following passage describes the problem of flooding on China's Chang River. It illustrates the decision-making process.

Look for information that points to a situation that requires a decision. Figures on the deadly toll of flooding show that a decision on damming was needed.

Predict possible consequences. The positive and negative results of the dam are listed.

Controlling the Chang River

In the past 100 years, more than 1 million people have died as a result of flooding along China's Chang (Yangtze) River. After devastating floods in the 1950s, Chinese leader Mao Zedong ordered studies to see whether damming the river was feasible. Finally, in the 1990s, construction began on the Three Gorges Dam, which—when completed—will be the largest dam in the world. In addition to providing flood control, the dam will be a source of hydropower. Its turbines are expected to produce up to one-ninth of China's electricity. The dam's series of locks will allow ocean-going ships to sail 1,500 miles inland.

Nevertheless, the project has serious drawbacks. For one thing, it will require the resettlement of an estimated 1.2 million people. Environmentalists warn of water pollution, as well as the eradication of migratory fish and rare plants. The dam is scheduled for completion in 2009. In the meantime, the Chinese government has already begun to address the problem of pollution with the building of at least one comprehensive sewage treatment plant.

Look for any options that are offered. Here, only the option of damming the river is considered.

Decide what the result was. The dam is scheduled to be completed in 2009.

THINKING ECONOMICALLY Making Decisions

1. What choice did the government have regarding the flooding of the Chang River?

2. What economic incentives do you think may have added to the government's decision?

3. What consequences of the decision might be contrary to economic growth? Explain your answer.

REVIEWING KEY CONCEPTS

1. 1. Explain the difference between these terms:

   a. *shock therapy*   **b.** *perestroika*

2. What makes privatization a challenge in transitional economies?

3. What role does infrastructure play in transitional economies?

4. Why are special economic zones important to the growth of the Chinese economy?

5. In what way(s) is privatization an element of China's shift to a market economy?

6. **Using Your Notes** Write a summary of the challenges of economic transitions and explain how they have been addressed in the former Soviet bloc and in China. Refer to your completed cluster diagram.

   Use the Graphic Organizer at **Online Review @ ClassZone.com**

Transition to a Market Economy

new challenges

CRITICAL THINKING

7. **Comparing and Contrasting Economic Information** What are three key differences between the economic transitions of the former Soviet bloc and China?

8. **Making Inferences and Drawing Conclusions** While China has welcomed western economic principles, it has continued to come down hard on political freedoms. For example, Deng crushed protesters in Tiananmen Square in 1989. Why do you think capitalism can grow in China under a restrictive government when in the former Soviet bloc it went hand in hand with political freedom?

9. **Applying Economic Concepts** Explain how life in the former Soviet bloc changed for each of the following during a transition to a market economy.

   a. factory worker   **b.** farmer   **c.** consumer   **d.** factory manager

10. **Challenge** Do businesses from foreign nations with strong anti-pollution laws have a responsibility to voluntarily limit pollution when located in a less developed country with less developed pollution laws? Give reasons for your answer.

ECONOMICS IN PRACTICE

Budapest, Hungary

Assessing Development
The chart below shows statistics from 2004 for Kyrgyzstan and Tajikistan, in Central Asia, and Hungary and Romania, in Eastern Europe.

	Kyrgyzstan	Tajikistan	Hungary	Romania
Gross national income ($ per capita)	268	154	4,913	1,729
Real GDP growth rate	6.0	10.5	3.9	8.1
Industrial production growth rate	6.0	8.2	9.6	4.0
Human development index (HDI)*	0.702	0.652	0.862	0.792

* Highest HDI is 1.0; lowest is 0.0.
Sources: CIA World Factbook; UNDP

Compare and Contrast Economic Information Write a paragraph comparing and contrasting the transition to a market economy in the selected Central Asian and Eastern European countries. Use the figures from the chart to explain the similarities and differences.

Challenge Why might the nation with the highest HDI, Hungary, also have the lowest real GDP growth?

Case Study

Economics Update
Find an update on this Case
Study at **ClassZone.com**

China's Campaign for Economic Power

Background Since 1978, when China's former leader, Deng Xiaoping, made the decision to adopt free-market reforms, China's economy has been steadily gaining momentum. Deng's "four modernizations" (agriculture, industry, science and technology, and defense) have helped China become a player in the global economy in less than a generation.

Its success is based in part on its encouragement of foreign investment, the establishment of a number of special economic zones, and the opening of 14 coastal cities to foreign investment in 1984. Also, in 2001, China joined the World Trade Organization. Today, China's economic impact is too big to ignore.

What's the issue? What accounts for China's successful transition to a market economy? Study these sources to discover what fuels China's economic growth and how it affects the rest of the world.

A. Magazine Article

This article discusses some of the underlying reasons for China's growing impact on the global economy.

The Dragon Awakes

China is changing the dynamics of the global economy.

[China's] contribution to global GDP growth since 2000 has been almost twice as large as that of the next three biggest emerging economies, India, Brazil and Russia, combined. Moreover, there is [a] crucial reason why China's integration into the world economy is today having a bigger global impact than other emerging economies, or than Japan did during its period of rapid growth from the mid-1950s onwards. Uniquely, China combines a vast supply of cheap labor with an economy that is (for its size) unusually open to the rest of the world, in terms of trade and foreign direct investment. The sum of its total exports and imports of goods and services amounts to around 75% of China's GDP; in Japan, India and Brazil the figure is 25–30%. . . . As a result, the dragon's awakening is more traumatic for the rest of the world.

Source: *The Economist*, July 28, 2005

Thinking Economically Identify the aspect of China's economy that, according to the article, has had the most significant impact on the global economy, and explain why its impact has been so great.

B. Political
Cartoon

The volume of
China's exports
has gotten a lot of
attention in recent
years.

caglecartoons.com/espanol

Thinking Economically
Why is it worth pointing
out that China's exporting
power seems to outstrip
that of other nations?

**C. Online
News Story**

China's economic
growth frequently
is referred to as an
"economic mira-
cle." The miracle,
however, is not
without problems.

China's Economic Miracle: the High Price of Progress

China's progress is uneven and sometimes problematic.

[China's] GDP is growing by 10 percent a year. Industrial production is galloping ahead at an annual rate of 17 percent. Its economy is now the second-biggest in the world, behind only the U.S., and there are predictions it will assume the top spot as early as 2020. . . .

China's explosive growth has come at a price. The economic gains have not been shared equally. Millions have become richer. But hundreds of millions have not. More than 60 percent of the population still toils in agriculture; the country's "economic miracle" has yet to make an appearance in much of the country. Corruption also remains well entrenched . . . [and] millions of workers have lost their jobs in the restructuring, prompting frequent protests. . . .

Source: **CBC News Online, April 20, 2005**

Thinking Economically Will China's economic growth alone increase the incomes of its poorest people? Why or why not?

THINKING ECONOMICALLY Synthesizing

1. All three documents point to China's success in international trade. What key element of financing development does document A cite as a component of China's success?

2. Documents A and B hint that the rest of the world is uneasy with China's economic growth, while document C discusses some of China's problems at home. Discuss these fears and problems in the context of what you've learned throughout Chapter 18.

3. Which factors do you think are most significant relative to China's economic growth? Explain why you think so. Use evidence from the documents in your answer.

Interactive Review

Review this chapter using interactive
activities at ClassZone.com

- **Online Summary**
- **Graphic Organizers**
- **Quizzes**
- **Review and Study Notes**
- **Vocabulary Flip Cards**

Online Summary

Complete the following activity either on your
own paper or online at **ClassZone.com**

**Choose the key concept that best completes
the sentence. Not all key concepts will be used.**

debt restructuring	per capita GDP
default	"shock therapy"
developed nations	stabilization program
infant mortality rate	privatization
International Monetary Fund (IMF)	World Bank
less developed countries (LDC)	

Nations with little industry and relatively low
GDP are said to be __1__ , while nations with a
market economy and higher standard of living are
known as __2__ . Economists measure the level of a
nation's development through such statistics as
__3__ , which allows for easy comparison with other
countries because it shows the nation's output in
relation to its population.

When nations set a course for development, they
often seek loans from other nations. Some heavily
indebted nations have gone into __4__ on their
loans, being unable to pay them back. In those
cases, nations can negotiate a __5__ plan to extend
the payback and/or lower the payback rate.

Some economies are moving from central
planning to an open market. These nations face
a number of challenges. For example, there are
questions about how to carry out __6__ , the transfer
of public property into individually owned
property. There are also questions about the
pace of change. __7__ involved suddenly removing
governmental restrictions on the economy.

CHAPTER **18 Assessment**

REVIEWING KEY CONCEPTS

Definitions of Development (pp. 544–551)

1. What are some features of a developed nation?

2. Name five measures economists use to gauge a
nation's level of development.

A Framework for Economic Development Objectives (pp. 552–561)

3. Describe the internal and external goals a
developing nation may set for itself.

4. In what ways can developing nations receive aid
from other countries?

Transition to a Market Economy (pp. 562–571)

5. Name five challenges nations face when moving
from a command economy to a market economy.

6. Briefly summarize the transition to a market economy
in the former Soviet bloc and in China

APPLYING ECONOMIC CONCEPTS

The graph below shows life expectancy in more
developed and less developed countries.

7. What is the general trend in both more developed
and less developed countries?

8. From 1980 to 2005, how much did life expectancy
increase for people in each group of countries?

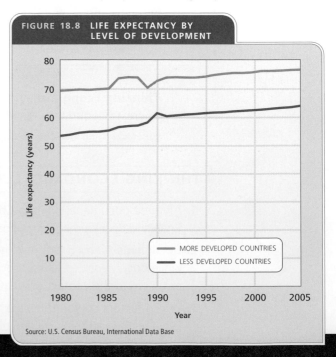

FIGURE 18.8 LIFE EXPECTANCY BY LEVEL OF DEVELOPMENT

Life expectancy (years) — Year

MORE DEVELOPED COUNTRIES
LESS DEVELOPED COUNTRIES

Source: U.S. Census Bureau, International Data Base

9. **Creating Graphs** Create a bar graph that illustrates the following data on the percentage of people living on $1 a day or less in different regions.

FIGURE 18.9 POVERTY TRENDS IN WORLD REGIONS

Region	1981	1990	2001
East Asia & Pacific	56.7	29.5	14.3
Latin America & Caribbean	10.1	11.6	9.9
Middle East & North Africa	5.1	2.3	2.4
South Asia	51.5	41.3	31.9
Sub-Saharan Africa	41.6	44.5	46.4

Source: U.N. Human Development Report, 2005

Use **SMART Grapher** @ ClassZone.com to complete this activity.

10. **Analyzing and Interpreting Data** Refer to the graph you created. In which region was the improvement in poverty most dramatic? In which regions did the situation worsen?

11. **Analyzing Cause and Effect** What might explain why this measure of poverty increased in Sub-Saharan Africa during this period?

12. **Making Inferences and Drawing Conclusions** For each dollar spent on foreign aid by members of OECD, $10 is spent on the military. What can you conclude about the OECD member nations' concerns for the future?

13. **Challenge** A recent study found that an increase of 10 mobile phones per 100 people raised GDP growth in a developing nation by 10 percent. What might explain this? What does it suggest as a way to speed development?

Work Toward Development Goals

In 2005, all the 191 members of the United Nations voted to adopt the Millennium Development Goals, with a target date of 2015 to have the goals realized.

Step 1 As a whole class, discuss the following eight goals that are part of this program:

1. Eradicate extreme poverty and hunger
2. Achieve universal primary education
3. Promote gender equality and empower women
4. Reduce child mortality
5. Improve maternal health
6. Combat HIV/AIDS, malaria, and other diseases
7. Ensure environmental sustainability
8. Develop a global partnership for development

Step 2 Break into eight small groups, one for each of the goals.

Step 3 Meet with your group and discuss your goal and why it is important. Then imagine concrete ways that the international community can contribute to meeting your goal. The international community includes the nations of the world as well as international organizations such as the World Bank.

Step 4 Present your recommendations to the rest of the class.

Step 5 After each presentation, hold a classroom discussion on the different ways of solving the problem. Try to decide which approach seems most likely to succeed.

1 Budgeting and Money Management

1.1 Budgeting

As an independent adult you have the freedom to make your own financial decisions. But with freedom comes responsibility. It takes planning and practice to learn how to use your income wisely, to pay your bills on time, and to have money left to save for the future.

What Would a Budget Do for Me?

Everyone has a limited amount of money. A **budget**—a plan for how to save and spend your income—can help you focus your limited financial resources on what's most important to you. It will help you pay for basics like food, clothing, and shelter. After those expenses are met, it can include optional items such as travel or entertainment. And with savings as part of your budget, you will be on the path to achieve your long-term financial goals.

How Do I Set Up a Budget?

Determine Your Income Make a list of all the steady income you receive, including your pay from after-school and summer jobs and occasional work such as mowing lawns. List only the money you take home after taxes have been withheld from your paycheck.

Track Your Expenses To learn where your money goes, keep a record of all your expenses for a month. Save your receipts, and carry a small notebook to jot down purchases when you make them. The list should cover a full month, because not all expenses occur every week.

Categorize Expenses When you have a record of your expenses, put them into categories, such as transportation, food, clothing, savings, and entertainment. Figure CPF 1 shows how monthly expenses might be categorized to help set up a budget.

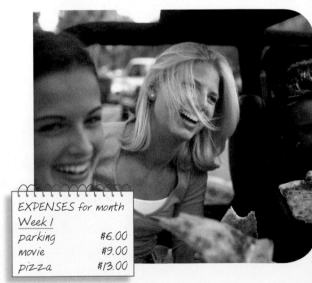

EXPENSES for month
Week 1
parking $6.00
movie $9.00
pizza $13.00

Figure CPF 1 Creating a Budget

(a) **Fixed Expenses** Your car payment and auto insurance are examples of fixed expenses.

(b) **Spending Wisely** Food is a necessity. But packing a lunch, cutting back on snacks, or eating out less often can help your budget.

(c) **Savings** Pay yourself each month. Limiting fixed expenses and reducing flexible expenses will help you meet your savings goals.

(d) **Flexible Expenses** Make room in the budget for entertainment, travel, and other fun stuff.

Monthly Expenses

Category	Current Expenses	Budget
Transportation		
Car payment	$200	$200
Insurance	70	70
Gas	60	40
Parking	6	0
Maintenance	50	25
Food		
School lunches	$85	$80
Snacks	35	30
Eating out	30	15
Savings	20	50
Clothing	100	50
Entertainment		
Movie tickets	$27	$18
Movie rentals	12	12
Recorded music	20	20
TOTALS	$715	$610

Determine Fixed and Flexible Expenses Identify which expenses must be paid every month and determine what portion of your income they take. Savings should be a fixed amount, not a flexible amount. Money from savings pays for emergencies, large insurance bills that only come due once or twice a year, and major investments such as cars or real estate. What's left is available for flexible expenses like entertainment.

Set Up a Spending Plan Now look at your income and expenses. Set out a plan for fixed expenses. Look at the amount left over and allocate it to cover the flexible expenses. If your flexible expenses are cutting into your savings or leading to debt, look for ways to cut your spending. For example, you might eat more meals at home instead of at restaurants, or rent DVDs to watch with friends instead of going out to the movies.

Check It Out!

✓ Create an emergency fund for unexpected expenses.

✓ Save in advance for holiday or birthday gifts.

✓ Resist the temptation of impulse buying.

APPLICATION Budgeting

1. Which of the expenses in Step 3 will be monthly bills?

2. **Planning a Budget** Suppose you have a job that brings in $1,150 a month after taxes. You contribute $350 toward rent and utilities each month for an apartment you share with two other people. You put $100 each month into a savings account, and you spend about $50 per month for a cell phone. Of course, you also eat, wear clothes, and go out with friends. You want to buy a car that will cost $300 per month for payments and insurance. Can you afford it? Plan a budget to see if you can take on this new fixed expense.

Budgeting and Money Management 575

1.2 Checking Accounts

Banks offer two basic types of accounts: checking and savings. Checking accounts are for immediate expenses. They can help you manage your expenses and pay your bills. The bank records deposits and withdrawals on your checking account, whether they are in the form of paper checks, automated teller machine (ATM) transactions, debit card purchases, or electronic transactions.

What Are the Benefits of Checking Accounts?

When you earn money on a regular basis, you should have a place to put it. Most people use checking accounts. Not only is your money safe in the bank, but a checking account makes it easy to pay your bills. In order to use electronic banking and ATMs, you need a checking account.

If you keep all your money as cash, your cash may be lost or stolen. It's also difficult to pay bills with cash. A checking account is safe and convenient.

Opening an Account By shopping around, you can find an account that suits your situation. Ask questions about fees, interest rates paid on the checking account, charges for printing checks, and any restrictions on the number or size of checks you write. Find out the bank's **minimum balance requirement**, which is the amount of money you must keep in the account in order to avoid fees. Most banks charge a high fee for an **overdraft**, a check or other withdrawal for more than the existing account balance.

You'll need several documents to open an account. Most banks require two forms of identification, one of which should have your photo on it. You must provide your Social Security number, address, and phone number. The bank may also ask for a personal or work reference. The money for an initial deposit may be in the form of cash or a check.

QUICK REFERENCE

A **minimum balance requirement** is the amount needed in an account to avoid fees.

An **overdraft** is a check that exceeds the account balance.

Figure CPF 2 Writing a Check

a Write the full name of the person or business receiving the check.

b Enter the amount in numbers and then in words on the next line.

c Sign the check to make it valid. Never sign a blank check.

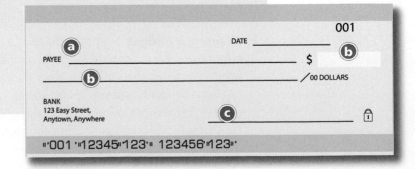

What's the Difference Between an ATM Card and a Debit Card?

Once you have a checking account, you have several options for making deposits and withdrawals. You could go to the bank, but that can be time-consuming, and some banks charge a fee for using a human teller. Instead, automated teller machines (ATMs) give you access to your checking account.

At ATMs Both ATM cards and debit cards allow you to use an ATM to access your checking account. You can withdraw cash, deposit cash or checks, or transfer money between linked accounts. Both cards require that you enter your personal identification number (PIN) when you use the ATM.

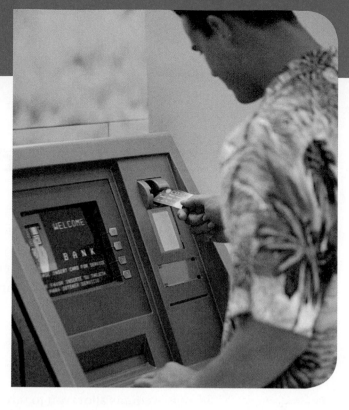

Using an ATM can cost you money. Most ATMs charge a service fee unless you have an account with that bank. Fees range from $1 to $3 or more. To avoid this expense, learn where your bank has ATMs near your home, school, and workplace.

At Stores You can also use ATM and debit cards at businesses to purchase goods and services. However, debit cards can be used like a credit card—the business swipes your card and you sign for the purchase. With an ATM card, the business must have a keypad for you to enter your PIN. In either case, the money comes directly out of your account. Some stores let you get cash back—with no additional charge—when you make a purchase. For example, if you buy $20 worth of groceries, you can charge your ATM or debit card $50 and receive the $30 difference in cash.

Register all the transactions you make with your ATM or debit card in your checkbook. These transactions will be recorded on the monthly account statement that the bank will send to you, but keep track of them as you go along to avoid overdrawing your account.

Check It Out!

☑ Research banking services at several banks.

☑ Immediately record your deposits and withdrawals—including checks, cash withdrawals, and purchases—in your checkbook register.

☑ Review your bank statement every month.

APPLICATION Checking Accounts

1. How is a debit card different from an ATM card?
2. **Finding a bank** Using the Internet, research checking accounts at three banks in your neighborhood. Create a table comparing the services offered and fees charged by the banks. Then write a paragraph identifying the bank you would choose if you wanted to open an account and why you would choose it.

1.3 Saving and Investing

What are your dreams? Do you want to go to college, to travel, to own a car and a home, or perhaps to retire early? Saving some of your income each month can help you achieve your dreams. Accidents and unforeseen problems happen to everyone, so it is good to have an emergency fund, too. When you save your money at a bank or invest in a company, they pay you for the privilege of using your funds. If you save and invest wisely, your money will grow, and you won't have to work as hard to achieve your dreams.

What Are the Benefits of Savings Accounts?

Savings accounts allow you to save money for future expenses. Your money grows in a savings account because banks pay **interest**, a fee for the use of your money. To open a savings account, you'll need the same kinds of identification and other information that you needed to open a checking account.

Types of Accounts Banks and credit unions offer a variety of savings accounts including standard accounts, money market deposit accounts, and certificates of deposit (CDs). The minimum balance, interest rates, and other features vary by type of account. Some banks offer better rates than others, so it's important to shop around for the best deal.

Deposits in these accounts are insured by the government. If the bank should fail, the Federal Deposit Insurance Corporation (FDIC) would make sure you got your money back. The FDIC insures each depositor up to $100,000 at each bank. Retirement accounts are insured up to $250,000.

Unlike stocks, bonds, and many other investments, you are guaranteed to get a positive return on your money in a government-insured account. Figure CPF 3 summarizes the features of the most common types of accounts used for savings.

QUICK REFERENCE

Interest is the price paid for the use of money.

Figure CPF 3 Government-Insured Accounts

Standard Savings Account	Money Market Account	Certificate of Deposit
A standard savings account requires a small initial deposit and allows you the most access to your money. However, it pays the lowest rate of interest.	A money market account pays higher interest and allows you to write a limited number of checks. But it also requires a higher minimum balance.	Certificates of Deposit (CDs) usually offer the highest interest rates. But you pay a penalty if you withdraw any money before the CD matures.

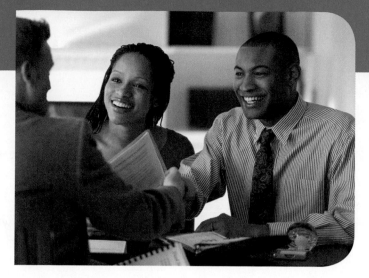

When Should I Start Investing?

The purpose of saving is to accumulate readily available cash. Most financial advisors recommend saving an emergency fund that would cover three to six months of expenses. After you have created your emergency fund, you can begin saving for short-term goals such as buying a car or paying for college tuition.

The purpose of investing is to build wealth—that is, to acquire assets that will grow in value over time and give you a pool of assets beyond the income you earn from a job. Building wealth comes from making your money work for you over a long period of time. It is never too early to start this process, even if you can only allocate a small portion of your income to investment. Investing even small amounts on a regular basis over a long period of time can lead to significant growth.

Before saving or investing, pay off any credit card debt. It is almost impossible to earn more from your investments than you are paying in interest on your debt. For example, if you are paying 15 percent interest on a loan, it doesn't make sense to put some of your money in a savings account that only pays 3 percent interest. Pay off the expensive loan first, then start saving.

Determining Risk As you learned in Chapter 11, there is an inverse relationship between risk and return—the riskier the investment, the greater the potential return. Figure CPF 4 shows this relationship, with the least risky investments at the bottom of the graph and the riskiest ones at the top.

Savings accounts and CDs carry little or no risk because the government insures the principal, and they pay a guaranteed rate of interest. Treasury bonds carry little risk because the U.S. government backs them. Corporate bonds carry greater risk because a company may go bankrupt and be unable to repay its creditors. Stocks offer higher possible returns but are subject to market risks and may decrease rather than increase in value.

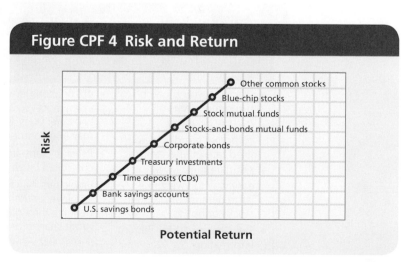

Figure CPF 4 Risk and Return

Risk (vertical axis), Potential Return (horizontal axis)

- Other common stocks
- Blue-chip stocks
- Stock mutual funds
- Stocks-and-bonds mutual funds
- Corporate bonds
- Treasury investments
- Time deposits (CDs)
- Bank savings accounts
- U.S. savings bonds

1 Budgeting and Money Management

How Should I Invest?

Consider your investment objective when choosing the type of investment. If you want to use the money to buy a house in five years, you would choose a different type of investment than if you are investing for your retirement. Generally, the sooner you plan to use the money, the more conservatively you should invest. Conversely, the longer you have before you need the money, the easier it will be to recover from any downturns. Figure CPF 5 shows different ways of investing to reach long-term goals.

There are three basic rules for building wealth: start early, buy and hold, and diversify.

Start Early By starting to invest early you have a longer time for wealth to build. A longer investment time frame also allows you to take more risks, because you can ride out the fluctuations in the market.

Buy and Hold The phrase "buy and hold" describes a disciplined approach to investing. Do research and talk to a financial adviser to make wise decisions, and then hold the investments you make for a long enough period of time to allow your wealth to build. Jumping in and out of the market can lead to significant losses of potential return.

Diversify Diversifying helps you maximize your returns and limit risks. You've probably heard the saying "Don't put all your eggs in one basket." Putting your money in different types of investments allows you to choose different levels of risk.

Figure CPF 5 Investment Options

Stocks, Bonds, and Mutual Funds	Employer-Sponsored Retirement Plans	Individual Retirement Accounts (IRAs)
• Stocks let you share in corporate profits. • Government and corporate bonds pay a fixed rate of interest. • Mutual funds are an easy way to invest in a large number of different stocks or bonds. • See Chapter 11 for more information.	• 401(k) plans let workers invest money for retirement and defer taxes. Employers may also contribute. • Pension plans are controlled by employers. • Employers may fund employee retirement benefits through profit sharing or stock ownership plans.	• Workers may invest money each year for retirement, tax deferred. • Traditional IRA contributions may be tax deductible. • Roth IRA contributions are not tax deductible but earn tax-free income. • Funds must be held until age 59½—with some exceptions.

FIGURE CPF 6 **THE POWER OF COMPOUNDING**

Year	Annual Investment (in dollars)	5 Percent Return (in dollars)	Year-end Balance (in dollars)
1	2,000.00	100.00	2,100.00
2	2,000.00	205.00	4,305.00
3	2,000.00	315.25	6,620.25
4	2,000.00	431.01	9,051.26
5	2,000.00	552.56	11,603.82
6	2,000.00	680.19	14,284.01
7	2,000.00	814.20	17,098.21
8	2,000.00	954.91	20,053.12
9	2,000.00	1,102.66	23,155.78
10	2,000.00	1,257.79	26,413.57

FIGURE CPF 7 **BUILDING WEALTH OVER TIME**

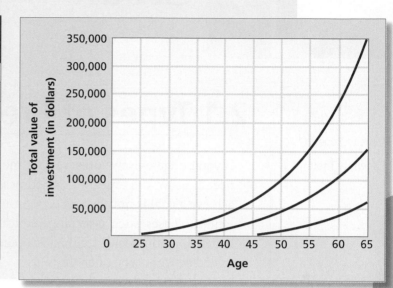

What Are the Benefits of Starting Early?

Figures CPF 6 and CPF 7 graphically illustrate the benefits of starting your investment program when you are young. The table, Figure CPF 6, shows how a savings account that pays 5 percent interest would grow. Investing $2,000 each year for 10 years—a total of $20,000—yields a balance of more than $26,000 through the benefits of compounding and reinvesting the earnings. If the investments continued at the same pace for 45 years, the total balance would reach almost $1 million.

The graph, Figure CPF 7, shows the benefits of starting to save for retirement early. The graph shows what happens to three people who invest $100 per month in a retirement account. It assumes they receive a return on their investments of 8 percent, which approximates the historical average return for the stock market. Someone who begins investing $100 per month at age 25 has over twice as much at retirement as someone who waits until age 35 and almost six times as much as someone who waits until age 45.

Check It Out!

☑ Make regular contributions to your savings account.

☑ Commit to investing for the long term.

☑ Diversify your investments.

Interactive ⊛ Review

Review Budgeting and Money Management using interactive activities at **ClassZone.com**

APPLICATION Saving and Investing

1. Suppose you have saved $1,000 toward the purchase of a car. Which type of savings plan would be best for this money until you are ready to use it? Why?

2. **Listing Financial Goals** Make a list of financial goals you might want to reach by the time you are 30 years old, then 50 years old, then at retirement age. Think about a plan that might help you achieve these goals. What sort of investments will you make? Write a summary paragraph describing your goals and plans.

2 Credit

2.1 Types of Credit

If you budget wisely and save your money, you will be able to buy what you need most of the time. But sometimes, waiting to accumulate the money to achieve a goal is not the best economic choice. Using credit to make important purchases, such as a college education or a home, often has economic benefits. If you decide to finance a purchase by using credit, you first need to decide what type of credit to use.

What Is Credit?

Credit is the practice of buying goods or services now and paying for them in the future. One form of credit is a **loan**, which is borrowed money that must be repaid with interest. Just as banks pay you interest for the use of your money in a savings account, you have to pay them interest if you want to use their money to buy something. Loans are usually used for large purchases such as a home, automobile, or school tuition.

Credit cards are like short-term loans, because they allow you to buy things without having the cash at the time of purchase. But you will be charged interest if the credit card balance is not paid in full each month, and credit cards usually charge higher interest rates than other loans.

QUICK REFERENCE

Credit is the practice of making a purchase now and paying for it in the future.

A **loan** is borrowed money repaid with interest.

How Much Does Credit Cost?

The cost of credit is called the **finance charge**. It includes the total amount of interest you will pay plus any service charges. The amount of interest you pay depends on the **annual percentage rate (APR)**, the length of the loan, and how often you make payments. With all of these variables, it can be challenging to figure out how much a loan actually costs. But all lenders are

QUICK REFERENCE

The **finance charge** is the total cost of the loan.

The **annual percentage rate (APR)** is the amount of interest charged per year.

Figure CPF 8 Costs of Borrowing $10,000

Loan	APR (in percent)	Length of Loan (in months)	Monthly Payment (in dollars)	Total Payments (in dollars)	Finance Charge (in dollars)
A	4	36	295.24	10,628.63	628.63
B	8	36	313.36	11,281.11	1,281.11
C	8	60	202.76	12,165.89	2,165.89

required to tell you the total finance charges and the APR. This information should allow you to understand how much a loan will cost and to compare offers from different lenders.

For example, suppose you want to borrow $10,000 to purchase a car. The finance charge will vary depending on the length of the loan and the interest rate. As you can see in Figure CPF 8, a longer loan might have a lower monthly payment, but it will also have the highest total cost.

How Do Lenders Decide If I Can Get Credit?

Lenders use three basic criteria to determine if you are creditworthy and can be trusted to repay a loan. The criteria—character, capacity, and capital—are often referred to as the three Cs. These three criteria are based on your past, present, and future financial situation.

Character refers to your past record of paying your bills on time. Lenders want to know if you can live within your means, which makes it more likely that you will be able to repay the loan. When you make car payments on time or pay off a department store charge card each month, you build a positive credit history. These actions show that you are financially responsible.

Capacity refers to your level of income relative to the size of the loan. A lender will check to see if you have a steady income and if the amount of your income is enough to make the loan payments. The lender may look at your past employment history to see if you are likely to keep your current job or may check with your employer to see if your income will remain steady over the projected term of the loan.

Capital—specifically, financial capital—includes your income, savings, and other investments. Lenders will consider how much money you have in the bank as well as assets such as a car or house. If you fail to repay the loan, the lender may be able to take these assets to recover the cost of the loan.

If you are weak on any of these criteria a lender might ask for a cosigner for the loan. A **cosigner** is a person who will assume responsibility for the debt if you fail to repay the loan. Taking out a loan with a cosigner but repaying it yourself is one way you can build up a positive credit history.

QUICK REFERENCE

A **cosigner** assumes responsibility for debt if a borrower doesn't repay.

Credit 583

2 Credit

What Should I Consider When Choosing a Credit Card?

Credit card companies are eager to get young adults to use their cards. But these companies offer a variety of terms, and some of them can be costly. Before you apply for a credit card, carefully examine the terms.

Annual Fee Many cards have no annual fee, but some charge $60 per year or more for membership.

Interest Rate The Truth in Lending Act requires that credit card companies state the interest rate in the form of an annual percentage rate (APR). Rates may be fixed, meaning that they will stay the same, or variable, meaning that they are tied to an index and likely to change frequently.

Grace Period The grace period is the time between your billing date and the date your payment is due. Late payments may result in stiff fees.

Minimum Payment The minimum payment may be a flat amount or a certain percentage of your balance. Paying this amount allows you to avoid paying penalties, but not interest.

Credit Limit The credit limit is the maximum amount you can charge. Your available credit is your credit limit minus any outstanding balance.

Other Fees There are usually fees for paying late or for spending over your credit limit. There may be a minimum finance charge or amount of interest due, or transaction fees for cash advances.

Bonuses Many credit cards offer to give you a bonus based on how much you charge as an incentive to use the card. Some cards offer "cash back"— a refund of a small percentage of your total purchases. Others offer discounts on merchandise or air travel.

What Should I Know About My Credit Card Statement?

When you pay by credit card, you will receive a record of what you have spent each month called a statement. It will also show any payments or credits to your account. Check your credit card statement right away to make sure all the purchases shown are ones that you made. Also check to be sure the credit card company received your last payment.

Figure CPF 9 points out some of the important information to notice on your credit card statement. Your new balance is the amount you must pay by the due date to avoid paying interest. The finance charge is the interest due on any unpaid balance from your last statement. Notice that the minimum payment is only a small percentage of your new balance. Credit card companies make money if you pay less than the full balance, because they charge you interest on the rest of your balance.

Figure CPF 9 Understanding Your Credit Card Statement

(a) The new balance includes all of your purchases for the month, plus any unpaid balance from the last month and interest, plus any fees. To avoid finance charges, pay the entire balance by the due date.

(b) If you cannot pay the entire balance, pay at least the minimum balance by the due date to avoid late fees. The minimum balance may be only a small percentage of your total balance but is usually at least $10.

(c) The periodic rate is the daily interest rate, that is, the APR divided by the number of days in the year.

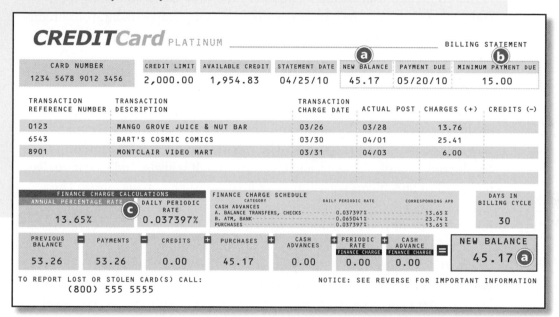

Pay at least the minimum balance by the due date. Most credit card companies charge high fees for late payments. Allow time for your payment to arrive and be processed before the due date.

How Is a Credit Card Different from a Debit Card?

Both cards can be used to make purchases. But when you use a credit card you create a loan to repay, while a debit card takes money directly from your checking account. You can use your debit card to get cash from your checking account at an ATM. But if you use your credit card to get cash, you are essentially taking out a loan. Interest begins accruing right away on the amount of the cash advance, and most cards charge an additional transaction fee. It is a very expensive way to get cash.

Check It Out!

☑ Determine all costs and fees for a credit card or loan.

☑ Check your statement every month for unauthorized expenses.

☑ Pay on time.

APPLICATION Types of Credit

1. What are the three Cs, and who uses them?

2. **Determining the Best Offer** Suppose you have offers from three credit card companies. Company A offers a fixed APR of 12 percent and has an annual fee of $60.00. Company B has no annual fee and offers an introductory rate of 9 percent—but it rises to 18 percent after the first 3 months. Company C offers a fixed APR of 15 percent with an annual fee of $30. If you pay off your balance each month, which offer is best for you?

2 Credit

2.2 Credit Reports

How you handle your finances can determine your ability to qualify for a loan or credit card, to be hired for a job, or to rent an apartment. Your credit report contains much of the information on the three Cs discussed earlier.

What's a Credit Report?

A **credit report** is a statement by a credit bureau that details a consumer's credit record. Equifax, Experian, and Trans Union are the three companies that handle most credit reporting. The report includes information on your employment, bank accounts, and credit history. It will also indicate if you've had any legal problems regarding your finances, such as bankruptcy. The report shows how well you have handled your financial obligations over the previous 7 to 10 years so lenders can determine if you are a good credit risk.

Credit agencies use the information in your credit report to assign you a **credit score**, a number that rates your credit worthiness. Different agencies use different scoring systems, but higher scores indicate a better credit history. Lenders may charge a lower interest rate to someone with a high credit score.

Where Do I Get My Credit Reports?	
online:	www.annualcreditreport.com
phone:	1-877-322-8228
mail:	Annual Credit Report Request Service P.O. Box 105281 Atlanta, GA 30348-5281 (print form at www.annualcreditreport.com)
Do not contact the three nationwide consumer credit reporting companies directly for free reports.	

Credit Report Users Lenders evaluate your credit report when you apply for a loan or a credit card. Buying the report from one of the three major companies saves them the time of contacting all your creditors to see how well you've paid your bills. Landlords may also check your credit report before agreeing to rent you an apartment. Some employers check credit scores before hiring people. Because so many people rely on these reports, you should verify the accuracy of the information in the report. Checking your credit reports also helps guard against identity theft. (See 2.3 Identity Theft for more information on this topic.)

How Do I Get a Copy of My Credit Report?

The Fair Credit Reporting Act makes it easy to access your credit reports (see "Where Do I Get My Credit Reports?" sidebar). By law, you may use this service to order one free copy from each company every 12 months. You provide your name, address, Social Security number, and date of birth. You may be asked other questions to verify your identity.

The government is the only legitimate source for free credit reports.

Figure CPF 10 How Does Your Credit History Rate?

Good Rating
• You pay bills in full
• You pay bills on time
• You can cover payments in case of emergency
• You can make payments if you lose your job

Danger
• More than 25 percent of your take-home pay goes to pay off debt
• You only make minimum payments
• You make payments after the due date
• You open new accounts because the old ones are maxed out
• Creditors harass you

Overextended
• Creditors repossess (take back) what you bought on credit
• Creditors garnish your wages (take money from your paycheck before you get it)
• You must declare bankruptcy

Avoid other sources that claim to offer free credit reports. Some of them want to sell you unnecessary services, and others want to steal your identity. Also avoid firms that promise to fix your credit rating. Only you can do that.

How Do I Solve Credit Problems?

The best cure is prevention. You can avoid credit problems by following your budget and paying off your bills on time. But if you recognize any of the signs of danger or overextension shown in Figure CPF 10, you can take action to avoid financial problems.

Self-Help These are the first steps for restoring your credit rating.
• Talk to your creditors and explain your situation and your desire to correct it.
• Cut up your credit cards and pay off your debts as soon as possible.
• Create a strict budget and follow it.

Professional Help If you are unable to resolve the problems yourself, see a professional counselor. Try nonprofit agencies first. The National Foundation for Credit Counseling can provide referrals. These agencies will provide services and help you to straighten out your debt problems.

Check It Out!
✔ Check your credit report yearly.
✔ Pay your bills on time.
✔ Watch for the danger signs, and act promptly to correct the problem.

APPLICATION Credit Reports

1. What groups might use your credit score?

2. **Paying Off Your Bills** Suppose you have a student loan, a car payment, and a credit card with debt. The student loan debt is $4,000 with interest at APR 8 percent. The car loan is $8,000 with APR of 4 percent. The credit card debt is $1,500 with APR of 18 percent. Your grandmother sends you a check for $1,000 for graduation. Which bill would you put the money towards?

2.3 Identity Theft

Your bank accounts, credit cards, and other financial tools are all tied to your name. You've seen what can happen if your credit report shows a poor credit history. What if a poor credit rating is not your fault?

What Is Identity Theft?

Identity theft is the use of personal information—such as Social Security numbers, credit card or bank account numbers—to commit fraud and other crimes. Identity thieves steal personal information to run up charges on existing accounts or to open new ones. They may withdraw money from your bank accounts, apply for loans, or use your telephone calling card. It takes victims weeks, months, and sometimes years to correct the damage done after their identity has been stolen.

How Can I Protect Myself?

If you know how these thieves operate, you can take measures to protect yourself. While some victims lose their identity through loss or theft of their wallet or purse, almost half of the victims don't know how the thief obtained their information. Here are some of the most common techniques.

Shoulder Surfing Identity thieves may watch you as you punch in a calling card or credit card number or your PIN. They might overhear you giving out an account number over the phone. Be conscious of those around you when you use an ATM or give out personal financial information.

Dumpster Diving Thieves look through the trash to find discarded credit card statements or other documents with financial information. Put such documents through a shredder before throwing them away.

Spamming or Phishing Identity thieves may send unsolicited e-mail (spam) that appears to be from a legitimate source. Or they may telephone and say there is a problem with your account or offer you some benefit if you confirm information.

Hacking Sometimes identity thieves will use programs that invade your computer and find your personal data. Or they might direct you to a fake Web site set up to look like that of a bank or other business. Security software can help prevent hacking, but you must pay attention when you give out credit card and other personal information over the Internet. Confirm that the site you visit is legitimate.

Where Do I Get More Information?	
Department of Justice	www.usdoj.gov
Federal Trade Commission	http://www.ftc.gov/ bcp/edu/microsites/ idtheft/
Consumer Action Web Site	www.consumeraction.gov

What If I Become a Victim?

If you learn that your personal information has been stolen, act immediately to limit the damage. Keep good records of all the steps you take. First, contact one of the three credit reporting companies to place a fraud alert on your credit report. The fraud alert will make it necessary for creditors to contact you before opening new accounts in your name. The Federal Trade Commission and Department of Justice Web sites (see "Where Do I Get More Information?" sidebar) provide toll-free phone numbers and Web site addresses for the credit reporting companies. When you notify one company it will notify the others to place a similar alert on their reports. Once you have placed such an alert, you may order free copies of your report to check for fraudulent activity.

Contact your creditors or banks to close out accounts that have been accessed by thieves or that have been opened without your permission. The FTC Web site also provides a form to dispute new accounts that you did not authorize. You may want to stop payment on any checks that have not cleared and change your ATM account and personal identification number (PIN).

File a report with the police and get a copy of the report or the report number. Provide as much information as you can. The report will provide proof to your creditors or financial institutions that a crime has been committed. Also file a report with the FTC, which maintains a database of reported cases of identity theft.

Check It Out!

Remember the word SCAM.

☑ Be **S**tingy. Only give personal information to people you trust.

☑ **C**heck your bank and credit card statements regularly.

☑ **A**sk for your credit report every 12 months.

☑ **M**aintain careful records of all your financial accounts.

Interactive ⟵ Review

Review Credit using interactive activities at **ClassZone.com**

APPLICATION **Identity Theft**

1. What are some ways that identity theft can occur?

2. Planning a Response Take a look in your wallet or purse. What items there could be the source of identity theft? How do you protect yourself from having these items stolen? Review how you would respond if these items were stolen.

3 Wise Choices for Consumers

3.1 Buying a Car

A car is a symbol of freedom and independence. It is convenient to be able to travel where and when you want. Yet owning a car includes financial obligations. Since it's expensive to own a car, first consider whether you really need one. Is good public transportation, such as a bus or a train, available to get you to work or school? Do you live close enough to ride a bike or to walk? If you don't need a car most of the time, would it make sense to rent a car occasionally or to join a car sharing plan?

What Should I Consider When Buying a Car?

If a vehicle is definitely in your future, take your time before you make a purchase. A car is a major investment, so it makes sense to do some research. Use the information in Figure CPF 11 as a starting point.

One decision is whether to buy a new car or a used car. New cars cost a lot and **depreciate**, or decrease in value, quickly. On average a new car loses 10 percent of its value as soon as you drive it off the lot. The biggest advantage new cars have is that they are covered by warranties. If something goes wrong, you probably won't have to dip into your savings to pay repair bills.

A used car will cost less but may be less reliable. Many experts suggest that cars that are two to three years old offer the best value. Certified used cars come with limited warranties to cover certain major repairs.

How Can I Finance the Purchase of a Car?

If you have not saved enough for the total purchase price of a car, you might consider applying for a car loan. Investigate loans before you shop for the car, so that you will know how much you can afford to spend. Call banks and credit unions and check out online banks to find the best interest rate. Find out the length of available loans, total finance charges, and the amount of your monthly payment. Most lenders will require that you have a down payment on the loan. You may also need a cosigner for your loan.

Beware of financing packages offered by car dealers. Combining price negotiations with financing terms generally results in a good deal for the dealer, not for you.

Research

- Decide what kind of vehicle best suits your needs and budget.
- Use Internet or library resources to find out such information as gas mileage, repair costs, safety record, and prices.
- If it's a new car, find out what the dealer paid for the car so you can negotiate a good price.
- If it's a used car, look up the average resale value in a "blue book" (used car price guide).

Looking for cars

- Visit dealer lots when they are closed to get an idea of what's available without sales pressure.
- Ask family and friends about their car-buying experiences. See if they know a reliable dealer or anyone selling a car.
- Check out "for sale" ads in newspapers, on local bulletin boards, or on Web sites.
- Look for dealer ads in newspapers or on the Internet.

Used cars

- Check the odometer. Avoid cars with an average of 15,000 miles per year or more.
- Look for rust, dents, and signs of the car having been in an accident.
- Review the vehicle's repair record. Check for regular maintenance such as oil changes.
- Find the vehicle identification number (VIN), and use it to research the car's history through an Internet service.
- Take a test drive. Test the air conditioner, heater, radio, and other equipment.
- Pay a mechanic you trust to examine the car and to list what needs to be repaired.

The buying experience

- Always go prepared with the information you have gathered.
- Know which options you want and which ones you can live without.
- Get any offer in writing. That way you are very clear on the exact costs.

What Should I Do After I Buy a Car?

Each state has laws about vehicle titles, taxes, registration, and insurance. You can learn what is required from a car dealership or your state's motor vehicle department. Call several insurance agencies to find out how much insurance for your vehicle will cost (also see 3.3 Getting Insurance). Keep the title, sales receipts, and other important documents in a safe place—not in the glove compartment. Only the registration and proof of insurance should be carried in the vehicle.

Check It Out!

- ✔ Consider whether you really need a car.
- ✔ Research the car and its price before you talk to a salesperson.
- ✔ Be sure you have all the necessary legal documents.

APPLICATION Buying a Car

1. Why should you do research on vehicles before you talk to a dealer?

2. **Planning a Purchase** Choose a particular model of car, new or used. Go to the library or look on the Internet and find information about the car from at least three different sources. Try to learn as much as you can about the car's features, reliability, and pricing, and write down what you learn.

3.2 Financing Your Education

Choosing to go on to college or vocational or technical school after graduation from high school is one of the biggest economic decisions you will make. Getting more schooling will cost you money, but it will pay off in higher salaries and a greater lifetime income. As you learned in Chapter 9, each additional amount of education you receive increases your chances of earning a higher income. More highly educated workers are also less likely to be unemployed. Although the costs of higher education can be daunting, there are many alternatives to help finance your education.

How Do I Decide About Higher Education?

What type of higher education do you want? Choices include college, vocational school, and technical school. Costs at different types of schools vary widely and may influence the type of education you choose. Generally, public colleges are less expensive than private ones, and community colleges are less expensive than four-year schools. Consider your career goals, interests, and aptitudes, and think about what type of school offers the best value that meets your needs.

Do you want to start right after high school? If you want to take a year off, think about what you will do and who will provide your financial support. Consider your income and expenses during that time and what kind of help your parents might give you. Postponing education postpones your future higher earnings and may lead to increased education costs.

Where do you want to go for schooling?
Are there schools in your state that would meet your needs? Out-of-state tuition is significantly higher than tuition at a public college in your own state. Going away to school generally means higher costs for housing, food, and travel, but it may be important for other reasons.

What Will Be the Total Cost of Going to School?

Paying for tuition to cover the costs of your coursework is just the beginning of school expenses. A variety of fees to cover student activities, connection to the school's computer network, and other costs are added to tuition. In the 2005–2006 school year, average tuition and fees ranged from about $2,200 at a public two-year college to about $5,500 at a public four-year college and more than $21,200 at a private four-year college. Room and board costs cover housing and food and average more than $6,600 per year at a public four-year college. You must also buy your textbooks, which may cost as much as $1,000 per year. Transportation for visits home as well as other personal expenses are also part of the costs of going to school.

Economics Update

Find an update on the cost of higher education at **ClassZone.com**

Where Can I Get the Money for Higher Education?

Once you have determined the costs of going to school, you can begin to make decisions about how to pay for your education. Here are some things to think about: Do I have the money to pay for it myself? Will my parents or family help me out? Can I work and study at the same time? Answers to these questions will help you decide if you need financial aid to go on to school.

All the costs of going to school can be daunting. Over 60 percent of students find that they need some financial help. In fact, most students pay much less than the published costs because of financial aid. There are three basic types of financial aid: grants and scholarships, loans, and work-study programs. Figure CPF 12 outlines the characteristics of each type of aid.

Figure CPF 12 Financial Aid Options

Grants	Scholarships	Loans	Work-Study Programs
• do not need to be repaid • usually based on need • sometimes based on academic merit • given by federal and state governments and colleges	• do not need to be repaid • usually based on academic merit or athletic or artistic ability • awarded by colleges, private groups, and the U.S. military	• must be repaid • federal loans for students • federal and private loans for parents • subsidized—based on need, some interest paid by government • unsubsidized—student pays all interest	• college helps student find a job • federal government helps pay the salary • earnings do not need to be repaid • students who work part-time often do better in school

3 Wise Choices for Consumers

How Much Aid Can I Get?

In general, the amount of aid you receive is determined by the difference between the cost of attending school and the amount you and your family can contribute. Schools consider the following when awarding financial aid:

- Income—yours and your parents. This is the single most important factor in determining financial aid based on need. Students and families with higher incomes are expected to contribute more.

- Number of higher education students in your family. A family with more than one student in college would be expected to contribute less for each one.

- Family assets and expenses. Students are expected to contribute a higher percentage of their savings than parents are, so it's better to have more savings in parents' accounts. In general, schools do not consider the value of retirement funds, a home, or personal assets such as automobiles in figuring out a family's contribution. Some schools do consider these assets, so it's important to know how the schools you are interested in figure their aid awards. Unusual medical expenses and other large expenses may be considered in determining a family's contribution.

- Pool of aid dollars at the school you want to attend. Schools award aid based on a combination of federal, state, and school funds. A wealthy private school may have more funds available than a state school.

- Number of students applying for aid at the school you want to attend. Since each school has a limited amount of funds available for aid, if more students apply for aid there may be less available for each student. The level of need of the students applying might also affect how much individual students receive.

How Do I Apply?

Start Early Meet with your guidance counselor and request financial aid information from schools at least a year before you plan to start school. Begin to research scholarships. Make note of all application deadlines.

Get a PIN A personal identification number (PIN) allows you to submit your Free Application for Federal Student Aid (FAFSA) online for faster results. Go to www.pin.ed.gov.

Gather All the Documents You Need You'll need income tax returns and W-2 forms for you and your parents, as well as information on nontaxable income. You'll also need your Social Security number and driver's license number, along with bank statements and information on mortgage payments and investments.

Complete the FAFSA Fill out a paper form or go to www.fafsa.ed.gov to apply online. Follow the instructions carefully. You only need to complete one form, which will be used by all the schools to which you are applying.

Fill Out Any Additional Aid Forms These forms may be required for some nonfederal aid such as state and school aid or private scholarships. Ask for recommendations from your teachers and other adults who know you well at least a month before scholarship application deadlines. Provide them any necessary forms and a stamped envelope for the recommender to send to the school.

Review Your Student Aid Report (SAR) This report is the result of your FAFSA application. Make sure all the information is accurate. Your SAR shows your Expected Family Contribution (EFC), which determines your eligibility for federal student aid based on need.

Contact Schools' Financial Aid Offices Make sure all schools you've applied to received all the information they need.

Compare Your Aid Awards After you receive responses, decide which school's aid package offers the best combination of grants, scholarships, loans, and work-study.

Where Do I Get More Information?	
Federal Student Aid Information Center	studentaid.ed.gov 1-800-4-FED-AID (1-800-433-3243)
FAFSA on the Web	www.fafsa.ed.gov
The College Board	www.collegeboard.com
SallieMae® loans	www.salliemae.com
Your school guidance counselor and the financial aid offices of the schools you are considering also have information.	

Check It Out!

✔ Get forms in on time.

✔ Photocopy all information or print copies of online applications.

✔ Make sure information is consistent on all forms.

APPLICATION Financing Your Education

1. What criteria are used to determine who gets financial aid?

2. **Using a Decision-Making Grid** Using the questions on page 592 and a decision-making grid, determine which type of schooling makes the most economic sense for you.

3.3 Getting Insurance

Insurance protects people from the financial effects of unexpected losses. When you buy insurance coverage, your money joins a pool of money from many different people who face similar risks. The system works because the risk is spread over a large group of people. The chances of any one individual suffering a loss are small.

What Are the Benefits of Insurance?

Most people take out insurance for problems that may be unlikely but would be expensive if they happened: medical treatment for a serious illness or accident, repairing a car damaged in an accident, or replacing valuables stolen from your residence. Such losses are potentially so large that it would be difficult to save enough in an emergency fund to pay for them. Insurance protects you financially against those kinds of losses.

What Kinds of Insurance Should I Get?

When you buy an insurance policy you purchase a certain amount of protection or coverage. Your payment for this protection is called an insurance **premium**. Many types of insurance require you to pay a **deductible**, which is the amount you pay before the insurance company pays on a loss. Some health insurance requires a **co-pay**, an amount you must pay each time you receive health care under your policy. When you have a loss you submit a **claim**, which is a request for payment, to the insurance company.

Most people start out with car insurance, health insurance, and renter's or personal property insurance. There are other options as well. See Figure CPF 13 for an overview of the basic types of insurance.

Most states require that you carry at least a minimum amount of car insurance in case of injury or property damage caused by your car. Premiums are based on the type of vehicle, your age, your driving record, and other related information. The more coverage you have the more the insurance will cost. If you carry a high deductible, it will reduce the premium.

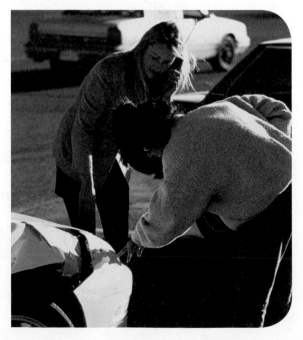

Figure CPF 13 Types of Insurance

Type of Insurance	Protects	Pays
Car	vehicle in case of accident or theft; occupants in case of accident	for property damage and bodily injury, legal costs, and related expenses
Health	policyholder in the event of illness or injury	for doctor and hospital visits, prescription drugs
Homeowner's	structures, land, and personal property	for damage due to fire, theft, or natural disaster
Renter's	personal property	for loss of or damage to personal items
Disability	income when a person cannot work	a percentage of income when a person is out of work due to injury or illness
Life	family when a wage-earner dies	money to the family to meet expenses after death

Health insurance is very costly. Your employer or school may offer insurance plans to cover some or all of your needs. In some states, you may be covered by your parents' health insurance until you graduate from college or reach age 25.

If you live in rented housing, you may want to protect your belongings with renter's insurance or with personal property insurance. Some policies cover the full replacement cost of insured items; others cover only the current value of the items. For example, actual cash value coverage will not cover the full cost of replacing a three-year-old bike that gets stolen.

Check It Out!

✔ Find out if you have insurance coverage at work or through your educational institution.

✔ See if your insurance covers the current value or the full replacement cost.

✔ Determine how much you can afford in deductibles.

What Questions Should I Ask an Insurance Agent?

• How much does the policy cover? Are there limits each year or for each accident or illness? Are there maximums for certain kinds of losses?

• What levels of deductibles are available? Higher deductibles lower the premiums.

• Are claims paid on actual cash value or on replacement value? The former may cost less, but you will receive less in the event of a loss.

• How often are premiums due—monthly or once or twice per year?

APPLICATION Getting Insurance

1. What reasons do people cite for getting insurance?

2. **Selecting Insurance** Explain how having insurance could help in each of the following situations. Case A: Your CD player and 10 CDs are stolen from your car. Case B: You have to have emergency surgery for a fractured leg. Case C: Your car is smashed up by a hit-and-run driver. The damage is well over $2,000.

3.4 Contracts: Reading the Fine Print

QUICK REFERENCE

A **contract** is a legally binding agreement.

Buying insurance, taking out a loan, signing up for a credit card—all of these involve a formal, legally binding agreement known as a **contract**. The contract may be in the form of a signed document or may be executed on a Web site when you download something from the Internet. These terms and conditions are called the "fine print" because they are often set in small type.

Why Should I Read the Fine Print?

There's an old saying: "Education is when you read the fine print. Experience is what you get when you don't." By reading the fine print, you will understand exactly what you are agreeing to when you sign a contract. The fine print often contains information about extra charges and fees that may not be displayed in marketing brochures or advertisements.

Consider Michele, a student who signed a cell phone service contract without reading it. When the first bill arrived, it was over $1,000. She checked the contract and found fine print stating that all text messaging both sent and received was subject to a charge. Even though Michele hadn't read these terms, she had signed the contract, and she had to pay the bill.

What Should I Do Before Signing a Contract?

- First, actually read the contract. If it is long or complicated, ask for a copy and take it home to read.

- Clarify all terms or provisions you don't understand. In a cell phone contract, for example, be clear on peak and off-peak hours, roaming charges, and the cancellation policy. Ask questions until you understand everything clearly. If there are parts you can't figure out, get advice from a friend before signing.

- Check all figures in the contract. Bring a calculator and figure the costs yourself—don't depend on the salesperson's math.

- Make sure any mistakes or omissions are corrected on the contract and initialed by the salesperson.

Source: www.CartoonStock.com

"Sign here to indicate you have no idea you've signed."

Figure CPF 14 A Cell Phone Contract

(a) Note how many minutes are included in the basic monthly price.

(b) Asterisks or footnotes often lead to small print that provides important information.

(c) If you exceed the allotted number of text messages, you pay a fee for each one.

(d) If you want to end your contract before it expires, you pay the cancellation fee.

(e) Your signature here shows that you have read and agree to the fine print.

CellPhone ———————— Service Agreement

Monthly calling plan	$24.95
Total minutes/month (peak)	**400** **(a)**
Unlimited off-peak	$5.95
Voice mail	Included* **(b)**
Additional minutes	$0.40/minute
Roaming charges (See coverage map and terms for details)	$1.00/minute
Text messaging	$3.95
Total outgoing messages/month	**100**
Additional outgoing messages	$0.10/each **(c)**
Incoming messages	Unlimited Free
Plus federal, state, and local taxes and fees	
Contract length	**24 months**
Cancellation fee	$150.00 **(d)**

(b) *Accessing voice mail through cellular phone accrues minutes like any other call.

I acknowledge that I have read and agree to the company's Terms and Conditions

(e) _____ (your signature)

What Should I Beware of?

- Don't let the salesperson rush you. Take your time and make sure you are certain of the terms of the contract. Even if the salesperson says certain desirable terms are about to expire, you should not sign anything you do not thoroughly understand and agree to.

- Never sign a contract with blank spaces. Make sure every blank on the contract is either filled in or marked through as being not applicable. If you leave blanks, someone might enter something after you sign that you did not want to agree to.

- Don't agree to verbal contracts. Make sure everything is in writing. If you agree to a verbal contract and run into a problem, you have no evidence of what the agreement was. Business agreements are generally too complex for either side to remember all the details.

- Don't leave without getting a copy of the contract. Keep the contract in a safe place. Check your first bill carefully to make sure everything matches the contract. If you have questions, call the company to resolve your concerns.

Check It Out!

✔ If it seems too good to be true, it probably is.

✔ Check all figures on the contract.

✔ Never sign a contract with blanks not filled in or crossed out.

Interactive ⟨← Review

Review Wise Choices for Consumers using interactive activities at **ClassZone.com**

APPLICATION Contracts

1. Why shouldn't you agree to a verbal contract?

2. **Evaluating an Offer** Study the ads or commercials for cell phone service. Suppose you are ready to sign a contract for cell phone service. Make a list of the questions you will ask before you sign the contract.

4 Getting Out on Your Own

4.1 Getting a Job

An important step to becoming an independent adult is getting a job. A job allows you to earn money, gain experience, and learn new skills. A career is more than a job. It is a work path that provides satisfaction, challenge, and opportunities for self-expression. Your first jobs help you learn about the world of work and what kind of career you might enjoy.

Where Can I Look for a Job?

Finding a job that suits your skills and helps advance you along your career path can be challenging. There are many sources of information about jobs, and the more you use, the better your chances of finding a good fit.

Friends and Family Talk to them to find out if they know of any job openings. They are the beginning of your network—people who will support you in what you attempt, and whom you support in turn.

School Guidance Counselor, or Career Planning or Placement Office These offices have listings of jobs and intern positions. You can also learn about different careers.

Internet Many Web sites offer job listings, places to post your resumé, and other services. America's Job Bank, managed through a partnership between federal and state governments, allows you to tap into career resources, look at job listings all over the country, and post a resumé.

Newspaper Want Ads Your local newspaper is a good source for jobs in your area.

Employment Agencies Your state and local governments may offer employment services. These public agencies often offer job counseling and training as well as job listings. Private agencies also offer job listings and placement, but they sometimes charge a fee for their services.

Job Fairs Job fairs offer the opportunity to talk to many employers in an area or a specific job category in a very short period of time.

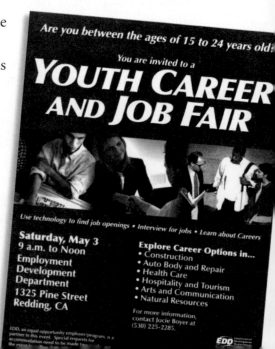

What Do I Need to Apply for a Job?

Before you apply for a job, you will need to prepare materials that introduce you to potential employers and tell them about your qualifications. You will need a resumé, a cover letter, and a list of references. References are people who know you and your work habits and are willing to talk to potential employers. Many jobs will also require that you fill out an application form.

Resumé A resumé is a record of your job history and education. It should be truthful and succinct—no more than one page long. Since employers judge you by your resumé, be sure it is visually appealing and free of errors. Figure CPF 15 shows a sample resumé for a recent high school graduate. If you apply for different kinds of jobs, you may want to develop more than one resumé.

Cover Letter A cover letter briefly explains why you want the job and how you are qualified for it. Address your letter to the specific individual who is

---

Cheryl A. Miller **ⓐ**
1909 E. Walnut St.
Long Beach, CA 90811
310-555-5678
camiller89@isp.net

ⓑ Objective To obtain an entry-level customer service position

Education Jefferson High School, 2003-2007

ⓒ Experience
September 2006–Present
Sales Associate, Electronics Super Center
• Advised customers on product features and helped them choose the ones that best met their needs
• Met or exceeded weekly sales quotas
• Developed promotional materials for in-store use
Summer 2006
Administrative Assistant, Oceanside Computer Center
• Tracked customer sales and repair orders to improve response time
• Responded to customer questions by phone and email
• Provided office support for staff of six
September 2005–June 2006
User support, Jefferson High computer lab
• Developed an orientation program for incoming students
• Helped students use a variety of software applications
• Led a workshop on Web page design

ⓓ Other Skills
• Proficient in a wide range of application software, including word processing, spreadsheet, database, and presentations
• Internet research

ⓔ Activities and Honors
• Member of varsity girls' track team
• Captain of debate team

References available upon request

Figure CPF 15
Writing a Resumé

ⓐ Include all the information an employer might need to contact you.

ⓑ Make your objective specific and succinct. Tailor it to the job you are applying for.

ⓒ List your work experience in reverse chronological order. Include volunteer work if you have little paid work experience. Focus on skills and accomplishments.

ⓓ List other skills you have that might be useful on the job, even if you have not been able to use them in previous jobs.

ⓔ Include a section that lists activities, honors, and community service.

4 Getting Out on Your Own

designated to receive applications. Open your letter with a strong statement of your interest in this particular job. In the body of the letter, use information from your resumé to explain why you are the best candidate. Close by restating your interest and indicate your intention to follow up to request an interview. Internet and library resources can give you samples of strong cover letters.

References Before you list someone as a reference, talk with him or her about your job hunt and ask their permission. The list of references should include the person's name, address (either business or home), telephone number, and an e-mail address, if they have one. It's also a good idea to indicate the person's position or relationship to you.

The people you choose as references should know you well enough to be able to describe your skills, experiences, and work habits. Choose people who will be enthusiastic about your abilities based on their experience with you. Typical references include former or current employers, teachers or coaches, or family friends who can vouch for your personal character. Stay in touch with your references during your job hunt. Let them know when they might expect to hear from an employer, and discuss what you would like them to emphasize when they are contacted.

Figure CPF 16 References

Cheryl A. Miller
1909 E. Walnut St.
Long Beach, CA 90811
310-555-5678
camiller89@isp.net

References

Barry Woods
Assistant Manager
Electronics Super Center
1234 Main St.
Long Beach, CA 90811
310-555-1357
bwoods@esc.com

Cynthia North
Director
Jefferson High Computer Lab
461 Grand Oak Boulevard
Long Beach, CA 90811
310-555-1234
c_north@jefferson.lb.ca.edu

Danielle Curran
Office Manager
Oceanside Computer Center
4916 Oceanside Road
Long Beach, CA 90812
310-555-2468
dmcurran@occ.com

Julie Barnes
Moderator
Jefferson High Debate Team
461 Grand Oak Boulevard
Long Beach, CA 90811
310-555-1345
j_barnes@jefferson.lb.ca.edu

How Can I Ace the Interview?

If an employer gets a good impression of you from your resumé and cover letter, they may invite you to come in for an interview. The interview is a chance for the employer to learn more about you and for you to learn more about the job and the company.

The Company and the Job Do some research on the company to which you are applying. A company's Web site will tell you more about the organization, but you might also find newspaper articles with information about the company. This research will help you to confirm that you are interested in working for the company. It will also show the company that you cared enough about the job to do some investigating before the interview.

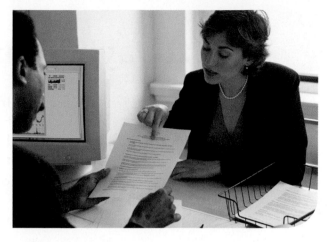

Use your research to prepare a set of questions about the organization and the job. Find out as much as you can about the job requirements and responsibilities before discussing such things as pay, hours, or benefits. In some cases, those topics may not come up until a later interview. Remember that both you and the employer want to confirm that you are a good fit for the job and the organization.

Presenting Yourself Be ready to answer questions about your qualifications and about how you will fit into the company. You may want to practice answering questions in front of a mirror or with a friend or family member. Make sure your answers are clear and succinct. Take time to think about your responses to unexpected questions. Books and online resources can provide examples of many common interview questions.

Dress appropriately for the job you are seeking. Don't show up to the interview in business attire if you are applying to work where you will get very dirty. By the same token, don't go to an interview for an office job dressed in jeans and a T-shirt. Always appear neat, clean, and well groomed.

Determine how long it will take to get to the interview. Plan to arrive about ten minutes early. Take weather conditions and traffic into consideration. If you are delayed, be sure to call and explain that you will be late.

Bring extra copies of your resume and list of references. You may want to bring a pad of paper to take notes during the interview. Be sure to get the name and title of each person who interviews you.

Check It Out!

☑ Learn about the company where you are applying.

☑ Prepare a list of questions about the job and the company.

☑ Bring extra copies of your resume and your list of references.

☑ Be on time for your interview.

Follow-Up Write a short thank-you note immediately after the interview to each interviewer. Thank the interviewer for spending time with you. If you still want the job, restate your interest in it. Refer to something you learned in the interview. Express your desire to learn more about the position.

APPLICATION Getting a Job

1. What is the purpose of a resume?

2. **Writing Your Resume** Study the resume in this section. Prepare a personal resume based on the model. Also assemble a list of people whom you might want to use as references.

4.2 Paying Taxes

Benjamin Franklin once said, "In this world nothing is certain but death and taxes." As you learned in Chapter 14, taxes provide the government with revenue to provide needed services. Recall that the Internal Revenue Service (IRS) is the government agency that collects the federal taxes owed by Americans. Most states also collect taxes. Taxes for the previous year must be paid by April 15 of the current year. For example, taxes for income earned in 2010 would need to be paid by April 15, 2011.

How Are My Taxes Determined?

The amount you pay in taxes is determined by your filing status and your taxable income. **Filing status** is based on your marital status or whether you have any dependents. A dependent is a child or relative in your household whom you support. People with more dependents have less tax withheld. Employers use the W-4 form, shown in Figure CPF 17, to determine your filing status for withholding taxes from your paycheck. You fill out a W-4 form when you begin a job. As long as you are still dependent on your parents, you claim only one withholding allowance.

The second determinant is your **taxable income**, which is the amount of income subject to taxation after all exemptions and deductions. The higher your income, the higher your taxes will be. Certain income may not be taxed. For example, money can be deducted from your paycheck before taxes to pay for health insurance. Income above a certain level is not subject to Federal Insurance Contributions Act (FICA) taxes for Social Security.

Figure CPF 17 The W-4 Form

(a) Instructions help you determine how many allowances to claim. A single person with one job who is claimed as a dependent gets one allowance.

(b) Your Social Security number is required on all IRS forms.

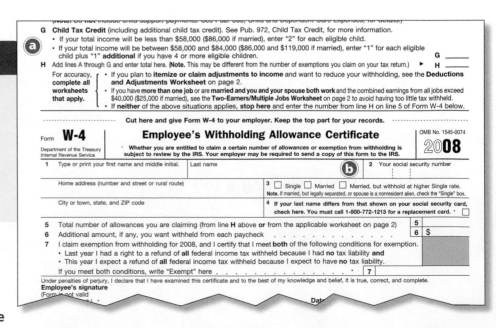

Where Do I Get Tax Forms?

Federal and state tax forms are available starting in January each year at post offices (federal forms only), libraries, banks, and IRS or state tax offices. They are also available through official Web sites, or you can order forms through the mail or by phone. The first year you file taxes, you will need to find the forms yourself. After that, you should receive forms in the mail from the state and federal governments at the end of each year. If your tax situation changes significantly from the previous year, you may need to pick up additional forms.

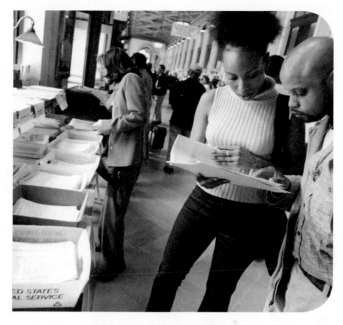

Form 1040 Most young adults do not have to file complicated tax forms. Generally, the 1040EZ form should be sufficient for your federal taxes. This is a one-page form that has only 12 lines to fill out. The back of the form explains who is eligible to use it. See Figure CPF 18 for a sample of a 1040EZ form.

If you receive more than $1,500 in interest, you cannot use the 1040EZ form. Likewise, if you receive any dividends or other income from stocks, bonds, or similar investments, you cannot use 1040EZ. Instead, you will need to use form 1040A or 1040. These forms have related forms, known as schedules, for reporting investment income.

Most state tax forms are simple because they are based on the results you obtain from filling out your federal forms.

The W-2 Form The W-2 form shows how much you earned during the year and how much you paid in taxes through withholding. The form shows your total gross earnings and the amount of earnings subject to taxation. The amount withheld for each type of tax is also shown, including federal income tax, Social Security and Medicare taxes, and state and local taxes.

At the end of each year, any employer that you have worked for that year must send you a W-2 form. Employers must send the forms in time to arrive at your home by January 31. The W-2 will include copies to file with your federal, state, and local tax returns, as well as one copy for your files.

Other Forms When you have savings or investments, your bank or financial institution will send you other forms. Form 1099-INT for savings interest and form 1099-DIV for investment gains should arrive about the same time as your W-2.

How Do I Fill Out a Tax Form?

Instruction booklets are available in most locations where you find tax forms. You may also download them for free from the IRS or state tax Web sites or request them by mail or phone. The instructions will take you through the steps to fill out the form line by line. They will also provide additional background information that may be helpful, as well as telling you where to go if you need help. Perhaps most important, the instructions contain the tax tables that will tell you how much tax you have to pay once you have determined your taxable income.

Follow the step-by-step instructions to complete each form. Always use correct and verifiable numbers. Making up numbers is considered tax fraud, which can be punishable with severe penalties. Figure CPF 18 shows a sample of a 1040EZ form.

Figure CPF 18 Filling Out the 1040EZ

(a) Use your W-2 form(s) to find the amount to enter here.

(b) The 1099-INT form shows how much interest you earned.

(c) The amount you enter here depends on your filing status. If you are a dependent, you get the standard deduction but not the personal exemption.

(d) The amount of tax withheld is found on your W-2 form along with earnings.

(e) If you had more withheld than you owe in taxes, you will get money back in the form of a refund. If you didn't have enough withheld, you will have to pay the amount you still owe to the U.S. Treasury.

How Do I File My Taxes?

Everyone who receives more than a certain amount of income during the year must file a tax return. Check the tax form instructions or the IRS Web site to determine if you are required to file. Even if you don't owe money, you must file a form if you meet the requirements. And, of course, you will not receive a refund for excess taxes withheld unless you file a tax return. See the "What if I get stuck?" sidebar to find out how to receive help with your taxes.

Before you send in your forms, double check your work. Confirm that you have entered the correct Social Security number; that your income, withholding, and tax figures are correct; and that you have signed your forms. Then make a photocopy of the forms for your own records.

When everything is ready, you can mail all the paperwork to the IRS service center listed on your form. You can also file your tax forms electronically. Electronically filed returns are generally more accurate, and refunds are processed more quickly. The IRS has formed a partnership with several tax software companies to offer the Free File service that allows most taxpayers to prepare and file their taxes electronically for free. You can find more information and instructions on e-filing options on the IRS Web site.

After you file your return, be sure to keep all your forms and copies in a safe place. Keep your tax returns and all related documents for at least three years—the limit if the IRS wants to contest your return.

Mistakes The IRS and state tax auditors usually catch simple math mistakes and inform you of them. They then recalculate your taxes and adjust the amount of your refund or taxes owed. If you discover a major error or omission on your form after you submit it, file an amended return as soon as possible. You must file an amended return within three years of the time when the original return was filed. You may have to pay a penalty depending on the type of error involved.

WHAT IF I GET STUCK?

- Ask a parent or other trusted adult. Most have many years of experience filling out tax forms.

- For federal tax help, go to the IRS Web site. For state tax help use the name of your state and the key words *tax help* to find the Web site.

- For additional help, call the local IRS office (1-800-829-1040) or your state tax office.

CONSUMER & PERSONAL FINANCE

Check It Out!

✔ The filing deadline is April 15, every year.

✔ Check everything on your form carefully before submitting it.

✔ Save your forms and copies for at least three years.

APPLICATION Paying Taxes

1. Where can you go to get tax forms?

2. Preparing to Do Your Taxes Make a list of the documents and information you will need to file federal and state income tax forms. Decide on a location where you will keep the list and the information until it is time to file your taxes.

4.3 Finding an Apartment

Most young adults will rent an apartment when they start out on their own because apartments are an affordable type of housing. Moving out of your parents' home or out of a college dormitory into an apartment will give you more freedom. But it also means more responsibilities. You will have to pay monthly bills, shop for groceries, fix meals, clean your apartment, and do laundry. With a little effort, you can find an apartment that suits you.

What Should I Consider About Renting an Apartment?

How much should I spend? Your housing expenses should amount to no more than about one-fourth to one-third of your take-home pay. These expenses include not only your rent, but also utilities, cable, and any other housing costs. Spending a higher proportion of your income on housing may not leave you enough to meet your other expenses or to have the money you want to enjoy life.

Should I live by myself or with roommates? If one-third of your take-home pay only pays rent for a storage locker, you may want to consider sharing a larger apartment with one or more roommates. Roommates can make living in an apartment cheaper and more fun, but they can become a problem if they are irresponsible or have a lifestyle that clashes with your own. Think about how to balance the desire for privacy and your own space with the desire for companionship and help with household expenses and chores. If you decide to live with roommates, consider looking for an apartment together. That way, everyone can commit to the same place, and people will be less likely to grow dissatisfied and leave.

How do I choose roommates? Look for individuals you are compatible with, whose personalities and lifestyles are similar to your own. Roommates should be people you can count on, whether it's to pay their share of the rent or to do their share of household chores. Living with other people can bring up conflicts about how to share expenses, use the living space, and keep it clean. You and your roommates will need to communicate to resolve such issues. Consider drawing up an agreement together that spells out the rules that everyone must obey and the responsibilities that each roommate accepts.

Figure CPF 19 Looking for an Apartment

Location
- Is it convenient to where you work?
- Is there nearby public transportation or parking?
- Are there grocery stores, self-service laundries, or other stores you need nearby?
- Is the neighborhood safe?

The Building
- Is it clean and well taken care of?
- Do the other tenants seem friendly?
- Are the lobby and stairwells safe?
- Are there sufficient parking spaces, laundry facilities, or bike rooms?

Space
- Is there enough room for the number of people living in the apartment?
- Is it suitable for your way of life?
- Are all the roommates happy with the living space and available storage?

Furnished or Unfurnished
- Do you want it furnished with furniture or do you want to use your own furniture?
- Can you get used furniture from family or friends or purchase inexpensive furniture?
- Does the apartment include appliances, such as a stove and refrigerator?

What Do I Need to Know About Signing a Lease?

- A **lease** is a contract for renting an apartment for a specific period of time. The contract is between you and your **landlord**, who is the owner of the rental property. A lease is a legal document that obligates you to pay rent and to follow certain rules for a specific period of time. The landlord has responsibilities as well. If you have roommates, whoever signs the lease is responsible even if other roommates fail to pay their part of the rent.

- You may be asked for the first and last months' rent, a security deposit, and possibly cleaning and key fees. When you move out, the landlord will inspect the property and return some or all of the security deposit and fees, depending on what repairs need to be done.

- You may need to provide character references—name, address, and phone number. Generally you should use three people who are not relatives, such as teachers, employers, or supervisors of volunteer work, who can vouch for you.

- You must provide your Social Security number and bank information. If you are employed you will provide employment information.

- If this is your first apartment or you are not employed, you may be asked to have a responsible adult act as a cosigner. This ensures that the landlord will be paid the rent due if you fail to pay.

QUICK REFERENCE

A **lease** is a contract for renting an apartment.

A **landlord** is the owner of rental property.

Check It Out!

✔ Provide a list of references.

✔ Be prepared for up-front costs such as a security deposit.

✔ Look at several places before committing to an apartment.

Interactive Review

Review Getting Out on Your Own using interactive activities at ClassZone.com

APPLICATION Finding an Apartment

1. What is a lease?
2. **Analyzing Your Needs** Decide if you would prefer to live alone or with others. If you prefer to live alone, write a paragraph explaining your decision. If you would like to live with others, create a list of roommate rules and responsibilities.

Holt McDougal

ECONOMICS
Concepts and Choices

Math Handbook

Table of Contents

Refer to the Math Handbook when you need help with the mathematical concepts that you might encounter in your study of economics.

1.1 Working with Decimals and Percents

Understanding the Skill

A decimal is a number that uses the base-ten value system where a decimal point separates the ones' and tenths' digits. Each place value is ten times the place value to its right. For example, 5.2 is five and two tenths and 12.45 is twelve and forty-five hundredths.

The word *percent* means "per hundred." For example, 5 percent means "5 per 100," or 5/100. If 5 percent of the population is unemployed, then, on average, 5 out of 100 people are unemployed.

To write a decimal as a percent, multiply by 100 percent. To write a percent as a decimal, divide by 100 percent.

Example 1: A company's February sales were 0.125 of its total annual sales. Express this as a percentage.

$0.125 \quad = 0.125 \times 100\%$ *Multiply by 100 percent.*

$\quad = 12.5\%$ *Move the decimal point two places to the right.*

Check your answer: 12.5 should be larger than 0.125 because you multiplied by 100.

Example 2: A company's workforce was 105 percent of what it was a year earlier. Express this as a decimal.

$105\% = \dfrac{105\%}{100\%}$ *Divide by 100 percent.*

$\quad = \dfrac{105}{100}$ *Cancel the % signs.*

$\quad = 1.05$ *To divide by 100, move the decimal point 2 places to the left.*

Check your answer: 1.05 should be smaller than 105 because you divided by 100.

Applying the Skill

1. In 2002, the total personal income in the United States was $8.922 trillion and the total personal taxes were $1.112 trillion. What percent of income were taxes? Round your answer to the nearest hundredth.

2. The GDP of the United States is $11.750 trillion and the GDP of the world is $55.500 trillion. What percent of the world's GDP is from the United States? Round your answer to the nearest tenth.

1.2 Calculating Averages

Understanding the Skill

There are three ways to express the average of a group of numbers. The most common way is to divide the total by the number of values. This kind of average is called the *mean*.

Mean, Median, and Mode Notice that, in Example 1, most workers earn much less than the mean of $27,000; the mean doesn't describe typical earnings well. Typical earnings are often described better by the two other kinds of average: the mode and the median. To determine the mode and the median of a group of numbers, write the numbers in order from smallest to largest. The *mode* is the most common value. The *median* is the middle value. If the number of values is even, the median is the mean of the two middle values.

Example 1: The annual earnings of five workers are shown below. Calculate the mean earnings.

    $14,000 $18,000 $14,000 $75,000 $14,000

Solution

Divide the total by the number of values. There are five numbers to average, so the number of values is 5.

$$\text{Mean} = \frac{\text{Total}}{\text{Number of values}}$$

$$= \frac{135,000}{5} \qquad \textit{Simplify the numerator.}$$

$$= \$27,000 \qquad \textit{Divide.}$$

The workers have mean   *Answer the question.*
earnings of $27,000

Example 2: Find the mode and the median of the earnings in Example 1.

Solution

Write the values in order from smallest to largest.

    $14,000   **$14,000**   **$14,000** $18,000 $75,000

The most common value is $14,000, so the mode is $14,000.

    $14,000 $14,000   **$14,000** $18,000 $75,000

The middle value is also $14,000, so the **median** is $14,000.

Applying the Skill

Calculate the mean, the median, and the mode of each group of numbers.

1. $40,000 $32,000 $38,000 $40,000 $40,000

2. $80,000 $50,000 $35,000 $35,000 $40,000 $60,000

1.3 Calculating and Using Percents

Understanding the Skill

As you recall, the term *percent* means "per hundred." For example, 25% is 25/100. To change a decimal to a percent, move the decimal point two places to the right and add the % symbol.

$$0.253 = 25.3\% \qquad 1.63 = 163\%$$

To calculate and use percents, first write a question. Then rewrite your question as an equation. Replace "percent" with /100, "of" with ×, and "is" with =. Replace the unknown value with a variable, like x.

Example 1: Sweden's gross domestic product (GDP) is $255,400,000,000. Agriculture accounts for about $5,108,000,000 of the GDP. What percent of the GDP is from agriculture?

Solution

What **percent of** the GDP **is** from agriculture?	*Write a question.*
What percent of $255,400,000,000 **is** $5,108,000,000?	*Substitute numbers.*
x**/100** × $255,400,000,000 = $5,108,000,000	*Rewrite as an equation.*
$x = \dfrac{\$5,108,000,000}{\$255,400,000,000} \times 100$	*Solve the equation.*
$x = 2$	*Use a calculator.*
Two percent of Sweden's GDP is from agriculture.	*Answer the question.*

Example 2: Sweden's unemployment rate is 5.6% and its labor force is 4.46 million. About how many people are unemployed?

Solution

5.6 **percent of** the labor force **is** how many people?	*Write a question.*
5.6 **percent of** 4.46 million **is how many**?	*Substitute numbers.*
5.6**/100** × 4,460,000 = x	*Rewrite as an equation.*
249,760 = x	*Use a calculator.*
About 250,000 people are unemployed.	*Round your answer.*

Applying the Skill

1. What is 10% of $65?

2. What is 150% of 256,000?

3. $3.75 is 15% of how much?

1.4 Using Ratios

Understanding the Skill

A ratio compares two numbers that have the same units of measure. For example, if Tina runs 8 miles per hour and Maria runs 7 miles per hour, the ratio of their speeds is 8 to 7, or 8:7. A ratio can also be written as a fraction: $\frac{8}{7}$.

You can simplify ratios in the same way that you simplify fractions.

Example 1: Raul runs 8 miles per hour and his little brother Ben runs 4 miles per hour. What is the ratio of Raul's speed to Ben's speed?

Solution

$$\frac{\text{Raul's speed}}{\text{Ben's speed}} = \frac{8}{4} \qquad \textit{Write a fraction.}$$

$$= \frac{8 \div 4}{4 \div 4} \qquad \textit{To simplify the fraction, divide both the top and the bottom by 4.}$$

$$= \frac{2}{1} \qquad \frac{2}{1} \textit{ means the same as 2:1 and "2 to 1."}$$

The ratio of Raul's speed to Ben's speed is 2 to 1.

Ratios are sometimes written as decimals. For example, a company's price-earnings ratio is the ratio of the price of a share of the company's stock to the earnings per share.

Example 2 Suppose a share of a company's stock costs $54.75 and the earnings per share are $2.73. What is the company's price-earnings ratio?

Solution

$$\text{Price-earnings ratio} = \frac{\text{Price of a share of stock}}{\text{Earnings per share}} \qquad \textit{Write a fraction.}$$

$$= \frac{\$55.75}{\$2.73} \qquad \textit{Substitute numbers.}$$

$$= 20.421245 \qquad \textit{Use a calculator.}$$

$$\approx 20.4 \qquad \textit{Round your answer.}$$

The company's price-earnings ratio is about 20.4.   *Answer the question.*

Applying the Skill

1. The GDP of the world is about $55 trillion and the GDP of the United States is about $11 trillion. What is the ratio of the GDP of the world to the GDP of the United States?

2. Suppose a share of a company's stock costs $26.24 and the earnings per share are $3.19. What is the company's price-earnings ratio?

1.5 Calculating Compound Interest

Understanding the Skill

For some savings instruments, interest is calculated and paid multiple times each year. To calculate the amount of each interest payment, you can use the following formula.

$$\text{Interest} = \frac{\text{Balance} \times \text{Interest rate}}{\text{Number of times calculated each year}}$$

If interest on your savings is *compounded,* that means the interest you earn is added to your total savings, and is included in future calculations of interest.

Notice that the interest for the second half of the year is greater than the interest for the first half of the year. In the second half of the year, you earn interest not only on your original balance, but also on the interest you earned in the first half of the year.

Compound interest on loans works the same as compound interest on savings. But for loans, if interest is compounded, you must *pay* interest on interest you haven't yet paid.

> **Example:** If interest on $1,000 is compounded biannually with an interest rate of 5 percent, how much interest do you earn for each compounding period in the first year?
>
> **Solution**
>
> If interest is compounded *biannually,* that means it is calculated **two** times a year and each compounding period is a half of a year. Calculate the interest for each half.
>
> **First half of year** $\text{Interest} = \dfrac{\text{Balance} \times \text{Interest rate}}{\text{Number of times calculated each year}}$
>
> $= \dfrac{\$1,000 \times 5\%}{2}$ *Substitute numbers.*
>
> $= \dfrac{\$1,000 \times 0.05}{2}$ *Convert the percent to a decimal.*
>
> $= \mathbf{\$25.00}$ *Use a calculator.*
>
> **Second half of year**
>
> First, calculate the new balance by adding the interest to the old balance.
>
> New balance = Old balance + Interest on old balance
>
> $= \$1,000 + \mathbf{\$25.00}$
>
> $= \mathbf{\$1,025.00}$
>
> $\text{Interest} = \dfrac{\text{New balance} \times \text{Interest rate}}{\text{Number of times calculated each year}} = \dfrac{\$1,025.00 + 5\%}{2} \approx \$25.63$
>
> The interest for the first half of the year is $25.00 and for the second half is $25.63.

Applying the Skill

1. If interest on $2,000 is compounded biannually with a rate of 6 percent, what is the interest for each compounding period in the first year? What is the total interest for one year?

2. If interest on $2,000 is compounded four times a year with a rate of 6 percent, what is the interest for each compounding period in the first year? What is the total interest?

3. Look at your answers to Questions 1 and 2. Do you earn more if the interest is compounded twice a year or if it is compounded four times a year?

1.6 Understanding Progressive Taxes

Understanding the Skill

The federal income tax is progressive: a person with a low income is taxed at a lower rate than a person with a higher income. The table at the bottom of the page shows the 2006 income tax brackets for a single person. If you file as single and your taxable income is **$7,125,** you are in the **10 percent** tax bracket because $7,125 is between **$0** and **$7,550.** If your taxable income is **$7,750,** then you are in the 15 percent tax bracket, but your tax is not 15 percent of $7,750. Instead, you pay 10 percent on the first $7,550 of your income. You pay 15 percent on the rest.

Example 1: Calculate tax in the 10 percent tax bracket on $7,125.

Tax = Tax rate x Income in bracket

   = **10%** × **$7,125**   *Substitute numbers.*

   = 0.10 × $7,125   *Write 10 percent as a decimal.*

   = $712.50   *Multiply.*

The tax on $7,125 is $713.   *Answer the question. Round to the nearest dollar.*

Example 2: Calculate tax in the 15 percent tax bracket on $7,550.

Pay **10 percent** on the first **$7,550.**

   Tax = Tax rate x Income in bracket = **10%** × **$7,550** = **$755.00**

Pay 15 percent on the rest of the income.

   Income in 15% bracket = Total income – **Income in 10% bracket**

   = **$7,750** – **$7,550**

   = **$200**

   Tax = Tax rate x Income in bracket = **15%** × **$200** = **$30.00**

Add the tax from the two brackets together to find the total tax.

   $755.00 + **$30.00** = **$785.00**

Applying the Skill

Using the tax bracket table on the right, calculate the taxes on the following taxable incomes:

A. $7,175   **B.** $17,225
C. $74,100   **D.** $98,975

2006 Federal Income Tax Brackets (Single)	
Income Bracket	Tax Rate
$0–$7,550	10%
$7,550–$30,650	15%
$30,650–$74,200	25%
$74,200–$154,800	28%

1.7 Creating Line Graphs

Understanding the Skill

A line graph is useful for showing how a value changes over time. You can use a spreadsheet or graphing software to make a line graph. In the example, type the years and inflation rates into the software. The software will do most of the above steps for you. See the software's tutorials or help feature for guidance.

United States Inflation Rate (in percent)									
1970	1971	1972	1973	1974	1975	1976	1977	1978	1979
5.7	4.4	3.2	6.2	11.0	9.1	5.8	6.5	7.6	11.3

Source: U.S. Bureau of Labor Statistics

❶ Write the title of the graph and make a grid under it.

❷ Write numbers along the left side, or verticle axis, of the grid with 0 at the bottom. The top number should be larger than the largest rate in the table. Label the axis.

❸ Write years from the table evenly along the bottom line, or horizontal axis, of the grid. Label the axis.

❹ Graph each point where the horizontal line from the **inflation rate** meets the vertical line from the **year.**

❺ Draw a straight line to connect each point to the point for the next year.

Example: Make a line graph showing the rate of inflation from 1970 to 1979. Find the largest rate in the table. It is **11.3.**

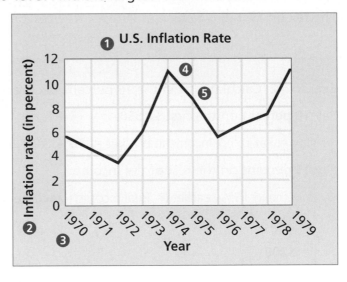

Applying the Skill

Make a line graph to show the unemployment rate from 1993 to 2002.

Unemployment Rate (in percent)									
1993	1994	1995	1996	1997	1998	1999	2000	2001	2002
6.9	6.1	5.6	5.4	4.9	4.5	4.2	4.0	4.7	5.8

Source: U.S. Bureau of Labor Statistics

1.8 Creating Bar Graphs

Understanding the Skill

A bar graph is useful for comparing different values. You can use a spreadsheet or graphing software to make a bar graph. In the example, type the oil consumption information into the software. The software will do most of the above steps for you. See the software's tutorials or help feature for guidance.

Leading Oil Consumers (in millions of barrels per day)							
United States	European Union	China	Japan	India	Brazil	Russia	Canada
20.0	14.6	6.4	5.6	2.3	2.1	2.8	2.2

Source: CIA World Factbook, 2005 data

❶ Write the title of the graph. Draw a box under it.

❷ Write numbers evenly along the vertical axis. The largest number should be larger than 20.0 and the smallest number should be 0. Label the axis.

❸ Write the names evenly along the horizontal axis. Label the axis.

❹ Draw each bar. Find the **oil consumption** on the vertical axis. Imagine a horizontal line from the oil consumption to directly above the **name.** Draw the bar as shown. Each bar should be the same width.

Example: Make a bar graph of the oil consumption of the three greatest oil consumers: the United States, the European Union, and China

Solution

Begin by finding the highest level of oil consumption—the United States with 20 million barrels a day. Then complete the following steps.

Applying the Skill

Use the information in the table at the top of the page to make a bar graph of the oil consumption of the three leading oil consumers in Asia: China, Japan, and India.

1.9 Creating Pie Graphs

Understanding the Skill

A pie graph is useful for showing the relationship of parts to the whole. The table at the right and the pie graph below show the GDP for various countries and the European Union. The graph makes it easy to see how each GDP contributes to the world's total GDP. The example shows how to make the pie graph.

GDP (trillions of U. S. dollars) and Population (millions of people) of Various Countries and the European Union					
Country	GDP	Population	Country	GDP	Population
United States	11.8	296	Russia	1.4	143
European Union	11.7	457	Canada	1.0	33
China	7.3	1,306	Mexico	1.0	106
Japan	3.7	127	South Korea	0.9	49
India	3.3	1,080	Indonesia	0.8	242
Brazil	1.5	186	Other	11.1	2,421

Source: CIA World Factbook, 2005 data

Example

❶ Write a title for the pie graph.

❷ Draw a circle. This represents the total GDP of all countries, or $55.5 trillion.

❸ Draw a wedge to represent each country or group of countries. Calculate the angle for each wedge using this formula:

$$\text{Angle} = \frac{\text{Country's GDP}}{\text{World GDP}} \times 360°$$

❹ Label each wedge with the country name and the amount of GDP. Wedges too small to draw easily can be grouped together and labeled "Other."

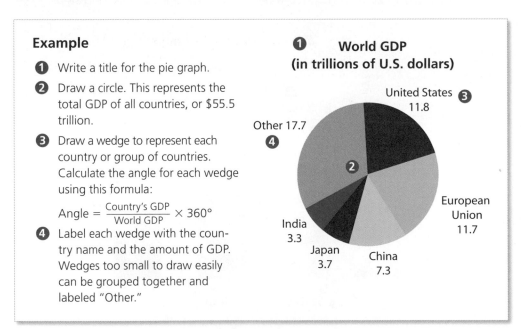

❶ World GDP (in trillions of U.S. dollars)

United States ❸ 11.8

Other 17.7 ❹

❷

European Union 11.7

India 3.3

Japan 3.7

China 7.3

Applying the Skill

Use the information in the table at the top of the page to make a pie graph of the populations of the world. Include wedges for the five largest countries, and one for all others.

1.10 Creating a Database

Understanding the Skill

A database is a large collection of information that can be organized and searched. You can use a spreadsheet to make a database. First enter information into the spreadsheet. Label each row and column, including units of measure. You can use the spreadsheet software to manipulate the information and answer questions.

Example Which country has the largest per capita oil consumption?

	A	B	C	D	E	F	G
1		United States	European Union	Japan	Russia	Canada	Mexico
2	Oil Consumption (**millions** of barrels per day)	20.0	14.6	5.6	2.8	2.2	1.8
3	Population (**millions** of people)	296	457	127	143	33	106

Solution

Per capita oil consumption is **oil consumption** divided by **population.** For the U.S. it is

$$\frac{20.0 \text{ million barrels per day}}{296 \text{ million people}} = \frac{20.0 \text{ barrels per day}}{296 \text{ people}} \approx 0.07 \text{ barrels per person per day.}$$

❶ Divide row 2 by row 3. Put the answer in row 4.

❷ Sort the whole database by row 4, from largest to smallest.

	A	B	C	D	E	F	G
1		United States	Canada	Japan	European Union	Russia	Mexico
2	Oil Consumption (**millions** of barrels per day)	20.0	2.2	5.6	14.6	2.8	1.8
3	Population (**millions** of people)	296	33	127	457	143	106
4	Per capita oil consumption (barrels/person/day)	0.07	0.07	0.04	0.03	0.02	0.02

Once the database is sorted, the United States and Canada are the first in the new order. So the United States and Canada are the countries in the database that have the greatest per capita oil consumption, with consumptions of 0.07 barrels per person per day.

Applying the Skill

Make a database of the information in the table on page R10, by entering the information into spreadsheet software. Multiply each GDP by 1 trillion so the units are "dollars" instead of "trillions of dollars." Multiply each population by 1 million so the units are "people" instead of "millions of people".

Contents

Refer to the Economics Skillbuilder Handbook when you need help in answering Application questions or questions in Section Assessments and Chapter Assessments. In addition, the handbook will help you answer questions about charts, graphs, databases, and economic models.

Skills for Understanding Economics

Using Print, Visual, and Technology Sources

1.1 Explaining an Economic Concept

EXPLAINING ECONOMIC CONCEPTS involves clarifying and communicating the basic ideas of economics. Some of these concepts are simple, while others are complex. Three basic steps will help you develop an explanation of a concept, regardless of its complexity.

Understanding the Skill

STRATEGY: Use the steps in the concept-explanation process. The following passage provides information on economic recessions. The table below that provides an analysis of the concept of economic recession based on the concept-explanation process.

1 **Identify and define the economic concept.**
2 **Describe the impact of the concept on the economy.**
3 **Give an example of the concept.** Providing an illustrative example will help underscore your explanation of the concept.

1 An economic recession may be defined as a downturn in the business cycle. During a recession, both production and employment decline. **2** As a result, the economy experiences little, if any, growth. **3** In 1990 and 1991, the United States experienced the greatest recession since the Great Depression. According to some economic analysts, the 1990–1991 recession caused the loss of 1.9 million jobs in 1992.

Make a Table

Use a table like the one shown here to help you explain an economic concept with the three-step process.

Explaining an Economic Concept	
Concept	Economic recession
Definition	A downturn in the business cycle, characterized by a decline in production and employment
Impact	Slows economic growth
Example	U.S. recession of 1990-1991

Applying the Skill

Turn to Chapter 7, Section 4, and read about deregulation on page 218. Use a table to explain the economic concept of deregulation with the three-step process.

1.2 Analyzing and Interpreting Data

DATA, or factual information, is the most basic tool of the economist. Economic data is most often in the form of statistics. Economists **ANALYZE** data to learn about economic conditions and trends. They **INTERPRET** data to draw conclusions or make predictions based on their analysis.

Understanding the Skill

STRATEGY: Analyze and interpret the data. Data usually is presented in visual form as a graph or a table like the one below.

① Read the title. The title provides a good indication of the kind of data shown. Here, the data concerns average food expenditures for several large cities in the Midwest of the United States.

② Determine how the data is organized. Here, data in each horizontal row provides information on a category of food expenditure. Each vertical column shows expenditures by food category for one of five metropolitan areas.

③ Ask what kinds of questions may be answered from the data. Answering such questions helps in the analysis and interpretation of the data.

① Average Annual Household Food Expenditures in Selected Midwestern Metropolitan Areas, 2003–2004 (in dollars)

	Chicago	Detroit	Milwaukee	Minneapolis-St. Paul	Cleveland
Cereals and Bakery	472	470	460	509	388
Meats, Fish, and Eggs	855	863	837	779	854
Dairy	366	339	309	431	310
Fruits and Vegetables	606	542	506	610	449
Other Foods at Home	1,128	1,073	950	1,236	822
Food Away from Home	2,597	2,439	2,126	2,983	1,765

Source: Consumer Expenditure Survey, 2003–2004, U.S. Bureau of Labor Statistics

Write a Summary

Summarize your analysis and interpretation of the data in the table

> Data in the above table reflects average annual household food expenditures for one year (2003-2004) for 5 Midwestern metropolitan areas. Food expenditures are shown according to type of food purchased: a food at home versus food away from home. The data may be analyzed and interpreted in a number of ways, including the following: comparing expenditures in different cities for foods in a single category or comparing expenditures for two or more food categories within a city; computation of percentages of total expenditure spent on specific food categories.

Applying the Skill

Turn to Chapter 14, Section 2, page 421, and study the table showing data on itemized tax deductions. Write a summary of your analysis and interpretation of data in the table.

1.3 Applying Economic Concepts

When attempting to understand complex economic behavior, economists make constant use of fundamental economic concepts, such as supply, demand, and price. By **APPLYING ECONOMIC CONCEPTS** to everyday situations, economists develop a better understanding of how the economy works.

Understanding the Skill

STRATEGY: Examine the information carefully. The news story below describes a fall in the price of crude oil. The supply and demand curves beneath it graphically illustrate this shift.

1 **Look for economic concepts as you read.** Such words as *prices, supplies, inventories,* and *capacity* indicate that the topic of this story is the relationship between supply and price.

2 **Look for relationships among concepts.** The story states that OPEC, the oil-producing cartel, has decided not to curtail production. It also notes that BP could restore lost oil production. So, even if demand remains constant, an increase in supply will cause the equilibrium price to fall.

3 **Express the relationship in graphic form.** Supply and demand curves provide a vivid picture of the impact of increased supply on price.

Crude Oil Prices Sink Below $66 a Barrel

1 Oil prices fell below $66 a barrel Monday as concerns over **1** supplies eased in expectation that **2** OPEC ministers would not change their production targets. . . .

1 Supplies remain ample. . . . OPEC maintains about 2 million barrels a day of spare **1** capacity, and stocks are high elsewhere; the U.S. Department of Energy said last week that **1** inventories have hit their highest levels since 1998. . . .

2 The possibility that [British Petroleum] could restore 180,000 barrels per day of lost Alaskan production at Prudhoe Bay by the end of October also calmed the market.

Source: Associated Press, September 11, 2006

Draw Demand and Supply Curves

Draw demand and supply curves to illustrate the situation described in the news story. Assume that demand stays constant. The increased supply shifts the supply curve to the right (from S1 to S2), causing prices to fall (from P1 to P2).

Applying the Skill

In the business section of a newspaper, find a story about a change in price. Analyze the information in the story to determine why the price changed. Then draw supply and demand curves that illustrate the shifts that caused such a change.

1.4 Creating and Interpreting Economic Models

CREATING an economic model involves using information and ideas to show an economic concept or situation in a visual way. An **ECONOMIC MODEL** might be a graph, a diagram, a three-dimensional representation, or a computer program. **INTERPRETING AN ECONOMIC MODEL** involves carefully studying the model in order to draw conclusions or make predictions based on the information it provides.

Understanding the Skill

STRATEGY: Create an economic model. The model below is a circular flow diagram. Economists use the circular flow model to help understand and describe how a market-based economy operates. Use the following steps to create an economic model.

1 **Gather the information you need to create an economic model.** In this case, you need to show the rules that govern the relationships between economic actors and economic markets in a market economy.

2 **Visualize and sketch an idea of your model.** The creator of this economic model used a circular diagram to convey the relationships between economic markets and economic actors.

3 **Think of symbols you may want to use.** Here, different colored arrows indicate the flow of money and the flow of resources and products.

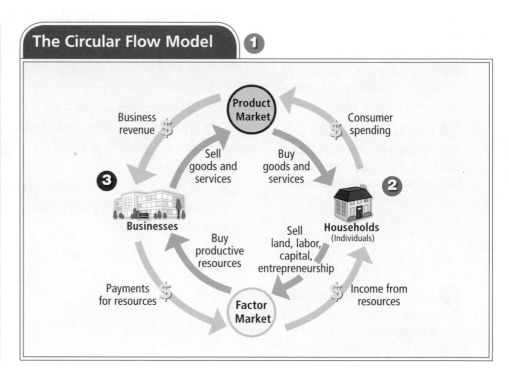

Interpret the Model

Write a summary of your interpretation of the information in the model.

> This model illustrates the interactions between businesses and individuals in the economy. The two main economic decision makers, businesses and households, are shown on the left and right of the model. The two main economic markets, product and factor, are shown at the top and bottom. The green arrows represent the flow of money between actors and through the markets. The blue arrows represent the flow of resources and products through the economy.

Applying the Skill

Turn to Chapter 7, Section 1, and read the information on perfect competition on pages 192–194. Create an economic model that shows the relationship between two actors—buyers and sellers—in a perfectly competitive market.

1.5 Using a Decision-Making Process

USING A DECISION-MAKING PROCESS involves choosing between two or more options or courses of action. Organized decision-making involves four steps: 1) identify the problem or situation that requires a decision; 2) identify options; 3) predict possible consequences of the decision; 4) put the decision into effect.

Understanding the Skill

STRATEGY: Use the steps in the decision-making process. The following passage describes how a Polish food producer used a decision-making process to introduce a new product into Poland's convenience food market. The flow chart organizes the elements of the process that was used.

1 Identify the decision that needs to be made. In this passage, the title offers a clue to the problem, which is stated more fully in the text.

2 Identify options. The company might have chosen to stay out of the convenience food market because most Poles did not own microwave ovens.

3 Identify possible consequences of the decision. Remember that there can be more than one possibility. Also look for factors that could affect the consequences.

4 Note what decision was made and the impact it had.

1 Polish Meals in the Microwave?

At the beginning of the current millennium, Pudliszki, a Polish firm owned by Heinz, was faced with a decision. **1** Should the company introduce full-course microwaveable meals into Poland's market for convenience foods? Poland's accession into the European Union promised to have a positive effect on both employment and disposable income. And with Polish workers averaging 40 hours on the job, projected demand for convenience foods appeared promising—a strong indication for the product's success. **2** However, households owning microwaves were very much in the minority, which could result in the product's failure. **3** Perhaps banking on an increase in household microwaves, Pudliszki introduced Meals from the Four Corners of the World. According to Euromonitor, an international market research firm, **4** Pudliszki's four full-course meals were "reasonably priced and accepted rather well by the market."

Source: Adapted from "Poland's EU Membership Presents Packaging Opportunities" by Chris Mercer. *Food Industry News*, February 2, 2005.

Make a Flow Chart

In a flow chart, state the decision to be made, its possible consequences, the actual decision, and the actual consequences of the decision.

Applying the Skill

Read the Chapter 1 Case Study, "The Real Cost of Expanding O'Hare Airport," on pages 32–33. From this information, identify the four steps of the decision-making process. Present your findings in a flow chart like the one shown at the right.

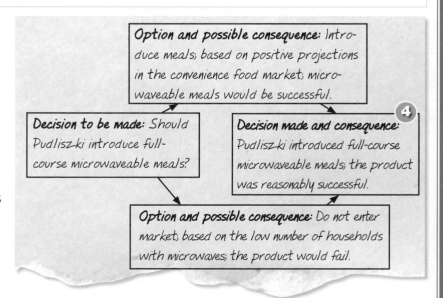

Option and possible consequence: Introduce meals; based on positive projections in the convenience food market; microwaveable meals would be successful.

Decision to be made: Should Pudliszki introduce full-course microwaveable meals?

Decision made and consequence: Pudliszki introduced full-course microwaveable meals; the product was reasonably successful. 4

Option and possible consequence: Do not enter market; based on the low number of households with microwaves; the product would fail.

1.6 Conducting Cost-Benefit Analyses

A **COST- BENEFIT ANALYSIS** involves determining the economic costs and benefits of an action and then balancing the costs against the benefits.

Understanding the Skill

STRATEGY: Look for the trade-offs that are a part of every economic decision.
The passage below describes the costs and benefits of a government-subsidized business development in Hong Kong. The decision-making grid beneath it summarizes the trade-offs in the project.

1 Identify the decision that is being made. The article notes that the Hong Kong government signed an agreement with a large private company to construct a new business.

2 Note the potential benefits of the decision. Here, government officials provide estimates of the economic benefits—jobs and money pumped into the economy.

3 Note the potential costs of the decision. The article focuses on the huge cost of the project to the government.

4 Determine if the decision is beneficial.

1 Hoping to jump-start their economy, government officials in Hong Kong inked an agreement with Walt Disney to build the U.S. company's third overseas theme park. . . . Government officials estimate that **2** construction of Hong Kong Disneyland will create 16,000 jobs. Another 18,400 jobs will be created once the park opens in 2005. Further, they hope that the park will draw millions of tourists to this city every year, raising more than US $1 billion a year.

Few doubt that the project will provide the city with a shot of confidence. Yet John Whaley, a Virginia-based economist, says the construction jobs provided by the project will be short-term positions, with little long-term economic impact. Also, since many tourists to Hong Kong are people of modest means from China, there is no guarantee that they will spend the money to go to the park.

3 Nevertheless, much of the costs for the new park will be paid by the Hong Kong government, which is spending more than US $2.83 billion to build the park. Estimates suggest the government is spending about US $100,000 for every new job it will create when the park is running.

Source: Adapted from "Disney-Park Deal May Not Wave A Magic Wand Over Hong Kong" by Jon E. Hilsenrath and Zach Coleman. *The Wall Street Journal*, November 4, 1999.

Make a Diagram

Summarize the costs and benefits of the Hong Kong government's decision in a diagram. Consider the wisdom of the decision by analyzing these costs and benefits.

Applying the Skill

Turn to page 125 and read the article titled "The Year of the Hybrid." Based on the information you find there, conduct a cost-benefit analysis of buying a hybrid automobile.

Decision: Hong Kong government partners with Disney to build a new theme park.

Potential benefits: Many new jobs; perhaps US $1 billion poured into the economy.

Potential costs: Huge initial outlay by the government; about half the jobs created are short-term.

Analysis: Too soon to tell, but the fact that potential audience for the park are of modest means does not guarantee success. **4**

1.7 Comparing and Contrasting Economic Information

Economists compare and contrast economic programs, concepts, and trends in order to understand them better. **COMPARING** involves finding both similarities and differences between two or more things. **CONTRASTING** means examining only the differences between them.

Understanding the Skill

STRATEGY: Look for similarities and differences. The following passage describes pension reform in Chile and in Britain. The Venn diagram that follows the passage shows some of the similarities and differences between the two economic programs.

① Compare: Look for features that two subjects or ideas have in common. Here, you learn that both Chile and Britain needed to reform their pension systems.

② Compare: Look for clue words indicating that two things are alike. Clue words include *all, both, as, likewise,* and *similarly.*

③ Contrast: Look for clue words that show how two things differ. Clue words include *different, however, unlike,* and *except.*

④ Contrast: Look for ways in which two things are different. Here you learn that the structure and the administration of the two programs were different.

Pension Reform in Chile and Britain

In the late 20th century, Chile and Britain faced **①** the same problem: how to reform their overburdened pension systems. **②** Both countries had social welfare budgets that were stretched to the limit. And both had pension systems that were nearly bankrupt. To provide for their aging population, Chile and Britain chose privatization as the means to reform their pension programs.

③ However, **④** the structure and administration of the two programs were very different. For example, in Chile a monthly payroll deduction became mandatory for all employees. The payments are administered by one of six private pension funds. In Britain, however, the plan was voluntary. Six million people chose the plan when it was first offered. They received a government rebate, along with responsibility for managing their own retirement money.

Source: Adapted from "In Britain and in Chile, Lessons for Social Security" by Mark Rice-Oxley and Jennifer Ross. *The Christian Science Monitor*, March 14, 2005

Make a Venn Diagram

Summarize similarities and differences in a Venn diagram like the one shown here. In the overlapping area, list characteristics shared by both subjects. Then, in one oval, list the characteristics of one subject not shared by the other. In the other oval, list characteristics unique to the second subject.

Applying the Skill

Turn to Chapter 8 and read Sections 1 and 2, pages 226–235. Construct a Venn diagram comparing and contrasting sole proprietorships and partnerships.

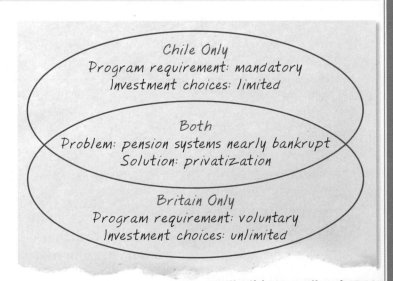

Chile Only
Program requirement: mandatory
Investment choices: limited

Both
Problem: pension systems nearly bankrupt
Solution: privatization

Britain Only
Program requirement: voluntary
Investment choices: unlimited

1.8 Analyzing Cause and Effect

CAUSES are the events, factors, and other reasons that lead to an event or condition. Causes happen before the event in time; they explain why it happened. **EFFECTS** are the results or consequences of the event. One effect often becomes the cause of other effects, resulting in a chain of events. Causes and effects can be both short-term and long-term.

Understanding the Skill

STRATEGY: Keep track of causes and effects as you read. The passage below describes factors leading to a shortfall of qualified staff in India's call centers. The diagram that follows the passage summarizes the economic chain of causes and effects.

1 Causes: Look for clue words that show cause. These include *due to*, *cause*, and *therefore*.

2 Look for multiple causes and multiple effects. Increased outsourcing to India caused the series of effects discussed in the rest of the article.

3 Effects: Look for results or consequences. Sometimes these are indicated by clue words such as *as a result* and *consequence*.

4 Notice that an effect may be the cause of another event. This begins a chain of causes and effects.

Each year, three thousand English speakers graduate from India's universities. **1** Largely due to this pool of job seekers fluent in English, India has been able to establish a highly successful business process outsourcing industry. **2** As businesses in more and more countries outsourced to India, call centers there have become increasingly successful. As a result, salaries for entry-level positions have continued to rise. An unintended **3** consequence of the **4** higher salaries has been a greater tendency of workers to job hop. Increasing success also has created increasing stress, as employees often are required to work long hours. Therefore, employment in call centers, once considered glamorous, has begun to lose its appeal. Analysts claim that such conditions will cause a shortfall of as many as 260,000 qualified workers by 2009.

Source: Adapted from "Busy Signals," *The Economist,* September 10, 2005

Make a Cause-and-Effect Diagram

Summarize cause-and-effect relationships in a diagram. Starting with the first cause in a series, fill in the boxes until you reach the end result.

Cause ⟶	Effect / Cause ⟶	Effect / Cause ⟶	Effect / Cause ⟶	Effect
Many of India's college graduates speak English.	Outsourcing industry enjoys success.	• Pay improves for entry-level jobs. • On-the-job stress increases.	• Workers change jobs often. • Fewer people apply.	There will soon be a shortage of qualified workers.

Applying the Skill

Turn to Chapter 2 and read "Under Pressure to Change" on page 40. Construct a Cause-and-Effect diagram summarizing the information you find.

1.9 Making Inferences and Drawing Conclusions

MAKING INFERENCES involves reading between the lines to extend the information provided.
DRAWING CONCLUSIONS involves analyzing what has been read and forming an opinion
about its meaning.

Understanding the Skill

STRATEGY: Develop inferences from the facts. Use the facts to draw conclusions. The
passage below describes the U.S. trade deficit in 2005. The diagram that follows shows how to
organize the facts and inferences to draw conclusions.

1 Read carefully to understand all the facts. Fact: The U.S. trade deficit rose almost 18 percent in 2005.

2 Use the facts to make an inference. Inference: It's unlikely that the United States will see a trade surplus in the foreseeable future.

3 Read between the lines to make inferences. Inference: Continued dependence on foreign oil will continue to increase the deficit.

4 Ask questions of the material. How can the United States reduce its trade deficit?

5 Use all this information to draw a conclusion. Conclusion: In order to reduce the deficit, the United States will need to reduce its dependence on foreign oil.

1 The U.S. trade deficit jumped nearly 18 percent in 2005, the government reported Friday, hitting its fourth consecutive record as consumer demand for imports increased, energy prices soared and the dollar strengthened against other currencies.

The $725.8 billion gap, **1** which is almost exactly twice the deficit in 2001, was driven by a 12 percent jump in imports and a more muted 10 percent increase in exports, the Commerce Department reported in Washington. **2** The nation last had a trade surplus, of $12.4 billion, in 1975.

3 The nation's deficit in trade for petroleum products accounted for 29 percent of the total gap, up from 25 percent in 2004. **4** Imports of petroleum goods climbed 39 percent, to $251.6 billion, after rising by 39 percent in 2004. Excluding oil and other petroleum products, the trade deficit would have grown 10 percent, to $537 billion.

Source: "The U.S. Trade Deficit Hit Record High in 2005" by Vikas Bajaj. *The New York Times,* February 10, 2006

Applying the Skill

Read the online news story "China's Economic Miracle; the High Price of Progress" on page 571. Use the chart at the right as a model for organizing facts, inferences, and conclusions about the passage.

Facts	Inferences	Conclusion about Passage
The U.S. trade deficit rose almost 18 percent in 2005. The deficit nearly doubled between 2001 and 2005.	The deficit is growing at a marked rate.	**5** In order to reduce the deficit, the United States will need to reduce its dependence on foreign oil.
Last trade surplus was in 1975.	Trade surplus is unlikely in foreseeable future.	
Trade in petroleum products accounted for 29 percent of deficit.	Continued dependence on foreign oil will continue to increase the deficit.	

1.10 Evaluating Economic Decisions

EVALUATING ECONOMIC DECISIONS means making judgments about decisions that individuals, businesses, and governments make on economic matters. Economists evaluate a decision based on its outcome and the choices available when that decision was made.

Understanding the Skill

STRATEGY: Look for choices and reasons. The following passage describes the marketing decisions Joe Sillett made to promote a cricket bat he had begun to manufacture. As you read the passage, look for alternative decisions he could have made.

1 **Look at decisions made by individuals or by groups.** Identify the decision Sillett made to market his company's product.

2 **Look at the outcome of the decisions.**

3 **Analyze a decision in terms of the choices that were possible.** Sillett could have chosen a marketing strategy that was less expensive and therefore less risky. Make a simple chart of your analysis.

Applying the Skill

Pages 234–235 of Chapter 8 describe Bart's decision to open his comic store as a partnership rather than a sole proprietorship. Make a chart like the one shown to summarize the pros and cons of his decision and your evaluation of that decision.

Marketing Woodworm

When Joe Sillett formed his company, Woodworm, to make cricket bats, he was up against stiff competition. . . Sillett had to decide how to break into the market. Should he utilize traditional marketing techniques, such as the development and purchase of print and media ads, to introduce his product? Or should he try something bolder? **1** Sillett decided to risk most of his marketing budget on a single idea: the sponsorship of two English heavy hitters—Andrew Flintoff and Kevin Pietersen. Sillett's idea proved to be a winner. **2** In just three years, Woodworm bats succeeded in capturing ten percent of the cricket bat market. **3** Sillett knew that a less expensive approach would have allowed him to grow his company over a more extended period of time. But because he believed that linking Woodworm bats with high profile players would quickly create brand recognition, Sillett risked the future of his company on a single marketing idea and won.

Source: Adapted from "The Benefits of Woodworm." *The Economist*, September 8th, 2005

3 Sillett's Choices	Pros	Cons	Evaluation
Sponsor popular players	Possible to gain market share quickly	Risky and expensive	In your opinion, which was the better choice? Why?
Pursue a less expensive marketing strategy	Less risky	Market share likely to grow slowly	

1.11 Synthesizing Economic Data

SYNTHESIZING ECONOMIC DATA is the skill economists use to develop interpretations of past economic events. Like detective work, synthesizing involves putting together clues from data to form an overall picture of an economic event.

Understanding the Skill

STRATEGY: Build an interpretation as you read. The passage below describes the collapse of Enron, a giant American energy company. Note how combining different data leads to a synthesis—an overall picture of Enron's fall and its significance.

1 **Read carefully to understand the data.** These statements explain why Enron borrowed money and how it succeeded in hiding $600 million in debt.

2 **Look for variables in the data that need an explanation.** Here, the data in the two statements present a puzzling picture. They lead one to question how a large company that tripled its profits could experience a loss of $638 million less than a year later.

3 **Form a synthesis based on the data.** This interpretation brings together the different pieces of data to arrive at a new understanding of the subject. Summarize your synthesis in a graphic organizer, such as a table or a cluster diagram.

Enron's Downfall

1 Enron began to borrow money to invest in new projects. Enron then created partnerships to keep the debt off its books. One partnership . . . allowed Enron to keep $600 million in debt off the books it showed to the government and to people who own Enron stock.
2 In December 2000, Enron claimed to have tripled its profits in two years.
2 The collapse began in October [2001], when Enron announced a loss of $638 million. In November, Enron said that it had overstated earnings for the past four years and it now owed over $6 billion. With these announcements, Enron's stock price took a dive.
3 Since Enron had made deals based on the assumption that the stock would go up, it suddenly had to repay lots of money. When Enron could not come up with the cash, it declared bankruptcy.
3 [One] consequence of [Enron's] failure may be new laws that change how much money big businesses can give politicians. Enron gave over $5 million to [political] campaigns since 1998. Lawmakers [also] are considering whether to make new laws to better regulate accounting practices.

Source: "Not Business as Usual," by Elisabeth Bauman. Online NewsHour Extra, January 30, 2002 (www.pbs.org)

Applying the Skill

Read the information on income distribution and income inequality on pages 390–391. Look for data to support a synthesis about the effectiveness and limitations of measuring income inequality. Organize your findings in a table or cluster diagram.

1.12 Generalizing from Economic Information

GENERALIZING involves making broad judgments based on information from more than one source. When you form generalizations, you need to be sure they are based on sufficient evidence and that they are consistent with the information given.

Understanding the Skill

STRATEGY: Look for common themes. The following three excerpts reflect concern regarding the economic deprivation of the elderly during the Great Depression.

1 **Determine what information the sources have in common.** All the sources suggest the need for a government program to provide pensions to the elderly.

2 **Form a generalization about the common information.**

3 **State your generalization in sentence form.** A generalization often needs a qualifying word, such as *most, many,* or *some,* to make it valid.

Plight of the Elderly

1 We also propose to give the old-age pensions to the old people . . . so that the people who reach the age of sixty can be retired from the active labor of life and given an opportunity to have surcease [rest] and ease for the balance of the life that they have on earth.
—*Governor Huey Long of Louisiana*

1 "Old age dependent pensions . . . are not gifts from charity. They are for compensation well earned."
—*Flyer attached to a letter written to President Franklin D. Roosevelt by a woman asking for help for her 81-year-old mother*

1 "It is estimated that the population of the age of 60 and above in the United States is somewhere between nine and twelve millions. I suggest that the national government retire all who reach that age on a monthly pension of $200 a month or more."
—*Francis E. Townsend*

Make a Web Diagram

Using a diagram can help you make generalizations. The diagram below records relevant information from the three statements that leads to a valid generalization.

Applying the Skill

Read the information under the headings "Changing Occupations" and "Changes in the Way People Work" on pages 268–271. Use a diagram like the one above to make a generalization about technology and work in the United States today.

1.13 Predicting Economic Trends

PREDICTING ECONOMIC TRENDS involves projecting the outcome or the continuation of an economic condition or trend. Economists use their knowledge of past economic events and conditions and related decisions to predict the outcome of current economic events and conditions.

Understanding the Skill

STRATEGY: Identify decisions. The following passage describes how the United States government, under the leadership of President Franklin D. Roosevelt, dealt with a nationwide banking crisis during the Great Depression.

1 To help you identify decisions, look for clue words. These words include *decide, decision,* and *chose.*

2 Notice how one economic decision often leads to others.

3 Notice that decisions may have positive or negative impacts.

4 Consider alternatives to the decisions that were made.

5 Make a chart to record decisions, suggest alternative decisions, and predict a possible outcome for each alternative decision.

During the Great Depression, many banks in the United States failed. In 1933 Americans, fearing the loss of their money, created "runs" on banks throughout the country. A bank run occurs when large numbers of people attempt to withdraw money within a short period of time. Banks did not have enough money to meet the demand.

In response, President Roosevelt **1** decided to temporarily shut down the nation's banks by proclaiming a bank holiday. **2** Congress **1** chose to pass a law in support of Roosevelt's decision. The law also provided for the rehabilitation of the nation's banking facilities. To avoid an epidemic of bank failures, **3** it was decided not to reopen all the banks at the same time. Instead, banks would open once they had been examined and judged to be sound. In addition, the government made the **1** decision to issue new currency—based on sound assets—so that banks, once reopened, would have enough currency to meet increased demand. Finally, it was decided to include state banks that were not members of the Federal Reserve in the rehabilitation process. The government response to the banking crisis served to stabilize the U.S. banking system.

Source: Franklin D. Roosevelt's First Fireside Chat, March 12, 1933

Applying the Skill

Read the document titled "Two American Entrepreneurs Start Out in a Garage" on page 252 and identify three business decisions that "the two Steves" made. Record them in a chart similar to the one shown for the passage above, along with an alternative decision for each. Then predict a possible outcome for each alternative decision.

5

Decisions	Alternative Decisions **4**	Prediction of Outcome
FDR proclaimed a nation-wide bank holiday.	FDR did not proclaim a bank holiday.	The run on banks continued.
Congress passed a law to rehabilitate banking facilities.	Congress passed no law to rehabilitate banking facilities.	Banks were not rehabilitated.
New currency was issued.	New currency was not issued.	There was not enough money to meet depositors' demands.
State banks would receive assistance.	Fed did not assist non-member state banks.	State banks failed to reopen.

2.1 Analyzing Political Cartoons

POLITICAL CARTOONS are drawings that express the artist's point of view about a local, national, or international situation or event. They may criticize, show approval, or draw attention to a particular issue, and may be either serious or humorous. Political cartoonists often use symbols as well as other visual clues to communicate their message.

Understanding the Skill

STRATEGY: Examine the cartoon carefully. The cartoon below was drawn as a comment on the process of globalization.

1 Look at the cartoon as a whole to determine the subject.

2 Look for symbols, which are especially effective in communicating ideas visually. Here, the cartoonist uses symbols that stand for a global economy. The arm in a suit stands for big business. The globe stands for Earth and its resources. The people represent consumers.

3 Analyze the visual details, which help express the artist's point of view. The Western-style house and clothing suggest that the people are Americans or Europeans. The people are smiling, indicating that they are happy about what is being offered to them.

Make a Chart

Summarize your interpretation in a chart. Look for details and interpret their significance. Then decide on the message of the cartoon.

Symbols and Visual Details	Significance	Message
Oversized arm in business suit	Corporations	Big business is the driving force behind globalization.
Disproportionately small Earth	Earth as the property of big business	
Happy people reaching out	Consumers	

Applying the Skill

Turn to page 283 and study the political cartoon. Note the clothing and apparent attitudes of the figures in the cartoon, as well as how they relate to one another. Then analyze the cartoon by making a chart like the one to the left.

2.2 Distinguishing Fact from Opinion

FACTS are events, dates, statistics, or statements that can be proved to be true. Facts can be checked for accuracy. **OPINIONS** are judgments, beliefs, and feelings of the writer or speaker.

Understanding the Skill

STRATEGY: Find clues in the text. The following excerpt describes economist Sir William Beveridge's 1942 recommendations for creating a welfare state in Great Britain.

1 Facts: Look for specific names, dates, statistics, and statements that can be proved. The first paragraph gives a factual account of the government's plan.

2 Opinion: Look for assertions, claims, hypotheses, and judgments. Beveridge expresses his opinion regarding provision for old age and for medical care.

3 Opinion: Look for judgment words that the writer uses to describe policies and events. Judgment words are often adjectives that are used to arouse a reader's emotions.

---

1 The coalition British Government has unveiled plans for a welfare state offering care to all from the cradle to the grave. The Beveridge report proposes a far-reaching series of changes designed to provide a financial safety net to ensure a "freedom from want" after the war is over. Everyone of working age would be expected to pay a weekly national insurance contribution. In return benefits would be paid to the sick, widowed, retired, unemployed and there would also be an allowance for families.

The architect of the report, economist Sir William Beveridge, drew on advice from various government departments. **2** He found provision for old age represented one of the most pressing problems. But there were other failings too. Medical provision was not universally available to all and Britain's achievement, in his words, "fell seriously short" compared with other countries of the world.

At a time when the war was destroying landmarks of every kind, [Beveridge] said, it was a **3** "revolutionary moment in the world's history, a time for revolutions, not for patching."

Source: BBC News

Make a Chart

Divide facts and opinions in a chart. Summarize and separate the facts from the opinions expressed in the passage.

Facts	Opinions
In 1942 the British government unveiled plans for a welfare state. The plan was based on a report by Sir William Beveridge and was designed to provide British citizens with a financial safety net.	• The British government's provision for old age represented one of the most pressing problems. • Britain's medical provision fell seriously short as compared to that of other countries. • It was a revolutionary moment in history.

Applying the Skill

Read "Government and Demand-Side Policies" on page 457. Using a chart like the one to the left, summarize the facts, opinions, and judgments stated. Look carefully at the language used in order to separate one from the other.

2.3 Evaluating Online Sources

EVALUATING ONLINE SOURCES involves making judgments about sites that are available on the Internet—a network of computers associated with universities, libraries, news organizations, government agencies, and other information providers. Each location on the Internet has a home page with its own address, or URL. The international collection of home pages, known as the **WORLD WIDE WEB,** is a good source of up-to-the-minute information as well as in-depth research on economic subjects.

Understanding the Skill

STRATEGY: Explore and evaluate the elements on the screen. The computer screen below shows "Treasury's Learning Vault," the education page of the United States Department of the Treasury.

1 Go directly to a Web page. Access the Internet using your Internet Service Provider (ISP). If you know the address of the Web site you want, type it in the address box at the top of your computer screen, then press ENTER or RETURN. (To access the page shown here, type in www.ustreas.gov/education.)

2 Explore the features and links. Click on any one of the images or topics to find out more about a specific subject. These links take you to other pages at this Web site. Some links take you to related information that can be found at other places on the Internet.

3 Evaluate the Web site. Use the information you gathered in Step 2 to evaluate the Web site. Ask yourself the following questions: Is the information provided by the site useful to an economist or a student of economics? How reliable is this information?

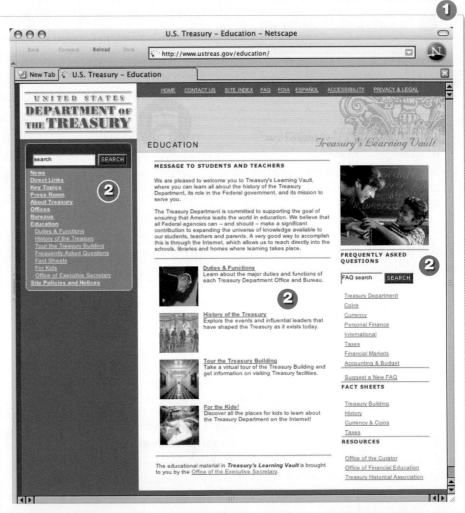

Applying the Skill

Access the Bureau of Labor Statistics (www.bls.gov) and the Census Bureau (www.census.gov) Websites through ClassZone.com. How useful do you think these sites might be to economists? How might economists use the information on these sites?

2.4 Interpreting Graphs

GRAPHS show statistical information in a visual manner. Economists use graphs to show comparative amounts, ratios, trends, and changes over time. Interpreting graphs will increase your understanding of economic trends and data. **LINE GRAPHS** can show changes over time, or trends. Usually, the horizontal axis shows a unit of time, such as years, and the vertical axis shows quantities. **PIE GRAPHS** are useful for showing relative proportions. The circle represents the whole, such as the entire population, and the slices represent the different groups that make up the whole. **BAR GRAPHS** compare numbers or sets of numbers. The length of each bar indicates a quantity. With bar graphs, it is easy to see at a glance how different categories compare.

Understanding the Skill

STRATEGY: Study all the elements of the graph. This double line graph shows the number of new firms started and the number of firm closures from 1994 to 2005.

1 **Read the title to identify the content of the graph.** Here, the title explicitly states the content of the graph—new firms and firm closures.

2 **Read the vertical and horizontal axes.** The vertical axis shows the number of firms, and the horizontal axis shows years.

3 **Look at the legend to understand what colors and symbols represent.** In this graph, different colored lines are used to represent new firms and firm closures.

4 **Summarize the information shown in each part of the graph.** What trend does each line show?

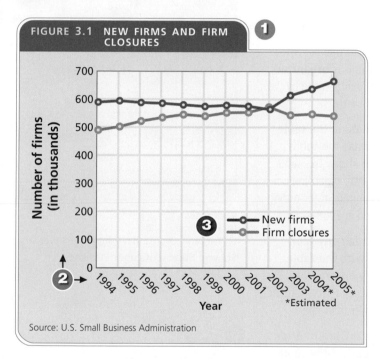

FIGURE 3.1 NEW FIRMS AND FIRM CLOSURES

Number of firms (in thousands)

New firms
Firm closures

Year
*Estimated

Source: U.S. Small Business Administration

Write a Summary

Write a summary paragraph to show what you have learned from the graph.

4 *Each year from 1994 to 2005, about 600,000 new firms opened in the United States. During the same time period, anywhere from 500,000 to about 575,000 firms closed. In 2002, there actually were more firm closures than new firm openings. The overall trend shows that nearly as many firms close as open each year.*

Applying the Skill

Turn to page 267 and study Figure 9.7, a graph that provides information on the U.S. labor force. Write a paragraph summarizing what you learn from the graph.

2.5 Interpreting Tables

TABLES present information in a visual form. Tables are created by simplifying, summarizing, and organizing information into a format that is easy to understand. Tables are the most commonly used charts in Economics books.

Understanding the Skill

STRATEGY: Study all the elements of the table. The table shown here provides statistical information about employment in the United States.

① **Read the title to identify the main idea of the table.** This table provides information on selected aspects of the United States labor force during 2006.

② **Read the headings to determine how the table is organized.** In this table, data is organized by category and by month.

③ **Study the data in the table to understand what the table was designed to show.** This table shows economic data regarding employment in the United States during a six-month period in 2006.

④ **Be sure to read any footnotes provided with the table. Footnotes clarify information.** For example, (P) indicates that a statistic is preliminary rather than final.

⑤ **Summarize the information shown in each part of the table.** Use the title and side headings to help you focus on what information the table is presenting.

Selected Labor Force Statistics, February to July, 2006 ①			
② **Month**	**Unemployment Rate (percent)**	**New Jobs Added (thousands)**	**Average Hourly Earnings[1] (in dollars)**
February	4.8	200	16.47
March	4.7	175	16.51 **③**
April	4.7	112	16.61
May	4.6	100	16.62
June	4.6	124P	16.69P
July	4.8	113P	16.76P

Footnotes: **④**
(P) Preliminary
(1) For production and nonsupervisory workers, in dollars and cents
Source: Bureau of Labor Statistics

⑤ *The table provides statistical information about employment in the United States. Statistics are given for each of six months, from February through July 2006. The unemployment rate fluctuated between 4.6 and 4.8 percent. There was an increase in the number of jobs each month, with the greatest increase occurring in June and the smallest in May. Average hourly earnings rose fairly steadily from $16.47 in February to $16.76 July.*

Applying the Skill

Turn to page 79 and study Figure 3.3. Then write a paragraph summarizing the information presented in the table.

2.6 Analyzing Databases

A **DATABASE** is a collection of data, or information, that is organized so that you can find and retrieve information on a specific topic quickly and easily. You can search for specific information without going through the entire database. A database provides a list of all information related to a specific topic.

Understanding the Skill

STRATEGY: Study the elements of the database. First identify the topic. The title "World's Top Oil Consumers" indicates the criterion for listing the six nations in the database. Look at the categories shown and pose questions about what you can learn from them. For example, in this database you could search for "countries consuming more than 10 million bbls (barrels) per day" and discover that the United States and the European Union fall into that category.

1 Determine the order of presentation of information. The six countries in this database are listed according to the amount of oil they consume, from most to least.

2 Identify the entries included under each heading. Here, the data in each row relates to one of the six countries listed.

3 Determine how the categories in the database relate to one another. This database includes the categories "oil production" and "proved oil reserves." Both relate to oil consumption. These related categories enable you, for example, to determine which countries, if any, produce less oil than they consume.

4 Read any labels or footnotes that clarify the nature of the data. In this database, the figures represent barrels (bbl) of oil. Also note that for purposes of providing statistical information, the EU is considered to be one country.

5 Note the source of the data. Is the source reliable? The source of data here is The CIA World Factbook, a respected and reliable source of data on the countries of the world.

World's Top Oil Consumers			
Country	Oil Consumption (Millions of bbl[1] / day)	Oil Production (Millions of bbl[1] / day)	Proved Oil Reserves (Billions of bbl[1])
United States	20.0	7.6	22.5
European Union[2]	14.6	3.4	7.3
China	6.4	3.5	18.3
Russia	2.8	9.1	69.0
Saudi Arabia	1.8	9.5	262.7
Iran	1.4	4.0	133.3

Footnotes: 4
(1) Barrels
(2) For data presentation, treated as a single country
Source: The CIA World Factbook, 2005 data **5**

Analyze the Database

Consider the kinds of information that you could quickly find from the database. For example, you can search for countries that produce or consume more or less oil than a specific number of barrels per day. Make a list of the kinds of information you could search for in this database.

Applying the Skill

Turn to page A12 in the Economic Atlas and Statistics and review the information in the two sets of graphs. Create a database for United States industry using statistics for the most recent year shown. Consider the steps listed above when creating your database.

Glossary

A

absolute advantage *n.* the ability of one trading nation to make a product more efficiently than another trading nation (p. 513)

aggregate demand *n.* the sum of all the demand in the economy (p. 360)

aggregate supply *n.* the sum of all the supply in the economy (p. 360)

antitrust legislation *n.* laws that define monopolies and give government the power to control or dissolve them (p. 214)

appropriations *n.* set amounts of money put aside for specific purposes (p. 431)

authoritarian *adj.* requiring absolute loyalty and obedience to authority (p. 43)

automated teller machine (ATM) *n.* an electronic device that allows bank customers to make transactions without seeing a bank officer (p. 308)

automatic stabilizer *n.* a feature of fiscal policy that works automatically to steady the economy (p. 447)

B

balanced budget *n.* a budget in which total government revenue is equal to total government spending (p. 436)

balance of payments *n.* a record of all the transactions that occurred between the individuals, businesses, and government units of one nation and those of the rest of the world (p. 529)

balance of trade *n.* the difference between the value of a country's imports and exports (p. 529)

bank exam *n.* an audit, conducted by the Federal Reserve, of a bank's financial practices (p. 481)

bank holding company *n.* a company that owns more than one bank (p. 481)

barrier to entry *n.* anything that hinders a business from entering a market (p. 198)

barter *n.* the exchange of goods and services without using money (p. 288)

bear market *n.* a situation in which stock market prices decline steadily over time (p. 335)

binding arbitration *n.* a process by which an impartial third party resolves disputes between management and unions (p. 280)

black market *n.* the illegal business of buying or selling goods or services in violation of price controls or rationing (p. 183)

Board of Governors *n.* the board of seven appointed members that supervises the operations of the Federal Reserve System and sets monetary policy (p. 476)

bond *n.* a contract a corporation issues that promises to repay borrowed money, plus interest, on a fixed schedule (p. 240)

bounced check *see* overdraft

break-even point *n.* a situation in which total costs and total revenues are the same (p. 142)

budget *n.* a plan for allocating income for saving and spending (p. 574)

budget deficit *n.* a situation in which the government spends more than it takes in (p. 462)

budget surplus *n.* a situation in which the government takes in more than it spends (p. 462)

bull market *n.* a situation in which stock market prices rise steadily over time (p. 335)

business cycle *n.* the series of growing and shrinking periods of economic activity, measured by increases or decreases in real gross domestic product (p. 358)

business organization *n.* an enterprise that produces goods or provides services, usually to make a profit (p. 226)

business structure *see* business organization

C

capital *n.* all the resources people make and use to produce and distribute goods and services (p. 8)

capital budget *n.* a plan for major expenses or investments (p. 436)

capital deepening *n.* an increase in the ratio of capital to labor (p. 371)

capital flight *n.* a situation in which capital from a country is invested outside the country (p. 558)

capital gain *n.* the profit made from the sale of securities (p. 330)

capitalism *n.* an economic system based on private ownership of the factors of production (p. 49)

capital market *n.* a market in which long-term financial assets are bought and sold (p. 322)

cartel *n.* a formal organization of sellers or producers who regulate the production, pricing, and marketing of a product (pp. 198, 535)

cease and desist order *n.* a ruling requiring a firm to stop an unfair business practice (p. 217)

central bank *n.* a nation's main monetary authority (p. 474)

centrally planned economy *n.* a system in which the society's leaders make all economic decisions (p. 42)

change in demand *n.* a situation in which a change in the marketplace prompts consumers to buy different amounts of a good or service at every price (p. 109)

change in quantity demanded *n.* a change in the amount of a product that consumers will buy because of a change in price (p. 108)

change in quantity supplied *n.* an increase or decrease in the amount of a good or service that producers are willing to sell because of a change in price (p. 146)

change in supply *n.* a situation in which a change in the marketplace prompts producers to offer different amounts for sale at every price (p. 148)

check clearing *n.* a service provided by the Federal Reserve to record receipts and expenditures of bank clients (p. 480)

circular flow model *n.* a visualization of all interactions in a market economy (p. 52)

civilian labor force *n.* people age 16 or older who are employed or actively looking for and available to do work (p. 266)

claim *n.* a request to an insurance company for payment on an insured loss (p. 596)

closed shop *n.* a business in which an employer can hire only union members (p. 279)

coincident indicators *n.* measures of economic performance that usually change at the same time as real gross domestic product changes (p. 364)

collective bargaining *n.* the process of negotiation between a business and its organized employees to establish wages and improve working conditions (p. 280)

command economy *n.* an economic system in which the government makes all economic decisions (p. 39)

commodity money *n.* money that has intrinsic value based on the material from which it is made (p. 291)

common stock *n.* a share of ownership in a corporation that gives the holder voting rights and a share of profits (p. 331)

communism *n.* an economic system in which there is no private ownership of property and little or no political freedom (p. 43)

comparative advantage *n.* the ability of one trading nation to produce something at a lower opportunity cost than that of another trading nation (p. 513)

competition *n.* the effort of two or more people acting independently to get business by offering the best deal (p. 49)

competitive pricing *n.* a situation in which producers sell goods and services at prices that best balance the twin desires of making the highest profit and luring customers away from rival producers (p. 174)

complements *n.* products that are used together, so the increase or decrease in demand for one will result in an increase or decrease in demand for the other (p. 112)

conglomerate *n.* a business composed of companies that produce unrelated goods or services (p. 243)

consumer *n.* a person who buys goods or services for personal use (p. 5)

consumer price index (CPI) *n.* a measure of changes in the prices of goods and services that consumers commonly purchase (p. 396)

consumer sovereignty *n.* the idea that consumers have the ultimate control over what is produced because they are free to buy what they want and refuse products they do not want (p. 50)

contingent employment *n.* temporary or part-time work (p. 270)

contract *n.* a formal, legally binding agreement (p. 598)

contraction *n.* a decrease in economic activity (p. 359); *see* business cycle

contractionary fiscal policy *n.* a plan to reduce aggregate demand and slow down the economy during a period of too-rapid economic expansion (p. 446)

contractionary monetary policy *n.* a plan to reduce the amount of money in circulation; also called tight-money policy (p. 492)

cooperative *n.* a type of business operated for the shared benefit of the owners, who are also its customers (p. 250)

co-pay *n.* an amount the insured owes when an insured receives health care (p. 596)

corporate income tax *n.* a tax based on a corporation's profits (p. 412)

corporation *n.* a business owned by shareholders, also called stockholders, who own the rights to the company's profits but face only limited liability for the company's debts and losses (p. 238)

cosigner *n.* a person who assumes responsibility for the debt if the borrower fails to repay the loan (p. 583)

cost-benefit analysis *n.* the practice of examining the costs and the expected benefits of a choice as an aid to decision making (p. 15)

cost-push inflation *n.* a situation in which increases in production costs push up prices (p. 399)

Council of Economic Advisers *n.* the three-member group that advises the President on fiscal policy and other economic issues (p. 452)

coupon rate *n.* the interest rate a bond-holder receives every year until the bond matures (p. 338)

craft union *n.* an organization of workers with similar skills who work in different industries for different employers (p. 274)

credit *n.* the practice of buying goods or services now and paying for them in the future (p. 582)

credit report *n.* a statement by a credit bureau that details a consumer's credit record (p. 586)

credit score *n.* a number that summarizes a consumer's creditworthiness (p. 586)

crowding-out effect *n.* a situation in which the government outbids private bond interest rates to gain loanable funds (p. 466)

currency *n.* paper money and coins (pp. 293, 475)

customs duty *n.* a tax on goods imported into the United States (p. 425)

customs unions *n.* agreements that abolish trade barriers among the members and establish uniform tariffs for non-members (p. 532)

cyclical unemployment *n.* unemployment caused by the part of the business cycle with decreased economic activity (p. 384)

D

debit card *n.* a card one can use like an ATM card to withdraw cash or like a check to make purchases (p. 308)

debt restructuring *n.* a method countries with outstanding debt obligations use to alter the terms of debt agreements to achieve some advantage (p. 559)

deductible *n.* the amount the insured pays before the insurance company pays (p. 596)

default *n.* the condition that occurs when a nation cannot pay interest or principle on a loan (p. 559)

deficit spending *n.* the government practice of spending more than it collects in revenue for a specific fiscal year (p. 462)

deflation *n.* a decrease in the general price level (p. 398)

demand *n.* the desire to have some good or service and the ability to pay for it (p. 98)

demand curve *n.* a graph that shows a demand schedule, or how much of a good or service an individual is willing and able to purchase at each price (p. 102)

demand deposits *n.* checking accounts, so called because checking accounts can be converted into currency "on demand" (p. 293)

demand-pull inflation *n.* a condition that occurs when total demand rises faster than the production of goods and services (p. 399)

demand schedule *n.* a table that shows how much of a good or service an individual is willing and able to purchase at each price (p. 100)

demand-side fiscal policy *n.* a plan to stimulate aggregate demand (p. 454)

deposit multiplier formula *n.* a mathematical formula that tells how much the money supply will increase after an initial cash deposit in a bank (p. 485)

depreciate *v.* to decrease in value (p. 590)

depression *n.* an extended period of high unemployment and reduced business activity (p. 359)

deregulation *n.* the reduction or elimination of government oversight and control of business (p. 218)

derived demand *n.* a demand for a product or resource based on its contribution to the final product (p. 259)

developed nations *n.* nations that have a market economy, a relatively high standard of living, a high GDP, industrialization, widespread private ownership of private property, and stable and effective governments (p. 544)

differentiated product *see* product differentiation

diminishing returns *n.* a situation in which new workers cause marginal product to grow but at a decreasing rate (p. 139)

discount rate *n.* the interest rate that the Federal Reserve charges when it lends money to other banks (p. 491)

discretionary fiscal policy *n.* actions taken by the federal government by choice to correct economic instability (p. 446)

discretionary spending *n.* spending that the government must authorize each year (p. 428)

disequilibrium *n.* a situation in which quantity supplied and quantity demanded are not in balance (p. 169)

disposable personal income (DPI) *n.* personal income minus taxes (p. 355)

diversification *n.* the practice of distributing investments among different financial assets to maximize return and limit risk (p. 327)

dividend *n.* the part of a corporation's profit that the company pays the stockholders (p. 238)

dumping *n.* the sale of a product in another country at a price lower than that charged in the home market (p. 521)

Dumpster diving *n.* technique used by identity thieves to gather personal information in the garbage (p. 588)

E

easy-money policy *see* expansionary monetary policy

economic cycle *see* business cycle

economic growth *n.* an increase in a nation's real gross domestic product (p. 358)

economic interdependence *n.* a situation in which producers in one nation depend on others to provide goods and services they do not produce (p. 510)

economic model *n.* a simplified representation of economic activities, systems, or problems (p. 18)

economics *n.* the study of how individuals and societies satisfy their unlimited wants with limited resources (p. 4)

economic system *n.* the way in which a society uses its scarce resources to satisfy its people's unlimited wants (p. 38)

economies of scale *n.* a situation in which the average cost of production falls as the producer grows larger (p. 201)

economize *v.* to make decisions according what is believed to be the best combination of costs and benefits (p. 12)

efficiency *n.* the condition in which economic resources are used to produce the maximum amount of goods and services (p. 20)

elastic *adj.* referring to a situation in which a change in price, either up or down, leads to a relatively larger change in the quantity demanded or the quantity supplied (pp. 117, 154)

elasticity of demand *n.* a measure of how responsive consumers are to price changes in the marketplace (p. 117)

elasticity of supply *n.* a measure of how responsive producers are to price changes in the marketplace (p. 154)

embargo *n.* a law that cuts off most or all trade with a specific country (p. 521)

entitlement *n.* a social welfare program with specific eligibility requirements (p. 428)

entrepreneurship *n.* the combination of vision, skill, ingenuity, and willingness to take risks that is needed to create and run new businesses (p. 9)

equilibrium price *n.* the price at which the quantity demanded equals the quantity supplied (p. 164)

equilibrium wage *n.* the wage at which the quantity of workers demanded equals the quantity of workers supplied; the market price for labor (p. 258)

estate tax *n.* a tax on the assets of a person who has died (p. 425)

European Union (EU) *n.* the economic and political union of European nations that was established in 1993 (p. 532)

euro *n.* the single currency of the European Union (p. 533)

excise tax *n.* a tax on the production or sale of a specific good or service (pp. 149, 425)

expansion *n.* an increase in economic activity (p. 358); *see* business cycle

expansionary fiscal policy *n.* a plan to increase aggregate demand and stimulate a weak economy (p. 446)

expansionary monetary policy *n.* a plan to increase the amount of money in circulation; also called easy-money policy (p. 492)

exports *n.* goods or services produced in one country and sold to other countries (p. 516)

externality *n.* a side effect of a transaction that affects someone other than the producer or buyer (p. 87)

F

factor market *n.* the market for the factors of production—land, labor, capital, and entrepreneurship (p. 52)

factors of production *n.* the economic resources needed to produce goods and services (p. 8)

federal budget *n.* a plan for spending federal tax money (p. 431)

federal funds rate (FFR) *n.* the interest at which a depository institution lends available funds to another depository institution overnight (p. 490)

Federal Insurance Contributions Act (FICA) *n.* a payroll tax that provides coverage for the elderly, the unemployed due to disability, and surviving family members of wage earners who have died (p. 423)

Federal Open Market Committee (FOMC) *n.* the Federal Reserve System board that supervises the sale and purchase of federal government securities (p. 477)

Federal Reserve System *n.* the central bank of the United States; commonly called the Fed (p. 474)

fiat money *n.* money that has no tangible backing but is declared by the government and accepted by citizens to have worth (p. 291)

filing status *n.* for filing taxes, based on marital status or support of dependents (p. 604)

financial asset *n.* a claim on a borrower's property (p. 319)

financial intermediary *n.* an institution that collects funds from savers and invests these funds in financial assets (p. 319)

financial market *n.* a situation in which buyers and sellers exchange financial assets (p. 319)

financial system *n.* all the institutions that help transfer funds between savers and investors (p. 318)

fiscal *adj.* of or relating to government revenue and spending (p. 446)

fiscal policy *n.* the federal government's use of taxing and spending to affect the economy (p. 446)

fiscal year *n.* a 12-month period for which an organization plans its expenditures (p. 431)

fixed costs *n.* expenses that business owners incur no matter how much they produce (p. 140)

fixed rate of exchange *n.* a system in which the currency of one nation is fixed or constant in relation to other currencies (p. 526)

flexible exchange rate *n.* a system in which the exchange rate for currency changes as supply and demand for the currency changes; also called the floating rate (p. 527)

focus group *n.* a moderated discussion with small groups of consumers (p. 208)

foreign exchange market *n.* a market in which currencies of different countries are bought and sold (p. 526)

foreign exchange rate *n.* the price of one currency in the currencies of other nations (p. 526)

franchise *n.* a business made up of semi-independent businesses that all offer the same products or services (p. 248)

franchisee *n.* a semi-independent business that pays a fee for the right to sell the parent company's products or services in a particular area (p. 248)

free contract *n.* a situation in which people decide for themselves which legal agreements to enter into (p. 73)

free enterprise system *n.* another name for capitalism, an economic system based on private ownership of productive resources (p. 70)

free rider *n.* a person who does not pay for a good or service but who benefits from it when it is provided (p. 85)

free-trade zone *n.* a specific region in which trade between nations takes place without protective tariffs (p. 532)

frictional unemployment *n.* the temporary unemployment of workers moving from one job to another (p. 384)

full employment *n.* a level of unemployment in which none of the unemployment is caused by decreased economic activity; generally marked by an unemployment rate of 4 to 6 percent (p. 383)

future *n.* a contract to buy or sell a stock on a specified future date at a preset price (p. 333)

G

general partnership *n.* a partnership in which each partner shares the management of the business and is liable for all business debts and losses (p. 233)

geographic monopoly *n.* a monopoly that exists because there are no other producers or sellers within a certain region (p. 201)

gift tax *n.* a tax on money or property given by one living person to another (p. 425)

glass ceiling *n.* an unseen, artificial barrier to advancement that women and minorities sometimes face (p. 262)

global economy *n.* all the economic interactions that cross international boundaries (p. 61)

gold standard *n.* a system in which the basic monetary unit is equal to a set amount of gold (p. 299)

goods *n.* physical objects, such as food, clothing, and furniture, that can be purchased (p. 5)

government monopoly *n.* a monopoly that exists because the government either owns and runs the business or authorizes only one producer (p. 201)

grant-in-aid *n.* a transfer payment from the federal government to state or local governments (p. 432)

gross domestic product (GDP) *n.* the market value of all final goods and services produced within a nation in a given time period (p. 350)

gross national product (GNP) *n.* the market value of all final goods and services produced by a country in a given time period (p. 355)

H

hacking *n.* technique used by identity thieves to gather personal information using computers and related technology (p. 588)

horizontal merger *n.* the joining of two or more companies that offer the same or similar products or services (p. 243)

human capital *n.* the knowledge and skills that enable workers to be productive (p. 261)

human development index (HDI) *n.* a combination of a nation's real GDP per capita, life expectancy, adult literacy rate, and student enrollment figures that indicates what life is like in a specific country (p. 547)

hyperinflation *n.* a rapid, uncontrolled rate of inflation in excess of 50 percent (p. 398)

I

identity theft *n.* the use of someone else's personal information for criminal purposes (p. 588)

imperfect competition *n.* a market structure that lacks one or more of the conditions needed for perfect competition (p. 195)

imports *n.* goods or services produced in one country and purchased by another (p. 516)

incentive *n.* a benefit offered to encourage people to act in a certain way (pp. 12, 176)

incidence of a tax *n.* the final burden of a tax (p. 415)

income distribution *n.* the way income is divided among people in a nation (p. 390)

income effect *n.* a change in the amount of a good or service a consumer will buy because his or her income (and therefore purchasing power) changes (p. 107)

income inequality *n.* the unequal distribution of income (p. 390)

increasing returns *n.* a situation in which hiring new workers cause marginal product to increase (p. 139)

independent contractor *n.* someone who sells his or her services on a contract basis (p. 270)

individual income tax *n.* a tax based on an individual's income from all sources (p. 412)

industrial union *n.* an organization of workers with many different skills who work in the same industry (p. 274)

inelastic *n.* a situation in which quantity demanded or quantity supplied changes little as price changes (pp. 117, 155)

infant industries *n.* new industries that are often unable to compete against larger, more established competitors (p. 523)

infant mortality rate *n.* the number of children who die within the first year of life per 1,000 births (p. 547)

inferior goods *n.* goods that consumers demand less of when their incomes rise (p. 110)

inflation *n.* a sustained rise in the general price level, or a sustained fall in the purchasing power of money (p. 396)

inflation rate *n.* the rate of change in prices over a set period of time (p. 397)

infrastructure *n.* the basic set of support systems—such as power, communications, transportation, water, sanitation, and education systems—needed to keep an economy and society going (pp. 86, 545)

input costs *n.* the price of the resources needed to produce a good or service (p. 148)

insourcing *n.* the practice of foreign companies establishing operations in, and therefore bringing jobs to, the United States (p. 269)

interest *n.* a fee a bank pays for the use of money (p. 578)

International Monetary Fund (IMF) *n.* the international organization established to promote international monetary cooperation, foster economic growth, and provide temporary financial assistance to countries to help ease balance-of-payments adjustment (p. 559)

investment *n.* the use of income today in a way that allows for a future benefit (p. 318)

investment objective *n.* a financial goal that is used to determine if an investment is appropriate (p. 324)

J

junk bond *n.* a high-risk, high-yield corporate bond (p. 339)

K

Keynesian economics *n.* the idea, first advanced by John Maynard Keynes, that the government needs to stimulate aggregate demand in times of recession (p. 454)

L

labor *n.* all the human time, effort, and talent used to produce goods and services (p. 8)

labor input *n.* the size of the labor force multiplied by the length of the workweek (p. 371)

labor productivity *n.* the amount of goods and services a person can produce in a given time (p. 149)

labor union *n.* an organization of workers that seeks to improve wages, working conditions, fringe benefits, job security, and other work-related matters for its members (p. 274)

Laffer Curve *n.* a graph that illustrates how tax cuts affect tax revenues and economic growth (p. 459)

lagging indicators *n.* measures of economic performance that usually change after real gross domestic product changes (p. 364)

laissez faire *n.* the principle that the government should not interfere in the economy (p. 49)

land *n.* all the natural resources on or under the ground that are used to produce goods and services (p. 8)

landlord *n.* the owner of rental property (p. 609)

law of comparative advantage *n.* the law stating that countries gain when they produce items that they are most efficient at producing and that are at the lowest opportunity cost (p. 514)

law of demand *n.* states that when the price of a good or service goes down, quantity demanded increases, and when the prices go up, quantity demanded falls (p. 99)

law of diminishing marginal utility *n.* states that the marginal benefit from using each additional unit of a good or service during a given time period tends to decline as each is used (p. 106)

law of increasing opportunity costs *n.* states that as production switches from one product to another, increasingly more resources are needed to increase the production of the second product, which causes opportunity costs to rise (p. 21)

law of supply *n.* states that producers are willing to sell more of a good or service at a higher price than they are at a lower price (p. 131)

leading indicators *n.* measures of economic performance that usually change before real gross domestic product changes (p. 364)

lease *n.* a contract for renting an apartment, vehicle, or other item for a specific period of time (p. 609)

legal equality *n.* a situation in which everyone has the same economic rights under the law (p. 73)

less developed countries (LDCs) *n.* countries with lower GDPs, less well-developed industry, and lower standards of living; sometimes called emerging economies (p. 545)

life expectancy *n.* the average number of years a person could expect to live if current mortality trends were to continue for the rest of that person's life (p. 547)

limited liability *n.* a situation in which a business owner's liability for business debts and losses is limited (p. 240)

limited liability partnership (LLP) *n.* a partnership in which all partners are not responsible for the debts and other liabilities of the other partners (p. 233)

limited life *n.* a situation in which a business ceases to exist if the owner dies, retires, or leaves (p. 228)

limited partnership *n.* a partnership in which at least one partner is not involved in running the business and is liable only for the funds he or she invested (p. 233)

literacy rate *n.* the percentage of people older than 15 who can read and write (p. 547)

loan *n.* borrowed money that is usually repaid with interest (p. 582)

Lorenz curve *n.* a curve that shows the degree of income inequality in a nation (p. 391)

M

macroeconomic equilibrium *n.* the point where aggregate demand equals aggregate supply (p. 361)

macroeconomics *n.* the study of the behavior of the economy as a whole; concerned with large-scale economic activity (p. 27)

mandatory spending *n.* government spending that is required by current law (p. 428)

marginal benefit *n.* the benefit or satisfaction gained from using one more unit of a good or service (p. 16)

marginal cost *n.* the additional cost of producing or using one more unit of a good or service (pp. 16, 140)

marginal product *n.* the change in total output that results from adding one more worker (p. 138)

marginal revenue *n.* the money made from each additional unit sold (p. 142)

market *n.* any place or situation in which people buy and sell goods and services (p. 48)

market allocation *n.* an agreement among or between competing businesses to divide up a market (p. 216)

market demand curve *n.* a graph that shows data from a market demand schedule, or how much of a good or service all consumers are willing and able to purchase at each price (p. 102)

market demand schedule *n.* a table that shows how much of a good or service all consumers are willing and able to purchase at each price in a market (p. 100)

market division *see* market allocation

market economy *n.* an economic system based on individual choice and voluntary exchange (p. 39)

market equilibrium *n.* a situation in which the quantity supplied and the quantity demanded at a particular price are equal (p. 164)

market failure *n.* a situation in which people who are not part of a marketplace interaction benefit from it or pay part of its costs (p. 84)

market research *n.* the gathering and evaluation of information about consumer preferences for goods and services (p. 208)

market share *n.* a company's percent of total sales in a particular market (p. 209)

market structure *n.* an economic model of competition among businesses in the same industry (p. 192)

market supply curve *n.* a graph that shows data from a market supply schedule (p. 134)

market supply schedule *n.* how much of a good or service all producers in a market are willing and able to offer for sale at each price (p. 132)

maturity *n.* the date when a bond is due to be repaid (p. 338)

Medicaid *n.* a government-run medical insurance program for low-income people (p. 429)

Medicare *n.* a government-run, national health insurance program mainly for citizens over age 65 (p. 423)

medium of exchange *n.* a means through which goods and services can be exchanged (p. 288)

merger *n.* the combining of two or more companies to form a single company (p. 214)

microeconomics *n.* the study of the behavior of individual players—such as individuals, families, and businesses—in an economy (p. 27)

minimum balance requirement *n.* the amount of money needed in an account to avoid fees (p. 576)

minimum wage *n.* the lowest amount, established by law, that an employer may pay a worker for one hour of work (pp. 182, 262)

mixed economy *n.* an economic system that has elements of traditional, command, and market economies; the most common economic system (p. 58)

modified free enterprise economy *n.* a mixed economic system that includes some government protections, provisions, and regulations to adjust the free enterprise system (p. 80)

monetarism *n.* an economic theory that suggests that rapid changes in the money supply are the main cause of economic instability (p. 496)

monetary *adj.* of or relating to money (p. 474)

monetary policy *n.* the Federal Reserve's actions that change the money supply to influence the economy (p. 490)

money *n.* anything that people will accept as payment for goods and services (p. 288)

money market *n.* a market in which short-term financial assets are bought and sold (p. 322)

monopolistic competition *n.* a market structure in which many sellers offer similar, but not standardized, products to consumers (p. 206)

monopoly *n.* a market structure in which only one seller sells a product for which there are no close substitutes (p. 198)

monopsony *n.* market structure in which there are many sellers but only one large buyer (p. 212)

multifactor productivity *n.* the ratio between an industry's economic output and its labor and capital inputs (p. 372)

multinational corporation *n.* a corporation with branches in several countries (p. 243)

mutual fund *n.* an investment company that gathers money from individual investors and uses the money to purchase a range of financial assets (p. 320)

N

NAFTA *n.* the North America Free Trade Agreement, which ensures free trade throughout the continent and constitutes the largest free-trade zone in the world (p. 533)

national accounts *see* national income accounting

national bank *n.* a bank chartered by the national government (p. 299)

national debt *n.* the total amount of money that the federal government owes (p. 462)

national income (NI) *n.* the total income earned in a nation from the production of goods and services in a given time period (p. 355)

national income accounting *n.* a way of analyzing a country's economy using statistical measures of its income, spending, and output (p. 350)

nationalize *v.* to change from private ownership to government or public ownership (p. 61)

natural monopoly *n.* a market situation in which the costs of production are lowest when only one firm supplies a product or service (p. 201)

near money *n.* savings accounts and other similar time deposits that can be converted into cash relatively easily (p. 293)

needs *n.* things such as food, clothing, and shelter that are necessary for survival (p. 4)

negative externality *n.* an externality that costs people who were not involved in the original economic activity (p. 87)

net national product (NNP) *n.* the gross national product minus depreciation of capital stock—in other words, the value of final goods and services less the value of capital goods that became worn out during the year (p. 355)

nominal GDP *n.* the gross domestic product stated in terms of the current value of goods and services (p. 352)

nonmarket activities *n.* services that have potential economic value but are performed without charge (p. 354)

nonprice competition *n.* the use of factors other than price—such as style, service, advertising, or giveaways—to try to convince customers to buy from one producer rather than another (p. 207)

nonprofit organization *n.* an institution that acts like a business but exists to benefit society rather than to make a profit (p. 250)

normal goods *n.* goods that consumers demand more of when their incomes rise (p. 110)

normative economics *n.* a way of describing and explaining what economic behavior ought to be, not what it actually is (p. 29)

not-for-profit *see* nonprofit organization

O

oligopoly *n.* a market structure in which only a few sellers offer a similar product (p. 209)

OPEC *n.* the Organization of Petroleum Exporting Countries, a regional trade group (p. 535)

open market operations *n.* the Federal Reserve's sale and purchase of federal government securities; the monetary policy tool most used by the Federal Reserve to adjust the money supply (p. 490)

open opportunity *n.* the ability of everyone to enter and compete in the market of his or her own free choice (p. 73)

operating budget *n.* a plan for day-to-day expenses (p. 436)

opportunity cost *n.* the value of something that is given up by choosing one alternative over another (p. 14)

option *n.* a contract giving an investor the right to buy or sell stock at a future date at a preset price (p. 333)

outsourcing *n.* the practice of contracting with an outside company, often in a foreign country, to provide goods or services (p. 269)

overdraft *n.* a check or other withdrawal that exceeds the existing account balance (p. 576)

P

par value *n.* the amount that a bond issuer promises to pay the buyer at maturity (p. 338)

partnership *n.* a business co-owned by two or more people, or "partners," who agree on how responsibilities, profits, and losses should be divided (p. 232)

patent *n.* a legal registration of an invention or a process that gives the inventor the exclusive property rights to that invention or process for a certain number of years (p. 202)

peak *n.* the end of an expansion in the economy (p. 359); *see* business cycle

per capita gross domestic product *n.* a nation's GDP divided by its total population (p. 546)

perestroika *n.* Russian leader Mikhail Gorbachev's plan to gradually incorporate markets into the Soviet Union's command economy (p. 564)

perfect competition *n.* the ideal model of a market economy; the market structure in which none of the many well-informed and independent sellers or buyers has control over the price of a standardized good or service (p. 192)

personal income (PI) *n.* the annual income received by a country's people from all sources (p. 355)

phishing *n.* technique used by identity thieves to gather personal information through deceptive telephone calls (p. 588)

PIN *n.* personal identification number (p. 577)

positive economics *n.* a way of describing and explaining economics as it is (p. 29)

positive externality *n.* an externality that benefits people who were not involved in the original economic activity (p. 87)

poverty *n.* the situation in which a person's income and resources do not allow him or her to achieve a minimum standard of living (p. 388)

poverty line *see* poverty threshold

poverty rate *n.* the percentage of people living in households that have incomes below the poverty threshold (p. 389)

poverty threshold *n.* the official minimum income needed to pay for the basic expenses of living (p. 388)

predatory pricing *n.* the setting of prices below cost for a time to drive smaller competitors out of a market (p. 216)

preferred stock *n.* a share of ownership in a corporation giving the holder a share of profits but, in general, no voting rights (p. 331)

premium *n.* an amount paid for insurance (p. 596)

price ceiling *n.* an established maximum price that sellers may charge for a product (p. 180)

price fixing *n.* conspiring among or between businesses to set the prices of competing products (p. 216)

price floor *n.* an established minimum price that buyers must pay for a product (p. 182)

price maker *n.* a business that does not have to consider competitors when setting its prices (p. 198)

price taker *n.* a firm that must accept the market price set by the interaction of supply and demand (p. 193)

primary market *n.* a market for buying newly created financial assets directly from the issuing entity (p. 322)

prime rate *n.* the interest rate that banks charge their best customers (p. 491)

private company *n.* a corporation that controls who can buy or sell its stock (p. 238)

private property rights *n.* the rights of individuals and groups to own resources and businesses (p. 48)

private sector *n.* the part of the economy that is owned by individuals or businesses (p. 432)

privatization *n.* the process of transferring state-owned property and businesses to individuals (p. 563)

privatize *v.* to change from government or public ownership to private ownership (p. 61)

producer *n.* a person who makes goods or provides services (p. 5)

producer price index (PPI) *n.* a measure of changes in wholesale prices (p. 397)

product differentiation *n.* the attempt to distinguish a product from similar products (p. 206)

product market *n.* the market in which goods and services are bought and sold (p. 52)

production possibilities curve (PPC) *n.* a graph used to illustrate the impact of scarcity on an economy (p. 18)

productivity *n.* the amount of output produced from a set amount of inputs (p. 372)

productivity, labor *see* labor productivity

profit *n.* the financial gain a seller makes from a business transaction (p. 49); the money left over after the costs of producing a product are subtracted from the income gained by selling that product (p. 78)

profit-maximizing output *n.* the point in production at which a business has reached its highest level of profit (p. 143)

profit motive *n.* the incentive that encourages people and organizations to improve their material well-being by seeking to gain from economic activities (p. 73)

progressive tax *n.* a tax that places a higher percentage rate of taxation on high-income earners than on low-income earners (p. 412)

property tax *n.* a tax based on the value of an individual's or a business's assets (p. 412)

proportional tax *n.* a tax that takes the same percentage of income from all taxpayers regardless of income level (p. 412)

protectionism *n.* the use of trade barriers between nations to protect domestic industries (p. 523)

protective tariff *n.* a tax on imported goods to protect domestic goods (p. 521)

public company *n.* a corporation that issues stock that can be freely traded (p. 238)

public disclosure *n.* a policy requiring businesses to reveal product information to consumers (p. 217)

public goods *n.* goods and services provided by the government and consumed by the public as a group (p. 84)

public transfer payment *n.* a transfer payment in which the government transfers income from taxpayers to recipients who do not provide anything in return (p. 89)

pure competition *see* perfect competition

Q

quota *n.* a limit on the amount of a product that can be imported (p. 520)

R

rational expectations theory *n.* the theory that states that individuals and business firms expect changes in fiscal policy will have particular effects and take action to protect their interests against those effects (p. 452)

rationing *n.* a system in which the government allocates goods and services using factors other than price (p. 183)

real GDP *n.* the gross domestic product corrected for changes in prices from year to year (p. 352)

real GDP per capita *n.* the real gross domestic product divided by total population (p. 369)

recession *n.* a prolonged economic contraction lasting two or more quarters (six months or more) (p. 359)

regressive tax *n.* a tax that takes a larger percentage of income from low-income earners than from high-income earners (p. 412)

regulation *n.* a set of rules or laws designed to control business behavior (pp. 150, 214)

representative money *n.* paper money that is backed by something tangible (p. 291)

required reserve ratio (RRR) *n.* the fraction of a bank's deposits, determined by the Federal Reserve, that it must keep in reserve so that it can loan out money (p. 484)

return *n.* the profit or loss made on an investment (p. 327)

revenue *n.* government income from taxes and nontax sources (p. 410)

revenue tariff *n.* a tax on imports specifically to raise money; are rarely used today (p. 521)

right-to-work laws *n.* legislation that makes it illegal to require workers to join unions (p. 279)

risk *n.* the possibility for loss on an investment (p. 327)

S

safety net *n.* government programs designed to protect people from economic hardships (p. 89)

sales tax *n.* a tax based on the value of goods or services at the time of sale (p. 412)

savings *n.* income not used for consumption (p. 318)

scarcity *n.* a situation that exists when there are not enough resources to meet human wants (p. 4)

seasonal unemployment *n.* unemployment linked to seasonal work (p. 384)

secondary market *n.* a market in which financial assets are resold (p. 322)

service *n.* work that one person does for another for payment (p. 5)

shadow economy *see* underground economy

share *n.* part of the stock of a corporation (p. 238); *see* stock

shock therapy *n.* an economic program involving the abrupt shift from a command economy to a free-market economy (p. 563)

shortage *n.* a situation in which demand is greater than supply, usually the result of prices being set too low (p. 167)

shoulder surfing *n.* technique used by identity thieves to gather personal information as you disclose private information in public (p. 588)

socialism *n.* an economic system in which the government owns some or all of the factors of production (p. 43)

Social Security *n.* a federal program to aid older citizens, orphaned children, and the disabled (p. 423)

sole proprietorship *n.* a business owned and controlled by one person (p. 226)

spamming *n.* technique used by identity thieves to gather personal information through deceptive e-mails (p. 588)

special economic zone (SEZ) *n.* a geographic region that has economic laws that are different from a country's usual economic laws, with the goal of increasing foreign investment (p. 567)

specialization *n.* a situation that occurs when individuals or businesses concentrate their efforts in the areas in which they have an advantage for increased productivity and profit (pp. 50, 138, 510)

spending multiplier effect *n.* a situation in which a small change in spending eventually results in a much larger change in GDP (p. 455)

stabilization programs *n.* programs that require troubled nations to carry out reforms such as reducing foreign trade deficits and external debt, eliminating price controls, closing inefficient public enterprises, and slashing budget deficits (p. 559)

stagflation *n.* a period during which prices rise at the same time that there is a slowdown in business activity (p. 359)

standardized product *n.* a product that consumers consider identical in all essential features to other products in the same market (p. 192)

standard of value *n.* the yardstick of economic worth in the exchange process (p. 289)

start-up costs *n.* the expenses that a new business must pay to enter a market and begin selling to consumers (p. 209)

state bank *n.* a bank chartered by a state government (p. 296)

statistics *n.* numerical data (p. 24)

stock *n.* shares of ownership in a corporation (p. 238)

stockbroker *n.* an agent who buys and sells securities for customers (p. 332)

stock exchange *n.* a secondary market where securities are bought and sold (p. 330)

stock index *n.* an instrument used to measure and report the change in prices of a set of stocks (p. 334)

stored-value card *n.* a card that represents money that the card holder has on deposit with the card issuer (p. 308)

store of value *n.* something that holds its value over time (p. 289)

strike *n.* a work stoppage used to gain negotiating power while attempting to convince an employer to improve wages, working conditions, or other work-related matters (p. 274)

structural unemployment *n.* unemployment that exists when the available jobs do not match the skills of available workers (p. 384)

subsidy *n.* a government payment that helps cover the cost of an economic activity that can benefit the public as a whole (p. 88)

substitutes *n.* products that can be used in place of other products to satisfy consumer wants (p. 112)

substitution effect *n.* the pattern of behavior that occurs when consumers react to a change in price of a product by buying a substitute product that offers a better relative value (p. 107)

supply *n.* the willingness and ability of a producer to produce and sell a product (p. 130)

supply curve *n.* a graph that shows data from a supply schedule (p. 134)

supply schedule *n.* a table that shows how much of a good or service an individual producer is willing and able to offer for sale at each price (p. 132)

supply-side fiscal policy *n.* a plan designed to provide incentives to producers to increase aggregate supply (p. 458)

surplus *n.* a situation in which supply is greater than demand, usually the result of prices being set too high (p. 167)

T

tariff *n.* a fee charged for goods brought into a country from another country (p. 521)

tax *n.* a mandatory payment to a government (p. 410)

taxable income *n.* the portion of income subject to taxation after all deductions and exemptions (pp. 421, 604)

tax assessor *n.* a government official who determines the value of property to be taxed (p. 437)

tax base *n.* a form of wealth—such as income, property, goods, or services—that is subject to taxes (p. 412)

tax incentive *n.* the use of taxes to encourage or discourage certain economic behaviors (p. 417)

tax return *n.* a form used to report income and taxes owed to the government (p. 421)

technological monopoly *n.* a monopoly that exists because a firm controls a manufacturing method, invention, or type of technology (p. 201)

technology *n.* the application of scientific methods and innovations to production (p. 149)

telecommuting *n.* the practice of doing office work in a location other than the office (p. 270)

telework *see* telecommuting

temp, temps, temping *see* contingent employment

thrift institution *n.* a financial institution that serves savers (p. 478)

tight-money policy *see* contractionary monetary policy

total cost *n.* the sum of fixed and variable costs (p. 140)

total revenue *n.* the income a business receives from selling its products (pp. 122, 142)

total revenue test *n.* a method of measuring elasticity by comparing the total revenue a business would receive when offering its product at various prices (p. 122)

trade barrier *n.* any law passed to limit free trade between nations (p. 520)

trade deficit *n.* an unfavorable balance of trade that occurs when a nation imports more than it exports (p. 529)

trade-off *n.* the alternative someone gives up when making an economic choice (p. 14)

trade surplus *n.* a favorable balance of trade that occurs when a nation exports more than it imports (p. 529)

trade union *see* labor union

trade war *n.* a succession of trade barriers between nations (p. 522)

trade-weighted value of the dollar *n.* a measure of the international value of the dollar that determines if the dollar is strong or weak as measured against another currency (p. 528)

traditional economy *n.* an economic system in which people make economic decisions based on customs and beliefs that have been handed down from one generation to the next (p. 38)

transfer payment *n.* money distributed to individuals who do not provide goods or services in return (pp. 89, 432)

transitional economy *n.* a country that has moved (or is moving) from a command economy to a market economy (p. 545)

Treasury bill (T bill) *n.* a short-term bond that matures in less than one year (p. 464)

Treasury bond *n.* a long-term bond that matures in 30 years (p. 464)

Treasury note *n.* an intermediate-term bond that matures in between two and ten years (p. 464)

trough *n.* the end of a contraction in the economy (p. 359); *see* business cycle

trust *n.* a group of firms combined in order to reduce competition in an industry (p. 214)

trust fund *n.* a fund held for a specific purpose to be expended at a future date (p. 465)

U

underemployed *n.* people employed part-time who want to work full-time, or those who work at a job below their skill level (p. 383)

underground economy *n.* market activities that go unreported because they are illegal or because those involved want to avoid taxation (p. 354)

underutilization *n.* the condition in which economic resources are not being used to their full potential, resulting in fewer goods and services (p. 20)

unemployment rate *n.* the percentage of the labor force that is jobless and actively looking for work (p. 382)

union *see* labor union

union shop *n.* a business in which workers are required to join a union within a set time period after being hired (p. 279)

unit elastic *adj.* relating to a situation in which the percentage change in price and quantity demanded are the same (p. 118)

unlimited liability *n.* a situation in which a business owner is responsible for all the losses and debts of a business (p. 228)

unlimited life *n.* a situation in which a corporation continues to exist even after a change in ownership (p. 240)

user fee *n.* money charged for the use of a good or service (p. 425)

utility *n.* the benefit or satisfaction gained from using a good or service (p. 12)

V

variable costs *n.* business costs that vary with the level of production output (p. 140)

vertical merger *n.* the combining of two or more businesses involved in different steps of producing or marketing a product or service (p. 243)

voluntary exchange *n.* a trade in which the parties involved anticipate that the benefits will outweigh the cost (p. 49)

voluntary export restraint (VER) *n.* a self-imposed limit on exports to certain countries to avoid quotas or tariffs (p. 521)

W

wage and price controls *n.* government limits on increases in wages and prices (p. 501)

wage-price spiral *n.* a cycle that begins with increased wages, which lead to higher production costs, which in turn result in higher prices, which result in demands for even higher wages (p. 400)

wage rate *n.* the established rate of pay for a specific job or work performed (p. 261)

wages *n.* the payments workers receive in return for work (p. 258)

wants *n.* desires that can be satisfied by consuming a good or service (p. 4)

welfare *n.* government economic and social programs that provide assistance to the needy (p. 392)

withholding *n.* the money taken from a worker's pay before the worker receives the pay (p. 421)

workfare *n.* a program that requires welfare recipients to do some kind of work in return for their benefits (p. 393)

World Bank *n.* a financial institution that provides loans, policy advice, and technical assistance to low and middle income countries to reduce poverty (p. 559)

World Trade Organization (WTO) *n.* an organization that negotiates and administers trade agreements, resolves trade disputes, monitors trading policies, and supports developing countries (p. 535)

Y

yield *n.* the annual rate of return on a bond (p. 338)

Spanish Glossary

A

absolute advantage [ventaja absoluta] *n.* capacidad de un país para hacer un producto más eficientemente que otro país (pág. 513)

aggregate demand [demanda agregada] *n.* suma de las demandas totales existentes en la economía (pág. 360)

aggregate supply [oferta agregada] *n.* suma de las ofertas totales existentes en la economía (pág. 360)

antitrust legislation [legislación antimonopolio] *n.* leyes que definen los monopolios y dan al gobierno el poder de controlarlos o disolverlos (pág. 214)

appropriations [asignaciones] *n.* cantidades fijas de dinero destinadas a fines determinados (pág. 431)

authoritarian [autoritario] *adj.* lo que exige una lealtad y una obediencia absolutas ante la autoridad (pág. 43)

automated teller machine (ATM) [cajero automático (ATM)] *n.* dispositivo electrónico que permite a los clientes de un banco hacer transacciones sin ver al personal del banco (pág. 308)

automatic stabilizer [estabilizador automático] *n.* característica de la política fiscal que actúa automáticamente para mantener estable la economía (pág. 447)

B

balanced budget [presupuesto balanceado] *n.* presupuesto en el que el total de ingresos del gobierno es igual al total de gastos del gobierno (pág. 436)

balance of payments [balanza de pagos] *n.* registro de todas las transacciones ocurridas entre las personas, las empresas y las unidades gubernamentales de un país y las del resto del mundo (pág. 529)

balance of trade [balanza de comercio] *n.* diferencia entre el valor de las exportaciones y el de las importaciones de un país (pág. 529)

bank exam [inspección bancaria] *n.* auditoría, realizada por la Reserva Federal, de las prácticas financieras de un banco (pág. 481)

bank holding company [compañía tenedora de acciones bancarias] *n.* compañía que posee más de un banco (pág. 481)

barrier to entry [barrera de entrada] *n.* todo factor que impide que una empresa entre en un mercado (pág. 198)

barter [trueque] *n.* intercambio de bienes y servicios sin utilizar dinero (pág. 288)

bear market [mercado a la baja (mercado "oso")] *n.* situación en la que los precios del mercado de valores bajan constantemente con el tiempo (pág. 335)

binding arbitration [arbitraje vinculante] *n.* proceso por el que un tercero imparcial resuelve los conflictos entre la dirección de una empresa y los sindicatos (pág. 280)

black market [mercado negro] *n.* compra o venta ilegal de bienes o servicios, violando los controles de precios o el racionamiento (pág. 183)

Board of Governors [Junta de Gobernadores] *n.* junta de siete miembros nombrados que supervisa las operaciones del Sistema de la Reserva Federal y establece la política monetaria (pág. 476)

bond [bono] *n.* contrato emitido por una sociedad anónima que promete reembolsar el dinero prestado, más intereses, según las fechas establecidas (pág. 240)

bounced check [cheque rebotado] véase overdraft [sobregiro]

break-even point [punto de equilibrio] *n.* situación en la que el total de costos y el total de ingresos son iguales (pág. 142)

budget [presupuesto] *n.* plan para asignar el ahorro y el gasto del ingreso (pág. 574)

budget deficit [déficit presupuestario] *n.* situación en la que los gastos del gobierno son mayores que los ingresos (pág. 462)

budget surplus [superávit presupuestario] *n.* situación en la que los ingresos del gobierno son mayores que los gastos (pág. 462)

bull market [mercado alcista (mercado "toro")] *n.* situación en la que los precios del mercado de valores suben constantemente con el tiempo (pág. 335)

business cycle [ciclo económico] *n.* serie de períodos de ascenso y descenso de la actividad económica, medida por los aumentos o las disminuciones del producto interior bruto real (pág. 358)

business organization [organización comercial] *n.* empresa que produce bienes o presta servicios, generalmente para obtener ganancias (pág. 226)

business structure [estructura comercial] véase business organization [organización comercial]

C

capital [capital] *n.* todos los recursos que se crean y utilizan para producir y distribuir bienes y servicios (pág. 8)

capital budget [presupuesto de capital] *n.* plan referente a los principales gastos o inversiones (pág. 436)

capital deepening [intensificación del uso del capital] *n.* aumento de la razón entre el capital y el trabajo (pág. 371)

capital flight [fuga de capitales] *n.* situación en la que capitales de un país se invierten fuera de dicho país (pág. 558)

capital gain [ganancias de capital] *n.* ganancias obtenidas de la venta de valores (pág. 330)

capitalism [capitalismo] *n.* sistema económico basado en la propiedad privada de los factores de producción (pág. 49)

capital market [mercado de capitales] *n.* mercado en el que se venden y compran activos financieros a largo plazo (pág. 322)

cartel [cártel] *n.* organización formal de vendedores o productores que regulan la producción, la fijación de precios y la comercialización de un producto (págs. 198, 535)

cease and desist order [orden de cese de actividades comerciales] *n.* decisión judicial que obliga a una compañía a dejar de realizar una práctica comercial injusta (pág. 217)

central bank [banco central] *n.* principal autoridad monetaria de un país (pág. 474)

centrally planned economy [economía de planificación centralizada] *n.* sistema en el que los dirigentes del país toman todas las decisiones económicas (pág. 42)

change in demand [cambio en la demanda] *n.* situación en la que un cambio en el mercado incita a los consumidores a comprar una cantidad diferente de un bien o de un servicio a cada precio (pág. 109)

change in quantity demanded [cambio en la cantidad demandada] *n.* cambio en la cantidad de un producto que los consumidores comprarán debido a un cambio en el precio (pág. 108)

change in quantity supplied [cambio en la cantidad ofertada] *n.* aumento o disminución de la cantidad de un bien o de un servicio que los productores están dispuestos a vender debido a un cambio en el precio (pág. 146)

change in supply [cambio en la oferta] *n.* situación en la que un cambio en el mercado incita a los productores a ofrecer para su venta una cantidad diferente a cada precio (pág. 148)

check clearing [compensación de cheques] *n.* servicio proporcionado por la Reserva Federal para registrar las entradas y las salidas de los clientes de los bancos (pág. 480)

circular flow model [modelo de flujo circular] *n.* visualización de todas las interacciones de una economía de mercado (pág. 52)

civilian labor force [fuerza laboral civil] *n.* personas de 16 años o mayores que trabajan o que buscan activamente un trabajo y están en condiciones para trabajar (pág. 266)

claim [reclamación] *n.* petición presentada ante una compañía de seguros para recibir un pago sobre una pérdida asegurada (pág. 596)

closed shop [compañía de sindicación obligatoria] *n.* compañía en la que el empleador sólo puede contratar miembros del sindicato (pág. 279)

coincident indicators [indicadores coincidentes] *n.* medidas del rendimiento económico que generalmente cambian al mismo tiempo que cambia el producto interior bruto real (pág. 364)

collective bargaining [negociación colectiva] *n.* proceso de negociación entre una empresa y sus empleados sindicalizados para establecer los salarios y mejorar las condiciones de trabajo (pág. 280)

command economy [economía autoritaria] *n.* sistema económico en el que el gobierno toma todas las decisiones económicas (pág. 39)

commodity money [dinero-mercancía] *n.* dinero que tiene un valor intrínsico basado en el material del que se compone (pág. 291)

common stock [acciones ordinarias] *n.* participación en la propiedad de una sociedad anónima que da al titular derecho a voto y parte de las ganancias (pág. 331)

communism [comunismo] *n.* sistema económico en el que no existe la propiedad privada y hay poca o ninguna libertad política (pág. 43)

comparative advantage [ventaja comparativa] *n.* capacidad de un país para producir algo a un costo de oportunidad más bajo que el de otro país (pág. 513)

competition [competencia] *n.* esfuerzo de dos o más personas que actúan independientemente por obtener clientes ofreciéndoles la mejor opción (pág. 49)

competitive pricing [fijación de precios competitivos] *n.* situación en la que los productores venden bienes y servicios a precios que intentan el mejor equilibrio entre dos deseos: obtener las mayores ganancias y atraer a los clientes de los productores rivales (pág. 174)

complements [complementarios] *n.* productos que se usan conjuntamente, de manera que el aumento y la disminución de la demanda de uno produzca el aumento o la disminución de la demanda del otro (pág. 112)

conglomerate [conglomerado] *n.* empresa compuesta de compañías que producen bienes o servicios no relacionados (pág. 243)

consumer [consumidor] *n.* persona que compra bienes o servicios para su uso personal (pág. 5)

consumer price index (CPI) [índice de precios al consumo (IPC)] *v* medida porcentual de los cambios en los precios de una cesta de los bienes y los servicios que los consumidores compran frecuentemente (pág. 396)

consumer sovereignty [soberanía del consumidor] *n.* idea de que los consumidores tienen el control definitivo sobre lo que se produce ya que son libres para comprar lo que quieren y para rechazar productos que no quieren (pág. 50)

contingent employment [empleo contingente] *n.* trabajo temporal o a tiempo parcial (pág. 270)

contract [contrato] *n.* acuerdo formal con fuerza jurídica (pág. 598)

contraction [contracción] *n.* reducción de la actividad económica (pág. 359); *véase* business cycle [ciclo económico]

contractionary fiscal policy [política fiscal restrictiva] *n.* plan para reducir la demanda agregada y desacelerar la economía durante un período de expansión económica demasiado rápido (pág. 446)

contractionary monetary policy [política monetaria restrictiva] *n.* plan para reducir la cantidad de dinero en circulación; también llamada política de dinero escaso (pág. 492)

cooperative [cooperativa] *n.* tipo de negocio dirigido a favor del beneficio compartido de los propietarios, que son también los clientes (pág. 250)

co-pay [copago] *n.* cantidad que el asegurado debe pagar cuando una persona asegurada recibe atención médica (pág. 596)

corporate income tax [impuesto de sociedades anónimas] *n.* impuesto basado en las ganancias de una sociedad anónima (pág. 412)

corporation [sociedad anónima] *n.* empresa que pertenece a los titulares de acciones, o accionistas, que poseen los derechos a las ganancias de la compañía pero cuya responsabilidad es limitada respecto a las deudas y pérdidas de la compañía (pág. 238)

cosigner [cofirmante, aval, avalista] *n.* persona que asume la responsabilidad de la deuda si el prestatario no reembolsa el préstamo (pág. 583)

cost-benefit analysis [análisis costo-beneficio] *n.* práctica de examinar los costos y los beneficios previstos de una opción, como ayuda en la toma de decisiones (pág. 15)

cost-push inflation [inflación de costos] *n.* situación en la que el aumento de los costos de producción hace subir los precios (pág. 399)

Council of Economic Advisers [Consejo de Consejeros Económicos] *n.* grupo de tres miembros que aconseja al Presidente sobre la política fiscal y otros asuntos económicos (pág. 452)

coupon rate [tasa de cupón] *n.* tasa de interés que el titular de un bono obtiene cada año hasta que vence el bono (pág. 338)

craft union [sindicato gremial] *n.* organización de trabajadores con aptitudes similares que trabajan en diferentes industrias para diferentes empleadores (pág. 274)

credit [crédito] *n.* práctica de comprar bienes o servicios en el presente y pagarlos en el futuro (pág. 582)

credit report [informe crediticio] *n.* documento emitido por una agencia de informes crediticios que explica detalladamente el historial de crédito de un consumidor (pág. 586)

credit score [calificación del riesgo crediticio] *n.* número que resume la reputación crediticia de un consumidor (pág. 586)

crowding-out effect [efecto de exclusión] *n.* situación en la que el gobierno supera la oferta de las tasas de interés de bonos privados para obtener fondos prestables (pág. 466)

currency [moneda] *n.* papel moneda y monedas metálicas (págs. 293, 475)

customs duty [derecho arancelario] *n.* impuesto aplicado en Estados Unidos a los bienes importados (pág. 425)

customs unions [uniones aduaneras] *n.* acuerdos que eliminan las barreras al comercio entre los miembros y establecen aranceles uniformes para los no miembros (pág. 532)

cyclical unemployment [desempleo cíclico] *n.* desempleo causado por la parte del ciclo económico que presenta una actividad económica reducida (pág. 384)

D

debit card [tarjeta de débito] *n.* tarjeta que se puede usar como tarjeta de cajero automático (ATM) para retirar dinero o como cheque para hacer compras (pág. 308)

debt restructuring [reestructuración de la deuda] *n.* método que utilizan los países con obligaciones de deuda pendientes para alterar los términos de los acuerdos de la deuda, a fin de conseguir alguna ventaja (pág. 559)

deduction [deducible] *n.* cantidad que el asegurado paga antes de que pague la compañía aseguradora (pág. 596)

default [incumplimiento] *n.* condición que se presenta cuando un país no puede pagar los intereses o el capital sobre un préstamo (pág. 559)

deficit spending [gastos deficitarios] *n.* práctica del gobierno de gastar más de lo que obtiene en ingresos en un determinado año fiscal (pág. 462)

deflation [deflación] *n.* disminución del nivel general de precios (pág. 398)

demand [demanda] *n.* deseo de obtener algún bien o servicio y la capacidad para pagarlo (pág. 98)

demand curve [curva de la demanda] *n.* gráfica que muestra una tabla de demanda, o la cantidad de un bien o de un servicio que una persona puede y está dispuesta a comprar a cada precio (pág. 102)

demand deposits [depósitos a la vista] *n.* cuentas corrientes, llamadas así porque las cuentas corrientes pueden convertirse en dinero "a la vista" (pág. 293)

demand-pull inflation [inflación de demanda] *n.* condición que se presenta cuando la demanda total sube más rápido que la producción de bienes y servicios (pág. 399)

demand schedule [tabla de demanda] *n.* tabla que muestra la cantidad de un bien o de un servicio que una persona puede y está dispuesta a comprar a cada precio (pág. 100)

demand-side fiscal policy [política fiscal sobre la demanda] *n.* plan para estimular la demanda agregada (pág. 454)

deposit multiplier formula [fórmula del multiplicador de depósitos] *n.* fórmula matemática que indica cuánto aumentará la oferta monetaria tras realizar un depósito inicial de dinero en un banco (pág. 485)

depreciate [depreciar] *v.* disminuir de valor (pág. 590)

depression [depresión] *n.* período prolongado con un alto nivel de desempleo y una reducción de la actividad económica (pág. 359)

deregulation [desregulación] *n.* reducción o eliminación de la vigilancia y el control de las empresas por parte del gobierno (pág. 218)

derived demand [demanda derivada] *n.* demanda de un producto o un recurso que se basa en su aportación al producto final (pág. 259)

developed nations [países desarrollados] *n.* países que tienen una economía de mercado, un nivel de vida relativamente alto, un PIB alto, industrialización, propiedad privada generalizada y un gobierno estable y efectivo (pág. 544)

differentiated product [producto diferenciado] *véase* product differentiation [diferenciación de productos]

diminishing returns [rentabilidad decreciente] *n.* situación en la que nuevos trabajadores hacen que el producto marginal aumente pero a un ritmo decreciente (pág. 139)

discount rate [tasa de descuento] *n.* tasa de interés que aplica la Reserva Federal cuando presta dinero a otros bancos (pág. 491)

discretionary fiscal policy [política fiscal discrecional] *n.* medidas que toma el gobierno federal a voluntad para corregir la inestabilidad económica (pág. 446)

discretionary spending [gastos discrecionales] *n.* gastos que el gobierno debe autorizar cada año (pág. 428)

disequilibrium [desequilibrio] *n.* situación en la que la cantidad ofertada y la cantidad demandada no se encuentran en equilibrio (pág. 169)

disposable personal income (DPI) [renta personal disponible (RPD)] *n.* renta personal menos los impuestos (pág. 355)

diversification [diversificación] *n.* práctica de distribuir las inversiones entre diferentes activos financieros para maximizar la rentabilidad y limitar el riesgo (pág. 327)

dividend [dividendo] *n.* aquella parte de las ganancias de una sociedad anónima que la compañía paga a los accionistas (pág. 238)

dumping [dumping] *n.* venta de un producto en otro país a un precio más bajo del que tiene en el mercado de origen (pág. 521)

Dumpster diving [buceo en la basura] *n.* técnica utilizada por los ladrones de identidad para recoger información personal en la basura (pág. 584)

E

easy-money policy [política de dinero barato] *véase* expansionary monetary policy [política monetaria expansiva]

economic cycle [ciclo económico] *véase* business cycle [ciclo económico]

economic growth [crecimiento económico] *n.* aumento del producto interior bruto real de un país (pág. 358)

economic interdependence [interdependencia económica] *n.* situación en la que los productores de un país dependen de otros para conseguir bienes y servicios que ellos no producen (pág. 510)

economic model [modelo económico] *n.* representación simplificada de las actividades, sistemas o problemas económicos (pág. 18)

economics [economía] *n.* estudio de cómo las personas y la sociedad satisfacen sus deseos ilimitados con recursos limitados (pág. 4)

economic system [sistema económico] *n.* forma en que la sociedad utiliza sus recursos escasos para satisfacer los deseos ilimitados de su población (pág. 38)

economies of scale [economías de escala] *n.* situación en la que el costo promedio de producción disminuye al crecer el productor (pág. 201)

economize [economizar] *v.* tomar decisiones según lo que se cree la mejor combinación de costos y beneficios (pág. 12)

efficiency [eficiencia] *n.* condición en la que los recursos económicos se utilizan para producir la cantidad máxima de bienes y servicios (pág. 20)

elastic [elástica] *adj.* situación en la que un cambio en el precio, ya sea para más o para menos, produce un cambio relativamente más grande en la cantidad demandada o en la cantidad ofertada (págs. 117, 154)

elasticity of demand [elasticidad de la demanda] *n.* medida de la reacción de los consumidores ante los cambios de los precios en el mercado (pág. 117)

elasticity of supply [elasticidad de la oferta] *n.* medida de la reacción de los productores ante los cambios de los precios en el mercado (pág. 154)

embargo [embargo] *n.* ley que prohíbe la mayor parte o todo el comercio con un país determinado (pág. 521)

entitlement [derechos sociales adquiridos] *n.* programa de asistencia social que tiene determinados requisitos de admisión (pág. 428)

entrepreneurship [capacidad empresarial] *n.* combinación de visión, aptitud, ingenio y disposición de asumir riesgos, necesaria para crear y dirigir nuevas empresas (pág. 9)

equilibrium price [precio de equilibrio] *n.* precio al que la cantidad demandada equivale a la cantidad ofertada (pág. 164)

equilibrium wage [salario de equilibrio] *n.* salario en el que la cantidad de trabajadores demandados equivale a la cantidad de trabajadores ofertados; precio de mercado de la mano de obra (pág. 258)

estate tax [impuesto de sucesiones] *n.* impuesto aplicado a los activos de una persona que ha muerto (pág. 425)

European Union (EU) [Unión Europea (UE)] *n.* unión económica y política de los países europeos, establecida en 1993 (pág. 532)

euro [euro] *n.* moneda única de la Unión Europea (pág. 533)

excise tax [impuesto sobre consumos] *n.* impuesto aplicado a la producción o a la venta de un bien o un servicio determinado (págs. 149, 425)

expansion [expansión] *n.* aumento de la actividad económica (pág. 358); *véase* business cycle [ciclo económico]

expansionary fiscal policy [política fiscal expansiva] *n.* plan para aumentar la demanda agregada y estimular una economía débil (pág. 446)

expansionary monetary policy [política monetaria expansiva] *n.* plan para aumentar la cantidad de dinero en circulación; también llamada política de dinero barato (pág. 492)

exports [exportaciones] *n.* bienes o servicios producidos en un país y vendidos a otros países (pág. 516)

externality [externalidad] *n.* efecto secundario de una transacción que afecta a alguien que no sea el productor o el comprador (pág. 87)

F

factor market [mercado de factores] *n.* mercado para los factores de producción: tierra, trabajo, capital y capacidad empresarial (pág. 52)

factors of production [factores de producción] *n.* recursos económicos necesarios para producir bienes y servicios (pág. 8)

federal budget [presupuesto federal] *n.* plan para gastar los ingresos obtenidos mediante los impuestos federales (pág. 431)

federal funds rate (FFR) [tasa de interés para fondos federales (TFF)] *n.* interés al que una institución de depósitos presta por un día fondos disponibles a otra institución de depósitos (pág. 490)

Federal Insurance Contributions Act (FICA) [Ley de Contribuciones al Seguro Federal] *n.* impuesto sobre nóminas que proporciona cobertura a las personas mayores, a los desempleados por incapacidad y a los familiares supervivientes de asalariados que han muerto (pág. 423)

Federal Open Market Committee (FOMC) [Comité Federal del Mercado Abierto] *n.* junta del Sistema de la Reserva Federal que supervisa la venta y la compra de valores del gobierno federal (pág. 477)

Federal Reserve System [Sistema de la Reserva Federal] *n.* banco central de Estados Unidos, llamado comúnmente la Fed (pág. 474)

fiat money [dinero fiduciario] *n.* dinero que no tiene respaldo tangible pero cuyo valor es declarado por el gobierno y aceptado por los ciudadanos (pág. 291)

filing status [estado personal] *n.* para la declaración de impuestos, se basa en el estado civil o en las cargas familiares (pág. 604)

financial asset [activo financiero] *n.* derecho de la propiedad del prestatario (pág. 319)

financial intermediary [intermediario financiero] *n.* institución que reúne fondos de los ahorradores e invierte estos fondos en activos financieros (pág. 319)

financial market [mercado financiero] *n.* situación en la que los compradores y los vendedores intercambian activos financieros (pág. 319)

financial system [sistema financiero] *n.* todas las instituciones que ayudan a transferir fondos entre los ahorradores y los inversionistas (pág. 318)

fiscal [fiscal] *adj.* lo relacionado a los ingresos y a los gastos del gobierno (pág. 446)

fiscal policy [política fiscal] *n.* uso que hace el gobierno federal de los impuestos y los gastos para afectar a la economía (pág. 446)

fiscal year [año fiscal] *n.* período de 12 meses en el que una organización planifica sus gastos (pág. 431)

fixed costs [costos fijos] *n.* gastos en los que incurren los propietarios de empresas, independientemente de cuánto produzcan (pág. 140)

fixed rate of exchange [tasa de cambio fija] *n.* sistema en el que la divisa de un país es fija o constante respecto a las otras divisas (pág. 526)

flexible exchange rate [tasa de cambio flexible] *n.* sistema en el que la tasa de cambio para una divisa fluctúa al fluctuar la oferta y la demanda de la divisa; también llamada tasa flotante (pág. 527)

focus group [grupo focal] *n.* discusión dirigida por un moderador y realizada con pequeños grupos de consumidores (pág. 208)

foreign exchange market [mercado de divisas] *n.* mercado en el que se compran y venden divisas de diferentes países (pág. 526)

foreign exchange rate [tasa de cambio de divisas] *n.* precio de una divisa expresado en las divisas de otros países (pág. 526)

franchise [franquicia] *n.* negocio formado por negocios parcialmente independientes que ofrecen todos los mismos productos o servicios (pág. 248)

franchisee [franquiciado] *n.* negocio parcialmente independiente que paga un cargo por el derecho a vender en una determinada zona los productos o servicios de la compañía matriz (pág. 248)

free contract [contrato libre] *n.* situación en la que las personas deciden por sí solas qué contratos legales aceptar (pág. 73)

free-enterprise system [sistema de libre mercado] *n.* otro nombre del capitalismo, sistema económico basado en la propiedad privada de los recursos productivos (pág. 70)

free rider [beneficiario gratuito] *n.* persona que no paga un bien o un servicio pero que se beneficia de él cuando se le da (pág. 85)

free-trade zone [zona de libre comercio] *n.* determinada región en la que el comercio entre los países se realiza sin aranceles proteccionistas (pág. 532)

frictional unemployment [desempleo friccional] *n.* desempleo temporal de los trabajadores que pasan de un puesto de trabajo a otro (pág. 384)

full employment [pleno empleo] *n.* nivel de desempleo en el que ninguna parte del desempleo se debe a la reducción de la actividad económica; por lo general, está marcado por una tasa de desempleo del 4 al 6 por ciento (pág. 383)

future [futuro] *n.* contrato para comprar o vender acciones en una fecha futura determinada y a un precio establecido (pág. 333)

G

general partnership [sociedad colectiva] *n.* sociedad en la que cada socio participa en la dirección de la empresa y es responsable de todas las deudas y pérdidas de la empresa (pág. 233)

geographic monopoly [monopolio geográfico] *n.* monopolio que existe debido a la ausencia de otros productores o vendedores en cierta región (pág. 201)

gift tax [impuesto sobre donaciones] *n.* impuesto aplicado al dinero o a las propiedades que una persona viva le da a otra (pág. 425)

glass ceiling [techo de cristal] *n.* barrera artificial e invisible que a veces afrontan las mujeres y las minorías y que les impide avanzar profesionalmente (pág. 262)

global economy [economía global] *n.* todas las interacciones económicas que cruzan las fronteras internacionales (pág. 61)

gold standard [patrón oro] *n.* sistema en el que la unidad monetaria básica es igual a una cantidad de oro establecida (pág. 299)

goods [bienes] *n.* objetos físicos, como los alimentos, la ropa y los muebles, que pueden comprarse (pág. 5)

government monopoly [monopolio gubernamental] *n.* monopolio que existe debido a que el gobierno posee y dirige esa empresa o autoriza un solo productor (pág. 201)

grant-in-aid [donativo del gobierno federal] *n.* pago de transferencia del gobierno federal a gobiernos estatales o locales (pág. 432)

gross domestic product (GDP) [producto interior bruto (PIB)] *n.* valor de mercado de todos los bienes y servicios finales producidos en un país durante un determinado período de tiempo (pág. 350)

gross national product (GNP) [producto nacional bruto (PNB)] *n.* valor de mercado de todos los bienes y servicios finales producidos por un país durante un determinado período de tiempo (pág. 355)

H

hacking [hacking] *n.* técnica empleada por los ladrones de identidad para recoger información personal mediante computadoras y tecnología relacionada (pág. 588)

horizontal merger [fusión horizontal] *n.* unión de dos o más compañías que ofrecen productos o servicios iguales o similares (pág. 243)

human capital [capital humano] *n.* conocimientos y aptitudes que permiten a los trabajadores ser productivos (pág. 261)

human development index (HDI) [índice de desarrollo humano (IDH)] *n.* combinación del PIB real per cápita, la esperanza de vida al nacer, la tasa de alfabetización de adultos y la tasa de matriculación de los estudiantes de un país y todo esto indica cómo es la vida en un país determinado (pág. 547)

hyperinflation [hiperinflación] *n.* tasa de inflación acelerada y no controlada superior al 50 por ciento (pág. 398)

I

identity theft [robo de identidad] *n.* uso de la información personal de otra persona con fines criminales (pág. 588)

imperfect competition [competencia imperfecta] *n.* estructura de mercado que carece de una o más de las condiciones necesarias para la competencia perfecta (pág. 195)

imports [importaciones] *n.* bienes o servicios producidos en un país y comprados por otro (pág. 516)

incentive [incentivo] *n.* beneficio ofrecido para estimular a las personas a que actúen de cierta manera (págs. 12, 176)

incidence of a tax [incidencia fiscal] *n.* carga final de un impuesto (pág. 415)

income distribution [distribución de la renta] *n.* forma en que la renta se divide entre las personas de un país (pág. 390)

income effect [efecto renta] *n.* cambio en la cantidad de un bien o de un servicio que un consumidor comprará debido a la variación de su renta (y por ello su poder adquisitivo) (pág. 107)

income inequality [desigualdad de la renta] *n.* distribución desigual de la renta (pág. 390)

increasing returns [rentabilidad creciente] *n.* situación en la que la contratación de nuevos trabajadores hace aumentar el producto marginal (pág. 139)

independent contractor [contratista independiente] *n.* alguien que vende sus servicios mediante un contrato (pág. 270)

individual income tax [impuesto sobre la renta personal] *n.* impuesto basado en las rentas que una persona recibe de todas las fuentes (pág. 412)

industrial union [sindicato industrial] *n.* organización de trabajadores con muchas y diversas aptitudes y que trabajan en la misma industria (pág. 274)

inelastic [inelástica] *n.* situación en la que la cantidad demandada o la cantidad ofertada cambia poco al cambiar el precio (págs. 117, 155)

infant industries [industrias nacientes] *n.* nuevas industrias que frecuentemente son incapaces de competir contra los competidores más grandes y establecidos (pág. 523)

infant mortality rate [tasa de mortalidad infantil] *n.* número de niños que mueren durante el primer año de vida por 1,000 nacimientos (pág. 547)

inferior goods [bienes inferiores] *n.* bienes que tienen menos demanda por parte de los consumidores cuando aumentan sus ingresos (pág. 110)

inflation [inflación] *n.* aumento persistente del nivel general de precios, o disminución persistente del poder adquisitivo del dinero (pág. 396)

inflation rate [tasa de inflación] *n.* tasa de variación de los precios durante un período de tiempo establecido (pág. 397)

infrastructure [infraestructuras] *n.* conjunto básico de los sistemas de soporte, como los sistemas energéticos, de comunicaciones, de transporte, de agua, sanitarios y de educación, que se necesitan para el funcionamiento de la economía y la sociedad (págs. 86, 545)

input costs [costos de los insumos] *n.* precio de los recursos necesarios para producir un bien o un servicio (pág. 148)

insourcing [uso de recursos internos] *n.* práctica de las compañías extranjeras que establecen operaciones en Estados Unidos y por lo tanto crean puestos de trabajo en este país (pág. 269)

interest [interés] *n.* cargo que paga un banco por el uso del dinero (pág. 578)

International Monetary Fund (IMF) [Fondo Monetario Internacional (FMI)] *n.* organización internacional establecida para promocionar la cooperación monetaria internacional, fomentar el crecimiento económico y proporcionar apoyo financiero temporal a los países para ayudar a mitigar el ajuste de la balanza-de-pagos (pág. 559)

investment [inversión] *n.* uso actual de la renta de manera tal que permita obtener un beneficio futuro (pág. 318)

investment objective [objetivo de inversión] *n.* meta financiera utilizada para determinar si una inversión es apropiada (pág. 324)

J

junk bond [bono basura] *n.* bono de empresa que es de alto riesgo y de alto rendimiento (pág. 339)

K

Keynesian economics [economía keynesiana] *n.* idea, propuesta inicialmente por John Maynard Keynes, de que el gobierno necesita estimular la demanda agregada en períodos de recesión (pág. 454)

L

labor [trabajo] *n.* todo el tiempo, esfuerzo y talento humano usado para producir bienes y servicios (pág. 8)

labor input [factor trabajo] *n.* magnitud de la fuerza laboral multiplicada por la duración de la semana laborable (pág. 371)

labor productivity [productividad del trabajo] *n.* cantidad de bienes y servicios que una persona puede producir en un tiempo determinado (pág. 149)

labor union [sindicato laboral] *n.* organización de trabajadores que trata de mejorar para sus miembros los salarios, las condiciones laborales, los beneficios suplementarios, la seguridad en el empleo y otros asuntos relacionados con el trabajo (pág. 274)

Laffer Curve [curva de Laffer] *n.* gráfica que ilustra cómo afecta la reducción de los impuestos a los ingresos fiscales y al crecimiento económico (pág. 459)

lagging indicators [indicadores retrasados] *n.* medidas del rendimiento económico que suelen cambiar después de cambiar el producto interior bruto real (pág. 364)

laissez faire [laissez faire] *n.* principio según el cual el gobierno no debe interferir en la economía (pág. 49)

land [tierra] *n.* todos los recursos naturales sobre o bajo el suelo que se utilizan para producir bienes y servicios (pág. 8)

landlord [propietario de una propiedad] *n.* dueño de una propiedad de alquiler (pág. 609)

law of comparative advantage [ley de la ventaja comparativa] *n.* ley según la cual los países se benefician cuando producen artículos cuya fabricación realizan con la mayor eficiencia y con el menor costo de oportunidad (pág. 514)

law of demand [ley de la demanda] *n.* establece que cuando el precio de un bien o de un servicio baja la cantidad demandada aumenta, y cuando los precios suben la cantidad demandada disminuye (pág. 99)

law of diminishing marginal utility [ley de la utilidad marginal decreciente] *n.* establece que el beneficio marginal obtenido al consumir cada unidad adicional de un bien o de un servicio durante un determinado período de tiempo tiende a disminuir tras el consumo de cada una (pág. 106)

law of increasing opportunity costs [ley de costos de oportunidad crecientes] *n.* establece que al pasar de fabricar un producto a fabricar otro, se necesitan cada vez más recursos para aumentar la fabricación del segundo producto, lo cual hace aumentar los costos de oportunidad (pág. 21)

law of supply [ley de la oferta] *n.* establece que los productores están dispuestos a vender más de un bien o de un servicio a un precio más alto que a un precio más bajo (pág. 131)

leading indicators [indicadores principales] *n.* medidas del rendimiento económico que generalmente cambian antes de que cambie el producto interior bruto real (pág. 364)

lease [contrato de arrendamiento financiero] *n.* contrato para alquilar un apartamento, vehículo u otro objeto durante un determinado período de tiempo (pág. 609)

legal equality [igualdad legal] *n.* situación en la que todo el mundo tiene los mismos derechos económicos bajo la ley (pág. 73)

less developed countries (LDCs) [países menos desarrollados (PMD)] *n.* países con un PIB más bajo, menos industrias bien desarrolladas y un nivel de vida menor; a veces, se llaman economías emergentes (pág. 545)

life expectancy [esperanza de vida al nacer] *n.* promedio de años que se prevé que una persona vivirá si las tendencias de mortalidad actuales continúan durante el resto de la vida de esa persona (pág. 547)

limited liability [responsabilidad limitada] *n.* situación en la que la responsabilidad del propietario de una empresa respecto a las deudas y a las pérdidas de la empresa es limitada (pág. 240)

limited liability partnership (LLP) [sociedad de responsabilidad limitada (SRL)] *n.* sociedad en la que no todos los socios son responsables de las deudas y de otras obligaciones de los otros socios (pág. 233)

limited life [vida limitada] *n.* situación en la que una empresa deja de existir si el propietario muere, se jubila o abandona la empresa (pág. 228)

limited partnership [sociedad limitada] *n.* sociedad en la que hay al menos un socio que no participa en la gestión de la empresa y es responsable sólo de los fondos que invirtió (pág. 233)

literacy rate [tasa de alfabetización] *n.* porcentaje de personas mayores de 15 años que saben leer y escribir (pág. 547)

loan [préstamo] *n.* dinero prestado que se reembolsa generalmente con intereses (pág. 582)

Lorenz curve [curva de Lorenz] *n.* curva que muestra el grado de desigualdad de la renta de un país (pág. 391)

M

macroeconomic equilibrium [equilibrio macroeconómico] *n.* punto donde la demanda agregada equivale a la oferta agregada (pág. 361)

macroeconomics [macroeconomía] *n.* estudio del comportamiento de la economía en su conjunto; lo relacionado a la actividad económica a gran escala (pág. 27)

mandatory spending [gastos obligatorios] *n.* gastos que debe realizar el gobierno según las leyes actuales (pág. 428)

marginal benefit [beneficio marginal] *n.* beneficio o satisfacción obtenido al consumir una unidad adicional de un bien o de un servicio (pág. 16)

marginal cost [costo marginal] *n.* costo adicional de producir o consumir una unidad adicional de un bien o de un servicio (págs. 16, 140)

marginal product [producto marginal] *n.* cambio en el producto total que es resultado de añadir un trabajador más (pág. 138)

marginal revenue [ingreso marginal] *n.* dinero obtenido al vender cada unidad adicional (pág. 142)

market [mercado] *n.* cualquier lugar o situación en que las personas compran y venden bienes y servicios (pág. 48)

market allocation [reparto de mercado] *n.* acuerdo entre dos o más empresas competidoras por el que se divide un mercado (pág. 216)

market demand curve [curva de demanda de mercado] *n.* gráfica que muestra datos de una tabla de demanda de mercado, o la cantidad de un bien o de un servicio que todos los consumidores pueden y están dispuestos a comprar a cada precio (pág. 102)

market demand schedule [tabla de demanda de mercado] *n.* tabla que muestra la cantidad de un bien o de un servicio que todos los consumidores pueden y están dispuestos a comprar a cada precio de un mercado (pág. 100)

market division [repartición de mercado] *véase* market allocation [reparto de mercado]

market economy [economía de mercado] *n.* sistema económico basado en la elección individual y el intercambio voluntario (pág. 39)

market equilibrium [equilibrio del mercado] *n.* situación en la que la cantidad ofertada y la cantidad demandada a un precio determinado son iguales (pág. 164)

market failure [fallo del mercado] *n.* situación en la que personas no participantes de una interacción del mercado se benefician de ella o pagan parte de sus costos (pág. 84)

market research [investigación de mercados] *n.* recogida y evaluación de información sobre las preferencias de los consumidores respecto a bienes y servicios (pág. 208)

market share [cuota de mercado] *n.* porcentaje del total de ventas de una empresa en un mercado determinado (pág. 209)

market structure [estructura de mercado] *n.* modelo económico de competencia entre las empresas de la misma industria (pág. 192)

market supply curve [curva de oferta de mercado] *n.* gráfica que muestra datos de una tabla de oferta de mercado (pág. 134)

market supply schedule [tabla de oferta de mercado] *n.* tabla que muestra la cantidad de un bien o de un servicio que todos los productores de un mercado pueden y están dispuestos a ofrecer para su venta a cada precio (pág. 132)

maturity [vencimiento] *n.* fecha en la que un bono debe reembolsarse (pág. 338)

Medicaid [Medicaid] *n.* programa de seguro médico gubernamental destinado a las personas de baja renta (pág. 429)

Medicare [Medicare] *n.* programa de seguro de salud nacional y gubernamental destinado principalmente a los ciudadanos mayores de 65 años (pág. 423)

medium of exchange [medio de intercambio] *n.* medio por el que se pueden intercambiar bienes y servicios (pág. 288)

merger [fusión] *n.* unión de dos o más compañías para formar una sola compañía (pág. 214)

microeconomics [microeconomía] *n.* estudio del comportamiento de los participantes individuales de una economía, como las personas, las familias y las empresas (pág. 27)

minimum balance requirement [requisito de saldo mínimo] *n.* cantidad de dinero que se debe mantener en una cuenta para evitar los cargos (pág. 576)

minimum wage [salario mínimo] *n.* la menor cantidad, según establece la ley, que un empleador puede pagar a un trabajador por una hora de trabajo (págs. 182, 262)

mixed economy [economía mixta] *n.* sistema económico que presenta elementos de las economías tradicional, autoritaria y de mercado; sistema económico más común (pág. 58)

modified free enterprise economy [economía de libre mercado modificada] *n.* sistema económico mixto que incluye algunas medidas protectoras, disposiciones y reglamentos del gobierno, para ajustar el sistema de libre mercado (pág. 80)

monetarism [monetarismo] *n.* teoría económica que sugiere que los cambios rápidos en la oferta monetaria son la causa principal de la inestabilidad económica (pág. 496)

monetary [monetario] *adj.* lo relacionado al dinero (pág. 474)

monetary policy [política monetaria] *n.* medidas de la Reserva Federal que cambian la oferta monetaria para influir en la economía (pág. 490)

money [dinero] *n.* todo lo que las personas aceptan como pago de bienes y servicios (pág. 288)

money market [mercado monetario] *n.* mercado en el que se compran y venden activos financieros a corto plazo (pág. 322)

monopolistic competition [competencia monopolista] *n.* estructura de mercado en la que un gran número de vendedores ofrecen a los consumidores productos similares pero no estandarizados (pág. 206)

monopoly [monopolio] *n.* estructura de mercado en la que un único vendedor vende un producto para el que no existen sustitutos adecuados (pág. 198)

monopsony [monopsonio] *n.* estructura de mercado en la que existe gran número de vendedores pero sólo un comprador grande (pág. 212)

multifactor productivity [productividad multifactorial] *n.* razón entre la producción económica de una industria y los factores trabajo y capital (pág. 372)

multinational corporation [empresa multinacional] *n.* sociedad anónima que tiene establecimientos en varios países (pág. 243)

mutual fund [fondo de mercado monetario, fondo mutual] *n.* compañía de inversión que reúne dinero de inversionistas individuales y lo utiliza para comprar una variedad de activos financieros (pág. 320)

N

NAFTA [NAFTA] *n.* Tratado de Libre Comercio con América del Norte, convenio que asegura el libre comercio por todo el continente y constituye la zona de libre comercio más grande del mundo (pág. 533)

national accounts [cuentas nacionales] *véase* national income accounting [contabilidad nacional]

national bank [banco nacional] *n.* banco autorizado por el gobierno nacional (pág. 299)

national debt [deuda pública] *n.* cantidad total de dinero que debe el gobierno federal (pág. 462)

national income (NI) [renta nacional (RN)] *n.* renta total percibida en un país por la producción de bienes y servicios durante un determinado período de tiempo (pág. 355)

national income accounting [contabilidad nacional] *n.* método de analizar la economía de un país usando medidas estadísticas de los ingresos, los gastos y la producción (pág. 350)

nationalize [nacionalizar] *v.* pasar de la propiedad privada a la propiedad gubernamental o pública (pág. 61)

natural monopoly [monopolio natural] *n.* situación del mercado en la que los costos de producción son más bajos cuando una única empresa proporciona un producto o un servicio (pág. 201)

near money [cuasidinero] *n.* cuentas de ahorro y otros depósitos a plazo similares que pueden convertirse en dinero de manera relativamente fácil (pág. 293)

needs [necesidades] *n.* objetos como los alimentos, la ropa y los lugares de vivienda, que son necesarios para la vida (pág. 4)

negative externality [externalidad negativa] *n.* externalidad que supone un costo para personas no participantes en la actividad económica original (pág. 87)

net national product (NNP) [producto nacional neto (PNN)] *n.* producto nacional bruto menos la depreciación del capital social. Es decir, es el valor de los bienes y los servicios finales menos el valor de los bienes capitales que quedaron desgastados durante el año (pág. 355)

nominal GDP [PIB nominal] *n.* producto interior bruto expresado en función del valor actual de los bienes y los servicios (pág. 352)

nonmarket activities [actividades no comerciales] *n.* servicios que tienen un valor económico en potencia pero que se prestan sin cobrar (pág. 354)

nonprice competition [competencia no basada en el precio] *n.* uso de factores distintos al precio, como el estilo, el servicio, la publicidad o los regalos, para tratar de convencer a los clientes para que compren algo de un productor y no de otro (pág. 207)

nonprofit organization [organización sin fines de lucro] *n.* institución que actúa como empresa pero que existe para beneficiar a la comunidad en lugar de obtener ganancias (pág. 250)

normal goods [bienes normales] *n.* bienes que tienen más demanda por parte de los consumidores cuando aumentan sus ingresos (pág. 110)

normative economics [economía normativa] *n.* forma de describir y explicar cómo debería ser el comportamiento económico y no cómo es en realidad (pág. 29)

not-for-profit [sin fines de lucro] *véase* nonprofit organization [organización sin fines de lucro]

O

oligopoly [oligopolio] *n.* estructura de mercado en la que un número reducido de vendedores ofrecen un producto similar (pág. 209)

OPEC [OPEP] *n.* Organización de Países Exportadores de Petróleo, grupo comercial regional (pág. 535)

open market operations [operaciones de mercado abierto] *n.* compraventa por parte de la Reserva Federal de valores del gobierno federal; instrumento de política monetaria de mayor uso por la Reserva Federal para ajustar la oferta monetaria (pág. 490)

open opportunity [oportunidad abierta] *n.* capacidad para que todo el mundo pueda entrar y competir en el mercado según su libre elección (pág. 73)

operating budget [presupuesto de operación] *n.* plan para los gastos diarios (pág. 436)

opportunity cost [costo de oportunidad] *n.* costo de elegir una alternativa económica en lugar de otra (pág. 14)

option [opción] *n.* contrato por el que se da al inversionista el derecho a comprar o vender acciones en una fecha futura y a un precio establecido (pág. 333)

outsourcing [subcontratación] *n.* práctica de contratar una empresa externa, a menudo en un país extranjero, para que proporcione bienes y servicios (pág. 269)

overdraft [sobregiro] *n.* cheque u otra forma de retirar fondos que excede del saldo existente en la cuenta (pág. 576)

P

par value [valor a la par] *n.* cantidad que el emisor de un bono promete pagar al comprador en la fecha de vencimiento (pág. 338)

partnership [sociedad] *n.* empresa que pertenece a dos o más personas, o "socios", que acuerdan la forma de repartir las responsabilidades, las ganancias y las pérdidas (pág. 232)

patent [patente] *n.* inscripción legal de un invento o de un proceso que da al inventor los derechos exclusivos de la propiedad sobre ese invento o proceso durante cierto número de años (pág. 202)

peak [punto máximo, pico] *n.* fin de una expansión de la economía (pág. 359); *véase* business cycle [ciclo económico]

per capita gross domestic product [producto interior bruto per cápita] *n.* PIB de un país, dividido por la población total (pág. 546)

perestroika [perestroika] *n.* plan del dirigente ruso Mijaíl Gorbachov de incorporar de forma gradual mercados en la economía autoritaria de la Unión Soviética (pág. 564)

perfect competition [competencia perfecta] *n.* modelo ideal de una economía de mercado; estructura de mercado en la que ninguno de los numerosos vendedores y compradores independientes y bien informados tiene control sobre el precio de un bien o un servicio estandarizado (pág. 192)

personal income (PI) [renta personal (RP)] *n.* renta anual recibida por el conjunto de personas de un país y procedente de todas las fuentes (pág. 355)

phishing [phishing] *n.* técnica empleada por los ladrones de identidad para recoger información personal mediante llamadas telefónicas engañosas (pág. 588)

PIN [PIN] *n.* número de identificación personal (pág. 577)

positive economics [economía positiva] *n.* forma de describir y explicar la economía tal como es (pág. 29)

positive externality [externalidad positiva] *n.* externalidad que beneficia a personas no participantes en la actividad económica original (pág. 87)

poverty [pobreza] *n.* situación en la que la renta y los recursos de una persona no le permiten obtener un nivel de vida mínimo (pág. 388)

poverty line [línea de pobreza] *véase* poverty threshold [umbral de pobreza]

poverty rate [tasa de pobreza] *n.* porcentaje de personas que viven en hogares cuya renta es inferior a la del umbral de pobreza (pág. 389)

poverty threshold [umbral de pobreza] *n.* renta mínima oficial necesaria para pagar los gastos básicos de la vida (pág. 388)

predatory pricing [establecer precios predatorios] *n.* fijar los precios por debajo del costo durante un tiempo para excluir de un mercado a los competidores de menor tamaño (pág. 216)

preferred stock [acciones preferentes] *n.* participación en la propiedad de una sociedad anónima que da al titular parte de las ganancias pero generalmente no da derecho a voto (pág. 331)

premium [prima] *n.* cantidad que se paga por un seguro (pág. 596)

price ceiling [precio máximo] *n.* precio máximo establecido que los vendedores pueden cobrar por un producto (pág. 180)

price fixing [imposición de precios] *n.* pactos entre dos o más empresas por los que fijan los precios de productos competidores (pág. 216)

price floor [precio mínimo] *n.* precio mínimo establecido al que los compradores deben pagar un producto (pág. 182)

price maker [fijador de precio] *n.* empresa que no tiene que tomar en cuenta a los competidores cuando fija sus precios (pág. 198)

price taker [tomador de precio] *n.* compañía que debe aceptar el precio de mercado fijado por la interacción de la oferta y la demanda (pág. 193)

primary market [mercado primario] *n.* mercado de valores para comprar activos financieros directamente del emisor (pág. 322)

prime rate [tasa preferencial] *n.* tasa de interés que los bancos aplican a sus mejores clientes (pág. 491)

private company [compañía privada] *n.* sociedad anónima que controla quién puede comprar o vender sus acciones (pág. 238)

private property rights [derechos a propiedad privada] *n.* derechos de las personas y de los grupos a poseer recursos y empresas (pág. 48)

private sector [sector privado] *n.* parte de la economía que pertenece a las personas o a las empresas (pág. 432)

privatization [privatización] *n.* proceso de transferir a las personas propiedades y empresas públicas (pág. 563)

privatize [privatizar] *v.* pasar de la propiedad gubernamental o pública a la propiedad privada (pág. 61)

producer [productor] *n.* persona que produce bienes o presta servicios (pág. 5)

producer price index (PPI) [índice de precios al por mayor (IPM)] *n.* medida de los cambios en los precios al por mayor (pág. 397)

product differentiation [diferenciación de productos] *n.* intento de distinguir un producto de otros productos similares (pág. 206)

product market [mercado de productos] *n.* mercado en el que se compran y venden bienes y servicios (pág. 52)

production possibilities curve (PPC) [curva de posibilidades de producción (CPP)] *n.* gráfica utilizada para ilustrar el efecto de la carencia sobre una economía (pág. 18)

productivity [productividad] *n.* cantidad de producto obtenido a partir de una cantidad establecida de insumos (pág. 372)

productivity, labor [productividad, trabajo] *véase* labor productivity [productividad del trabajo]

profit [ganancias] *n.* ganancias financieras que obtiene un vendedor al realizar una transacción comercial (pág. 49); dinero que queda tras restar los costos de fabricar un producto a los ingresos obtenidos al vender ese producto (pág. 78)

profit-maximizing output [nivel de producción de máxima ganancia] *n.* punto de la producción en el que una empresa ha alcanzado su mayor nivel de ganancias (pág. 143)

profit motive [afán de lucro] *n.* incentivo que estimula a las personas y a las organizaciones para que mejoren su bienestar material buscando obtener ganancias de actividades económicas (pág. 73)

progressive tax [impuesto progresivo] *n.* impuesto que aplica una tasa impositiva más alta a las personas de alta renta que a las personas de baja renta (pág. 412)

property tax [impuesto sobre la propiedad] *n.* impuesto basado en el valor de los activos de una persona o de una empresa (pág. 412)

proportional tax [impuesto proporcional] *n.* impuesto que extrae el mismo porcentaje de renta a todos los contribuyentes, independientemente de su nivel de renta (pág. 412)

protectionism [proteccionismo] *n.* uso de barreras al comercio entre los países para proteger las industrias nacionales (pág. 523)

protective tariff [arancel proteccionista] *n.* impuesto aplicado a los bienes importados para proteger los bienes nacionales (pág. 521)

public company [empresa que cotiza en Bolsa] *n.* sociedad anónima que emite acciones que pueden negociarse libremente (pág. 238)

public disclosure [divulgación pública] *n.* política que exige que las empresas revelen a los consumidores información sobre sus productos (pág. 217)

public goods [bienes públicos] *n.* bienes y servicios proporcionados por el gobierno y consumidos por el público como grupo (pág. 84)

public transfer payment [pago de transferencia público] *n.* pago de transferencia por el que el gobierno transfiere ingresos de los contribuyentes a los beneficiarios sin que éstos den nada a cambio (pág. 89)

pure competition [competencia pura] *véase* perfect competition [competencia perfecta]

Q

quota [cuota] *n.* límite sobre la cantidad de un producto que puede importarse (pág. 520)

R

rational expectations theory [teoría de las expectativas racionales] *n.* teoría según la cual las personas y las empresas prevén que los cambios en la política fiscal tendrán efectos determinados y actúan para proteger sus intereses contra esos efectos (pág. 452)

rationing [racionamiento] *n.* sistema en el que el gobierno asigna bienes y servicios aplicando factores distintos al precio (pág. 183)

real GDP [PIB real] *n.* producto interior bruto corregido respecto a los cambios en los precios de un año a otro (pág. 352)

real GDP per capita [PIB real per cápita] *n.* producto interior bruto real dividido por la población total (pág. 369)

recession [recesión] *n.* contracción económica prolongada que dura dos o más trimestres (seis meses o más) (pág. 359)

regressive tax [impuesto regresivo] *n.* impuesto que extrae un mayor porcentaje de renta a las personas de baja renta que a las personas de alta renta (pág. 412)

regulation [regulación] *n.* serie de reglas o leyes diseñadas para controlar el comportamiento comercial (págs. 150, 214)

representative money [dinero representativo] *n.* papel moneda respaldado por algo tangible (pág. 291)

required reserve ratio (RRR) [coeficiente de reservas exigidas (CRE)] *n.* fracción de los depósitos de un banco, tal como lo determina la Reserva Federal, que debe tener en forma de reservas para poder dar préstamos de dinero (pág. 484)

return [rentabilidad] *n.* ganancias o pérdidas derivadas de una inversión (pág. 327)

revenue [ingresos] *n.* renta gubernamental procedente de los impuestos y de fuentes no impositivas (pág. 410)

revenue tariff [arancel financiero] *n.* impuesto aplicado a las importaciones específicamente para recaudar fondos; actualmente se usa muy poco (pág. 521)

right-to-work laws [leyes de libertad de sindicación]
n. legislación que hace ilegal exigir que los trabajadores se asocien a los sindicatos (pág. 279)

risk [riesgo] *n.* posibilidad de sufrir pérdidas en una inversión (pág. 327)

S

safety net [red de protección] *n.* programas gubernamentales diseñados para proteger a las personas de las dificultades económicas (pág. 89)

sales tax [impuesto sobre las ventas] *n.* impuesto basado en el valor de los bienes o los servicios en el momento de la venta (pág. 412)

savings [ahorros] *n.* ingresos que no se utilizan para el consumo (pág. 318)

scarcity [carencia] *n.* situación en la que los recursos no son suficientes para satisfacer los deseos humanos (pág. 4)

seasonal unemployment [desempleo estacional] *n.* desempleo asociado al trabajo estacional (pág. 384)

secondary market [mercado secundario] *n.* mercado en el que los activos financieros se venden de nuevo (pág. 322)

service [servicios] *n.* trabajo que una persona realiza para otra a cambio de un pago (pág. 5)

shadow economy [economía sumergida] *véase* underground economy [economía subterránea]

share [acción] *n.* unidad del conjunto de acciones de una sociedad anónima (pág. 238); *véase* stock [acciones]

shock therapy [terapia de choque] *n.* programa económico en el que se pasa abruptamente de una economía autoritaria a una economía de libre mercado (pág. 563)

shortage [escasez] *n.* situación en la que la demanda es mayor que la oferta y la causa suele ser la fijación de precios excesivamente bajos (pág. 167)

shoulder surfing [navegar por el hombro] *n.* técnica utilizada por los ladrones de identidad para recoger información personal cuando se revela información privada en público (pág. 588)

socialism [socialismo] *n.* sistema económico en el que el gobierno posee algunos o todos los factores de producción (pág. 43)

Social Security [Seguridad Social] *n.* programa federal que proporciona ayuda a los ciudadanos mayores, a los niños huérfanos y a los incapacitados (pág. 423)

sole proprietorship [empresa unipersonal] *n.* empresa que pertenece a una sola persona y que es controlada por esa persona (pág. 226)

spamming [spamming] *n.* técnica utilizada por los ladrones de identidad para recoger información personal mediante correos electrónicos engañosos (pág. 588)

special economic zone (SEZ) [zona económica especial (ZEE)] *n.* región geográfica que tiene leyes económicas diferentes de las leyes económicas normales de un país, con el objetivo de aumentar las inversiones extranjeras (pág. 567)

specialization [especialización] *n.* situación en la que las personas o las empresas centran sus esfuerzos comerciales en los campos en que presentan una ventaja para una mayor productividad y mayores ganancias (págs. 50, 138, 510)

spending multiplier effect [efecto multiplicador de los gastos] *n.* situación en la que un pequeño cambio en los gastos acaba produciendo un cambio mucho más grande en el PIB (pág. 455)

stabilization programs [programas de estabilización] *n.* programas en los que los países en dificultades se ven obligados a realizar reformas, como reducir el déficit comercial exterior y el endeudamiento externo, eliminar los controles de precios, cerrar las empresas públicas ineficientes y bajar radicalmente el déficit presupuestario (pág. 559)

stagflation [estanflación] *n.* períodos durante los que suben los precios a la vez que se reduce la actividad económica (pág. 359)

standardized product [producto estandarizado] *n.* producto que los consumidores consideran idéntico en todas sus características esenciales a otros productos del mismo mercado (pág. 192)

standard of value [patrón de valor] *n.* forma de medir el valor económico en el proceso de cambio de divisas (pág. 289)

start-up costs [costos de puesta en marcha] *n.* gastos que una nueva empresa debe pagar para entrar en un mercado y empezar a vender a los consumidores (pág. 209)

state bank [banco estatal] *n.* banco autorizado por el gobierno de un estado (pág. 296)

statistics [estadísticas] *n.* datos numéricos (pág. 24)

stock [acciones] *n.* participaciones en la propiedad de una sociedad anónima (pág. 238)

stockbroker [agente de bolsa] *n.* agente que compra y vende valores para los clientes (pág. 332)

stock exchange [bolsa de valores] *n.* mercado secundario donde se venden y compran valores (pág. 330)

stock index [índice bursátil] *n.* instrumento utilizado para medir e informar sobre el cambio en los precios de un conjunto de acciones (pág. 334)

stored-value card [tarjeta de valor almacenado] *n.* tarjeta que representa dinero que el titular tiene en forma de depósito con la compañía emisora (pág. 308)

store of value [depósito de valor] *n.* algo que conserva su valor con el paso del tiempo (pág. 289)

strike [huelga] *n.* paralización del trabajo utilizada para ejercer presión en las negociaciones mientras se trata de convencer al empleador de que mejore los salarios, las condiciones laborales u otros asuntos relacionados con el trabajo (pág. 274)

structural unemployment [desempleo estructural] *n.* desempleo que existe cuando los puestos de trabajo disponibles no se corresponden con las aptitudes de las personas en condiciones de trabajar (pág. 384)

subsidy [subsidio] *n.* pago gubernamental que ayuda a cubrir el costo de una actividad económica que puede beneficiar al público en su conjunto (pág. 88)

substitutes [sustitutos] *n.* productos que se pueden usar en lugar de otros productos, para satisfacer los deseos de los consumidores (pág. 112)

substitution effect [efecto sustitución] *n.* patrón de comportamiento que se presenta cuando los consumidores, al reaccionar ante un cambio en el precio de un producto, compran un producto sustitutivo que ofrece un mejor valor relativo (pág. 107)

supply [oferta] *n.* disponibilidad y capacidad para producir y vender un producto (pág. 130)

supply curve [curva de la oferta] *n.* gráfica que muestra los datos de una tabla de oferta (pág. 134)

supply schedule [tabla de oferta] *n.* tabla que muestra la cantidad de un bien o de un servicio que un productor individual puede y está dispuesto a ofrecer para su venta a cada precio (pág. 132)

supply-side fiscal policy [política fiscal sobre la oferta] *n.* plan diseñado para ofrecer incentivos a los productores para que aumenten la oferta agregada (pág. 458)

surplus [excedente] *n.* situación en la que la oferta es mayor que la demanda y la causa suele ser la fijación de precios excesivamente altos (pág. 167)

T

tariff [arancel] *n.* cargo aplicado a los bienes transferidos a un país procedentes de otro país (pág. 521)

tax [impuesto] *n.* pago obligatorio a un gobierno (pág. 410)

taxable income [renta gravable] *n.* aquella parte de la renta sujeta a impuestos después de descontar todas las deducciones y exenciones (págs. 421, 604)

tax assessor [asesor fiscal] *n.* funcionario gubernamental que determina el valor de una propiedad sujeta a impuestos (pág. 437)

tax base [base imponible] *n.* forma de riqueza, como la renta, la propiedad, los bienes o los servicios, que está sujeta a impuestos (pág. 412)

tax incentive [incentivo fiscal] *n.* uso de impuestos para estimular o desalentar ciertos comportamientos económicos (pág. 417)

tax return [declaración de la renta] *n.* formulario utilizado para declarar la renta y los impuestos que deben pagarse al gobierno (pág. 421)

technological monopoly [monopolio tecnológico] *n.* monopolio que existe debido a que una empresa controla un método de fabricación, un invento o un tipo de tecnología (pág. 201)

technology [tecnología] *n.* aplicación de métodos e innovaciones científicos a la producción (pág. 149)

telecommuting [trabajo a distancia] *n.* práctica de realizar el trabajo de oficina en un lugar distinto a la propia oficina (pág. 270)

telework [teletrabajo] *véase* telecommuting [trabajo a distancia]

temp, temps, temping [trabajo temporal] *véase* contingent employment [empleo contingente]

thrift institution [entidad de ahorros] *n.* institución financiera que sirve a los ahorradores (pág. 478)

tight-money policy [política de dinero escaso] *véase* contractionary monetary policy [política monetaria restrictiva]

total cost [costo total] *n.* suma de los costos fijos y variables (pág. 140)

total revenue [ingreso total] *n.* ingreso que recibe una empresa al vender sus productos (págs. 122, 142)

total revenue test [prueba del ingreso total] *n.* método para medir la elasticidad comparando el ingreso total que obtendría una empresa al ofrecer su producto a diferentes precios (pág. 122)

trade barrier [barrera al comercio] *n.* toda ley aprobada para limitar el libre comercio entre los países (pág. 520)

trade deficit [déficit comercial] *n.* balanza de comercio desfavorable que se produce cuando un país importa más de lo que exporta (pág. 529)

trade-off [compensación] *n.* alternativa que se rechaza al tomar una decisión económica (pág. 14)

trade surplus [superávit comercial] *n.* balanza de comercio favorable que se produce cuando un país exporta más de lo que importa (pág. 529)

trade union [sindicato] *véase* labor union [sindicato laboral]

trade war [guerra comercial] *n.* serie de barreras al comercio entre los países (pág. 522)

trade-weighted value of the dollar [valor ponderado del dólar] *n.* medida del valor internacional del dólar que determina si el dólar es fuerte o débil al compararse con otra divisa (pág. 528)

traditional economy [economía tradicional] *n.* sistema económico en el que las personas toman decisiones económicas basándose en costumbres y creencias que se han pasado de una generación a la siguiente (pág. 38)

transfer payment [pago de transferencia] *n.* dinero enviado a personas que no dan bienes o servicios a cambio. (págs. 89, 432)

transitional economy [economía transicional] *n.* país que ha pasado (o está pasando) de una economía autoritaria a una economía de mercado (pág. 545)

Treasury bill (T bill) [letra del Tesoro] *n.* bono a corto plazo cuyo vencimiento es de menos de un año (pág. 464)

Treasury bond [bono del Tesoro a largo plazo] *n.* bono a largo plazo cuyo vencimiento es de 30 años (pág. 464)

Treasury note [pagaré del Tesoro] *n.* bono a medio plazo cuyo vencimiento es de entre dos y diez años (pág. 464)

trough [punto mínimo] *n.* fin de una contracción de la economía (pág. 359); *véase* business cycle [ciclo económico]

trust [grupo de empresas] *n.* grupo de compañías que se combinan para reducir la competencia en una industria (pág. 214)

trust fund [fondo fiduciario] *n.* fondo creado para un fin determinado y para un uso futuro (pág. 465)

U

underemployed [subempleados] *n.* personas que trabajan a tiempo parcial pero que quieren trabajar a tiempo completo, o personas que tienen un trabajo que requiere una capacidad inferior a la suya (pág. 383)

underground economy [economía subterránea] *n.* actividades de mercado que no se declaran por ser ilegales o porque los participantes quieren evitar pagar impuestos (pág. 354)

underutilization [infrautilización] *n.* condición en la que los recursos económicos se usan por debajo de su potencia total, dando lugar a menos bienes y servicios (pág. 20)

unemployment rate [tasa de desempleo] *n.* porcentaje de la fuerza laboral que no tiene empleo y que está buscando activamente un trabajo (pág. 382)

union [sindicato] *véase* labor union [sindicato laboral]

union shop [compañía de exclusividad sindical] *n.* empresa en la que los trabajadores están obligados a asociarse a un sindicato durante un período de tiempo establecido después de ser contratados (pág. 279)

unit elastic [elasticidad unitaria] *n.* situación en la que el cambio porcentual del precio y el de la cantidad demandada son iguales (pág. 118)

unlimited liability [responsabilidad ilimitada] *n.* situación en la que el propietario de una empresa es responsable de todas las pérdidas y deudas de la empresa (pág. 228)

unlimited life [vida ilimitada] *n.* situación en la que una sociedad anónima continúa existiendo aun después de un cambio de propietario (pág. 240)

user fee [cargo de usuario] *n.* cantidad de dinero que se cobra por el uso de un bien o servicio (pág. 425)

utility [utilidad] *n.* beneficio o satisfacción obtenido del consumo de un bien o un servicio (pág. 12)

V

variable costs [costos variables] *n.* costos comerciales que varían con el nivel de producción (pág. 140)

vertical merger [fusión vertical] *n.* combinación de dos o más empresas relacionadas con diferentes fases de la producción o de la comercialización de un producto o un servicio (pág. 243)

voluntary exchange [intercambio voluntario] *n.* intercambio en el que las partes participantes prevén que los beneficios serán más importantes que el costo (pág. 49)

voluntary export restraint (VER) [retricción voluntaria a la exportación (RVE)] *n.* autolimitación sobre las exportaciones a ciertos países para evitar cuotas o aranceles (pág. 521)

W

wage and price controls [controles de precios y salarios] *n.* limitaciones gubernamentales sobre el aumento de los precios y los salarios (pág. 501)

wage-price spiral [espiral de precios y salarios] *n.* ciclo que empieza con el aumento de los salarios, lo cual da lugar a costos de producción más altos, que a su vez produce precios más altos; esto provoca la demanda de salarios incluso más altos (pág. 400)

wage rate [escala de salarios] *n.* salario establecido para un determinado puesto de trabajo o tarea realizada (pág. 261)

wages [salarios] *n.* pagos que reciben los trabajadores a cambio de su trabajo (pág. 258)

wants [deseos] *n.* deseos que pueden satisfacerse mediante el consumo de un bien o un servicio (pág. 4)

welfare [asistencia social] *n.* programas económicos y sociales del gobierno que proporcionan ayuda a los necesitados (pág. 392)

withholding [retención] *n.* dinero descontado del pago de un trabajador antes de que reciba ese pago (pág. 421)

workfare [programa de empleo público] *n.* programa que obliga a los beneficiarios de la asistencia social a realizar algún tipo de trabajo a cambio de sus beneficios (pág. 393)

World Bank [Banco Mundial] *n.* institución financiera que proporciona préstamos, consejos relacionados con la política y ayuda técnica a países de ingresos bajos o medios, para reducir la pobreza (pág. 559)

World Trade Organization (WTO) [Organización Mundial del Comercio (OMC)] *n.* organización que negocia y gestiona acuerdos comerciales, resuelve conflictos comerciales, supervisa las políticas comerciales y apoya los países en vías de desarrollo (pág. 535)

Y

yield [rendimiento] *n.* tasa de rentabilidad anual sobre un bono (pág. 338)

Index

Page numbers in **bold** indicate that the term is defined on that page. Page numbers in *italics* indicate an illustration. A letter after a number indicates a specific kind of illustration: *c* – chart; *i* – photograph; *m* – map. An *a* after an italicized page number indicates an Animated Economics feature.

lagging indicators, 364

laissez faire, 49

land, *A4m, A9m* **8,** *9,* 555

Land, Edwin, 202

landlord, 609

Landrum-Griffin Act, 277

Latvia, 565

law enforcement, 86

law of comparative advantage, 514

law of demand, *99,* 99

law of diminishing marginal utility, 106–107, *107*

law of increasing opportunity costs, 21

law of supply, *131,* 131

leading indicators, 364

lease, 609

legal equality, 73, *74*

lending. *See* loans.

less developed country (LDC), 545, 553–559

Lewis, John L., 277

life expectancy, 547, 551

life insurance company, 320–321

limited liability, 240–241

limited liability partnership (LLP), 233

limited life, 228–229, 235

limited partnership, 233

line graph, 25–26, *26,* 47, 303, R8, R29, S10–S11

liquidity, 325

literacy rate, 547, 551

Lithuania, 565, *565*

loans, 305, **582**

    car, 590

    credit history and, 583

    to developing nations, 559

    Federal Reserve System and, 475, 480–481

financial crisis and, 307, 313, 344

inflation and, 402

student, 593–595, *593*

local taxation and spending, 437–438

Lorenz curve, *391,* **391**

luxury, 120

lysine, 216

M

MacGuineas, Maya, 426, *426i*

macroeconomic equilibrium, 361

macroeconomics, 27–28, *28,* 352. *See also* economic indicators.

Madison, James, 297

Majoras, Deborah Platt, *215i*

Malthus, Thomas Robert, 374, *374*

mandatory spending, 428–429

manufacturing sector, 209, 268, 278, 390

Mao Zedong, 568

maps

    United States, *A2m–A5m*

    world, *A6m–A11m*

marginal analysis, 142, R18

marginal benefit, 16

marginal costs, 16, **140**–141

marginal product, **138**–139

marginal product schedule, *139,* 139

marginal revenue, 142–143

market, 48–49. *See also* financial markets.

    allocation, **216**

    division, 216

    equilibrium, **164,** *166*

    factor, *80,* 81

    failure, **84**

    free, 30, 54

    labor, 266–271, 273

    product, *80,* 81

research, 101, 133, 208

share, **209**–210

size, 110–111

types of, 322

market demand curve, 102–103, *103,* 105, 166, *166, 337*

market demand schedule, 100–101, *101,* 165, *165a*

market economy, 39, 43, 48–55, *51, 57*

    circular flow in, **52**–53, *53*

    command economy and, 56, 562–563

    competition and, **49**–50, 55

    specialization and, **50**–51

    transition to, 562–567, 569

market structures, 191–218

    comparing, 211, *211*

    deregulation, **218,** 300, 306

    imperfect competition, **195,** 212

    monopolistic competition, **206**–208, 211–212

    monopoly, **198**–205

    oligopoly, **209**–210, 211–212

    perfect competition, **192**–195, *194,* 197

    regulation, **150, 214**–217, 241–242, 306–307

    types of, 213

market supply curve, **134**–135, 137, 147

market supply schedule, **132**–133

Marx, Karl, 43–44

Mary Kay Cosmetics, 230

maturity, **338**

Mazda Motor Corporation, 62

mean, R3

"means tested" program, 429

Meany, George, 277

median, R3

Medicaid, 392, 429, **429**

underutilization, 20

unemployment, 365–366, 382–386

compensation, 90, 393, 423, 429

rate, **382**–383, *383, 386*

types of, 384–385, 387

Uniform Partnership Act (UPA), 235

unions. *See* labor unions.

union shop, 279

United Autoworkers Union (UAW), 276–277

United Farm Workers, *277*

United Kingdom, 61

United Mine Workers, *277*

United Nations Development Program (UNDP), 559

United States

antitrust legislation, 214–215

automobile industry, 124–125

average tax rates, *90*

banking in, 296–302, 365

China and, 529, *529*

consumer price index, *397*

employment, *268,* 365–366, 517, *A12–A13*

energy use, 549

GDP, A12, *351,* 351–352, *352,* 546, *A12*

imports and exports, 518, *518*

income distribution, 391, *391*

industrialization, 55

inflation, 404–405

interest rates, *A14*

labor force, *261, 267, 267, 272*

market economy and, 59

money supply, 293–294, *294*

national debt, **462,** *465,* 465–466, *A14*

online purchases, *441*

population, A5m, A16

Postal Service, 201

poverty rate, *389*

productivity, *372*

rationing in, 183

right-to-work states, *279*

social spending, *90*

sugar industry, 538–539

trade balance, 530, *530,* R21

unemployment rates, *383, 386*

union membership, *278*

world economy and, A15, 518

United States maps

household income, *A5m*

land use, *A4m*

natural resources, *A4m*

political, *A2m–A3m*

population density, *A5m*

unit elasticity, 118

unlimited liability, 228–229, 235

unlimited life, 240–241

unskilled worker, 261

U.S. Agency for International Development (USAID), *559*

U.S. Department of Agriculture (USDA), 538

user fee, 425

utility, 12, 106–107, *107*

Utopia, 38

V

variable cost, 140

Venn diagram, R19

vertical merger, 243–244

veterans' benefits, 429

Viacom, 244

Vietnam, A15

Volkswagen, 124

voluntary exchange, 49

voluntary export restraint (VER), 521

W

wage and price controls, 501

wage-price spiral, *400,* **400**

wage rate, 261–263

wages, 258–263

calculating, *263*

equilibrium wage, **258,** 260, 265

minimum wage, *182,* **182, 262**–263

Wagner Act, 276

Wang, Vera, 104, *104i*

wants, 4–5

water company, 201

Wealth of Nations, The, 30, 39

web diagram, R24

welfare, 90, **392**–393

W-2 form, 605

W-4 form, *604,* **604**

wildcat banking, 298–299

Wilson, Woodrow, *299*

withholding, 421

women

in labor force, 267, *267,* 556

wage discrimination and, 262

wool production, 511

workfare, 90, **393**

working conditions, 262, 270–271

work stoppage, 274, 280

World Bank, **559,** 560

world data table, *A15*

world maps

GDP per capita, *A11m*

land use, *A9m*

natural resources, *A8m*

political, *A6m–A7m*

population density, *A10m*

world markets, *336*

world population, *A16*

World Trade Organization (WTO), 535

Text Acknowledgments

Chapter 1, page 32: Excerpts from "O'Hare International Airport (ORD/KORD), Chicago, IL, USA," from the Airport-Technology Web site. Reprinted by permission of SPG Media Limited.

Chapter 1, page 33: Excerpt from "Organization and Introduction," from the AReCO Web site. Reprinted by permission of The Alliance of Residents Concerning O'Hare, Inc. (AReCO).

Chapter 2, page 64: Excerpt from "The North Korean Famine," from *Peace Watch,* June 2002. Reprinted by permission of the United States Institute of Peace.

Chapter 2, page 65: Excerpt from "Masters of the Digital Age," by Rana Foroohar and B. J. Lee, *Newsweek,* October 18, 2004. Copyright © 2004 *Newsweek,* Inc. All rights reserved. Reprinted by permission.

Chapter 3, page 92: Excerpt from "The Industry: Message in a Bottle" by Matt Lee and Ted Lee, *The New York Times,* June 28, 2005. Copyright © 2005 by The New York Times Co. Reprinted with permission.

Chapter 3, page 93: Excerpt from "Growing Occupation: Being Your Own Boss" by Stacey Hirsh, *Baltimore Sun,* April 21, 2006. Copyright © 2006 The Baltimore Sun. Reprinted by permission.

Chapter 4, page 124: Excerpts from "Volkswagen Tries 12 Months of Free Car Insurance to Lure Buyers" by Jeff Green, December 31, 2004, Bloomberg Web site. Copyright © 2004 Bloomberg L.P. All rights reserved. Reprinted by permission of Bloomberg L.P.

Chapter 4, page 125: Excerpt from "2005 – The Year of the Hybrid," from the InvoiceDealers Web site. Reprinted by permission of Dealix Corporation, a Division of The Cobalt Group.

Chapter 5, page 144: Excerpt from "Why is the Supply of Cement Falling Short of Demand?" from the Portland Cement Association Web site. Reprinted by permission of the Portland Cement Association.

Chapter 5, 158: Excerpts from "Robots for Babies: Toyota at the Leading Edge" by Burritt Sabin, Japan Inc. Web site. Reprinted by permission of Japan Inc.

Chapter 5, page 159: Excerpt from "Cake Decorating" from the EPSON Robots Web site. Reprinted by permission of EPSON America Inc.

Chapter 6, page 187: Figure 1 from "The Economics of Real Superstars: The Market for Concerts in the Material World" by Alan B. Krueger, *Journal of Labor Economics,* 23(1), 2005. Reprinted by permission of The University of Chicago Press.

Chapter 7, page 220: Excerpts from "Anyone for Telly?," The Economist, September 10, 2005. The Economist Newspaper Ltd. All rights reserved. Reprinted with permission. Further reproduction prohibited. www.economist.com.

Chapter 7, page 221: Excerpt from "Gartner Says Mobile Phone Sales Will Exceed One Billion in 2009," from the Gartner Web site. Reprinted with permission.

Chapter 8, page 248: "World's Leading Franchises," from Franchise Facts. Copyright © International Franchise Association. Reprinted by permission of the International Franchise Association.

Chapter 8, page 252: Excerpt from "Steve Jobs and Steve Wozniak: The Personal Computer" from the Lemelson-MIT Program Web site. Courtesy of Inventor of the Week, Lemelson-MIT Program, http://web.mit.edu/invent.

Chapter 8, page 253: Excerpts from "Interview with Evelyn Richards" by Wendy Marinaccio, appearing on the "Making the Mac/Technology and Culture in Silicon Valley" Web page, Stanford University Library. Reprinted by permission of the Stanford University Library.

Chapter 8, page 253: "Highlights in Apple Company History" adapted from Apple timeline appearing in *Macworld,* February 2004. Copyright © 2004 Mac Publishing LLC. All rights reserved. Reprinted by permission.

Chapter 8, page 255: "Mergers in the United States" *MergerStat Review,* 2004. Copyright © 2004 Mergerstat Holdings, LLP. Reprinted by permission of FactSet Mergerstat LLC.

Chapter 9, page 282: Excerpt from "Subcontinental Drift" by Nandini Lakshman, *Business Week,* January 16, 2006. Copyright © 2006 by The McGraw-Hill Companies, Inc. Reprinted by special permission.

Chapter 9, page 283: Excerpt from "Foreign Firms Come Bearing Jobs" by Mike Meyers, *Star Tribune,* September 5, 2004. Copyright © 2004 Star Tribune. All rights reserved. Reprinted by permission of the Star Tribune, Minneapolis – St. Paul, Minnesota.

Chapter 10, page 312: Excerpt from "Las Vegas House 'Flipping Boom' Goes Bust," The Associated Press, April 27, 2007. Copyright © 2007 The Associated Press. All rights reserved. Reprinted by permission of The Associated Press.

Chapter 10, page 313: Excerpt from "From Subprime to the Ridiculous" by Peter Schiff, Forbes, March 15, 2007. Copyright © 2007 Forbes.com LLC. All rights reserved. Reprinted by permission of Forbes.com LLC.

Chapter 11, page 334: "Dow Jones Industrial Average, 1988-2008" from Yahoo! Finance Web site. Copyright © 2009 Yahoo! Inc. YAHOO! and the YAHOO! logo are trademarks of Yahoo! Inc. Reprinted by permission of Yahoo! Inc.

Chapter 11, page 342: "Apple Computer (AAPL-Q)," from *The Globe and Mail,* April 19, 2006. Reprinted by permission of the Globe and Mail

Chapter 11, page 345: Excerpt from "Time to Unravel the Knot of Credit-Default Swaps" by Gretchen Morgenson, The New York Times, January 25, 2009. Copyright © 2009 by the New York Times Co. All rights reserved. Used by permission and protected by the Copyright Laws of the United States. The printing, copying, redistribution, or retransmission of the Material without express written permission is prohibited.

Chapter 12, page 364: "U.S. Leading Economic Indicators (LEI) and Real GDP". The Conference Board, United States Bureau of Economic Analysis, National Bureau of Economic Research. Reprinted by permission of The Conference Board Inc.

Chapter 12, page 376: Excerpts from "Europe's Capitalism Curtain" by Steve Pearlstein, *The Washington Post,* July 23, 2004. Copyright © 2004, The Washington Post. Excerpted with permission.

Chapter 12, page 377: Excerpts from "Reaping the European Union Harvest," *The Economist,* January 8, 2005. The Economist Newspaper Ltd. All rights reserved. Reprinted with permission. Further reproduction prohibited. www.economist.com.

Chapter 13, page 404: Excerpt from "The Search for a New Economic Order" by Robert Tolles, *Ford Foundation,* New York, 1982, p. 24. Reprinted by permission of the Ford Foundation.

Chapter 13, page 405: Excerpts from "Open Editorial" by Bernice Davidson, *The New York Times,* September 29, 1972. Copyright © 1972 by The New York Times Co. Reprinted with permission.

Chapter 14, page 440: Excerpts from "iPod Tax Planned for Music Downloads?" from the CNET Web site, March 10, 2006. Copyright © 2006 CNET Networks, Inc. All rights reserved. Reprinted by permission of Reprint Management Services.

Chapter 14, page 441: Excerpt from "Internet Sales Tax," from *The New York Times,* July 5, 2005. Copyright © 2005 by The New York Times Co. Reprinted with permission.

Chapter 15, page 468: Excerpts from "Federal Budget Deficit Sparks Worries," *The Associated Press,* January 15, 2006. Copyright © 2006 The Associated Press. All rights reserved. Reprinted by permission of Reprint Management Services.

Chapter 15, page 469: Excerpt from "Snow Sets Sights on Deficits" by Edward Alden, Andrew Balls, and Holly Yeager, *Financial Times,* November 4, 2005. Copyright © The Financial Times Ltd. 2005. Reprinted with permission.

Chapter 16, page 504: Excerpts from "Fed Expected to Boost Key Interest Rates," *The Associated Press,* May 10, 2006. Copyright © 2006 The Associated Press. All rights reserved. Reprinted by permission of Reprint Management Services.

Chapter 16, page 505: Excerpts from "Bernanke Talks Tough on Inflation" by Edmund L. Andrews, *The New York Times,* June 6, 2006. Copyright © 2006 by The New York Times Co. Reprinted with permission.

Chapter 17, page 521: "Tariffs are Falling," from the *Human Development Report,* 2005, United Nations Development Programme. Reprinted by permission of the United Nations Publications Department.

Chapter 17, page 538: Excerpt from "Sugar Daddies" by Jason Lee Steorts, *National Review,* July 18, 2005. Copyright © 2005 National Review. Reprinted by permission.

Chapter 17, page 539: Excerpts from "Sweetener Impact on US Economy," from the American Sugar Alliance Web site. Copyright © 2005 American Sugar Alliance. Reprinted by permission.

Chapter 18, page 570: Excerpt from "From T-shirts to T-bonds," *The Economist,* July 28, 2005. The Economist Newspaper Ltd. All rights reserved. Reprinted with permission. Further reproduction prohibited. www.economist.com.

Chapter 18, page: Excerpts from "China's Economic Miracle: The High Price of Progress," from CBC News, April 20, 2006, Canadian Broadcasting Corporation Web site. Copyright © CBC 2006. Reprinted by permission.

Skillbuilder Handbook

Page R15: Excerpts from "Crude Oil Prices Sink Below $66 a Barrel," *The Associated Press,* September 11, 2006. Copyright © 2006 The Associated Press. All rights reserved. Reprinted by permission of Reprint Management Services.

Page R21: Excerpt from "U.S. Trade Deficit Hit Record High in 2005"by Vikas Bajaj, *The New York Times,* February 10, 2006. Copyright © 2006 by The New York Times Co. Reprinted with permission.

Page R23: Excerpt from "Not Business as Usual" by Elizabeth Bauman, *Online NewsHour Extra,* January 30, 2002. Copyright © 2002 MacNeil-Lehrer Productions. Reprinted by permission.

Page R27: Excerpt from "1942: Beveridge Lays Welfare Foundations," from BBC Web site. Copyright © BBC. Reprinted by permission.

Art Credits

Frontmatter

cov *top* © Randy Faris/Corbis; *bottom left* © Peter Horree/Alamy Images; *top right* © Scott Olson/Getty Images; *center right* © Jochem D. Wijnands/Getty Images; *bottom right* © ShutterStock; iii *top* © Mark Lewis/Getty Images; *second from top* © Paul A. Souders/Corbis; *third from top* © Veer; *third from bottom* © Joeseph Sohm-Visions of America/Getty Images; *second from bottom* © Jack Dagley Photography/ShutterStock; *bottom* © Jose Luis Pelaez, Inc./Corbis; iv *Sally Meek* Photo courtesy of Isaac Portrait Photography, Dallas, Texas, isaacphotography.com; *Mark Schug* Photo courtesy of Diana Johnson, Northwestern University; *John Morton* Photo courtesy of Kathryn S. Morton; 4 © Getty Images.

Unit 1

2–3 © Charles Gupton/Corbis; 5 AP/Wide World Photos; 6 AP/Wide World Photos; 7 *left* © Kazuyoshi Nomachi/Corbis; *right* © Bill Stormont/Corbis; 8 © Karen Kasmauski/Corbis; 11 © PictureQuest; 12 © Michelle Pedone/zefa/Corbis; 13 *right* © GDT/Getty Images; *center* © RNT Productions/Corbis; *left* © Getty Images; 14 © Nancy Ney/Getty Images; 16 *left* © Getty Images;*center* © Corbis; *right* © Peter Mason/Getty Images; 17 © Bryan Bedder/Getty Images; 18 © C Squared Studios/Getty Images; 21 *left* © Frank Rossoto Stocktrek/Getty Images; *right* © David Hancock/Alamy Images; 23 AP/Wide World Photos; 25 AP/Wide World Photos; 27 © Tim Boyle/Getty Images; 29 © Matthew Mcvay/Corbis; 30 *left* The Granger Collection, New York; *right* The Granger Collection, New York; 31 © Bettmann/Corbis; 32 © Lawrence Manning/Corbis; 33 © CartoonStock; 36 © Keren Su/Corbis; 39 *left* © Frans Lanting/Corbis; *center* © Peter Turnley/Corbis; *right* © Burt Glinn/Magnum Photos; 40 © Frank Herholdt/Alamy Images; 41 © Robert Harding Picture Library Ltd/Alamy Images; 44 *bottom* © Dagli Orti/The Art Archive; *center* The Granger Collection, New York; 46 *left* © Thomas Hoepker/Magnum Photos; *right* © Wolfgang Kaehler/Corbis; 47 © Peter Turnley/Corbis; 48 © Rolf Bruderer/Corbis; 50 *left* © Getty Images; *center* © Tim Boyle/Getty Images; *right* © Mario Tama/Getty Images; 52 © Juan Silva/Getty Images; 54 © Sue Cunningham Photographic/Alamy Images; 55 © image100/Getty Images; 57 © Stockbyte/Getty Images; 59 © David Woods/Corbis; 61 © Martin Guhl/CartoonStock; 62 © Rubberball/Jupiter Images; 63 © Fotosearch Stock Photography; 64 Lasse Norgaard/Red Cross/AP/Wide World Photos; 67 © Cathrine Wessel/Corbis; 68–69 © Cohen/Ostrow/Getty Images; 70 Photo courtesy of Monica Ramirez; 72 © Russell Gordon/Danita Delimont; 73 © Al Freni/Getty Images; 75 *center* © Jeff Greenberg/age fotostock america, inc.; *right* © Susan Van Etten/PhotoEdit; *left* © Getty Images; 76 *bottom* © Roger Ressmeyer/Corbis; *book image* © John Labbe/Getty Images; *book cover Free to Choose*, © 1980 by Milton Friedman and Rose Friedman, reproduced by permission of Harcourt, Inc. This material may not be reproduced in any form or by any means without prior written permission of the publisher.; 77 © Veer Wild Bill Melton/Getty Images; 78 © Creatas/Alamy Images; 83 © Time Life Pictures/Getty Images; 84 Seth Joel/Getty Images; 85 © Joe Drivas/Getty Images; 86 *left* © Getty Images; *center* © Gideon Mendel/Corbis; *right* © David McNew/Getty Images; 87 © Ashley Cooper/Corbis; 88 © LADA/Photo Researchers, Inc.; 89 © David Young-Wolff/PhotoEdit; 91 © Gabe Palmer/Corbis; 92 © Ben Stechschulte/Redux; 95 © Niall McDiarmid/Alamy Images.

Unit 2

96-97 © Ryan McVay/Getty Images; 97 © Issei Kato/Reuters/Corbis; 98 © Jupiter Images; 99 © Getty Images; 102 © Scott Barbour/Getty Images; 104 *bottom* © Matthew Peyton/Getty Images; *center* Thomas Iannaccone/Fairchild Publications/AP/Wide World Photos; 107 © Getty Images; 108 © Getty Images; 110 *left* © Getty Images; *center* © Getty Images; *right* © Ron Kimball/Ron Kimball Stock; 112 *left* © Getty Images; *center* © Benjamin Rondel/Corbis; *right* © Martyn Goddard/Corbis; 114 © Kevin Kallaugher, www.kaltoons.com; 115 © Corbis; 116 © Vehbi Koca/Alamy Images; 117 *left* © Getty Images; *bottom inset* © Corbis; *bottom right* © Wayne Eastep/Getty Images; 119 *left* © Altrendo images/Getty Images; *center* © Getty Images; *right* Photograph by Tricia Bauman/Clik Photography; 123 © Mark E. Gibson; 124 © David Young-Wolff/Getty Images; 125 *top* © Brian Duffy/The Des Moines Register; *center* © Issei Kato/Reuters/Corbis; 128-129 © AFP/Getty Images; 129 © Lucas Schifres/Corbis; 130 © Mason Morfit/Getty Images; 131 © Jupiter Images; 132 © Chris Thomaidis/Getty Images; 136 © Martin Thiel/Getty Images; 137 © Spencer Grant/PhotoEdit; 138 © David A. Barnes/Alamy Images; 140 *clockwise from top left* © Michael Goldman/Getty Images; © Brownie Harris/Corbis; © Corbis; © Danish Khan/ShutterStock; © Todd S. Holder/ShutterStock; © Image Source/Getty Images; 142 © C Squared Studios/Getty Images (Royalty-Free); 145 © David McNew/Getty Images; 146 *left* © James L. Amos/Corbis; *right* © David Young-Wolff/PhotoEdit; 149 *left* © Albo/ShutterStock; *right* © Doug Priebe/ShutterStock; 152 *bottom* AP/Wide World Photos; *center* Stephen Chernin/AP/Wide World Photos; 153 © Getty Images; 154 AP/Wide World Photos; 156 *left* © Getty Images; *center* © David Joel/Getty Images; *right* © Jupiter Images; 157 © Thinkstock; 158 © Lucas Schifres/Corbis; 159 © John Morris/CartoonStock; 162–163 © Peter M. Fisher/Corbis; 163 © Tim Mosenfelder/Getty Images; 164 ©

Eric Futran/FoodPix/Jupiter Images; 168 AP/Wide World Photos; 171 © Danny Lehman/Corbis; 173 © Dennis Wise/Getty Images; 174 © Tom Stewart/Corbis; 177 *center* © Yoshikazu Tsuno/AFP/Getty Images; *right* © Getty Images; *left* © Getty Images; 178 *top* Harry Cabluck/AP/Wide World Photos; *center* © Bob Riha, Jr./Dell/Handout/Reuters/Corbis; *bottom* © Elipsa/Corbis; 179 © Sally and Richard Greenhill/Alamy Images; 180 © David Bergman/Corbis; 183 © Corbis; 184 © Forrest Anderson/Getty Images; 185 © Scott Sinklier/AgStock Images/Corbis; 186 © Tim Mosenfelder/Getty Images; 190–191 © Chuck Pefley/Alamy Images; 191 Kai-Uwe Knoth/AP/Wide World Photos; 193 © Veer; 195 © Sandra Ivany/Botanica/Jupiter Images; 197 © Brigitte Sporrer/zefa/Corbis; 198 © Dave G. Houser/Post-Houserstock/Corbis; 201 © Will & Deni McIntyre/Corbis; 202 *top left* © Getty Images; *top right* © BananaStock/Alamy Images; *top center* © Dynamic Graphics Group/i2i/Alamy Images; *bottom right* © istockphoto.com; 203 © Rob Leiter/MLB Photos via Getty Images; 204 © Harley Schwadron/CartoonStock; 205 © Royalty-Free/Corbis; 206 © Judy Griesedieck/Corbis; 207 © Matt Bowman/Foodpix/Jupiter Images; 208 © Justin Kase/Alamy Images; 209 © Chuck Savage/Corbis; 210 © Sue Cunningham Photographic/Alamy Images; 212 © Peter Lofts Photography; 213 © Royalty-Free/Corbis; 214 © Stock Montage/Getty Images; 215 Caleb Jones/AP/Wide World Photos; 218 © 2006 by R. J. Matson/Caglecartoons.com. All rights reserved.; 219 © Joseph Sohm/Visions of America/Corbis; 220 Kai-Uwe Knoth/AP/Wide World Photos; 221 © Richard Sly/CartoonStock; 223 © Hans-Peter Merten/Digital Vision/Getty Images.

Unit 3

224–225 © Comstock Images/Jupiter Images; 225 Paul Sakuma/AP/Wide World Photos; 226 © Getty Images; 227 © Stockbyte Platinum/Alamy Images; 228 © Brand X Pictures/Alamy Images; 230 Photo courtesy of Mary Kay Inc.; 231 © Viviane Moos/Corbis; 232 © Yuri Arcurs/ShutterStock; 233 © Arthur Tilley/Getty Images; 235 © Creasource/Corbis; 237 © Michael Keller/Corbis; 241 © Chris Wildt/CartoonStock; 244 © John Morris/CartoonStock; 246 © Lynn Goldsmith/Corbis; 247 © LWA-Dann Tardif/Corbis; 249 *top left* © Getty Images; *top right* © Thinkstock/Alamy Images; *top center* © Douglas Freer/ShutterStock; 250 *bottom* Courtesy of Salvation Army; *top* Reprinted with permission © 2007 American Lung Association. For more information about the American Lung Association or to support the work it does, call 1-800-LUNG-USA (1-800-586-4872) or log on to www.lungusa.org; 251 Alan Diaz/AP/Wide World Photos; 252 Paul Sakuma/AP/Wide World Photos; 253 © Bernard Gotfryd/Corbis; 255 © Dave G. Houser/Post-Houserstock/Corbis; 256–257 © Bruce Avres/Getty Images; 257 © Andrew Toos/CartoonStock; 258 © Ariel Skelley/Corbis; 262 © Roger Ressmeyer/Corbis; 264 *right* Joshua Lott/AP/Wide World Photos; *left* Human Capital: A Theoretical and Empirical Analysis with Special Reference to Education, by Gary S. Becker. © 1993. Reprinted with permission of The University of Chicago Press.; 265 © Brenda Prince/Photofusion Picture Library/Alamy Images; 266 © Getty Images; 269 *top right* © Robert Llewellyn/Corbis; *top left* © H. Armstrong Roberts/Corbis; 270 *bottom left* © Getty Images; *bottom center* © David Sacks/Getty Images; *bottom right* © Terry McCormick/Getty Images; 271 © Charles Thatcher/Getty Images; 273 © Alamy Images; 275 © Time Life Pictures/Getty Images; 276 *left* © Hulton Archive/Getty Images; *second from right* © Bettmann/Corbis; *right* The Granger Collection, New York; *second from left* The Granger Collection, New York; 277 *left* © Ted Streshinsky/Corbis; *right* © Roger Ressmeyer/Corbis; 280 © Jeff Kowalsky/AFP/Getty Images; 281 © H. P. Merten/zefa/Corbis; 282 © Jagadeesh/Reuters/Corbis; 283 © Andrew Toos/CartoonStock.

Unit 4

286–287 © George Diebold Photography/Getty Images; 287 © Grizelda/CartoonStock; 288 © Comstock Images/Alamy Images; 290 © Lowell Georgia/Corbis; 291 © W. Perry Conway/CORBIS; 292 © Dennis Galante/Corbis; *all flags this page* © FOTW Flags of the World website at http://flagspot.net/flags; 295 © Klaus Hackenberg/zefa/Corbis; 296 Counting House (about 1375–1400). British Library, London. Photo © HIP/Art Resource, New York; 297 *center* © Archivo Iconografico, S.A./Corbis; *bottom right* The Granger Collection, New York; 298 *top left* © The Granger Collection, New York; *bottom right* The Granger Collection, New York; *top right* © The British Museum; *right* The Granger Collection, New York; 299 *left* © Getty Images; *top* © Bettmann/Corbis; *right* © Wally McNamee/Corbis; 301 © JRC, Inc./Alamy; 303 © Don Smetzer/PhotoEdit; 308 © Brandtner & Staedeli/Getty Images; 309 *right* © Chuck Savage/Corbis; *bottom left* © Altrendo images/Getty Images; *center* © Chuck Savage/Corbis; 310 © Michael Keller/Corbis; 311 © Ryan McVay/Getty Images; 312 © David J. Phillip/AP/Wide World Photos; 313 © Grizelda/CartoonStock; 315 © Antonio M. Rosario/The Image Bank/Getty Images; 316–317 © Jean Miele/Corbis; 317 © Piero Tonin/CartoonStock; 318 © Graca Victoria/ShutterStock; 320 © Free Agents Limited/Corbis; 322 © Susan Van Etten/PhotoEdit; 323 © White Packert/Getty Images; 324 © Marc Romanelli/Getty Images; 325 *top left* © Getty Images; *top center* © Peter Adams/zefa/Corbis; *top right* © Chuck Savage/Corbis; 328 © Peter Kramer/Getty Images; 328 *top left* © Altrendo images/Getty Images; *top center* © Royalty-Free/Corbis; *top right* © Alan Schein/zefa/Corbis; 329 © Robert Mizerek/ShutterStock; 330 © Alan Schein/zefa/

Corbis; **331** © Harley Schwadron/CartoonStock; **332** © Scott Barrow, Inc./SuperStock; **333** © Tonis Valing/ShutterStock; **336** © The Cover Story/Corbis; **337** © Ethan Miller/Getty Images; **339** *right* © Glowimages/Getty Images; *top* © Peter Bowater/Alamy Images; *center* © Zina Seletskaya/ShutterStock; **341** © Jim Sizemore/CartoonStock; **343** © Kai Hecker/ShutterStock; **345** © Piero Tonin/CartoonStock; **347** © Royalty-Free/Corbis.

Unit 5

348–349 © Royalty-Free/Corbis; **349** © Wojtek Laski/East News via Getty Images; **350** © Jason Hawkes/Corbis; **354** © Ariel Skelley/Corbis; **357** © Royalty-Free/Corbis; **358** © Best of Latin America/Caglecartoons.com; **362** © Andersen Ross/Getty Images; **363** © Stan Honda/AFP/Getty Images; **365** *top* © Archive Holdings Inc./Getty Images; *bottom* The Granger Collection, New York; **371** © Ed Kashi/Corbis; **374** The Granger Collection, New York; **375** © Gary Braasch/Corbis; **376** © Wojtek Laski/East News via Getty Images; **377** © Peter Schrank; **380–381** © David Trood/Getty Images; **381** © Time & Life Pictures/Getty Images; **382** © Chris Hondros/Getty Images; **384** © Adam Crowley/Getty Images; **385** © AFP/Getty Images; **387** © Cleo Photography/PhotoEdit; **392** © Justin Sullivan/Getty Images; **393** © Photofusion Library/Alamy Images; **394** *top* © Cecilia Durand/*El Comercio*, Lima, Peru; *bottom* © Getty Images; **395** © Khaled El Fiqui/epa/Corbis; **396** © Dave Einsel/Getty Images; **400** © Stephanie Davis/ShutterStock; **401** *right* © Danny Bailey/istockphoto.com; *center* © James Leynse/Corbis; *left* © Getty Images; **402** © James Leynse/Corbis; **404** © Time & Life Pictures/Getty Images; **405** © Larry Katzman/CartoonStock; **407** © David Lees/Getty Images.

Unit 6

408–409 © Philip Gould/Corbis; **411** Frank and Ernest reprinted with permission of Thaves; **416** © Ljupco Smokovski/ShutterStock; **419** Phil Coale/AP/Wide World Photos; **420** © Tim Boyle/Getty Images; **422** © Myrleen Ferguson Cate/PhotoEdit; **423** © Harley Schwadron/CartoonStock; **426** Photo courtesy of Sarah Brennan; **427** © Elizabeth Simpson/Getty Images; **428** © George Mattei/Photo Researchers, Inc.; **429** © Spencer Platt/Getty Images; **430** *left* © Getty Images; *center* © Jose Luis Pelaez, Inc./Corbis; *right* © Mark Wilson/Getty Images; **432** © Royalty-Free/Corbis; **433** Rachel Denny Clow/Corpus Christi Caller-Times/AP/Wide World Photos; **436** © Mike Lane/Caglecartoons.com; **438** © Dan Brandenburg/istockphoto.com; **439** © Michael Newman/PhotoEdit; **440** © G. Schuster/zefa/Corbis; **444–445** © I. Vanderharst/Getty Images; **445** © Harley Schwadron/www.CartoonStock.com; **447** © Joel Stettenheim/Corbis; **448** © John Humble/Getty Images; **452** © Larry Wright/Caglecartoons.com; **453** © Jeff Metzger/ShutterStock; **454** The Granger Collection, New York; **456** From *The General Theory of Employment, Interests, and Money,* by John Maynard Keynes (1997), book cover. (Amherst, NY: Prometheus Books). Book cover © 1997 by Prometheus Books. Reprinted with permission of the publisher.; *Time cover* © Time Life Pictures/Getty Images; **457** © Hulton-Deutsch Collection/Corbis; **460** *left* © Altrendo images/Getty Images; *center* Mel Evans/AP/Wide World Photos; *right* © Jim West/Alamy Images; **461** © Charles Luzier/Reuters/Corbis; **462** © Harley Schwadron/www.CartoonStock.com; **467** © Peter Beck/Corbis; **468** © Stan Honda/AFP/Getty Images; **469** © Harley Schwadron/www.CartoonStock.com; **472–473** © Brooks Kraft/Corbis; **475** The Granger Collection, New York; **478** *bottom* © Kitt Cooper-Smith/Alamy Images; *top* © James Leynse/Corbis; **479** © Louie Psihoyos/Corbis; **480** © Janis Christie/Getty Images; **483** *top* U. S. Treasury/AP/Wide World Photos; *bottom* U. S. Treasury/AP/Wide World Photos; **486** David Zalubowski/AP/Wide World Photos; **489** © Jim Pathe/Star Ledger/Corbis; **492** Frank and Ernest reprinted with permission of Thaves.; **494** © Time & Life Pictures/Getty Images; **496** © James Leynse/Corbis; **497** © Don Mason/Corbis; **498** © Royalty-Free/Corbis; **501** *left* © Getty Images; *center* © Greg Henry/istockphoto.com; *right* © Sharon Meredith/istockphoto.com; **503** © Stocksearch/Alamy Images; **504** © Joshua Roberts/Reuters/Corbis; **505** © Harley Schwadron/www.CartoonStock.com.

Unit 7

508–509 © William Caram/Alamy; **509** © Jack Kurtz/ZUMA/Corbis; **510** *left* © KCNA/epa/Corbis; *right* © Benelux Press/Getty Images; **511** *left* © Altrendo images/Getty Images; *center* © Tom Stewart/Corbis; *right* © Anita Patterson Peppers/ShutterStock; **512** The Granger Collection, New York; **513** *left* © Robert Garvey/Corbis; *right* © Royalty-Free/Corbis; **515** © Barry Mason/Alamy Images; **517** © Andrew Brookes/Corbis; **519** © Gordon Swanson/ShutterStock; **520** © Stephane Peray/Caglecartoons.com; **523** © Pierre Verdy/AFP/Getty Images; **524** © images-of-france/Alamy Images; **525** © Karl Weatherly/Getty Images; **526** *top* © Danita Delimont/Alamy Images; *center* © B.A.E. Inc./Alamy Images; *bottom* © Pacific Press Service/Alamy Images; **527** © You Sung-Ho/Reuters/Corbis; **528** *left* © Getty Images; *center* © Blue Line Pictures/Getty Images; *right* © Jerry Arcieri/Corbis; **531** © Alan Schein Photography/Corbis; **532** Mindaugas Kulbis/AP/Wide World Photos; **535** *right* Gautam Singh/AP/Wide World Photos; *second from right* © Ralph Orlowski/Getty Images; *second from left* © Chung Sung Jun/Getty Images; *left* Newscast/AP/Wide World Photos; **537** © PhotoLink/Getty Images; **538** © Jack Kurtz/ZUMA/Corbis; **541** *left* © Royalty-Free/Corbis; *right* © Steven

Collins/ShutterStock; **542–543** © Mark Daffey/Getty Images; **543** © Best of Latin America/Caglecartoons.com; **545** *left* © Ed Kashi/Corbis; *right* © Justin Guariglia/Corbis; **547** © Caroline Penn/Corbis; **549** © MedioImages/Getty Images; **550** © Juda Ngwenya/Reuters/Corbis; **551** © Rafiqur Rahman/Reuters/Corbis; **552** © Royalty-Free/Corbis; **554** © Bill Fritsch/Age Fotostock America, Inc.; **555** *right* © SW Productions/Getty Images; *left* © Three Lions/Hulton Archive/Getty Images; **556** © Penny Tweedie/Alamy Images; **558** © AP/Wide World Photos; **560** © Dieter Nagl/AFP/Getty Images; **561** James Marshall/Corbis; **562** © Javier Larrea/Age Fotostock; **564** © Christo Komarnitski/Caglecartoons.com; **565** © Jon Hicks/Corbis; **566** *left* © Panorama Media (Beijing) Ltd./Alamy Images; *right* © Raymond Gehman/NGSImages.com; **569** © Directphoto.org/Alamy Images; **570** © Best of Latin America/Caglecartoons.com; **571** © Best of Latin America/Caglecartoons.com; **573** © Bob Krist/Corbis; **574** © George Shelley/Corbis; © Getty Images; **576** © Tara Urbach/ShutterStock; **577** © Digital Vision/Getty Images; **579** © Ariel Skelley/Corbis; **582** *top left* © Getty Images; *bottom right* © Mike Lane/Caglecartoons.com; **588** © BananaStock/Jupiter Images; **590** *top left* © Getty Images; *right* © Gabe Palmer/Corbis; **591** © Alexander Walter/Getty Images; **592** © David Young-Wolff/PhotoEdit; **594** © Mike Lane/Caglecartoons.com; **596** © Colorstock/Getty Images; **598** © John Morris/www.CartoonStock.com; **600** *top left* © Getty Images; *bottom right* Reprinted with permission of the Employment Development Department, State of California; **603** © Creatas Images/Jupiter Images; **605** © Mario Tama/Getty Images; **606** © Ken Reid/Getty Images; **608** © PM Images/Getty Images.

Backmatter

R26 © Stan Eales/CartoonStock.

Maps (except Economic Atlas and Statistics maps)

© GeoNova Group.

Trademark Acknowledgments

AMERICAN RED CROSS design is a trademark of American Red Cross Inc.
AMOCO design is a registered trademark of Amoco Oil Company
BET.COM design is a trademark of Black Entertainment Television, Inc.
DELL design is a registered trademark of Dell Inc.
FANTASTIC SAM'S is a registered trademark of Fantastic Sam's Franchise Corporation
HABITAT FOR HUMANITY design is a registered trademark of Habitat for Humanity International, Inc.
INTERNATIONAL MONETARY FUND design is a trademark of The International Monetary Fund
MASTERCARD design is a registered trademark of MasterCard International Incorporated
MICROSOFT is a registered trademark of Microsoft Corporation
NASDAQ is a registered trademark of NASDAQ Stock Exchange, Inc.
NEWSWEEK is a registered trademark of Newsweek, Inc.
NOKIA is a registered trademark of Nokia Corporation
NYSE is a registered trademark of New York Stock Exchange, Inc.
PIONEER is a registered trademark of Pioneer Kabushiki Kaisha DAB Pioneer Electronic Corporation
SALVATION ARMY design is a registered trademark of The Salvation Army
SAMSUNG is a regisered trademark of Samsung Electronics Co., Ltd.
The **SHELL** emblem is a trademark of Shell International Limited
TIME design is a registered trademark of Time, Inc.
TYCO is a trademark of Mattel, Inc.
U.S. NEWS & WORLD REPORT design is a registered trademark of U.S. News & World Report, L.P.
VAIO design is a registered trademark of Sony Kabushiki Kaisha TA Sony Corporation
VISA design is a registered trademark of Visa International Service Association
WWF design is a registered trademark of World Wide Fund for Nature

All other trademarks are property of their respective owners and are in no way affiliated with, connected to or sponsored by Holt McDougal, a division of Houghton Mifflin Harcourt. Trademarks, trade names, logos and graphics are shown in this book strictly for illustrative purposes.